KINGFISHERS
BEE-EATERS & ROLLERS

KINGFISHERS
BEE-EATERS & ROLLERS
A Handbook

C Hilary Fry and Kathie Fry
Illustrated by Alan Harris

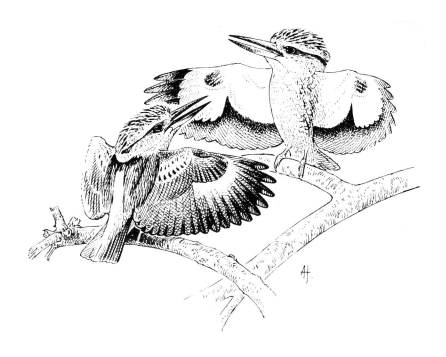

Princeton University Press

Princeton, New Jersey

© 1992 C Hilary Fry, Kathie Fry and Alan Harris

Published by Princeton University Press,
41 William Street, Princeton, New Jersey 08540

Library of Congress Cataloging-in-Publication Data available

ISBN 0-691-08780-6

Printed in Italy

For our children
and Hanne and Jens

CONTENTS

Introduction   x

Acknowledgements   xi

Explanation of Plates, Maps and Text   1

Characters and Relationships   6

Food and Foraging   12

Nesting   17

Social and Breeding Behaviour   19

Distribution and Derivation   21

Island Rarities   24

Colour Plates   25

Systematic Section   107

KINGFISHERS

1	Celebes Green Kingfisher	*Actenoides monachus*	107
2	Regent Kingfisher	*Actenoides princeps*	107
3	Moustached Kingfisher	*Actenoides bougainvillei*	109
4	Hombron's Wood Kingfisher	*Actenoides hombroni*	110
5	Spotted Wood Kingfisher	*Actenoides lindsayi*	111
6	Rufous-collared Kingfisher	*Actenoides concretus*	112
7	Common Paradise Kingfisher	*Tanysiptera galatea*	113
8	Numfor Paradise Kingfisher	*Tanysiptera carolinae*	116
9	Aru Paradise Kingfisher	*Tanysiptera hydrocharis*	117
10	Buff-breasted Paradise Kingfisher	*Tanysiptera sylvia*	118
11	Red-breasted Paradise Kingfisher	*Tanysiptera nympha*	120
12	Brown-headed Paradise Kingfisher	*Tanysiptera danae*	121
13	Lilac Kingfisher	*Cittura cyanotis*	122
14	Hook-billed Kingfisher	*Melidora macrorrhina*	123
15	Shovel-billed Kingfisher	*Clytoceyx rex*	125
16	Banded Kingfisher	*Lacedo pulchella*	127
17	Rufous-bellied Kookaburra	*Dacelo gaudichaud*	128
18	Spangled Kookaburra	*Dacelo tyro*	130
19	Blue-winged Kookaburra	*Dacelo leachii*	131
20	Laughing Kookaburra	*Dacelo novaeguineae*	133
21	White-rumped Kingfisher	*Halcyon fulgida*	136
22	Stork-billed Kingfisher	*Halcyon capensis*	137
23	Celebes Stork-billed Kingfisher	*Halcyon melanorhyncha*	139
24	Brown-winged Kingfisher	*Halcyon amauroptera*	140
25	Ruddy Kingfisher	*Halcyon coromanda*	141
26	White-breasted Kingfisher	*Halcyon smyrnensis*	143
27	Java Kingfisher	*Halcyon cyanoventris*	145
28	Chocolate-backed Kingfisher	*Halcyon badia*	146
29	Black-capped Kingfisher	*Halcyon pileata*	147

30	Grey-headed Kingfisher	*Halcyon leucocephala*	149
31	Brown-hooded Kingfisher	*Halcyon albiventris*	152
32	Striped Kingfisher	*Halcyon chelicuti*	154
33	Blue-breasted Kingfisher	*Halcyon malimbica*	155
34	Woodland Kingfisher	*Halcyon senegalensis*	157
35	African Mangrove Kingfisher	*Halcyon senegaloides*	159
36	Black-sided Kingfisher	*Halcyon nigrocyanea*	161
37	Winchell's Kingfisher	*Halcyon winchelli*	162
38	Moluccan Kingfisher	*Halcyon diops*	164
39	Lazuli Kingfisher	*Halcyon lazuli*	165
40	Forest Kingfisher	*Halcyon macleayii*	166
41	New Britain Kingfisher	*Halcyon albonotata*	168
42	Ultramarine Kingfisher	*Halcyon leucopygia*	169
43	Chestnut-bellied Kingfisher	*Halcyon farquhari*	170
44	Lesser Yellow-billed Kingfisher	*Halcyon torotoro*	171
45	Mountain Yellow-billed Kingfisher	*Halcyon megarhyncha*	173
46	Sombre Kingfisher	*Halcyon funebris*	174
47	Mangrove Kingfisher	*Halcyon chloris*	175
48	Micronesian Kingfisher	*Halcyon cinnamomina*	181
49	Beach Kingfisher	*Halcyon saurophaga*	183
50	Sacred Kingfisher	*Halcyon sancta*	185
51	Timor Kingfisher	*Halcyon australasia*	188
52	Red-backed Kingfisher	*Halcyon pyrrhopygia*	189
53	Pacific Kingfisher	*Halcyon tuta*	190
54	Tahiti Kingfisher	*Halcyon venerata*	192
55	Niau Kingfisher	*Halcyon gertrudae*	193
56	Marquesas Kingfisher	*Halcyon godeffroyi*	194
57	African Dwarf Kingfisher	*Ceyx lecontei*	195
58	African Pygmy Kingfisher	*Ceyx pictus*	196
59	Oriental Dwarf Kingfisher	*Ceyx erithacus*	198
60	Philippine Dwarf Kingfisher	*Ceyx melanurus*	200
61	Celebes Dwarf Kingfisher	*Ceyx fallax*	201
62	Madagascar Pygmy Kingfisher	*Ceyx madagascariensis*	201
63	Variable Dwarf Kingfisher	*Alcedo lepida*	202
64	White-bellied Kingfisher	*Alcedo leucogaster*	204
65	Malachite Kingfisher	*Alcedo cristata*	206
66	Madagascar Malachite Kingfisher	*Alcedo vintsioides*	208
67	Silvery Kingfisher	*Alcedo argentata*	209
68	Philippine Pectoral Kingfisher	*Alcedo cyanopecta*	209
69	Caerulean Kingfisher	*Alcedo coerulescens*	210
70	Blue-banded Kingfisher	*Alcedo euryzona*	211
71	Shining-blue Kingfisher	*Alcedo quadribrachys*	213
72	Azure Kingfisher	*Alcedo azurea*	214
73	Bismarck Kingfisher	*Alcedo websteri*	215
74	Little Kingfisher	*Alcedo pusilla*	216
75	Blue-eared Kingfisher	*Alcedo meninting*	217
76	River Kingfisher	*Alcedo atthis*	219
77	Half-collared Kingfisher	*Alcedo semitorquata*	222
78	Great Blue Kingfisher	*Alcedo hercules*	223
79	American Pygmy Kingfisher	*Chloroceryle aenea*	224
80	Green-and-rufous Kingfisher	*Chloroceryle inda*	225
81	Green Kingfisher	*Chloroceryle americana*	226
82	Amazon Kingfisher	*Chloroceryle amazona*	228
83	Crested Kingfisher	*Megaceryle lugubris*	229
84	Giant Kingfisher	*Megaceryle maxima*	231
85	Ringed Kingfisher	*Megaceryle torquata*	233
86	Belted Kingfisher	*Megaceryle alcyon*	234
87	Pied Kingfisher	*Ceryle rudis*	236

BEE-EATERS

88	Red-bearded Bee-eater	*Nyctyornis amicta*	241
89	Blue-bearded Bee-eater	*Nyctyornis athertoni*	242
90	Celebes Bee-eater	*Meropogon forsteni*	244
91	Black-headed Bee-eater	*Merops breweri*	246
92	Blue-headed Bee-eater	*Merops muelleri*	247
93	Black Bee-eater	*Merops gularis*	249
94	Swallow-tailed Bee-eater	*Merops hirundineus*	251
95	Little Bee-eater	*Merops pusillus*	253
96	Blue-breasted Bee-eater	*Merops variegatus*	255
97	Cinnamon-chested Bee-eater	*Merops oreobates*	257
98	Red-throated Bee-eater	*Merops bullocki*	259
99	White-fronted Bee-eater	*Merops bullockoides*	262
100	Somali Bee-eater	*Merops revoilii*	264
101	White-throated Bee-eater	*Merops albicollis*	265
102	Boehm's Bee-eater	*Merops boehmi*	267
103	Little Green Bee-eater	*Merops orientalis*	269
104	Blue-cheeked Bee-eater	*Merops persicus*	271
105	Madagascar/Blue-tailed Bee-eater	*Merops superciliosus*	273
106	Rainbow Bee-eater	*Merops ornatus*	275
107	Blue-throated Bee-eater	*Merops viridis*	277
108	Bay-headed Bee-eater	*Merops leschenaulti*	279
109	European Bee-eater	*Merops apiaster*	281
110	Rosy Bee-eater	*Merops malimbicus*	283
111	Carmine Bee-eater	*Merops nubicus*	285

ROLLERS

112	Rufous-crowned Roller	*Coracias naevia*	287
113	Indian Roller	*Coracias benghalensis*	289
114	Celebes Roller	*Coracias temminckii*	291
115	Racket-tailed Roller	*Coracias spatulata*	292
116	Lilac-breasted Roller	*Coracias caudata*	294
117	Abyssinian Roller	*Coracias abyssinica*	296
118	European Roller	*Coracias garrulus*	298
119	Blue-bellied Roller	*Coracias cyanogaster*	300
120	Blue-throated Roller	*Eurystomus gularis*	301
121	Broad-billed Roller	*Eurystomus glaucurus*	303
122	Dollarbird	*Eurystomus orientalis*	305
123	Azure Roller	*Eurystomus azureus*	308

| Bibliography | | | 309 |
| Index | | | 318 |

INTRODUCTION

The Kingfisher, *Alcedo atthis*, not just a European species but one that is found as far away as the Solomon Islands, has a special place in the affections of Europeans: in history and folklore this lovely bird goes back at least as far as the ancient Greeks and the legend of the Halcyon. It may come as a surprise to learn that there are a great many more kinds of kingfishers in the world than just this one: 86 more to be precise, every one of them a feathered jewel. Although they really belong to the Old World tropics, a few – the green and some of the giant kingfishers – fill the New World from the Arctic to Tierra del Fuego. It is America's loss that that is not the case with two smaller families of equally beautiful birds, kingfishers' cousins: the bee-eaters and rollers. Their 36 species also belong mainly to the Old World tropics, especially Africa, and each has a representative in Europe as well as in Australia.

Rollers and bee-eaters are varied, vocal and vivacious animals and with their spectral colours are real 'birders' birds'. Kingfishers, if rather more stolid, are also among nature's lovelier creations and are just as delightful to watch and study. Resplendent in every imaginable shade of emerald, commonly with scarlet bill and legs, they have in fact been evolutionarily rather conservative in the array of their plumages. This makes it tempting to try to perceive relationships between geographically separated kinds, and that is one of the things that many years ago attracted us to these birds.

In the 1970s J M Forshaw was preparing the ground for his great monograph on kingfishers and related families. Knowing that we were already interested in understanding relationships among kingfishers, he asked us to revise their classification. Our studies, of skins in the British Museum (Natural History) with a literature review of the biology of species, were eventually published in *The Living Bird* and *Ibis*, and in due course the findings were incorporated in Forshaw's *Kingfishers and Related Birds*. The kingfisher volumes of that treatise appeared in 1983 and 1985, followed by the bee-eater volume in 1987; the work has now been completed with the roller volume (1991, but not yet seen by us). Published in limited edition, it is a collectors' set that is unfortunately not at all readily available to most people. That is why we have written this *Kingfishers, Bee-eaters & Rollers*.

Other quite closely related families are the American todies and motmots, the Madagascan ground-rollers, and the Cuckoo-roller of the Comoro Islands. Altogether we have watched and admired over 60 species of kingfishers, bee-eaters and rollers in the field. But, because we know only a handful of todies and motmots (and because their identification and biology have already been treated in other books), we are not dealing with those families here. Nor do we yet have any experience of ground-rollers and the Cuckoo-roller, although we make passing reference to them in relation to nearby Africa's true rollers. Many kingfisher species, and several rollers and a few bee-eaters, remain very poorly known because of their rarity and inaccessibility on remote islands. It is our hope that this guide, which illustrates every one of the 123 species and attempts to summarise everything of consequence that is known about each of them, will encourage birders not only to seek out these exquisite birds for themselves, but also to discover new things about them – a quest that will surely bring its own rich rewards.

ACKNOWLEDGEMENTS

Ever since first meeting Joe Forshaw in Australia nearly 20 years ago we have enjoyed a free and full exchange of information with him about kingfishers. For his unstintingly-given knowledge and friendship, as well as for his generous gift of *Kingfishers and Related Birds*, we are deeply and truly indebted. Our information about bee-eaters has been drawn from *The Bee-eaters* (Fry 1984), and about African kingfishers and rollers from our reviews in the *Atlas of Speciation in African Non-passerine Birds* (Snow 1978) and *The Birds of Africa* Vol. III (Fry, Keith and Urban 1988). For information about most other kingfishers, however, we freely acknowledge an almost total reliance upon J M Forshaw's compendious work. Without it, and without the national bird-skin collection at the British Museum (Natural History) in Tring, this book could scarcely have been contemplated.

We and Alan Harris warmly thank the Trustees and staff of the British Museum (Natural History), in particular Peter Colston and Graham Cowles, for making skins available to us and on numerous occasions for being of much help in other ways. Alan Harris also thanks Kamol Komolphalin and Paul Tout for their help. Also for the loan of study skins, we thank G F Mees of Rijksmuseum van Natuurlijke Historie in Leiden and Richard Sloss of the American Museum of Natural History in New York. For their help in providing field observations, critical comment, photographs and other source material we are most grateful to John Ash, Linda Birch, Duncan Brooks, Humphrey Crick, Paul Leader, Trevor Poyser, Paul Roper, Philip Round, Uthai Treesucon and Reginald Victor.

We thank especially Hanne Eriksen and Jens Eriksen for providing the photographs from which many of the text drawings were made, for valuable computing help, and for their good company on a hundred field trips in Oman.

C Hilary Fry and Kathie Fry   *Sultan Qaboos University,*
                                                 Oman, May 1991

KINGFISHERS
BEE-EATERS & ROLLERS

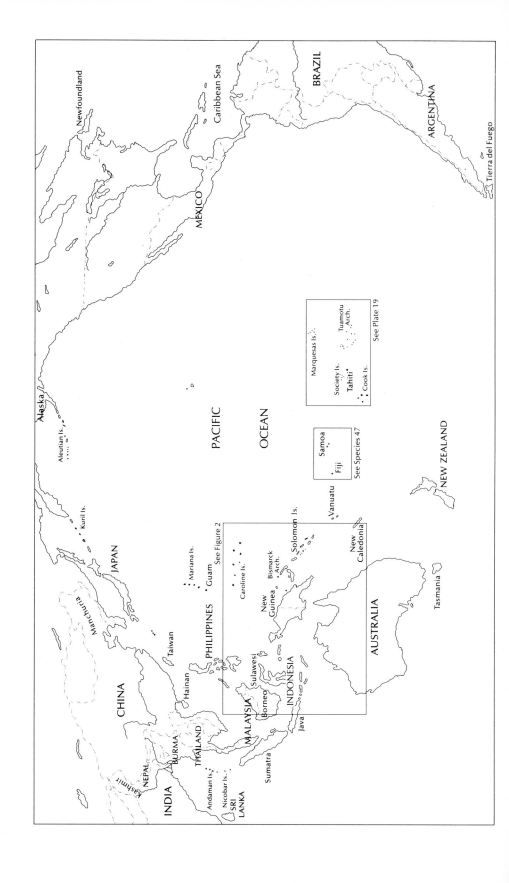

NEWFOUNDLAND

BRAZIL

CARIBBEAN SEA

ARGENTINA

MEXICO

TIERRA DEL FUEGO

ALASKA

Aleutian Is.

PACIFIC

OCEAN

Marquesas Is.

Tuamotu
Arch.

Society Is.

Tahiti

Cook Is.

See Plate 19

Kuril Is.

Samoa

Fiji

See Species 47

NEW ZEALAND

JAPAN

Vanuatu

Manchuria

Mariana Is.

Guam

See Figure 2

Solomon Is.

New
Caledonia

Taiwan

PHILIPPINES

Caroline Is.

Bismarck
Arch.

CHINA

Hainan

Sulawesi

New
Guinea

AUSTRALIA

Tasmania

NEPAL

BURMA

THAILAND

MALAYSIA

Borneo

INDONESIA

Kashmir

Java

INDIA

Andaman Is.

Sumatra

Nicobar Is.

SRI
LANKA

EXPLANATION OF PLATES, MAPS AND TEXT

The Plates   The 40 plates show all of the 123 full species of kingfishers, bee-eaters and rollers that we recognise. Males, females and juveniles are illustrated separately wherever there are marked sex and age differences in plumage; but in the majority of species sex differences are trivial or non-existent (although many female kingfishers are about 5% heavier than males), while juvenile and immature birds are nearly always like their adults but for rather duller plumage and faint scallop markings. Juveniles of red- and yellow-billed species generally have brown bills, and juveniles of tail-streamered species have short streamers or lack them completely.

About a third of the species are monotypic, that is to say they have no subspecies (or races, as they are often called). Two-thirds are polytypic, with two or more subspecies; several species have over ten subspecies each, and one, the Mangrove Kingfisher, has 50 subspecies. Altogether the polytypic species encompass nearly 350 subspecies. Although all are mentioned in the text, it has proved possible to illustrate only the nominate subspecies (i.e. the one possessing the same racial name as the species: *Alcedo atthis atthis* is the nominate race of the River Kingfisher) and the better-marked racial variations of it. All birds have been portrayed from skins, and their posture and shape from personal experience and photographs. Within any one taxon (species, subspecies) there is always a degree of individual variation; birds with typical plumages were selected for painting, and appropriate remarks have been made in the facing-page legends in instances where atypical but common variants are likely to be encountered in the field.

The birds in any one plate are all portrayed to the same scale. Since the largest of our birds, however, are 50 times as heavy and five times as long as the smallest, the individual plates are painted to several different scales. Sizes of every species are given in the text.

Maps   The geographical distributions of essentially resident or sedentary species are shown in **green**. Regions where a species is a breeding visitor are in **yellow**, and those where it is a non-breeding visitor are in **blue**. The small scale of the maps inevitably simplifies situations which in many cases are complex, either because a species inhabits numerous small islands or because of migration. Maps should always be interpreted in conjunction with details of range, density and migration given in the text.

Several of the maps are of a region (the Indonesian island of Sulawesi, for instance) with which the reader may not be familiar. Such regions can readily be identified by reference to maps of the Pacific and its bordering lands (Figure 1) and of the main islands from Borneo to the Solomons (Figure 2).

Legends   For convenience, species are numbered from 1 to 123 in the text, and the plate legends deal with them in sequence (except that kingfisher 3 is portrayed on Plate 8 and roller 114 on Plate 40). One of the maps opposite Plate 14 shows two species, and two maps for

Figure 1. The Pacific Ocean and bordering lands. Kingfishers occur in all of the named localities.

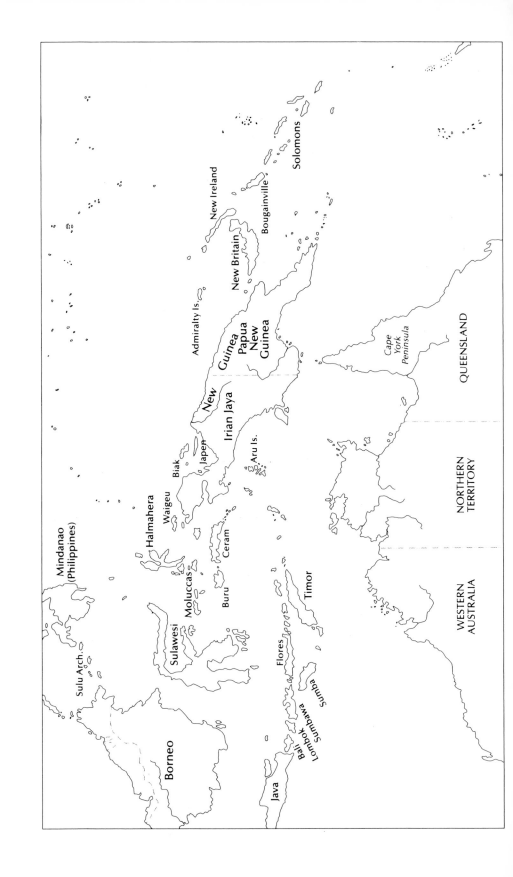

Solomons

New Ireland

Bougainville

New Britain

Admiralty Is.

New
Guinea

Papua
New
Guinea

QUEENSLAND

Cape
York
Peninsula

Irian Jaya

Biak

Japen

Aru Is.

Waigeu

Halmahera

NORTHERN
TERRITORY

Ceram

Mindanao
(Philippines)

Buru

Moluccas

Timor

Sulawesi

WESTERN
AUSTRALIA

Flores

Sulu Arch.

Sumba

Sumbawa

Borneo

Lombok

Bali

Java

Plate 20 have two species each. With few exceptions each of the plates 'reads' in species-number sequence from top to bottom.

Legends simply state range and habitat of each bird and give its principal field identification features.

Species Texts
Sequence

Within each of the families, the sequence of genera and species is broadly from primitive to derived and specialised. The sequence of the families themselves is arbitrary.

Vernacular Names

The birds that have long been known in Britain simply as The Kingfisher, The Bee-eater and The Roller need adjectival modifiers to distinguish them from their many relatives. Here we use European Bee-eater and European Roller, because these species' world ranges are more or less West Palearctic or European. 'European Kingfisher' is not, however, at all apt for a bird that breeds across Europe and Asia to New Guinea and the Solomons, and therefore we call it the River Kingfisher. ('European Bee-eater' is a name that has already become established; what a pity, as was observed in *The Bee-eaters* (Fry 1984), that the more apposite and romantic Russian name 'Golden Bee-eater' has escaped adoption in the English-speaking world.)

English names of American, African, Indian and Australian species are for the most part well established. But that is certainly not the case with the numerous kingfishers endemic to islands and archipelagos from the Philippines and Indonesia to New Guinea and the Pacific. For each of them we have chosen what seems to be the best established, most appropriate and least confusing name from the array available in such works as Fry (1980a), Forshaw (1983, 1985), Coates (1985), Pratt *et al*. (1987), White and Bruce (1986) and van Marle and Voous (1988).

Scientific Names

Scientific or systematic names of animal species are binomial: a generic name and a specific epithet. Generic allocations of all of the bee-eater and roller species are nowadays broadly agreed and stabilised; those of many of the kingfishers that we have placed in *Actenoides*, *Halcyon* or *Alcedo* are not (see Relationships, below). Specific epithets are more stable, although such a bird as the Azure Roller, which is here treated as a full species, *Eurystomus azureus*, would have to be known as *E. orientalis azureus* if regarded as a race of the Dollarbird *Eurystomus orientalis*.

Certain systematic names of kingfishers are of etymological interest. The generic name *Halcyon* is from the ancient Greek *alkuon*, meaning kingfisher (almost certainly referring to the River Kingfisher *Alcedo atthis*, rather than to the other Mediterranean kingfishers *Halcyon smyrnensis* or *Ceryle rudis*, both of which are at the western extremity of their Palearctic ranges in the Greek Dodecanese islands). According to legend, (H)alcyone, daughter of the wind god Æolus, threw herself into the sea out of devotion for her shipwrecked husband Ceyx. Both were transformed into kingfishers, who nested on a sea becalmed for the purpose by Æolus for the seven 'Halcyon days' at the winter solstice. The literal translation of *Halcyon* or *Alcyone* is 'the sea-blue one'; the name *Ceyx* has also been given to a genus of kingfishers.

Figure 2. Principal islands and archipelagos from Borneo to the Solomons.

Quite a different interpretation of the Halcyon and Sirens of classical mythology has been proposed by Bourne *et al.* (1988), who identify them as the two species of Mediterranean shearwaters. Andrew (1990), however, traces Halcyon back through Ovid and Homer to the Greek Αλκυονη and aspirated ἁλκυων, and in so doing convincingly returns the legend to the kingfisher.

Alcedo, the type genus of the Alcedinidae, is a Latinised form of *alkuon*; the genera *Dacelo* and *Lacedo* are anagrams of it. *Atthis*, incidentally, is Greek for a woman of Athens, while *Ceryle* derives from the Latin *caeruleus*, 'deep blue', and so is an unfortunate misnomer when applied to the only group of kingfishers entirely lacking that colour.

Field Identification

For the most part, the birds of these families do not present difficult identification problems. Indeed, many island species of kingfisher will have their identity determined simply by the birder knowing what island he or she is on! The specific identity of bee-eaters, rollers and kingfishers in large landmasses where many kinds occur, will seldom be in much doubt when a good view can be obtained. But occasionally even experienced ornithologists can make an error: the Blue-breasted Kingfisher would have been added to Ethiopia's list many years ago, were it not for easily understandable confusion with the commoner Woodland Kingfisher.

Voice

Coracias rollers with their raucous 'kaarsch' cries all sound much alike to our ears. Bee-eaters are also vocal birds, some, such as the Carmine, distinctively so but many others having the pleasant rolling 'prruik' notes of the European and Rainbow Bee-eaters. On the whole kingfishers are a good deal less vocal, although many halcyons have loud, structured songs – often a long trill or series of clear whistles – that are frequently repeated by day and in some species by night, and, once known, readily identify the caller hidden in trees. Calls and songs of a number of kingfishers are not at all well known: another area where the traveller with a tape-recorder can easily add to knowledge. Several kingfishers' calls appear to vary geographically to a considerable extent.

Geographical Variation

This section lists the races (subspecies) that we recognise and states their characters. The first race listed is generally the nominate one, described in detail at the end of each species account. Additional races have their characters given briefly and comparatively.

Habitat and Range

These are dealt with together, since the geographical range of a species is often determined in part by the distribution of the habitat that it requires. Most rollers and many bee-eaters are birds of open countryside and have probably benefited and extended their ranges as ever more land is taken for agriculture. In contrast, most kingfishers belong to undisturbed tropical forests and woodlands, and such is the continuing destruction of tropical forest worldwide that the ranges of many of them are likely to be more patchy and fragmented than indicated.

Population

Density and abundance are discussed only for those few species for which there are good enough data for meaningful population estimates to be made.

Migration

Nearly all tropical species are essentially sedentary, although their juveniles may disperse locally and a few species move altitudinally. Those breeding at higher tropical latitudes in seasonal habitats such as wooded savannas, and nearly all species that extend into temperate latitudes, are partially or wholly migratory. Eastern Palearctic species tend to winter near the Equator in southeast Asia; western ones tend to cross the Equator and winter in southern Africa. Australia's roller and bee-eater, and several of its kingfishers, winter north to the Equator. A Madagascan roller and bee-eater winter in Africa. Species that are latitudinally widespread, such as the Carmine Bee-eater that breeds both north and south of the Equator in Africa, can have complicated migrations in which northern populations move southward after breeding and southern populations (which breed six months later) move northward. Colour maps of such species will show yellow zones symmetrically disposed north and south of a green zone.

Some comments on migratory performance are included in this section.

Food
Remarks here are mainly an inventory of the principal foods known to be eaten, sometimes quantified. Foraging behaviour is usually described under Habits.

Habits
The length of the Habits paragraph gives some indication of the sum total of knowledge about the biology of each species. A book of this kind cannot be fully comprehensive, and sufficient is now known about a few of the species dealt with here – for instance, the Laughing Kookaburra, River Kingfisher, Belted Kingfisher, Pied Kingfisher, Red-throated Bee-eater, White-fronted Bee-eater and European Bee-eater – for each to deserve a book-length monograph. The more interesting habits are summarised in the essays on Food and Foraging, and Social and Breeding Behaviour.

Description
Plumage descriptions of adults and juveniles of the nominate race are intended to be sufficiently detailed to preclude any possibility of misidentification of a bird in the hand or a well-viewed one in the field. Measurement ranges (in millimetres), and weights (in grams) where known, are given at the end.

References
Citations in the species accounts, and salient references at the end, are intended to serve as an entrée to literature that is copious for some species but sparse for others. All references are cited in full in the Bibliography at the end of the book.

CHARACTERS AND RELATIONSHIPS

Nearly 30 orders of birds are traditionally recognised, and kingfishers, bee-eaters and rollers with various other families compose one of them, the Order Coraciiformes. Coraciiform birds are large-headed, short-necked, short-legged, and mostly large- or long-billed. Their feet are rather weak and their toes short, with the middle one of the three forward-pointing toes united with the inner one at its base and with the outer one for most of its length. Generally the tail is moderately long and often it has long streamers. Plumages are bright, mainly in iridescent or pigmentary greens and blues; there is seldom much sex or age variation in plumage within a species. All coraciiform birds are hole-nesters and have unmarked white eggs. Young hatch blind and naked, the lower mandible overshooting the upper, and the legs fleshy with horny papillae on the heels. Half-grown nestlings look like hedgehogs, with rows of long grey feather papillae, quite spiny until they start to break open.

In most of these features coraciiforms converge strongly with another assemblage of hole-nesting birds, the toucans and their allies. In the past, the classification and mutual affinities of both groups have been controversial, but molecular and other modern evidence now indicates that five orders should be recognised. Distantly allied with coraciiforms are trogons (Trogoniformes), and at increasingly further remove are hoopoes and hornbills (Bucerotiformes), jacamars and puffbirds (Galbuliformes), and toucans, barbets, honeyguides and woodpeckers (Piciformes).

The orthodox scheme of bird classification has been turned on its head in recent years as a result of the extensive genetical studies of Charles Sibley and Jon Ahlquist and their colleagues in the USA. The Order Coraciiformes, however, has remained relatively unscathed. These are ancient perching birds, in a sense prototypes or early forebears of the songbirds, and it is now clear that the various coraciiform families are more distantly related to each other than appearances suggest. Conventionally the kingfishers, for instance, have composed a single family divided into three subfamilies: the Daceloninae for the species here numbered 1-56, Alcedininae for 57-78 and Cerylinae for 79-87. But it is now evident that ceryline and dacelonine kingfishers diverged from one another even longer ago than did pelicans and storks, or swallows and treecreepers. The three kingfisher subfamilies should therefore be upgraded to family level, as the Dacelonidae, Alcedinidae and Cerylidae (Sibley, Ahlquist and Monroe 1988). The Order Coraciiformes thus comprises nine families, grouped as follows:

Suborder	Dacelonidae	kookaburras and halcyons
Alcedini	Cerylidae	green and giant kingfishers
	Alcedinidae	small blue-and-rufous kingfishers
	Momotidae	motmots
	Todidae	todies
	Meropidae	bee-eaters
Suborder	Coraciidae	true rollers
Coracii	Brachypteraciidae	ground-rollers
	Leptosomidae	Cuckoo-roller

By 'hybridising' the genetic material of pairs of species, Sibley and his team show that kingfishers are more closely related to motmots and todies than to bee-eaters. They also show that dacelonid and cerylid kingfishers are more closely allied to each other than to alcedinid kingfishers, and that alcedinids appear to be the original stock from which the others derived. The last finding comes as a surprise, since it has generally been believed that dacelonids, with their unspecialised sit-and-wait foraging methods, represent the more primitive stock, and that the alcedinid and cerylid kingfishers, seemingly more specialised, evolved from them later. But a simple explanation offers itself. Alcedinid kingfishers are small, so they probably begin to breed earlier in life than do the much larger dacelonids and cerylids. There is already a little evidence for that actually being the case. With quicker generation turnover, the genetic clock will run faster for alcedinids than for larger

Figure 3. *Puerto Rican Tody* Todus mexicanus *(left) and Blue-crowned Motmot* Momotus momota *(right). (Drawing not to scale).*

kingfishers, so that alcedinids may not be as ancient as the genetic evidence indicates. Indeed, they could quite easily be younger, derived from and more 'modern' than dacelonids, and that is the inference from zoogeographical and biological studies.

Of the nine coraciiform families, this book deals with five. It excludes the todies, five species of diminutive 'flycatchers' in the Caribbean, and the eight motmots, a family of Neotropical forest birds. Representatives are portrayed in Figure 3. Also excluded from full treatment are the ground-rollers of Madagascar, family Brachypteraciidae. Their five species are shown in Figure 4. They are small birds, not well known, and appear to have habits half way between those of pittas (which the Blue-headed Ground-roller *Atelornis pittoides* convergently resembles) and roadrunners (which the Long-tailed Ground-roller *Uratelornis chimaera* looks a little like): quite long-legged ground-dwelling birds that make short dashes to catch insect and small vertebrate prey. They do not have joined toes. The ninth family contains a single species, the Cuckoo-roller, *Leptosomus discolor*, endemic to the Comoro Islands between Madagascar and Africa (Figure 5). Chameleons feature in its diet to a large extent, and this roller is further exceptional for a coraciiform bird in having marked sexual dimorphism, tinted eggs and downy nestlings.

Relationships within each of the five families of kingfishers, bee-eaters and rollers are best understood in terms of the adaptive radiation and presumptive history of these birds. The 123 species and 18 genera that we recognise are listed under Contents at the front of the book. They are distributed among the families as follows:

Kingfishers (Dacelonidae)	56 species in 8 genera	(*Actenoides, Tanysiptera, Cittura, Melidora, Clytoceyx, Lacedo, Dacelo, Halcyon*)
Kingfishers (Alcedinidae)	22 species in 2 genera	(*Ceyx, Alcedo*)
Kingfishers (Cerylidae)	9 species in 3 genera	(*Chloroceryle, Megaceryle, Ceryle*)
Bee-eaters (Meropidae)	24 species in 3 genera	(*Nyctyornis, Meropogon, Merops*)
Rollers (Coraciidae)	12 species in 2 genera	(*Coracias, Eurystomus*).

Generic boundaries among the rollers are not contentious, and there now appears to be a fair degree of concurrence about the generic division of bee-eaters (Fry 1984). But that is not the case with kingfishers. In this book we adopt the revision of Fry (1978, 1980a, 1980b) except that, for simplicity, we merge the genus *Corythornis* (three red-billed African and Madagascan forms) with *Alcedo*: *Corythornis* is almost exactly intermediate between the fishing *Alcedo* kingfishers and the smaller, insectivorous *Ceyx* species.

Dacelonid kingfisher genera are morphologically fairly uniform. *Actenoides* and *Halcyon* are often merged, but some subgenera among the 36 species of *Halcyon* are commonly raised to generic status (storkbills as *Pelargopsis*, yellowbills as *Syma*, Pacific flatbills as *Todiramphus*). They are all essentially sit-and-wait predators of small ground animals, with some kinds specialising more on fishing or flycatching or – the crepuscular *Melidora* and *Clytoceyx* – grubbing in soil. The amazing Shovel-billed Kingfisher *Clytoceyx rex*, or Earthworm-eating Kingfisher as it is often called, has the most surprising diet and foraging habits of any of the kingfishers. Dacelonids vary in plumage colours and patterns: *Tanysiptera* species are streamer-tailed, and kookaburras (*Lacedo, Dacelo*) are sexually dimorphic. They vary in size (and in sizes of their preferred prey), and the storkbills and kookaburras are giants. But mainly they vary in foraging behaviour, which has its principal morphological correlate in the structure of the bill, as can be seen in the drawings of bills in the texts on the Rufous-collared Kingfisher (6), Hook-billed Kingfisher (14), Shovel-billed Kingfisher (15), Laughing Kookaburra (20), Stork-billed Kingfisher (22) and Sacred Kingfisher (50).

Affinities within the alcedinid kingfishers remain obscure. All authors recognise the two genera *Ceyx* and *Alcedo*, but there is little agreement upon their boundaries. In each, some species are three-toed and others four-toed, and several other genera are often discriminated (in parentheses in the table below). Toe-count in these little insect- or fish-eating kingfishers seems to be neither adaptive nor significant systematically.

		Number of toes
African Dwarf	*Ceyx (Ispidina) lecontei*	4
African Pygmy	*C. (Ispidina) pictus*	4
Oriental Dwarf	*C. erithacus*	3
Philippine Dwarf	*C. melanurus*	3
Celebes Dwarf	*C. fallax*	3½ *
Madagascar Pygmy	*C. (Ispidina) madagascariensis*	4
Variable Dwarf	*Alcedo (Ceyx) lepida*	3
White-bellied	*A. (Corythornis) leucogaster*	4
Malachite	*A. (Corythornis) cristata*	4
Madagascar Malachite	*A. (Corythornis) vintsioides*	4
Silvery	*A. (Ceyx) argentata*	3
Philippine Pectoral	*A. (Ceyx) cyanopecta*	3
Caerulean	*A. coerulescens*	4
Blue-banded	*A. euryzona*	4

cont.

Figure 4. (a) Crossley's Ground-roller Atelornis crossleyi, (b) Blue-headed Ground-roller A. pittoides, (c) Scaly Ground-roller Brachypteracias squamigera, (d) Short-legged Ground-roller B. leptosomus, (e) Long-tailed Ground-roller Uratelornis chimaera.

(a)

(b)

(c)

(d)

(e)

4

Figure 5. Cuckoo-roller: female (left) and male.

		Number of toes
Shining-blue	A. quadribrachys	4
Azure	A. (Alcyone) azurea	3
Bismarck	A. (Alcyone) websteri	3
Little	A. (Alcyone) pusilla	3
Blue-eared	A. meninting	4
River	A. atthis	4
Half-collared	A. semitorquata	4
Great Blue	A. hercules	4

* C. fallax has three complete toes and a vestigial one.

Superficially the cerylid kingfishers, feeding from water, seem to be more nearly related to the alcedinids than to the dacelonids. That is evidently the case: minutely detailed anatomical investigation by Miller (1912) showed that the Amazon Kingfisher Chloroceryle amazona, the Pied Kingfisher Ceryle rudis and the Belted Kingfisher Megaceryle alcyon are equidistantly related to each other, and that the three smaller species of Chloroceryle are intermediate between Ceryle and Megaceryle on the one hand and alcedinids on the other.

Relationships within the American green kingfishers of the genus Chloroceryle are, for once, easy to interpret. There are four species, and they are clearly the product of a double dichotomy in their evolution from a common ancestor. As can be seen in Plate 26, males and females differ in plumage and the species divide into two pairs: the smallest one (American Pygmy C. aenea, 79) is very like the second-largest (Green-and-rufous C. inda, 80), and the second-smallest (Green C. americana, 81) is just as similar to the largest (Amazon C. amazona, 82). Among birds, except perhaps brood-parasites, the process of species multiplication is utterly dependent upon geographical isolation. Some geographical barrier must have intervened to divide the ancestral green kingfisher into two populations, which in due course speciated and then spread back into each other's range. A later geographical event (probably a recurrence of the same one) separated the common range of the two species into two parts again, and further speciation and range extensions produced the four species which are today sympatric, with much the same distribution.

Their size differences are most instructive. Two closely-related bird species of immediately common descent can penetrate each other's ranges and become wholly sympatric only if they can minimise competition by such a stratagem as evolving different sizes, so that they can take different-sized food. The average bill lengths of the four green kingfishers are in the ratio $1 : 1\frac{1}{2} : 2 : 2\frac{1}{2}$, and the birds' weights approximate to the ratio $1 : 2 : 4 : 8$.

Our interpretation is that, after the first speciation event, the 'rufous' aenea-inda ancestor and the 'white' americana-amazona ancestor evolved respective weights of, say, 30 grams and 60 grams. Then the rufous ancestor gave rise to aenea at half (15 g) and inda at twice its weight (60 g), and the white one similarly produced americana (30 g) and amazona (120 g). The four, and the Ringed Kingfisher (which weighs over 300 g), live together by the same forest streams and doubtless exploit the complete size range of smaller fishes there (Remsen 1991).

FOOD AND FORAGING

Kingfishers

Many kingfishers spend much of their time in quiet surveillance of their surroundings from a perch low down in the forest or a mangrove swamp or at the edge of a pond. Sitting stolidly, they wait until they see prey below them and then swoop or dive on to it. This method of feeding seems neither versatile nor skilled; all the same, it enables them to catch a variety of animals on the ground or at the surface of water. Most prey items are still or slow-moving invertebrates and small vertebrates: with few exceptions kingfishers do not pursue their prey in a predatory chase. A prey item is grabbed in the bill and the bird usually then returns to its perch, where the hapless animal is beaten to one side and the other, insects' legs and wings sometimes being knocked off in the process, until immobile; what is left is then swallowed whole.

Far more specialised a foraging technique is deep-diving into water to seize a small fish. The bird must cope with bright light reflected from the surface, and its retina is adapted to change instantaneously from air vision to water vision. Its plunge must carry it to an appropriate depth, and the bird must anticipate the fish's likely escape route in the instant after the water surface is broken. Only the cerylids and *Alcedo* species are true fishers; nearly all other kingfishers have unspecialised diets or are primarily insectivorous, although there are several incipient foraging specialisations.

In the humid lowland rainforests of New Guinea, the Hook-billed Kingfisher feeds largely at night and the Shovel-billed Kingfisher by twilight and by day, the latter by ploughing a square metre of leaf-littered earth with the bill and seizing any grub, worm, snail, centipede or lizard that is revealed. Earthworms are the main food of the Shovel-bill, which thrusts its huge conical beak into the soil and works it from side to side for a minute at a time. If a particularly large worm is found, the bird is said to pull it out by degrees, lifting its head like a thrush and bracing itself with its tail. Ruddy Kingfishers, more aquatic birds, take a wide range of insects, crustaceans, lizards, frogs, fish and offal, and in the Philippines they evidently eat large land snails, smashing them open at regularly used 'anvil' stones on the forest floor.

Many halcyons are dry-land birds living in open woodlands or arid thornbush country and seldom if ever feeding from water. Grasshoppers feature importantly in the diet of the Red-backed Kingfisher of Australia's arid interior. Africa's diminutive Striped Kingfisher carries a grasshopper held head-forward to its young, much like an *Alcedo* carrying a fish to the nest. Larger African halcyons catch termites on the wing, pluck skinks from tree trunks, catch mice and small birds when they can, and occasionally dive into shallows for shrimps and fish; but their main prey items are large arthropods caught on the ground, often quite difficult or dangerous ones such as scorpions, camel spiders, centipedes and millipedes. The kookaburras of New Guinea and Australia are even more predatory; in keeping with their large size, they take more land vertebrates than the halcyons, and quite often tackle lengthy snakes which can be dropped on to the ground from a height to stun them.

Several halcyon species in the western Pacific are mainly insectivorous and catch a significant proportion of their food on the wing, by 'flycatching'. The Chestnut-bellied Kingfisher of Vanuatu is exclusively insectivorous (if spiders are counted as insects), and subsists largely on small moths and beetles taken in flight or snatched from among foliage. Like true flycatchers, flycatching kingfishers have the bill somewhat flattened dorsoventrally, but purely fishing ones like the cerylids have dagger-like bills flattened laterally.

Although several dacelonids are aquatic – riverside birds such as the Black-capped Kingfisher, inhabitants of mangrove, or seashore-dwellers such as the Beach Kingfisher – not one member of this large family has really specialised as a fisher. The best attempt is by the Beach Kingfisher, a bird of reefs and coral cliffs in Micronesia. It feeds less on fish than on crabs, which it catches by hovering momentarily and plunge-diving into rock-pools and surf, even 100 m offshore.

Small insects and spiders are the mainstay of the tiny *Ceyx* kingfishers. One of them, the African Pygmy, often occurs in dry country well away from any standing water, but for the most part the *Ceyx* species are neither dry-land nor properly aquatic birds. Rather, the forest species live among dank, dripping vegetation with rain puddles recharged daily on the forest floor, so that, unsurprisingly, they catch watery food, tadpoles, small frogs and mayfly nymphs, to supplement their non-aquatic diet. They flycatch to some extent and hover to take a spider from its web. Accordingly, *Ceyx* bills are compressed dorsoventrally, and markedly so in the African Dwarf Kingfisher, whose tody-like, square-tipped bill doubtless relates with some unknown food or foraging habits. *Ceyx* bills are bright red, like the bills of many dacelonids and a few *Alcedo* species that are more insectivorous than piscivorous. One wonders if a red beak is somehow an adaptation to a dryish-land, insect diet; or could it be that *black* bills are adapted for fishing?

The River Kingfisher is a typical *Alcedo* with a mainly black, laterally compressed dagger-like fishing bill and a diet to match. In Britain, fish comprise 40% of its prey in June and 80% in November, insects vary from 10% to 30%, and shrimps, tadpoles, worms and the odd spider and lizard make up the rest. Minnows and sticklebacks are their favourites; fish-prey length averages 23 mm, but in Kashmir River Kingfishers take young pike up to 125 mm long. They plunge for fish from a waterside perch, and rarely they hover briefly and then dive.

Cerylid kingfishers are also perch-fishers, but diving from hovering flight is an increasingly used option. Belted Kingfishers quite commonly fly 500 m out from the lakeshore and hover 3-15 m above the surface, plunging vertically into the water to a depth of 60 cm for a fish 9 cm or more long. But one other species is pre-eminent in its reliance upon hovering when feeding: the Pied Kingfisher. It hunts from lakeside perches – fishermen's boats and poles – but hover-hunting allows it to extend its feeding territory well offshore. When the water is choppy, up to 80% of its feeding is by hover-diving, and on Africa's great lakes it hunts up to 3 km away from land. Other evolutionary firsts in its foraging tactics are mentioned in the Pied Kingfisher account (p. 238), and it is difficult to resist the view that this species is the most advanced and specialised kingfisher of them all.

Bee-eaters   Small bee-eaters are, like many kingfishers, sit-and-wait predators of insects, but with the difference that bee-eaters give lively chase to fast-fleeing prey. A further distinction is that all bee-eaters eat bees and such other dangerously venomous insects as wasps and hornets, and that requires them to master a highly specialised de-stinging technique. Larger bee-eaters are also wait-and-see hunters that hawk for passing insects from a treetop or telegraph wire, but in addition they tend to seek out their prey actively, travelling some distance to a likely source of food and then pursuing swarming insects, catching them one by one and eating them on the wing until satiated. Kingfishers are rather passive birds; bee-eaters are very active.

Both kingfishers and bee-eaters regurgitate neat pellets of the indigestible parts of their food, but for various reasons bee-eaters' pellets are much easier to collect and study. For that reason much is known about their diets; much is also known about their foraging biology (Fry 1984).

Bee-eaters are opportunists. Keeping lively watch at their perch, they will pursue practically any sort of insect airborne within about 20 m, whether a hardly visible speck of a fruit-fly, a dragonfly darting about with clattering wings, honeybees at flowers, hatching termites rising like smoke, or a large chafer droning at speed through the airspace. Within the vast spectrum of flying insect life probably only a few very fast or large ones are ignored, and besides stinging wasps bee-eaters eat warningly coloured, distasteful butter-flies and even blister-beetles. But an insect crawling on the ground, or one that escapes pursuit by landing on a leaf, is totally ignored. So geared are bee-eaters to making their livelihood *on the wing* that the ignored insect proves irresistible the moment it takes to the air. Tackling everything that flies does not, however, mean that bee-eaters are totally unselective. In fact, if given the choice they are highly selective, and wasps, hornets, bumble-bees, sweat-bees and in particular honeybees are much sought after.

Honeybees predominate in the diet. In 20 separate studies of the diet of 16 kinds of bee-eaters, Hymenoptera (ants, bees and wasps) comprised from 20% to 96% of all insects eaten, and honeybees formed on average about one-third of the Hymenoptera. There are four species of honeybee in the world; beekeeping has made one of them almost cosmopolitan (its natural distribution was Europe and Africa), and the other three are Asiatic. Put together, their four ranges are nearly congruent with the range of the bee-eater family, which suggests that for aeons the birds have evolved in relation to honeybees, as their predators. Bee-eaters are attracted to apiaries, and sometimes then shot as pests; but they also consume a large number of bee-wolves and other honeybee-eating insects, so that in the long run beekeepers may be doing themselves a disservice by destroying them.

No special technique seems to be employed to catch a honey-bee: normally the bee-eater simply seizes it with the tips of its long mandibles, gripping it sideways across the thorax. By contrast, the Blue-tailed Bee-eater in Malaysia can see a small wasp or a fierce hornet flying 80-100 m away against a backdrop of distant trees (what amazing vision) and the bird typically flies on a course to pass immediately below its victim, at the last moment reaching up with its bill to seize it with deft precision from below. Although tropical hornets can give a fierce sting by bending the abdomen down and forward, it is likely that this method of seizing from below, with head thrown back and bill pointing straight up, is some special adaptation for capturing these large and dangerous insects.

All venomous Hymenoptera that are caught are brought back to the perch, where they are devenomed, immobilised and eaten.

Bending to one side, the bee-eater violently strikes the bee's head against the perch a few times; then the insect is juggled until held by the tip of its tail, and the bird bends to the other side, closes its eyes and subjects the bee's tail with sting to several bouts of rapid rubbing. Bowel-fluid and venom, and often the sting itself, are discharged, wetting the perch, and then the bee's head is beaten again and the insect tossed back and swallowed.

Like kingfishers, bee-eaters have a number of other foraging peculiarities. Carmine Bee-eaters come from miles away to a bush fire and hawk fleeing insects in and out of the smoke. They specialise particularly upon grasshoppers and locusts, and in the Inundation Zone of the River Niger, in Mali, Carmines migrate in time with swarms of migratory locusts, desert locusts and other grasshoppers, feeding upon them. Carmine Bee-eaters follow people, tractors and grazing mammals, catching insects disturbed from the grass, and they have the engaging habit of riding on the back of an Ostrich, bustard, stork, Secretary-bird, goat, camel, antelope, zebra or warthog, dashing away every few moments to catch an insect put to flight, and returning to incapacitate it by beating it against the antelope's horns or the Ostrich's back.

Even more remarkable an association between bird and beast is that of White-throated Bee-eaters and forest squirrels in West Africa. This bee-eater breeds along the borders of the Sahara, but in winter it has a completely different habitat and lives in and above the canopy of the rainforest. Like many other animals there, squirrels relish the nutritious flesh of oil-palm nuts, but to get at it they have to strip away the fibrous, oily skin. Narrow strips of skin rain down beneath a squirrel feeding in the crown of an oil palm, and bee-eaters, waiting animatedly in the fronds below, catch them as adroitly as they catch wasps. No other bee-eater ever eats vegetable matter, and perhaps the White-throated does so only because the strip is momentarily airborne.

In their desert breeding grounds White-throated Bee-eaters occasionally pounce upon small lizards, and in winter flocks spend much time feeding on high-flying ants and termites. Boehm's Bee-eater is an incipient fly specialist, and Blue-cheeked Bee-eaters catch large numbers of dragonflies. In Oman, European and Blue-cheeked Bee-eaters take numerous cicadas, perhaps because other sorts of insects are scarce. All bee-eaters plunge on to the surface of still water from time to time, doubtless to bathe, but at least three species are now known to take fish on rare occasions. It is an interesting thought that kingfishers will also sometimes eat bees!

Rollers

What *Coracias* rollers lack in the way of foraging skills and specialisations shown by bee-eaters and fishing kingfishers they make up for in the range of animal foods that they can successfully tackle. They, too, are sit-and-wait hunters, living in open countryside rather than closed forest, keeping watch from any elevated station – tree, lamp post, fence or building – and sailing down to land by the prey, which is grabbed in the bill and dismembered and eaten back at the perch. A characteristic of their diets is the inclusion of noxious prey that other birds generally leave alone, such as hairy caterpillars and warningly coloured grasshoppers, and rollers often eat scorpions, centipedes and small snakes. They will in fact eat practically all invertebrates encountered on the ground, including maggots, spiders, ants, wasps, worms, molluscs and mantises, and a wide range of vertebrates, too: lizards, toads, shrews, rodents and young birds. Rollers forage well into dusk, and sometimes feed at night near street lights. Rather surprisingly they do not eat vegetable matter, although in West Africa Blue-bellied Rollers do sometimes eat oil-palm fruits.

With regard to foraging, the broad-billed rollers (*Eurystomus*) are altogether different. They hunt on the wing, taking a large variety of beetles, bugs, crickets and wasps captured in powerful, falcon-like flight as the birds wheel, swoop and dash around the treetops. A few prey items are caught on the ground and eaten there, but all insects taken in the air are consumed on the wing, and the birds' beaks, short, deep and very wide, scoop up an insect and doubtless crush it in the instant.

Not much is known about the feeding behaviour of the Dollarbird and nothing about that of the Azure Roller, but the two African broad-billed rollers are unusual and fascinating. They exploit the huge swarms of winged termites and ants which, after rain, rise in smoky columns from every pore in the ground. Throughout much of the tropics, humid mornings produce thunderclouds by midday and rainstorms in the afternoon. Millions of termites and ants are on the wing towards dusk, and the rollers, having sat around all day not doing very much, then search out a swarm where tens or hundreds of other rollers will gather. Silently and purposefully the birds perform magnificent evolutions as, in the hour before nightfall, each one catches up to 800 insects until, replete, it retires to roost.

NESTING

Ovenbirds, weaverbirds, penduline tits – birds of many families in fact – go to great lengths to build the safest nests that they can. Coraciiform birds have settled for safe nests that do not need too much time and trouble to make, but are all too often not totally safe either: they nest in holes. Tree holes are the usual site for dacelonid kingfishers, but they excavate a nesting cavity themselves only if the woody tissue is rotten, friable or pulpy. They can probably never make a suitable hole in hard, living wood as woodpeckers and some other birds will, but if a pair of kingfishers finds such a hole untenanted they will take it over. Being territorial and quite aggressive in defence of their nesting territory, kingfishers often compete successfully with barbets, starlings or parakeets showing an interest in an old woodpeckers' hole at the time.

Any tree hole will do, provided it keeps the weather out, has a large enough entrance and is not so deep that the nestlings could not scramble out. A pair will use one hole for many years in succession, with only the minimum of refurbishment and never with any attempt to bring any nesting material in. Eggs are simply laid on whatever vegetable matter has accumulated over the years. Soft or rotting wood can be quite extensively excavated, however, and Sacred Kingfishers and others can successfully make a nest hole in the 'coconut matting' fibrous trunks of certain palms.

Many kingfishers use the earthen tree-nests of termites, structures up to a metre long built high up against the side of a rainforest tree trunk or among the foliage. Termite nests have crusty surfaces and aerated, flaky interiors, easily dug out by the kingfisher but firm enough to make a strong, safe enclosure for the eggs. Obligingly, the termites adapt to the destruction by putting a crust around the interior walls of the hole, which must make it almost ideal for the kingfishers. Some *Halcyon* species seem to nest exclusively in arboreal termitaria, although others are more adaptable and will use wood holes, termitaria and earthen banks equally.

Rollers nearly always use tree holes. Alcedinid and cerylid kingfishers and all bee-eaters nest in holes that they generally dig out for themselves in earthen banks, slopes or flat ground. With their hard sharp beaks used as a pick or chisel, the three families are about equally suited for the task, and, according to the nature of the earth, nest holes can be up to 2-3 m long. Generally they are more or less straight, and they always end in an ovoid chamber. No nesting material is used, and the eggs, which in all coraciiform birds are white and subspherical, are laid on bare earth. Tunnel diameter is no greater than is needed to accommodate the adult crouching with its head forward but running quite rapidly on its very short legs. There may be a piston effect, a bird helping to ventilate the chamber every time it enters or leaves. Certainly ventilation would seem to be needed, for bee-eater nests quickly accumulate a blackish carpet of trodden-down pellets and dropped insects which, with the whitewash of nestlings' faeces voided against the walls, give it a characteristic pungent ammoniacal odour. Older nestlings, particularly of kingfishers, whose droppings are more liquid and smelly than bee-eaters', squirt their faeces out of the tunnel entrance; but by then the damage is done, and kingfisher nests stink even more offensively than nests of bee-eaters.

If short legs and weak feet are adapted to scuttling along a tunnel, they also come in useful, at least for bee-eaters, in excavation. Earth is loosened by pecking with the bill; but to spade it out of the growing hole the bee-eater supports its weight on bill-tip and 'wrists', lifts its body and thus frees the legs to scrabble loose earth backwards with a bicycling action. Often several tunnels are started, but abandoned if stones or roots are encountered. In their definitive nest some bee-eater species construct an inclining burrow, with a hump before the terminal chamber to reduce the chance of eggs rolling out. Other bee-eaters make a declining burrow, which precludes accidental egg loss but can let rain in.

Clutch size varies from about four eggs in the tropics to eight at high latitudes. Most species lay their eggs at one-day intervals, and all of them start incubating as soon as the first egg is laid. It follows that the eggs hatch at one-day intervals, so that broods of kingfishers, bee-eaters and rollers are always staggered, with the oldest nestling up to a week older than the youngest. There is an important consequence: when food is scarce, only the older nestlings are fed. There is always squabbling among the nestlings for every insect or fish that their parents bring, and the oldest ones soon learn to scuttle out of the chamber and along the tunnel when they perceive a parent entering with food. Since two nestlings cannot enter the tunnel abreast, only one, usually the eldest unless it is already replete, wins the race. This selfish procedure ruthlessly ensures a cut-off point within the staggered brood. The 'haves' survive and the 'have-nots' starve and die, a simple mechanism that relates the number of survivors to the amount of food that their parents can provide in a given season.

Coraciiform birds hatch pink, naked, blind and helpless. Even before their eyes begin to open they become very mobile, moving forwards and backwards with equal facility on legs which at that age are proportionately well developed. Like a human being, and unlike all adult birds with their elevated tarsi (foot bones), young bee-eaters and kingfishers stand on their heels, which have horny papillae used like the ridged soles of running shoes. At about one week of age, their unopened feathers grow from the skin as long grey spines, and for a few days the nestlings are like wizened little grey hedgehogs. But soon the spines begin to sprout, and the feather vanes unfurl in almost the same glorious colours as those of the adults. Plumage grows fast, and in its fifth week of life the nestling is 10% or so heavier than its parents and ready to leave – but not until it is starved for a day or two by way of encouragement. As the youngsters take their first flights over the space of one or two days, the adults stay in the vicinity and call concernedly, accompanying the fledglings as their flying rapidly improves, marshalling them and bringing food in response to their begging. In spite of parental attention, however, this is a dangerous time, and many young kingfishers perish in their first water-diving attempts.

SOCIAL AND BREEDING BEHAVIOUR

Not many kingfishers, or rollers, have been studied at the depth that is needed to unravel the complexities of mating systems and demographic structure. But with a few exceptions they seem to be essentially monogamous, a pair breeding solitarily in a defended territory from which their young are in due course expelled and in which the pair, if not migratory, will probably base their whole lives. The exceptions – three species of kookaburras, Pied and Striped Kingfishers, and perhaps Blue-bellied Rollers – have a sort of qualified monogamy, and young of the year are not expelled from the parental territory. Instead they stay in it perhaps for years, and their social and even sexual roles become almost indistinguishable from those of their parents. This group-living system, with its proven corporate survival advantages, is known as cooperative breeding, and it is a system, with helpers-at-the-nest, which has been developed particularly by bee-eaters.

Although only seven bee-eater species (nos. 95, 98, 99, 101, 106, 109 and 111) have been studied at all adequately in this regard, it seems likely that in the family as a whole the degree of cooperative breeding correlates with nesting coloniality. In solitary-nesting bee-eater species the pair rears its young unaided, whilst among gregarious ones the majority of broods in the colony are brought up by their parents assisted by up to five helpers.

Why are some bee-eaters solitary breeders, when others are loosely gregarious or nest in compact colonies of a few dozen birds, or hundreds, or thousands, or (Rosy Bee-eaters) ten-thousands? A few cerylid kingfishers are weakly colonial; but why are no rollers or kingfishers strongly so? Ecologists usually answer such questions in terms of food availability. If a patch of land generates enough food to satisfy the needs of a pair of birds and their young, and is small enough for the pair to defend, then defended it will be and the species will be dispersed in solitary, territorial pairs. But birds whose food is distributed patchily (in space or time) will have to forage distantly and cannot defend their food supply; and, if the advantages of coloniality – strength in numbers – outweigh such benefits of solitary nesting as being concealed from predators, then colonial they will become. Weak-flying small bee-eaters live among bushes, long grass or in forest where a small patch suffices for their needs. Strong-flying large ones become colonial because they do not have to nest close to their food supply and it may be more important for them to find a safe, if distant, haven for breeding.

In short, large bee-eaters of open countryside tend to forage and nest gregariously; and colonial breeding, without territoriality and social exclusion, is one of the factors that promotes the evolution of helping-at-the-nest behaviour. Among cooperative-breeding bee-eaters and kingfishers, most helpers are the offspring from a previous nesting of the pair that they are currently helping. Sometimes a helper is more distantly related, however, and can even come from another colony. Helpers look exactly like breeders and are themselves sexually mature. They tend to be long-lived, and a bird often alternates between breeding and helping in successive years, as social and ecological circumstances demand. Helpers assist in all reproductive duties: they help to dig the nest, incubate the eggs and, most importantly, to feed the young. Bee-eater broods with helpers have the starvation cut-off point changed, such that fully twice as many fledge as from unhelped nests.

Bee-eater societies are complex in other regards as well. Red-throated Bee-eaters, for instance, live year-round in extended families or clans of about a dozen birds. A clan roosts together, and in the morning flies as a flock to a feeding territory of a few hectares, 2-3 km away. Clan members spend the day foraging around the territory, each bird keeping close to its mate and helper sons and daughters and in somewhat looser touch with other members. The clan defends its territory against incursion by bee-eaters from other clans. In autumn, about the end of the summer rainy season, clans repair to their breeding cliff and dig new nest holes, or refurbish old ones, while the earth is still fairly moist and soft. Then they leave the immediate area, but return in December as the prelude to egg-laying in January. A clan may embrace two to four breeding pairs and their helpers. Altogether there may be 100 or more nest holes and pairs or breeding units of birds in the colony, and a perpendicular cliff is riddled with definitive nest holes and 'false starts' in an area of only 2-3 m^2. Breeding members of one clan do not necessarily nest adjacently, but they are each other's 'closest friends' and there is a great deal of visiting at nests of other members of the clan.

By this time the colony is a frantically active crowd of bee-eaters coming and going, bickering, chasing, displaying, copulating, males and helpers bringing insects to 'courtship-feed' the incubating females. Society is not entirely nice and cooperative, however. A male spends much time guarding his nest hole from entry by a non-clan female and guarding his own female when out of the nest to ensure that no other male copulates with her. At the same time the male in question has an eye to the main chance and will chase and copulate with any other unguarded female if he can. Nor are females entirely innocent. Females constantly visit other nest holes in the colony, and will lay an egg in another pair's clutch if opportunity affords. Many more fascinating details of White-fronted Bee-eater society are given by Emlen (1990), Emlen and Wrege (1991), and Wrege and Emlen (1991).

Laughing Kookaburras and Pied Kingfishers have similarly complex societies with helping behaviour, and their systems, too, are essentially selfish rather than altruistic. Although kingfishers and rollers are much less gregarious than some bee-eaters, there is every reason to suppose that their social behaviours are as interesting. They should be easier to study, for few birds are more conspicuous than the territorial pair of Woodland or Grey-headed or White-breasted Kingfishers chasing around the trees and displaying with ringing calls, pivoting on a treetop perch and flashing the patterned wings open and shut. As for rollers, they are equally vociferous and even more aggressively territorial, advertising their territories with patrolling flights intended to show off their striking plumage, and defending them with spectacular and intimidating rolling dives.

DISTRIBUTION AND DERIVATION

All five families are essentially tropical. One of them, Cerylidae, is mainly American, with five species in the American tropics, one in North America, one in Africa, one common to Africa and Asia and one in the Orient. In the other four families the great majority of species are Afrotropical (i.e. Africa south of the Sahara, Madagascar and southwest Arabia), or Oriental, or Australasian (i.e. Australia, New Zealand, New Guinea, and islands from Lesser Sundas and Moluccas to Solomons and Vanuatu). The table below emphasises the different foci of distribution, with dacelonid species mostly in Australasia, Alcedinidae in the Oriental and Afrotropical regions, and Meropidae and Coraciidae in the Afrotropics. Numbers between the main columns are of species shared between the regions shown to left and right. 'Other' species are: Dacelonidae, Mangrove Kingfisher (Red Sea to Samoa); Alcedinidae, Variable Dwarf Kingfisher (Philippines to Solomons) and River Kingfisher

	American	Afrotropical		Oriental		Australasian	Pacific	Other
Dacelonidae		7		15		28	5	1
Alcedinidae		8		9		3		2
Cerylidae	6	1	1	1				
Meropidae		14	3	5		1		1
Coraciidae		7		2	1	1		1

(Britain to Solomons); Meropidae, European Bee-eater (West Palearctic); and Coraciidae, European Roller (West Palearctic). Kingfisher distribution patterns can be seen more readily in Figure 6, which shows the numbers of dacelonids (6a) and alcedinids and cerylids (6b) in greater regional detail.

Whether the five families originated in those regions where they are found most abundantly today is open to question. It is a reasonable inference that they did, although quite a different picture might emerge if there had been much extinction elsewhere in the meantime. Dacelonidae, for instance, seem to have arisen in or around New Guinea, where many of what are thought to be rather primitive species live; but, if we knew that African forests had once held numerous other primitive dacelonids, we might infer that the family had arisen there and not in New Guinea.

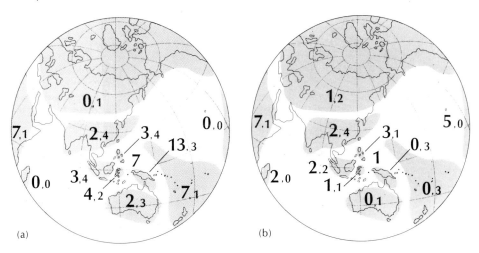

(a)　　　　　　　　　　　　(b)

Figure 6. Kingfisher distribution. In each of the shaded regions the bold figure is the number of endemic species (found nowhere else) and the small figure the additional number of non-endemic species. The bold number 7 in (a) and number 1 in (b), north of New Guinea, refer to island endemics not in any of the shaded regions (a) Dacelonidae, (b) Alcedinidae and Cerylidae.

Fossils could provide a clue, but hardly any fossil Coraciiformes are known and those that do exist add nothing to an understanding of the families' histories. The only other data to go on are relationships between species, geographical pathways that can be inferred from them, and deductions from relict and primitive distributions. Conclusions from such analyses in the past (Fry 1978, 1980a, 1980b, 1984) are as follows.

Kingfishers

The family Dacelonidae is indeed thought to have originated in that region where most species still live: the ancient tropical forests of northern Australasia and adjacent archipelagos. The Alcedinidae probably arose further west, in the south and southeast Asia of 40 or 50 million years ago, also as rainforest insectivores. Several lineages from each family evolved to occupy more open habitats: the dacelonids becoming predators of large arthropods and small vertebrates in tropical woodlands and savannas, with some propensity for feeding from shallow water, and the alcedinids taking to fishing and moving into all freshwater habitats. Some dacelonids radiated westward into Africa, several moved north, and many moved south into Australia and east into the Pacific. With alcedinids the main thrust was westward, but 5 or 10 million years ago some spread across the Bering Strait into the New World, where they gave rise to the Cerylidae. From the Americas, a green kingfisher crossed the Atlantic in the Pliocene (2-5 million years ago) to become the Pied Kingfisher, and a giant kingfisher followed it probably within the last million years and gave rise to the Giant and Crested Kingfishers.

Africa's rich kingfisher fauna seems to be the product of no fewer than eight separate invasions from the Orient and two from America. Fairly recently a southeast Asian dwarf kingfisher colonised Madagascar, not via Africa but by direct transoceanic flight; it became the Madagascar Pygmy Kingfisher. Madagascar's other kingfisher arrived very recently from Africa.

Bee-eaters

Again, the family seems to have arisen in the forests of southeast Asia. Adapting itself to open countryside, it invaded Africa long ago and there has given rise to most of its contemporary species. Whether the European and Bay-headed Bee-eaters, which are sister-species, ever had an African ancestry is uncertain; perhaps they have always been Mediterranean-Asian stock. The South African breeding population of European Bee-eaters is certainly very recent, perhaps little more than 100 years old. Incidentally, the European Bee-eater is monotypic (without any geographical variation or subspecies) because, inhabiting the temperate zone, it is necessarily migratory, and it happens that pairing takes place on the wintering grounds in Africa where the various Eurasian populations mix. A Spanish bird is as likely to find an Asian as a European mate; every year western and eastern genes thereby mix, which prevents the species from differentiating geographically. The corollary is that sedentary tropical species subspeciate easily.

Of the four *Merops* bee-eaters in southeast Asia, two are also found in Africa while two (Bay-headed and Blue-throated) are endemic. Only one kind inhabits Australasia, the Rainbow Bee-eater. It is clearly derivative of the Blue-cheeked/Madagascar/Blue-tailed Bee-eater complex (which has evolved not so much in Africa as in African, Arabian and Asiatic hot deserts), and the Blue-throated Bee-eater is quite closely allied to it, too. Obviously the genus *Merops* in the Orient and Australia has come from the west.

Rollers   With only 12 species and two genera, one generalised and one specialised, the geographical radiation of rollers is not easy to interpret. *Coracias* is largely African; *Eurystomus* is half African, half Oriental/Australasian. As with bee-eaters and kingfishers, one species is fully European in its range. The presence of two other roller families adjacently to Africa, in the Comoros and Madagascar, suggests that the Coraciidae is primitively African, not Asiatic.

ISLAND RARITIES

No species of kingfishers, bee-eaters or rollers with mainland distributions are endangered (but some Madagascan ground-rollers may well be). Island species and races of bee-eaters and rollers, such as the Azure and Celebes Rollers and the Bay-headed Bee-eater of the Andaman Islands, are probably not in any great danger of extirpation either, being inhabitants of open countryside. Some island kingfishers, however, are greatly endangered; indeed, two, the Miyako Kingfisher *Halcyon (cinnamomina) miyakoensis* and the Gambier Kingfisher *H. (tuta) gambieri*, are extinct. The Miyako's close relative, *H. c. cinnamomina* of Guam Island, is teetering on the brink and may already be extinct in the wild, although there is a small captive breeding population. The Ponapé Island *H. c. reichenbachii* has become scarce and its population may possibly be less than 1,000 strong, which is certainly the case with the Niau Kingfisher *H. gertrudae* and may be also with the Marquesas Kingfisher *H. godeffroyi*. Twenty years ago there were fewer than 100 Pacific Kingfishers *H. t. tuta* on Bora Bora Island, and, although the subspecies is said to be plentiful still on other islands, it is extinct on Tupai Island. Another subspecies, *H. t. ruficollaris*, confined to Mangaia Island, is very much at risk. Difficult as the task would be, all of these isolated-island forest-dwelling birds should be closely monitored, and thought given to setting aside large woodland reserves for them.

One of the most striking kingfishers in the world, the large, red-billed, orange, purple and olive Moustached Kingfisher *Actenoides bougainvillei* is known only from Bougainville and Guadalcanal Islands in the Solomons. One subspecies has not been seen for 40 years and the other for 60. Bougainville is a large island; so are Luzon and Mindanao in the Philippines, Halmahera, Ceram, New Britain and many others with their own endemic kingfishers, inhabitants of native forest and hence very much at risk.

It would be a pity to conclude our introduction to such lovely birds pessimistically, by suggesting that the world may lose a dozen of them in the next 20 or 30 years. Instead we conclude on an optimistic note. Kingfishers are all easy to save, by conserving their habitats and by captive-breeding: what a wonderfully worthwhile task, to get out there and do it.

PLATES 1–40

PLATE 1   SULAWESI ORNATE KINGFISHERS

1 Celebes Green Kingfisher *Actenoides monachus*   **Text page 107**

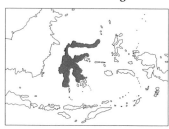

Sulawesi (Indonesia): lowland forest.
a Adult male *A. m. monachus* (north Sulawesi): red bill, blue crown and cheeks, green back, wings and tail, rufous collar and underparts.
b Adult female *A. m. monachus*: red bill, rufous cheeks.
c Juvenile *A. m. monachus*: yellowish-horn bill, rufous cheeks.
d Adult male *A. m. capucinus* (east and south Sulawesi): black head.

2 Regent Kingfisher *Actenoides princeps*   **Text page 107**

Sulawesi (Indonesia): montane forest.
a Adult male *A. p. princeps* (northeast Sulawesi): yellowish bill and collar, blue head, buff-scalloped brown back and wings, finely barred pale underparts.
b Adult female *A. p. princeps*: buffy eyebrow and moustachial stripe.
c Adult female *A. p. regalis* (southeast Sulawesi): orange bill, greenish crown and rump, rufous collar; no bars on back, few on underparts. (Male *A. p. regalis* unknown.)
d Adult male *A. p. erythrorhamphus* (central Sulawesi): red bill, rufous collar.
e Juvenile *A. p. princeps*: bill dark brown with pale tip; heavily scalloped and barred.

PLATE 2   SPOTTED KINGFISHERS

4 Hombron's Wood Kingfisher *Actenoides hombroni*   **Text page 110**

Mindanao (Philippines): montane forest.
a Adult male: red bill, blue head, rufous collar and underparts, blue-green back, wings and tail.
b Adult female: red bill, dull crown, buff-spotted olive back
   and wings.

5 Spotted Wood Kingfisher *Actenoides lindsayi*   **Text page 111**

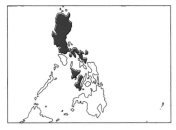

Philippines: undisturbed forest.
a Adult male *A. l. lindsayi* (north Philippines): black-and-
   yellow bill, rufous cheeks, collar and throat, blue moustache, heavily buff-spotted green back, pale underparts
   with green scallops.
b Adult female *A. l. lindsayi*: cheeks and throat whitish.
c Juvenile male *A. l. lindsayi*: buffy cheeks, turquoise eyebrow and moustache.
d Adult male *A. l. moseleyi* (central Philippines): blues and
   greens darker, and more heavily spotted.

6 Rufous-collared Kingfisher *Actenoides concretus*   **Text page 112**

Burma to Sumatra and Borneo: lowland forest.
a Adult male *A. c. concretus* (Malaysia, Sumatra): yellowish bill, rufous collar and breast, blue moustache, back,
   wings and tail, pale belly.
b Adult female *A. c. concretus*: differs from female Spotted
   Wood Kingfisher in having plain underparts.

PLATE 3   PARADISE KINGFISHERS (1)

7 Common Paradise Kingfisher *Tanysiptera galatea*

Text page 113

Moluccas (Indonesia) and New Guinea: lowland forest.

a Adult *T. g. galatea* (west New Guinea): red bill, blue upperparts, white underparts, long blue tail.

b Juvenile *T. g. galatea*: brown bill and upperparts, scalloped underparts; long superciliary stripe, rufous on very young bird, becoming pale blue on older one (shown here).

c Adult *T. g. rosseliana* (Rossel Island): white tail.

d Adult *T. g. naïs* (south Moluccas): bright blue upperparts, silvery-blue eyebrow and lesser wing-coverts.

e Adult *T. g. ellioti* (Kofiau Island): tail white, central feathers broad.

f Adult *T. g. sabrina* (Kayoa Island): white patch on back.

g Adult *T. g. emiliae* (Rau Island): crown silver-blue, crested; upper back white.

h Adult *T. g. riedelii* (Biak Island): pale blue head, stout bill. Sometimes regarded as a distinct species.

8 Numfor Paradise Kingfisher *Tanysiptera carolinae*

Text page 116

Numfor Island, Indonesian New Guinea: forest and wooded farmland.

The only paradise kingfisher on Numfor Island, where the adult is unmistakable. The juvenile (not shown) is also distinctive: head, back and wings dark blue, rump white but tail blackish, underparts mainly rufous.

PLATE 4   PARADISE KINGFISHERS (2)

9 Aru Paradise Kingfisher *Tanysiptera hydrocharis*   Text page 117

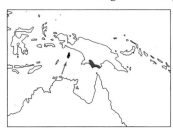

Aru Islands (Indonesia) and south New Guinea: rainforest.
a Adult: like the Common Paradise Kingfisher (Plate 3), with which it occurs in south New Guinea, but smaller, with slight differences in the crown and tail (see text).
b Juvenile: not safely distinguishable from juvenile Common Paradise Kingfisher, but underparts appear striped rather than scalloped.

10 Buff-breasted Paradise Kingfisher *Tanysiptera sylvia*   Text page 118

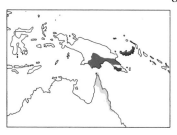

Australia and south New Guinea: forest.
a Adult *T. s. sylvia* (northeast Australia, winters in New Guinea): white spot on back, white rump, orange underparts.
b Juvenile *T. s. sylvia*: white mark on back separates it from juvenile Common Paradise (Plate 3) and Aru Paradise Kingfishers.
c Adult *T. s. leucura* (Umboi Island) (and *T. s. nigriceps*, not shown, New Britain): cap and scapulars black, underparts pale; tail white on *leucura*, blue and white on *nigriceps*.

11 Red-breasted Paradise Kingfisher *Tanysiptera nympha*   Text page 120

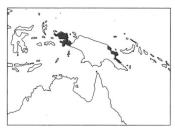

North New Guinea: lowland forest.
a Adult: blackish crown, back and wings, pink rump.
b Juvenile: bill orange with brown saddle; underparts tinged pink.

12 Brown-headed Paradise Kingfisher *Tanysiptera danae*   Text page 121

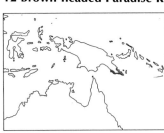

East New Guinea: lowland forest.
a Adult: upperparts mainly rufous; bright pink rump.
b Juvenile: bill orange with brown saddle, rump rufous, underparts rather plain.

PLATE 5   THREE ABERRANT KINGFISHER GENERA

13 Lilac Kingfisher *Cittura cyanotis*   **Text page 122**

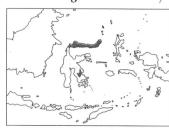

Sulawesi (Indonesia): lowland forest.

a Adult male *C. c. cyanotis* (north Sulawesi): red bill, brown back and blue wings with whitish line between them, rufous rump and tail. Adult female (not shown) has mask and upperwing-coverts black, not blue.

b Adult female *C. c. sanghirensis* (Sangihe Islands): forehead black, ear-coverts long, stiff, bright lilac, back rufous-brown, breast mauve.

14 Hook-billed Kingfisher *Melidora macrorrhina*   **Text page 123**

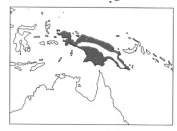

New Guinea: lowland forest.

a Adult male *M. m. macrorrhina* (Western Papuan Islands): heavy bill, spotted blue crown, white collar and underparts, buff-spangled back. Feeds on ground at dusk, sings at night.

b Adult female *M. m. macrorrhina*: forehead yellowish, underparts buffy.

15 Shovel-billed Kingfisher *Clytoceyx rex*   **Text page 125**

New Guinea: lowland and hill forest.

a Adult male *C. r. rex* (most of New Guinea): massive pale conical bill, often caked with mud, dark head, back and wings, rufous collar and underparts, blue rump and tail. Forages in leaf-litter and soil.

b Adult female *C. r. rex*: rufous tail.

PLATE 6   KOOKABURRAS (1)

16 Banded Kingfisher *Lacedo pulchella*   **Text page 127**

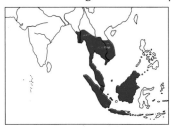

Southeast Asia: lowland forest.

a Adult male *L. p. pulchella* (peninsular Malaysia, Sumatra, Java): red bill, rufous forehead and cheeks, bright blue cap, black back, wings and tail heavily banded with bright blue, whitish underparts. Constantly raises and lowers crest, slowly and evenly.

b Adult female *L. p. pulchella*: black-and-rufous-banded upperparts are shrike-like, but red bill makes it unmistakable.

c Adult male *L. p. melanops* (Borneo): forehead and cheeks black.

17 Rufous-bellied Kookaburra *Dacelo gaudichaud*   **Text page 128**

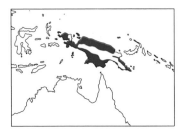

New Guinea: forest and woodland.

a Adult male: large whitish bill, black cap and back, white collar, blue wings, rump and tail, rufous underparts. Territorial, noisy and conspicuous.

b Adult female: tail rufous.

18 Spangled Kookaburra *Dacelo tyro*   **Text page 130**

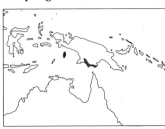

Aru Islands and New Guinea: forest and woodland.

Adult *D. t. tyro* (Aru Islands): black-and-white bill, buff-spotted head and mantle, black scapulars, blue wings, rump and tail, whitish underparts.

D. t. archboldi (not shown) (New Guinea): underparts buffy.

16a

16b

16c

17a

17b

18

PLATE 7   KOOKABURRAS (2)

19 Blue-winged Kookaburra *Dacelo leachii*　　　　　Text page 131

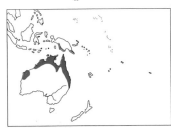

Australia and New Guinea: woodland.
a Adult male *D. l. leachii* (Broom to Cooktown and Brisbane): crow-sized; white or yellowish eye, whitish head and underparts, blue wings, rump and tail. Loud song. Often in small territorial flocks.
b Adult female *D. l. leachii*: rufous tail.
c Wing pattern conspicuous in flight.
d Adult *D. l. cliftoni* (west Australia): white head.
e Adult female *D. l. intermedia* (New Guinea): streaked head, blackish back, unbarred underparts (same on blue-tailed male, not shown).
f Adult female *D. l. cervina* (Northern Territory coast): streaked head, dark back, buffy breast (same on blue-tailed male, not shown).

20 Laughing Kookaburra *Dacelo novaeguineae*　　　　　Text page 133

Australia: woods, farms, parks, gardens.
a Adult male *D. n. novaeguineae* (Australia except Cape York Peninsula): crow-sized; whitish head and under-parts, dark eye and mask, dark back and wings with only little pale blue in wing-coverts and rump, rufous tail. Female (not shown) is like male but has even less blue in rump. Loud laughing song. In pairs or loose flocks.
b In flight looks darker than Blue-winged Kookaburra.

19a

19d

19b

19e

19c

19f

20a

20b

AH.

PLATE 8   MOUSTACHED AND WHITE-RUMPED KINGFISHERS

3 Moustached Kingfisher *Actenoides bougainvillei*   **Text page 109**

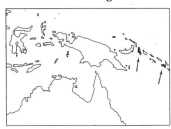

Bougainville Island (Papua New Guinea) and Guadalcanal Island (Solomons): forest. Very rare.

a Adult male *A. b. bougainvillei* (Bougainville Island): red bill, rufous head, mantle and underparts, blue moustache, eye-stripe, back, wings and tail, pale blue rump.

b Adult female *A. b. bougainvillei*: back olive-green.

c Adult female *A. b. excelsus* (Guadalcanal Island): pale underparts. Male is not known.

21 White-rumped Kingfisher *Halcyon fulgida*   **Text page 136**

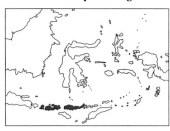

Lesser Sunda Islands (Indonesia): forest.

Barely known, but must be unmistakable: red bill and eye-ring, black head, blue back, wings and tail, snow-white rump and underparts.

3a

3b

3c

21

PLATE 9   STORKBILLS AND RUDDY KINGFISHER

22 Stork-billed Kingfisher *Halcyon capensis* Text page 137

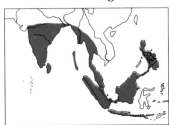

South and southeast Asia: rivers, lakes, wooded seashores.
a Adult *H. c. capensis* (India, Sri Lanka): large red bill, grey head, buffy collar and underparts, blue back, wings and tail, azure rump, red feet.
b Adult *H. c. intermedia* (Nicobar Islands): head buff.
c Adult *H. c. gigantea* (Sulu Islands): head, collar and underparts white.
d Adult *H. c. malaccensis* (Malay Peninsula): dark grey cap, rufous-buff collar and underparts.

23 Celebes Stork-billed Kingfisher *Halcyon melanorhyncha* Text page 139

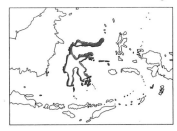

Sulawesi (Indonesia): creeks, wooded seashores.
a Adult *H. m. melanorhyncha* (Sulawesi): large black bill, whitish head and underparts, dusky face, dark back, wings and tail, white rump, dark red feet.
b Adult *H. m. dichrorhyncha* (Banggai Islands): bill largely red.

24 Brown-winged Kingfisher *Halcyon amauroptera* Text page 140

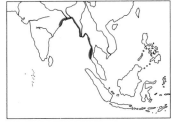

Southeast Asia: mangrove, creeks and rivers.
Lacks the capped appearance of many races of the Stork-billed Kingfisher, and differs from that species in having dark brown back, wings and tail.

25 Ruddy Kingfisher *Halcyon coromanda* Text page 141

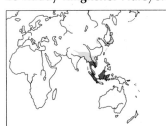

Japan, Taiwan and southeast Asia: montane forest, coastal woods, mangrove.
A secretive, rather uncommon migratory kingfisher, told by its lilac-washed rufous plumage, silvery-blue rump, and red bill and legs. Race shown is *H. c. coromanda*; eight other races differ in rufous and lilac hues and in size. Sexes alike; juveniles darker and less violaceous.

22a

22b

22c

22d

23a

23b

24

25

AH.

PLATE 10   MAINLY ASIATIC HALCYONS

26 White-breasted Kingfisher *Halcyon smyrnensis*   Text page 143

Turkey to Philippines: woods, farms, gardens, palms, forested coasts.

a Adult *H. s. smyrnensis* (Turkey to northwest India): chestnut head and belly, white throat and breast, red bill, bright blue back, wings and tail. Noisy; perches conspicuously on treetop, post or palm frond.

b Strongly patterned wings are conspicuous in flight.

c Adult *H. s. gularis* (Philippines): only the throat is white.

27 Java Kingfisher *Halcyon cyanoventris*   Text page 145

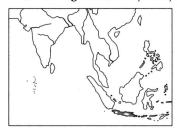

Java and Bali: woods, paddyfields, scrub.

a Adult: an easy-to-watch dark-headed halcyon with deep rufous collar and breast, purple body, bright blue in wings and tail. Noisy.

b Black-tipped white primaries show in flight but not at rest.

28 Chocolate-backed Kingfisher *Halcyon badia*   Text page 146

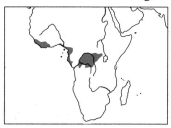

Africa: lowland rainforest.

a Adult: small; red bill, dark chestnut upperparts, white underparts, bright azure rump, and azure in wings and tail.

b In flight, brilliant blue rump and speculum, contrasting with dark upperparts, make the bird distinctive.

29 Black-capped Kingfisher *Halcyon pileata*   Text page 147

Asia: forested rivers and streams, creeks, palms, bamboos, paddyfields, wooded seashores.

a Adult: large red bill, black head, white collar and throat, purple-blue back, rump and tail, black shoulders, pale rufous underparts.

b In flight a very conspicuous white patch in wing; underwing-coverts pale rufous.

c Juvenile: duller and buffier; small buff loral spot, scaly breast.

PLATE 11   AFRICAN HALCYONS (1)

30 Grey-headed Kingfisher *Halcyon leucocephala*   **Text page 149**

Africa: thorny and grassy woodland.

a Adult female *H. l. leucocephala* (northern tropics): red bill, pale grey head and breast, rufous belly, black back, black and azure-blue wings, bright blue rump and tail.

b Adult male *H. l. leucocephala*: usually brighter and cleaner-looking than female; black parts glossy, not matt; breast whiter (at least in Ghana). Species is migratory; sings often, but song weak, a trill.

c Juvenile *H. l. leucocephala*: dusky bill, scaly head and breast, pale rufous or buff belly.

d Adult *H. l. actaeon* (Cape Verde Islands): head whitish, underparts pale orange.

e Adult *H. l. pallidiventris* (southern tropics): head and belly paler than on *leucocephala*.

31 Brown-hooded Kingfisher *Halcyon albiventris*   **Text page 152**

Africa: woodland, bushy grassland, cultivation.

a Adult male *H. a. albiventris* (Cape Province, Natal): red bill, brown-striped pale head, breast and belly, black back, black and turquoise wings and tail, bright blue rump. Female (not shown) has browner back and streakier crown and underparts.

b Juvenile *H. a. albiventris*: dusky bill, streaky hindneck, back of very young birds scalloped with buff.

c Adult female *H. a. vociferans* (Zimbabwe, Transvaal): paler and more lightly streaked than *albiventris*; white collar. Male (not shown) has blacker back.

PLATE 12   AFRICAN HALCYONS (2)

32 Striped Kingfisher *Halcyon chelicuti*

Text page 154

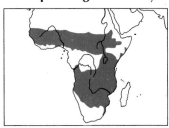

Africa: dry woodlands, thornbush.

Adult male *H. c. chelicuti* (most of sub-Saharan Africa) (illustrated): small and inconspicuous, but at times sings constantly and displays on treetop with outstretched, pied wings. Heavily striped crown, whitish collar and underparts, dark mantle, blue back and rump, greenish tail, striped flanks, bill with red base. Female (not shown) is browner, rather less streaky. Juvenile (not shown) is buffier, with hardly any blue.

33 Blue-breasted Kingfisher *Halcyon malimbica*

Text page 155

Africa: rainforest and dense woods.
a Adult *H. m. malimbica* (Cameroon to Uganda and Zambia): large; ringing voice; red-and-black bill, blue hindneck and breast, black mantle and shoulders, blue rump and tail, much blue in wing.
b Juvenile *H. m. malimbica*: green wash on crown, buffy wash on flanks.

34 Woodland Kingfisher *Halcyon senegalensis*

Text page 157

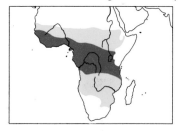

Africa: woodlands, gardens.
a Adult *H. s. senegalensis* (northern tropics): much more widespread and familiar than Blue-breasted Kingfisher, and told from it by having mantle and scapulars grey-blue (not black) and breast grey-white (not blue). Song a ringing trill, uttered often. Pair displays on treetop, turning from side to side with outstretched wings and singing. Underside of wing white. Migratory.
b Juvenile *H. s. senegalensis*: dusky bill; head and breast finely vermiculated.
c Adult *H. s. cyanoleuca* (southern Africa): black wedge behind eye.

35 African Mangrove Kingfisher *Halcyon senegaloides*

Text page 159

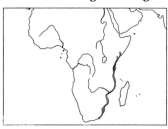

Africa: east coast mangrove and woodland.
Adult: bill all red and larger than on Woodland Kingfisher; underside of wing white, with small black patch at 'wrist'.

32

33a

33b

34a

34b

34c

35

PLATE 13   BLUE-AND-WHITE HALCYONS (1)

36 Black-sided Kingfisher *Halcyon nigrocyanea*   **Text page 161**

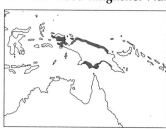

New Guinea: forest, forested waterways.
a Adult male *H. n. nigrocyanea* (west New Guinea): blue and black, with white chin, white breast spot.
b Adult female *H. n. nigrocyanea*: white belly.
c Juvenile male *H. n. nigrocyanea*: creamy throat and breast spot, rufous breast and belly, blackish sides.
d Juvenile female *H. n. nigrocyanea*: whitish underparts, pale rufous breast, black sides.
e Adult male *H. n. stictolaema* (south New Guinea): white-speckled throat, black-speckled flanks.
f Adult male *H. n. quadricolor* (north New Guinea): chestnut belly.

37 Winchell's Kingfisher *Halcyon winchelli*   **Text page 162**

Philippines: forest.
a Adult male *H. w. winchelli* (Basilan Island): blue upperparts, white underparts, rufous loral spot and collar.
b Adult female *H. w. winchelli*: pale orange wash on breast.
c Adult female *H. w. nesydrionetes* (Tablas, Sibuyan and Rombon Islands): orange wash on breast (male, not shown, like male *H. w. winchelli*).
d Juvenile *H. w. winchelli*: cheeks and back blackish, collar and breast freckled.

38 Moluccan Kingfisher *Halcyon diops*   **Text page 164**

Northern Moluccas (Indonesia): forest, woods, gardens, mangrove.
a Adult male: dark blue head, wings and tail, light blue back and rump, white loral spot, collar and underparts.
b Adult female: no white collar; mantle dark blue; broad breast-band.
c Juvenile male and female: rufous loral spot and collar; breast often fawnier than shown.
d In flight, adult shows pale blue rump and white patch in wing.

PLATE 14   BLUE-AND-WHITE HALCYONS (2)

39 Lazuli Kingfisher *Halcyon lazuli*   **Text page 165**

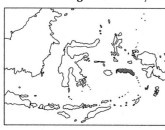

Southern Moluccas: forest, mangrove.
a Adult male: pale blue, with dark blue ear-coverts, wings and tail, white loral spot, incomplete collar, and breast.
b Adult female: pale blue breast.
c Juvenile male and female: buffy loral spot, white collar freckled with blackish, throat buffy, breast speckled.

40 Forest Kingfisher *Halcyon macleayii*   **Text page 166**

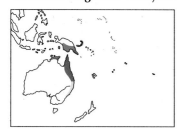

Australia and New Guinea: open forest and waterside woods.
a Adult male *H. m. macleayii* (Northern Territory): black ear-coverts, white collar.
b Adult female *H. m. macleayii*: hindneck blue, white collar incomplete.
c Juvenile male and female: like adult male, but most white parts washed with rufous.
d Adult male *H. m. incincta* (Queensland): back greenish.
e A white wing-patch shows in flight, larger on *macleayii* (illustrated) than on other races.

41 New Britain Kingfisher *Halcyon albonotata*   **Text page 168**

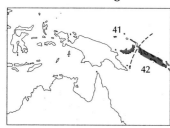

New Britain: lowland forest.
a Adult male: white mantle, back and rump.
b Adult female: white mantle, dark blue back and rump.
Juvenile male and female (not shown): see text.

42 Ultramarine Kingfisher *Halcyon leucopygia*   **Text page 169**

Bougainville and Solomon Islands: forest, woods, gardens, scrub.
a Adult male: dark blue with white collar and underparts, lilac rump and rufous undertail-coverts.
b Adult female: white back.
c Juvenile male: collar freckled, wing-coverts pale-tipped, underparts buffy. Juvenile female (not shown) the same but with whitish back.

43 Chestnut-bellied Kingfisher *Halcyon farquhari*   **Text page 170**

Vanuatu: upland woods and forest.
a Adult male: breast, belly and undertail-coverts orange.
b Adult female: belly white.

PLATE 15   YELLOWBILLS AND SOMBRE KINGFISHER

44 Lesser Yellow-billed Kingfisher *Halcyon torotoro*   **Text page 171**

New Guinea and Australia: lowland forest, plantations, mangrove.

a Adult male *H. t. torotoro* (New Guinea): yellow bill and legs, rufous head, pale rufous underparts, black patch on nape, dark green back, wings and tail.

b Adult female *H. t. torotoro*: dark crown.

c Adult male and female *H. t. ochracea* (D'Entrecasteaux Islands): rufous underparts (female lacks dark crown of female of nominate race).

45 Mountain Yellow-billed Kingfisher *Halcyon megarhyncha*   **Text page 173**

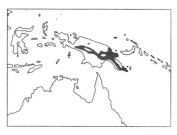

New Guinea: montane forest.

a Adult male *H. m. megarhyncha* (most of New Guinea): larger than Lesser Yellowbill, larger black mark in front of eye, ridge of bill dusky.

b Adult female *H. m. megarhyncha*: blackish crown, dusky culmen.

H. m. sellamontis (Huon Peninsula) (not shown) has an all-yellow bill, but differs from Lesser Yellowbill in body size and eye-patch size.

46 Sombre Kingfisher *Halcyon funebris*   **Text page 174**

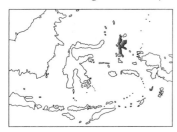

Northern Moluccas (Indonesia): woods, cultivation.

a Adult male: readily distinguished from Mangrove Kingfisher (of which the nominate race occurs in the Moluccas) (Plate 16) by the long white eyebrow.

b Adult female: much duller than male.

44a

44b

44c

45a

45b

46a

46b

PLATE 16   MANGROVE KINGFISHER (1)

47 Mangrove Kingfisher *Halcyon chloris* (See also Plate 17).   **Text page 175**

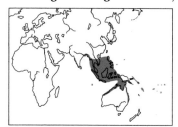

Red Sea coasts to Samoa: mangrove, seashores, woods, cultivation.

Throughout its immense range the Mangrove Kingfisher varies geographically to such an extent that it is not practicable to characterise it in a few words. The 50 races are described in the text. Their habitats vary also: some races are restricted to mangrove, others occur commonly in gardens and woodland. Fortunately, nearly all of the races are sedentary, so only one will occur on any particular island or mainland coastline. Mangrove Kingfishers can be confused with several other species that live alongside them regionally, including Winchell's (37), Forest (40), New Britain (41), Lesser Yellow-billed (44), Sombre (46), Micronesian (48), Beach (49), Sacred (50), Timor (51) and Red-backed Kingfishers (52). The 14 races illustrated here and in Plate 17 have been chosen to show the range of plumage variation:

a Adult *H. c. abyssinica* (Red Sea).

b Adult *H. c. occipitalis* (Nicobar Islands).

c Adult *H. c. humii* (Bangladesh to Singapore and north-east Sumatra).

d Adult *H. c. sordida* (south New Guinea, north Australia).

e Adult *H. c. chloris* (Indonesia: Lombok and Sulawesi to west New Guinea).

f Juvenile *H. c. chloris*: juveniles of all races have most white parts faintly buff-washed, freckled neck and breast, and pale-tipped wing-coverts.

g Adult *H. c. albicilla* (southern Mariana Islands).

h Adult *H. c. matthiae* (St Matthias Islands): white-crowned variant.

i Adult *H. c. matthiae*: dark-crowned variant.

j Adult *H. c. tristami* (New Britain).

PLATE 17   MANGROVE KINGFISHER (2) AND ALLY

47 Mangrove Kingfisher *Halcyon chloris* (See also Plate 16)   **Text page 175**

k Adult male *H. c. alberti* (Bougainville and Solomon Islands).

l Adult female *H. c. alberti*: belly white, not rufous (and see text). Other sexually dimorphic races, most not illustrated, are *orii* (Rota Island), *amoena* (Rennell Island, Bellona Island), *brachyura* (Reef Islands), *vicina* (Duff Island), *santoensis* (Vanuatu), *vitiensis* (Fiji) and *pealei* (Samoa).

m Adult *H. c. ornata* (Santa Cruz and Tinakula Islands).

n Adult *H. c. utupuae* (Utupua Island).

o Adult *H. c. melanodera* (Vanikoro Island).

p Adult *H. c. juliae* (Vanuatu).

q Adult female *H. c. vitiensis* (Fiji).

48 Micronesian Kingfisher *Halcyon cinnamomina*   **Text page 181**

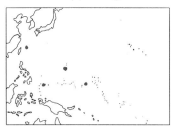

Pacific: Palau, Caroline and Guam Islands: woods.

a Adult male *H. c. cinnamomina* (Guam): rufous head and underparts, dark line through eye, blue-green upperparts.

b Adult female *H. c. cinnamomina*: underparts mainly white.

c Adult male and female *H. c. pelewensis* (Palau Islands): white neck and underparts.

47k

47l

47m

47n

47o

47p

47q

48a

48b

48c

PLATE 18 SACRED KINGFISHER AND ALLIES

49 Beach Kingfisher *Halcyon saurophaga*   **Text page 183**

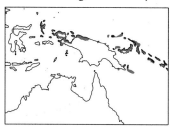

Northern Moluccas (Indonesia) to Solomon Islands: mangrove, beaches, reefs.
a Adult *H. s. saurophaga* (Moluccas to Solomons): large; black-and-white bill, white head and underparts, bright blue back, wings and tail.
b Adult *H. s. admiralitatis* (Admiralty Islands): crown varies from blue to white.

50 Sacred Kingfisher *Halcyon sancta*   **Text page 185**

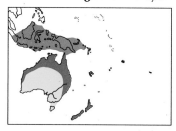

Australia, New Zealand (wintering in Indonesia, Solomons), Samoa: woods, parkland, scrub.
a Adult male *H. s. sancta* (Australia, Solomons): buffy suffusion in loral spot, collar and flanks. For distinctions from Mangrove Kingfisher, see text.
b Juvenile *H. s. sancta*: freckled cheeks, collar, breast and flanks.
c Adult male *H. s. recurvirostris* (Western Samoa): bill flattened dorsoventrally; collar and flanks often more cinnamon-washed than shown.

51 Timor Kingfisher *Halcyon australasia*   **Text page 188**

Lesser Sunda Islands: woodland.
a Adult male *H. a. australasia* (Lombok, Timor and Wetar): blue-green crown, rufous forehead, eyebrow, collar and underparts.
b Adult male *H. a. interposita* (Leti Islands): rufous crown.

52 Red-backed Kingfisher *Halcyon pyrrhopygia*   **Text page 189**

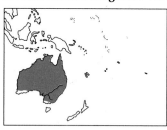

Australia: dry woodland, desert scrub.
a Adult male: stripy green crown and tertials, rufous back and rump.
b Adult female: duller than male, forehead streakier; collar and flanks sometimes buffier than shown.
c Juvenile: collar and breast buffy, dark-freckled; flanks sometimes buffy.

49a

49b

50a

50b

51a

51b

50c

52a

52b

52c

PLATE 19   PACIFIC FLAT-BILLED HALCYONS

53 Pacific Kingfisher *Halcyon tuta*   Text page 190

Society, Cook and Gambier Islands: forest, cultivation.
a Adult *H. t. tuta* (Society Islands): the only kingfisher in its range except on Tahiti, where 54 occurs.
b Juvenile *H. t. tuta*: distinguished from juvenile Tahiti Kingfisher by its pale eyebrow, blue back, and lack of breast-band.
c Adult *H. t. ruficollaris*: Mangaia Island, where the sole kingfisher.
d Adult *H. t. atiu*: Atiu Island, where the only kingfisher.
e Adult *H. t. gambieri*: Mangareva Island, where the only kingfisher.

54 Tahiti Kingfisher *Halcyon venerata*   Text page 192

Tahiti and Moorea: woods and gardens.
a Adult *H. v. venerata* (Tahiti): lack of white forehead, eyebrow and collar distinguishes it from nominate Pacific Kingfisher (53a).
b Juvenile *H. v. venerata*: brown and white; see 53b (above).
c Adult *H. v. youngi* (Moorea): pallid brown.

55 Niau Kingfisher *Halcyon gertrudae*   Text page 193

Niau Island (Tuamotu Archipelago): woods, cultivation. The sole kingfisher on Niau.

56 Marquesas Kingfisher *Halcyon godeffroyi*   Text page 194

Marquesas Islands: forest.
a Adult: there are no other kingfisher species in the Marquesas.
b Juvenile.

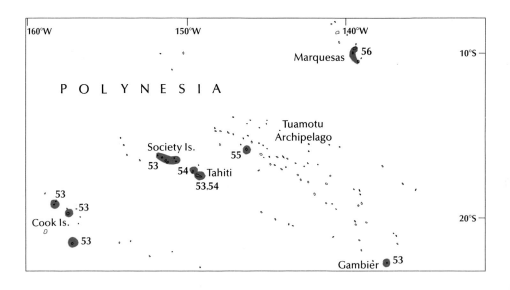

53a

53b

53c

53d

53e

54a

54b

54c

55

56a

56b

PLATE 20 DWARF AND PYGMY KINGFISHERS

57 African Dwarf Kingfisher *Ceyx lecontei*   Text page 195

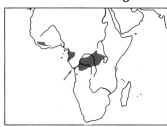

Africa: forest.
a Adult: tiny; red bill with square-ended tip, black fore-head, rufous lore, crown and underparts, dark blue back, wings and tail.
b Juvenile: bill and cheeks dusky, crown and back black, spangled with light blue.

58 African Pygmy Kingfisher *Ceyx pictus*   Text page 196

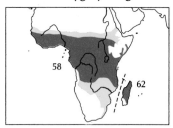

Africa: shrubby grassland, cultivation.
a Adult *C. p. pictus* (northern tropics): very small; banded blue crown, broad rufous eyebrow, lilac cheek.
b Adult *C. p. natalensis* (southern Africa): orange eyebrow wider than on *pictus,* blue spot on side of neck.

59 Oriental Dwarf Kingfisher *Ceyx erithacus*   Text page 198

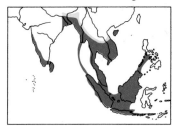

Southeast Asia: forest.
a Adult *C. e. erithacus* (India to Hainan and Sumatra): black-backed form: black spot on forehead, violaceous-orange head, rump and tail, blue-and-white neck mark, black back, blue wings, pale orange underparts.
b Adult *C. e. erithacus*: rufous-backed form.

60 Philippine Dwarf Kingfisher *Ceyx melanurus*   Text page 200

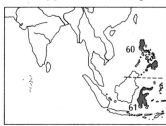

Philippines: lowland forest.
a Adult *C. m. melanurus* (Luzon, Polillo Islands): lilac-rufous, with black wings, black line on scapulars, and blue-and-white neck mark.
b Adult *C. m. platenae* (Basilan, Mindanao): lacks blue mark on neck; wing-coverts rufous.

61 Celebes Dwarf Kingfisher *Ceyx fallax*   Text page 201

Sulawesi: lowland forest. Map above.
a Adult *C. f. fallax* (Sulawesi): banded blue crown, broad rufous eyebrow, lilac cheek, brown back.
b Adult *C. f. sangirensis* (Sangihe Island): larger blue speckles on crown.

62 Madagascar Pygmy Kingfisher *Ceyx madagascariensis*   Text page 201

Madagascar: grassy woodland, scrub. Map above. Illustrated is the lilac-washed adult *C. m. madagascariensis*.

PLATE 21   VARIABLE DWARF KINGFISHER

63 Variable Dwarf Kingfisher *Alcedo lepida*   Text page 202

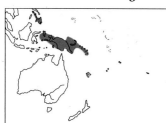

Philippines to Solomons: lowland forest.

a Adult *A. l. lepida* (southern Moluccas): red bill, orange loral spot, black head and wings spotted with dark blue, orange underparts, blue back, silvery-blue rump.

b Adult *A. l. cajeli* (Buru Island): loral spot and underparts yellow-orange, back silvery-blue.

c Adult pale-phase *A. l. margarethae* (southern Philippines): upperparts cobalt-blue, malar stripe orange, belly yellow. Dark-phase birds (not shown) have ultramarine-blue upperparts.

d Adult *A. l. mulcata* (New Hanover, New Ireland): bill black.

e Adult male *A. l. meeki* (Bougainville, Solomons from Choiseul to Santa Ysabel Islands): black bill, buffy-yellow loral spot, neck mark and underparts, pink feet. Female (not shown) has orange-yellow underparts.

f Adult male *A. l. dispar* (Admiralty Islands): silvery-blue back and rump, rufous breast, red feet.

g Adult female *A. l. dispar*: head mainly orange.

h Adult *A. l. sacerdotis* (New Britain): dusky upper mandible, ultramarine rump, pale belly and undertail-coverts.

i Adult *A. l. gentiana* (San Cristóbal Island): black bill, white loral spot and underparts.

For confusion species in various parts of the range of the Variable Dwarf Kingfisher, see text.

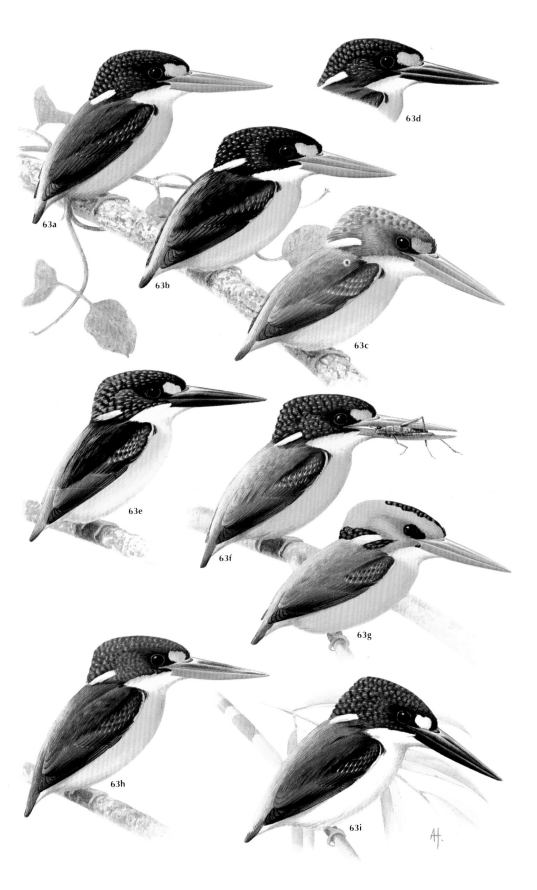

63a

63b

63c

63d

63e

63f

63g

63h

63i

PLATE 22   MALACHITE KINGFISHERS AND ALLY

64 White-bellied Kingfisher *Alcedo leucogaster*   **Text page 204**

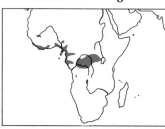

Africa: forest.

a Adult *A. l. leucogaster* (Nigeria to Angola): red bill, banded non-crested blue crown, ultramarine back, wings and tail, chestnut cheeks and underparts, latter white in midline.

b Juvenile *A. l. leucogaster*: bill black, mantle spangled like crown, speckled moustache.

c Adult *A. l. nais* (Principe Island): no rufous eyebrow, breast rufous.

d Juvenile *A. l. nais*: bill black with white tip, speckled moustache.

65 Malachite Kingfisher *Alcedo cristata*   **Text page 206**

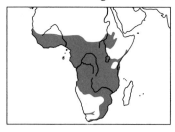

Africa: rank waterside vegetation, reeds.

a Adult *A. c. cristata* (south of Limpopo River): red bill, straggly crest of narrow blue-and-black-banded feathers, blue upperparts, rufous cheeks, pale rufous underparts.

b Adult *A. c. cristata*: raises forehead crest when excited or alarmed. *A. c. galerita* (tropics) (not shown) is like nominate *cristata* but with deep orange underparts.

c Juvenile *A. c. cristata*: black bill, dusky face, blackish back.

d Adult *A. c. thomensis* (São Tomé Island): short crown feathers, rufous cheeks and underparts, dark blue rump.

e Juvenile *A. c. thomensis*: blackish.

66 Madagascar Malachite Kingfisher *Alcedo vintsioides*   **Text page 208**

Madagascar and Comoro Islands: rank vegetation, reeds, mangrove.

A. v. vintsioides (Madagascar) is shown. Differs from Madagascar Pygmy Kingfisher (Plate 20) in its black bill, black-and-green crest, and dark blue upperparts.

PLATE 23   PHILIPPINE KINGFISHERS AND ALLIES

67 Silvery Kingfisher *Alcedo argentata*   **Text page 209**

Philippines: forest streams.
a Adult *A. a. argentata* (Negros, Panay, Basilan, Cebu, Dinagat, Siargao Islands): unmistakable; dark blue and white, with red feet and silvery line down back.
b Adult *A. a. flumenicola* (Samar, Leyte, Bohol Islands): creamy throat, purple breast.

68 Philippine Pectoral Kingfisher *Alcedo cyanopecta*   **Text page 209**

Philippines: forested streams, swamps, mangrove.
a Adult male *A. c. cyanopecta* (north Philippines): black-and-red bill, distinctive double breast-band.
b Adult female *A. c. cyanopecta*: single incomplete blue breast-band. It can be told from Variable Dwarf Kingfishers (Plate 21), which overlap on Sibuyan Island only, by its black (not red) upper mandible, small loral spot, and partial breast-band.
c Adult male *A. c. nigrirostris* (central Philippines): black bill, single complete breast-band, dark rufous belly. Female (not shown) like female of nominate race, but belly is darker.

69 Caerulean Kingfisher *Alcedo coerulescens*   **Text page 210**

Sumatra to Sumbawa Islands (Indonesia): streams in cultivated land, mangrove.
The only small kingfisher in its range without any rufous in its plumage. Adult male is shown; female is duller, with a less distinct breast-band.

70 Blue-banded Kingfisher *Alcedo euryzona*   **Text page 211**

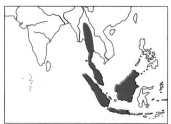

Southeast Asia: forest streams.
a Adult male *A. e. euryzona* (Java): blackish bill, dark blue upperparts with silvery back and rump, white underparts with blue breast-band.
b Adult female *A. e. euryzona*: red lower mandible, dark brown upperparts, orange underparts.
c Adult female *A. e. peninsulae* (Burma to Sumatra, Borneo): breast orange. Male (not shown) is like male of nominate race, but the breast-band is mottled.

PLATE 24   AZURE KINGFISHER AND ALLIES

71 Shining-blue Kingfisher *Alcedo quadribrachys*   Text page 213

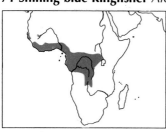

Africa: forested rivers, reeds, mangrove.
a Adult male *A. q. quadribrachys* (West Africa): black bill, dark blue upperparts, white throat, blue patch at side of breast, rufous breast and belly.
b Juvenile *A. q. quadribrachys*: white tip to bill, underparts pale, mottled.

72 Azure Kingfisher *Alcedo azurea*   Text page 214

Australia, New Guinea: wooded rivers and lakes, mangrove.
a Adult male *A. a. azurea* (east Australia): very like the African Shining-blue Kingfisher, but only three toes.
b Adult male *A. a. lessonii* (New Guinea): pale underparts.
c Adult male *A. a. ruficollaris* (north Australia): smaller but brighter than nominate race.

73 Bismarck Kingfisher *Alcedo websteri*   Text page 215

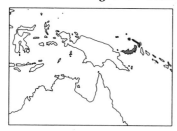

Bismarck Archipelago: forest streams.
One of the largest *Alcedos*. Sexes alike: adult (illustrated) uniformly blue above, white below.

74 Little Kingfisher *Alcedo pusilla*   Text page 216

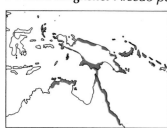

Australia, New Guinea, Solomons: wooded pools, swamps, mangrove.
a Adult *A. p. pusilla* (New Guinea, northeast Australia): tiny; dark blue upperparts, white underparts.
b Juvenile *A. p. pusilla*: duller blue, face blackish, freckled breast.
c Adult *A. p. bougainvillei* (west Solomon Islands): freckled breast.
d Adult *A. p. richardsi* (central Solomon Islands): blue breast-band.
e Juvenile *A. p. ramsayi* (Northern Territory, Australia): greyish-blue; freckled breast-band. Adult (not shown) has breast-patches forming a broken band.

71a

71b

72a

72c

72b

73

74a

74b

74c

74d

74e

PLATE 25   RIVER KINGFISHER AND ALLIES

75 Blue-eared Kingfisher *Alcedo menintinğ*   **Text page 217**

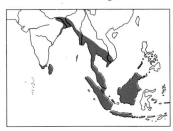

South and southeast Asia: forest streams, mangrove.
a Adult male *A. m. meninting* (Sumatra to west Philippines): red-and-black bill, banded crown, blue upperparts with brilliant back and rump, white throat and neck mark, orange underparts.
b Adult female *A. m. meninting*: more red on bill.
c Juvenile *A. m. meninting*: rufous ear-coverts, dusky breast.
d Adult male *A. m. rufigaster* (Andaman Islands): lighter blue, paler orange.

76 River Kingfisher *Alcedo atthis*   **Text page 219**

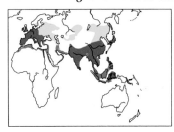

Europe to Solomons: clearwater streams, reeds, mangrove.
a Adult male *A. a. atthis* (Europe): black bill, rufous ear-coverts, greenish-blue malar stripe and upperparts with brilliant pale blue back and rump, rufous loral spot and underparts.
b Adult female *A. a. atthis*: reddish lower mandible.
c Adult male *A. a. hispioides* (Sulawesi, New Guinea, Bismarck Archipelago): ear-coverts and upperparts blue.

77 Half-collared Kingfisher *Alcedo semitorquata*   **Text page 222**

Africa: woodland streams and rivers, reeds.
  Adult male: black bill, blue upperparts and breast-patch, brilliant back and rump, buffy underparts. Female (not shown) has reddish base to lower mandible.

78 Great Blue Kingfisher *Alcedo hercules*   **Text page 223**

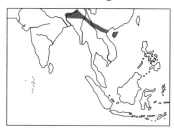

Sikkim to Hainan: forest streams.
  Adult male: large; stout black bill, banded crown, blue upperparts and breast-patch, rufous loral spot and underparts. Female (not shown) has red base to lower mandible.

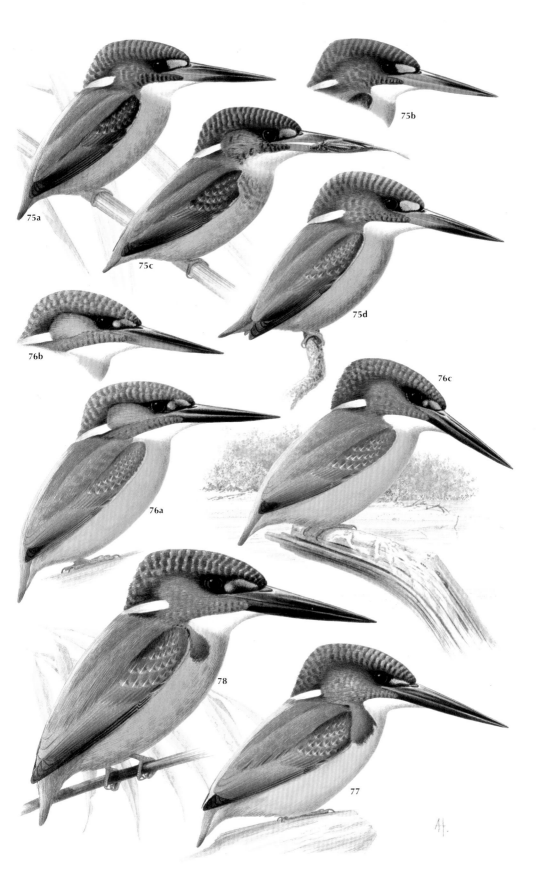

75a

75b

75c

75d

76b

76c

76a

78

77

PLATE 26   AMERICAN GREEN KINGFISHERS

79 American Pygmy Kingfisher *Chloroceryle aenea*　　　Text page 224

Tropical America: forest, and forest streams.
a Adult male *C. a. aenea* (South America): tiny; green upperparts, yellowish-rufous chin and collar, rufous underparts, white belly and undertail-coverts.
b Adult female *C. a. aenea*: green breast-band.
c Juvenile *C. a. aenea*: no breast-band; speckles on wings and flanks; rufous parts pale.

80 Green-and-rufous Kingfisher *Chloroceryle inda*　　　Text page 225

Tropical America: forest streams, swamps.
Like American Pygmy Kingfisher but four times as heavy.
a Adult male: narrow buffy collar, underparts wholly rufous, wings more spotted than in American Pygmy Kingfisher.
b Adult female: narrow buffy collar, green breast-band, rufous belly, wings more spotted than those of American Pygmy Kingfisher.

81 Green Kingfisher *Chloroceryle americana*　　　Text page 226

Tropical America: all brackish and freshwater habitats.
a Adult male *C. a. americana* (northern South America): green upperparts with white collar and spotted wings, white throat and belly, chestnut breast, barred flanks.
b Adult female *C. a. americana*: buffy throat and breast with speckled green breast-band.

82 Amazon Kingfisher *Chloroceryle amazona*　　　Text page 228

Tropical America: lowland rivers.
Like Green Kingfisher but three times as heavy.
a Adult male: green upperparts, shaggy crest, white collar, throat and belly, chestnut breast; differs from Green Kingfisher in having unspotted wings and streaked (not barred) flanks.
b Adult female: shaggy crest, white throat and breast with green patch at side, streaked flanks, wings not spotted.

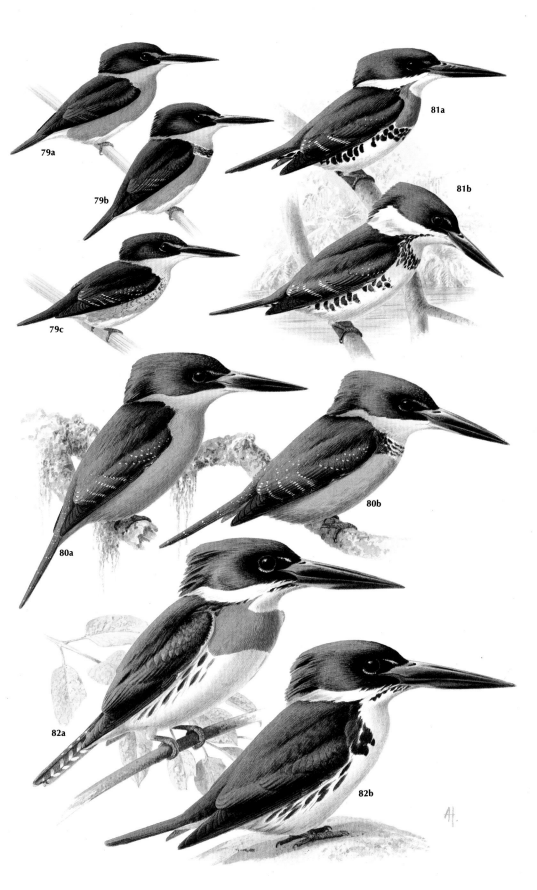

79a

79b

79c

81a

81b

80a

80b

82a

82b

PLATE 27   CRESTED KINGFISHERS (1)

83 Crested Kingfisher *Megaceryle lugubris*   **Text page 229**

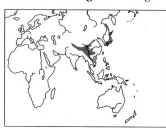

Afghanistan to Japan: turbulent mountain rivers.

a Adult male *M. l. lugubris* (Japan): unmistakable; pepper-and-salt upperparts, shaggy crest with two distinct white areas in it, white collar and underparts with rufous-speckled breast-band, barred tail.

b Adult male *M. l. lugubris*: white wing-lining.

c Adult female *M. l. lugubris*: moustache and breast-band of black speckles.

d Adult female *M. l. lugubris*: pale rufous wing-lining.

84 Giant Kingfisher *Megaceryle maxima*   **Text page 231**

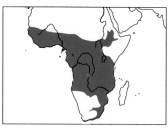

Africa: wooded rivers and lagoons.

a Adult male *M. m. maxima*: huge and unmistakable; loud call, shaggy crest, finely spotted blackish upperparts, chestnut breast, barred white belly.

b Adult male *M. m. maxima*: white wing-lining.

c Adult female *M. m. maxima*: black-speckled breast, unbarred chestnut belly and undertail-coverts.

d Adult female *M. m. maxima*: chestnut wing-lining.

83b

83d

83a

84d

83c

84c

84b

84a

PLATE 28 CRESTED KINGFISHERS (2)

85 Ringed Kingfisher *Megaceryle torquata*   **Text page 233**

Tropical America: rivers, lakes, mangrove.

a Adult male *M. t. torquata* (Mexico to Argentina): huge, shaggily crested; grey upperparts with white collar, rufous underparts with white undertail-coverts and wing-lining.

b Adult female *M. t. torquata*: grey breast-band, rufous undertail-coverts and wing-lining.

86 Belted Kingfisher *Megaceryle alcyon*   **Text page 234**

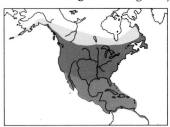

North America: rivers, lakes, ponds.

a Adult male: large, shaggily crested; grey upperparts and breast-band, white collar and belly.

b Adult female: rufous lower breast-band and flanks.

c Juvenile male: tawny breast-band.

d Juvenile female: tawny breast-band, and on older birds a pale rufous lower breast-band.

87 Pied Kingfisher *Ceryle rudis*   **Text page 236**

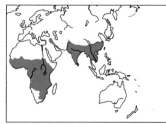

Africa, Asia: lakes, rivers, estuaries.

a Adult male *C. r. rudis* (Africa, Israel, Iraq): unmistakable, noisy, often gregarious, shaggily crested; pied above and below, double breast-band.

b Adult female *C. r. rudis*: single breast-band, deep at sides, broken in midline.

c In flight appears even more pied; commonly hovers when hunting.

85a

85b

86a

86c

86b

86d

87b

87a

87c

PLATE 29   ASIATIC BEARDED BEE-EATERS

88 Red-bearded Bee-eater *Nyctyornis amicta*   Text page 241

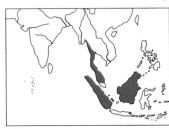

Southeast Asia: forest.
a Adult male: unmistakable; green, with decurved bill, pink forecrown, scarlet beard, and black-and-yellow underside of the tail.
b Adult female: less pink and more scarlet on forehead.
c Juvenile: throat and breast green, belly and underside of tail yellowish, tail lacks black tip.

89 Blue-bearded Bee-eater *Nyctyornis athertoni*   Text page 242

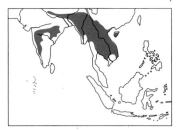

India to Indochina, Hainan: hill forest, dry woods.
a Adult *N. a. athertoni* (India to Indochina): green, with pale blue forehead and beard, green-streaked buff belly; long tail, green above, yellow below.
b Sailing flight on rather rounded wings.

90 Celebes Bee-eater *Meropogon forsteni*   Text page 244

Sulawesi (Indonesia): forest clearings.
a Adult male: slender bill, purple head and beard, green back and wings, and green-and-chestnut tail with long streamers; underside of tail russet.
b Adult female: forebelly dark red-brown (not purple).
c Juvenile: forehead and breast feathers green-fringed, tail lacks streamers.
d Chestnut in tail can be seen in flight; rather rounded wings.

PLATE 30   AFRICAN FOREST BEE-EATERS AND SWALLOWTAIL

91 Black-headed Bee-eater *Merops breweri*   Text page 246

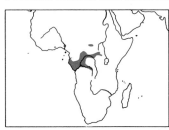

Africa: forest edges and clearings, savanna woodland.
a Adult: black head, crimson eye, green back, wings and long central tail feathers, narrow cinnamon breast-band, buff belly.
b Sailing flight, wings rounded, tail shows cinnamon.
c Juvenile: greenish crown, tail lacks streamers.

92 Blue-headed Bee-eater *Merops muelleri*   Text page 247

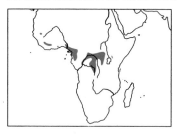

Africa: forest.
a Adult *M. m. muelleri* (Cameroon to west Kenya): white forehead, pale blue crown, black face, scarlet chin, chestnut back and wings, purple-blue tail and belly. Adult *M. m. mentalis* (not shown) (Mali to Cameroon) has dark blue forehead and crown, blue cheeks, and short clubbed tail-streamers.
b Juvenile *M. m. muelleri*: purple-blue parts are dusky turquoise, chestnut parts duller than on adult; chin bluish, usually with a few red barbs.

93 Black Bee-eater *Merops gularis*   Text page 249

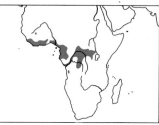

Africa: clearings in tall forest.
a Adult *M. g. gularis* (Sierra Leone to Nigeria): black, with scarlet chin and throat, streaked breast, pale blue eyebrow, belly, undertail-coverts and rump, rufous primaries. Adult *M. g. australis* (Cameroon, Zaïre, Angola) (not shown) lacks pale blue eyebrow.
b Juvenile *M. g. australis*: dull, greenish-black, throat pale orange, breast and belly unstreaked.

94 Swallow-tailed Bee-eater *Merops hirundineus*   Text page 251

Africa: mature savanna woodland.
a Adult *M. h. hirundineus* (Angola to South Africa): green upperparts, yellow throat, narrow blue breast-band, green breast, blue-green belly, long forked blue tail.
b Juvenile *M. h. hirundineus*: whitish throat, no breast-band.
c Adult *M. h. chrysolaimus* (West Africa): blue forehead and eyebrow, greenish tail.
d In flight, wings look green and rufous with black trailing edges; tail deeply forked, white-tipped.

91c

91a

91b

92a

92b

93b

93a

94d

94b

94a

94c

PLATE 31   AFRICAN LITTLE BEE-EATERS

95 Little Bee-eater *Merops pusillus* **Text page 253**

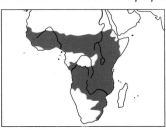

Africa: grassland.
a Adult *M. p. pusillus* (West Africa): small; green upper-parts, rufous in wings, yellow throat, red eye, black gorget, cinnamon upper breast, buffy belly; tail green and rufous, black-ended, sharp-cornered.
b Juvenile *M. p. pusillus*: breast greenish, faintly streaked, without a gorget; eye brown.
c Adult *M. p. cyanostictus* (Ethiopia, Kenya): pale blue eyebrow, narrow purple line above gorget.
d Adult *M. p. meridionalis* (Uganda, southern Africa): short blue eyebrow, narrow whitish line above gorget.

96 Blue-breasted Bee-eater *Merops variegatus* **Text page 255**

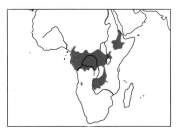

Africa: marshes, grassy hills, forest edge.
a Adult *M. v. bangweoloensis* (mainly Zambia): larger than Little Bee-eater, throat yellow becoming white at side of neck, greenish belly; wetter habitats.
b Adult *M. v. variegatus* (Congo Basin): blue gorget.
c Adult *M. v. lafresnayii* (Ethiopian highlands): larger; forehead, eyebrow and gorget deep blue, sides of neck white.
d Juvenile *M. v. lafresnayii*: breast green, streaky, without a gorget.

97 Cinnamon-chested Bee-eater *Merops oreobates* **Text page 257**

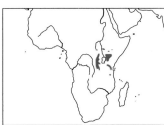

Montane East Africa: wooded hillsides, grassy clearings.
a Adult: green upperparts, red eye, throat yellow becoming white at side of neck, broad black gorget, cinnamon breast, dark buff belly.
b Adult in flight shows rufous primaries, wings with black trailing edge, tail with black wedges and white tip.

95a

95b

95c

95d

96a

96b

96c

96d

97b

97a

PLATE 32   AFRICAN RED- AND WHITE-THROATED BEE-EATERS

98 Red-throated Bee-eater *Merops bullocki*   Text page 259

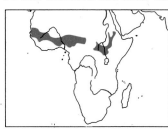

Northern tropics: wooded savannas, sandy cliffs.
a Adult *M. b. bullocki* (West Africa): green upperparts with buffy hindneck, scarlet throat, buff breast and belly, blue thighs and undertail-coverts; colonial, noisy.
b An uncommon variant has the throat bright yellow.
c Adult *M. b. frenatus* (Nile countries): blue streak above and below black mask.
d Wing with black trailing edge, tail showing warm buff.

99 White-fronted Bee-eater *Merops bullockoides*   Text page 262

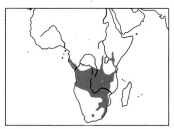

Southern tropics: wooded savannas, sandy cliffs.
a Adult: mealy-white forecrown, white chin and cheek, warm buff hindcrown and neck, scarlet throat, blue rump, thighs and undertail-coverts; colonial, noisy.
b Wing with black trailing edge, rump blue, tail all green.

100 Somali Bee-eater *Merops revoilii*   Text page 264

Horn of Africa: arid thorn scrubland.
a Adult: small, slender, often scruffy; looks attenuated and leggy in the heat; white throat, no gorget, buff breast and belly, pale blue undertail-coverts, no tail-streamers.
b Bright cobalt-blue rump is conspicuous in flight.

101 White-throated Bee-eater *Merops albicollis*   Text page 265

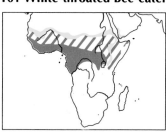

Northern tropics: desert in summer, forest in winter; migrants occur not only in West Africa but also in East, as shown by hatching.
a Adult: unmistakable; strikingly pied head, red eye, buff hindneck, green back, wings and tail, long streamers, pale green underparts; usually gregarious, noisy.
b Green and rufous wings with black trailing edge.

PLATE 33   GREEN BEE-EATERS

102 Boehm's Bee-eater *Merops boehmi* — Text page 267

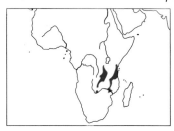

Southeast Africa: park-like woodland.
a Adult: green, with rufous crown and throat, pale blue cheek line, black-tipped tail with long streamers.
b Adult in flight mainly green; wings rounded, with blackish trailing edge. Juvenile like adult, but lacks streamers.

103 Little Green Bee-eater *Merops orientalis* — Text page 269

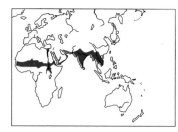

Africa, south Asia: varied habitats (see text).
a Adult *M. o. ferrugeiceps* (Assam to Indochina): green, with rufous crown and hindneck, red eye, narrow black gorget, long streamers.
b Adult *M. o. orientalis* (India, Sri Lanka): crown and hindneck golden-green.
c Adult has rounded wings with black trailing edge, long streamers.
d Adult *M. o. viridissimus* (Africa): very long streamers; crown, hindneck and throat grass-green, but in Sudan throat often yellow.
e Adult *M. o. beludschicus* (Iraq to Punjab): crown and hindneck golden-green, throat pale blue, gorget a thin black bar.
f Adult *M. o. cyanophrys* (Yemen, Oman, Dead Sea valley): blue forehead, eyebrow and throat, large blackish gorget, short streamers.

104 Blue-cheeked Bee-eater *Merops persicus* — Text page 271

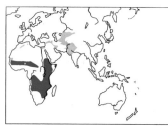

Africa, Asia: desert, woodland near water, cultivation.
a Adult *M. p. persicus* (Asia, winters in Africa): large, long-winged, elegant, gregarious, vocal; burnished green with whitish forehead, pale blue eyebrow and cheek, red-brown eye, yellow chin, rufous throat, long streamers. Like Madagascar Bee-eater (Plate 34), but crown green, and blue on face.
b In flight, upperparts uniformly green but underwing-coverts bright rufous.
c Juvenile *M. p. persicus*: mottled, duller than adult, tail lacks streamers.

102a

102b

103a

103c

103b

103e

103f

103d

104b

104a

104c

PLATE 34   AUSTRALIAN BEE-EATER AND ALLIES

105 Madagascar/Blue-tailed Bee-eater *Merops superciliosus*   **Text page 273**

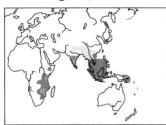

Africa, Madagascar, southeast Asia: plains, marshes, woods, forest, farmland.

a Adult *M. s. superciliosus* (East Africa, Madagascar): like Blue-cheeked Bee-eater (Plate 33), but cheeks, chin and eyebrow are white (or yellowish, but not bluish), and crown olive-brown (not green).

b Long pointed wings, long tail, rufous underwings, and elegant swooping flight are all as Blue-cheeked Bee-eater's.

c Adult *M. s. philippinus* (India to New Guinea): like Blue-cheeked Bee-eater, but forehead and eyebrow green, rump and tail blue.

106 Rainbow Bee-eater *Merops ornatus*   **Text page 275**

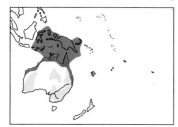

Australia, winters mainly in New Guinea: pasture, woodland, forest.

a Adult male: black gorget, thin streamers.

b Adult: green, with burnished head, black-bordered rufous-and-green wings, blue rump, black tail.

c Adult female: black-and-blue gorget, streamers shorter than on male and clubbed.

d Juvenile: dull olive-green above; lacks gorget, blue cheek stripe and streamers.

107 Blue-throated Bee-eater *Merops viridis*   **Text page 277**

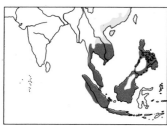

China, southeast Asia: forest, sandy clearings, gardens.

a Adult *M. v. viridis* (not Philippines): green, with chestnut crown and mantle, red eye, blue throat and belly, long streamers.

b Flying adult shows brilliant blue back and rump.

c Adult *M. v. americanus* (Philippines): green throat.

d Juvenile, both races: green crown, greenish throat, tail lacks streamers.

105a

105b

105c

106a

106c

106d

106b

107a

107b

107c

107d

PLATE 35   EUROPEAN BEE-EATER AND ALLY

108 Bay-headed Bee-eater *Merops leschenaulti*   **Text page 279**

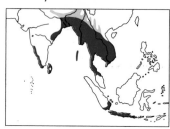

Southeast Asia: forest, grassland, cultivation.

a Adult *M. l. leschenaulti* (mainland and Sri Lanka): green, with rufous crown and mantle, pale blue back and rump, yellow throat, black-and-rufous gorget; no streamers. Gregarious.

b Adult *M. l. quinticolor* (Java, Bali): mask rufous, thin black gorget, throat and breast yellow.

c Adult *M. l. andamanensis* (Andaman Islands): mask mainly rufous; rufous lower throat joins rufous of mantle.

d Adult, all races: black trailing edge, brilliant blue rump.

e Juveniles of all races have green crowns.

109 European Bee-eater *Merops apiaster*   **Text page 281**

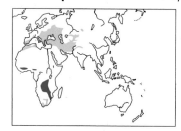

Europe, west Asia, winters in Africa: all open habitats.

a Adult male: the only bee-eater with golden-yellow scapulars and parti-coloured chestnut-and-green wings.

b Adult female: scapulars suffused with green, less chestnut in wing.

c Adult male: golden scapulars form a V with golden rump; inner half of wing chestnut, outer half green, underside of wing pale rufous.

d Juvenile: scaly pale green back and wings, crown and mantle green, scapulars silvery-green.

108a

108c

108b

108e

108d

109a

109b

109c

109d

PLATE 36   ROSY AND CARMINE BEE-EATERS

110 Rosy Bee-eater *Merops malimbicus*   **Text page 283**

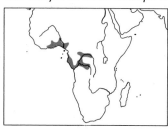

West Africa: large sandy rivers, forest.
a Adult: unmistakable, highly gregarious, noisy; slate-grey
  upperparts, vivid pink underparts, white cheek line, red
  eye, reddish tail, short streamers.
b Against bright white sky, upperparts can look black; pink
  throat distinguishes it from local Carmine Bee-eater (*M.
  n. nubicus*).
c Juvenile: paler than adult, less pink.

111 Carmine Bee-eater *Merops nubicus*   **Text page 285**

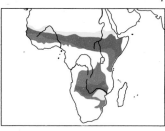

Africa: rivers, savanna woodland.
a Adult *M. n. nubicus* (northern tropics): carmine upperparts, green-blue head and throat, vivid pink breast, pale
  blue undertail-coverts.
b Adult *M. n. nubicoides* (southern tropics): throat pink.
c,d In flight, wings red with dusky trailing edge, back and
  rump brilliant pale blue, tail red, long streamers, wing-
  lining pale buff (c, *nubicus*; d, *nubicoides*).
e Juvenile: upperparts mainly rufescent-brown, wings and
  tail reddish, throat greyish-blue on *nubicus*, usually pinkish
  on *nubicoides*, breast mottled with buff, short streamers.

PLATE 37   INDIAN AND TWO AFRICAN ROLLERS

112 Rufous-crowned Roller *Coracias naevia*   Text page 287

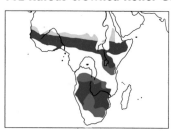

Africa: savanna woodland and farmland with large trees.
a Adult *C. n. naevia* (northern tropics): pink-rufous crown and hindneck, conspicuous white eyebrow, white mark on nape, olive-green back, mainly purple wings and tail, pink-and-white-striped cheeks and underparts.
b Juvenile *C. n. naevia*: head and underparts greener.
c Adult *C. n. mosambica* (southern tropics): crown and hindneck olive-green, underparts purplish.
d Adult *C. n. naevia* in flight shows strikingly purple-and-lilac wings; heavy, crow-like flight.

113 Indian Roller *Coracias benghalensis*   Text page 289

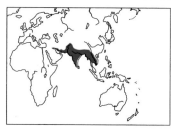

South Asia: parks, woods, cultivation.
a Adult *C. b. benghalensis* (Iraq to Bangladesh): blue crown, yellow skin around eye, brown back, pink cheeks and breast with white streaks, pale blue belly.
b Juvenile *C. b. benghalensis*: head and body much duller than adult, but wings and tail as bright.
c Adult *C. b. affinis* (southeast Asia): an unmistakable blue, olive-green and purple bird.
d In flight, all races (*benghalensis* illustrated) have brilliant blue in tail, on wing-coverts, and in wide band across purple primaries.

115 Racket-tailed Roller *Coracias spatulata*   Text page 292

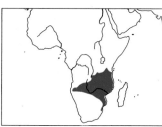

Southern Africa: miombo and mopane woodland.
a Adult *C. s. spatulata* (Angola to south Mozambique): whole underparts pale blue, tail with clubbed streamers.
b Adult *C. s. spatulata* has dark purple wings with brilliant pale blue stripe, and rufous greater coverts.
c Juvenile *C. s. spatulata*: see text for distinctions from juvenile Lilac-breasted Roller.
d Adult *C. s. weigalli* (north of Zambezi River): face and breast pink, striped with white.

PLATE 38   ABYSSINIAN ROLLER AND ALLIES

116 Lilac-breasted Roller *Coracias caudata*   Text page 294

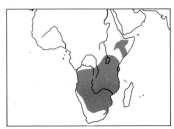

Eastern Africa: lightly wooded savannas.

a Adult *C. c. caudata* (Kenya to South Africa): lilac throat and breast; told from Racket-tailed Roller *C. s. weigalli* (Plate 37) by the shape of the streamers.

b Adult *C. c. lorti* (Ethiopia, Somalia, north Kenya): unique combination of lilac throat and blue breast.

c Both races have pale blue forewing, purple primaries and secondaries.

d Juvenile *C. c. caudata*: very like juvenile Racket-tailed Roller (see text).

117 Abyssinian Roller *Coracias abyssinica*   Text page 296

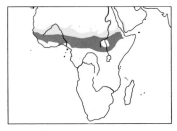

Northern tropics: woodland, parks, gardens.

a Adult: pale blue, with brown back and long tail-streamers; aggressive and noisy.

b In flight adult resembles Lilac-breasted Roller, but throat blue, uppertail-coverts dark blue, and streamers longer.

c Juvenile: pale, brownish hindneck; wings as adult; no streamers.

118 European Roller *Coracias garrulus*   Text page 298

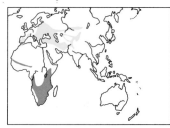

West Palearctic, winters in Africa: all open habitats with trees.

a Adult *C. g. garrulus* (Morocco to Siberia): blue head and underparts, brown back, no streamers.

b Primaries and secondaries mainly black, tail partly light blue with black mark at corners.

c Juvenile *C. g. garrulus*: browns and blues are pale. In Africa, told from juvenile native rollers by its black primaries.

PLATE 39 BLUE-BELLIED AND BROAD-BILLED ROLLERS

119 Blue-bellied Roller *Coracias cyanogaster*   Text page 300

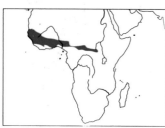

Northern tropics: mature *Isoberlinia* woodland.
a Adult: unmistakable; dark blue, with whitish head and breast.
b Shows brilliant pale blue wing-stripe and tail.

120 Blue-throated Roller *Eurystomus gularis*   Text page 301

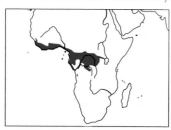

Africa: forest.
a Adult *E. g. gularis* (Guinea to Nigeria): like a stubby falcon, with short yellow bill, chestnut body, and small blue throat patch.
b Adult *E. g. neglectus* (Congo Basin): larger, underparts more lilac.
c In flight, both races show mainly dark blue wings; blackish and light blue tail is shallowly forked.
d Juvenile *E. g. gularis*: dusky bill, brown throat, grey-blue underparts.

121 Broad-billed Roller *Eurystomus glaucurus*   Text page 303

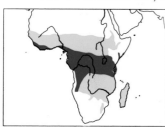

Africa and Madagascar: forest, woodland, cultivation.
a Adult *E. g. glaucurus* (Madagascar, winters in East Africa): larger than *E. gularis neglectus*; lilac throat, blue-grey undertail-coverts.
b Adult *E. g. suahelicus* (southern Africa): smaller; undertail-coverts pale blue.
c Adult *E. g. glaucurus*: wings mainly purple-blue, rump blue (blue and brown in West African *E. g. afer*), tail light blue and blackish, forked.
d Juvenile *E. g. glaucurus*: like juvenile Blue-throated Roller but larger.

119a

119b

121a

121c

121d

121b

120a

120c

120b

120d

PLATE 40   DOLLARBIRDS AND CELEBES ROLLER

122 Dollarbird *Eurystomus orientalis*   Text page 305

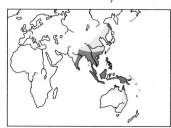

Asia, Australia: lowland forest, woodland, plantations.

a Adult *E. o. orientalis* (India, southeast Asia): dark greenish-blue, head often looks blackish, stout scarlet bill, red eye-ring, blue throat, red feet.

b,c In flight, adults appear blackish below (b) and mainly blue above (c), with very conspicuous pale blue patch in wing.

d Juvenile *E. o. orientalis*: upper mandible dusky, lower mandible yellow, entire underparts slaty-blue, wing-patches smaller and not so clearly defined, yellowish feet.

e Adult *E. o. pacificus* (Australia): head brown, underparts pale.

f Juvenile *E. o. pacificus*: black-and-yellow bill, yellowish feet.

123 Azure Roller *Eurystomus azureus*   Text page 308

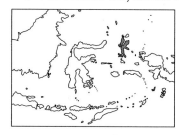

Northern Moluccas (Indonesia): plantations, woodland, forest edge.

a,b Adult: uniformly glossy dark blue, except for pale blue patch in wing and red bill, eye-rim and feet.

114 Celebes Roller *Coracias temminckii*   Text page 291

Sulawesi (Indonesia): cultivated lowlands.

a,b Adult: unmistakable; large, pale blue and purple with olive back.

122b

122a

122d

122c

122e

122f

123b

114b

123a

114a

TOPOGRAPHY

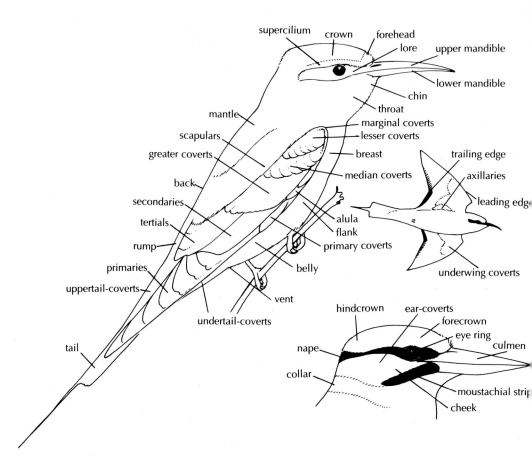

supercilium crown forehead
lore upper mandible
lower mandible
chin
throat
mantle
scapulars marginal coverts
lesser coverts
greater coverts breast
median coverts
back
secondaries trailing edge
tertials axillaries
rump leading edge
primaries alula
uppertail-coverts flank
primary coverts
belly
tail vent underwing coverts
undertail-coverts

hindcrown ear-coverts
forecrown
eye ring
nape culmen
collar
moustachial strip
cheek

1 CELEBES GREEN KINGFISHER (Blue-headed Wood Kingfisher)
Actenoides monachus
Plate 1

Halcyon monachus Bonaparte, 1850, Consp. Genera Avium, 1, p. 154, Celebes.

Field identification Length 31 cm (12 in). A large kingfisher, confined to the lowland forests of Sulawesi, with a rather short scarlet bill, black or blue head, dark green back, wings and tail and rufous collar and underparts. Males have blue and females chestnut cheeks. *Confusion species:* the Regent Kingfisher (2) of Sulawesi is montane and the two species seem to be separated altitudinally, though some overlap is possible. Regent is smaller, with dark brown back and wings heavily scalloped with buff, the male with buffy underparts and whitish belly and the female with buffy forehead, eyebrow and scaly white underparts.

Voice A long melodious whistle, low-pitched, rising towards the end. A netted bird uttered a harsh 'rark-rark-kraaa' on release (Watling 1983).

Geographical variation There are two races, differing in head colour and in the rufous hue of breast and belly.

A. m. monachus Northern Sulawesi (Celebes), and some offshore islands. Head rich dark blue, breast deep rufous, belly orange-rufous, tail tinged with blue.

A. m. capucinus South, southeast and eastern Sulawesi. Head black, breast and belly the same orange-rufous hue, no blue tinge to tail.

Habitat and range The species inhabits dense lowland rainforest, from the coast up to about 900 m. It is confined to Sulawesi, where it appears to range in all parts where primary forests remain. Doubtless it is sedentary.

Food Large centipedes and beetles.

Habits A quiet, solitary bird of rainforests, very poorly known. A nest with eggs found in the 19th century, in March, was a hole which the birds had excavated in a tree termitarium. Recently-fledged youngsters have been seen in April.

Description *A. m. monachus* **Adult male:** forehead blackish, crown rich, deep turquoise-blue; lores black; ear-coverts, cheeks and malar area blue, slightly paler than the crown, and sharply defined from the white chin and throat. A narrow hindneck-collar is deep rufous, broken in the middle where the blue hindcrown reaches the mantle. Mantle, back, wings and tail dark olive-green. Breast deep rufous, confluent with the collar; belly, flanks and undertail-coverts a rather paler rufous. Underwing-coverts cinnamon-buff. Bill bright red; eye dark brown; legs and feet orange-red. **Adult female:** like the male, except that the forehead and short but wide superciliary stripe are light orange-rufous, and ear-coverts and cheeks are dark chestnut, some feathers with blue tips. **Juvenile:** like the adult female, but underparts (particularly the breast) duller, chin dirty buff, and the bill yellowish-horn. **Measurements:** wing of male 138-150, of female 142-152; tail of male 101-120, of female 104-119; bill of male 47-58, of female 49-57; tarsus of male 20-24, of female 21-24.

References Forshaw (1985), White and Bruce (1986).

2 REGENT KINGFISHER (Bar-headed Wood Kingfisher)
Actenoides princeps
Plate 1

Monachalcyon princeps Reichenbach, 1851, Handb. Spec. Orn., p. 38, Celebes.

Field identification Length 24 cm (9½ in). Like the Celebes Green Kingfisher (1), this is a splendid rainforest bird endemic to Sulawesi and is very poorly known in the field. *Confusion species:* there is supposedly a gap of some 600 m altitudinally between the lowland-forest Celebes Green Kingfisher and the highland-forest Regent Kingfisher, but in reality the two may overlap somewhat. Males of both species have blue heads and dark rufous collars, and females have buffy foreheads. Regent, however, is distinguished by its buff-scalloped dark brown back in all plumages (back of Celebes Green Kingfisher uniform dark green) and by its underparts being buffy-white (male) or heavily barred (female); the underparts of Celebes Green Kingfisher are dark rufous, which should prevent confusion. In northwest and central Sulawesi the bill of the Regent Kingfisher is red, in the northeast it is horn-coloured, and in the southeast it is brown and orange.

Voice A series of soft, mournful whistles, the first notes rolling, later ones rising in pitch and then falling away.

Geographical variation Three subspecies are recognised; the male of one is unknown, and males of the other two differ in the intensity of buff and rufous.
A. p. erythrorhamphus Northwest and central Sulawesi. Red bill, rich rufous collar, slight barring at the sides, and back and wing feathers with broad rufous margins. The male has an all-blue head, white supraloral spot, and buff breast and belly with slight barring at the sides; the female has a rufous eyebrow and moustache, and barred rufous underparts.
A. p. princeps Northeast Sulawesi. Yellowish-brown bill, yellowish-buff collar, and back and wing feathers with narrow buff margins. Male has buffy supraloral spot and finely barred underparts, and female has buff eyebrow and moustache and heavily barred white underparts.
A. p. regalis Southeast Sulawesi. Male unknown. The female has greenish crown, rump and primaries, rufous collar, unbarred back and wings, plain rufous underparts, dark brown upper mandible and orange-red lower mandible.

Habitat and range Montane rainforest in Sulawesi, at altitudes from about 900 to 1800 m. It keeps to the interior of undisturbed forest, where it may be rather less scarce than records suggest. Like the Celebes Green Kingfisher, it ranges throughout the island, and has been found as low as 250 m.

Food Beetles. A cicada nymph was once eaten; doubtless the bird takes numerous different arthropods.

Habits It perches solitarily in the forest understorey and can be difficult to locate in the usual poor light. Calling is more frequent at dawn than during the day. In short flights the wings make a loud whirring. No nests have been discovered recently, but burrows in an earth bank in 1983 probably belonged to this species. A clutch of four eggs was taken in the 19th century.

Description A. p. erythrorhamphus **Adult male:** head dark purple-blue, almost black on the forehead and lores; hindneck rich dark rufous; feathers of mantle to rump, and upperwing-coverts, dark brown with broad rufous-buff tips and narrow black subterminal band; tail, primaries and secondaries dark brown; underwing-coverts rufous-buff, with dusky barring. Chin and throat white; belly buffy-white; rest of underparts warm buff, becoming rufous at the sides of breast and flanks, where the feathers have dusky fringes. Bill orange-red; eye dark brown; legs and feet yellowish-brown. **Adult female:** like the male, but some forehead feathers tipped with rufous, a long rufous superciliary stripe from nostril to behind the ear-coverts, and a broad rufous stripe from gape to the side of the neck; throat rufous-buff, breast rufous, and belly, flanks and undertail-coverts rufous-buff. All underparts except the chin and throat are dark-barred, narrowly on the breast, broadly on the flanks. **Juvenile:** like the adult female, but with extensively buffy forehead, broader and brighter rufous bars on the back and wings, and narrower bars on the underparts; the bill is dark brown with a pale tip. **Measurements:** (A. p. princeps) wing of male 110-118, of female 114-124; tail of male 77-90, of female 75-91; bill of male 40-51, of female 43-48; tarsus of male 18-21, of female 18-21.

References Forshaw (1985), White and Bruce (1986).

Actenoides bougainvillei

Halcyon bougainvillei Rothschild, 1904, Bull. Brit. Orn. Club, 15, p. 5, Bougainville Island.

Field identification Length 32 cm (12½ in). Unmistakable: a large, orange kingfisher with red bill and purple-blue moustache, wings and tail. Three other halcyon kingfishers, the Ultramarine (42), Mangrove (47) and Beach Kingfishers (49), occur in its island homes of Bougainville and Guadalcanal, but they are quite different in appearance and habitat.

Voice A loud, ringing laugh, 'ko-ko-ko-ko'.

Geographical variation There are two subspecies, one paler and less rufous than the other.
　A. b. bougainvillei Bougainville Island, Papua New Guinea. Strikingly rufous and purple-blue, the male with rufous and the female with olive-green scapulars and upper back. Immature plumage unknown.
　A. b. excelsus Guadalcanal in the Solomon Islands, about 600 km southeast of Bougainville. Adult male unknown. Adult female is more olive-green on the upper back, scapulars and tertials, and has much paler orange underparts, than the nominate female. An immature male specimen has the upper back, scapulars and tertials very dark olive-green.

Habitat and range It inhabits lowland forest and hill forest in southern Bougainville, and hill and mist forest at between 550 and 1250 m in Guadalcanal. The Moustached Kingfisher is a very rare bird, a candidate for the Red Data Book, given as 'Vulnerable' by Johnson and Stattersfield (1990); it was first described in 1904, and a dozen specimens were collected in southern Bougainville in the late 1930s, since when the species has not been recorded there. In 1941 *excelsus* was described on the basis of a single specimen from Guadalcanal, and two more were obtained there in 1953.

Food The diet is known to include stick-insects and frogs.

Habits Nothing is known about this magnificent kingfisher. In the 1950s, local people said that its nest burrows were holes in riverbanks or in the ground in forest.

Description *A. b. bougainvillei* **Adult male:** forehead, crown, cheeks and mantle dark tawny-orange; a narrow, clearly delineated purple-blue line runs from behind the eye to the nape, and another, broader one forms a long moustachial stripe from the lower mandible, curving under and behind the cheeks and ear-coverts. Upper back, scapulars, wings, sides of rump, and tail dark purple-blue; lower back and centre of rump and uppertail-coverts brilliant pale azure-blue. Underparts orange-rufous, paler on chin, belly and undertail-coverts than on breast and flanks. Bill red; eye dark brown; legs and feet red, nails brown. **Adult female:** like the male, but upper back, scapulars and tertials are olive-green and the head darker rufous, merging into the mantle. **Juvenile:** unknown. **Measurements:** wing of male 127-136, of female 127-133; tail of male 85-95, of female 91-96; bill of male 49-58, of female 46-51; tarsus of male 19-21, of female 19-21. Weight (two females of *excelsus*): 160, 215.

Reference Forshaw (1985).

4 HOMBRON'S WOOD KINGFISHER   Plate 2
Actenoides hombroni

Actenoides hombroni Bonaparte, 1850, Consp. Genera Avium, 1, p. 157, Oceania (error for Philippine Islands).

Field identification Length 27 cm (10½ in). Five other halcyons live on Mindanao, in the range of Hombron's Wood Kingfisher. They are the Stork-billed (22), Ruddy (25), White-breasted (26), Winchell's (37) and Mangrove Kingfishers (47), but there should be no mistaking them for this species with its blue or green cap and tail, rufous cheeks and underparts, reddish bill and blue-green back.

Voice Although this kingfisher is locally quite common, its voice is not known.

Geographical variation Populations in west and east Mindanao seem to be separated by a gap of some 100 km. The chin and throat are white in the west of the island and pale rufous in the east, and eastern birds are in general a trifle darker, but the differences appear to be clinal and we do not recognise any subspecies.

Habitat and range Hombron's Wood Kingfisher inhabits undisturbed rainforest in hilly districts, mainly between 1000 and 2000 m altitude. Thirty years ago it was reportedly quite common, at least locally, but since then there has been massive and widespread destruction of native forest and today the range is likely to be fragmented and the bird much less common. In western Mindanao it occurs from the Zamboanga Peninsula to about Ozamiz, and in the east from Mount Apo to Davao, Surigao del Sur and Mount Hilong-hilong. There are no reports of migration, and it is doubtless sedentary, like nearly all tropical rainforest birds.

Food Large insects and other animals: grasshoppers, locusts, beetles, larvae, snails, frogs and small reptiles.

Habits Like its close relative the Spotted Wood Kingfisher (5) of the northern Philippine Islands, Hombron's lives solitarily or in pairs in deep forest, perching in the lower storey and probably feeding by landing on the ground to seize prey. Practically nothing is on record, however, about its foraging or its breeding behaviour. No nests have been found.

Description *Adult male:* cap deep purple-blue, darkest on the forehead, and delineated by a band of more brilliant blue running from behind the eye to the nape. From the lower mandible a broad, oval, purple-blue moustache extends along the edge of the white chin and throat. Between moustache and cap is a large area of rich orange-rufous, extending from below the eye to the hindneck and side of the breast, the feathers on the hindneck and upper mantle fringed with dark blue. Lower mantle, scapulars, tertials and upperwing-coverts dark green-blue with small rufous spots; lower back, rump and uppertail-coverts brilliant azure-blue; tail cobalt-blue. Breast, belly, flanks and undertail-coverts rufous. Bill red, darkening to brownish-black on the culmen; eye dark brown; legs and feet dark pinkish olive-brown. *Adult female:* cap dull green, suffused with rufous on the forehead and above the lores, and encircled by a band of greenish-blue from behind the eye to the nape. Moustachial area orange-rufous with some small greenish spots. Mantle, scapulars, tertials and upperwing-coverts dull olive-green, each feather with a buffy mark. Tail greenish-blue. *Juvenile:* like the adults but duller. *Measurements:* wing of male 116-131, of female 118-131; tail of male 85-99, of female 83-101; bill of male 46-54, of female 45-52; tarsus of male 18-20, of female 18-19. Weight: male 108-124, female 106-147.

Reference Forshaw (1985).

5 SPOTTED WOOD KINGFISHER

Plate 2

Actenoides lindsayi

Dacelo Lindsayi Vigors, 1831, Proc. Zool. Soc. London, pt 1, 1830-1831, p. 97, Manila, Philippine Islands.

Field identification Length 26 cm (10 in). The same five halcyons occur in the range of the Spotted Wood Kingfisher in the northern Philippines as are found in the range of Hombron's Wood Kingfisher (4) in the southern Philippines: namely, Stork-billed (22), Ruddy (25), White-breasted (26), Winchell's (37) (on Negros Island), and Mangrove (47). Spotted Wood Kingfishers, however, are quite unlike all of them, and can readily be distinguished by the green upperparts with copious large buffy spots on the back and wings and by the strikingly scalloped breast and flanks. The male has a bright orange neck and pale azure-blue moustache, and the female has a black line from eye to nape and a green moustache.

Voice It is probably this bird which utters a wavering whistle sometimes heard in dense forest.

Geographical variation Birds on Negros Island are more strongly marked than those of Luzon.

A. l. lindsayi Northern Philippines: Luzon, Catanduanes and Marinduque.

A. l. moseleyi Central Philippines: Negros and Panay Islands (Gonzales and Rees 1988). Has darker greens than *lindsayi*, and the male also darker blues, brighter orange throat, darker blackish-green back, and larger buff spots.

Habitat and range An uncommon and easily overlooked bird of deep, undisturbed rainforest, sometimes living near forest streams, in lowland and hilly districts. There are records from many parts of Luzon Island, and the kingfisher was probably widespread before so much forest was cut. It occurs on Luzon, Catanduanes, Marinduque, Panay and Negros.

Food Insects and snails.

Habits Almost nothing is on record about the species. It lives solitarily or in pairs, perching quite low down in the forest, and probably taking its prey from the ground. It is thought to excavate its nest holes in arboreal termitaria, although other species of *Actenoides* seem to prefer tree holes and ground holes.

Description *A. l. lindsayi* **Adult male:** forehead and crown feathers dark green with lighter green tips; some buffy suffusion on the forehead, and sometimes a pale rufous patch above the lores. A line of brilliant pale blue from above or behind the eye to the nape, and below it a band of black. A long, oval, bright blue moustachial mark, bordered above and below by orange-rufous, confluent with a broad dark rufous hindneck-collar. Mantle, back, scapulars, tertials and upperwing-coverts dark green, each feather with a large buff teardrop mark at its tip. Rump and uppertail-coverts uniform bright green; tail dark olive-green, with dark rufous bars on the outer feathers. Chin and throat orange-rufous; feathers of breast and flanks white, with dark green borders, wider at sides than at tip; belly and undertail-coverts mainly white. Underwing-coverts cinnamon-buff. Upper mandible black, with narrow but distinct yellow line along the culmen from base to tip; lower mandible orange-yellow; eye dark brown; legs and feet pale green. **Adult female:** not so bright as the male, but still a very striking bird. Forehead buffier; line encircling crown emerald-green; moustache brownish-green; feathers of hindneck-collar rufous-brown with black border; chin white; throat white with green scallops. **Juvenile:** male like the adult female, but ear-coverts are buffier, supercilium and moustachial stripe turquoise; female duller, greens browner, throat buffy, bill grey-brown with yellow tip and yellow-horn base to the lower mandible. **Measurements:** wing of male 107-113, of female 105-114; tail of male 78-92, of female 74-92; bill of male 40-47, of female 40-48; tarsus of male 17-19, of female 17-19.

Reference Forshaw (1985).

Actenoides concretus

Dacelo concreta Temminck, 1825, Planch. Col., 58, p. 346, Sumatra.

Field identification Length 24 cm (9½ in). A fine, boldly marked kingfisher of lowland forest, stolid, unobtrusive and shy. *At rest:* male with green cap, black band through eye and around nape, large blue moustache, rufous collar and underparts, and blue back and tail; female the same, but for dark green back and wings with pale spots. *In flight:* brilliant pale blue rump; rounded wings, rather heavy, whirring flight. *Confusion species:* none of the many other kingfishers in its range has its distinctive head pattern with large moustache.

Voice A rising whistle, 'kwi-i', repeated at the rate of nine calls in 10 seconds. Also low chuckling noises.

Geographical variation There are three subspecies, differing slightly in body size, hue and spot size.

A. c. concretus Sumatra, Belitung, Bangka, Singapore and the Malayan Peninsula north to Trang, Thailand.

A. c. peristephes From Trang in peninsular Thailand to about Tavoy, 14°N in Burma. Rufous and buff parts slightly paler than on nominate subspecies, and female with larger buff spots on wings. Larger: wing 110-124 (average 115) and tail 55-65 (average 60.5).

A. c. borneanus Borneo. Upperparts darker than on nominate subspecies, the female with more prominent spots. Tail length as *concretus* but wing length as *peristephes*.

Habitat and range Rufous-collared Kingfishers inhabit dense, undisturbed forest, from Tenasserim (south Burma) to Johore (Malaysia), Sumatra and Borneo. They are not common, or at least are not commonly encountered; but they are easily overlooked, and where suitable habitat remains are probably actually common. When forest disappears they are locally exterminated (and may well now be extinct in Singapore). In mainland southeast Asia they range from lowlands up to 800 m, but on Mount Kinabalu in Borneo

they occur up to 1700 m and seem to be commoner above than below 1000 m. They keep to dense growth, by rivers and streams or far from water, and also occur in moss forest; they often perch on standing or fallen dead timber. The species is sedentary.

Food Large invertebrates and small vertebrates: cicadas, longicorn beetles, mantises, spiders, scorpions up to 9 cm long, snails, small fish, blind-snakes (*Typhlops*), ground-snakes (*Maticora*), and lizards.

Habits This kingfisher hunts solitarily or in pairs, perching in the lower storey of the forest, keeping still but for slow fore-and-aft wagging of the tail and alert cocking of the head as it searches foliage and the ground for prey. Most food seems to be taken from the ground. A bird was once seen on a log floating in a river; they also perch in vegetation overhanging rivers, and may fish rather more than is supposed. Some evidence suggests that they may be able to remove the stings of scorpions (Burton 1978). *Nesting:* only about six nests have been found, most in burrows in low banks, but one a hole in a rotten trunk. Ground-nests are usually near a stream, and are horizontal holes 10 cm in diameter and 60 cm long, ending in an oval egg chamber 20 cm in diameter. The clutch is of two eggs, and the nestling period about 22 days. *Laying months:* Malaysia (Selangor), April-May/June; Sumatra, March; Borneo, December-March.

Description *A. c. concretus* **Adult male:** cap dark green, the feathers dusky blackish with green tips; forehead blackish, hindcrown greener, both brighter at the sides. A broad black line from the nostril through the eye, curving down to where it crosses the nape; above it, a narrow buffy line from forecrown to just behind the eye. Cheeks, chin and throat pale yellowish-orange; between them, a well-defined purple-blue moustache from the lower mandible, broadening under the ear and

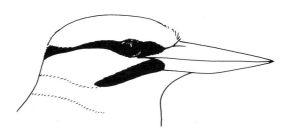

with the lower feathers elongated and usually meeting the mantle. Hindneck-collar and breast tawny-rufous. Mantle blackish; upper back and wings dark purple-blue, the feathers black, broadly fringed blue. Lower back and rump brilliant pale blue; tail purple-blue. Belly, flanks, undertail-coverts and underwing-coverts pale rufous. Bill yellowish-horn, becoming dark brown along the culmen; eye dark brown, eyelids pale; legs and feet pale yellow-green. *Adult female:* like the male, except that the buffy superciliary stripe is a little broader, and upper back, scapulars, tertials and wings are dark olive-green (not purple-blue), each feather with a large, pale yellow-green teardrop-shaped spot at its tip. *Juvenile:* like the adults but duller, males with the back heavily spotted; bill grey-brown, with base of the lower mandible and tip yellowish. *Measurements:* wing of male 105-113, of female 102-117; tail of male 49-59, of female 53-65; bill of male 44-51, of female 44-54; tarsus of male 17-19, of female 17-19. Weight (*A. c. borneanus*): male 70-89, female 70-90.

References Burton (1978), Forshaw (1985), Fry (1980a), Medway and Wells (1976), Smythies (1981).

7 COMMON PARADISE KINGFISHER   Plate 3
Tanysiptera galatea

Tanysiptera galatea G.R. Gray, 1859, Proc. Zool. Soc. London, pt 27, p. 154, Dorey (= Manokwari), New Guinea.

Field identification Length 22 cm (8¹/₂ in), excluding tail-streamers of up to 20 cm (8 in) in length. The six paradise kingfishers can readily be told from the many other kingfishers in their range — New Guinea, New Britain and northeast Australia — by their streamered central tail feathers. Even recently-fledged youngsters have markedly long, graduated tails, although in other plumage characters juveniles differ markedly from their adults. The Common Paradise Kingfisher is the only one, apart from the Aru Paradise (9), with white underparts (adults). *At rest:* from in front it looks all white, including the underside of the tail; from behind it is dark blue, with pale blue crown, shoulders and tail, white rump, and large white spatulate tips to the central tail feathers. While the bird calls the tail is jerked up high. When the streamered and racketed central pair of tail feathers is moulted, the rest of the tail, which is strongly graduated, looks disproportionately short. Young birds are brown, with rufous superciliary stripe, cinnamon-fringed forehead and mantle feathers, uniformly brown rump and tail, and buff breast with black streaks or scallops. *In flight:* the white rump and white tail-rackets of the adult are conspicuous, as usually are the white edges to the base of the tail. *Confusion species:* in south New Guinea, this kingfisher's range overlaps that of the Aru Paradise Kingfisher. The latter also has white rump, tail-rackets and underparts, but it is smaller, with dark blue (not pale blue) crown, and the tail, other than the central pair of feathers, is dark blue. On the Common Paradise, the outer four tail feathers are white with narrow blue outer edges.

Voice The song is a series of 1-4 separated, mournful whistles on the same pitch, rapidly accelerating into a short trill (Coates 1985), and lasting about 1½ seconds. It is also described as a loud, rising, accelerating, whistled trill, preceded by a longer, rather nasal note (Forshaw 1985). Other calls are shrill squawks, a rasping chatter and sometimes a single low, mournful whistle 'wheeyou', either downslurred and lasting 1½ seconds or upslurred and lasting 2-3 seconds (Coates 1985).

Geographical variation There are two subspecies in mainland New Guinea, four on offshore islands, and 11 on different islands in the Moluccas, between New Guinea and Sulawesi. They differ in the hue and brilliance of blue on crown and wing-coverts, in the amount of white in the tail, and in the colour of the upper back (black, blue or white). Two of the island forms, of Biak Island and Kofiau Island, are often treated as distinct, full species. Birds from Keyoa, Morotai and Rau Islands, off Halmahera, resemble the Buff-breasted Paradise Kingfisher (10) in having a white patch high on the back.

T. g. galatea Western Papuan Islands (except Misoöl and Kofiau) and west New Guinea, east to eastern Geelvink Bay and Triton Bay.

T. g. minor South New Guinea, from Digul River (Irian Jaya) to Kumusi River (Papua New Guinea), and on some offshore islands. Like *galatea*, but with bluer upperwing-coverts and a shorter, finer bill.

T. g. meyeri North New Guinea, from Mamberamo River (Irian Jaya) to Lae (Papua New Guinea), inland to Jimi River, and on some offshore islands. Like *galatea*, but with the crown brighter, paler blue, the back and wings bluer, and bases of the central tail feathers white.

T. g. riedelii Biak Island, in Geelvink Bay, northern Irian Jaya. Forehead, crown, cheeks, ear-coverts, hindneck, mantle, upper back and lesser wing-coverts pale azure-blue; feather shafts are particularly bright blue, and everywhere the black feather bases show through. Scapulars dark blue-black, as on *galatea*. The Biak

Paradise Kingfisher is often treated as a separate species (e.g. Forshaw 1985). It is slightly shorter-winged and shorter-tailed than *galatea*, but larger-billed and heavier (weight: 63-70). This bird is a candidate for the Red Data Book and is listed as 'Vulnerable' by Johnson and Stattersfield (1990).

T. g. vulcani Manam Island, off Bogia, north Papua New Guinea. Like *meyeri* but larger: male wing averages 113, tail (without streamers) 121, and bill 40.

T. g. rosseliana Rossel Island, east of Louisiade Archipelago, easternmost New Guinea. Like *meyeri*, but upperparts deeper purple-blue and tail almost entirely white. Tail long: average (without streamers) 113 on males and 110 on females.

T. g. naïs Ceram (Seram), Ambon, Manipa, Manawoka and Gorong Islands, south Moluccas, Indonesia. Upperparts brighter blue than on *galatea*; line of feathers encircling crown, and lesser wing-coverts, pale silvery-blue. Tail like that of *meyeri*, with black shafts to the central feathers. Same size as *galatea*.

T. g. boanensis Boano Island, northwest Ceram. Like *naïs*, but crown pale azure-blue.

T. g. acis Buru Island, west of Ceram. Like *galatea* but upperparts blackish, and some dark streaks in white rump.

T. g. obiensis Central Moluccas: Obi and Obi Latu Islands, south of Halmahera. Like *galatea* but larger, crown and lesser wing-coverts bright cobalt-blue, and rump feathers white with blue edges.

T. g. margarethae Batjan (Bacan) Island, between Obi and Halmahera. Like *galatea*, but crown purple-blue encircled by broad line of cobalt-blue, rump feathers white with broad blue edges, and tail mainly blue. Very young birds have dark brown crowns. Small: male wing averages 96, tail (excluding streamers) 85 and bill 36.5.

T. g. brunhildae Doi Island, off northwest Halmahera, north Moluccas. Like *margarethae*, but tail blue with white sides.

T. g. browningi Halmahera Island, north Moluccas. Like *margarethae*, but crown deep blue encircled by narrow line of cobalt.

T. g. sabrina Kayoa Island, between Batjan and Halmahera. Like *galatea* but for a white patch in the middle of the upper back; and outer tail feathers entirely white.

T. g. doris Morotai Island, north of Halmahera. Entire upper back white.

T. g. emiliae Rau Island, between Halmahera and Morotai Island, north Moluccas. Like *doris*, but crown silvery green-blue, prominently crested.

T. g. ellioti Kofiau Island, one of the Western Papuan Islands, between Salawati, Misoöl, Halmahera and Waigeu. Tail entirely white, the central pair of feathers long but not as narrow as on other races. Treated as a full species by many authors, and as a threatened species by Mountfort (1988).

Habitat and range A common, widespread bird of primary lowland rainforest and monsoon forest, from sea level up to 300 m, locally up to 600 m and on Karkar Island up to 820 m. Outside the main forests it occurs in gallery forests in grassy valleys, and in small forest isolates in open countryside; less commonly it is found in secondary forest and old teak plantations. The species inhabits all of the Moluccan islands except for Ternate, Tidore and Ambon, and occurs in the Western Papuan Islands of Salawati, Batanta, Waigeu, Gebe and Kofiau, almost throughout lowland New Guinea, and on some offshore islands (Biak, Walis, Manam, Karkar, Bagabag, Rossel). It may be absent between Etna Bay and Digul River and between Astrolabe Bay and Kumusi River, although it does occur near Lae and on the north side of Huon Peninsula. In most of its range it is strictly sedentary, but it vacates monsoon forest in the dry season. Where sedentary, ringing shows that adults seldom stray more than 100 m; but young birds are evicted from parental territories, and may disperse a few kilometres afield. A vagrant has occurred on Darnley Island in Torres Strait.

Population Common Paradise Kingfishers are indeed common; they can be one of the most numerous birds in the forest. Where sedentary, a pair maintains a territory of 0.3-0.5 ha; at a site near Brown River, there were once estimated to be 15 individuals in 3 ha (Bell 1980).

Food Earthworms, snails, beetles, grasshoppers, caterpillars, centipedes and lizards have been recorded, earthworms the most commonly.

Habits This bird is a sit-and-wait predator, perching semi-concealed in the dark forest understorey, and darting to the ground for prey, which is seized in the bill and taken back to a branch; there it is beaten against the perch until suitably dismembered or immobilised. The kingfisher also snatches insects from foliage. Earthworms are obtained by the bird landing on damp ground, working through surface litter and then digging and probing with its bill, which soon becomes caked with mud; the worm is dragged out and carried to a low branch, where it is struck repeatedly and worked in the bill for up to a minute. With tail pointing down, the bird sits upright, perching for long periods with little movement but for turning its head to search for prey and occasionally sweeping its tail up and down. It bathes by splashing onto the surface of a forest puddle and returning directly to its perch to preen. In the breeding season this kingfisher is vigorously territorial. It chases away intruders and sings often, answered by several other territory-owners at once; when singing it sits upright with bill agape, pointing up at 30° to the horizontal, tail pointing straight down and vibrating with the trilling, and white rump feathers conspicuously fluffed out. *Nesting:* the nest is a hole excavated by both sexes in the active carton termitarium of *Microcerotermes biroi*. This abundant termite makes its earthen nest on the side of a forest tree, 3-4.5 m above the ground. Birds of a pair take turns to fly at the chosen termitarium, striking it with the mandibles, and later clinging to it and pecking. Many trial burrows are started on different termitaria, before one is selected. One entrance tunnel was 15 cm long, ending in an egg chamber 13 cm in diameter. The clutch is of five eggs. Both sexes provide for the nestlings; at one nest many earthworms were brought for them, one at a time. Young birds are left to fend for themselves soon after leaving the nest, and adult plumage is acquired very rapidly, within 3-4 months. *Laying months:* about November-March (Brown River: Bell 1980; Coates 1985).

Description *T. g. galatea* Sexes alike. *Adult:* forehead dark purple-blue, grading through royal-blue on the forecrown to

115

light, bright azure-blue on the hindcrown. Lores blackish; cheeks and ear-coverts purple-blue; sides of neck, nape, hind-neck, mantle, scapulars and back blue-tinged black. Primaries blackish, median and lesser wing-coverts bright azure-blue, rest of upperwing purple-blue. Rump and uppertail-coverts white. Central pair of tail feathers blue, greatly elongated, with white rackets at the tip; other tail feathers white, with blue outer edges. Chin to undertail-coverts white. Axillaries and adjacent underwing-coverts black, re-maining underwing-coverts white. Bill red; eye dark brown; legs and feet yellowish-brown. *Juvenile:* head feathers very dark brown, with yellowish fringes on lores and forehead and rufous fringes elsewhere, and occasional feathers edged blue. A long, rufous superciliary stripe.

From nape to uppertail-coverts plain dark brown. Wings dark brown, most upperwing-coverts edged with bright rufous. Tail brown, central feathers washed with blue. Underparts buffy, the feathers edged (but not tipped) with black, giving a heavily streaked and scalloped effect at the sides of the throat and across the breast. Bill grey-brown, with pale tip. *Measurements:* wing of male 100-112, of female 102-114; tail (excluding streamers) of male 75-119, of female 75-119; bill of male 32-40, of female 32-39; tarsus of male 17-19, of female 17-19. Weight: male 58-65, female 55-69; other races range from 40 to 78.

References Bell (1980), Coates (1985), Forshaw (1985), Fry (1980a), White and Bruce (1986).

8 NUMFOR PARADISE KINGFISHER   Plate 3
Tanysiptera carolinae

Tanysiptera Carolinae Schlegel, 1871, Ned. Tijdschr. Dierk., 4, p. 13, Numfor Island.

Field identification Length 26 cm (10 in) excluding tail-streamers. Adult unmistak-able: a magnificent kingfisher confined to Numfor Island in Geelvink Bay, northwest New Guinea; purple-blue, with scarlet bill and white tail. Juveniles are very different, with rufous-and-buff underparts and blackish tail; but, as on the adult, the rump and uppertail- and undertail-coverts are white, which, with the typical kingfisher large-headed shape, serves to distinguish it with certainty. **Confusion species:** none; there are no other paradise kingfishers on Numfor, and only four other kookaburra and kingfisher species there, none looking in the least like this one.

Voice There is an old statement in the literature that the call is like that of a Common Cuckoo *Cuculus canorus*. That seems unlikely.

Geographical variation None.

Habitat and range Forest and open habi-tats on Numfor Island, north Irian Jaya.

The species is said to be common and widespread (Forshaw 1985).

Food Grasshoppers, beetles and snails.

Habits From what very little is known, its habits seem to be like those of the Common Paradise Kingfisher (7). **Nesting:** unknown.

Description Sexes alike. **Adult:** head, body and wings purple-blue, brightest on the crown and at the bend of the wing, darkest – almost blackish – on scapulars and tertials. Lower back, rump, uppertail-coverts and undertail-coverts white. Tail white; the middle pair of rectrices long, the shafts unwebbed and dark blue for about 12 cm, but ending in large white rackets. Underwing-coverts black. Bill red; eye dark brown; legs and feet dull olive-brown. **Juvenile:** head and upper-parts purple-blue; rump and uppertail-coverts white, with rufous wash and narrow black shaft-streaks; tail blackish, with blue wash and narrow white shaft-streaks; chin and throat cinnamon, breast and belly pale rufous, with a few purplish-black feathers; undertail-coverts white. **Measurements:** wing of male 103-112, of female 102-113; tail (excluding streamers) of male 89-110, of female 87-103; bill of male 38-44, of female 39-44; tarsus of male 18-20, of female 18-20.

Reference Forshaw (1985).

9 ARU PARADISE KINGFISHER (Lesser Paradise Kingfisher)
Plate 4

Tanysiptera hydrocharis

Tanysiptera hydrocharis G.R. Gray, 1858, Proc. Zool. Soc. London, pt 26, p. 172, Aru Islands.

Field identification Length 19 cm (7½ in) excluding tail-streamers. A blue-tailed version of the Common Paradise Kingfisher (7), found on Aru Islands and 650 km away in south New Guinea, where it occurs in the same forests as the Common Paradise. **Confusion species:** the Aru Paradise is smaller than the Common Paradise, and the adult differs from the latter in having the crown dark blue (not pale blue) encircled by mid blue, and the tail, seen from in front, dark blue (not white) or, seen from behind, dark blue with broad white sides to the middle two feathers (rather than blue with mainly white sides). Juvenile Aru Paradise Kingfishers are quite unlike the adult, dark brown above including rump and tail, with rufous-tinged wing feathers, and heavily striped underparts. Like juvenile Common Paradise, they have a rufous superciliary stripe; the best distinction is in the throat and breast, which are buffy-white with continuous black stripes on Aru, and pale buff with delicate black scallops on Common. Very young Aru Paradise Kingfishers have the crown mainly brown.

Voice Not known.

Geographical variation None: mainland and Aru Islands individuals are exactly alike.

Habitat and range Dense lowland rainforest, in Aru Islands and also in the Trans-Fly region of southern New Guinea, between Fly River to the north, Oriomo River to the east (Papua New Guinea) and to the west Merauke River or perhaps Digul River (Irian Jaya). Formerly the species was said to be common in the islands, but its present status there is unknown. On the mainland it is either rare or overlooked (it has certainly been confused with the Common Paradise): there are only about six records, and none since the late 1950s. The two species have been found at the same localities, at Wuroi and Lake Daviumbu.

Food Insects and insect larvae.

Habits Prey is taken in foliage and from the ground; otherwise this bird's habits are unknown. **Nesting:** local people say that it nests in holes in tree termitaria, like the Common Paradise Kingfisher. **Laying months:** Aru Islands, ?April (a very young bird taken in May).

Description Sexes alike. **Adult:** feathers of forehead and crown black with narrow pale blue margins; indistinct pale blue superciliary stripe; lores, cheeks, ear-coverts, hindneck, mantle, scapulars and upper back black; lower back, rump and uppertail-coverts white. Tail dark blue; central pair of feathers long, attenuated, with narrow or broad white edges proximally and ending in a large white racket. Wings purple-blue; underwing-coverts black. Underparts from chin to undertail-coverts white. Bill red; eye dark brown; legs and feet olive-grey. **Juvenile:** forehead and crown feathers brown with black margins; ear-coverts, hindneck, mantle, scapulars, back and rump uniform dark brown. Wings dark brown, the coverts with rufous edges and tips. Tail dark brown, the central pair of feathers blue-brown. Chin and throat buffy-white, margined with two long black and two long buff lines; breast buff, the feathers with blackish edges which form long streaks; belly whiter, unmarked. Upper mandible dark brown, lower mandible pale brown. *Measurements:* wing of male 82-91, of female 86-92; tail (excluding streamers) of male 56-72, of female 56-65; bill of male 28-31, of female 28-31; tarsus of male 15-17, of female 15-17.

References Coates (1985), Forshaw (1985).

10 BUFF-BREASTED PARADISE KINGFISHER (White-tailed Paradise Kingfisher)   Plate 4
Tanysiptera sylvia

Tanysiptera sylvia Gould, 1850, in Jardine's Contrib. Orn., p. 105, Cape York Peninsula, Queensland.

Field identification Length 23 cm (9 in), or 30-35 cm (12-14 in) including streamers. Unmistakable throughout its range, having a white back in all plumages. *At rest:* black scapulars and tertials conceal parts of the white back, but white is always visible as a large patch on the upper back. Orange or yellow-buff underparts further distinguish the adult from all other paradise kingfishers. Red bill, black or blue cap, and long tail, which varies geographically from all white to mainly blue, complete the picture. Juveniles have brown bills and short tails. *In flight:* the long white line from back to rump is diagnostic; on some individuals it is interrupted by black feathers in the lower back. *Confusion species:* the Red-breasted Paradise Kingfisher (11) differs in all plumages in having pink-red on the breast, rump and undertail-coverts.

Voice In eastern Papua New Guinea the song is a subdued rapid trill on one pitch, usually decelerating, like a referee's whistle blown softly (Coates 1985); it differs from the song of Common Paradise Kingfisher (7) in being faster, lower-pitched, not accelerating, and lacking any introductory whistles. Other calls are squawks, rattles, a high-pitched 'see' and a shrill, descending series of four up-slurred notes: 'krei, krei, krei, krei' or 'kiu, kiu, kiu, kiu'. In Australia the song is a soft, liquid, downward trill, or a steady ascending trill with upwardly-inflected notes, 'ch-kow, ch-kow...' or 'chop, chop...', repeated 4-5 but up to 14 times (Gill 1964).

In New Britain the song is a rising and then falling series of songbird-like chirps, accelerating to a trill up to 7 seconds long.

Geographical variation There are two pairs of subspecies, differing in hue of the underparts, crown colour (purple-blue or glossy black), and in the amount of blue in the tail. The two black-headed forms, from Bismarck Archipelago, are somewhat larger than the others and have paler underparts, broader streamers, much longer tails (excluding the streamers), and a different song. They may well constitute a separate species, the Black-headed Paradise Kingfisher, *T. nigriceps* (Coates 1985).

T. s. sylvia Northeast Australia, wintering in east Irian Jaya and south Papua New Guinea. Crown purple-blue, underparts rich cinnamon-buff, central tail feathers white, outer ones dark blue.

T. s. salvadorina Southeast Papua New Guinea, from Angabunga River to Kemp Welch River; resident. Like *sylvia* but underparts paler.

T. s. nigriceps Bismarck Archipelago (Papua New Guinea): New Britain and Duke of York Island. Cap black; scapulars black without blue wash, breast pale yellowish-buff, chin, throat and belly very pale; tail grey-blue except for shafts, inner webs and tips of the two central feathers; legs dull yellow. Tail (except streamers) 87-102 long on males, 71-102 on females. Weight: 43-74.

T. s. leucura Umboi Island, between New Guinea and New Britain. Like *nigri-*

ceps but tail entirely white; tail length (except streamers) 93-112 on males, 97-117 on females.

Habitat and range Buff-breasted Paradise Kingfishers inhabit forested lowlands and foothills and monsoon forest, generally keeping near to watercourses; termite mounds, for nesting, are a necessary component of the habitat. They tend to perch higher than Common Paradise Kingfishers, in the mid-storey and lower canopy, and come to the ground to feed. In Australia they ascend to 900 m and in New Britain to 1560 m. Locally common in parts of New Guinea and Queensland, they are unexpectedly absent from some areas and scarce in others. In some localities they occur alongside Common Paradise Kingfishers; in others the two species seem to be mutually exclusive. A density of eight pairs in 10 ha has been found at Innisfail, Queensland (Gill 1964).

Migration Populations breeding in New Guinea are probably resident, but *T. s. sylvia*, confined as a breeding bird to Australia, is a summer visitor to Queensland and winters in New Guinea. In Australia the breeding range is from Cape York Peninsula south on the eastern seaboard to about 20°S. Arrival around Townsville is in the first half of November, but on Cape York Peninsula it is three or four weeks later, which suggests immigration from separate wintering grounds. In December large flocks arrive suddenly in Cape York, perhaps from the northwest; other birds come across the Coral Sea at night, and some are killed by striking lighthouses on the Great Barrier Reef. Adults depart in the first week of April, and juveniles a week or two later.

Food Invertebrates and small vertebrates: beetles, grasshoppers, mantises, cicadas, larvae, spiders, earthworms, snails, lizards and frogs (Forshaw 1985).

Habits Buff-breasted Kingfishers catch prey on the ground and also in foliage. Mud-caked bills suggest that they dig for earthworms and larvae, perhaps in the manner of a Shovel-billed Kingfisher (15). Snails given to nestlings have the shells removed: perhaps the bird smashes snail shells at anvils as Ruddy Kingfishers (25)

are thought to do. **Nesting:** in New Britain a nest was found in a tree hole 5 m above the ground, but in Australia and mainland New Guinea the birds invariably use termitaria, sometimes in trees, but commonly on the ground. In the latter site, tunnels are 4 cm wide, 15-20 cm long, with the entrance about 16 cm above the ground and leading to an unlined egg chamber about 14 cm high and 17 cm across. The three eggs are incubated and the young brooded and fed by both parents; at one nest, 56 feeding visits were recorded in 7½ hours (Forshaw 1985). As soon as they hatch, the young keep up an almost continuous squeaking, which becomes louder in response to the slightest stimulus. At about five days of age they are already covered with down, and they grow very quickly thereafter. Later they become aggressive, constantly quarrelling and pecking at each other. The same termitarium may be used for eight years or more. **Laying months:** New Britain, May, June and probably December; mainland Papua New Guinea, February; Queensland, November, December and January.

Description *T. s. sylvia* Sexes alike. **Adult:** forehead and lores black, forecrown blue-black, paling to bright blue on the hind-crown. Cheeks, ear-coverts, hindneck and upper mantle black. Lower scapulars and tertials bluish. Lower mantle and a narrow line down the back white, rump and uppertail-coverts white. Tail dark blue, except for the long central pair of feathers, which are white. Wings blue-black above, brightest near the 'wrist', and rufous-buff below. Underparts from chin to undertail-coverts bright cinnamon-buff. Bill red; eye dark brown; legs and feet pink-red. **Juvenile:** like the adult, but forehead buffy, wing feathers buff-tipped, back black with a large buffy-white patch above it, white rump feathers fringed with blue, and orange-buff feathers of underparts edged and tipped with black; bill brown, legs and feet yellowish. **Measurements:** wing of male 89-103, of female 88-102; tail (excluding streamers) of male 55-74, of female 56-77; bill of male 30-38, of female 30-38; tarsus of male 15-17, of female 15-17. Weight: male 40-66, female (one) 54.

References Coates (1985), Forshaw (1985), Gill (1964).

11 RED-BREASTED PARADISE KINGFISHER

Plate 4

Tanysiptera nympha

Tanysiptera Nympha G.R. Gray, 1840, Ann. Mag. Nat. Hist., 6, p. 238, New Guinea, = Vogelkop Peninsula.

Field identification Length 23 cm (9 in), excluding streamers of up to 8 cm (3 in). *At rest:* a typical paradise kingfisher in shape and behaviour, with red bill, blue-black cap and upperparts, steeply graduated blue tail, and long central tail feathers ending in white rackets; but the bright pink-red breast, rump and undertail-coverts render it unmistakable in all plumages. *In flight:* pink rump and white rackets are conspicuous. Underwing-coverts rufous. Flight swift, not undulating. *Confusion species:* the Brown-headed Paradise Kingfisher (12) also has pink-red breast, rump and undertail-coverts, but its head, mantle and back are warm brown, not glossy blue-black. The ranges of the two species do not overlap.

Voice Said to be like that of the Brown-headed Paradise Kingfisher.

Geographical variation None.

Habitat and range Lowland forest mainly below 900 m, occasionally up to 1500 m, forested hills, tall secondary growth, and mangrove. The species is restricted to northern New Guinea, where it is known in Irian Jaya from the Vogelkop Peninsula east to Etna Bay in the south and Geelvink Bay in the north, and in Papua New Guinea from Huon Peninsula and Gulf, Adelbert Mountains and Bulolo and Watut River valleys. Although patchily distributed, it is locally quite common (Beehler 1978).

Food Insects, larvae, and perhaps earthworms.

Habits Poorly known, because of the little ornithological exploration in its range and because it is shy and wary. The few data suggest that it is much like the other paradise kingfishers in habits. *Nesting:* unknown, although an undated clutch of two eggs from Huon Peninsula exists (Forshaw 1985).

Description Sexes alike. *Adult:* forehead blue-black, crown dark blue. Lores, cheeks, ear-coverts, hindneck, mantle, back, scapulars and wings blue-black, except for the forewing which is bright cobalt- or azure-blue. Rump bright pink. Tail dark blue, the long central pair of feathers with broad white spatulate tips and sometimes narrowly white-edged bases. Chin and throat buff; breast, belly and undertail-coverts bright pink-red, flanks buffy, underwing-coverts rufous. Bill red; eye dark brown; legs and feet pink-red. *Juvenile:* like the adult, but the forehead is buffy, blue-black parts of the adult plumage are dark brown, with wing-coverts broadly tipped rufous, and pink-red parts are paler and less extensive. The belly is buff, and buff feathers of the throat and sides of the neck are narrowly black-fringed. Bill orange, with a brown saddle at the base of the culmen. *Measurements:* wing of male 92-99, of female 89-98; tail (excluding streamers) of male 75-80, of female 65-86; bill of male 33-36, of female 33-38; tarsus of male 15-18, of female 15-18. Weight: male (one) 57, female 47-57.

Reference Forshaw (1985).

Tanysiptera Danae Sharpe, 1880, Ann. Mag. Nat. Hist., (5), 6, p. 231, Milne Bay, New Guinea.

Field identification Length 23 cm (9 in), excluding streamers of up to 9 cm (3½ in). Confined to easternmost mainland New Guinea, where it inhabits the same forests as Common and Buff-breasted Paradise Kingfishers (7, 10) and is readily separated from them by its pink-red (not white or orange) breast, rump and uppertail-coverts. **Confusion species:** it is much more like the Red-breasted Paradise Kingfisher (11), but their ranges do not overlap and appear to approach no closer to each other than about 100 km, between Garaina (Brown-headed) and upper Watut River (Red-breasted). Adults differ from adult Red-breasted only in having the head and back rich brown, not blue-black. Juvenile Brown-headed and Red-breasted Paradise Kingfishers are separable only by the crown being brown on the former and bluish on the latter; juvenile Common and Buff-breasted Paradise Kingfishers lack any pink in the plumage, have blue caps, brown (rather than orange) bills, and (Common only) a white patch on the back.

Voice The song is very like that of the Common Paradise Kingfisher, but quicker: 1-4 mournful whistles on the same pitch, accelerating into a slightly nasal trill. A mournful call, 'wheeyou', is exactly like that of the Common Paradise Kingfisher (Coates 1985).

Geographical variation None.

Habitat and range Brown-headed Paradise Kingfishers inhabit dark primary forest, mainly on hills up to 800 m in altitude; less commonly they occur in gallery forest, alluvium forest, *Castanopsis* forest, forest edges and secondary growth. They are restricted to southeast New Guinea, from Waria River in the north and Aroa River in the south to near Alotau in the east. Although easily overlooked, they are quite common in some places but seem to be scarce in others. Near Port Moresby they occur higher in the hills than Common Paradise Kingfishers, but at Popondetta they range as low as 150 m and outnumber Common Paradise Kingfishers by five to one (Coates 1985).

Food Insects, including beetles and caterpillars.

Habits Solitary or in pairs, perching quietly in lower and middle storeys of the forest; not shy. Strongly territorial, three or four birds chasing each other from branch to branch and, when perching, sitting upright with the bill pointing up at about 30° to the horizontal, the tail pointing straight down, and the rump feathers puffed out. The mandibles gape apart, even a little when the bird sings, as it often does in this posture. Foraging behaviour has not been studied; the bird occasionally comes to the ground. **Nesting:** unknown; judging from frequency of singing, breeding is about May-October (Coates 1985).

Description Sexes alike. **Adult:** forehead, crown, lores, cheeks, ear-coverts, hindneck, mantle and scapulars are warm rufous-brown. Rump and uppertail-coverts bright pink-red. Tail steeply graduated and dark purplish-blue; central pair of feathers long, attenuated, mid-blue, with narrow white outer edges near the base and with white rackets. Chin and throat pale buffy-pink, breast and belly bright pink-red, flanks buffy-brown, undertail-coverts buffy-pink. Wing flight feathers blackish, their greater coverts deep blue, and median and lesser coverts pale azure, particularly along the shafts; underwing-coverts buff. Bill red; eye dark brown; legs and feet pink or orange. **Juvenile:** browns duller and less rufescent than on the adult; upperwing-coverts browner, less blue, and broadly margined with pale brown; feathers at sides of throat and breast with brown edges and tips, making the underparts look scaly; rump pale rufous. Belly and undertail-coverts paler and buffier than on the adult. Bill orange, with a dark brown saddle at the base of the culmen. *Measurements:* wing of male 81-93, of female 84-96; tail (excluding streamers) of male 62-79, of female 62-80; bill of male 31-37, of female 32-36; tarsus of male 15-17, of female 15-17. Weight: male 37-46, female 42-50.

References Coates (1985), Forshaw (1985).

13 LILAC KINGFISHER (Celebes Flat-billed Kingfisher)   Plate 5
Cittura cyanotis

Dacelo cyanotis Temminck, 1824, Planch. Col., 44, pl. 262, Sumatra (error for Sulawesi).

Field identification Length 28 cm (11 in). A quite large, rufous-brown and buff bird of rainforest in Sulawesi, with red bill, eye and legs, black mask, purple-blue wings and pink-lilac cheeks and ear-coverts. *In flight:* underside of the wings white, with a black patch near the 'wrist'. *Confusion species:* none. Other large land kingfishers in Sulawesi are the Celebes Green (1), Regent (2), Celebes Stork-billed (23) and Ruddy (25).

Voice A very rapid 'ku-ku-ku-ku', repeated every few minutes, likened to the cry of a falcon, cuckoo, or paradise kingfisher, and possibly given in duet (Forshaw 1983).

Geographical variation Two subspecies have been recognised on mainland Sulawesi, differing in the depth of lilac of the cheeks, and a third on Sangihe Island, a striking bird with white chin and lilac ruff of stiffened feathers.
  C. c. cyanotis Northern Sulawesi. Forehead brown, throat yellowish-buff, chin buffy-white; ear-coverts stiff, pink-lilac.
  C. c. modesta Eastern and southeastern Sulawesi. Forehead brown, chin buffy-white, throat rufous-lilac; ear-coverts less stiff than on *cyanotis*, lilac on males and rufous on females. This subspecies was not recognised by White and Bruce (1986).
  C. c. sanghirensis Great Sangihe and Siau, in the Sangihe Island group between Sulawesi and Mindanao. Brighter, more rufous; forehead black; black feathers at the base of the bill; white lines above and below the black mask; chin white, throat

lilac-buff; ear-coverts long, stiff, bright lilac; breast lilac-mauve in a broad band continuous with the ear-coverts. Tail 7%, wing 10% and bill 15% longer than on the mainland forms.

Habitat and range Lowland rainforest and drier types of forest on mountain slopes up to 1000 m in altitude in the Sangihe Islands and the 'pan-handle' of northern Sulawesi. It is widespread and quite frequently encountered in Sangihe and the northern peninsula, but has been recorded from only a few other areas: near Luwuk in east Sulawesi, near Masamba in south-central Sulawesi, and in the southeastern peninsula. It is common in Tangkoko-Batuangus Reserve.

Food Large insects: mantises, cicadas, grasshoppers, leafhoppers, beetles; also millipedes.

Habits It perches solitarily at low levels in the forest, keeping patient watch for prey on the ground below, almost motionless except for occasional turns of the head. Calling birds sit higher in the canopy. Nothing else of substance is known, and no courtship or territorial behaviour has been observed nor nests found.

Description *C. c. cyanotis* **Adult male:** forehead, crown, hindneck, mantle, back and scapulars olive-brown. Rump rufous-brown; tail foxy, quite long, and strongly graduated. Folded wing mainly purple-blue, in contrast to adjacent plumage; primaries and secondaries and their greater coverts blackish, lesser and median coverts purple-blue; outer webs of scapular feathers pale buff, forming a distinct line. A narrow superciliary line of pointed feathers is pinkish. Lores brown, almost bare, and lore and eye have narrow blue-black lines above and below, forming a mask through and behind the eye. Cheeks and sides of neck pale buffy-brown, chin buffy-white, throat and breast yellowish-buff, the whole area suffused with lilac. The buffy-pink-lilac ear-coverts are elongated, stiff, and sparsely barbed. Belly, flanks and undertail-coverts yellowish-buff; underwing-coverts yellowish-white, with the greater underwing-coverts forming a black patch. Bill red; eye dark red; legs and feet red,

nails dark brown. The bill is strongly flattened dorsoventrally. ***Adult female:*** like the male, but mask and all upperwing-coverts are black, and the superciliary line is black with white speckles. ***Juvenile:*** like the adults but duller and browner; wing-coverts broadly tipped olive-brown; bill grey-brown. ***Measurements:*** wing of male 95-106, of female 94-103; tail of male 84-95, of female 79-93; bill of male 36-42, of female 36-40; tarsus of male 15-17, of female 15-17.

References Forshaw (1983), Fry (1980a), White and Bruce (1986).

14 HOOK-BILLED KINGFISHER   Plate 5
Melidora macrorrhina

Dacelo macrorrhinus Lesson, 1827, Bull. Univ. des Sci. et de l'Ind., Sect. 2, Sci. Nat. et Géol., 12, p. 131, Dorey Harbour, New Guinea.

Field identification Length 27 cm (10½ in). Quite a large, dumpy forest kingfisher of New Guinea, told by its green-blue or yellow-green cap (male and female respectively), blackish mask, large black-and-yellowish bill, white collar, dark brown upperparts heavily scalloped with buff, and white underparts. ***At rest:*** looks large-headed, large-eyed and heavy-bodied; the sides of the head are stripy; the cutting edges of the bill are markedly recurved and the upper mandible is

strongly hook-tipped. The white collar is concealed when the neck is drawn in. ***In flight:*** the combination of white collar and brown rump is distinctive; the flight is heavy and direct, the bird looking rather short-tailed; underwing-coverts are white. ***Confusion species:*** the only other deep-forest-dwelling kingfishers in New Guinea with white underparts are the Common Paradise (7) in the north and the Aru Paradise (9) in the south. Both have a general plumage similarity to the Hook-

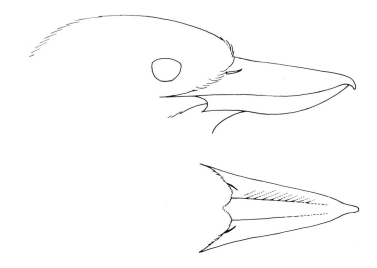

billed, but are smaller and slighter birds, without the white collar, and with white rumps and long, attenuated tails. Young of these two paradise kingfishers have the back, wings and rump brown, but the underparts are buffy, scalloped with black, and the tail long and bluish.

Voice Hook-billed Kingfishers call and sing mainly at night. The commonest call is a plaintive liquid whistle followed by 1-4 (usually 2-3) short notes at higher pitch: 'teuw-tu-tu' or 'tooo-too-too'. Sometimes there are 2-3 initial plaintive whistles; and the final short note may be trilled. The call lasts about 1 second, and resembles a short, loud Common Paradise Kingfisher song. A second call or song is an irregular series of 3-5 plaintive notes, downslurred and then upslurred, lasting 2-5 seconds (Coates 1985). The alarm is a repeated chatter, like a paradise kingfisher.

Geographical variation Three subspecies are recognised, two differing only in size and the third with its females black-crowned.

M. m. macrorrhina Western Papuan Islands (Indonesia): Misoöl, Batanta and Salawati, and the whole of New Guinea except where *jobiensis* occurs.

M. m. waigiuensis Western Papuan Islands: Waigeu. About 5% larger than *macrorrhina* in all measurements.

M. m. jobiensis Japen (Yapen) Island and from the east shores of Geelvink Bay (northern Irian Jaya, Indonesia) to Astrolabe Bay (northern Papua New Guinea). Male like male *macrorrhina*, but female lacks the yellowish-green fringes to the crown feathers, which are blackish.

Habitat and range A common bird of lowland forests and dense stands of timber in cleared areas. It occurs mainly at elevations below about 700 m, and locally it lives up to 1280 m. It inhabits primary and secondary rainforest, gallery forests in open countryside, scrub, older plantations of teak and rubber, partly cleared areas, and stands of trees in such towns as Lae. Its range is the whole of lowland New Guinea, and the adjacent islands of Japen, Waigeu, Batanta, Misoöl and Kolepom; possibly also Goodenough Island. Ringing studies show it to be sedentary, with birds recovered up to 5½ years later at the same site where ringed.

Population It is more often heard than seen, but is widely distributed and clearly common: for instance near Port Moresby and in Baiyer River Sanctuary, where a dozen can be heard calling at a time (Mackay 1980).

Food Large insects including stick-insects, and frogs.

Habits A solitary, crepuscular and nocturnal bird of forest and dense woods. It calls at nightfall, occasionally throughout dark nights, and particularly just before dawn. On bright moonlit nights it calls constantly. Birds respond to each other's calls and to human imitations of them; many individuals can be heard answering each other at night. During the breeding season they are active during the day, and sometimes they call by day. Songs are given mainly from the crown of a tall, leafy forest tree. Two or more birds countersinging, presumably territorially, call every few seconds; at other times a bird gives voice only at long intervals. Diet and foraging behaviour are surprisingly poorly known; individuals often have the bill caked in mud, so they probably dig on surface soil for prey, like a Shovel-billed Kingfisher (15). By day Hook-billed Kingfishers are generally encountered singly, perching unobtrusively low down in dark-shaded vegetation. They are not shy, and when flushed fly no great distance to another low perch, perhaps calling on landing, with the crown feathers raised and lowered. *Nesting:* the nest is a chamber excavated by the birds in an active termite nest 3-6 m above the ground on the trunk of a tree, the nest site being leafy and shaded. One nest burrow sloped upward from the side of the termitarium to near the top, where the egg chamber was 11-12 cm across. The clutch is of two eggs, which hatch at different times. Evidently the male helps to incubate or brood, at least during the day. *Laying months:* in the Port Moresby and Trans-Fly regions this kingfisher breeds in the late dry season, with eggs laid from about July to October.

Description *M. m. macrorrhina* **Adult male:** feathers of forehead and crown black, with buff fringes at the side of the forehead and with blue or turquoise fringes elsewhere. The side of the head —

lores, cheeks, most ear-coverts, and a band running around the nape – is black, but there is a narrow buff line from nostril to gape, broadening behind the gape into a streak of buff across the central ear-coverts. Below the black nape-band is a narrow white collar, sometimes broken by black in the middle of the hindneck. Mantle, back, wings, rump and tail are dark brown, with all feathers except the primaries and outer secondaries broadly tipped and fringed with yellowish-buff. Underparts from chin to undertail-coverts, and the underwing-coverts, are white, often lightly or strongly suffused with buff, pink or yellow; some chin, throat and breast feathers are delicately margined with black. Upper mandible blackish, lower mandible horn-coloured; eye very dark brown; legs and feet greenish-grey.

Adult female: like the male, but forehead and crown feathers are fringed yellowish-green, not blue, except at the sides of the crown where there is a prominent turquoise band encircling the head. The underparts are buffy, seldom pure white. *Juvenile:* like the adults, but cap darker, with narrower greenish feather fringes; hindneck-collar and underparts rufous-buff, pink-buff or yellow-buff, throat and breast feathers with fine dusky margins. *Measurements:* wing of male 112-125, of female 113-126; tail of male 81-92, of female 78-93; bill of male 44-50, of female 43-50; tarsus of male 17-21, of female 18-21. Weight: male 90-110, female 85-110.

References Coates (1985), Forshaw (1983).

15 SHOVEL-BILLED KINGFISHER
Clytoceyx rex

Plate 5

Clytoceyx rex Sharpe, 1880, Ann. Mag. Nat. Hist., (5), 6, p. 31, East Cape, New Guinea.

Field identification Length 31-34 cm (12-13½ in). A large, heavy-looking, brown-and-rufous kookaburra of hill forest in New Guinea, with a short, broad, rounded bill. As often as not it is encountered on the ground, and when flushed it usually flies to a horizontal limb in the lower or mid storeys. The flight is laboured. *At rest:* capped appearance, dark brown back and wings, broad rufous collar and rufous underparts with clearly delineated white throat. Short, robust bill, with dark upper and pale lower mandible. Tail green-blue (male) or dark rufous (female). *In flight:* the rump is conspicuously pale blue, serving to distinguish the Shovel-billed from the Hook-billed Kingfisher (14) and paradise kingfishers (7-12). *Confusion species:* in dim forest light it could be mistaken for the same-sized Rufous-bellied Kookaburra (17), which, however, has a black cap, pale bill, white mark behind the eye, white collar, and bright blue wings. (The Spangled Kookaburra (18) could also be taken for it, but its range is well to the south.)

Voice The call described by Diamond (1972) is a series of three, sometimes four, far-carrying clear liquid notes descending the scale, lasting about 1 second, the last note slightly apart. It is given mainly after dawn, from the crown of a tall tree, and with each note the tail is jerked upward. A second call (Beehler 1978) is a monotonous series of 8-10 upwardly-inflected whistles, all on the same pitch, at 1-second intervals: 'wu, wu, wu, wu...'.

Geographical variation Birds from the southern foothills of the Djajawidjaja Mountains in eastern Irian Jaya are larger than others.

C. r. rex Forested hills and mountains of New Guinea, from the Vogelkop (west Irian Jaya) to the Finisterre and Stanley Ranges (east Papua New Guinea).

C. r. imperator Irian Jaya, between Noord River and Mount Goliath. Like *rex* but larger; one specimen has wing 178, tail 135, bill 52 and tarsus 26 (Forshaw 1983).

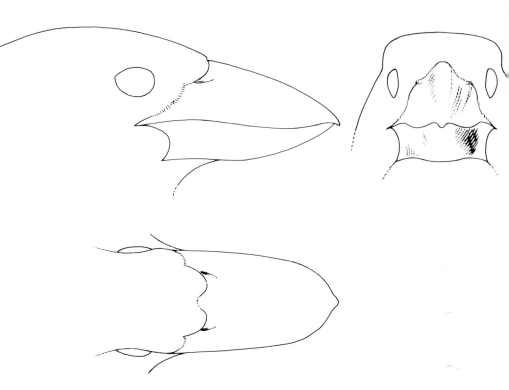

Habitat and range Shovel-billed Kingfishers inhabit lowland and hill rain-forest up to 2400 m altitude. The species is quite widespread, and commoner in hills and mountains than in low-lying forest; it keeps to wet forests, with constant cloud cover and damp soil, favouring forest edges, gardens and steep, densely wooded valleys and ravines with streams. The range is the interior of New Guinea, from Vogelkop (Irian Jaya) to the eastern extremity of mainland Papua New Guinea.

Food The diet is not well known, but the principal prey seems to be large earth-worms. Insects, larvae, snails, lizards and a snake have also been recorded.

Habits It forages on the ground, often near the buttress roots of large forest trees, where the earth over an area averaging 20 x 30 cm is ploughed up completely by the bird to a depth of 8 cm (Bell 1981). One oft-quoted observation was as follows: 'Its feet were firmly planted and the neck flattened out as it thrust its bill into the ground at a very slight angle. Then it would push, tail straight out or down, the head moving occasionally from side to side. It would be

at this for as long as a minute, perhaps; then the head would be jerked up. It shook the mud off, snapping its bill a few times. Then erect and motionless with the alert look that kingfishers have for a few seconds, then another vigorous shovel-full. Indeed, I was impressed with the effort shown in the process. David saw one get hold of a long worm and lifting its head drag out the captive sideways' (Mayr and Rand 1937). Mist-netted birds invariably have the bill caked inside and out with damp earth; although digging has only rarely been watched, shovelling would appear to be the main mode of foraging. **Nesting:** no nests have been found by ornithologists, nor any courtship displays observed. A fledgling purchased in a market near Wau in October was said to be one of two in a tree-hole nest (Forshaw 1983).

Description *C. r. rex **Adult male:*** cap dark brown, sharply demarcated from the orange neck. Forehead slightly paler, tinged with rufous, and featherlets behind the nostril are orange. A narrow but well-defined line behind the eye, running to above the ear, is orange. Chin and throat white; hindneck and sides of neck orange.

Mantle and back black, scapulars and wings very dark brown; upperwing-coverts narrowly edged with rufous, inner-most lesser wing-coverts fringed with pale blue. Rump and uppertail-coverts brilliant pale azure. Tail dark blue-brown. Breast, underwing-coverts, flanks, belly and undertail-coverts orange. Bill of massive construction, short, arched, rounded, upper mandible dark brown, lower mandible horn-coloured; eye dark brown; legs and feet dull yellow-brown. *Adult female:* like the male, but tail rufous-brown. *Juvenile:* like the adult female but duller;

upperwing-coverts prominently margined with rufous; orange neck and breast feathers fringed with dusky brown. *Measurements:* wing of male 156-171, of female 156-174; tail of male 111-132, of female 107-125; bill of male 44-54, of female 47-52; tarsus of male 24-27, of female 22-28. Weight: male 245-310, female 247-325.

References Bell (1981), Coates (1985), Forshaw (1983), Fry (1980a), Mayr and Rand (1937).

16 BANDED KINGFISHER   Plate 6
Lacedo pulchella

Dacelo pulchella Horsfield, 1821, Trans. Linn. Soc. London, 13, pt 1, p. 175, Java.

Field identification Length 20 cm (8 in). A quite small forest kingfisher of southeast Asia, with striking sexual dimorphism. The male, with its red bill, mauve-blue crown, chestnut head, banded blue-and-black upperparts and pale underparts, is like no other bird, and so is readily recognised. So is the female, once known, yet when first encountered its tiger-striped upperparts can bring to mind some quite different bird, such as a Bay Woodpecker *Blythipicus pyrrhotis* or Tiger Shrike *Lanius tigrinus*. The underside of the tail is conspicuously barred with black and silver. Individuals at rest in the forest canopy constantly raise and lower the crest, a curious habit which is diagnostic.

Voice A long whistle, 'wheeeoo', followed after a brief pause by 15 short whistles in 17 seconds. The short whistles begin as trisyllables, 'chiwiu', and either the 'chi' part gradually fades away (birds that we heard in Thailand in 1990) or the 'wiu' part does (in Malaysia: Medway and Wells 1976). Also a sharp 'wiak', repeated once or twice. These kingfishers can easily be called up by a person imitating the song.

Geographical variation There are three subspecies, males with sides of the head either rufous or black, and with or without

a hindneck-collar, females with some variation in barring.

L. p. pulchella Malay Peninsula south of about 7°N, Sumatra, Java, Riau Archipelago and North Natuna Islands (Indonesia). Male with sides of head and hindneck rufous.

L. p. amabilis Malay Peninsula north of about 7°N; Thailand, southern Burma and Indochina. Male like male *pulchella*, but hindneck the same mauve-blue as crown; female more rufous above than female *pulchella*, and with heavier black bars on the crown. Slightly larger than *pulchella*, and longer-tailed.

L. p. melanops Borneo, and Bangka Islands (off Sumatra). Like *pulchella*, but on males the sides of head and hindneck-collar are black and the forehead blackish.

Habitat and range A bird of lowland rain-forest, never very common, but quite widespread in the Malay Peninsula and Tenasserim, Burma, ranging from near sea level up to 625 m. In Borneo it occurs much higher, up to 1700 m, and on Mount Kinabalu it is commoner above 800 m than in the lowlands. In Java it is rare, and in Sumatra very rare. Evidently it does not need pools or streams in its forest habitat as many other 'dry-land' kingfishers do.

Food Insects: grasshoppers, katydids, crickets, cicadas, stick-insects, beetles and larvae. Occasionally small lizards are captured, too.

Habits Banded Kingfishers live singly or in pairs in the lower storeys of dark, damp forest. Some fieldworkers have reported them to be exceptionally sluggish for a kingfisher, others exceptionally active: probably they are territorial and much more active when breeding than at other seasons. They hawk for insects in the undercanopy and among foliage, and sometimes come down to fallen trees and the forest floor. Birds which we watched in Thailand constantly raised and lowered the crest (all of the forehead and crown feathers) at a rate of four times per 10 seconds. The crest is opened and closed slowly and evenly; when it is open the crown feathers look quite long but thin and stringy. Both sexes incessantly flaunt the crest in this manner. *Nesting:* only five or six nests have been found, in holes mostly in rotting tree trunks, up to 3 m above ground level, but twice in the globular nest of the tree-termite *Eutermes*. The clutch is of 2-5 eggs. *Laying months:* Thailand, February and May; Sumatra, May; Java, March; Borneo, January.

Description *L. p. pulchella* **Adult male:** forehead, lores, malar area, cheeks, ear-coverts and a narrow collar around the hindneck are bright chestnut, distinctly demarcated from adjacent parts. Crown mauve-blue, with black feather bases making the forecrown darker than the hindcrown. Behind the head, the entire upperparts except primaries and secondaries are banded with black and bright azure-blue; the tail has a blue tip and about six other evenly spaced narrow blue bands. Primaries blackish; secondaries blackish crossed with two narrow white bars, and with narrow white tips. Chin and throat white; breast, flanks and undertail-coverts pale orange, centre of belly white, underwing-coverts buff. Bill red; eye yellowish-brown; legs and feet pale pinkish-brown. **Adult female:** entire upperparts rufous, tiger-banded with black: black bands are narrow but distinct on the head and upperwing-coverts, and much broader and spaced out across the back and scapulars; the tail is rufous, with about six evenly spaced narrow black bands crossing all feathers. Chin and throat white; remaining underparts white or buffy-white, with narrow, irregular but distinct black bars on the breast and flanks. **Juvenile:** like the adults but duller; male with dusky bars on the cheeks and some fine dusky barring on the breast, and female with heavier black barring below than on the adult. Upper mandible mainly brown and lower mandible orange; tip of bill pale. **Measurements:** wing of male 79-86, of female 82-88; tail of male 58-66, of female 61-77; bill of male 37-42, of female 37-43; tarsus of male 13-15, of female 14-15.

References Forshaw (1983), Fry (1980a), Medway and Wells (1976).

17 RUFOUS-BELLIED KOOKABURRA   Plate 6
Dacelo gaudichaud

Dacelo Gaudichaud Quoy and Gaimard, 1824, Voyage d'Uranie, Zool., I, p. 112, pl. 25, Papuan Islands.

Field identification Length 28-31 cm (11-12 in). A large, conspicuous, strikingly marked kingfisher, common and widespread throughout New Guinea. Unmistakable. Even in poor forest light the whitish bill, broad white collar, and white streak behind the eye are diagnostic. Cap black, wings and rump bright azure, breast and belly chestnut. Tail blue on males, rufous on females.

Voice Seven calls have been described by Coates (1985). The commonest are (a) a repeated, loud 'tok' or 'chok', very like the call of a green barbet *Megalaima* sp.; (b) 'toktoktok' or 'kukukuk', so rapid as sometimes to sound like 't'k'k', repeated regularly every 2 seconds; and (c) a series on one pitch of 5-20 loud, hoarse, high-pitched barks, uttered at about one bark per second or up to twice as fast. Calls (a) to (c) all stimulate nearby birds to call also. (d) A staccato rattle, usually in flight, can become a laughing 'kikikikik-haw-haw-haw-haw-haw' when the bird alights. Other calls are (e) 3-6 slow, high-pitched shrieks, 'elew elew elew'; (f) a rasp, like that of a catbird *Ailuroedus* sp., used in chasing other bird species away; and (g) a weak whistle. Several birds calling together can sound very like chorusing Blue-winged Kookaburras (19).

Geographical variation None.

Habitat and range It keeps largely to the lower canopy of monsoon and riverine forests, but also enters primary rainforest, floodplain-forest, parklands, secondary growth, thick coastal palm scrub, mangrove, and gardens. Patches of timber left standing in otherwise cleared country are occupied, and sometimes plantations of rain trees or teak as well. Rufous-bellied Kookaburras are one of the commonest and most widely spread of all New Guinea kingfishers, strictly sedentary, mainly in lowlands below 500 m altitude, but found up to 1300 m on Mount Bosavi. They also inhabit several small inshore islands, Kolepom, Aru, Misoöl, Batanta, Salawati and Waigeu, and all of the islands in Geelvink Bay.

Food Arthropods and small vertebrates: grasshoppers, locusts, beetles, larvae, stick-insects, large spiders, crabs, small frogs and lizards.

Habits This kookaburra forages mainly in the lower canopy, snatching lizards and large insects on tree limbs and among foliage. Occasionally it comes to the ground, where one was once watched digging. Another attacked small birds entangled in a mist-net. It may well prey on songbird nestlings, for the species is often mobbed by passerines. Rufous-bellied Kookaburras are noisy, conspicuous birds, occurring singly or in pairs. When not foraging they move to an exposed outer branch or dead treetop to call, and calling often provokes neighbours to

join in. They are strongly territorial, chasing their own species and being aggressive towards some others. Territories are 2-2.5 ha in extent, defended by the male; sometimes a kookaburra seems to keep largely to a single large tree (Bell 1981). The flight is direct and swift, with deliberate even beats, but birds are capable of speedy twisting and turning in pursuit of a rival. *Nesting:* the nest is a cavity excavated by both members of a pair, in the side of a large earthen termitarium high up in a forest tree. In various parts of New Guinea, nest-digging has been seen in May, June, August and September, eggs found in October, and nestlings in January and February: the species breeds mainly in the wet season. The clutch seems to be of two eggs.

Description *Adult male:* a broad white collar encircles the neck, suffused with buffy-yellow near the mantle. Above it the cap is black, slightly glossy, with two small but distinct white patches, one along the base of the bill and one behind the eye. Below it the entire underparts are rich cinnamon, except for the underwing-coverts which are yellowish-buff. Mantle, upper back, scapulars and tertials are black, lower back, rump and uppertail-coverts bright azure-blue, the tail dark blue with dusky tip, and the wing feathers black, broadly edged with cobalt-blue (primaries and secondaries and their greater coverts) or broadly tipped with brilliant cobalt or azure (median and lesser coverts). Bill whitish-horn colour or pale yellowish-grey, sometimes with the culmen blackish; eye dark brown; legs and feet dark grey. *Adult female:* like the male, but tail rich rufous or chestnut. *Juvenile:* like the adult female, except that feathers at the base of the upper mandible are orange-buff, the hind half of the collar pale orange, and the collar and breast feathers have narrow dusky margins. Bill dark grey. *Measurements:* wing of male 131-147, of female 131-150; tail of male 87-100, of female 89-103; bill of male 51-64, of female 53-62; tarsus of male 16-21, of female 17-21. Weight: male 110-161, female 138-170.

References Bell (1981), Coates (1985), Forshaw (1983).

Dacelo tyro

Dacelo tyro G.R. Gray, 1858, Proc. Zool. Soc. London, pt 26, p. 171, pl. 133, Aru Islands.

Field identification Length 33 cm (13 in). The only kookaburra or large kingfisher in Aru Islands. It also occurs in the Trans-Fly region of southern New Guinea, where head pattern, mantle markings and breast colour prevent confusion with the Rufous-bellied Kookaburra (17), but care must be taken to distinguish it from the Blue-winged Kookaburra (19). *At rest:* head blackish, flecked with buff; dark eye; upper mandible black, lower whitish. The back looks mainly black, but the mantle is buff with black scallops and plenty of bright blue shows in wing-coverts and tail. Underparts white or buffy. *In flight:* the head looks mealy and the back and wings mainly blackish, with large areas of bright blue on rump and forewing, quite like a Blue-bellied Roller (119). *Confusion species:* very like the Blue-winged Kookaburra but smaller, with relatively short bill, darker head, dark eye, buffy brindled mantle, and dark blue tail without a white tip. There is no sexual dichromatism (as there is in the Blue-winged).

Voice Very like that of the Blue-winged Kookaburra, a series of loud, throaty 'kurk' notes.

Geographical variation Two subspecies, the Aru Islands one having much darker underparts. They are the same size.

D. t. tyro Aru Islands, Indonesia.

D. t. archboldi Southern New Guinea: Bian River and Pulau Habé (Irian Jaya) to Wassi Kussa River and Dimissisi (Papua New Guinea). Buffs and blues of upper-parts paler than on *tyro*, and underparts mainly white. Undertail-coverts buff; throat sometimes washed with buff.

Habitat and range Spangled Kookaburras frequent well-wooded, dry savannas, open deciduous forest, monsoon forest, and patches of tall scrub on open plains. Nearly all of 300 sightings by Stronach (1989) near Bensbach were in one of three habitats: riverine forest, narrow thickets of

Dillenea alata at the edges of swamps, and mosaics of monsoon forest, thickets and *Melaleuca* savanna woodland. The bird spends most of the time in the under-storey, and makes more use of exposed perches than does the Blue-winged Kookaburra. The range is as that of the Aru Paradise Kingfisher (9): the Trans-Fly region of southern New Guinea, and the Aru Islands well to the west.

Population There are no recent reports from Aru, but in its restricted range in New Guinea this is a common bird. The range is only 250 km from west to east, and most records of this kookaburra are within 50 km of the coast.

Food Insects, including beetles, ants and stick-insects (one 12 cm, or nearly 5 in, long).

Habits It forages by perching low down, only 1-4 m above ground level, patiently scanning around, moving only the head and occasionally cocking the tail, then making a shallow flight to the ground, seizing its prey in the bill, and flying up with it to another perch (Coates 1985). Also, and surprisingly for such a large bird, it flutters about on the edge of a tree, catching winged ants in the air and among the foliage (Forshaw 1983). Like the Blue-winged Kookaburra, it lives singly or in parties of up to five, which suggests that it may have the same social complexity as the two Australian kookaburras, with helpers-at-the-nest. It often forms mixed flocks with Blue-winged Kookaburras, and even calls in unison with them (Bell 1981). *Nesting:* only two nests have been reported, both containing young in March: these were holes in the sides of hemispherical tree termitaria about 45 and 60 cm in diameter, some 5 m high on the trunks of *Alstonia scholaris* and *Acacia mangium* trees (Stronach 1989).

Description *D. t. tyro* Sexes alike. *Adult:* feathers of the whole head (except chin and throat), hindneck and mantle pale yellow-buff with distinct black margins; the forehead and mantle look buff marked with black, and the crown black spangled with buff; there is often a buffy line from lore to below the eye. Back, scapulars and tertials black; rump and uppertail-coverts bright cobalt-blue; tail blue-black, bluer towards the base and sides. Wings purple-blue, lesser and median coverts edged with bright cobalt or azure-blue; primaries black. Chin and throat whitish, breast and belly warm yellow-buff, flanks and undertail-coverts pale orange. Underwing-coverts yellow-buff, underside of tail blackish. Upper mandible black, lower mandible pale horn-coloured with darker base; eye dark brown; legs and feet grey or greenish-grey. *Juvenile:* like the adult but duller, head duskier, mantle more conspicuously marked with black, throat and breast feathers narrowly margined with black. **Measurements:** wing of male 144-153, of female 145-154; tail of male 105-112, of female 107-118; bill of male 47-57, of female 49-56; tarsus of male 20-22, of female 20-23. Weight (*D. t. archboldi*): male 128-145, female 148-165.

References Bell (1981), Coates (1985), Forshaw (1983), Fry (1980a), Stronach (1989).

19 BLUE-WINGED KOOKABURRA   Plate 7
Dacelo leachii

Dacelo leachii Vigors and Horsfield, 1826, Trans. Linn. Soc. London, 15, pt 1, p. 205, Keppel Bay, Australia.

Field identification Length 38-41 cm (15-16 in). A very large kingfisher of wooded savannas in northern Australia and southern New Guinea. *At rest:* pale streaked head with large bill, white eye and white ear-coverts, dark brown back, blue wings and rump, white or buffy underparts, and blue (male) or rufous (female) tail make it a distinctive bird. *Confusion species:* in New Guinea, its greater size, more massive bill, pale eye and dark brown mantle distinguish it from the Spangled Kookaburra (18); also, its flight is slower and more buoyant and its habitat more open and park-like. Some calls of the two species are indistinguishable. In Australia, the Blue-winged Kookaburra can be told from the Laughing Kookaburra (20) by its longer bill, pale eye, white ear-coverts, large amount of pale blue in the wings and on the rump, and by the voice; birds with blue tails are Blue-winged Kookaburras, but those with rufous tails could be either species.

Voice The territorial song is delivered by two or three birds more or less in unison: a demented, maniacal, far-carrying, screeching cackle, 'kuk-kuk-kuk-kuk', developing into loud 'ow's and trills and then ceasing abruptly. In duets one bird commonly calls at higher pitch than the other. The trills and 'ow' calls can also be uttered separately, and several other short, strident calls, barks and hoarse screeches have been described.

Geographical variation Five subspecies are recognised, one in New Guinea and the rest in Australia. They vary in the amount of shaft-streaking in the crown, the hue of browns and blues in the upperparts, and in the underparts colour/pattern (white or yellow-buff, plain or faintly barred).

    D. l. leachii From Broome and Derby, Kimberley Division, across north Australia to Cooktown, Queensland, southeast rarely to Brisbane; just into New South Wales (Byron Bay).

    D. l. kempi Cape York Peninsula, south to about Cooktown and Mitchell River (15-16°S). Upperparts darker.

    D. l. cervina Melville Island and the humid coastline of Van Diemen Gulf, north Northern Territory. Darker above and below than *leachii*, the breast pale orange, and about 10% smaller (wing 170-195).

    D. l. cliftoni The Pilbara region, west Australia, from De Grey River to Wooramel River and Shark Bay, east to

Lake Dora. It is separated from *leachii* by Eighty Mile Beach and the Great Sandy Desert. Like *leachii*, but with buffy underparts and much narrower shaft-streaks on the crown, making the head whiter. Slightly larger than *leachii*.

D. l. intermedia Southern New Guinea, from Mimika River (Irian Jaya) to the mouths of Fly River (Papua New Guinea) and again in coastal lowlands from Eloa River to Amazon Bay. Like *leachii*, but browns of upperparts darker, blues brighter, head more heavily streaked, and underparts whiter. Papua New Guinea birds are the size of *leachii*, but Irian Jaya ones seem to be markedly larger (wing 202-216).

Habitat and range Blue-winged Kookaburras inhabit open woodland, park-like wooded savannas, tall trees and woods along watercourses, riverine forests, cultivated land with stands of timber, outer urban gardens, plantations, eucalypt forest on plains and in broken country (northwest Australia) and mangrove (Irian Jaya). In such habitats they range over northern Australia from the coast to 400 km inland, south to 25-26°S, and the coastal lowlands of southern New Guinea (up to 600 m high on Sogeri Plateau, rarely up to 900 m). Over most of this great range the Blue-winged Kookaburra is frequent or common; in eastern Cape York Peninsula it is extremely abundant. The drier the countryside, the less common it becomes, and in most of Queensland south of 15°S it is only half as plentiful as the Laughing Kookaburra. It is sedentary, apart from some local movements according to season (for instance near Darwin: Crawford 1979).

Food Large arthropods taken mainly on the ground, and small vertebrates: grasshoppers, cicadas, beetles, insect larvae, centipedes, scorpions, crayfish, snails, earthworms, frogs, lizards, snakes, terrapins, small fish, small birds, birds' eggs, and disabled birds up to the size of small doves.

Habits Blue-winged Kookaburras live year-round in family parties of up to 12 birds: a pair, with their adult progeny from previous matings. Often, however, the 'party' consists of the pair only, and many individuals live solitarily until breeding

commences. Birds occupy a territory varying in size according to its productivity, and all group members help to establish and defend the territory and to provide for the nestlings. Blue-winged and Laughing Kookaburras are interspecifically territorial, at least occasionally (Frith 1976). Territories are advertised by singing, with several birds joining in to make a loud cacophony, in Australia more at dawn and dusk than during the day, in New Guinea at any time from before dusk until after dark. When calling, the bird points the bill skywards and cocks the tail over the back. Foraging is passive, the kookaburra perching stolidly on a branch, telegraph wire or similar perch, 2-4 m above open ground, waiting for prey to appear. From time to time it moves to a new perch some distance away. If while flying it sees some small animal, it alights precipitately, gauges its prospects, then flies down rapidly to seize the prey. The species is opportunistic, coming to bush fires to feed on fleeing animals, or trying to eat a bird caught in a mist-net. It is wary, difficult to approach, never becoming as familiar as Laughing Kookaburras. **Nesting:** eggs are laid in cavities excavated in termitaria, and in unlined tree holes. In Northern Territory, Australia, nest holes are commonly made in the large ground-level termitaria of the termite *Nasutitermes triodiae*. Earthen nests of different species of termites, from 4.5 to 30 m high in trees, are used in New Guinea. Tree-hole sites are usually at least 2 m above ground level. The clutch is generally of two eggs, but up to five are known, the circumstances suggesting that they may be laid by more than one female of the social group. **Laying months:** New Guinea, about September-January; Australia, September-December.

Description *D. l. leachii* **Adult male:** feathers of forehead, crown, cheeks and ear-coverts lanceolate, white (or near the bill buffy) with thin dark brown shaft-streaks; lores and malar area white with dark streaks. Chin white; throat, sides of neck and hindneck buffy-white, finely marked with pale grey-brown vermiculations; breast, belly, flanks and undertail-coverts the same but more or less strongly suffused with yellowish-buff. Mantle, upper back, scapular and tertial feathers dark brown, tipped paler; lower back, rump and uppertail-coverts bright azure-blue. Tail purple-blue, the central pair of feathers narrowly and the others broadly tipped with white, and the outer feathers barred. Primaries and secondaries dark brown with purple-blue outer webs, the secondaries slightly pale-tipped; primary and greater secondary coverts and alula purple-blue; median and lesser coverts bright azure-blue, sometimes with the blackish feather centres showing. Underwing-coverts white, margined with dark brown. Upper mandible brownish-black, lower mandible pale horn or whitish; eye white or very pale yellow, orbital skin white; legs and feet pale greenish-grey. *Adult female:* slightly larger than the male, and uppertail-coverts and tail are rufous, barred with black and tipped with buff. *Juvenile:* like the adult female, but the crown looks paler and breast feathers are narrowly margined with dusky brown. *Measurements:* wing of male 182-205, of female 189-209; tail of male 111-130, of female 114-134; bill of male 71-88, of female 74-92; tarsus of male 25-29, of female 25-30. Weight: male 250-322, female 260-370.

References Coates (1985), Forshaw (1983), Frith (1976), Fry (1980a).

20 LAUGHING KOOKABURRA   Plate 7
Dacelo novaeguineae

Alcedo novae Guineae Hermann, 1783, Tabl. Affin. Anim., p. 192, New Guinea, *ex* Daubenton, Planch. enlum., 1783, pl. 663, = New South Wales.

Field identification Length 39-42 cm (15^1/$_2$-16^1/$_2$ in). The world's largest kingfisher, some females reaching nearly 0.5 kg. It is a common and familiar woodland and city-parks bird of eastern Australia, Tasmania and the southwest, and is found also near Auckland, New Zealand. It can readily be told even at a distance by its solid shape, large, whitish head with dark brown ear-coverts, white underparts, brown back and black-barred rufous tail. *Confusion species:* it overlaps with the Blue-winged Kookaburra (19) from Cape York Peninsula to near Brisbane, and is distinguished from it by its dark eye, dark ear-coverts, and vestigial blue areas in wing and rump (conspicuously bright blue on the Blue-winged). The bill is shorter, more conical and less tip-tilted than on the Blue-winged. Voices differ.

Voice The famous laugh is the territorial song, delivered by two or three birds at once, mainly about dawn and dusk. A single bird's laugh lasts 5-8 seconds, starting and finishing with low chuckles and with a comedian's side-splitting laugh in the middle: 'koo-hoo-hoo-hoo-hoo-ha-ha-ha-HA-HA-hoo-hoo-hoo'. It is repeated many times. There are six short calls (Parry 1970): (a) a chuckling 'koo-hoo-hoo', used all year as a location call; (b) a location call 'hoo', used in the breeding season only; (c) a squawk, used by begging juveniles, and by adult females food-begging during courtship; (d) the courtship call is a soft squawk; (e) 'koo-aa', warning of danger; and (f) the 'ha-ha-ha-ha' component of the song on its own, which signals aggression.

Geographical variation There are two subspecies, differing only in size.
D. n. novaeguineae The whole range of the species excepting Cape York Peninsula.
D. n. minor Cape York Peninsula, south to about Cooktown. Smaller: wing of males 186-212 and of females 191-207; tail 127-153, bill 58-73.

Habitat and range Laughing Kookaburras inhabit open, dry eucalypt forest, woodland, wooded farmland and watercourses, homesteads, city parks, and gardens. The natural range at the time of European settlement was eastern Australia from Cape York Peninsula, east and west of the Great Dividing Range, to Victoria, west to Flinders Range and Cape Otway. Multiple introductions were made, which ultimately led to successful colonisation, into the southwest first in 1897, Tasmania about 1905, Kangaroo Island in 1926 and Flinders Island in 1940. Several attempts were made to colonise New Zealand, with introductions between 1866 and 1880, but Laughing Kookaburras survive only along the west coast of Hauraki Gulf, between Cape Rodney and Whangaparaoa Peninsula; vagrants sometimes occur elsewhere in New Zealand, but whether they originate in the north or in Australia is unknown. In Australia Laughing Kookaburras are for the most part common, and locally very common. Where their range overlaps that of the Blue-winged Kookaburra, the two species tend to be mutually exclusive. In Magnetic Island off Townsville, they are interspecifically territorial; elsewhere the two kookaburras can be seen sharing telegraph wires, watching for prey in the sugarcane fields. Around Cooktown, the Laughing favours large eucalypts near water and the Blue-winged keeps to drier woodland savanna. Further south, Laughing Kookaburras inhabit a variety of wooded and forested country, in Tasmania sclerophyll forest and savanna woodland, and everywhere they seem to have benefited from human settlement and urbanisation. They are strictly sedentary.

Laughing Kookaburra 'laughing'

Population Seven estimates of density in New South Wales and Victoria vary from 0.05 to 0.8 individuals per ha (Blakers *et al*. 1984). Taking the average, 0.30 per ha,

and extrapolating to the high-density areas of the total range gives a population estimate of 66.5 million birds. (See also Sacred Kingfisher (50).)

Food Laughing Kookaburras are predators of a large variety of animals; at birdtables they are also very fond of cheese and raw meat. Near Melbourne, the diet of breeding birds is 35% lizards and snakes, 32% insects, 15% earthworms, 8% crayfish, 1% rodents, and 7% birdtable scraps (Parry 1970). Elsewhere frogs, fish and adult and nestling birds are eaten. Snakes feature importantly in the diet; ones 20-30 cm long are commonly fed to nestlings, and an adult once ate a snake about 1 m long, probably a venomous copperhead *Austrelaps superbus* (Ralph and Ralph 1973).

Habits Nearly all of the food is captured on the surface of the ground. Some food is obtained in shallow water, and occasionally kookaburras take fish from garden ponds. They forage by waiting for long periods on a branch, roof or powerline: when prey appears below, the bird swoops down, lands by it and at the same instant strikes or seizes it with the bill; it then usually returns to its perch, against which it beats the prey repeatedly until it is immobilised, and then swallows it whole. The kookaburra sometimes beats its prey, especially a snake, against the ground; snakes are also dropped from a height to stun them. Laughing Kookaburras are strictly territorial, and a pair stays year-round in its territory. Commonly the pair is accompanied by its grown young, up to four or five in number, each kookaburra requiring on average 1.25 ha of land, so that a group territory becomes larger with each additional young helper allowed to remain in it. Such a group defends its large territory corporately, and the 'helpers', non-breeding adults, assist the breeding pair in nesting duties: incubating the eggs, brooding and feeding the chicks. By day the pair and helpers keep in sight or sound of each other, and at night they roost in a leafy treetop in a dense cluster. A bird can 'help' for up to four years; eventually either it finds a mate and moves out to nest elsewhere, or it remains to breed in the family territory, replacing a parent who has died. In this regard kookaburra society is very like that of Pied Kingfishers (87) and of several bee-eaters (98, 99, 101, 106, 109). All of these cooperative-breeding species tend to be long-lived; Laughing Kookaburras are known to have lived wild for at least 10 and 12 years. **Nesting:** the birds pair for life. Courtship is not elaborate, and is marked by the male beginning to feed the female, six weeks before egg-laying, and by both sexes spending much time in or by the selected nest site, a hole in a tree or tree termitarium. Courtship-feeding becomes more frequent until egg-laying commences, and stops a few days later. Nest holes, which are occasionally also in masonry, are generally several metres above ground level, with an entrance 15 cm wide opening directly into the egg chamber, which is usually about 30 cm across and 25 cm high. A pair or group of birds can use the same nest hole for many years. Two or three eggs comprise the clutch, and when up to five occur it is likely that some have been laid by a female helper. All members of the group develop brood-patches, and helpers incubate for up to one-third of the time. The young hatch after 24-26 days over a period of a few days, and are ready to leave the nest after a further 33-39 days. Thereafter they depend totally on their parents and helpers for food for at least two months (Parry 1970). **Laying months:** southeast Australia, September-December.

Description *D. n. novaeguineae* **Adult male:** forehead and crown feathers a mixture of pale buff and tawny-brown, barred with dark brown; sides of the crown white, with pale brown vermiculation; nape dark brown. Lores dusky; ear-coverts and cheeks dark brown with a russet wash. Malar area, sides of the neck and hindneck buffy-white with some pale brown vermiculation. Mantle, back, scapulars and wings dark brown, but lesser and median upperwing-coverts have dull pale blue tips and in the folded wing the bases of the outer primaries form a small whitish mark. A pale blue patch in centre of rump, variable in size. Uppertail-coverts rufous, banded with black. Tail rufous, with 6-7 variable dusky bands; central feathers tipped with white, and outer feathers have narrow white outer edges. Chin and throat white; remaining underparts white, with pale grey vermiculation on the breast and pale brown banding on the flanks. Underwing-coverts

white with brown margins. Underside of tail white with dusky bands. Upper mandible brownish-black, lower mandible pale horn with the base brown; eye dark brown; legs and feet pale greenish. *Adult female:* larger than the male, and with less blue in the rump. *Juvenile:* plumage as that of the adult female, but slightly darker and more barred. *Measurements:* wing of male 211-228, of female 216-237; tail of male 128-166, of female 146-170; bill of male 62-72, of female 62-85; tarsus of male 24-27, of female 25-29. Weight: male 310-345, female 355-480.

References Forshaw (1983), Fry (1980a), Parry (1970, 1973).

21 WHITE-RUMPED KINGFISHER (Glittering Kingfisher) Plate 8
Halcyon fulgida

Halcyon fulgidus Gould, 1857, Proc. Zool. Soc. London, pt 25, p. 65, Lombok.

Field identification Length 30 cm (12 in). Unmistakable, given any but the most fleeting of views. The head is black, with scarlet iris and orbital ring and long red bill, and is sharply demarcated from the white chin and throat. Mantle, wings and tail are dark blue, often looking black in the poor light of the bird's tropical-forest home, and contrasting sharply with the snowy-white back and rump. The entire underparts of the adult are white (except for the blackish vent, which cannot generally be seen in the field), and legs and feet are bright red. The tail is rather long and a little graduated, greyish-black below. Juveniles differ from adults chiefly in having a buffy wash on breast and flanks. *At rest:* the white rump may not always be visible, yet the blue-black upperparts, white underparts, and scarlet or orange-red soft parts are diagnostic. *In flight:* the white back and rump rule out confusion with any other similarly shaped bird. The voice is unknown.

Geographical variation Two subspecies, differing slightly in measurements and form of the bill. The species is confined to the Lesser Sunda Islands, Indonesia, and its characters seem to link it with *Tanysiptera* as well as with *Halcyon*.
  H. f. fulgida Restricted to Lombok and Sumbawa Islands.
  H. f. gracilirostris Flores Island. Poorly differentiated, but averages 4 mm longer in the wing and 2 mm longer in the tail than the nominate form, and its bill is a little narrower (i.e. more compressed laterally).

Habitat and range The White-rumped Kingfisher inhabits rainforests and bamboo forests on the three Lesser Sunda islands of Lombok, Sumbawa and Flores, east of Bali and south of Borneo and Sulawesi, in Indonesia. Nothing is known about its population density there, nor about its ability, if any, to adapt to disturbed or secondary forest. It is doubtless quite sedentary, and its numbers are likely to have been greatly diminished by deforestation in recent decades.

Food An old record of stomach contents lists insects and insect larvae.

Habits Almost nothing is on record, except that White-rumped Kingfishers occur solitarily or in pairs, and sit patiently and unobtrusively on a vantage point low down in the forest. If it is at all like the other supposedly primitive forest-dwelling halcyons of the Wallacean region, it will plunge down from its perch to grab an insect or perhaps a small vertebrate on the forest floor – but that is pure speculation. *Nesting:* all that is known is what can be inferred from the capture of a single female in a nest burrow in an earthen bank, and from the fact that a clutch of two eggs has been taken and on another occasion a single nestling. *Laying months:* Flores, March and (by inference) January; Sumbawa (by inference) February or March.

Description Sexes alike. *Adult:* forehead, crown, hindneck, lores and cheeks glossy black, with a wash of purple-blue on the hindcrown and nape; mantle and scapulars deep purplish-blue; lower back and rump lustrous or pearly white; tail deep purplish-blue above and glossy dark grey below; upperwing-coverts, primaries and secondaries mainly blackish, more or less broadly edged and tipped with glossy purple-blue; tertials entirely purple-blue, like the scapulars. Chin and throat to flanks, belly and undertail-coverts snowy-white, the feathers with dusky bases which sometimes show through; a small patch around the vent is blackish. Inner greater underwing-coverts white, outer ones black, and all lesser underwing-coverts black. Bill bright red; eye and

orbital skin red or orange-red; legs and feet bright red or orange-red. *Juvenile:* like adult, but upperparts less glossy, slaty rather than coal-black, without so much purplish suffusion; breast and flanks tinged buff or rufous-buff, and breast feathers narrowly and inconspicuously fringed with brown-grey. Bill yellow-orange, eye light brown. *Measurements:* (*H. f. fulgida*) wing of male 124-140, of female 127-135; tail of male 105-118, of female 111-112; bill of male 48-52, of female 48-53; tarsus of male 20-22, of female 21-22.

Reference Forshaw (1985).

22 STORK-BILLED KINGFISHER   Plate 9
Halcyon capensis

Alcedo capensis Linnaeus, 1766, Syst. Nat., ed. 12, I, p. 180, Cape of Good Hope (error for Chandernagore, Bengal).

Field identification Length 35 cm (14 in). The large size alone serves to distinguish this red-billed, bluish-backed kingfisher from all others in its range except the Brown-winged Kingfisher (24), which has dark brown (not blue) back, wings and tail. *At rest:* very large scarlet bill; blue back, wings and tail; head and underparts rufous or creamy; some races are grey-capped. *In flight:* brilliant azure rump and orange underwing-coverts, as on many other kingfishers. The bird is large and heavy-looking, and the flapping flight is laboured; the large head and very large bill give it a top-heavy appearance. *Confusion species:* Brown-winged Kingfisher (see above), a coastal bird ranging from Bengal to south Thailand.

Voice The call, given frequently at perch and in flight, is a loud, raucous cackle, 'ke-ke-ke-ke....', the first syllable explosive and sometimes uttered on its own. Another call (the territorial song?) is a pleasant 'peer...peer...purr' (Forshaw 1983).

Geographical variation Fifteen subspecies are recognised, some of them only poorly differentiated, varying in hue of the back and wings, colour of the head and under-

parts (rufous, buff or creamy – several subspecies being markedly capped), and size (wing averages being from 142 to 164 mm).

H. c. capensis India and Sri Lanka. Cap clearly defined, dark olive-brown; collar yellowish-buff, paler on the chin and throat; remaining upperparts mainly dull greenish-blue and underparts rich orange-buff. Male wing averages 155.

H. c. osmastoni Andaman Islands. Paler than nominate race and smaller: male wing averages 147.

H. c. intermedia Nicobar Islands. Like *capensis* but not capped; head, neck and underparts rich yellowish-buff.

H. c. burmanica From Burma to about Isthmus of Kra in Malay Peninsula. Paler than *capensis*, cap greyer and darker, underparts richer. Male wing averages 151; relatively short-billed.

H. c. malaccensis Malay Peninsula, Riau and Lingga Archipelagos. Like *burmanica* but cap darker and olive; underparts darker. Small: male wing averages 145, tail 88 and bill 80.

H. c. cyanopteryx Sumatra, Bangka Island, Belitung Island and Borneo. Like *malaccensis*, but cap paler and buff-washed, upperparts bluer and underparts paler.

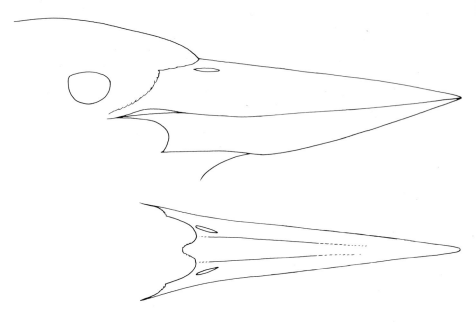

H. c. simalurensis Simeulue Island (south of Banda Atjeh, northwest Sumatra). Slightly duller than *cyanopteryx*.

H. c. sodalis Banyak (Banjak) Island, between Simeulue and Sumatra. Like *simalurensis* but female larger, wing averaging 161; the male has not yet been described.

H. c. nesoeca Nias Island and Batu Islands, southeast of Simeulue Island, off Sumatra. Cap and underparts paler than on *simalurensis* and back, wings and tail bluer.

H. c. isoptera Mentawai Islands, southeast of Batu Islands, Sumatra. Underparts much paler than on *simalurensis*, and rump green-blue. Larger: size of *burmanica*. Van Marle and Voous (1988) do not separate *isoptera* and *nesoeca* from *sodalis*.

H. c. javana Java. Like *cyanopteryx*, but cap light buffy-brown, remaining upperparts greenish-blue and underparts deep yellow-buff.

H. c. floresiana Bali, Lombok, Sumbawa and Flores Islands. Like *javana*, but sides of the head are suffused with green. Larger: size of *capensis*.

H. c. gouldi Northern Philippine Islands. Like *intermedia*, but blues paler and greener, and buffs richer. Females much larger than males: male wing averages 145, tail 83, bill 83; female wing 154, tail 92, bill 84.

H. c. smithi Southern Philippines, from southeast Luzon and Masbate to Basilan and Mindanao. Like *gouldi* but buffs yellower. Same size as female *gouldi*.

H. c. gigantea Sulu Archipelago, between Mindanao and Borneo. Head and underparts creamy-white. Large: male wing averages 158, female wing 164.

Habitat and range On small islands and sometimes elsewhere it inhabits wooded seashores, but the major habitat is the forested edges of streams, canals, broad placid rivers, reservoirs, lakes, and mangrove. It keeps to lowlands, up to 800 m in altitude, but is found occasionally as high as 1200 m in India and Borneo. The species has a great range, from Gulf of Cambay and Ahmadabad in Gujarat, India, to Indochina, Malaysia, Sumatra, Java, the Lesser Sunda Islands, Borneo, Palawan and the Philippines. On the whole it is rather sparsely distributed, but locally can be quite common, for instance in west Thailand, tidal forests of Java, the coasts of Simeulue Island and north Borneo, and mangroves in the Philippines. It occurs deep in primal rainforest, and sometimes wanders onto open coconut plantations and paddyfields. Ringing shows the species to be sedentary.

Food Freshwater, brackish and seashore fishes up to 10 cm long, crabs taken from mudflats, crustaceans, frogs, lizards, rodents, young birds, insects and insect larvae.

Habits Stork-billed Kingfishers are solitary, shy and (their size notwithstanding) inconspicuous birds which spend much time perching quietly, half concealed on a branch overhanging water or on a mangrove stilt root, looking out for prey. They sit motionless but for bobbing the head about seven times per minute, and wagging the tail fore and aft a little. Prey is carried back to the perch and struck against it to right and left a few times until immobilised. Territory-holders are aggressive and chase away other birds, including storks and eagles. **Nesting:** the species is monogamous and territorial. Both sexes dig the nest hole, striking the chosen spot in flight with the tip of the bill to loosen earth or wood, then clinging and working the site by pecking and prising. The nest hole is made in a riverbank, decayed tree trunk, or tree termitarium. Sometimes a natural tree hollow is taken over. Once a pair spent weeks trying without success to bore a burrow into a brick wall (Forshaw 1983). There are 2-5 eggs, and the bird is single-brooded, or sometimes double-brooded (or it lays replacement clutches in the same nest). **Laying**

months: India, January-September; Sri Lanka, January-May and August-September; Nicobar Islands and Burma, April; Malaysia, March and April; Singapore, about May and June; Java, January or February; Philippines, April.

Description *H. c. capensis* Sexes alike. **Adult:** forehead, crown, lores, cheeks and ear-coverts dark olive-brown; collar around hindneck and sides of neck dark yellow-buff. Mantle, back, scapulars, tertials and tail dull greenish-blue; upperwing-coverts slightly brighter blue; primaries and secondaries dark brown, edged with blue; lower back and rump brilliant pale azure-blue. Chin and throat pale yellow or buff; rest of underparts including underwing-coverts rich orange-buff. Bill scarlet, darker towards the tip; eye dark brown; legs and feet orange-red. **Juvenile:** like the adult, but with narrow dusky fringes to the feathers of hindneck and breast. **Measurements:** wing of male 150-160, of female 152-167; tail of male 96-99, of female 96-111; bill of male 84-94, of female 81-90; tarsus of male 18-20, of female 18-20. Weight (*H. c. gouldi*): male 143-180, female 182-225.

Reference Forshaw (1983).

23 CELEBES STORK-BILLED KINGFISHER (Great-billed Kingfisher)   Plate 9
Halcyon melanorhyncha

Alcedo melanorhyncha Temminck, 1826, Planch. Col., 66, pl. 391, Celebes.

Field identification Length 35 cm (14 in). Confined to Sulawesi and its offshore islands, where it is much the largest kingfisher and, with its huge black bill and dark greenish-brown and buffy-white plumage, is unmistakable.

Voice A loud 'kak-kak-kak' or repeated 'ke-kak'.

Geographical variation Besides the mainland form, there are two island subspecies which are larger, with partly red bills.
H. m. melanorhyncha Sulawesi and its southern islands, Wowoni, Butung, Muna, Kabaena and Salajar (Indonesia).

H. m. dichrorhyncha Banggai Archipelago, east of Sulawesi. Like *melanorhyncha*, but base of the bill dark red; wing and tail longer, bill noticeably larger.
H. m. eutreptorhyncha Sula Islands, east of Banggai Archipelago, Indonesia. Intermediate between the two foregoing subspecies in size and in the amount of dark red on the bill.

Habitat and range It inhabits rivers, estuaries, creeks, mangrove, wooded seashores, shrubby sea-cliffs, and trees in coastal villages, and ranges mainly in coastal Sulawesi and its southern and eastern islands. It is quite common, at least in the Togian Islands, and on larger rivers in Dumoga and Morowali Reserves. Inland, it has been recorded in Lore Lindu Reserve, at 575 m (Watling 1983).

Food Mainly crabs; also crayfish.

Habits It feeds solitarily or in pairs, perching above shallows and plunging down for crabs. The bird is wary, and when disturbed flies off into the forest. Almost nothing is known of its biology; those on Butung and Muna Islands are in breeding condition in September.

Description *H. m. melanorhyncha* Sexes alike. *Adult:* head, neck, mantle, rump and entire underparts creamy-white, with a buffy-yellow wash on belly and undertail-coverts; lores dusky, and the feathers of the forehead, malar area, cheeks and ear-coverts have dusky brown centres, giving the whole face a dusky appearance. Uppertail-coverts dusky brown, with cream-white fringes. Back, scapulars, wings and tail dark dull greenish-brown, clearest green on secondaries and tail; some lesser wing-coverts are narrowly pale-fringed. Bill black, sometimes with a small dark red spot at the base; eye dark brown; legs and feet dark red-brown. *Juvenile:* like the adult, but feathers of the hindneck and breast are narrowly fringed with dark brown. *Measurements:* wing of male 142-158, of female 143-156; tail of male 87-95, of female 85-94; bill of male 76-84, of female 72-89; tarsus of male 16-19, of female 17-19. Weight: one male 184, one female 203.

References Forshaw (1983), Watling (1983).

24 BROWN-WINGED KINGFISHER   Plate 9
Halcyon amauroptera

Halcyon Amauropterus Pearson, 1841, J. Asiat. Soc. Bengal, 10, pt 2, p. 635 (Calcutta, India).

Field identification Length 35 cm (14 in). A fine large coastal kingfisher ranging from the Bay of Bengal to the Thailand-Malaysian border, readily identified by its large red bill, pale orange head and underparts, dark brown back, wings and tail, and brilliant blue rump. Legs and feet red. Loud, raucous voice. **Confusion species:** the Stork-billed Kingfisher (22) is sympatric, slightly larger, with an even more massive red bill and the same pale orange neck and underparts and brilliant blue rump; but it is grey-capped, and mantle, scapulars, wings and tail are blue (not dark brown). Three other halcyons with all-red bills occur in the range of the Brown-winged, but they are all readily told by their colloquial-name features: the Ruddy (25), White-breasted (26) and Black-capped Kingfishers (29).

Voice A harsh cackling 'chak-chak-chak-chak-chak', uttered frequently.

Geographical variation None.

Habitat and range It is almost entirely coastal, keeping to mangrove, mudflats, estuaries and brackish creeks, but occasionally it wanders a few kilometres inland on larger rivers. From northeast India (the northerly mouths of Mahanadi River, Orissa) through the Bangladeshi Sundarbans and Burmese coast and coastal islands, the Gulf of Martaban and west coast of peninsular Thailand including Mergui Archipelago, to Ladang, Langkawi, Tarutao and Dayang Bunting Islands on the Malaysia border. Locally common; probably sedentary.

Food No detailed studies; mainly crabs and fish.

Habits It hunts from perches quite high in mangrove trees, keeping intent watch and then dropping, levelling out and flying low, to land on mud and seize a crab in the same instant, or to plunge into water with the wings momentarily uplifted (Forshaw 1983). Larger prey items are carried in the bill to a low perch and struck against it with slow, deliberate sideways swings of the head. The bird tosses its head once to reposition a fish in its bill and again to swallow it, then wipes the bill against the perch. It occurs singly or in pairs, plunging mainly into still water, but sometimes into rough surf. It scratches itself with a foot over the drooped wing (Forshaw 1983); all movements at perch seem laboured. The flight is strong, mainly with steady beats low over the water but with some rapid double beats interspersed as it ascends and banks through mangrove. It calls at perch and in flight. **Nesting:** few nests have been described; one was excavated by the birds near the top of a 5-m-high mud cliff by a creek, the burrow 10 cm wide and 30 cm long, opening into an egg chamber 20 cm in diameter. Another burrow was 60 cm long. The clutch is of 3-4 eggs, which measure 33.1-36.0 × 29.1-30.2. **Laying months:** India, March-April.

Description Sexes alike. **Adult:** head, neck, upper mantle, and entire underparts including underwing-coverts orange or deep orange-buff, but small forehead feathers have dusky centres, and lores and featherlets immediately below and behind the eye are blackish with orange fringes. Lower mantle, scapulars, wings, uppertail-coverts and tail dark brown; inner webs of flight feathers pale orange. Back and rump brilliant glossy azure-blue. Bill scarlet, dusky towards the tip; iris dark brown, orbital skin red; legs and feet scarlet, nails blackish. **Juvenile:** like the adult, but upperwing-coverts (and on very young birds mantle and scapular feathers) narrowly pale-fringed, and breast feathers dark-fringed, giving a scalloped effect. **Measurements:** wing of male 141-152, of female 143-155; tail of male 84-96, of female 83-98; bill of male 78-90, of female 75-87; tarsus of male 18-19, of female 18-19.

References Baker (1934), Forshaw (1983).

25 RUDDY KINGFISHER   Plate 9
Halcyon coromanda

Alcedo coromanda Latham, 1790, Index Orn., I, p. 252, Coromandel, India.

Field identification Length 25 cm (10 in). A shy and secretive kingfisher which keeps to dense woody cover in mangrove or forest, and is more often heard than seen. Usually the only encounter is a glimpse of a silver- or pale-blue-rumped orange bird as it flies away swiftly through the trees. If a view is obtained, its large red bill and overall bright rufous plumage, with pale silvery-azure rump, preclude confusion with any other species.

Voice In India a high-pitched shrill monosyllable, quite like the flight call of a River Kingfisher (76); in Japan, a tremulous fluty 'pyorr, pyorr ...' repeated at intervals – perhaps a territorial song.

Geographical variation Nine subspecies,

differing mainly in depth of rufous coloration and degree of pink, violaceous or buff suffusion. Migratory northern races have more pointed wings than resident tropical ones. Regional variations in plumage are real enough but are difficult to convey in writing and are best appreciated in museum series.

H. c. coromanda Nepal, Sikkim, Bhutan, Bihar, West Bengal, Bangladesh, northern Burma and southwest China east to Macao; winters in part in Malay Peninsula, Sumatra and Java. See Description. Wing 108-118 (average 113), bill 54-63 (average 56 on males, 59 on females).

H. c. mizorhina Andaman Islands, southwest of Burma. Upperparts dark rufous with bright violaceous sheen;

underparts much darker than on *coromanda*, breast washed with violet. Bill longer (63-66).

H. c. major Japan from Hokkaidō to about Kyoto, South Korea, and northeast China mainly in coastal lowlands of Liaoning, Hopei and Shantung; migrants occur in eastern China, Taiwan, Ryukyu Islands, Philippines, Sulawesi and (rarely) Borneo. Upperparts paler than on *coromanda* and much less violaceous, rump-patch blue, reduced to a narrow stripe; underparts buffier and much paler than on *coromanda*. Bill more slender, wing longer (119-130, average 124).

H. c. bangsi Ryukyu Islands, east of Taiwan, wintering in the Philippines south to Talaud Islands (Indonesia). Upperparts much darker and more violaceous; underparts darker, and base of bill deeper than on *coromanda*; wing long (120-129, average 124).

H. c. minor From about 10° N in Malay Peninsula south to Singapore, Riau Archipelago, Sumatra, Mentawai, Bangka and Beliton Islands, west Java, and Borneo. Upperparts darker and underparts much darker than on *coromanda*, rich chestnut, the crown, mantle and breast glossy and washed with violet; silvery rump-patch large. Wing short (96-111, average 103 on males and 105 on females).

H. c. linae Palawan Island and Tawitawi Islands (southwest Philippines). Like *minor*, but slightly darker above and below; mantle and breast almost plum-coloured.

H. c. rufa Sulawesi and its offshore islands of Sangihe, Buton and Muna. Like *minor*, but not quite so dark; rump lustrous pale blue. Wing long (111-121, average 116); bill long (58-64); tail short (Mees 1991).

H. c. pelingensis Peleng Island (Sulawesi, Indonesia). Like *rufa*, but rump silver.

H. c. sulana Sula Islands, east of Peleng Island. Like *coromanda*, but more violaceous and wing long (117-122, average 120); bill long (61-65).

Habitat and range In the Himalayas, northeast China and Japan, Ruddy Kingfishers occur on and near mountain streams in dense evergreen forests up to 1800 m in altitude, but in the tropics they keep to wooded coastal regions and particularly mangrove, *Nipa* palms and tidal forest. Near Tōkyō they favour wet, cool *Cryptomeria* groves (Forshaw 1985). The breeding range is from the eastern Himalayas and northeast India to western (and eastern?) Indochina, Andaman Islands, Malayan Peninsula, Singapore, Sumatra, Java, Borneo, Sulawesi east to Sula Islands, Palawan, Philippines and southwest China, and from northeast China, South Korea and Japan to the Ryukyu Islands.

Population Uncommon or rare almost everywhere in its range, but locally common in south Thailand, in Ryukyu Islands (on passage?) and in Sabah, Borneo, in mangrove. As it is a secretive bird of dense cover, its scarcity may, however, be more apparent than real: 45 stuffed Ruddy Kingfishers were found in a dealer's shop in Taiwan (Mees 1977).

Migration Ruddy Kingfishers from Japan and northeast China migrate through eastern China, the Ryukyu Islands and Taiwan to winter in the Philippines and Sulawesi. Those from India, Nepal, Bhutan and Burma move through the Malayan Peninsula to wintering grounds mainly in Sumatra. A very few remain on their Indian and perhaps even their Korean breeding grounds all year. Migrants keep to forest, and move at night. In spring this species migrates through Taiwan from late April to late May, and it is present on the breeding grounds in Korea and Japan from May to September or (Honshū) early October. Any return through Taiwan in autumn has not been documented, but birds winter in the Philippines from late September until mid May. The race *bangsi*, which also winters in the Philippines, summers in the Ryukyus from early April to mid September.

Food According to habitat this kingfisher eats large insects (beetles, grasshoppers, locusts, larvae), small arthropods and small land snails and lizards, or littoral fish, crabs and offal. Freshwater prey includes crayfish, frogs and tadpoles. One lizard eaten was 8 cm long.

Habits Because it is so shy and retiring little is known about this species. It occurs solitarily or in pairs and is quite vocal, which suggests that it is territorial like other halcyons. During his extensive migration studies, McClure (1974) found that individuals resident in Malaysia keep to the same locality for at least six years and that migrants return in successive years to the same regions in the Philippines. The known diet suggests that Ruddy Kingfishers forage like their congeners, by sitting patiently in trees and scanning the ground and puddles nearby. Perched, they flick the tail up briefly and bob the head from time to time, like all kingfishers. Birds were once seen flying from beach-front trees in Borneo, diving into the surf, and returning with their captures to the woods (Smythies 1981). There is strong circumstantial evidence that in the Philippines they commonly eat large land snails, smashing them open on regularly used anvil stones on the forest floor (Rand 1954). **Nesting:** most nests in India and in Ryukyu Islands are burrows excavated by the birds in steep earthen banks, but in Japan they are in tree holes (up to 3 m above ground) or in village mud walls; one nest in Borneo was a hole in a mud termitarium against the trunk of a whistling-pine tree. The nest is generally concealed behind leafy vegetation; the entrance is 5 cm across, the tunnel 45-100 cm long, and the terminal egg chamber about 15 cm wide and 12 cm high. The clutch is of 4-6 eggs; both sexes attend the nest (Baker 1934). **Laying months:** South Korea, June; Japan, June-July and perhaps August; India, April-May and perhaps March; Malaysia, May (Tioman Island); Sabah, Malaysia (Borneo), February or March and May; Sulawesi, February-March.

Description *H. c. coromanda* Sexes alike. **Adult:** entire upperparts except for the rump-patch deep rufous-chestnut, rather paler and more orange on forehead, fore-crown, lores, ear-coverts, and malar area below the eye. The hindcrown, hindneck, mantle, scapulars, wings and tail are of a rare and beautiful shade, owing to a strong, glossy violet or mauve suffusion. A long oval or diamond-shaped patch in the middle of the lower back and rump is silvery or very pale azure-blue. Sides of rump and uppertail-coverts chestnut. Chin pale yellow, quite well demarcated from rufous malar area, and becoming darker yellow on throat and pale rufous on upper breast; remaining underparts buffy dark orange, darkest across the breast, which can be cinnamon-rufous. Underwing-coverts rufous. Bill red or orange-red; iris very dark brown, orbital skin red; legs and feet scarlet. **Juvenile:** like the adult, but darker and duller, almost without any violet wash, and with the rump-patch dark royal-blue; breast scalloped with dusky feather fringes. Bill brown-orange. **Measurements:** wing of male 110-117, of female 108-118; tail of male 60-66, of female 59-66; bill of male 54-59, of female 57-63; tarsus of male 15-17, of female 15-17. Weight: males, of various subspecies, 73-80.

References Forshaw (1985), Fry (1980a), McClure (1974), Smythies (1981).

26 WHITE-BREASTED KINGFISHER (White-throated Kingfisher)
Halcyon smyrnensis

Plate 10

Alcedo smyrnensis Linnaeus, 1758, Syst. Nat., ed. 10, I, p. 116, Africa and Asia, = Smyrna.

Field identification Length 27-28 cm (10½-11 in). A strikingly handsome kingfisher, unmistakable anywhere in its range. **At rest:** red bill, chestnut head and body with white throat and breast (in the Philippines, white throat only), and brilliant blue wings, rump and tail. **In flight:** median wing-coverts black; primaries blackish with white bases, the white forming a large, conspicuous patch on both upperwing and underwing. Noisy.

Voice The call, uttered commonly as the bird takes flight, is a loud cackle or laugh, 'chake ake ake-ake-ake-ake'. The song is a loud trill or tremulous whistle, 'klilililili', repeated at short intervals from the very top of a palm or tree.

Geographical variation Four subspecies are generally recognised, differing in the hue of green-blues, the intensity of chestnut, and the extent of white.

H. s. smyrnensis From about Izmir (Smyrna) in west Turkey, and Cairo, Egypt, to the south Caspian, northern Persian Gulf, Pakistan, Afghanistan and northwest India; casual in Greece (three records) and Cyprus. Chin, throat and breast white.

H. s. fusca India and Sri Lanka to Taiwan and Hainan, Indochina, Malay Peninsula and Sumatra. Slightly darker; blues less green-tinged.

H. s. saturatior Andaman Islands. Like *smyrnensis*, but the browns are darker.

H. s. gularis Philippines. Like *fusca*, but only the chin and throat are white; there is more black in the forewing.

Habitat and range This kingfisher occupies a wide range of habitats: oil-palm plantations, roadside trees, ricefields, large gardens, dams, ponds, canals, light-industrial sites, beaches with coconut palms and trees, creeks, *Nipa* palm swamps, mudflats, the edges of mangrove, farmland, bamboo forest and dry deciduous forest. It is fairly common throughout much of its range, for instance in Jordan, Israel, Iraq, Kashmir, India, Sri Lanka, Burma, Thailand, peninsular Malaysia, and Vietnam. Locally it is abundant, as in Carey Island, Malaysia. It is less common above 2000 m, but sometimes ascends to 5000 m in Nepal. It colonised Sumatra 50 years ago, and is now rapidly replacing the Mangrove Kingfisher (47) in cultivated areas there. It nested for the first time in Egypt, near Cairo, in 1986 and in Java, near Gunung Cileueur, in 1972; but it is very rare in both countries.

Migration White-breasted Kingfishers are partial migrants, but move almost entirely within their breeding range. Some migration, with seasonal variations in abundance, is evident in Iraq, India, Burma and Hong Kong (Forshaw 1985). Vagrants have appeared in Saudi Arabia as far south as Riyadh, and in Egypt and Java.

Food Mole-crickets, grasshoppers, bee-

tles, mantises, termites, crabs, fish, frogs, skinks, chameleons, snakes up to 65 cm long, nestling birds, voles and mice. Vertebrate prey items usually weigh 2-10 g. In Bengal, fish comprise 19% of the diet by weight in the dry season and 43% in the wet season. In Israel, White-breasted Kingfishers catch and eat tired spring migrants such as Chiffchaffs *Phylloscopus collybita*.

Habits This kingfisher is a sit-and-wait predator, perching for long periods on a fence or telegraph wire alongside canals and roads, occasionally bobbing the head or wagging the tail back and forth. It catches termites on the wing but feeds mainly on the ground, diving swiftly down at a 45° angle. It strikes the surface of a puddle feet-first, but in deeper water it dives head-first. It can hover momentarily over water. Often it forages along seashores: in Israel and Malaysia, for instance. The bird occurs singly or in pairs. It is strongly territorial, and vocal at all times but particularly when breeding. *Nesting:* in the breeding season there is a conspicuous display, a bird singing on a treetop, perching upright and intermittently spreading the wings, undersides facing forwards to show the white patches. In an apparent display flight, one was once seen several times flying up to about 60 m, calling loudly, then spiralling downwards into the tops of palms (Forshaw 1985). The nest is a chamber at the end of a level burrow 7 cm in diameter and 50 cm long, excavated by the birds in the earthen bank of a ditch, stream, pond or road cutting. Uncommon sites are termitaria, tree holes and mud walls (Harrison 1961). The clutch is of 4-7 eggs. *Laying months:* Egypt, about June; Israel, May; Iraq, May; India, January-May; Sri Lanka, December-April; Thailand, April; Malaysia, December-May; Sumatra, April; Philippines, March and April.

Description *H. s. smyrnensis* **Adult male:** entire plumage rich chestnut, except: chin, throat and centre of breast white; mantle, back, scapulars and wings turquoise-blue, the wing with mainly black median and lesser coverts and blackish primaries with white bases; rump brilliant blue; tail greenish-blue above, black below. Bill red; orbital skin red, eye dark brown; legs and feet dusky red. **Adult**

female: like the male, but brown parts not quite so dark. *Juvenile:* like the adult, but duller, with fine dark scallops on the white breast. Bill brown, or yellowish on fledglings. *Measurements:* wing of male 119-131, of female 121-131; tail of male 74-91, of female 78-87; bill of male 59-69, of

female 59-69; tarsus of male 16-18, of female 16-17. Weight (*H. s. fusca*): male 78-83, female 79-85.

References Cramp (1985), Forshaw (1985).

27 JAVA KINGFISHER (Blue-bellied Kingfisher)   Plate 10
Halcyon cyanoventris

Halcyon cyanoventris Vieillot, 1818, Nouv. Dict. Hist. Nat., 19, p. 42, Java.

Field identification Length 27 cm (10½ in). A very dark-looking purple-and-brown, red-billed halcyon confined to Java and Bali. *At rest:* it shows dark chestnut throat, upper breast and collar and dark purple belly; other plumage features are as White-breasted and Black-capped Kingfishers (26, 29). *In flight:* it shows the same large white wing-panel as on those two species. *Confusion species:* five other halcyons occur in Java, and all except the Mangrove Kingfisher (47) are similarly red-billed. The Ruddy Kingfisher (25) is instantly told by its rufous plumage, the Stork-billed (22) by its size and buffy head, the Black-capped by its white collar, and the White-breasted by its white throat and breast. Only the last-named can really be confused with the Java Kingfisher, which differs in its chestnut (not white) breast, blackish (not chestnut) head, purple (not chestnut) belly, purple-blue (not dark brown) mantle and back, and purple-blue (not turquoise) rump. Juvenile Java Kingfishers have buff-white throats, making them even more like White-breasted Kingfishers.

Voice (a) A loud penetrating scream, (b) a loud 'tjie-rie-rie-rie-rie' and (c) a repeated 'tjeu-wii, ii', or 'tschrii, ii' (Hoogerwerf 1970).

Geographical variation None.

Habitat and range This distinctive kingfisher is endemic to Java and Bali and some of their small outlying islands. It is not a waterside bird, but inhabits a wide variety of wooded and cultivated country, pasture, fishponds, paddyfields, dried-up marshes, coastal scrub, mangrove, and

open dry forest. It avoids humid forest with closed canopy, although it may penetrate forest for some distance along roadsides and bushy paths. Although it sometimes occurs in municipal gardens and parks, the bird is not really suburban. It ranges from coasts and coastal lowlands up to about 1500 m and is moderately common, although 50 years ago it was evidently commoner.

Food Mainly insects taken from dry ground, but also fish, freshwater shrimps, dytiscid water-beetle larvae, and frogs.

Habits Java Kingfishers live singly or in pairs, perching conspicuously on treetops or, when foraging, on exposed side-branches or on telephone wires and posts. They are rather shy, and often call when put to flight. Birds watched feeding by the ponds of a fish farm flew down to catch frogs and insects from the ground at the water's edge or from shallows, but did not catch any of the abundant fish in deeper water. Twice an individual clumsily hovered and plunged into a pond, but failed to make a catch. *Nesting:* burrows at least 1 m long are dug by both of the pair in open, sunny places: the bank of a ditch or road cutting, or an earthen wall. There are 3-5 glossy white eggs. *Laying months:* Java, February-September.

Description Sexes alike. *Adult:* head brownish-black, some feathers across the nape tipped purple-blue; chin, throat, broad hindneck-collar and breast chestnut-brown, a little paler on the chin, and with small black streaks on chin, throat and sides of the neck. Mantle, back, scapulars, rump and uppertail-coverts

145

purple-blue. Lesser and median coverts and inner greater coverts black; remaining upperwing-coverts, and those parts of the primaries, secondaries, and tertials visible in the folded wing, bright turquoise-blue. Folded tail similarly turquoise-blue. All primaries except the outermost have white proximal halves, forming a white patch in the spread wing. Axillaries and underwing-coverts black. Bill red; iris dark brown, orbital ring of skin red; legs and feet dark red. *Juvenile:* like adult but duller, blues dull greenish rather than bright turquoise or rich purple; throat buffy-white and bill brownish-orange. *Measurements:* wing of male 119-131, of female 121-131; tail of male 74-91, of female 78-87; bill of male 59-69, of female 59-79; tarsus of male 16-18, of female 16-17. Weight: one female 93.

References Forshaw (1985), Fry (1980a), Hoogerwerf (1970).

28 CHOCOLATE-BACKED KINGFISHER   Plate 10
Halcyon badia

Halcyon (Cancrophaga) badia Verreaux and Verreaux, 1851, Rev. Mag. Zool., (2) 3, p. 264, Gabon.

Field identification Length 21 cm (8¼ in). Dumpy kingfisher shape, dark upperparts and sharply demarcated snowy underparts serve to distinguish it from all other African rainforest birds, including dumpy broadbills and flycatchers. The bill is red or brownish-red (or dusky black with a small orange tip on juveniles), but not particularly large. It perches solitarily and quietly in the lower or low-middle storey of low-lying forest, flying to the ground for prey. Like many rainforest birds, this kingfisher can probably be most easily located by learning its distinctive voice from published recordings. *At rest:* in poor forest light the upperparts can look blackish, although head and shoulders are in fact rich dark brown. In side view a bright azure-blue panel in the wing is generally conspicuous, and from behind the tail is blue. *In flight:* the white underparts, white underwing, and brilliant kingfisher-blue rump are obvious.

Voice The song, given frequently at least in the breeding season (November-March in Gabon), is a high, not very audible 'pee' followed after 1 second by 12-17 long, fluty, pure-toned notes. The notes are evenly spaced, quite loud and far-carrying through dense trees, and last 5-7 seconds in all, the pitch rising barely perceptibly in the first half and falling a little towards the end. The final two notes are sometimes quieter, low-pitched and mournful. The alarm is a very harsh, scolding screech.

Geographical variation None, other than a gradual increase in size from west to east.

Habitat and range A bird of lowland forests, where it perches at middle height – 6-10 m – in places where its view is relatively unobstructed. It is not a waterside kingfisher and in fact is not associated with water at all, not even rain pools on the forest floor; nor is it attracted to human habitations. One habitat requirement is earthen termite or ant nests several metres up in trees, for nesting. It ranges through the west and central African rainforest zone, in Sierra Leone, Liberia, south Ivory Coast and south Ghana, then (beyond the 'Dahomey savanna gap') from southwest Nigeria through Bioko Island, south Cameroon, Rio Muni, Gabon except in the east, and Zaïre except north of River Uele or in Katanga Province. It seems to be absent from the Republic of Congo. It just enters Angola on the River Cuango and in Cabinda, and west Uganda in Maragambo, Bwamba, Bugoma and Budongo Forests. It is found from sea level up to 1400 m.

Population A common bird in Ituri, eastern Zaïre, and locally common in

Uganda. In the west, it is frequent in Liberia and uncommon in Ghana and Nigeria, where it is now confined to forest reserves and national parks. In the rest of its range, although easily overlooked, it is probably common wherever undisturbed forest still stands.

Food Mainly grasshoppers and beetles, also mantises, cicadas, bugs, dragonflies, earwigs, termites, caterpillars, spiders and lizards.

Habits Not well known; studied chiefly in Gabon. In pairs. It spends much time sitting quietly, quite high in trees, overlooking a clear space, and from time to time flies out to catch an insect in mid-air, or, more commonly, it flies down swiftly to seize prey on the ground. It attends driver-ant columns, perching low down, and feeding either on the ants themselves or on insects which they flush. **Nesting:** unfloodable sites seem to be surprisingly scarce for earth-burrowing rainforest birds; Chocolate-backed Kingfishers get around the problem by habitually using the large, round, half-hanging earth nests of *Nasutitermes* termites. Typically, such nests or termitaria are firmly fixed to a woody liane or sloping bough, about 4-5 m above the forest floor. The birds excavate the nest hole horizontally from one side, and can dig away the greater part of the termitarium. Evidently the termites react only by sealing themselves off. Hanging ant nests, made of earth, in trees are also sometimes used. **Laying months:** Gabon, October, January and February;

Cameroon, June and October; Liberia and Nigeria, about March; Bioko Island, about November; northern Zaïre, about September.

Description Sexes alike. *Adult:* the head, down to the moustachial region and hind-neck, is dark mahogany-brown; mantle brownish-black, back black, rump brilliant shiny azure-blue; uppertail-coverts black, tail dull azure-blue, the feathers with black shafts and dusky tips. Primary feathers blackish, secondaries black with proximal half of the outer web shiny azure-blue; upperwing-coverts black, tipped mahogany-brown. The entire underparts are white except for a small black patch on the upper edge of the flanks, sharply demarcated from the upperparts, and the underwing-coverts are also white. Bill red or brownish-red; eye dark brown with a narrow red orbital ring; legs and feet dark purple-red. *Juvenile:* much like the adult, except that the breast is buffy, scalloped with fine dark crescents, and the flank feathers are finely marked with black; there is less azure-blue in the tail, and on very young birds the bill is black with a small orange tip. *Measurements:* male and female are the same size. Wing 87-94 in Liberia and Ghana, 91-97 in Cameroon and Gabon, 92-105 in northeast Zaïre and Uganda; in Liberia, tail 53-67, bill 42-47, tarsus 12.5-14.5. Weight: male 54-65, female 47-65.

References Brosset and Darchen (1967), Forshaw (1985), Fry *et al.* (1988).

29 BLACK-CAPPED KINGFISHER   Plate 10
Halcyon pileata

Alcedo pileata Boddaert, 1783, Table Planch. enlum., p. 41, China, ex Daubenton, Planch. enlum., 1783, pl. 673.

Field identification Length 28 cm (11 in). Even if it gives only a brief view, this kingfisher, with its bold, colourful markings in all plumages, can hardly present a problem: large red bill, black head sharply demarcated from broad white collar, purple-blue back, and rufous belly. It is rather shy, but often perches in the open. *At rest:* in combination, the above-

mentioned features are unique among kingfishers. All upperparts behind the neck are purple-blue except for the upperwing-coverts, which form a large area of solid black. *In flight:* the wings appear black and blue above and black and rufous below, with a large white patch formed by white bases of primaries; being on the inner webs, the white marks make a patch better defined on the underside than the upperside of the wing. **Confusion species:** none in its range. Elsewhere, the White-breasted Kingfisher (26) is the same size, occupies similar habitats, has a red bill, blue, black and chestnut plumage, and in flight shows a conspicuous white patch in the wing, but it lacks any white collar. Two others, the Rufous-bellied Kookaburra (17) and the Chestnut-bellied Kingfisher (43), happen to have black heads, white collars and rufous bellies (but not red bills), but even in winter the migratory Black-capped Kingfisher does not penetrate their southeasterly ranges.

Voice A distinctive ringing cackle, 'kikik-ikikiki', like the call of the White-breasted Kingfisher but higher-pitched.

Geographical variation None. In some regards it seems to be a northerly-breeding Oriental ally of the White-breasted Kingfisher, but there is evidence that in fact much its nearest relative is in Africa, the Grey-headed Kingfisher (30) (Fry 1980b).

Habitat and range This is the most northerly halcyon, breeding as far north as Korea and Manchuria and vagrant in USSR near Vladivostok. Because of the presence of wintering individuals its southern breeding limit is not so well known: the most southerly nests known are in Mysore, India, south Burma, Indochina, Hainan and Hong Kong, with a possible one at Paknampho in Thailand. The species is, however, resident south of Mysore, in Kerala. The westernmost point in its range is the Indian coastal lowlands south of Bombay. In eastern India and in Bangladesh it again tends to be coastal, but it occurs at up to 500 m in southern India and up to 1000 m in Nepal. Since the bird is very common in parts of its wintering grounds, it must breed abundantly somewhere in the north, probably in the interior of China. In winter it ranges south to Sri Lanka, Malaysia, Borneo, Sumatra and Java, and the wintering range extends at least as far north as Hong Kong. The Black-capped Kingfisher is vagrant to Ryukyu Islands and to Kyūshū and west Honshū, Japan. This species inhabits deciduous forest near water, wooded riverbanks and pools in small forest streams in Korea and China, and in the tropics rice-fields, creeks, mangrove, wooded seashores, *Nipa* palm groves, lagoons, estuaries, willow jungles (Burma), forest clearings, streams in lowland bamboo forest, and open cultivated land.

Population Evidently it is rare as a breeding visitor as far north as Korea and Manchuria, but widespread in coastal and inland provinces of China. In Bengal and Bangladesh it is common in the mouths of the Ganges, and it is extremely abundant along the coast of Burma; wintering birds are very common also on Thailand's coast. It is fairly common in peninsular Malaysia, Singapore and Vietnam, mainly on passage, abundant as a winter visitor to Borneo, but scarce in Sulawesi, Sumatra and Java.

Migration In China and Korea the Black-capped Kingfisher is a breeding summer visitor from May to October. In Sri Lanka, Thailand, Indochina, Malaysia and Indonesia it is a winter visitor (although a few may breed in the north). Between these two regions – in India and from Bangladesh and Burma to Hainan and Hong Kong – the species is resident and a partial migrant. Autumn passage through southwest Thailand and at Fraser's Hill, Pahang, Malaysia, is from late September to late November and spring passage is in March (mainly) and April. Wintering in Borneo is from September to April. Some or all of these birds move at night. Individuals are faithful to given routes: many migrants caught in Selangor, Malaysia, have been recaptured in subsequent years, once six years later.

Food In coastal habitats fish and crabs are the staple, but elsewhere mainly insects: dragonflies, dragonfly nymphs, water boatmen, locusts, grasshoppers, crickets, leaf-insects, beetles, bees and wasps. A few frogs and reptiles are taken. Those wintering along Borneo's great rivers take insects but rarely fish, even when they hunt from branches actually overhanging water.

Habits Mainly solitary on migration and in winter, and paired in defence of a territory on its breeding grounds. Black-capped Kingfishers are rather quiet and shy birds, but conspicuous because they perch

148

openly at the edges of mangrove, along wooded riverbanks, and on telegraph wires where a road runs through forest. In such places they hunt actively, changing perches or changing viewing directions at one perch more often than do Mangrove or Stork-billed Kingfishers (47, 22), for instance (Burton 1978). When disturbed they usually fly away silently, not perching again for several hundred metres. Within a territory the same lookout perches are used day after day, the bird making sorties into foliage or to the ground, but only rarely plunging into water. **Nesting:** the patterned-winged halcyon kingfishers of Africa and Asia have a very conspicuous territorial song display, opening the wings wide so as to display them and swivelling to left and right on a treetop perch; but no such display has yet been observed in this species. The nest is a burrow usually dug by male and female in a stream bank or earth cutting, and once (in Hong Kong) between the stones of an old plaster-and-gravel wall; on another occasion a termite mound was used. The clutch is of 4-5 eggs; there seems to be but a single brood each summer. **Laying months:** Korea, June; Hong Kong, May-June; Mysore, April and probably until July; Burma, April.

Description Sexes alike. **Adult:** head black; chin, throat, upper breast and broad collar around neck white. Lesser and median wing-coverts and inner greater coverts black; leading edge of the wing from 'wrist' to alula buff. Remaining parts of the upperwing and the mantle, scapulars, back, rump and tail all deep purple-blue, with the rump and uppertail-coverts slightly paler and brighter than the back and tail. A large white patch in the wing, not visible when the wings are folded, is formed by white bases to all primaries; on the inner primaries the white reaches nearly to the feather tips. Underwing-coverts pale rufous. Lower breast, belly, flanks and undertail-coverts deep orange-rufous. Bill scarlet; iris very dark brown, orbital skin black; legs and feet dull carmine, claws black. **Juvenile:** like the adult, but blue parts duller, a small rufous-buff loral spot, buffy collar, and white feathers at the sides of the throat have black shafts and those on the breast have narrow dusky fringes. Sometimes the breast scaling is extensive. Bill brownish-orange. **Measurements:** wing of male 124-136, of female 125-137; tail of male 73-83, of female 75-84; bill of male 55-68, of female 60-70; tarsus of male 15-17, of female 15-17. Weight: 85-88.

References Burton (1978), Forshaw (1985), Fry (1980a,b), Smythies (1981).

30 GREY-HEADED KINGFISHER (Chestnut-bellied Kingfisher)
Halcyon leucocephala

Plate 11

Alcedo leucocephala P.L.S. Müller, 1776, Natursyst., Suppl., p. 94, Senegal.

Field identification Length 22 cm (8¹/₂ in). A rather small halcyon, lively, flighty and conspicuous, with scarlet bill and legs, pale grey or light brown head and breast, black back and shoulders, brilliant cobalt or violet-blue rump, tail, primaries and secondaries, and rufous or chestnut belly and underwing-coverts. **At rest:** the rufous belly distinguishes it at a glance from all other kingfishers in its range. **In flight:** the underwing is conspicuously patterned, with rufous lining and a large white patch at the base of the primaries, showing on

Underwing pattern

the upperside as a pale blue window. **Confusion species:** see Brown-hooded Kingfisher (31) for distinctions, particularly of juveniles.

Voice The song is a weak trill, sibilant or squeaky, of 5-7 notes falling in pitch, lasting half a second: 'siiiiiu', 't's's's'iu' or 'ji-ji-ji-ji-chi'. Sometimes alternating with it is a second song, a slower trill on one pitch. Other calls are a clear 'piuu, piuu, piuu', each note downslurred, a long chatter, and scolding 'tch' notes.

Geographical variation The three African subspecies vary in their blue and rufous hues; a fourth race in Arabia is poorly differentiated, and a fifth one in the Cape Verde Islands is white-headed.

H. l. leucocephala The northern tropics of Africa, from Senegambia to Eritrea and Somalia, south to Gabon, northeast Zaïre, Lake Victoria basin and north Tanzania.

H. l. hyacinthina South Somalia, coastal Kenya, Tanzania south to Dar es Salaam and inland to Pare Mountains and Kilosa. Wing and tail violet-blue rather than royal-blue.

H. l. pallidiventris The southern tropics: south Zaïre and Tanzania to north Namibia and (just) Natal; winters north to the Equator. Like *leucocephala*, but head paler grey and belly and undertail-coverts pale rufous.

H. l. acteon Cape Verde Islands: Fogo, Brave and São Tiago. Head greyish-white, wings and tail dark ultramarine-blue, belly and undertail-coverts pale chestnut.

H. l. semicaerulea Southwest Arabia, north to about Mecca (Saudi Arabia) and east to Taqa (Oman); a summer visitor, wintering probably in Somalia. Very like *leucocephala* but blues not green-tinged.

Habitat and range Breeding pairs inhabit woodland, bushy grassland, thickets, thornbush, parkland and cultivated areas, from sea level up to 2400 m. Migrants occur in almost any open habitat, including gardens and desert palmeries, but avoid thick forest and very arid regions. Its abundance varies, but on the whole the Grey-headed Kingfisher is fairly common, and locally it can be plentiful on migration. It breeds in all parts of its range, which is from Cape Verde Islands, Senegal and south Mauritania to Eritrea, 46°E in Somalia, and southwest Arabia (east to

south Oman), and south throughout Africa, except in densely forested regions, to north Namibia, north and east Botswana, Zimbabwe, Mozambique, east Transvaal and northeast Swaziland. It is rare in southeast Botswana, a scarce non-breeding visitor to Zanzibar and Pemba, and in Natal it occurs only at Ndumu.

Migration Populations in Cape Verde Islands are resident, and so perhaps are some in equatorial Africa. In Arabia the Grey-headed Kingfisher is a breeding summer visitor in about April-November, and it is a well-defined migrant at higher latitudes in Africa. Its movements in West Africa are probably representative. There its breeding range is from derived savannas near the coastal forests (nesting in January and February, the dry season) north to the desert-edge sahel zone (nesting in July and August, the wet season, north to 15°N in Mali and 15½°N in Chad). In derived savannas it is exclusively a dry-season visitor and it migrates north for the wet season, whereas in sahel savannas it is exclusively a wet-season visitor, moving south for the dry season; whether pairs nest twice a year, in January in the south and July in the north, is unknown. Individuals breeding in middle latitudes have an unusual three-stage migration: they nest about March-June and then evidently move to the far north, where they moult in the rainy season, then migrate to the far south for the dry season, and finally return a short distance back north to their breeding latitudes (Nigeria: Skinner 1968, Elgood *et al.* 1973). Grey-headed Kingfishers visit Zimbabwe from early September to early May and Natal in August-April. In Malaŵi, a few reside all year and breeding visitors are commonest in October-March. In Zambia, breeding migrants occur from late August to June and are common in October-May; a few stay in the dry season. *H. l. pallidiventris* breeds north to Tabora, northwest Tanzania, and is a seasonal visitor to Rwanda and Burundi in April-October and Kenya in April-September. The coastal *hyacinthina* is resident but is a sporadic visitor to Zanzibar and Pemba Islands. Locally-breeding populations of *H. l. leucocephala* in East Africa are augmented by migrants from Ethiopia in winter; the subspecies visits Serengeti in August-February and Tsavo East National Park in

November-April. The species migrates at night, when some are attracted to lights at Ngulia Lodge, Kenya. In Nigeria, juveniles migrate 1-2 weeks later than adults. Some individuals move far: ringed birds have been recovered 1430 km distant in southern Africa (Malaŵi to Zaïre) and 960 and 1750 km distant in eastern Africa (both from Ethiopia to Kenya).

Food Mainly grasshoppers; also locusts, crickets, mole-crickets, cockroaches, mantises, bugs, ants, beetles, moths, caterpillars, spiders, scorpions up to 50 mm long, slow-worms and small lizards. The species has been known to eat mice, frogs, fish, and nestling birds.

Habits Single birds can be rather timid but in the Cape Verdes the species is very tame. Family parties of six individuals keep together, and loose aggregations occur on migration; otherwise it lives singly or in pairs. About 24 once roosted together at night in a large tree, where 130 different individuals were netted in a short period after breeding (Nigeria: Jones 1980). When resting this kingfisher sits hunched, sometimes bobbing its head. When actively searching for food, it scans fixedly in one direction then another, and just before diving down on to prey it moves its head jerkily up and down, as if checking the prey's exact position. Small food items are swallowed whole; larger ones are whacked against the perch to one side then the other, insects' legs flying off.

Sometimes an insect is caught in flight or a fish taken by flying low over water, but most prey is captured on the ground. **Nesting:** the species digs nest tunnels in riverbanks, irrigation ditches, erosion gullies, ground termitaria and Aardvark (Antbear) tunnels. It is territorial; dry watercourses in Nigeria have 1-2 pairs per km, and in Kenya riverine territories can be only 100 m apart, extending 250 m back from the riverbank. Displaying involves the pair circling around in flight above the trees, calling constantly, then diving down to perch on a topmost twig, where both sexes may sing, flicking the wings open in the vertical plane to show their patterned undersides, and pivoting the body from side to side with the outspread wings vibrating before being snapped shut; on the ground they also sometimes aggressively adopt the wing-spread posture. Nest burrows are straight, horizontal, 5 cm wide and 40-100 cm long, and 2-6 eggs (usually four) are laid. Males courtship-feed females, and both sexes care for the young. Nests are often parasitised by Greater Honeyguides *Indicator indicator*. **Laying months:** Cape Verde Islands, July-April; Senegal, Gambia and Mali, May-October; Nigeria, January-June according to latitude (see above); Sudan, May-June; Ethiopia, October-June; East Africa, all months, mainly in the wet season; Angola, August-September; Zambia, September-February, mainly October-November; Malaŵi, mainly November; Zimbabwe,

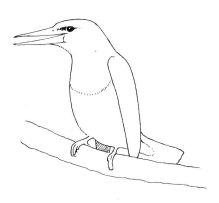 

Grey-headed Kingfisher displaying

September-December, mainly October-November; Natal, October-November.

Description *H. l. leucocephala* **Adult male:** lores are black, but the rest of the head, neck, upper mantle and breast are ash-grey, sometimes brown-tinged, darkest on the crown and palest on the throat, and sharply demarcated from the back and belly. Lower mantle, scapulars and upperwing-coverts black; rump, uppertail-coverts and tail brilliant azure-blue, washed with violet. Secondaries black, with azure outer webs; primaries black, the proximal halves white on the inner and azure on the outer webs. Belly, flanks, undertail and underwing-coverts bright orange-chestnut. Undersides of the tail and wing are black, with a large white patch in the primaries. Bill red; eye dark brown; legs and feet red. **Adult female:** like male but evidently slightly duller, head and breast greyer and rufous parts paler. **Juvenile:** like the adult, but azure parts are a duller and softer blue, the crown, ear-coverts and hindneck dark buff, and the underparts warm buff where the adult is chestnut; moustachial area, breast and flanks are marked with numerous fine dark crescents. Bill and legs are dusky red. **Measurements:** wing of male 98-109, of female 100-107; tail of male 55-64, of female 52-63; bill of male 42-49, of female 39-49; tarsus of male 14-16, of female 14-16. Weight: 35-61 (males averaging 42, females 43).

References Cramp (1985), Forshaw (1985), Fry *et al.* (1988), Jones (1980).

31 BROWN-HOODED KINGFISHER   Plate 11
Halcyon albiventris

Alcedo albiventris Scopoli, 1786, Del. Flor. et Faun. Insubr. 2, p. 90, Cape of Good Hope.

Field identification Length 22 cm (8½ in). **At rest:** a small to medium-sized African halcyon with red bill and legs, streaky brown crown, and blackish mantle and shoulders separated from the dark head-top by a broad whitish or buffy collar. Wings and tail are dull turquoise, the rump brilliant azure-blue, and the underparts creamy, buffy or pale rufous-brown with breast and flanks moderately or heavily streaked with dark brown. **In flight:** wing bluish, with black forewing, an indistinct whitish window at the base of the primaries, and buffy-white wing-lining. **Confusion species:** the Grey-headed Kingfisher (30) differs in not being streaky; adults have the hood pale grey or brownish, the belly and wing-lining chestnut and the blues violaceous; in flight its wing shows a large white window. Juvenile Grey-headed can be very like Brown-hooded but is not streaky. Both species are variable, the most consistent difference being the pale-collared look of Brown-hooded and the wing-window of Grey-headed. The only other streaky African halcyon is the Striped Kingfisher (32), which is much smaller, with brownish bill, strongly patterned wings and distinctive song.

Voice The song is a weak trill, 'tiiiu' or 'ki-ti-ti-ti', on its own or repeated regularly up to 20 times in 17 seconds. Other calls are a sharp 'cheerit' of alarm and a low-pitched trilling when mates greet each other.

Geographical variation Four subspecies are recognised, intergrading somewhat, varying in tone and streakiness.
H. a. albiventris Southwest Cape Province to Natal; some winter north to southeast Zimbabwe. The darkest and streakiest race.
H. a. vociferans East Botswana and east Zimbabwe, south Mozambique, Swaziland, just into Natal and Orange Free State. Paler, with crown and breast more lightly streaked; females are conspicuously white-collared.
H. a. orientalis Coastal lowlands from Mozambique to south Somalia, inland to Malaŵi, south Zambia and north

Botswana. Pale; underparts unstreaked. Wing 5% and tail and bill 10% shorter than on *albiventris*.

H. a. prentissgrayi Angola, Gabon, Congo, Zaïre, north Zambia, west Tanzania and south Kenya. Crown generally unstreaked; underparts of female are tawny. The same size as *orientalis*.

Habitat and range It inhabits woodland, wooded grassland, cultivation, scrub, forest clearings and edges, parks and gardens, from the coast up to 1800 m. Over most of its range – from Congo to Angola, from south Somalia to Zimbabwe, and from Mozambique and Swaziland to Swellendam – it is common in open country, sometimes associated with water but often well away from it.

Migration Most Brown-hooded Kingfishers are sedentary, but members of the South African subspecies occur regularly in central and southeast Zimbabwe about June-August. Seasonal fluctuations in abundance have been noticed in Malaŵi; and in Tsavo National Park, Kenya, the species occurs only in October-May.

Food Mainly insects, but it preys on a variety of large invertebrates, including scorpions up to 65 mm long, and on small vertebrates, snakes and lizards up to 25 cm long and sometimes young songbirds, rodents and fishes.

Habits Brown-hooded Kingfishers occur solitarily or in pairs, and after breeding the family roosts together for a few weeks. Foraging and aggressive territorial habits are like those of Grey-headed Kingfishers; most food is obtained from the ground, but some is found in trees. On the whole these small halcyons are more active than larger ones. When singing, at the side or top of a tree, the bird perches upright with the wings held loosely and vibrating. Two displaying birds face each other singing continuously, spasmodically flicking the wings open in the vertical plane, vibrating them to display vestiges of the pattern which is much bolder in other African halcyons. **Nesting:** the species is a monogamous, solitary nester, digging its 1-m burrow in earthen road cuttings, stream banks and gullies. The nest hole is sometimes overhung by vegetation. As with other kingfishers, the brood chamber soon becomes foul with faeces, pellets, dropped food, and moulted feathers. Well-grown nestlings void their faeces out of the burrow entrance. **Laying months:** South Africa, September-April, mainly September-December; Zimbabwe and adjacent parts of Mozambique, September-December, mainly November; Malaŵi and Zambia, October-February; Katanga, September-October; Kenya and Tanzania, February-March, June, and September-November.

Description *H. a. albiventris* **Adult male:** forehead to hindneck brown, streaked blackish, pale just above the lore and eye, and buffy towards the mantle and sides of the neck; lores and just behind the eye black; sides of head grey-brown, lightly streaked. Mantle, scapulars and most upperwing-coverts brownish-black; lower back and rump bright azure-blue; uppertail-coverts and tail dark greyish-blue. Primaries dark brown with very pale blue basal halves; primary coverts and secondaries mainly turquoise or greyish-blue, with brown tips and some buffy-white on the inner webs of the secondaries. Chin white, throat white or slightly buffy, breast pale tawny with a few narrow dark shaft-streaks, flanks pale orange with a few conspicuous blackish streaks, belly and undertail-coverts buffy. Wing-lining creamy-buff. Bill red with dark brown tip; eye dark brown; legs and feet carmine. **Adult female:** differs from the male in having the crown darker, the upperparts dark brown, and the underparts more tawny and streaky. **Juvenile:** blues and browns are duller than on the adult female, the hindneck streaky, flanks and undertail-coverts yellow-buff and the rest of the underparts white, with some streaks and narrow feather-tip scallops. Bill dark. **Measurements:** wing of male 101-110, of female 105-111; tail of male 62-69, of female 63-70; bill of male 45-54, of female 45-51; tarsus of male 16-17, of female 16-17. Weight (*H. l. vociferans*): male 48-53, female 54-58.

References Forshaw (1985), Fry *et al.* (1988).

32 STRIPED KINGFISHER

Plate 12

Halcyon chelicuti

Alaudo Chelicuti [Stanley], 1814, in Salt's Voyage to Abyssinia, App. IV, p. lvi, Chelicut.

Field identification Length 17 cm (6½ in). Much the smallest halcyon in Africa, like the Brown-hooded Kingfisher (31) in plumage but only half its weight. It is rather drab, without much blue, the red lower mandible seldom showing well in the field. It is more commonly heard than seen, the distinctive song far-carrying and loud for so small a bird. **At rest:** the dark brown crown and mantle are separated by a clear-cut whitish collar; back and rump are bright blue, the tail dull blue, and underparts whitish, striped on the flanks. **In flight:** fast wingbeats, underwings conspicuously pied. **Confusion species:** it differs from the Brown-hooded Kingfisher as follows: the brown crown has long white streaks (not short black ones); cheeks are white (not brown); the white collar and sides of the head are more distinct, and separated from the crown by a blackish line from eye to nape; upper mandible brown (not red); lesser and median coverts are fringed with white; sides of the breast and flanks are more heavily striped; and the underside of the wing is boldly patterned in black, white and grey.

Voice A loud, high-pitched, ringing 'keep-kirrrrr' lasting 1.2 seconds, less disyllabic in east than in west or southern Africa; at a distance the trilling quality is lost and it sounds like 'pee-hee' or 'cheer-oh'.

Geographical variation Two subspecies.

H. c. eremogiton The sahel zone, from Mali (about Mopti) to Sudan (White Nile). Crown and mantle grey-brown; underparts almost unstreaked.

H. c. chelicuti South of *eremogiton* (which intergrades with it), from south Mauritania to northwest and south Somalia, northeast Namibia, Botswana and Natal. Crown and mantle dark brown; breast and flanks streaked.

Habitat and range Striped Kingfishers inhabit dry woodlands and thornbush almost throughout sub-Saharan Africa,

north to about 17°N in Mauritania and Sudan, east to about 46°E in Somalia, and south to about 16°S on the Angola coast and to Mtunzini in Natal. They are absent from the rainforest zone of West Africa and the Congo Basin, but range throughout Ethiopia and East Africa including Zanzibar and Mafia Islands, south to Botswana (except the southwest), lowveld Transvaal, and Swaziland, with three records in Orange Free State. From sea level they range up to 2300 m. The species avoids intensively farmed land, is not water-dependent, and is not migratory.

Food Principally grasshoppers, then beetles, larvae and butterflies. Mantises, cicadas, termites, small lizards, snakes and rodents are taken occasionally.

Habits It lives solitarily or in pairs or trios, and is strongly territorial, often giving chase to a shrike, dove or roller. One territory was 3 ha in extent and contained 100 tall trees. The territory-owner sings from a treetop, sometimes sitting just into the foliage, starting before sunrise and singing at intervals until the early afternoon. Distant individuals respond, and particularly in the evening a chorus of 'pee-hee' calls can be heard. Striped Kingfishers keep watch for prey from a perch about 3 m high, and shift their stance or bob the head before flying fast down to the ground, where nearly all food is taken; prey is carried back to the perch, where small items are swallowed directly but large ones are first knocked vigorously. A bird plunges for prey up to ten times a minute, and four out of five dives are successful. Sometimes termites are caught on the wing. Mated individuals display by facing each other on a treetop in erect posture, tails cocked high, singing repeatedly, and rapidly flicking the wings open and shut. The wings are spread for ½-2 seconds, and wingspreads are not synchronised with singing: the two birds may start in unison but finish by alternating. The 'pee-hee' song soon gives way to a series of half-second trills and half-second pauses (Greig-Smith 1978b). **Nesting:** eggs are laid in abandoned holes of barbets or woodpeckers high up in trees. Most Striped Kingfishers are monogamous, but in Kenya four territories out of 20 held a female with two males, both of which copulated with her and helped to rear the young (Reyer 1980b): cooperative breeding as in other kingfishers and bee-eaters. The male courtship-feeds his mate, but refuses to release the item and makes the female tear it piece by piece. Eggs are incubated by either sex during the day, but at night only by the female. The species is double-brooded. In Kenya a

Pair of Striped Kingfishers displaying

quarter of all nests are parasitised by honeyguides. **Laying months:** Senegal, June-September; Mali, September-October; Nigeria, March-April; Ethiopia, January-October; East Africa, all months; Malaŵi and Zimbabwe, mainly September-October; Zambia, October-November; Natal, September-November.

Description *H. c. chelicuti* **Adult male:** forehead and crown heavily streaked with brown, blackish and buffy-white in about equal parts, the streaks being long and almost unbroken. Lores, area around eye, and a broad band from eye to nape are black. Cheeks, ear-coverts and neck creamy, grey-white or buffy-white, with tiny dark shaft-streaks. Mantle and scapulars are dark brown, back, rump and uppertail-coverts azure-blue, and tail greenish-grey-blue. Upperwing-coverts dark brown, edged white; alula pale blue and white, primary coverts dull blue; tertials bluish-brown, secondaries greenish-blue with dusky tips and inner webs and concealed white bases, primaries dark brown shading to grey at the tips, the outer webs blue with white bases (showing as a small white patch in the closed wing). Chin, throat, belly and undertail-coverts are white, breast buffy-white with dark streaks mainly at the sides, and flanks buffy-white, heavily streaked with brown. Underside of wing white, with a large dark patch near the 'wrist', broad grey trailing edge and broad black subterminal band. Underside of tail silvery-grey. Upper mandible purple- or red-brown, lower mandible red with a brown tip; eye dark brown; legs and feet dull dark red. **Adult female:** like the male, but the crown is browner and less streaky, and the underside of the wing has a smaller dark wrist-patch and lacks a black subterminal band across the flight feathers. **Juvenile:** the crown is plainer, blues are paler with only vestiges in wing and tail, and breast, flanks and belly are buffier than on the adult, the breast feathers narrowly dark-fringed. **Measurements:** wing of male 74-86, of female 75-84; tail of male 39-48, of female 38-45; bill of male 31-37, of female 30-38; tarsus of male 12-14, of female 12-14. Southern African individuals average about 5% larger. Weight: male 30-41, female 37-50.

References Forshaw (1985), Fry *et al.* (1988), Greig-Smith (1978b), Reyer (1980b). Stop press: see also Clancey, P.A. (1991), *Durban Mus. Novit.,* 16: 22-24.

33 BLUE-BREASTED KINGFISHER   Plate 12
Halcyon malimbica

Alcedo Malimbica Shaw, 1811, Gen. Zool. 8, pt I, p. 66, Malimba, Portuguese Congo.

Field identification Length 25 cm (10 in). This is the largest halcyon in Africa, a forest bird with a distinctive voice, more often heard than seen. **At rest:** a mainly turquoise-blue kingfisher with bright red upper mandible, black lower mandible, grey crown, short black mask, black back and shoulders, and white throat and belly. **Confusion species:** the Woodland Kingfisher (34) has the breast pale grey (not blue) and the mantle and scapulars greyish-blue (not black); it is smaller and more flighty than the Blue-breasted, with a different song. Habitats differ, although there is some overlap. Blue-breasted Kingfishers keep to deep shade, where the only other African forest halcyon, the Chocolate-backed Kingfisher (28), with its all-red bill and striking plumage, cannot be mistaken for it.

Voice The song begins with a single 'ti' or 'chiu' followed, after a second's pause, by up to ten clipped piping whistles uttered in 2-2½ seconds, the first ones short and quick, later ones longer and more emphatic: 'chiu; pu-pu-pu pu ku ku, ku, ku'. The alarm, commonly used, is a raucous, echoing 'tchup, tchup-tchup-tchup' lasting 1½ seconds.

Geographical variation Six subspecies have been named, varying in size and slightly in hue; we recognise four.

H. m. torquata Senegal, Gambia, Guinea-Bissau, and just into west Mali.

H. m. forbesi Sierra Leone to Nigeria; Bioko Island, and Mt Cameroon. Blues less green-tinged than in *torquata*, and forehead and crown slightly paler.

H. m. malimbica Cameroon to Uganda and Zambia. Breast, rump and hindneck rich blue, darker than in *forbesi* and without any green tinge; forehead and crown brown-grey, washed with blue-green. Although the same size as *torquata*, *malimbica* is much heavier, averaging 116 g (range 108-121) compared with the 83 g of *torquata*. The small population recently discovered in Ethiopia (see below) will probably prove to belong to this subspecies.

H. m. dryas Principe Island and formerly São Tomé Island. Like *forbesi* but crown as *malimbica*; larger, with very large bill (wing 121-128, tail 79-86, bill 56-62; weight 110-130).

Habitat and range Blue-breasted Kingfishers inhabit secondary forest, mangrove, rainforest, gallery forest (dense woods growing along watercourses in savanna country), riverine woodland, and thick savanna woodland dominated by *Anogeissus leiocarpus* trees. They keep mainly, although not invariably, in deep shade, perching typically in open airspace below the leafy canopy. In such habitats they range from sea level up to 1800 m, from Senegal to extreme south Sudan (Aloma Plateau, Tambura, Kagelu), south Uganda (east to Mabira Islands in the northwest of Lake Victoria), west Ethiopia (Legedema River, Didessa River), northwest Tanzania, Salujinga and South Kasiji River in northwest Zambia, and northern districts of Angola (Lunda, Malanje, Cuanza Norte, Cabinda). Only two individuals have been seen on Legedema River in Ethiopia (de Castro and de Castro 1990); but J. S. Ash (1991) has supplied us with details of kingfishers that he netted nearby on Didessa River 20 years ago, and weights and measurements clearly show that these were Blue-breasted Kingfishers, and not Woodland Kingfishers as Dr Ash assumed at the time. There are further records in Guidimaka, Mauritania (two), Rwanda (one), and in the Kinyinya-Malagarazi region of Burundi (a few). The species occurs commonly on Bioko and Principe Islands, but is now rare or extinct on São Tomé Island. It is common in mangrove and rainforest, and becomes progressively more local and less common in drier savannas at higher latitudes (in Nigeria it occurs north to 11½°N).

Migration It is resident, but in savannas the range contracts somewhat during the dry season. In Nigeria the most northerly records are all in the wet season, May-September. In Ghana it is mainly a wet-season visitor in April-July to the Accra Plain forest outliers, and it is widespread in Gambia during the summer rains but retreats into riverine woods on the upper Gambia River in the dry season.

Food It eats some vegetable matter, including fruits of the oil-palm *Elaeis guineensis* (sought after by all birds, even hawks and some insectivores), but mainly invertebrates: roaches, grasshoppers, termites, wasps, beetles, mantises, spiders, millipedes, whip-scorpions, crabs, and molluscs (*Columna flaminea*). Mudskippers, frogs, toads, lizards, mice and a White-bellied Kingfisher (64) are also known prey.

Habits The species lives solitarily or in pairs. It is wary, disappearing into the forest when disturbed, usually calling in alarm as it takes flight (but on Principe Island it is tame). It searches for food by perching on a large branch some 5 m up, and diving down to alight and snatch its prey; sometimes it stays grounded for a few moments, but generally it returns with its prey directly to its perch. Like other halcyons this one is territorial. Both sexes sing, frequently, throughout the day, perched in the forest and sometimes in flight over the treetops. They display by perching near the top of a tree, singing, pointing the bill up, rapidly opening the wings in the vertical plane and closing them, and simultaneously jerking the tail up. Using the same heraldic posture, males courtship-feed females with 8-cm lizards (Brosset and Erard 1986). **Nesting:** not many nests have been found, but all were holes excavated into the side of an arboreal termitarium, usually of *Microcerotermes*, 6-10 m up. Four such nests in Gabon contained clutches or broods of two, one of which, while under observation, was raided by Chimpanzees. **Laying months:** Guinea-Bissau, August-September; Ghana, March-April; Nigeria, January-June; Cameroon, August; Gabon, December-June; Principe Island, October-December; Uganda, April.

Description *H. m. torquata* Sexes alike. **Adult:** forehead pale grey-brown, with a narrow whitish stripe above the lores; crown dark brown; lore and a triangular patch behind the eye black; hindneck, upper mantle, ear-coverts, cheeks and sides of the neck blue; lower mantle, upper back, scapulars and forewing black; lower back and rump bright azure-blue; tail darker blue. Primaries, secondaries, primary coverts and alula bright blue, with broad black ends. Chin and throat white, breast greenish-blue, flanks and undertail-coverts greyish, belly white. The underwing is white, with black greater primary coverts and shiny grey-black ends to the primaries and secondaries. The underside of the tail is glossy black. Upper mandible bright red with black tip and long black triangle by the gape, lower mandible black; eye dark brown; legs and feet dark red. **Juvenile:** like the adult, but crown washed with blue-green, blues of the head and underparts are greener, and the underparts are pale buff (palest on chin and belly, and with the breast green-blue). Legs brown, feet red, brown on top of toes. Very young birds have the bill reddish-brown with a pale tip. **Measurements:** wing of male 112-120, of female 110-122; tail of male 78-90, of female 78-86; bill of male 55-63, of female 54-66; tarsus of male 16-18, of female 16-18. Weight (*H. m. malimbica*): male 66-94, female 70-93.

References Brosset and Erard (1986), Forshaw (1985), Fry *et al.* (1988), de Naurois (1980).

34 WOODLAND KINGFISHER   Plate 12
Halcyon senegalensis

Alcedo senegalensis Linnaeus, 1766, Syst. Nat., ed. 12, I, p. 180, Senegal.

Field identification Length 23 cm (9 in). The only blue-backed African halcyon except for the African Mangrove Kingfisher (35). The bill, with red upper and black lower mandible, distinguishes adults from all halcyons other than the Blue-breasted Kingfisher (33). **At rest:** a medium-sized woodland kingfisher with black shoulders, but otherwise softly patterned with greyish head, blue upperparts and greyish-white underparts. The bill is red and black on adults and dusky on young birds; legs and feet are black. **In flight:** looks white below and bright blue above, with black shoulder-patches, dusky wingtips, and white bases to some primaries making a window (usually apparent only in transmitted light). **Confusion species:** very like the African Mangrove Kingfisher and quite like the Blue-breasted: for distinctions, see under those species. In Malaŵi some Woodland Kingfishers have red patches in the lower mandible, making them even harder to distinguish from African Mangrove Kingfishers (Fry 1983; Hanmer 1984, 1989).

Voice Very vocal. The song is a single sharp 'tiu', followed by a loud fast trill lasting $2^{1}/_{2}$-$3^{1}/_{2}$ seconds, slowing and falling a little towards the end. It is repeated about ten times (occasionally up to 40 times) at intervals of 5-10 seconds. A pair flies around its territory trilling incessantly: 'tirrrrr-tirrrrr-tirrrrr-tirrrrr...'. The alarm is a fast 'kee-kee-kee-kee-kee'.

Geographical variation The three subspecies differ slightly in hue; one has a small black triangle behind the eye (like the Blue-breasted Kingfisher) which the other two lack.

H. s. senegalensis Northern tropical savannas. Crown pale; no eye-patch. It intergrades with *fuscopilea* at the forest/savanna interface and with *cyanoleuca* in northwest Tanzania. Slightly larger in East than in West Africa.

H. s. fuscopilea West African and Congo Basin forests. Crown dark brown-grey; mantle and breast greyer than on *senegalensis*; slightly smaller; no eye-patch.

H. s. cyanoleuca Africa south of Congo Basin and Kenya; a non-breeding visitor north to south Sudan. Crown, hindneck and mantle paler blue than on *senegalensis*; a black wedge behind the eye; faint bluish wash on breast. About 10% larger than West African *senegalensis*.

Habitat and range This is a common bird of woodlands, forests, and wooded places around human habitation throughout sub-Saharan Africa, north to 17°N in Mauritania and 16°N in Sudan. It is absent only from Somalia, Kenya east of the Rift Valley (but it occurs at Lake Baringo), Namibia except near the Angola border, central and southwest Botswana, Lesotho, Orange Free State, Cape Province, and land above 2000 m; it is uncommon above 1500 m. It occurs on Bioko but not on Zanzibar or other islands. Woodland Kingfishers inhabit forest clearings and edges, but in savannas they avoid closed cover and prefer open areas with scattered trees, farmland, parks and large gardens. A single large leafy tree left in cleared land is enough to attract a pair to nest. They often nest on or around houses.

Migration *H. s. fuscopilea* is sedentary. Savanna populations are resident within about 8° of the Equator, but are progress-ively more migratory towards the northern and southern extremities of their range. In West Africa great numbers visit the sahel zone north to 17°N in July-October, but around 10°N the species is a visitor from April to November. It is a breeding visitor to Zambia, Okavango (Botswana), low-land Zimbabwe, and Natal south to Umzimvubu River, from September or October to April. Some southern birds cross the Lake Victoria basin to 'winter' north at least to Baro River and Lake No in Sudan. Migrants travel at night, solitarily or in loose groups.

Food Insects, mainly grasshoppers, locusts and beetles. Also: dragonflies, cicadas, roaches, mantises, moths, butterflies, larvae, ants and termites; scorpions, milli-pedes, shrimps, crabs, fish, frogs, lizards, snakes, and occasionally small birds.

Habits Woodland Kingfishers live in pairs and are strongly territorial, a pair pro-claiming its territory by constant singing. Noisy territorial disputes are frequent, and one or two pairs sometimes fly at treetop height, pursuing each other and calling incessantly. Other hole-nesting birds, small hawks and human beings are aggressively chased away. When not breeding it spends 70-95% of the daytime quietly perching in semi-shade and scan-ning around for food, sitting upright with the tail pointing down and sometimes wagging back and forth, and from time to time head-bobbing. Prey is seized on or near the ground and eaten back at the perch, where a large item is first held crosswise in the bill and beaten to left and right. The average lookout perch is 2.6 m high; from a much higher perch the bird spirals slowly down, briefly hovers, then plunges directly on to the prey. Sometimes it catches a termite in flight, or crashes into shallow water for a fish. The species bathes by plunging recklessly on to the surface or by diving headlong into deep water, then shaking itself, scratching and preening vigorously at perch. *Nesting:* be-fore and during the breeding season the bird displays by trilling from a treetop with bill half open and pointing upward. Then it sits very erect, suddenly opens its wings wide in the vertical plane, and turns the body from side to side, pivoting on its legs; seen from in front, the white wing-lining contrasts conspicuously with the black flight feathers. Wing-spreading usually lasts for 1-2 seconds but can last for 7 seconds and be repeated 15 times, with the wings opening progressively to their full extent in three or four movements while the tail is fanned and cocked. Often two mated birds display together, sitting facing each other, pivoting with outstretched wings and singing in duet. Migrants return to use the same nest hole for several years running. Nests are nearly always in tree holes, either fresh ones or old holes of barbets, woodpeckers or starlings; rarely they are in nestboxes, under eaves, in arboreal termitaria, or in swifts' holes. Only once has a Woodland Kingfisher been known to hollow out its own nest hole. Nest holes are 5 m above ground on average. The clutch is of 2-4 eggs, usually three, the incubation period 13-14 days and the nestling period 22-24 days. Young are cared for by both parents, and accompany them for up to five weeks after leaving the nest. **Laying months:** across the northern tropics this kingfisher breeds from March (about 7°N) until September and perhaps October (about 15°N), and south of the Equator from November until March (once October, in Katanga).

Description *H. s. senegalensis* Sexes alike. **Adult:** forehead brown-grey, becoming blue-grey on crown and blue on nape; a narrow white stripe from bill to eye. Lores and narrow orbital ring of feathers and skin black; ear-coverts and sides of neck pale grey-blue. Mantle and scapulars blue, with grey feather bases sometimes showing. Rump and tail bright blue. Upperwing-coverts black; secondaries bright azure-blue with dusky tips, primary coverts blue, primaries black with white bases and mainly blue outer webs. Chin and throat white; breast pale grey (actually white with very fine grey vermiculation) with a green-blue wash; belly, flanks and undertail-coverts white, sometimes with greyish wash. Underside of the wing with coverts and base of the primaries snowy-white, but secondaries and distal halves of primaries glossy black. Underside of the tail black. Upper mandible bright red with a small blackish patch near the gape, lower mandible black; eye dark brown; legs and feet blackish. **Juvenile:** like the adult, but forehead, supercilium, cheeks, and underparts except chin and throat are washed with yellowish-buff and finely vermiculated with dark grey; sometimes a blackish mark behind the eye. Both mandibles are blackish with red bases and, on very young birds, white tips. **Measurements** (East Africa): wing of male 98-110, of female 100-111; tail of male 58-71, of female 57-69; bill of male 42-50, of female 43-48; tarsus of male 14-16, of female 14-16. Weight: male 41-60, female 55-64.

References Forshaw (1985), Fry (1980a,b, 1983), Fry *et al.* (1988), Greig-Smith (1978a, 1979), Hanmer (1984, 1989), Milstein (1962).

35 AFRICAN MANGROVE KINGFISHER Plate 12
Halcyon senegaloides

Halcyon Senegaloides A. Smith, 1834, S. Afr. Quart. J., 2 (2), p. 144, near Port Natal.

Field identification Length 22 cm (8¹/₂ in). A poorly-known bird of the east and southeast African seaboard, overlapping with the Woodland Kingfisher (34) from Dar es Salaam or Lindi to about East London, and distinguishable from it only by voice, bill, and underwing pattern. The bill is all-red (not with black lower mandible as on the Woodland Kingfisher) and is slightly longer, deeper-keeled and wider. Under the wing there is a black patch near the 'wrist' (white on Woodland), as on Striped and Blue-breasted Kingfishers (32, 33), normally visible only in wing-spreading display. Legs and feet are said to be browner than on Woodland Kingfishers. Its size increases gradually from Somalia to South Africa. East African populations are about the same size as Woodland Kingfishers there, slightly shorter-winged and shorter-tailed but 10% heavier, with the bill a little longer and over 1½ times wider at the base (average 18.4 mm wide, as against 11.6 mm on Woodland). Woodland Kingfishers also increase in size towards South Africa, where African Mangrove Kingfishers are shorter-winged (102-112; 105-120 in the Woodland) and only slightly wider-billed (average 14.4; 11.6 in Natal Woodland Kingfishers). A further distinction in southeast but not East Africa is that African Mangrove Kingfishers lack the blackish mark behind the eye of Woodland Kingfishers. In Malaŵi some Woodland Kingfishers show characters of African Mangrove Kingfishers, with red patches in the lower mandible and a trace of black in the greater under primary coverts, and the two species may possibly interbreed nearby in Mozambique.

Voice The song is a raucous 'tchi, tchi tcha tcha tcha-tch-ch-ch-ch...' accelerating into a slightly descending trill, lasting 6-7 seconds.

Geographical variation Southern populations, somewhat longer-winged but narrower-billed than northern ones, and slightly less bright blue, have sometimes been treated as a separate subspecies.

Habitat and range African Mangrove Kingfishers do not nest in mangrove, but inhabit nearby low-lying woodland and open country with wooded rivers. They move into wooded estuaries and mangrove in the non-breeding season, and occur on wooded seashores and in cultivated areas, thornveld, deciduous and light evergreen forest, city parks, fishponds and gardens. They keep mainly within 20 km of the coast, from about 3°N in Somalia to about 33°S in east Cape Province (south to Great Kei River and perhaps Great Fish River estuaries), but extend up to 150 km inland in Juba River valley, along the Zambezi to Sena, Mozambique, and occasionally into Kruger National Park (records at Malelane and Skukuza). They occur at altitudes of up to 300 m.

Migration These kingfishers are partial migrants, vacating coastal woods and mangrove in late September and early October and moving 5-50 km inland to breed.

However, they visit Zanzibar in September-January to nest, and seem to be year-round residents on Tumbatu Island (Zanzibar) and Pemba Island. In February and March migrants from inland return to the coast, when juveniles are sometimes killed by colliding with wires and buildings in Durban.

Food Crabs, prawns, fishes, lizards and insects.

Habits They fish more regularly and efficiently than do Woodland Kingfishers, and are more aquatic in habitat and diet. When not breeding they are not very vocal, and can be elusive, particularly in mangrove. They are known to have a wing-spreading treetop song display, like the Woodland, but it has not been studied in detail. **Nesting:** nest holes have been found high in a dead tree, a living mango, and in riverbanks. **Laying months:** Kenya, October; Tanzania (Pemba Island), December; Cape Province, November-December. In East Africa this kingfisher sings from August to January and in South Africa from September to April (mainly October-December), doubtless indicating the breeding seasons there.

Description Sexes alike. **Adult:** forehead, crown and hindneck dark grey-brown; a narrow white line from nostril to above eye; lores black; ear-coverts, cheeks, and sides of neck brown-grey. Breast and flanks vermiculated grey, sometimes with a buffy wash. Greater under primary coverts black. Otherwise the plumage is almost exactly like that of the Woodland Kingfisher. Bill red, the lower mandible with a dusky tip; eye dark brown; legs and feet dark grey-brown. **Juvenile:** like the adult, but blues duller, breast and flanks more coarsely vermiculated and washed with yellowish-buff. Bill dark brown, with a white tip on very young birds. **Measurements:** wing of male 98-108, of female 98-112; tail of male 50-66, of female 57-66; bill of male 47-55, of female 44-55; tarsus of male 14-16, of female 14-16. Weight (Kenya): 57-66.

References Clancey (1965), Forshaw (1985), Fry et al. (1988).

36 BLACK-SIDED KINGFISHER

Plate 13

Halcyon nigrocyanea

Halcyon nigrocyanea Wallace, 1862, Proc. Zool. Soc. London, p. 165, pl. 19, northwest peninsula of New Guinea, = Manokwari.

Field identification Length 23 cm (9 in). This kingfisher is confined to New Guinea, in three distinct subspecies, with the added identification problem of males, females and juveniles being dissimilar. The habitat is not distinctively different from that of many other New Guinea kingfishers, and the voice is like that of some others; but this is the only kingfisher there possessing (on adults) a complete, broad, blue breast-band that is sharply contrasted with white chin and throat and with at least some white on the lower breast (the belly can be blue-black, rufous or white). In southern New Guinea, however, males of the race *stictolaema* are blue-black, apart from white mottling on the throat, a pale blue, almost azure, streak behind the eye, and (like adults of all subspecies) bright pale blue rump. Juveniles resemble the adult female in each race, described below, except that white parts are suffused with orange-buff, and dark blue areas in the breast and belly of adult females are dusky burnt orange on the juveniles.

Voice The song consists of three notes at increasingly high pitch, the last run into a loud descending trill; it lasts 3 seconds and is like the songs of the Hook-billed Kingfisher (14) and some of the paradise kingfishers (7-12). Females utter a 'cheez'.

Geographical variation Males of the three races are strikingly different in plumage, but with insignificant variation in size. The female of *quadricolor* is not known; females of the other two subspecies are alike.

H. n. nigrocyanea Irian Jaya, from Geelvink Bay (near Kwatisore) in the north and Princess Marianne Straits in the south, west to Vogelkop, Batanta and Salawati Islands; absent from the Vogelkop Mountains. The male, described in detail below, is purple-blue and black with white chin and throat, a white lozenge across the lower breast, and azure back. Female: like the male, but lower breast

and belly white; flanks and thighs black.

H. n. quadricolor Northern New Guinea, from Geelvink Bay (near Nuboai) and Japen Island, east to about Madang and Astrolabe Bay. Males differ from males of the nominate race as follows: white lozenge on lower breast reduced to a narrow transverse band, belly chestnut, back purple blue. The female has not been described; it is probably like females of other subspecies.

H. n. stictolaema Southern New Guinea, from southeast Irian Jaya to about Mount Cameroon, southeast Papua New Guinea. The ranges of the three races appear not to meet. Male: purple-blue and black, feathers in centre of throat white with broad black tips; upperparts as *nigrocyanea*, back azure. Female: like female *nigrocyanea,* hence quite different from male *stictolaema*.

Habitat and range Lowland forests, often near rivers; also seen in *Eucalyptus* forest, *Melaleuca* swamps, thickets by creeks, near small forested streams, in partly flooded forest, and coastal village gardens. From the coast, Black-sided Kingfishers range well into the interior, to the forested lower slopes of New Guinea's spinal ranges of mountains. In the Vogelkop Peninsula, Salawati, Batanta and Japen Islands – that is to say, in the west of its range – this kingfisher is common, but it seems to become progressively less so to the east, and is scarce throughout much of Papua New Guinea. Hence the races *quadricolor* and *stictolaema* are known to ornithologists much less well than is the nominate *nigrocyanea*. The species is doubtless sedentary.

Food Consonant with the bird's evident fondness for the proximity of water, its food is partly aquatic. Of three specimens collected for museums, one stomach contained crabs, one fishes and one a 10-cm lizard.

Habits Nothing more is known than has been mentioned above. Nest and eggs have not been described, and its breeding and social biology are entirely unknown.

Description *H. n. nigrocyanea* ***Adult male:*** forehead and crown purple-blue; sides of crown brighter, paler blue, forming long superciliary stripes which meet on the nape. Lores, ear-coverts, malar area, cheeks, sides of neck, hindneck and sides of breast black; mantle, scapulars and tertials also black, the last with purple-blue outer edges. Back bright pale azure-blue, which darkens over rump to become purple-blue on uppertail-coverts and tail. Wings purple-blue, the flight feathers blackish with purple-blue outer edges. Underside of tail black; underside of wing grey-black, but outermost greater underwing-coverts edged white. Chin and throat white, breast caerulean-blue in a well-defined broad band, lower breast white, belly caerulean-blue, and flanks, thighs, vent and undertail-coverts black, the last tinged blue. Bill black, with small area of horn colour along arms of lower mandible; eye dark brown, orbital skin black; legs and feet greyish-black. ***Adult female:*** differs from the male in having the belly white, confluent with white lower breast, and the upperparts blacker. ***Juvenile:*** male very distinct, looks like a different species. Upperparts like those of the adult but duskier, the blues less intense and most feathers, particularly upperwing-coverts and supraloral feathers, fringed with orange-buff. Chin and throat creamy, strongly suffused at the edges with orange-buff; lower breast the same. Upper breast burnt orange, scalloped with narrow dusky tips to the feathers. Upper belly tawny, lower belly buff, some feathers at sides of belly broadly tipped blackish. Sides of breast, flanks and undertail-coverts black. The juvenile female is like the juvenile male, but lower breast, belly and undertail-coverts are buffy-white. ***Measurements:*** wing of male 90-99, of female 92-101; tail of male 56-68, of female 59-69; bill of male 46-55, of female 45-53; tarsus of male 16-18, of female 16-18. Weight: male 51-54, female 55-57.

Reference Forshaw (1985).

37 WINCHELL'S KINGFISHER   **Plate 13**
Halcyon winchelli

Halcyon Winchelli Sharpe, 1877, Trans. Linn. Soc. London, (2), 1, p. 318, pl. 47, Isabella, Basilan, Philippines.

Field identification Length 25 cm (10 in). A splendid, large, dark blue, white and rufous kingfisher of forests in the southern Philippines, unmistakable in close view. Views are, however, apt to be distant and fleeting. *At rest:* male told by very dark blue upperparts (looking black in poor light), with large orange-rufous supraloral spot and broad hindneck-collar, and entirely white underparts, except that in central Philippines there is a large black patch at the side of the breast. The bill is mainly black, and the rump is azure. Upperparts of the female are the same, but her underparts are buff, cinnamon or tawny-orange, varying geographically. *In flight:* the main impression is of a dark-backed, white-breasted (male) or orange-breasted (female) bird, obviously a kingfisher because of the azure rump, and told as Winchell's if the chestnut supraloral spot and hindneck-collar can be seen.

Voice The only description is of a loud squawking, near dawn and dusk.

Geographical variation We recognise five subspecies.

H. w. mindanensis Mindanao, the main island of the south Philippines.

H. w. winchelli Basilan Island, southwest of Mindanao and very close to it. Like *mindanensis*, but hue of purple-blue parts less rich, and blacker; black mask washed with blue. Juveniles lack the the blue wash on crown, mantle and wing-coverts of juvenile *mindanensis*.

H. w. alfredi Tawitawi and Jola Islands,

and perhaps still a few other islands in the Sulu Archipelago (between Basilan and Borneo) large enough to retain forest. Like female *mindanensis,* but females have much paler buff underparts; juveniles like juvenile *winchelli.*

H. w. nigrorum Central Philippines: Samar, Calicoan, Bohol, Leyte, Negros, Siquijor; not certainly still surviving on Cebu. Like *mindanensis,* but purple-blue parts duller and blacker (more so than on nominate *winchelli*), and a conspicuous black patch at the side of the breast, usually washed purple-blue. Juveniles like *mindanensis* juveniles, but not so strongly blue-washed.

H. w. nesydrionetes Northwest-central Philippine islands of Tablas, Sibuyan and Romblon only. Like *mindanensis,* but females have the breast bright orange or orange-buff, the colour joining the hind-collar and mask to enclose the whitish chin and throat; belly whitish. Juveniles like adult females, but the tawny-orange breast-band is even better demarcated.

Habitat and range Undisturbed or little-disturbed forest in the southern Philippine Archipelago, from Mindanao, Basilan and the Sulu Islands in the south to Samar and Tablas in the north; it seems to be absent from the intervening large islands of Panay and Masbate, and may now be extinct on Cebu. It is reported to spend much time perching exposed or hidden on branches in the upper canopy, but it also perches, presumably to hunt, down to a height of 4 m, and is occasionally encountered on the ground. Winchell's Kingfisher occurs at up to 750 m altitude on Bohol Island. It is surely resident and sedentary. Mountfort (1988) regards the species as a candidate for the Red Data Book.

Population In general it seems to be rare, which is often the case with rainforest birds frequenting the canopy, but it may have been widely overlooked. Late in 1971, a joint American-Filipino expedition found Winchell's Kingfisher to be 'common' in some densely forested islands in the Sulu Archipelago.

Food Large insects (cicadas, grasshoppers, beetles, larvae) and spiders.

Habits Food is taken on the ground and also, reportedly, high in trees. Prey is battered by the bird in the usual way. Nest and eggs are unknown.

Description *H. w. mindanensis* **Adult male:** forehead and crown in the midline blackish, paling through deep purple-blue to bright blue at the edges of the crown. Large, oval, bright orange-rufous supra-loral spot, from nostrils to eye; lores, upper cheeks and ear-coverts blue-black. Broad, bright orange-rufous hindneck-collar, bordered by blackish feathers above and below. Feathers of mantle, upper back, scapulars, tertials and wings black, fringed with dark purple-blue; lower back, rump and uppertail-coverts pale bright azure-blue. Tail purple-blue above, blackish below. Wing-lining buffy-white; undersides of primaries and secondaries blackish. Chin, throat, sides of neck and breast to undertail-coverts white; irregular blue-black mark at sides of breast, mostly concealed by the folded wing, formed by broad crescentic fringes to the feathers there. Bill black, rami of lower mandible yellowish-horn; eye dark brown, orbital skin black; legs and feet greyish-black, soles yellower. **Adult female:** upperparts as on male; underparts warm buff, with cinnamon wash on breast, belly paler in midline. **Juvenile:** like the adult female but duller, purple-blues of upperparts less vivid, hindneck-collar pale rufous, underparts not so rich a buff. **Measurements:** wing of male 95-102, of female 98-101; tail of male 65-70, of female 67-76; bill of male 48-49, of female 50-53; tarsus of male 15-17, of female 15-17. Weight (*H. w. nigrorum*): male 60-64, female 67-80.

Reference Forshaw (1985).

38 MOLUCCAN KINGFISHER (Blue-and-white Kingfisher)
Halcyon diops

Plate 13

Alcedo diops Temminck, 1824, Planch. Col., 46, pl. 272, Amboina, Timor and Celebes (error for Ternate).

Field identification Length 19 cm (7½ in). All members of the group of eight species to which this kingfisher belongs have marked sexual disparity of plumage. In appearance male and female, even if quite different, are equally striking. This species, endemic to the northern Moluccan Islands between Sulawesi and New Guinea, south of the Philippines, is purple-blue above and white below, with azure-blue back and rump and a large, round, white supraloral spot. Males have a broad white collar and entirely white underparts; females have the hindneck and breast purple-blue. **Confusion species:** of the seven kinds of kingfishers that inhabit the Moluccas, this and the Mangrove (47) are the only halcyons. The female Moluccan Kingfisher is readily distinguished from the Mangrove by its purple-blue hindneck and well-demarcated breast-band. Males are rather alike, but the Moluccan can be told immediately by its having an all-black bill (black-and-horn on Mangrove) and by its white supraloral spot being larger than the eye (much smaller on Mangrove). The diminutive Little Kingfisher (74), with its purple-blue upperparts, white underparts and white supraloral spot, is also superficially like the Moluccan, but its rump is dark blue, not azure, and it has a white neck-flag.

Voice A warbling 'tu-tu-tu-ti-ti'.

Geographical variation None.

Habitat and range What was the original habitat is open to question, but in the heavily populated northern Moluccas today this kingfisher is found in a variety of situations: woods, wooded gardens, lowland orchards, the edges of mangrove, coconut groves, at the edges of cut-about forest, and in all manner of cultivated land. It is a common bird, not only on the main island Halmahera, but on Morotai, Ternate, Obi, Bisa and the three Batjan Islands.

Food Known to eat grasshoppers. Doubtless it preys on other large invertebrates and small vertebrates, as its congeners do.

Habits Very little is on record, and its breeding behaviour, nest and eggs have not been described. It perches on telegraph wires. Almost certainly its habits will prove to be very like those of its well-known close ally the Forest Kingfisher (40).

Description *Adult male:* centre of forehead and forecrown blackish, rest of crown deep purple-blue; sides of forehead white, forming a large, discrete, circular or somewhat triangular supraloral spot abutting the nostril. Lores, malar area, ear-coverts and upper cheeks black, extending as a black band around the nape; sometimes a few white feathers above the black nape-band. Broad white collar. Mantle, upperwing-coverts, tertials and tail deep purple-blue, paling through scapulars and back to bright pale blue on rump and uppertail-coverts. Entire underparts white. Underwing-coverts white, but outermost greater underwing-coverts blue. Primaries and secondaries blackish above, washed purple-blue along outer edges, and greyish-black below. Underside of tail greyish-black. Bill black; eye dark brown, orbital skin black; legs and feet greyish-black, soles yellowish. *Adult female:* like the male, but hindneck, sides of neck and cheeks blue-black, and breast deep purple-blue. *Juvenile:* like the adult male, but supraloral patch, collar, sides of throat and whole of breast tawny-rufous, the throat and breast feathers with dusky tips; flanks sometimes buffy. *Measurements:* wing of male 84-93, of female 85-96; tail of male 43-53, of female 41-56; bill of male 38-46, of female 38-46; tarsus of male 13-15, of female 13-15. Weight: male 41-45, female 42-65.

Reference Forshaw (1985).

39 LAZULI KINGFISHER (Lazuline Kingfisher)   Plate 14
Halcyon lazuli

Alcedo lazuli Temminck, 1830, Planch. Col., 86, pl. 508, Sumatra (error for Amboina).

Field identification Length 22 cm (8½ in). A fine, unmistakable kingfisher with deep purple-blue crown, wings and tail, azure-blue back, rump and belly, and white throat. On males the breast is white, on females azure-blue. *Confusion species:* in its home, Ceram and its small offshore islands in the southern Moluccas, between Sulawesi and New Guinea, the only other halcyon kingfisher is the Mangrove (47). The two are rather alike, but the Mangrove Kingfisher has a pale blue crown and white belly. No other bird in Ceram has any resemblance to the Lazuli Kingfisher.

Voice Not known.

Geographical variation None.

Habitat and range Its habitat requirements are not at all well known; it has been found in mangrove, and in inland forest. The range is Ceram and its satellite islands, Amboina (Ambon) and the Saparuas (Haruku), southern Moluccas. A candidate for the Red Data Book (Mountfort 1988).

Food Grasshoppers and beetles (Cerambycidae) have been found in stomachs.

Habits Virtually nothing is on record. Four recently-fledged birds were once being fed by both parents, in early December. Nest and eggs are unknown.

Description *Adult male:* forehead and mid-crown black, washed with blue; small white supraloral spot, behind which sides of the crown are dark blue. Lores, malar region, upper cheeks and ear-coverts black, washed with blue, continuing as blue-black band around nape; a few white feathers on hindcrown above the black nape. Broad white collar, the hindneck feathers tipped blue-black. Mantle feathers blackish with blue fringes, scapulars blackish with broad pale blue fringes; back and rump silvery-blue or azure. Tertials and upperwing-coverts mainly purple-blue, inner lesser wing-coverts brighter blue, primaries and secondaries blackish with deep blue outer edges. Tail purple-blue. Chin, throat, sides of neck, breast and forebelly white; belly, flanks and undertail-coverts azure-blue. Underwing-coverts mainly grey, with some white or dull blue. Upper mandible black, lower mandible yellowish-horn, with brown-black cutting edges and tip; eyes dark brown, orbital skin black; legs and feet brownish-black. *Adult female:* differs from the male in having hindneck and sides of neck purple-blue and breast azure-blue (concolorous with belly), leaving a well-defined white chin-and-throat patch; underwing-coverts grey and dark blue. *Juvenile:* like the adult male but blues duller, particularly the azure-blues; white collar heavily marked with dusky blue. Whites of supraloral spot, throat and collar washed with buff; sides of breast scalloped, the feathers being narrowly tipped with black. *Measurements:* wing of male 91-99, of female 93-99; tail of male 52-57, of female 52-58; bill of male 40-44, of female 40-45; tarsus of male 13-15, of female 13-15.

Reference Stresemann (1914).

40 FOREST KINGFISHER

Plate 14

Halcyon macleayii

Halcyon Macleayii Jardine and Selbȳ, 1830, Illustr. Orn., 2, pl. 101 and text, no locality (Port Essington, Berlepsch, 1911).

Field identification Length 20 cm (8 in). A black, white and two-toned blue kingfisher of forests in north and east Australia, south and east New Guinea, adjacent parts of Indonesia,· and the Bismarck Archipelago. *At rest:* the large white supraloral spot, between bill and eye, is visible from afar. In shade or poor light the rest of the cap of males can appear black, cleanly divided from the blue back by a broad white collar. Females can also seem white-collared, although the collar is incomplete, the hindneck being blue. *In flight:* shows a conspicuous white patch in the wing, formed by white bases to the outer secondaries and all except outer primaries. *Confusion species:* in Australia, the large white supraloral spot serves to distinguish it from all other kingfishers except the diminutive Little Kingfisher (74), which occurs within the same range but has quite different neck markings. Their black mask and white collar make Forest Kingfishers look like Mangrove (47), Sacred (50) and Red-backed Kingfishers (52), but the first and second are mainly olive-green above and the last has an orange rump. Female Forest Kingfishers sometimes have buffy flanks, like Sacred. Fledglings of the Mangrove and Forest Kingfishers only a few weeks old are very alike: distinguish them by accompanying parents, or in close view by olive (Mangrove) rather than bluish (Forest) crown and mantle. In and adjacent to New Guinea several subspecies of Mangrove Kingfisher occur in the range of the Forest Kingfisher, the principal one being *H. c. sordida*, which is larger than Forest (more than twice its weight) and dark brown-olive where Forest is blue. Male Moluccan Kingfishers (38) are very like male Forest (females are quite different), but their ranges approach no nearer than Obi Island (northern Moluccas) and Kai Island (Aru Islands) respectively.

Voice A harsh, strident 'scissor-weeya scissor-weeya', a chattering 'kreek-kreek-kreek-kreek', and loud whistles and screeches.

Geographical variation Involves shades of blue on back and rump, and length of the ? white wing-patch. Variation in size is barely significant.

H. m. macleayii Breeds in Australia at the Top End, from about Victoria River to Melville, Crocodile, Sir Edward Pellew Islands and Groote Eylandt. A partial migrant, and records from Sermata and Aru Islands, Indonesia, probably refer to migrants and not to any population resident there.

H. m. incincta Breeds in northeast Australia, from Cape York Peninsula and some Torres Strait islands to about Macleay in New South Wales; rare west of Great Dividing Range, vagrant to east Victoria. A partial migrant, some wintering in Indonesia and New Guinea. Like *macleayii* but fractionally smaller, with the mantle and rump darker blue, the back, scapulars and tertials greener, and five outer primaries (rather than only three) lacking white bases.

H. m. elisabeth Resides in east Papua New Guinea and perhaps as far east as New Ireland. Like *macleayii* but bluer, the upperparts almost without green tinge.

Habitat and range A bird of woodlands and open forest, particularly near fresh water. Its preferred habitat seems to vary regionally, and in New Guinea and New Britain winter visitors may occupy rather more open situations than the resident population. In Australia it occurs in forest adjacent to swamps and *Pandanus* (screwpine) savanna, at the edges of wet sclerophyll forest, in lightly wooded country including farmland, pasture, cropland, wooded swamps and creeks, open *Eucalyptus* forest, mangrove, wet *Melaleuca* stands, and monsoon forest. In New Guinea the species inhabits forest edges and clearings, and all humid well-timbered places up to about 1600 m elevation: it is even common in Kimbe township in New Britain. In such habitats Forest Kingfishers range from northeast New South Wales, mainly east of the Great Dividing Range, to Cape York Peninsula, and Northern Territory from Melville Island, Darwin and Victoria River to Cape Arnhem and Groote Eylandt, islands in Torres Strait, and eastern Papua New Guinea from Astrolabe Bay and Hall Sound to at least western parts of Bismarck Archipelago.

Population A measure of the abundance of this species is that, in a traverse of the eastern coast of Australia in the winter of 1960, about 1,900 individuals were counted in the 160 km from Ingham northwards (12 birds per km).

Migration Winter records south of the Tropic of Capricorn are rare: nearly all of the New South Wales and southern Queensland population leaves in March and April and returns in September and October. North of the Tropic, in northern Queensland, passage at those times has been noted at several localities, and the kingfisher is less common from May to August than in summer. It winters in Kai and Tanimbar Islands, Indonesia, and from Mimika River, Irian Jaya, through southern Papua New Guinea to Louisiade Archipelago, New Britain and perhaps New Ireland. *H. m. elisabeth* is resident and so is *H. m. macleayii*, although records of the latter from Sermata and Aru Islands may refer to migrants.

Food Invertebrates and small terrestrial vertebrates: grasshoppers, *Aeshna* dragonflies, beetles, larvae, spiders, frogs, tadpoles and lizards. In one brood, nestlings were fed on tree-frogs, mosquito-fish *Gambusia* and lizards; the two nestlings ate 12-20 frogs and lizards daily, but rejected insects.

Habits Forest Kingfishers generally occur in pairs. They hunt by perching patiently on some elevated vantage point such as a bare branch or telegraph wire, and plunging down to the ground, sometimes striking it with breast and legs, to pounce on to prey. Food is seized in the bill, and the bird flies back to its perch to immobilise it by vigorous beating. Particularly in defence of a breeding territory, they are showy and noisy birds. Pairs evidently re-

turn to the same territory in consecutive years, and establish winter as well as summer territories. A male displays to its mate by standing upright on a telegraph pole or fence post, fanning and cocking the tail, drooping the wings, and calling with bill pointing skyward. Calling can be so vigorous that the bird's whole body vibrates. *Nesting:* nests are excavated by male and female of a pair in arboreal termitaria. Other sites occasionally used are natural tree hollows, and soil compacted between the roots of fallen trees. There is a short, inclining entrance burrow, leading to an egg chamber about 23 cm in diameter. The clutch is of 3-6 eggs. Both parents feed the young. *Laying months:* New South Wales, October-December; Queensland, August-December; Northern Territory, September-November; New Guinea, January.

Description *H. m. macleayii* **Adult male:** centre of forehead, crown, upperwing-coverts, tertials and tail deep purple-blue. A large and well-defined round supraloral spot at the side of the forehead; lores and ear-coverts black. Hindneck white; mantle royal-blue, becoming turquoise on the back and cobalt-blue on the uppertail-coverts. Sides of neck, chin, throat, breast, flanks, belly and undertail-coverts white; flanks sometimes suffused with buff. Wing-lining white. Upper mandible blackish-brown, lower mandible yellowish-horn with blackish-brown cutting edge and distal half; eye dark brown, orbital skin black; legs and feet greyish-black. **Adult female:** differs from the male in the hindneck being dark blue, concolorous with crown and mantle; flanks usually buffy. **Juvenile:** like the adult male, but supraloral spot buff, blue parts of plumage less intense, feathers of crown and especially of upperwing-coverts fringed with buff, breast feathers buffy with dusky fringes, flanks and belly washed with buff, scapulars and back grey-blue or dusky, and some white feathers of collar with dusky tips. **Measurements:** wing of male 85-91, of female 82-92; tail of male 48-59, of female 50-57; bill of male 36-42, of female 37-44; tarsus of male 13-15, of female 13-14. Weight: male 33-42, female 29-40.

References Bell (1981), Forshaw (1985), Mees (1982), Storr (1973), Tubb (1945).

41 NEW BRITAIN KINGFISHER (White-mantled Kingfisher)
Halcyon albonotata

Plate 14

Halcyon (Cyanalcyon) albonotata Ramsay, 1885, Proc. Linn. Soc. N.S.W., 9, p. 865, New Britain.

Field identification Length 16 cm (6¼ in). Small for a woodland kingfisher (*Halcyon*), but unlikely to be confused with the larger alcedinine kingfisher on New Britain, the Bismarck Kingfisher (73). *At rest:* the light blue cap with white supraloral spot, blackish mask, dark purple-blue wings and tail and entirely white trunk of the male are most distinctive. Females have the collar and mantle white also, but the lower back and rump are purple-blue, not white. *In flight:* the impression of a blue-capped white-bodied bird with disembodied dark blue wings and tail (the male) is even more compelling. On the female, however, the dark blue of wings and tail are joined across the back and rump, leaving a large white area on neck and mantle, conspicuous as she flies away. Wing-lining white. *Confusion species:* other kingfishers in its range are Buff-breasted Paradise (10), Forest (40), Mangrove (47), Beach (49), Variable Dwarf (63), Bismarck, Little (74) and River (76). The Beach Kingfisher, present on New Britain and adjacent islands in several subspecies, shares with the present species its white collar and underparts but, variable as the Beach is, it is much larger and greener, and all populations have the mantle olive-green, never white. Forest Kingfishers, however, are very similar to the New Britain: they have purple-blue (not pale blue) crown, purple-blue (not white) mantle, purple-blue hindneck (female), and blue back and rump (male), the last character being shared with female New Britain Kingfisher. No other kind of bird in the Bismarck Archipelago is remotely similar.

Voice A light cackling trill, 'ki-ki-ki-ki', like the call of Mangrove Kingfisher but softer, the individual notes not so discrete.

Geographical variation None.

Habitat and range Forest, mainly primary formations of the coastal lowlands, but also disturbed, logged forest, secondary forest, and evidently on occasion deforested areas, too. The species is confined to New Britain, the principal island in the Bismarck Archipelago, immediately to the east of New Guinea. It is seldom encountered, and poorly known. It appears to spend much time in the upper canopy of trees (which may make it seem rarer than it really is), and is probably the most forest-canopy-bound of all *Halcyon* kingfishers – perhaps through competition for food with the similar-sized, understorey-dwelling Buff-breasted Paradise Kingfisher (Diamond and Marshall 1977). New Britain Kingfishers will also, on occasion, perch low down, scan the ground, and pounce on to an insect there. Like its close relatives Winchell's Kingfisher (37) and the Lazuli Kingfisher (39), it is a candidate for the Red Data Book (Mountfort 1988).

Population Perhaps commoner in undisturbed forest than appearances suggest (see above). Whether this kingfisher can adapt to man-induced habitat change is not known.

Food Large insects, including crickets and grasshoppers.

Habits New Britain Kingfishers, poorly known as they are, seem to live in pairs year-round. They are noisy birds, more often heard than seen, and are generally found high up in the canopy, male and female sitting near each other and calling back and forth in short outbursts. Sometimes one perches conspicuously on some high dead branch. One observation suggests that they are very active early in the morning. Prey is immobilised by beating it against a stout perch. *Nesting:* one nest was in an arboreal termitarium 2 m above the ground in secondary forest, by a clearing. The clutch is of at least 2-3 eggs. *Laying months:* September and (by inference) August and October.

Description *Adult male:* centre of forehead and crown light blue; sides of crown brighter blue, sometimes making a superciliary stripe; conspicuous and well-defined white supraloral spot; lores and ear-coverts black, washed with dark blue; narrow dark blue band from rear of ear-coverts across the nape, with an irregular narrow white band above it. Neck white, mantle, back and rump white, in sharp contrast with purple-blue wings and tail. Entire underparts from chin to undertail-coverts white. Bill black, usually with small horn-coloured area at base of lower mandible; eye dark brown, orbital skin black; legs and feet greyish-black. *Adult female:* like the male, but lower back and rump purple-blue; uppertail-coverts are white, but concealed by long rump feathers. *Juvenile:* each sex like its adult, but all white parts except the mantle are buffy; most blue parts are duller; and upperwing-coverts are scaly, with narrow buff fringes. *Measurements:* wing of male 79-84, of female 80-86; tail of male 48-52, of female 47-53; bill of male 33-39, of female 33-39; tarsus of male 12-14, of female 12-14. Weight: 32 (one male).

References Forshaw (1985), Gilliard and LeCroy (1967).

42 ULTRAMARINE KINGFISHER   Plate 14
Halcyon leucopygia

Cyanalcyon leucopygius J. Verreaux, 1858, Rev. Mag. Zool., (2) 10, p. 305, Solomon Islands.

Field identification Length 21 cm (8¼ in). Confined to Bougainville and the Solomon Islands, where unmistakable: the only bird with deep blue upperparts, white collar and underparts, and lilac-rufous rump and undertail-coverts. Males have the back white, females deep blue. *Confusion species:* no birds in the area, except a few kingfishers, have remotely similar plumage. Other kingfishers in the region are Moustached (3), Mangrove (47), Beach (49), Variable Dwarf (63), Little (74) and River (76). The last three are small waterside fishers, not to be mistaken for the forest-dwelling Ultramarine Kingfisher. The Moustached Kingfisher is the only other high-forest form, a rufous-and-blue bird with red bill. The aptly named Beach Kingfisher is white-headed, leaving the Mangrove Kingfisher as the only one likely to cause confusion. It has numerous subspecies in the range of the Ultramarine, but they differ in having the upperparts green-blue rather than deep purple-blue, with a supraloral spot and/or superciliary stripe, and light blue (never violet) rump.

Voice Usual call at perch and in flight is a repeated, rattling 'kidek-kidek-kidek', rather high-pitched and rapid. Other calls are 'chew-cho-tew', descending the scale, the 'tew' falling away, and a quiet, nasal 'kee-kowl'.

Geographical variation None.

Habitat and range Ultramarine Kingfishers inhabit dense lowland primary and secondary rainforest in Bougainville Island (Papua New Guinea) and the adjacent Solomon Islands, east to Guadalcanal and the small Florida Islands; they may also be present on Nissan Island, northwest of Bougainville. They range up to about 2000 m, and also occur at forest margins, in wooded gardens, whistling-pine trees and regenerating scrubland. Widespread but nowhere abundant, the species appears to be at its most plentiful in not-too-disturbed forest in foothills, valleys and coastal districts. In forest, these kingfishers utilise mainly the middle and upper storeys, often perching in dense shade, but also spending much time exposed to view near the tops of trees. They also forage near the ground, using telegraph wires as vantage points.

Food Insects and spiders have been found in stomachs.

Habits Ultramarine Kingfishers are generally encountered singly or in pairs, perching quietly and unobtrusively on trees or wires, on the lookout for prey. Although essentially birds of forest, they are not particularly shy and often occur near human habitation, along roadsides and in large gardens, sometimes near Mangrove Kingfishers. They are quite vocal. A greeting or courtship display involves the pair in reciprocal bowing. **Nesting:** the nest is excavated by the birds in earthen arboreal termitaria. **Laying months:** by inference, September and October in Bougainville Island.

Description *Adult male:* forehead and crown deep purple-blue, a little brighter at the sides than in the centre. Lores, ear-coverts, cheeks and a narrow band across the nape black. Hindneck white, in a broad band confluent with the white sides of the neck. Upper mantle dark purple-blue, in a band joining the purple-blue scapulars; lower mantle and back white.

Rump purple-blue in the centre, with a large violet patch at each side; uppertail-coverts purple-blue; tail blue-black. Upperwing-coverts and tertials purple-blue, primaries and secondaries blackish, the latter washed with deep blue on the outer webs. Underwing-coverts white. Chin and throat to flanks and belly white; undertail-coverts bright rufous. Bill black or greyish-black; eye dark brown, orbital skin black; legs and feet blackish. *Adult female:* differs from the male only in having the back and lower mantle purple-blue, not white. *Juvenile:* like the adult, but underparts somewhat buffy, and feathers of breast and collar with narrow blackish tips forming dusky crescents. *Measurements:* wing of male 84-93, of female 84-95; tail of male 52-64, of female 52-61; bill of male 38-45, of female 38-45; tarsus of male 13-15, of female 13-15. Weight: male 35-52, female 44-61.

References Forshaw (1985), Schodde (1977).

43 CHESTNUT-BELLIED KINGFISHER Plate 14
Halcyon farquhari

Halcyon farquhari Sharpe, 1899, Bull. Brit. Orn. Club, 10, p. 29, Malikolo and Espiritu Santo, New Hebrides.

Field identification Length 21 cm (8¼ in). Unmistakable: a handsome bird with black cap, dark blue back, white forehead spot and collar, and chestnut-and-white underparts. This and the Mangrove (47) are the only kingfishers in Vanuatu (formerly the New Hebrides Islands, northeast of New Caledonia). Several subspecies of the Mangrove Kingfisher inhabit Vanuatu, the principal ones in the northern and central islands being *H. c. santoensis* and *H. c. juliae*, which are readily told from the Chestnut-bellied by their long cinnamon superciliary stripes and greenish upperparts.

Voice The territorial song is distinctive, a high-pitched piping that starts slowly and speeds up while rising in pitch. The alarm is a harsh 'cach, cach', like that of the Mangrove Kingfisher.

Geographical variation None.

Habitat and range Chestnut-bellied Kingfishers are confined to the three adjacent islands of Espiritu Santo, Malo and Malekula in central Vanuatu. Their habitat, in relation to that of Mangrove Kingfishers, was studied on Malo Island in 1979-80 by Graham Robertson of Aberdeen University, who found that the two species occur together over much of the island. The Chestnut-bellied was absent from the coast, and scarce in low-lying gardens, farmland and coconut groves a short distance inland; it became progressively commoner towards the deep forest in the interior, above 200 m, and in a walk from the coast to the summit of Pic Malo he found 8-10 pairs, their territories about 200 m apart. (Mangrove Kingfishers, by contrast, were commonest at the coast, plentiful in gardens and coconut plantations, and less common – but still commoner than Chestnut-bellied – in inland forest.) In the other two islands a similar habitat distinction has been noted (Diamond and Marshall 1977), but the two species are almost entirely segregated, with Chestnut-bellied confined to closed forest in the uplands and Mangrove confined to coastal and lowland cleared ground. Chestnut-bellied Kingfishers occupy both the canopy and the understorey of forest.

Food Insects, caught in flight or within foliage or snatched from tree trunks, branches and the ground; also spiders. Small grasshoppers, ants, moths and – commonly – beetles have been recorded.

Habits Like many of its congeners, this kingfisher lives year-round in territorial pairs. It perches well above head height in trees, sitting quietly for as much as 30 minutes while intently scanning for prey. Often it is concealed from easy view in thick canopy, where flycatching is a major mode of foraging. Among kingfishers in general, there appears to be an adaptive correlation in bill form, from laterally flattened in fishers, to robust in ground-pouncers, and dorsoventrally flattened bills in 'flycatching' species; true to trend, this kingfisher has a flat bill. It also forages on the ground, probing into forest litter and upturning soil in search of insects. When perched, it slowly raises and lowers the tail, and from time to time about-faces on its perch. It calls frequently, and can make itself conspicuous in hawking from an overhead branch for flying insects, but otherwise it is unobtrusive, and in a lengthy study Robertson did not notice any wing-spreading or other visual territorial display. **Nesting:** pairs excavate nesting holes in arboreal termitaria, or use tree holes; Robertson found 24 nests in termitaria and 13 in holes in palms and tree-ferns. **Laying months:** Espiritu Santo, December.

Description *Adult male:* forehead and crown blue-washed dull black, the former with a large, round white or buff supraloral spot at the side, and the latter bordered by deep purple-blue in a band from above the eye back towards the nape. Lores, ear-coverts and upper cheeks black, this extending backwards to form a black band around the nape; above the nape a few midline feathers have white bases, which show through. Chin, throat, sides of neck and hindneck white, forming a broad collar. Mantle purple-blue (blackish next to the white collar); wings, back, rump and tail purple-blue, the flight feathers blacker. Breast yellow-orange, darkening through orange-rufous to rich chestnut on belly and undertail-coverts. Underwing-coverts orange-rufous. Upper mandible greyish-black, lower mandible pale horn; eye dark brown, orbital skin black; legs and feet greyish-black. *Adult female:* like the male, except that the belly is white; breast and undertail-coverts orange, as on the male. *Juvenile:* like the adult, but blues less intense, and supraloral spot, superciliary stripe and hindneck-collar strongly suffused with rufous. *Measurements:* wing of male 85-95, of female 84-96; tail of male 54-62, of female 54-67; bill of male 35-43, of female 36-40; tarsus of male 14-16, of female 14-16. Weight: male 32-42, female 35-42.

References Forshaw (1985), Fry (1980a).

44 LESSER YELLOW-BILLED KINGFISHER   Plate 15
Halcyon tororo

Syma tororo Lesson, 1827, Bull. Sci. Nat. Géol., 2, II, p. 443, Dorey (= Manokwari), New Guinea.

Field identification Length 20 cm (8 in). This kingfisher is very like the following one, also of New Guinea, but the two are readily distinguished from all other kingfishers. *At rest:* the bright yellow bill, yellow legs, and rich rufous head and breast with large black patch on the nape make the two yellow-billed kingfishers unmistakable. Females have a dark crown-patch. On both sexes the long, dense crown feathers are often raised, making the bird's head look as large as its body. The all-yellow bill is conspicuous even in poor forest light. *In flight:* back green, tail blue; wings blackish-green, unmarked except for yellow-buff lining. *Confusion species:* the Mountain Yellow-billed Kingfisher (45) is larger, but is safely distinguishable only when its dark culmen line can be seen. On Huon Peninsula, however, even that character is lacking, and the two species are inseparable in the field. Their voices are very similar.

Voice The song is a loud clear trill like a blast on a referee's whistle; either lasting 1-2 seconds, descending slightly and ending abruptly, or lasting 5-6 seconds, falling slightly in pitch, then gradually rising and falling again before tailing off. The second song type has variations: it may keep at one pitch then fall to a slightly lower pitch; or the whole trill may fall slowly and evenly (Coates 1985). Two birds may counter-sing, using different songs. Often an individual, before it starts to sing, utters a single short sharp note, repeated regularly for half a minute or more at intervals of rather less than 1 second; these notes may or may not accelerate into the song (Coates 1985). An uncommon call is a laugh recalling that of a kookaburra (17-20) or paradise kingfisher (7-12).

Geographical variation There are three subspecies, varying in overall hue and in the extent of the female's crown-patch.

H. t. torotoro Lowland New Guinea, usually up to 500 m in altitude but locally up to 1100 m (e.g. in Karimui basin, Chimbu Province); also Aru Islands, Western Papuan Islands, and Japen (Yapen) Island. Slightly paler and smaller birds in southeast New Guinea have been separated by some authors as *H. t. meeki*; females also have smaller crown-patches.

H. t. ochracea D'Entrecasteaux Archipelago, off southeast New Guinea. 8% larger than *torotoro*; uniformly dark yellow-rufous below; female with large black patch on crown.

H. t. flavirostris Cape York Peninsula, Queensland. Upperparts considerably paler than in *torotoro*.

Habitat and range It inhabits primary and secondary rainforest, clearings, edges, mature teak and rubber plantations, gallery forest, and locally mangrove forest. This is a common bird throughout lowland New Guinea, from Western Papuan and Aru Islands to D'Entrecasteaux Islands, and in Cape York Peninsula. It is much commoner below than above 500 m, and in forest near Port Moresby there were estimated to be ten individuals per 10 ha (Bell 1982). The species is not migratory.

Food Grasshoppers, mantids, cicadas, dragonflies, larvae, earthworms, small lizards and eggs.

Habits Lesser Yellow-billed Kingfishers forage by perching in the lower canopy, peering intently at the ground, and pouncing down on to prey. When searching, they sway from side to side, perhaps the better to judge distance. On diving down, they hit the ground with an audible thump (Coates 1985). Some food is caught among foliage or in the air, and rarely prey such as a tadpole is taken at the edge of water. Sometimes they spend a few moments digging in soaked leaf litter and topsoil. They commonly divebomb into water, but that is to bathe, not to feed. These kingfishers occur solitarily or in pairs and are not particularly shy. A bird is said to look away, so that its two black neck-patches look like eyes (Bell 1981), but that has been disclaimed by Coates (1985). Like other halcyons, this one flicks its tail up, and may hold it cocked when about to fly. It is a vocal bird, singing from a high perch at any time of day. *Nesting:* nest holes are excavated by the birds into the side of an active termite nest, 3 m or more up in a tree or palm, or sometimes low down. One cavity was 12 cm deep, 9 cm wide and 9.5 cm high, with the entrance 4 cm wide and 4 cm long. The clutch is of 3-4 eggs. *Laying months:* Queensland, November-January; Papua New Guinea, September-October (probably August-March).

Description *H. t. torotoro* **Adult male:** head and hindneck bright rufous; lores black, joining with a narrow black band just above and below the eye; a large black patch at each side of the hindneck. Mantle black, scapulars and tertials dark green; lower back, rump and uppertail-coverts greenish-blue; tail dark purple-blue. Wing feathers black, mostly with green-blue or bluish edges and tips. Chin and throat white, breast rufous-orange paling to yellowish ·or creamy-buff on flanks, belly, undertail-coverts and underwing-coverts. Underside of tail dull black. Bill bright yellow, the cutting edges serrated towards the tip of the upper mandible; eye deep brown; legs and feet yellow, nails dark brown. *Adult female:* like the male, but with the crown black except at the sides, and with the two black neck-patches joined by a line across the hindneck; flanks, belly and undertail-coverts usually paler than on the male. *Juvenile:* like the female, but black crown feathers narrowly edged with rufous, a wider black area around the eye, and feathers of cheeks and breast dusky-tipped. Bill grey-black. *Measurements:* wing of male 70-86, of female 70-83; tail of male 48-65, of female 53-62; bill of male 36-44, of female 34-44; tarsus of male 14-15, of female 14-15. Weight: male 32-50, female 30-52.

Reference Forshaw (1985).

45 MOUNTAIN YELLOW-BILLED KINGFISHER   Plate 15
Halcyon megarhyncha

Syma megarhyncha Salvadori, 1896, Ann. Mus. Civ. Stor. Nat. Giacomo Doria, 36, p. 70, Moroka, New Guinea.

Field identification Length 24 cm (9½ in). Mountain Yellow-billed Kingfishers are very like Lesser Yellowbills (44), but are larger and heavier, have a larger black mark around the front of the eye, and females have a larger area of black in the crown. Except for subspecies *sellamontis* on Huon Peninsula (Papua New Guinea), Mountain Yellowbills differ also in having a dark line along the culmen. Lesser Yellowbills occur from sea level up to 500 m, locally up to 1140 m, Mountain Yellowbills from 760 to 2200 m (Coates 1985).

Voice Song and calls are indistinguishable from those of Lesser Yellowbills (which see). The song resembles those of Chestnut-breasted Cuckoo *Cacomantis castaneiventris* and Fan-tailed Cuckoo C. *pyrrhophanus*, but is louder (Coates 1985).

Geographical variation There are three subspecies.
H. m. megarhyncha Mountains of New Guinea, excluding the ranges of the following two subspecies, from Sudirman Range (Irian Jaya) to Owen Stanley Range (Papua New Guinea).
H. m. sellamontis Mountains of Huon Peninsula, northern Papua New Guinea.

Bill, including culmen, yellow. Slightly smaller than *megarhyncha*.
H. m. wellsi Snow and Weyland Mountains, west Irian Jaya. Back and tertials darker than in *megarhyncha*, chin and throat buffy, and other underparts darker. Slightly larger than *megarhyncha*, but bill shorter.

Habitat and range It occurs deep in dense forest, mainly between 1200 and 2200 m in altitude, where in some carefully worked areas it is known to be common (Diamond 1972); it has also occurred down to 760 m.

Food Insects, larvae, and small lizards.

Habits A shy and retiring kingfisher which lives solitarily or in pairs deep in primary forest, keeping mainly to the mid- and upper storeys. Even when singing, it is exasperatingly difficult to locate (Forshaw 1985). *Nesting:* only one nest has been found, a hole with two eggs in an earth bank on Mt Simpson, Papua New Guinea, in December (Harrison and Frith 1970). It is said also to use tree holes (Majnep and Bulmer 1977).

Description *H. t. megarhyncha* **Adult male:** head and hindneck bright rufous;

lores black, joining with a black band just above and below the eye; a large black patch at each side of the hindneck. Mantle black, scapulars and tertials dark green; lower back, rump and uppertail-coverts greenish-blue; tail dark purple-blue. Wing feathers black, mostly with green-blue or bluish edges and tips. Chin and throat white or buff, breast deep rufous-orange paling to yellowish or creamy-buff on flanks, belly, undertail-coverts and underwing-coverts. Underside of tail dull black. Bill bright yellow, with the culmen and tip of the upper mandible dark grey-brown, cutting edges serrated; eye very dark brown; legs and feet yellow, nails dark brown. *Adult female:* like the male, but with the crown black, and with the two black neck-patches joined by a line across the hindneck. Flanks, belly and undertail-coverts usually paler than on the male. *Juvenile:* like the female, but black crown feathers narrowly edged with rufous; a whitish hindneck-patch with black-tipped feathers, a wider black area around the eye, and feathers of cheeks and breast dusky-tipped. Bill grey-black. *Measurements:* wing of male 83-91, of female 83-91; tail of male 55-72, of female 60-68; bill of male 43-53, of female 42-49; tarsus of male 15-18, of female 15-18. Weight: male 52-60, female 49-63.

References Coates (1985), Forshaw (1985).

46 SOMBRE KINGFISHER (Olive-backed Kingfisher)   Plate 15
Halcyon funebris

Todiramphus funebris Bonaparte, 1850, Consp. Genera Avium, 1, p. 157, Celebes (error for Moluccas).

Field identification Length 30 cm (12 in). Only two other halcyons occur in its range: the Mangrove (47) and Beach Kingfishers (49). From the former the Sombre Kingfisher is readily distinguished by its long white superciliary stripe. Beach Kingfishers are quite different, being white-headed. *At rest:* the Sombre is a black-and-white-looking bird, with dark olive-green or blackish (male) or dark brown (female) upperparts interrupted by a broad white hindneck-collar, white supraloral spot and long white supercilium, and with white underparts. The bill is bicoloured, as on Beach and Mangrove Kingfishers. *In flight:* the rump is much less conspicuously blue than on the others.

Voice A distinctive, slow 'ki...ki...ki...ki', readily separated from the calls of Mangrove and Beach Kingfishers.

Geographical variation None.

Habitat and range Endemic to Halmahera and Ternate Islands, northern Moluccas, between Sulawesi and New Guinea (Indonesia). It inhabits open, cultivated low-lands, gardens and coconut plantations near forest, and is evidently quite common, at least on Halmahera. Doubtless sedentary.

Food Large arthropods, including grass-hoppers and centipedes.

Habits Very little is on record. Sombre Kingfishers occur singly or in pairs and are thoroughly arboreal, keeping to the middle levels of trees, and plunging to the ground for prey. Nothing is known about their breeding behaviour, and no nests have been found.

Description *Adult male:* forehead and crown black with a greenish wash. Lores, malar area, cheeks and ear-coverts black, extending as a black band around the hindneck. A large white supraloral spot and, starting above the eye, a broad white superciliary stripe, suffused with blue where it meets the black crown, narrowing as it extends backwards across the nape. Lower hindneck white; mantle greenish-black; back, scapulars, tertials and upperwing-coverts dark olive-green, the coverts edged with green-blue. Rump

174

and uppertail-coverts green-blue and tail bluish olive-green. Underparts from chin to undertail-coverts white, rather dingy-looking, except for a black patch at the side of the breast. Primaries and secondaries dark brown with blue-green outer webs. Underwing white, the outer greater underwing-coverts broadly edged with black. Upper mandible black, lower mandible yellowish-horn with blackish cutting edges and distal half; iris very dark brown; legs and feet blackish. *Adult female:* much duller and browner than the male; crown dull black, mantle and tail dark brown, most feathers edged with olive; wings and rump brownish olive-green. *Juvenile:* even browner than the adult female, lacking any olivaceous tinge. Feathers of the white hindneck-collar and breast have dark brownish margins. Bill tipped whitish. *Measurements:* wing of male 110-125, of female 110-124; tail of male 80-90, of female 78-93; bill of male 52-60, of female 51-60; tarsus of male 17-20, of female 17-20.

Reference Forshaw (1985).

47 MANGROVE KINGFISHER (Collared Kingfisher, White-collared Kingfisher) Plates 16 and 17
Halcyon chloris

Alcedo Chloris Boddaert, 1783, Table Planch. enlum., p. 49, Cape of Good Hope, *ex* Daubenton, Planch. enlum., 1783, pl. 783.

Field identification Length 23-25 cm (9-10 in). Very variable throughout its immense geographical range: a distance of 16,000 km from the Red Sea to the eastern Samoan islands. There are 50 subspecies, making the Mangrove Kingfisher one of the most polymorphic of all bird species. Some races are confined to mangrove, others occupy a variety of coastal, man-made and natural inland habitats. In general the bird has blue, blue-green or olive-green upperparts and white supraloral spot or long superciliary stripe, complete white collar, and white underparts, but in many forms the 'white' parts are buff or pale orange. Some subspecies are white-crowned. Others have incipient sexual dimorphism. A constant feature, and a usefully confirmatory one (although not diagnostic) is the bill: large, with black upper mandible and mainly yellowish-horn lower mandible. *Confusion species:* rather than giving a lengthy discussion here, we refer the reader to the plates and maps. Mangrove Kingfishers are mentioned as confusion species in many species accounts, and the characteristics of the apposite races are given. Suffice here to list those kingfishers the most in need of careful discrimination: Sacred (50), Sombre (46), Micronesian (48), Timor (51), Beach (49), Lesser Yellow-billed (44), Red-backed (52), Winchell's (37), Forest (40), and New Britain (41).

Voice Some regional variation. The main call is a harsh or ringing, metallic 'ki', 'kee', 'kip', 'krerk' or 'aank' repeated 3-5 times, usually when the bird takes flight. In Palau the flight call is a repeated 'tchup-weee', and in the Marianas 'caw-heee' and a loud barking 'kip-kip-kip'. In Samoa the last call is higher-pitched and a drawn-out 'kreeeep' is uttered. In Borneo and Vanuatu 6-7 different calls have been recognised (Smythies 1981; G. Robertson in Forshaw 1985), including a piping 'pirpph', repeated up to 27 times (territorial song, given from high perch), a harsh 'cack-cack-cack' descending the scale and decelerating (alarm), 'chirrup-chirrup' (individual alighting next to another), and various other quiet or squeaking notes.

Geographical variation The process of subspeciation of Mangrove Kingfishers will repay much further study, not only of museum characters but also of laboratory ones such as genetic relationships and biological ones such as voice and pair-formation – several lifetimes of research. It would probably lead to revised taxonomy. In the meantime we follow Forshaw (1985) in recognising and delineating 50 races which differ slightly in size and greatly in colour.

H. c. chloris Sulawesi, Sangihe Islands (between Sulawesi and Mindanao), Peleng and Sula Islands (east of Sulawesi), all Lesser Sunda Islands west to Lombok, Moluccas (Morotai, Halmahera, Batjan, Obi, Buru, Ceram, Kai, Tanimbar and smaller islands), Western Papuan Islands (Waigeu, Misoöl, Batanta, Salawati) and coasts of the Vogelkop and Onin Peninsulas in Irian Jaya. See Plate 16 and Description below.

H. c. enigma Talaud Islands, southeast of Mindanao. Like *chloris* but 15% smaller. *H. c. chloris* also occurs in these islands, perhaps as a non-breeding migrant. If *chloris* and *enigma* both breed there, then presumably *enigma* should be given specific status.

H. c. palmeri Java, Bali, Bawean, and Kangean Islands. Like *chloris* but brighter blue; ear-coverts and nape-band blue rather than black.

H. c. laubmanniana Sumatra, Borneo, Bangka and Belitung Islands, and all or nearly all lesser islands and archipelagos between Sumatra, Singapore, peninsular Malaysia and Borneo. Like *chloris*, but back blue rather than green; ear-coverts and nape-band blue rather than black.

H. c. chloroptera Islands southwest of Sumatra (except Enggano), and adjacent mainland coasts. Like *laubmanniana* but 5% larger.

H. c. azela Enggano Island. Duller, greener and 10% smaller than *chloroptera*.

H. c. humii Coasts of northeast Sumatra, Singapore, peninsular Malaysia and Thailand, Burma, Bangladesh and West Bengal; Tioman and Mergui Archipelagos. Like *chloris* but bluer, and white supraloral spot extends backwards to above eye, forming a short superciliary stripe. Crown, band below eye, back, wings and tail bright blue, washed with green on mantle and below eye. Flanks and sides of breast and of neck washed with buff. Smaller than *chloris*.

H. c. armstrongi Interior of Thailand and Burma; Indochina. Greener than *humii*, but otherwise like it.

H. c. davisoni Cocos Islands and Andaman Islands. Like *humii* but 10% smaller, cheeks and ear-coverts blackish-green, mantle dusky olive where it borders the white collar, and underparts buffy.

H. c. vidali From Ratnagiri (west coast of India, 120 km south of Bombay) south to Kerala; confined to coastal districts. Like *humii* but mantle greener, wings

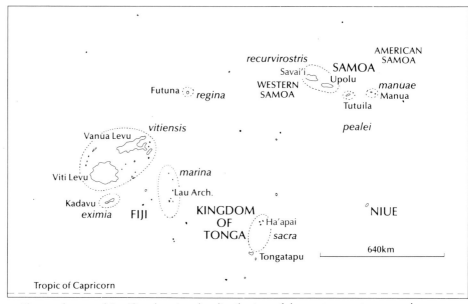

The south-central Pacific, showing the distribution of the easternmost seven subspecies of Mangrove Kingfisher Halcyon chloris (vitiensis, marina, eximia, sacra, regina, pealei *and* manuae) *and of the easternmost subspecies of Sacred Kingfisher* H. sancta recurvirostris.

brighter blue, area under eye with cheeks and ear-coverts blue-green, and very broad white hindcollar. Same size as *chloris*.

H. c. occipitalis Nicobar Islands. A distinctive subspecies, with long, broad, buff superciliary stripes meeting on the nape; otherwise like *vidali* but darker, crown green, underparts buffy, with belly deep buff. 5% smaller than *vidali*.

H. c. kalbaensis Khawr Kalba, a mangrove lagoon between Fujayrah (United Arab Emirates) and Shnass (Oman), with around 50 birds in 1968. Occasionally wanders to Shnass, Liwa and Sohar (Oman). Forehead, crown, mantle, back, scapulars and tertials sea-green; rump bluer; wings and tail blue; broad white collar, white underparts, long superciliary stripe from above lores nearly to nape, slightly speckled behind the eye; blackish-green band from base of bill to cheeks, ear-coverts and lower nape. About the size of *humii*.

H. c. abyssinica Patches of mangrove on west coast of Red Sea: Dahlac Archipelago, Massawa (Lunga Islands), Sulla and Assab Bay (Ammennamus Island) (all off Eritrea, Ethiopia). An old record from Suakin, Sudan; and in Somalia an old and a recent record from Saad-ed-Din Island, Zeila. Like *kalbaensis* but rump bright blue, white superciliary stripe shorter, only from lore to above eye, and bill about 10% longer, averaging 50 mm.

H. c. collaris Philippines, Palawan and Sulu Archipelago. Like *chloris* but greener; black collar across lower nape narrower.

H. c. teraokai Palau Islands (east of Philippines and northwest of New Guinea). Like *collaris* but slightly greener.

H. c. orii Rota Island, in the south of the Marianas Islands, northeast of Palau. Supraloral spot larger than in *teraokai*, buffy, and extends backward to above eye as a short superciliary stripe. Nape streaked with white; back washed with olive-green, particularly on females, and not clear blue-green as in *chloris*.

H. c. albicilla Saipan and Tinian Islands, in southern Marianas. Crown and nape white, lores black, ear-coverts black with green wash, cheeks white, white hindneck-collar very broad. Otherwise like *chloris*, with green-blue wings but oily or olivaceous-green mantle. Large:

wing 111-121 mm, bill 51-60 mm. On young birds the crown and nape are buffy, with green streaks.

H. c. owstoni Northern Marianas: Asuncion, Pagan, Agrihan and Almagan Islands. Like *albicilla*, but nape and hind-crown blue-green; slightly smaller.

H. c. sordida North Australian and south New Guinean coasts. In Australia, Derby, Admiralty Gulf, more commonly from Anson Bay and Melville Island to Groote Eylandt and the Sir Edmund Pellew Group, Wellesley Island, and almost continuously around Cape York Peninsula, along the Queensland Pacific coast, and into New South Wales at Cape Byron; in New Guinea, from Mimika River (Irian Jaya) to China Straits (Papua New Guinea); also Aru Islands (Indonesia) and Torres Strait islands. Like *chloris*, but dull dark oily olive-green where *chloris* is bright green-blue. Wings and tail dull blue-green, where *chloris* is purple-blue. Lores, cheeks and ear-coverts black; white supraloral spot, sometimes extending towards eye; inconspicuous white spot on nape, like *chloris*. Wing shorter than in *chloris*, 100-117 mm, but bill longer, 49-62 mm.

H. c. pilbara Western Australia, from DeGrey River mouth to Exmouth Gulf, with records from Shark Bay. Upperparts duller, browner and paler than in *sordida*; white hindneck-collar narrower; bill narrower.

H. c. colona Southeastern Papua New Guinea: Louisiade Archipelago. Duskier than *sordida*; wing 5% shorter, bill longer than in *sordida*.

H. c. stresemanni Witu (Vitu) Islands, Umboi, Sakar, Long, Tolokiwa and some smaller islands, between New Britain and mainland Papua New Guinea. Like *sordida* but rump, wings and tail bluer, belly pale cinnamon, and crown variably flecked with white; crown varies from all dark olive-green to nearly all white. Wing longer and bill shorter than in *sordida*.

H. c. tristami New Britain (Papua New Guinea). Chin and middle of belly white, but all other 'white' parts are pale cinnamon-buff. Buff supraloral spot sometimes forms a short, buff, superciliary stripe. Forehead and upper mantle blackish-green; band at sides of crown, from behind eye to nape, blue; lores, cheeks, ear-coverts, and narrow band across lower nape black. Remaining upperparts as in *chloris*, except that the rump is bright blue. Wing longer and bill shorter than in *sordida*.

H. c. novaehiberniae Southwest New Ireland (Papua New Guinea). Head like *tristami* (but supraloral spot and collar white), body like *sordida*.

H. c. nusae New Ireland (except southwest), New Hanover, islands between the two, and Feni Islands (between New Ireland and Green Island), all in Papua New Guinea. Head like *tristami*, but supraloral spot white and crown blackish; collar and sides of breast often buffy; rest of body like *sordida*.

H. c. matthiae St Matthias Islands, northeast Papua New Guinea. Like *nusae*, but top of head, from forehead to black band across lower nape, varies from all dark green, through an equal mixture of green and white, to white with a few scattered dark green spots. On white-crowned birds, black band around nape is generally narrow and broken. Hindneck-collar and sides of breast white, never buffy as in *nusae*. White of crown is buffy on young birds.

H. c. bennetti Nissan Island, east of New Ireland (Papua New Guinea). Like *nusae*, but crown and mantle not so blackish, and flanks tinged with buff.

H. c. alberti Bougainville and Buka Islands (Papua New Guinea) and Solomon Islands east to Guadalcanal and the Florida group, but absent from intervening Russell Islands. Sexually dimorphic. Female like *tristami*, but crown dull green, blue band behind eye dull, and breast and collar paler than in *tristami*; mid-breast and belly whitish. Male has crown brighter green, with bright blue band from eye to nape, the breast whitish and collar pale cinnamon-buff, and flanks, belly and undertail-coverts yellow-rufous. Back, wings and tail green-blue. On both sexes rump brighter blue than that of *tristami*.

The following ten subspecies, *pavuvu* to *melanodera* inclusive, are from the Solomon Islands, *pavuvu* in the central and the remainder in the southeastern Solomons.

H. c. pavuvu Pavuvu Island in the Russell group. Like *alberti* but buff supraloral spots much larger.

H. c. mala Malaita Island. Compared with *alberti*, upperparts brighter and bluer, underparts paler, less richly buff.

H. c. solomonis San Cristóbal Island

and adjacent islands except for the Olu Malaus. Crown green-blue, bordered by broad rufous superciliary stripe running from supraloral spot usually to nape; lores black, cheeks, ear-coverts and narrow band across lower nape green-blue. Chin and throat white, collar and breast faintly buffy; belly, flanks and undertail-coverts cinnamon-buff. Underwing-coverts pale cinnamon. Back, wings and tail like *alberti*.

H. c. sororum Malaupaina and Malaulaulo Islands in the Olu Malau group. Like *solomonis*, but superciliary stripes always meet on nape; male has paler buff underparts than *solomonis*.

H. c. amoena Rennell and Bellona Islands. Like *solomonis*, but superciliary stripe narrower, rufous on males, buffy-white on females; throat, collar and sides of breast pale buff; chin, belly, flanks and undertail-coverts white. Upperparts darker and bluer than in *solomonis*. Small: wing 84-92 mm, bill 41-47mm.

H. c. brachyura Fenualoa and Lomlom in the Reef Islands. Like *solomonis*, but superciliary stripe paler rufous on males and almost white on females; chin, throat, collar, breast and middle of belly white, flanks and underwing-coverts cinnamon. Back, wings and tail darker and bluer than in *solomonis*.

H. c. vicina Duff Islands. Like *solomonis*, but underwing-coverts paler, and underparts of female entirely white.

H. c. ornata Santa Cruz and Tinakula Islands. Like *solomonis*, but collar and flanks bright rufous; breast, belly and undertail-coverts cinnamon-buff. Back and wings green-blue, rump bright blue, tail deep blue.

H. c. utupuae Utupua Island in the Santa Cruz group. Like *solomonis*, but rufous supraloral patches so large as sometimes to meet across the forehead, and rufous superciliary stripe very broad. Collar and underparts white, sometimes tinged buffy. Back, wings and tail greener than in *solomonis*.

H. c. melanodera Vanikoro Island in the Santa Cruz group. A distinctive subspecies, somewhat like *solomonis*, but with a small supraloral patch and practically no superciliary stripe; forehead blackish; breast and underwing buffy-white, the feathers narrowly black-tipped.

The following five subspecies, *torresiana* to *erromangae* inclusive, are from

Vanuatu (formerly New Hebrides).

H. c. torresiana Hiu, Lo and Toga Islands in the Torres group. Small, buffy supraloral spot, becoming a poorly defined superciliary stripe, often not extending as far as the nape. Ear-coverts and band across lower nape green-blue, collar and underparts white.

H. c. santoensis Banks Islands to Espiritu Santo and Malo. Like *solomonis*, but superciliary stripe always extends to nape; upperparts greener and duller, with olive wash on females; collar and underparts white.

H. c. juliae Maewo and Aoba to Efate Island. Forehead blue-green, crown bright blue; long, rufous superciliary stripe, from nostrils to nape; cheeks, ear-coverts and band across lower nape dark blue. Collar and underparts buffy.

H. c. tannensis Tanna Island. Differs from *juliae* in having broader rufous superciliary stripe, and collar and underparts cinnamon.

H. c. erromangae Erromanga Island. Cinnamon-rufous parts paler than in *tannensis*.

The following and last seven subspecies have some of the characters of Sacred Kingfishers (50) (*vitiensis, eximia, regina*) and of Pacific Kingfishers (53) (*marina, sacra, pealei, manuae*) (Pratt *et al*. 1987).

H. c. vitiensis Fiji Islands: Viti Levu, Koro, Ovalau, Ngau, Vanua Levu and Taveuni. Crown bright green-blue; supraloral spot rufous; superciliary stripe white, becoming buffy at nape; collar and underparts white, tinged buffy on females and more extensively so on males; back, wings and tail deep blue, rump brilliant blue.

H. c. marina Fiji Islands: Lau Archipelago. Greener above and whiter below than *vitiensis*; supraloral spot larger and superciliary stripe broader.

H. c. eximia Fiji Islands: Kadavu Group. Like *vitiensis* but supraloral spot buff-white.

H. c. sacra Central and southern Tonga Islands. Like *vitiensis*, but supraloral spot larger and buff-white, and crown and entire upperparts deep blue. Larger than *vitiensis*.

H. c. regina Futuna Island, midway between Fiji and Samoa. Crown and mantle green, wings and tail green-blue; large cinnamon supraloral spot and broad cinnamon superciliary stripe, becoming deep

rufous across nape; collar and underparts pale buff, grading into cinnamon on flanks and underwing-coverts.

H. c. pealei Tutuila Island, Samoa. Crown blue; forehead white on females, buffy-white on males, continuing as a very broad white superciliary stripe to upper nape; ear-coverts and band across lower nape greenish-blue; collar and underparts white; mantle green-blue, rump brilliant blue, wings and tail deep blue.

H. c. manuae Tau, Olosega and Ofu Islands, in the Manua group, Samoa. Like *vitiensis*, but supraloral spot larger, and superciliary stripe wider, becoming tawny or cinnamon at nape. Underwing-coverts buffy.

Habitat and range In Ethiopia, Oman and India the Mangrove Kingfisher is confined to mangrove, keeping to edges bordering tidal creeks and foraging mainly for crabs at low water. In southeast Asia, from Burma and Vietnam to Singapore, it inhabits mangrove, creeks, beachfront vegetation and adjacent coconut groves and gardens, and also coastal roadsides, where it freely uses telegraph wires. It is common in suburban gardens of Singapore, and occurs at least 26 km inland in Malaysia. In Borneo and throughout the Philippines, Indonesia and southern New Guinea it occupies similar habitats – mangrove, and plantations and woods backing onto beaches; but is even more prone to use cultivated land – ricefields, open coconut and palm fields, gardens, marshes and dry grassland with scattered trees, and other types of cleared, open country with regrowth in farms and gardens, usually within 5 km of the coast. On smaller islands in this region and throughout the Pacific, the habitat is influenced by the presence of other halcyons: if there are competitors Mangrove Kingfishers remain coastal, but if none they range inland, for instance into savannas and forested hills of Babelthaup Island (Palau group). On Rota Island in the Marianas group they live in closed forest, sometimes feeding along the adjacent shoreline, using rocks and coral platforms. They ascend in open country to about 1500 m in Sumatra and Java, and on larger islands throughout Indonesia and the Solomons the species inhabits a wide variety of land, from mangrove, coconut groves and coastal suburbs to cultivated uplands, second-growth vegetation and rainforest.

Population In the main part of their range, Mangrove Kingfishers are common or abundant along coasts and in coastal lowlands. Although seldom straying further than a few kilometres from tidal creeks and the shoreline, they often seem to be one of the commonest of all birds there because they perch conspicuously on telegraph wires, powerlines, palm fronds and trees around buildings – as in Sulawesi, for instance. An estimate on Malo Island, off Espiritu Santo (Solomons), gave 200-225 pairs, with pair-territories 250 m apart in the areas of highest density (coasts with mixed palms, trees and open spaces); they were scarce in deep forest above 200 m altitude in the middle of Malo, where Chestnut-bellied Kingfishers (43) were commonest (G. Robertson, pers. comm.). They are uncommon throughout much of their Australian range, and even where quite common, in northern mangrove, they are much less plentiful than Sacred Kingfishers. Pair-territory sizes were 7-10 ha near Brisbane, Australia, in 1934 and 1.5 ha in mangrove at the mouth of Brisbane River in 1957.

Migration Mainly resident and sedentary, but post-breeding dispersal is noticeable in some places, and there is plenty of evidence of longer movement by some individuals. A few night-migrating Mangrove Kingfishers have been netted on Fraser's Hill, Malaysia; and three recoveries of ringed birds in the Philippines were 152, 256, and 304 km away. Seasonal occurrences in Malaysia, Borneo and New Guinea suggest regular migration by a small proportion of the population for a few hundreds of kilometres. Some appear to migrate in Australia, arriving in Cape York in mid September and in southern Queensland in late September; but there is no real evidence of migration in the Torres Strait, and the bird is present year-round as far south as Brisbane.

Food Mangrove and coastal populations take mainly small crabs (carapace width 1-2 cm), also shrimps, mudskippers and other small fish. Inland, the species takes invertebrates and small vertebrates: cicadas, beetles, carpenter bees, wasps, grasshoppers, earthworms, snails, land crabs, spiders, frogs and snakes, and less commonly mice and small birds' eggs and nestlings. Lizards and snakes are up to 11 cm long. A total of 54 prey items in Vanuatu comprised equal numbers of skinks, locusts and beach-pool fish, eight butterflies and other insects and a crab (G. Robertson).

Habits Mangrove Kingfishers occur singly or in pairs, and adults are strongly territorial. Territories are defended year-round from invaders, and the owners are generally noisy, bold and conspicuous, male and female keeping in contact by calling at all hours from dawn to dusk. Sometimes, however, these birds are shy and silent and easily overlooked. Territories are 200-400 m across, and one pair regularly used 13 perches in its territory. The birds perch mainly 1-3 m up and can be rather inactive, sitting for long periods with little movement other than a jerky cocking of the tail from time to time. Perching posture on thin branches is fairly upright but on rocks is more horizontal. Flight is swift and direct, low over water and mangrove, the beats mainly regular but suddenly speeding for two or three beats every 20 beats or so. Adults and chicks regurgitate pellets of indigestible food remains. *Nesting:* little is known about this species' breeding behaviour. Birds pursue each other in territorial courtship flights low over trees, and males are known to courtship-feed the females. Copulation is generally immediately preceded by such a feeding. Nest holes are excavated by both birds, in arboreal termitaria, rotten trunks and stumps, or earthen banks. Unaltered natural tree holes appear to be used quite often, and old woodpecker holes can be taken over. In trees, nest holes are 2-30 m above the ground. Of 68 nest holes that G. Robertson found in Vanuatu, 38 were in termitaria in trees and coconut palms, 18 in rotten trunks of tree-ferns and 12 in sound trunks of other trees and palms. There are usually two or more nestings each season. In Borneo a pair started to bore eight holes in tree trunks, finishing two or three of them, and reared two broods in quick succession from different holes (T.H. Harrisson in Smythies 1981). The clutch is of 2-5 eggs. Average egg dimensions in various localities are 27.8 × 24.4 mm, 29.2 × 22.7 mm and 31.1 × 25.3 mm. The period from egg-laying to the chick leaving the nest is about 44 days. *Laying months:* Ethiopia, April-July; United Arab Emirates/Oman, June; northeast India and Bangladesh, March-August (mainly April-May); Andaman Islands, March-May; Nicobar Islands, February-March; Burma, April; Thailand, March-July; peninsular Malaysia, December-August; Philippines and Borneo, about May-June; Mariana Islands, July-August; Sumatra and Java, March-November; Papua New Guinea, October-March; Solomon Islands, August-November; Vanuatu, about October; Fiji, December; Australia, September or October to about February (mainly October).

Description *H. c. chloris* Sexes alike. *Adult:* crown and forehead blue or greenish-blue, rather brighter towards sides of crown and greener towards nape; lores, cheeks, ear-coverts and a broad band running back to upper hindneck are black, washed with blue near the eye, and forming a conspicuous blackish mask. There is a small white supraloral spot between nostril and eye, and a partly concealed white patch behind the crown and just above the black hindneck-band. A broad white collar around neck, joining the white of chin, throat, breast, flanks and undertail-coverts. Mantle, back, scapulars and tertials blue-green; back and rump bright azure-blue; tail purplish-blue; upperwing-coverts blue; primaries and secondaries dark grey with purplish-blue outer webs. Underwing-coverts white. Upper mandible greyish-black, waxy and shiny, lower mandible yellowish-horn with dark brown cutting edges and tip; iris very dark brown, orbital skin black; legs and feet dark grey, soles yellowish. *Juvenile:* like the adult, but upperparts greener-tinged and duller, and white parts washed with buff except in the midline from chin and throat to belly. Upperwing-coverts narrowly fringed with buff; breast feathers narrowly fringed with dark grey. *Measurements:* wing of male 104-121, of female 105-118; tail of male 61-74, of female 62-73; bill of male 45-56, of female 46-53; tarsus of male 16-18, of female 16-18. Weight: male 51-90, female 54-72.

References Blakers *et al.* (1984), Forshaw (1985), Fry (1980a), McClure (1974), Medway and Wells (1976), Smythies (1981).

48 MICRONESIAN KINGFISHER   Plate 17
Halcyon cinnamomina

Halcyon cinnamomina Swainson, 1821, Zool. Illustr., 2, text to pl. 27, no locality, = Marianas Islands.

Field identification Length 20 cm (8 in). This kingfisher is restricted to three islands or island groups in the southwest Pacific, on only one of which does another kingfisher species occur. A subspecies on a fourth group of islands was exterminated 70 years ago. The Micronesian Kingfisher is a small, woodland species with rufous crown, blackish-green mask extending around the nape, dark blue-green upperparts, purplish-blue wings, and cinnamon-rufous wing-linings, with the rest of the body (hindneck, sides of neck, chin to undertail-coverts) rufous in one subspecies and white in two others. The upper mandible is dark brown and the lower mainly horn-coloured; eye dark brown, legs blackish. On females and young birds the rufous parts are pale and the belly whitish. *Confusion species:* in the Palau group of islands in Micronesia, east of the Philippines and northwest of New Guinea, the population of Micronesian Kingfishers found on most of the better-wooded islands (*H. cinnamomina pelewensis*) has white neck and underparts (the juvenile with pale rufous throat and breast). It inhabits woods and forests in the interior. Also occurring on most islands is the coastal Mangrove Kingfisher (47) *H. chloris teraokai*, which has a blue or green-blue crown and a small white spot at the side of the forehead; otherwise the two species are very alike.

Voice On the Palau Islands the call is a raucous, rolling 'creee', like the call of Mangrove Kingfishers there, and uttered at night as well as by day.

Geographical variation The two southerly subspecies have white neck and underparts, and the two northerly ones have those parts rufous. The extinct *miyakoensis* differed further in having red legs and possibly also a red bill: it is known only from a single specimen, lacking its billsheath, collected in 1887; if the bill was red, then *miyakoensis* would be better treated as a full species, as originally described (*Halcyon miyakoensis*).

H. c. pelewensis Palau Islands. Rufous crown, black mask, white neck, bluegreen mantle and rump, purple-blue wings and tail, white underparts, black and pale horn bill, brown eye, blackish legs.

H. c. reichenbachii Ponapé Island (in Caroline Islands, far to the east of Palau Islands). Like *pelewensis*, but crown paler rufous; sometimes a few white feathers in the nape, at least on females; wing 10 mm longer than in *pelewensis*, tail 10-13 mm longer, bill 2.0-2.5 mm longer.

H. c. cinnamomina Guam Island (in the Marianas Archipelago, north of a line between Palau and Ponapé). Male differs from *pelewensis* in having cinnamon-rufous neck and underparts; female like *pelewensis* (see Description). Slightly larger than *reichenbachii*.

H. c. miyakoensis Extinct; formerly endemic to Miyako Jima, in the Ryukyu Islands, between Japan and the Philippines. Like *cinnamomina* but slightly smaller; legs and feet red, and it lacked the black line across the nape. Colour of bill unknown.

Habitat and range Micronesian Kingfishers inhabit forest, woods, and marginal areas between natural woodland and country cleared for farming and settlement. In north Guam they lived in what is left of native forest on limestone soils and in mixed upland woods; they occur in wooded coastal lowlands, among coconut palms, at the edges of mangrove swamps, and in spacious gardens with plenty of timber. They often perch on telegraph wires. Their range is Guam, Ponapé, the Palau Islands, and formerly Miyako Jima.

Population In the Ryukyu Archipelago the endemic bird, of which only a single specimen was ever encountered, is evidently extinct. On Guam it was common and widespread or even abundant 40 years ago, but, with the growth of the great US Airbase, the economic development of the island with much of the original forest destroyed, and with the introduction of brown tree-snakes, it has declined dramatically. In 1976 only 150 pairs were thought to exist in Guam, in the north; in 1985 a mere ten pairs and ten solitary males could be found, and the only pair that bred successfully used a snake-proofed site. The Micronesian Kingfisher will soon be extinct in Guam; but it is breeding successfully in captivity, and the bird is to be reintroduced to Guam as soon as the population of brown tree-snakes can be controlled (Marshall 1989). On Ponapé it seems to be much less common now than formerly, although it is not greatly endangered there (King 1981). The Palau Islands are the headquarters of the species; it is absent from small islands, but is still quite common on well-wooded large ones. Mangrove Kingfishers are commoner, however, and not necessarily confined to the coast.

Food Like its congeners, this kingfisher subsists on a diet of large terrestrial insects and small vertebrates. It is known to catch and eat large grasshoppers, cicadas and other insects, also skinks and geckos.

Habits An unobtrusive bird, it spends much time sitting on an exposed branch low down on the outside of a large tree, or on a telegraph wire, horizontal forest vine or other such place, where it waits patiently for prey to appear on the ground nearby. Micronesian Kingfishers generally occur in pairs; they call from time to time, which serves to locate them – otherwise they are not easy to find in their wooded habitat. They are doubtless quite sedentary. **Nesting:** male and female share the task of nest-making, by excavating a hole usually at least 3 m (but up to 8 m) up in a tall tree or coconut palm. Sometimes the pair uses a natural tree hollow, with one or two entrances, and limit their attentions to cleaning it out. Several nest holes may be owned by the pair, although only one is used. Both parents attend the chicks. **Laying months:** Guam, December-July; Ponapé, August.

Description *H. c. pelewensis* **Adult male:** forehead and crown light orange-rufous; lores black, narrow line of feathers below eye black, and upper ear-coverts black tinged green, the black extending backwards as a narrow band which crosses the nape, dividing rufous crown from white hindneck. Broad white collar around the neck, sometimes suffused with buff on the hindneck. Mantle dark blue-green, becoming nearly black adjacent to the white collar; back and scapulars blue-green; rump, tertials, and inner upperwing-coverts green-blue or blue, a brighter shade; tail green-blue; outer upperwing-coverts purple-blue; remiges blackish-brown with green-blue outer edges. Chin, throat, cheeks, breast, flanks, belly and undertail-coverts white. Upper mandible greyish-black, tip and cutting edge of lower mandible the same, rest of lower mandible pale horn; iris dark brown, orbi-tal skin black; legs and feet greyish-black. **Adult female:** like the male (but in *H. c. cinnamomina*, in which the male has uniformly cinnamon-rufous underparts and underwing-coverts, the female has white underwing-coverts and rufous breast paling towards the chin, and paling to almost white on the lower belly). **Juvenile:** juveniles of *H. c. pelewensis* resemble adult females of *H. c. cinnamomina*, with pale rufous throat and buffy or whitish belly, and feathers from chin to lower breast have narrow dusky fringes. **Measurements:** wing of male 88-91, of female 88-91; tail of male 57-62, of female 58-67; bill of male 44-49, of female 43-49; tarsus of male 14-16, of female 14-15. Weight (*H. c. cinnamomina*): male 56-62, female 58-74.

References Baker (1951), Jenkins (1983), Pratt *et al.* (1980).

49 BEACH KINGFISHER   Plate 18
Halcyon saurophaga

Halcyon saurophaga Gould, 1843, Proc. Zool. Soc. London, pt 11, p. 103, near Cape d'Urville, New Guinea.

Field identification Length 30 cm (12 in). A bird of mangrove coasts and offshore islands from the Moluccas and northern New Guinea coast to islands around the Bismarck Sea and the Solomons. White, with blue back, wings and tail; indistinct blackish line behind eye. Bill like that of Mangrove Kingfisher (47), black, with large area of horn colour on proximal half of lower mandible, but longer and heavier. On Wuvulu, Ninigo, Hermit, Anchorite and Admiralty Islands, a varying proportion of the population has blue or partly blue crown recalling the Mangrove Kingfisher; the latter does not, however, occur there. Both species occur in northern Moluccas around Ceram Sea, on Western Papuan Islands and around West Irian's Vogelkop and Bomberai Peninsulas, where the Mangrove Kingfisher is readily distinguished by its solid blue crown and broad black mask from bill to nape. To the east, only the Beach Kingfisher ranges along the north New Guinea coast and only the Mangrove along the south, east of Port Moresby to Hula. Then the Beach occurs less than 50 km away at Marshall Lagoon. Both species inhabit Milne Bay area and Louisiade Archipelago at the eastern extremity of Papua New Guinea, where the Mangrove is white and dark olive-green. Both species are found also in New Britain, New Ireland and the Solomons, where most Mangrove subspecies are white and blue or green with a broad buffy superciliary stripe; also on Mussau and Emira Islands in the St Matthias group, northwest of New Ireland, where the Mangrove Kingfisher subspecies *matthiae* has a white crown (with variable amounts of green on adults) and is best told from the Beach Kingfisher by its smaller size.

Voice Like that of Mangrove Kingfisher but louder and deeper, 'kill kill', 'kee-kee-kee' or 'kiokiokiokio'.

Geographical variation Four subspecies, with crowns varying from white to green-blue. This species is a large version of the Mangrove Kingfisher; the two are very closely related and over much of their ranges their distributions are complementary.

H. s. saurophaga Range of the species, except for Admiralty, Hermit, Anchorite and Ninigo Islands. Crown always white.

H. s. admiralitatis Admiralty Islands, northeast of New Britain (Papua New Guinea). Crown white (60% of population), green-blue (8%) or mixed (32%).

H. s. anachoreta Hermit and Ninigo Islands, west-northwest of Admiralty Islands, Papua New Guinea. Crown white in about half of the population and green-blue in half.

H. s. subsp. Anchorite Islands, north of Hermit group. Crown always blue-green. This race requires formal naming. It and *anachoreta* were included in *admiralitatis* by Forshaw (1985).

Habitat and range Beach Kingfishers inhabit mangrove swamps, open shores and beaches with driftwood and a few elevated perches, coral cliffs and pools, seaside coconut plantations, rocky islets just offshore, tidal reefs, shorelines with plentiful vegetation and trees overhanging water, and rocky coasts and headlands. They occur in northern Moluccas (Morotai, Halmahera, Batjan, Obi), Western Papuan Islands (Salawati, Waigeu, Gebe), on the south coast of West Irian east to Kamrau Bay, around Vogelkop Peninsula and Geelvink Bay, on Biak, Japen and Numfor Islands, at places on the north coast of New Guinea, and islands including Wuvulu, Manam, Kairiru and Madang, around Bismarck Sea on Crown, Long, Tolokiwa, Umboi, New Britain, Witu, Lolobau, Watom, Duke of York, New Ireland, New Hanover, Tabar, Lihir, Tanga, Feni, Tench, Mussau and Emira in the St Matthias group, Manus, Lou, San Miguel, Rambutyo, Nauna and Los Reyes in the Admiralty Islands; the Anchorites, Hermits, and Ninigos; Nuguria and Nissan Islands east of New Ireland; in southeast mainland Papua New Guinea at Kupiano (Marshall Lagoon), Coutance Island, Heath Island, and in D'Entrecasteaux and Louisiade Archipelagos on Goodenough, Egum Atoll, East Island and Misima (Coates 1985); and they are widespread along coasts of Bougainville, also on Buka Island and Shortland Island (Solomons), and in most Solomon Islands east to San Cristóbal.

Population Distribution is patchy, determined partly, it seems, by that of the Mangrove Kingfisher: where one is common the other is rare or absent. Quite common in Western Papuan Islands. Rare or extremely local in mainland New Guinea and mainland New Britain, but common on islands only a few kilometres (and more distantly) offshore. Very common on Wuvulu, Ninigo, Hermit and Admiralty Islands: 30 pairs were counted on Menam, a tiny island of only 20 ha in the Ninigos, and eight pairs along 2 km of shoreline on Luf (Hermit Islands) (Bell 1970b). Common on Nissan Island, locally common on Bougainville.

Migration A seasonal visitor from offshore islets to the mainland coast of Papua New Guinea or Madang, but that hardly amounts to migration (Forshaw 1985).

Food Crabs, fishes, insects, insect larvae, and lizards.

Habits A quite large, noisy bird, solitary or in pairs, conspicuous by reason of the white plumage and the species' free use of prominent perches. It hunts from the outer branch of a tree overhanging mud, rock-pools, coral, or a sandy beach, or from a large piece of driftwood, rock or post, plunging down to the ground or shallows for prey. At low tide it feeds mainly on crabs, and at high tide keeps more to vegetation behind the beach, catching lizards (hence 'saurophaga') and insects in and below the trees. It sometimes hovers momentarily above water and plunge-dives for a fish in surf or rock-pools, at times hunting 100 m offshore. *Nesting:* few nests have been found. Nests are in tree holes, and probably also in fibrous tissue in the heads of coconut palms. One clutch on Misima Island (Louisiade Archipelago) was of four eggs, averaging 27.7 × 22.5 mm. Five other eggs averaged 32.5 × 25.8 mm. *Laying months:* Irian Jaya and eastern Papua New Guinea, December; various evidences point to laying there as early as August.

Description *H. s. saurophaga* Sexes alike. *Adult:* head white, with some dark grey feather bases occasionally showing through in the hindcrown, and with a thin blackish line extending backwards from the eye above the ear-coverts. Neck, upper mantle, and entire underparts including underwing-coverts white. The lower mantle and back are green-blue, rump and uppertail-coverts bright azure-blue, tail greenish-blue, upperwing-coverts bright blue, and primaries and secondaries dark grey with purple-blue outer webs. Upper mandible black, lower mandible yellowish-horn with dark brown cutting edges and tip; iris very dark brown, orbital skin black; legs and feet blackish. *Juvenile:* like the adult, but blues are duller; upperwing-coverts, tertials and lower mantle feathers narrowly fringed with buff; breast feathers narrowly fringed with dark grey; and crown, breast, belly, underwing- and undertail-coverts tinged buffy. *Measurements:* wing of male 115-134, of female 118-133; tail of male 74-86, of female 71-88; bill of male 57-67, of female 58-70; tarsus of male 18-20, of female 18-20. Weight: male 90-146, female 110-146.

References Coates (1985), Forshaw (1985), Fry (1980a).

50 SACRED KINGFISHER   Plate 18
Halcyon sancta

Halcyon sanctus Vigors and Horsfield, 1827, Trans. Linn. Soc. London, 15, pt 1, p. 206, New Holland, = New South Wales.

Field identification Length 22 cm (8½ in). Told by the combination of buff loral spot, green crown and back, black mask, absence of eye-stripe, buffy hindneck-collar with narrow black band above it, white throat, buffy or ochre underparts, and blue wings, rump and tail. *Confusion species:* the Sacred Kingfisher overlaps geographically with many other halcyons. Its buffy-white collar distinguishes it from all but the Mangrove and Red-backed Kingfishers (47, 52). Mangrove is larger, with a relatively more massive bill, and many of its subspecies differ from Sacred Kingfishers in having white (not buff) underparts; other, buffy subspecies (*tristami, bennetti* and *alberti*, which inhabit New Britain, Nissan, Bougainville and the Solomon Islands, where Sacred Kingfishers are winter visitors) are very like Sacred, but are larger.

Voice Four or five loud staccato notes, sometimes up to 12, slightly descending the scale: 'kik-kik-kik-kik'; repeated monotonously. Also, two or three squealing or rasping notes, 'schssk, schssk'. At the nest it emits a chuckling 'ch-rrr-k', and a loud 'skreeek' in defence.

Geographical variation There are five subspecies, differing unimportantly in size and plumage shade. One island race has the bill somewhat flattened dorsoventrally, and another more so. On that account the latter has generally been regarded as a separate species, *H. recurvirostris*, the Flat-billed Kingfisher.

H. s. sancta Australia, and Guadalcanal and the San Cristóbal group in the eastern Solomon Islands. Australian breeders winter throughout Indonesia and Melanesia, from eastern Sumatra and Borneo to New Guinea, Bismarck Archipelago and the Solomons. The wing averages 93 mm and bill 43 mm.

H. s. canacorum New Caledonia and Isle of Pines. Resident. Like *sancta* but wing shorter, averaging 91 mm.

H. s. macmillani Loyalty Islands (northeast of New Caledonia). Like *canacorum*, but upperparts darker and underparts deeper buff or cinnamon. Bill slightly flattened dorsoventrally, and shorter, averaging 38.5 mm.

H. s. recurvirostris Western Samoa: Apolima, Upolu and Savai'i Islands. Like *macmillani*, but a deeper cinnamon on collar and flanks, and smaller, the wing averaging 81 mm. The bill is flatter and shorter than that of *macmillani*, averaging 36 mm.

H. s. vagans New Zealand, and Lord Howe, Norfolk and Kermadec Islands.

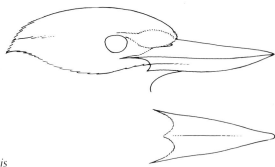

H. s. recurvirostris

Like *sancta*, but duller, and crown and mantle duskier; underparts yellowish-buff. Larger: wing averages 101 mm and bill 46 mm.

Habitat and range This is the common woodland kingfisher of Australia, where its mapped breeding distribution co-incides neatly with regions of over 50 mm of summer rainfall (Blakers *et al*. 1984). It is a summer visitor up to about 1800 m in altitude in all parts, a few staying in winter in mangrove near Sydney, for example, and large numbers remaining in the north. Sacred Kingfishers are widespread in eucalypts and all types of woodland, par-ticularly near water, and are especially common in red gum woods *Eucalyptus camaldulensis* and in mangrove, along seashores and onshore islands. They range throughout much of the *Acacia* scrub country of Western Australia and *Melaleuca* swampland in the north, but avoid the spinifex, mallee and saltbush zones; some occur in tussock grassland where there are stands of timber, and they breed not only commonly around the periphery of the continent (except the Great Australian Bight and Tasmania, where they are rare visitors mainly in win-ter) but in the epicentre, at Alice Springs and in the Macdonnell Ranges. In their winter quarters they especially favour 'parkland' – cleared, open country with mown grass and short cover, where birds can perch in trees or on wires to scan the ground below for food. They are common along wooded roadsides and forest edges, as well as in mangrove and other vege-tation bordering seashores, gardens, around human habitation, swamps and savannas. Sacred Kingfishers are wide-spread in New Zealand, in habitats like their Australian ones. Rather surprisingly, New Zealand breeders are not migratory, although there is marked altitudinal move-ment between summer and winter quarters (Taylor 1966). Other resident populations inhabit Kermadec Islands, Lord Howe Island, Norfolk Island, New Caledonia, Loyalty Islands, Guadalcanal and San Cristóbal Islands, and possibly Timor. In the non-breeding season, Australian birds are widespread and com-mon in more open parts of Papua New Guinea, Bismarck Archipelago and the Solomons. Further west, they are also common in West Irian, the Moluccas, parts of Sulawesi, most of the Lesser Sunda Islands, and the northern coastal lowlands of Java. They are regular but uncommon migrants to the whole of Borneo, and are rare visitors to Bangka, eastern Sumatra, and Sangihe and Talaud Islands. A few winter in all parts of Australia, but they are common then only along the northern coasts.

Population Sacred Kingfishers are fre-quent to common throughout the major part of their breeding range, and some birders rate them locally abundant. Similarly, they are common in wooded but partly cleared country throughout at least the eastern part of their wintering range. Densities measured at five places in New South Wales and Victoria are quite similar: 5-18, 12, 17-19, 31 and 40 indi-viduals per km^2. There were once about 90 birds on a 4-ha airstrip in west Papua New Guinea forest-edge habitat, and 10 pairs along 600 m of road in southeast Papua New Guinea (Bell 1981). In area Australia is 7,690,000 km^2. Sacred Kingfishers are at high density in just one-third of that area, at low density in one-third, and absent from one-third (Blakers *et al.* 1984). If their high density is the average of the values given above, 22.5 individuals per km², and their low density a tenth of that figure, the total Australian population will be some 63.4 million birds.

Migration A few birds remain for the ensuing winter in all parts of their Australian breeding range, but the great majority migrate northward to winter near the north Australian coast and in Indonesia, Borneo, Sulawesi, New Guinea, Bismarck Archipelago and Solomons. New Zealand breeders do not migrate, except altitudinally. One recovery of a Sacred Kingfisher ringed in New South Wales was 2700 km away, in Trobriand Islands, Papua New Guinea, but some individuals probably migrate nearly 4000 km. Northward migration in Papua New Guinea is in March and April, and southward from late September to late October. Sacred Kingfishers move at night, and cross Torres Strait in large numbers; but the lack of other obvious concentrations suggests that migration over the Arafura and Coral Seas is on a broad front.

Food Numerous opportunistic observations of Sacred Kingfishers catching prey, as well as analyses of regurgitated pellets and of the contents of birds killed on roads, show that they eat a variety of arthropods and small vertebrates. Insects are the most important prey: locusts, grasshoppers, dragonflies, cockchafers, longhorn, carabid and click beetles, grubs and caterpillars. Spiders, freshwater fish and crayfish, tadpoles and frogs, and sometimes mice and small birds are eaten, and crabs taken from brackish and saltwater shallows and from rocks exposed at low tide are also common prey.

Habits The species is territorial, quite aggressively so, a pair calling vigorously and chasing other kingfishers and many other birds away from summer and winter territories. Although singletons are often seen, occurrence in pairs is the norm. Some evidence suggests that a pair returns to the same territories in its breeding and its wintering grounds year after year. Although the annual mortality is doubtless high (many are killed against windows and by traffic), it thus seems likely that the

pair remains faithful, migrating and living together year-round. These birds use vantage points for hunting, where they are conspicuous, sitting patiently on a post, fence, outer branch, telegraph wire, treetop or clothes-line, in a hunched posture, or alertly moving the head to scan for prey, from time to time flicking the tail upwards. Most food is taken from the ground, but birds sometimes plunge into water for prey (they can be unwelcome at fishponds), and those living on beaches dive onto sand, mud and into water wherever prey is seen. Sacred Kingfishers often catch insects in flight, and they sometimes briefly hover to snatch a meal from foliage. **Nesting:** these kingfishers excavate nest holes or use little-altered natural hollows. There is rather marked regional variation in site, perhaps a matter of availability rather than of tradition. In west Australia they nearly always use tree holes, and on Rottnest Island they dig into the fibrous 'bark' or frond bases of palm trunks. In the east a regular site is earth banks by streams and creeks. On the central New South Wales coast, however, tree termitaria are always used (Forshaw 1985). In an area of North Island, New Zealand, where there is a dearth of suitable clay banks, the birds use holes in dead trees. In New Caledonia and on Norfolk Island nearly all nests are in road embankments or seaboard earthen banks, and in the Solomons arboreal termitaria 1-3 m above the ground are commonly used. Burrows in banks are generally about 30 cm long, the clutch of 3-6 eggs being laid in a cavity at the end. Incubation, mainly by the female, lasts about 18 days, and the nestling period is about 24 days. Two broods are commonly reared in succession. One tree nest hole in New Zealand was used for 17 years. *Laying months:* Australia, mainly September-October, but in the north also December and January; New Zealand, October-January; New Caledonia, December; Norfolk Island, October-December.

Description *H. s. sancta* **Adult male:** forehead and crown dark green, slightly paler and bluer towards the sides of the crown; side of forehead buff, forming a supraloral spot or a narrow line extending from nostril to above the eye. Lores black, with cheeks and ear-coverts forming a black mask which extends backwards as a narrower black line across the nape; there is sometimes a small patch of white above the black nape line. Chin and throat white or very pale buff, and collar around neck buff or pale orange. Upper mantle dark olive-green, lower mantle, back and scapulars green or dark green; upperwing-coverts blue-green, primaries and secondaries blackish, with blue outer webs; rump bright blue; tail blue, washed with purple in centre and with green at the sides. Breast buff or light orange, the colour deepening on the underwing-coverts, flanks, belly and undertail-coverts. Upper mandible blackish, lower mandible pale horn with blackish cutting edges and tip; iris very dark brown, orbital

skin black; legs and feet black, slaty or dark pinkish-brown. *Adult female:* duller and greener than the male, particularly on the wings and rump. *Juvenile:* duller than adult female; forehead buffier; dusky fringes to breast feathers and sometimes neck feathers, and buff fringes to all upperwing-coverts. *Measurements:* wing of male 88-99, of female 88-98; tail of male 50-62, of female 55-63; bill of male 39-48, of female 39-47; tarsus of male 13-16, of female 13-15. Weight: male 28-58, female 39-55.

References Bell (1981), Forshaw (1985), Fry (1980a), Moon (1989), Ralph and Ralph (1977).

51 TIMOR KINGFISHER (Lesser Sundas Kingfisher)   Plate 18
Halcyon australasia

Alcedo australasia Vieillot, 1818, Nouv. Dict. Hist. Nat., 19, p. 419, no locality.

Field identification Length 21 cm (8¼ in). Confined to some (not all) of the Lesser Sunda Islands, Indonesia. From the Mangrove Kingfisher (47, nominate subspecies), the only other halcyon in its range, the Timor Kingfisher can readily be distinguished by its broad orange superciliary stripe (the Mangrove has no stripe) and its orange or rufous collar and underparts (white on Mangrove). Any vocal differences are unknown – the voice of Timor Kingfisher has not been described.

Geographical variation The five subspecies differ mainly in the amount of green on the forehead and crown. White and Bruce (1986) did not recognise *tringorum* or *interposita*.

H. a. australasia Lombok Island, east of Bali, and, 750 km further east, the islands of Timor (550 km long) and, just north of it, Wetar (120 km long). Forehead and crown green.

H. a. tringorum Roma (Romang), a small island east of Wetar. Forehead and forecrown rufous, hindcrown green.

H. a. dammeriana Damar Islands, 100 km east-northeast of Roma, and Babar Islands, 250 km east-northeast of Timor and 130 km southeast of Damar. Forehead and crown rufous, with some dull green stripes in the forehead (particularly on males) and a small green patch in centre of crown.

H. a. interposita Moa, Lakar and other Leti Islands (but not Sermata), between Timor and Babar. Like *dammeriana*, but rufous parts paler, and green patch on crown smaller or absent.

H. a. odites Tanimbar Islands, 150 km east of Babar. Like nominate *australasia*, but rufous parts paler and crown more blue than green. Small: wing 73-77 mm, tail 45-51 mm, bill 38-40 mm.

Habitat and range Nusateng Gara or the Lesser Sunda Islands: Lombok, and continuously from Timor to Wetar, Roma, Leti Islands, Damar, Babar and the Tanimbar group; the chain of large and lesser islands from Sumbawa, Sumba and Flores to Alor, however, is not occupied by this species. The habitat appears to be woodland, and on Lombok the bird occurs in open rainforest at 500 m altitude. Only locally is it at all common. This is a potential Red Data Book species, listed as 'Vulnerable' by Johnson and Stattersfield (1990).

Food Insects and insect larvae.

Habits Nothing is on record.

Description *H. a. australasia* ***Adult male:*** forehead, forecrown and hindcrown oily green; a few rufous flecks in forehead. A broad superciliary stripe runs from nostril to nape, buffy or pale orange above the lore and deep cinnamon-orange behind the eye. Lores, cheeks, ear-coverts, and a narrow line across the hindneck are black with a green tinge. Chin buffy-white; throat, entire underparts and sides of neck orange, hindneck-collar cinnamon-orange. Mantle, scapulars and upper back oily dark green, lower back blue-green, rump and uppertail-coverts bright pale blue. Wings blue-green, lesser and median coverts bluer, and primaries edged purplish-blue. Tail blue-green, but central pair of feathers dark purplish-blue.

A small patch of greenish-black at side of breast, concealed under folded wing. Underwing-coverts rufous. Upper mandible brownish-black, lower mandible straw-coloured, darker towards tip; iris dark brown, orbital ring of minute featherlets buff; legs and feet blackish. ***Adult female:*** like the male, but slightly duller. ***Juvenile:*** like the adult female, but breast and flank feathers are narrowly fringed with black, and upperwing-coverts fringed with buff. The bill is pale-tipped. ***Measurements:*** wing of male 78-84, of female 78-86; tail of male 50-58, of female 53-62; bill of male 40-45, of female 40-44; tarsus of male 14-16, of female 14-16.

References Forshaw (1985), Fry (1980a), White and Bruce (1986).

52 RED-BACKED KINGFISHER   Plate 18
Halcyon pyrrhopygia

Halcyon pyrrhopygia Gould, 1841, Proc. Zool. Soc. London, pt 8, 1840, p. 113, New South Wales.

Field identification Length 22 cm (8½ in). A woodland halcyon endemic to Australia. **At rest:** the streaky cap and rufous rump are diagnostic. **In flight:** a large patch of rufous shows on the back as well as the rump. **Confusion species:** its green-and-white-streaked head top and rufous back and rump distinguish it from the similar Mangrove and Sacred Kingfishers (47, 50). The Forest Kingfisher (40), with its white forehead spots and dark blue cap, is not likely to be confused with the Red-backed. Red-backed is the quietest and least obtrusive of these Australian halcyons.

Voice A loud, mournful whistle, 'pee-eee' or 'ter-ep', repeated monotonously in the breeding season. Otherwise this is rather a silent bird, except for a churring and harsh chattering of alarm (Forshaw 1985).

Geographical variation None.

Habitat and range It inhabits dry woodlands and arid *Acacia* scrub throughout Australia except for the southwest (south

of a line from Perth to Eyre) and Tasmania: mallee, open mulga, and dry coolabah-lined riverbeds. There are a few records in Gibson Desert, Great Victorian Desert, or within 100 km of the New South Wales coast; otherwise it is a moderately common bird, quite uniformly distributed (Blakers *et al.* 1984).

Migration Red-backed Kingfishers are mainly winter visitors in Cape York Peninsula but resident or partially migrant in the remainder of the northern half of Australia. Further south they are mainly breeding summer visitors, from August to April (September to March in the far south). At many localities their appearance is sporadic, however, common in some years and absent in others, and no very clear picture of migration emerges. Locally, movement in winter from the interior to the coast is sometimes more evident than north/south migration.

Food Locusts and grasshoppers, including *Austracis guttulosa, Chortoicetes terminifera* and *Choryphistes* spp.; also beetles and other insects, spiders, centipedes, frogs, tadpoles, lizards, mice, and small birds' eggs and nestlings (Forshaw 1985).

Habits Surprisingly little is on record; our own observations suggest that this is a typical halcyon in its behaviour, feeding largely from the surface of the ground, like the arid-lands African species (30-32). Like other birds of Australia's arid centre, it migrates and breeds opportunistically, in response to rainfall (Chinner 1977). *Nesting:* burrows are excavated by both birds of a pair in earth cliffs, sand banks, ground termitaria, and sometimes in tree termitaria or earth in an uprooted tree; the burrow is about 120 cm long. The clutch is of 4-6 eggs. Red-backed Kingfishers are double-brooded. *Laying months:* Northern Territory, September-January; Queensland, September-February; Western Australia, August-November; South Australia, November; New South Wales, September-March.

Description *Adult male:* forehead and crown green, flecked and striped with white, and with a suggestion of a white superciliary line. Lores, ear-coverts, and a narrow band across the nape are black; hindneck, cheeks, chin, throat and entire underparts including underwing-coverts are white. Mantle, scapulars and upper back green, very dark next to the white collar; some upper back feathers have whitish edges, making it look streaky. Lower back and rump bright rufous; uppertail-coverts buffy-rufous, with some greenish feather centres. Tail dark blue, greener at the sides. Upperwing-coverts light blue; tertials and secondaries dark blue with narrow white ends; primaries blackish with green outer webs. Bill greyish-black, with a large horn-coloured area in the lower mandible; eye dark brown; legs and feet grey-olive. *Adult female:* like the male, but all greens and blues are duller, washed with grey or brown; forehead and crown are streakier, and the white collar and flanks are sometimes suffused with buff. *Juvenile:* like the female, but hindneck and flanks pale rufous-buff, and feathers of neck and breast are narrowly tipped dusky. Median and lesser wing-coverts are buff-tipped. *Measurements:* wing of male 97-107, of female 98-106; tail of male 59-72, of female 60-70; bill of male 38-49, of female 38-48; tarsus of male 14-16, of female 14-16. Weight: male 45-58, female 41-62.

Reference Forshaw (1985).

53 PACIFIC KINGFISHER (Polynesian Kingfisher, Chattering Kingfisher) Plate 19
Halcyon tuta

Alcedo tuta Gmelin, 1788; Syst. Nat., I, pt I, p. 453, no. 28, Tahiti.

Field identification Length 22 cm (8½ in). In the Society Islands Pacific Kingfishers resemble diminutive Beach Kingfishers (49) of the green-capped form. Juveniles, without much white on the head and with the breast heavily black-barred, are distinctly different from the white and blue-green adults. This species occurs on many islands but overlaps with another kingfisher only on Tahiti: Pacific Kingfishers have a white superciliary stripe and collar; Tahiti Kingfishers (54) do not. Three races inhabit some of the Cook Islands, where there are no other kingfishers: two have the white parts buffy, and so they look rather like Sacred Kingfishers (50), and the third has much orange about the collar and eyebrow. See also *H. (t.) gambieri*, below.

Voice A rapid, staccato 'kee-kee-kee-kee', repeated after a few seconds or accelerating into a rattling chatter; also 'ke-kow, ke-kow, ke-kow' (or 'ki-wow') and various other notes – shrill hissing shrieks, harsh cackles and soft chuckles. The alarm is a loud 'shriii' or 'scriii'. Calls of Mangaia individuals differ somewhat from those of other populations (Holyoak 1974a,b).

Geographical variation Subspecies vary in the extent of green on the crown and the degree of buff or orange-rufous suffusion of the white parts. The limits of this species are not at all certain. It is closely allied to the Mangrove (47) and Sacred Kingfishers, and the birds of eastern Fiji (*marina*), Tonga (*sacra*) and American Samoa (*manuae, pealei*), which we have treated here as Mangrove Kingfishers, may in fact be Pacific Kingfishers (Pratt *et al*. 1987). The kingfisher of Mangaia in Cook Islands (*ruficollaris*), named as a separate species when it was described in 1974, and which we treat below as a subspecies of Pacific Kingfisher, presents an equally good case for being classed as a Sacred Kingfisher.

Four thousand kilometres to the east of Mangaia is the island of Mangareva in the Gambier group, Tuamotu Archipelago. A bird variously known as the Mangareva, Gambier or Tuamotu Kingfisher formerly inhabited it but became extinct about 1922 (Thibault 1973; Holyoak and Thibault 1977). It has generally been treated as a separate species, *H. gambieri*, which is reasonable in view of its isolation, but we think its differences from *H. tuta* warrant only subspecific recognition.

H. t. tuta Society Islands (South Pacific, 151°-153°W): Bora Bora, Maupiti, Huahine, Raiatea, Tahaa, Tupai and Tahiti. No buff wash: plumage entirely white and dark green. Much white on forehead; white superciliary stripe rather narrow.

H. t. atiu Cook Islands (South Pacific, 157°W): Atiu. Crown white, faintly buffy, with green streaks in centre of the forecrown and a green patch on the hindcrown; collar, sides of breast, and flanks washed with buff.

H. t. mauke Cook Islands: Mauke, northwest of Atiu. Like *tuta*, but forehead, collar and sides of breast buffy or pale rufous; superciliary stripe and flanks faintly buffy.

H. t. ruficollaris Cook Islands: Mangaia, 300 km south of Atiu. Crown green, with narrow buff line at side of forehead, joining with a narrow buff or light orange superciliary stripe. Collar orange-rufous; breast washed with orange, strongly at the sides. A candidate for the Red Data Book (Johnson and Stattersfield 1990).

H. (t.) gambieri Gambier Islands (Tuamotu Archipelago): Mangareva. Extinct. Like *atiu*, but crown green and rufous, not green and buffy-white; collar and under-parts white, without any buff suffusion.

Habitat and range South Pacific: Society Islands, Mauke, Atiu and Mangaia in the Cook Islands, and formerly Mangareva in the Gambier Islands. It inhabits primary forest, particularly in highland stream valleys; also secondary forest, old plantations, wooded and cultivated land and gardens.

Population Pacific Kingfishers have been adversely affected by deforestation and increasing human populations. They are common or even abundant in montane forest on Raiatea, up to 800 m, and plentiful in farmland and around habitations down to sea level. They are still common in the remaining woodland of Atiu, Mauke and Mangaia. But they are now uncommon on Tahiti, where they are restricted to montane forests above 1000 m; and on Bora Bora there were thought to be fewer than 100 in 1972 (mainly in montane forest between 300 m and 600 m). The bird is apparently extinct on Tupai, where none has been seen since the 1890s.

Food Insects, insect larvae, small reptiles, small freshwater fish and crustaceans (freshwater shrimps 5-6 cm long).

Habits This kingfisher keeps mainly to mid and upper levels of trees, where it hawks insects, many caught in flight. It is quite vocal, and in forest is heard more often than seen, although in coconut groves and more open woods around villages it perches conspicuously, is not particularly shy, and is easy to watch. Prey is captured also on branches and among foliage. Seldom is food taken from the ground, although the bird does sometimes fish in shallow streams from some low perch. Pacific Kingfishers are territorial, calling from treetops, with the bill pointing skywards, to advertise a territory. **Nesting:** one nest with a set of two white eggs was excavated by the birds in the rotten trunk of a *Hibiscus* tree. As usual with kingfishers, there is no nest-lining. **Laying months:** Society Islands, December-January.

Description *H. t. tuta* Sexes alike. **Adult:** crown dark blue-green; forehead and superciliary stripe white, confluent with the white hindneck. Lores black; cheeks and ear-coverts greenish-black. Chin, throat, collar, and entire underparts including underwing-coverts are white. The broad white hindneck-collar is bisected by a thin black line joining the ear-coverts. Mantle and scapulars dark blue-green; wings, rump and tail dark greenish-blue, brightest on rump. Upper mandible black, lower mandible straw-coloured with black-brown cutting edges and tip; iris dark brown, orbital skin black; legs and feet slaty-grey or black, soles dull yellow. *Juvenile:* forehead feathers dark green with buffy-white margins; crown green, darker than on the adult; superciliary area finely streaked with green and white. Chin and throat white, finely black-

barred at sides. Hindneck blackish, with white collar hidden by black fringes. Mantle black or blackish-green. Upperwing-coverts broadly fringed with buff, each feather with a narrow black subterminal crescent. Breast heavily barred with black and white; belly creamy. Remaining parts as on the adult. *Measurements:* wing of male 98-103, of female 98-102; tail of male 70-76, of female 68-73; bill of male 37-41, of female 37-43; tarsus of male 15-17, of female 15-17.

References Forshaw (1985), Fry (1980a), Holyoak (1974a,b).

54 TAHITI KINGFISHER   Plate 19
Halcyon venerata

Alcedo venerata Gmelin, 1788, Syst. Nat., I, pt I, p. 453, no. 29, 'Insula amici', = Society Islands.

Field identification Length 21 cm (8¼ in). The only kingfisher in the South Pacific Society Islands besides the Pacific Kingfisher (53). Only on Tahiti do both species occur sympatrically, represented respectively by the subspecies *H. v. venerata* and *H. t. tuta*. Both have mainly green upperparts and white underparts. Adults are readily distinguished by the white forehead, superciliary stripe and hindneck of the Pacific, whereas on the Tahiti the whole head is brownish blue-green and there is no hindneck-collar. Tahiti Kingfisher males have a rusty breast-band and females a dark brown one. Young Pacific Kingfishers can lack a white collar, have an indistinct streaky superciliary stripe, and the breast can be heavily barred with black. From such birds adult Tahiti Kingfishers are best distinguished by the dusky breast being streaked rather than black-barred. Tahiti Kingfishers are slightly smaller than Pacifics and have appreciably shorter bills; the bill is flat and broad at the base. On Moorea, where there are no other kingfishers, the Tahiti Kingfisher is plain, with brown upperparts and mainly white underparts.

Voice Moorea and Tahiti populations sound alike. Their calls are like those of Pacific Kingfishers, but the two can be separated with experience. The commonest call is a rattling 'ki-ki-ki-ki-ki-ki' or 'ki-ki-ki-ki-koo'; there is a high, double-noted whistle, and various raucous and croaking monosyllables. The repertoire is more limited than that of Pacific Kingfishers (Holyoak 1974a).

Geographical variation There are two subspecies, one green above and one brown, sufficiently distinct to have been treated as separate species in the past.

H. v. venerata Tahiti. Upperparts dull olive, with bright glossy aquamarine above and behind the eye and on the ear-coverts; wings and tail brighter and greener than back. Underparts white, with a broad rufous (male) or blackish (female) breast-band.

H. v. youngi Moorea (20 km northwest of Tahiti). Upperparts brown, most contour feathers with pale buff, almost pinkish-buff, fringes; a narrow vestigial whitish collar. Outer webs of primaries and greater wing-coverts washed with dull green. Tail brown, suffused with dull green. Underparts white, some feathers at the sides of throat and breast with buffy or dusky fringes. Juveniles have the chin, throat and breast heavily marked with soft dark brown stripes. Slightly larger than the nominate subspecies.

Habitat and status On Tahiti widespread in wooded lowlands and particularly *Purao* woods, also in gardens and plantations; it is also quite plentiful in montane forests up to 1700 m, its territories sometimes abutting those of Pacific Kingfishers. On Moorea it is uncommon except in one area where it is abundant (Holyoak 1974a), occurring in primary and secondary forests up to 300 m. Neither population is regarded as endangered.

Food Insects, insect larvae, small lizards, fish and crustaceans.

Habits Tahiti Kingfishers live year-round in pairs but are often encountered singly, perching at mid levels in forest, or conspicuously on outer branches of a solitary tree affording unimpeded flights after prey. Although food is taken from the surface of the ground and from shallow freshwater puddles, the species also commonly catches insects in flight or among foliage. In that regard it behaves like some large leaf-gleaning flycatcher, and its broad, flat bill is befitting. Birds spend much time perching stolidly, looking out for prey. Pairs are markedly territorial, and often chase other kingfishers and even swallows, monarchs and pigeons. Territories are advertised vocally, birds calling frequently all day, particularly after dawn and before dusk, and all year. **Nesting:** nests are in holes excavated by the birds in rotting branches and trunks, up to 11 m

from the ground. The clutch is of three eggs. **Laying months:** Tahiti, October-December.

Description *H. v. venerata* **Adult male:** forehead, crown, hindneck and mantle feathers dark brown with slightly paler olive margins; at the sides of the crown the margins are broader, glossy and blue-green. Lores blackish; cheeks and ear-coverts glossy aquamarine-green. Back and scapulars brownish-green, with some dark feather centres showing through. Rump and uppertail-coverts bluish-green, tail olive-green. Upperwing-coverts and flight feathers dark brown with broad bluish-green margins or outer webs. Chin white; throat white, with dark brown shaft-streaks and feather bases towards the sides of the throat, where feathers have buff or rufous margins. Breast variable, white with black streaks at the sides, buffy, or rusty-orange with black shaft-streaks and dusky crescents. Belly white; flanks white or buffy; undertail-coverts white, sometimes with dark bars; underwing-coverts white. Upper mandible black, lower mandible horn-coloured with blackish cutting edges and tip; iris dark brown, orbital skin black; legs and feet black. **Adult female:** like the male, but aquamarine parts duller, and breast-band blackish. **Juvenile:** like the adult female but upperparts browner; breast-band streakier, with lower throat streaky; flanks and belly buffy. **Measurements:** wing of male 94-101, of female 94-103; tail of male 65-73, of female 62-72; bill of male 33-37, of female 32-37; tarsus of male 15-17, of female 15-16.

References Forshaw (1985), Fry (1980a), Holyoak (1974a).

55 NIAU KINGFISHER (Tuamotu Kingfisher)   Plate 19
Halcyon gertrudae

Todiramphus gertrudae Murphy, 1924, Amer. Mus. Novit., no. 149, p. 1, Niau Island, Tuamotu Archipelago.

When the Whitney South Seas Expedition visited Niau Island, in French Polynesia about 600 km east-northeast of Tahiti, and discovered this distinctive kingfisher in 1921, it was common, perching in trees and bushes around villages, and even in the village streets. In 1974 there was still a healthy population, estimated by J. C.

Thibault at between 400 and 600 birds throughout the island. It is a candidate for the next Red Data Book (Johnson and Stattersfield 1990), and we join J. Forshaw (1985) in thinking that 'consideration should be given to translocation of some birds, so that supplementary populations can be established on other islands'. Such visits as ornithologists have made to nearby wooded islands such as Rangiroa, Makatea and Fakarava have failed to find any kingfishers there. Nothing is known about the habits of Niau Kingfishers. Most recent authorities have made it conspecific with the Mangareva Kingfisher, naming them together the Tuamotu Kingfisher, *Halcyon gambieri*. All South Pacific kingfishers seem to be very closely related and the taxonomic status of the Mangareva, now extinct, is academic (see 53). We know of no evidence that any kingfishers ever occurred in the Tuamotu Archipelago between Niau and Mangareva, which are 1250 km apart with scores of islands in between.

Description Sexes alike. *Adult:* head and neck buffy-cream, with some rufous feather bases showing through, except as follows: variable amount of blue feathers on crown, on some birds forming an irregular blue patch on hindcrown, on others forming an almost wholly blue crown with creamy-white forehead and broad buffy superciliary band running from above the eye to the nape; lores blackish and ear-coverts clear or dusky blue; sometimes a few blue feathers on the otherwise pale orange-buff hindneck, forming a broken line joining the ear-coverts. Mantle, back, rump, wings and tail blue, brightest on the rump, suffused with green on mantle and scapulars and with purple on wings and tail. Chin and throat white; sides of neck and sides of breast creamy-buff or very pale orange; remaining underparts and underwing-coverts white. Upper mandible black, lower mandible straw-coloured with black-brown cutting edges and tip; iris dark brown, orbital skin black; legs and feet slaty-grey or black. *Juvenile:* not known. *Measurements:* wing of male 91-92, of female 90-93; tail of male 63-66, of female 63-65; bill of male 36-38, of female 36-38; tarsus of male 15-16, of female 15-16.

References Forshaw (1985), Fry (1980a), Holyoak and Thibault (1977).

56 MARQUESAS KINGFISHER   Plate 19
Halcyon godeffroyi

Halcyon godeffroyi Finsch, 1877, Proc. Zool. Soc. London, p. 408, Marquesas Islands.

Field identification The only kingfisher in the Marquesas Islands. It resembles the Pacific Kingfisher (53, subspecies *atiu*) in size and the flat bill, the Mangrove Kingfisher (47, subspecies *albicilla*) in the white crown and bright blue upperparts, and both of them in the dark mask and thin black band across a white hindneck. Its distinctive feature is the buff triangle on the upper mantle. Juveniles are very different, with blue crown and black hindneck and breast.

Voice A regularly repeated, short, very deep 'kiau', which can be speeded up into a loud chatter. Call also described as a soft 'treeet-tee-tee'.

Geographical variation None.

Habitat and status Endemic to the south-eastern Marquesas Islands of Hivohoa, Tahuata and Fatuhiva (South Pacific, 139°W). It inhabits primary forest, occurring mainly near streams, and recently has been found only in a few remote valleys. When first discovered it seemed to be rare or uncommon, although a decade later it was described as common on all three islands (Adamson 1939). It is a candidate for the next Red Data Book and is given 'Vulnerable' status by Johnson and Stattersfield (1990).

Food Insects, including beetles and large grasshoppers. Small bones found in one specimen could have been of lizards or fishes.

Habits Solitary or in pairs; rather shy. A vocal bird in its forest habitat. It evidently forages by flycatching within foliage and by diving from a lookout perch to the ground. *Nesting:* two nests have been found: one was in a hole 5 m from the ground in an old mango tree; the other was a hollow with two entrances, dug out by the kingfishers, 2 m up in a decayed screw-pine trunk. *Laying months:* Hivahoa, September-November (by inference).

Description Sexes alike. *Adult:* forehead and crown white, with thin dark shaft-streaks. Lores black; upper ear-coverts blue-black, joined by a narrow black or blue-black band across the nape, deepest in the midline. A thin line of white feather-lets below the eye, bordering the orbital skin. Collar and entire underparts are white; the white of the hindneck extends onto the upper mantle, where it becomes creamy-buff. Lower mantle and remaining upperparts bright blue, brightest and palest on the rump, and tinged with purple on wings and tail. Upper mandible black, lower mandible straw-coloured with black-brown cutting edges and tip; iris dark brown, orbital skin black; legs and feet slaty-grey or black. *Juvenile:* forehead and crown blue-green, pale above the eye, darker on the forecrown. Ear-coverts, cheeks and malar area greenish-black; sides of neck, hindneck and upper mantle black; a small white patch on the nape. Remaining upperparts greener than on the adult, the upperwing-coverts fringed with buffy-white. Chin and throat white, softly striped towards the sides with dark grey; breast black, the larger feathers margined with blue-green; belly and undertail-coverts whitish; flanks white, with dusky marks. *Measurements:* wing of male 96-102, of female 95-102; tail of male 67-71, of female 67-70; bill of male 39-43, of female 38-44; tarsus of male 15-16, of female 15-16.

References Adamson (1939), Forshaw (1985), Holyoak (1975).

57 AFRICAN DWARF KINGFISHER
Ceyx lecontei

Plate 20

Ispidina Lecontei Cassin, 1856, Proc. Acad. Nat. Sci. Philadelphia, 8, p. 158, Moonda River, Gabon.

Field identification Length 10 cm (4 in). The world's smallest kingfisher, a tiny bird of African rainforest. *At rest:* distinguished by its rufous crown and broad black line from eye to eye across the forehead, the adult is otherwise like other small kingfishers, with red bill, dark blue upper-parts, rufous underparts, and a white blaze on the side of the neck. The bill has a curiously flattened, square-ended tip, sometimes obvious in the field but at other times hard to discern. *Confusion species:* the only small African kingfisher with a rufous crown; the African Pygmy Kingfisher (58) is very similar, but has a dark blue crown. Juveniles of both species differ markedly from the adults: the head top and the upperparts are blue-spangled black, bill black with whitish tip, lores, cheeks and underparts buff, moustache blackish and throat white. Juvenile African Dwarf, however, lacks the lilac wash on cheeks and hindneck found on African Pygmy, and it has a bluer rump and dusk-ier moustache than the latter.

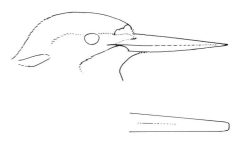

Voice A high-pitched bat-like squeak.

Geographical variation None.

Habitat and range This minute gem of a kingfisher keeps mainly low down inside dark rainforest. It also inhabits dense undergrowth in riverine forest, secondary growth around clearings and at the edge of forest, and sometimes rather more open areas such as waterlogged oil-palm plantations. It occurs from Mt Nimba (Liberia) to south Ghana, from southwest Nigeria (Ife, Benin, Sapele) to west Gabon, and from about 16°E in the Congo Basin to the Western Rift Valley and Mabira Forest in Uganda; there are isolated records from near the mouth of River Congo, from Roca Canzele in north Angola, and from Bengengai in Sudan. Over most of its range it seems to be uncommon, even rare, but it is common in Gabon and in Bwamba, Budongo and Lugalambo Forests in Uganda. It is not migratory, and occurs from sea level up to 1400 m.

Food Small insects, including damselflies, mantises, beetles, beetle larvae, ants, and large flies.

Habits Solitary, or in territorial pairs. This kingfisher perches quietly 1-2 m above the forest floor, and when alarmed readily flies off low down, disappearing into thick undergrowth. It hunts from a low perch for prey, taken from the ground and on the wing; sometimes it attends at ant columns. In courtship, two birds perch facing each other and sing in duet, the bills pointing almost vertically upwards: then the male moves around the still female, keeping about 50 cm away, and trying to keep parallel with her; after a few circuits he suddenly flies rapidly in a tight circle around her, then perches and sings again

(Brosset and Erard 1986). **Nesting:** the burrow, in a low earth bank, is about 15 cm long and ends in a chamber some 15 cm long and 5 cm high. **Laying months:** Cameroon, February; Gabon, November-February.

Description Sexes alike. **Adult:** lores and line around eye black; oval area between eye and nostril pale orange; forehead black; crown rufous, the feathers with small, shiny lilac tips. Sides of head and hindneck lilac, with a large white patch on the side of the neck. Mantle to uppertail-coverts dark purple-blue; tail black; wings black, the larger feathers with narrow purple edges and the upperwing-coverts with bright ultramarine tips. Chin and throat white; remaining underparts and underwing-coverts yellowish-rufous. Bill red-orange; eye dark brown; legs and feet orange-red. **Juvenile:** forehead black; crown feathers black with blue tips, upperwing-coverts the same; mantle and scapular feathers the same, but more blue than black; back and rump bright blue. Lores and ear-coverts buff; moustachial area dusky; chin and throat white, breast greyish-rufous and belly buff. Bill black with whitish tip (not square-tipped as on adults), base of lower mandible reddish; legs brown-orange. **Measurements:** wing of male 45-50, of female 47-55; tail of male 18-22, of female 19-23; bill of male 25-31, of female 25-30; tarsus of male 7-9, of female 8-9. Weight: male 9-11, female 9.5-12.

References Brosset and Erard (1986), Forshaw (1983), Fry (1980b), Fry et al. (1988).

58 AFRICAN PYGMY KINGFISHER   Plate 20
Ceyx pictus

Todus picta Boddaert, 1783, Table Planch. enlum., p. 49, Juida (= St Louis), Senegal.

Field identification Length 12 cm (5 in). A very small kingfisher of dry grassy woodland; only the African Dwarf Kingfisher (57) is smaller. **At rest:** the most distinctive features are the lilac-washed sides of the head, and blue crown with broad rufous eyebrow. **Confusion species:** the aquatic

Malachite Kingfisher (65) has the same red bill and legs, dark blue upperparts, rufous cheeks and breast, and white throat and neck blaze, but its long, narrow forehead and crown feathers are banded pale blue and black and it lacks any rufous eyebrow. The African Dwarf Kingfisher is very like the African Pygmy except in forehead and crown colour; moreover, the two species' habitat preferences, respectively forest and savanna, make their ranges practically exclusive.

Voice A thin, high-pitched 'tseet, tseet'.

Geographical variation There are two similar subspecies in the northern tropics and a rather more distinct one in the southern.

C. p. pictus Senegal to Eritrea, south to Uganda.

C. p. ferrugineus Forest edges and clearings and lush grassland from Guinea-Bissau to west Uganda, south to central Angola, northwest Zambia and north Tanzania. Like *pictus* but darker.

C. p. natalensis Breeds in savannas south of *pictus*, from south Angola to Zanzibar (and perhaps Pemba), Mozambique and east Cape Province; a partial migrant, wintering north to Uganda and south Sudan. Area of blue in crown smaller than in *pictus*, hence a wider rufous eyebrow; a small, bright blue spot above the white neck-flag; underparts paler than in *pictus*.

Habitat and range African Pygmy Kingfishers occur in dry grassland with thickets and trees, often near streams, in thornveld, lush riparian elephant-grass, swampy forest, thick evergreen forest, plantations, fields, large gardens, pasture and arable land. They are widespread throughout sub-Saharan Africa, commonest in tall-grass savannas, penetrating open areas of the equatorial rainforest zone, and uncommon towards their northern and southern limits. The species is absent from east Ethiopia, northeast Kenya, Somalia (except Juba and Webbi Shebelle valleys), and from Namibia, most of Botswana, and South Africa except in the east down to Port Elizabeth. In southern Africa it ranges up to 1500 m and in eastern Africa up to 2000 m.

Migration These kingfishers are breeding visitors to South Africa from October to April or May, Zambia in August-May (commonest in October-March), and Katanga in September-May. In south Malawi they occur all year, although winter and summer populations differ. Southern African birds 'winter' in Rwanda

in March-August and north Zaïre in April-August, some moving as far north as Talanga, Sudan, in June-July. The northern tropical subspecies is a breeding visitor north of 12°-13°N from June to October (north to 17°N in Mauritania), and is resident and partially migrant south of 9°N. They migrate at night, and great numbers are stunned in South Africa and Zimbabwe by colliding with buildings.

Food Grasshoppers, moths, flies, beetles, caterpillars, spiders, small millipedes, small frogs and some aquatic invertebrates.

Habits A quiet, solitary, unobtrusive bird, which hunts from a perch often only 1 m high. It sits patiently for long periods, sometimes bobbing the head or flicking the tail. It drops down to the ground and returns to its perch to treat prey, or pursues an insect in flight, or with a small splash takes prey from the surface of still water. The flight is rather weak but direct, less than 1 m above bare ground. Adults are territorial, using a few favourite perches for weeks on end. In the hand they sometimes twist the neck like a Malachite Kingfisher (which see). **Nesting:** nest burrows are 30-60 cm long, dug by male and female into the banks of streams, erosion gullies and pits, the sides of Aardvark lairs, and into ground termitaria. Four or five eggs are laid at low latitudes and six at high latitudes. Both sexes care for the young; at least in captivity, a pair can raise several broods in quick succession. **Laying months:** Mauritania and Mali, September-November; further south in West Africa, March-October; East Africa, January, March-June and October-November; Zaïre and Angola, January-March, August-October; in the rest of southern Africa, October-December and occasionally until March.

Description *C. p. pictus* Sexes alike. **Adult:** forehead and crown black, the feathers tipped with glossy blue. A wide area above the lore, eye and ear-coverts is rufous. Lores blackish; sides of head lilac, with a large white or buffy patch on the side of the neck; hindneck bright rufous. Mantle to uppertail-coverts dark purple-blue; tail black; wings black, the larger feathers with narrow purple edges and the upperwing-coverts with bright purple tips.

Chin and throat white; remaining under-parts and underwing-coverts yellowish-rufous. Bill red; eye dark brown; legs and feet orange-red. *Juvenile:* like the adult but duller, blues paler, mantle and back mottled, dusky tips to moustachial and breast feathers; bill black with yellowish tip, legs and feet pink. *Measurements:* wing of male 49-53, of female 49-54; tail

of male 22-26, of female 21-26; bill of male 26-28, of female 25-29; tarsus of male 8-9, of female 8-9. Weight: male 11-16, female 9-15.

References Forshaw (1983), Fry (1980a,b), Fry *et al.* (1988), Hanmer (1979, 1980), Jones (1984), Prigogine (1973).

59 ORIENTAL DWARF KINGFISHER   Plate 20
Ceyx erithacus

Alcedo erithaca Linnaeus, 1758, Syst. Nat., ed. 10, I, p. 115, Bengal.

Field identification Length 14 cm (5½ in). Over much of southeast Asia two forms of dwarf kingfisher occur, both orange-yellow below, one lilac-rufous above and the other with dark blue back and wings, a blue-black mark on the forehead and a patch of blue above the white neck blaze. Some authorities treat them as separate species, respectively the Rufous-backed Dwarf Kingfisher *Ceyx rufidorsus* and the Black-backed Dwarf Kingfisher *C. eritha-cus*. The two forms hybridise widely in Borneo, where there is every gradation between rufous- and black-backed forms. There is also some hybridisation in Sumatra and peninsular Malaysia, and for that reason we treat these kingfishers as a single dimorphic species; all the same, north of about Kuala Lumpur black-backed populations are migratory, red-backed ones are sedentary, there is but little hybridisation, and the two forms be-have as distinct species. The red bill, yellow underparts, and violet-rufous upperparts with or without a blue-black back, make Oriental Dwarf Kingfishers impossible to confuse with any other birds in their range.

Voice A high-pitched, shrill or soft 'tsriet-tsriet' in flight.

Geographical variation Three subspecies of black-backed birds are recognised, varying in the amount of lilac suffusion. The first two have rufous-backed forms in Malay Peninsula south of 3°N and in Sumatra and Borneo, where blue and rufous forms freely hybridise (see above).

Van Marle and Voous (1988) recognise two further races from islands lying off Sumatra.

C. e. erithacus Sri Lanka, southwest India north to Bombay, northeast India, Sikkim, Nepal, Burma, Thailand, Indochina and Hainan, south to Singapore, Sumatra and its offlying islands.

C. e. motleyi Borneo, Palawan to Mindoro and Panay (Philippines), and Java to Sumbawa and Flores (Indonesia). Like *erithacus*, but more lilac-washed on the mantle. Only black-backed birds occur in Java to Sumbawa and in the west-ern Philippines except Mindoro.

C. e. macrocarus Nicobar and Andaman Islands, and Nias Island, off west Sumatra. Crown darker and more lilac-washed than in *erithacus*; black spot on forehead sometimes absent.

Habitat and range Oriental Dwarf Kingfishers inhabit primary and secondary forest, deciduous and evergreen, and differ from their African congeners in keeping near forest streams and ponds. They keep low down, and commonly perch and fly within 1-2 m of the forest floor. They range from Bombay to Hainan and the western Philippines, south to Sri Lanka and Java. In several countries they are said to be scarce even in such forests as remain, and they are absent from India except for the southwest and northeast. They are difficult to find, however, like many deep-forest birds, and mist-netting can often show them to be commoner than supposed. In general they seem to be more abundant near the Equator than at higher latitudes; they are rare in Thailand except the south, and are common throughout forested lowland Borneo, ranging up to about 1000 m.

Migration Perhaps its increase in reported abundance from north to south results in large part from the northern birds wintering in southern parts of the breeding range. It is a well-known migrant in southern peninsular Malaysia, where in August-December large numbers of night-flying birds have been found at Fraser's Hill, and a few at Maxwell's Hill and at light stations on many islands up to 60 km off the west coast. The main movement is in August-September, with the return in March. Whether the most northerly parts of the range are entirely vacated in winter is uncertain. In India it is a breeding visitor to many areas, but movements have not been worked out.

Food Mantises, grasshoppers, flies, water-beetles, spiders, and small crabs, frogs and fishes.

Habits Oriental Dwarf Kingfishers forage solitarily, perching on rocks or low down in vegetation and diving into water without submerging to take small animals at or just below the surface. Much prey is taken from the ground. They feed also by flying out to snatch an insect among leaves or in flight low over the surface of water, and have been seen trying to take spiders from their webs (one kingfisher died after being caught in a spider's web). In a ritual dispute, probably territorial, two birds sat upright 20 cm apart on a horizontal twig, facing away, slowly dipped their bodies with heads stretched forwards, then raised and lowered themselves in a long series of alternating bows, one bow every 1-1½ seconds; one bird flew at the other, which seized it by its bill and held it suspended and fluttering below the perch. The entire sequence was repeated twice more, the same individual the aggressor each time (Ali and Ripley 1970). **Nesting:** both birds of a pair excavate the nest burrow, which is about 1 m long when made in a stream-bank or road earth cutting well away from water, but shorter when dug into a ground termite-hill or soil in the roots of a fallen tree. One pair dug 25 cm of their burrow, in sand, in only 40 minutes. The burrow ends in an unlined chamber 13-15 cm wide and 5-7 cm high. The clutch is of 3-7 eggs. **Laying months:** Sri Lanka, February-June; southwest India, July-September; northeast India, April-May; Malaysia, May; Java, December-May; Sumatra, March.

Description *C. e. erithacus* Sexes alike. ***Adult, black-backed form:*** head top and hindneck rufous with strong lilac wash and some feathers tipped with violet. A small black patch in the middle of the forehead; lores black, frontal area pale buff. Ear-coverts, cheeks, malar region and sides of the neck orange. A yellowish-white blaze on the side of the neck, with a same-sized dark blue patch just above it. Mantle rufous; upper back dark blue, lower back rufous, rump and uppertail-coverts lilac, tail rufous. Scapulars and tertials deep blue; wings black, most coverts blue-fringed. Chin and throat white or pale yellow; remaining underparts and underwing-coverts bright rufescent yellow. Bill red; eye dark brown, orbital skin blackish; legs and feet red, only three toes. ***Adult, rufous-backed form:*** the same, except that all blue parts are violet-washed rufous. ***Juvenile:*** like the adults but duller, with much less lilac wash; chin, throat and belly white; tail sometimes dusky-tipped; bill yellow-orange with a pale tip. Juveniles of the black-backed form lack blue, except in the scapulars and wing-coverts. ***Measurements:*** wing of male 53-60, of female 54-64; tail of male 20-24, of female 20-26; bill of male 35-38, of female 30-40; tarsus of male 9-10, of female 9-10. Weight: male 14-20, female 14-16.

References Forshaw (1983), Fry (1980a), van Marle and Voous (1988), Medway and Wells (1976).

60 PHILIPPINE DWARF KINGFISHER

Plate 20

Ceyx melanurus

Alcedo melanura Kaup, 1848, Verh. Naturh. Ver. Grosshurz. Hessen, 2, p. 74, Philippines.

Field identification Length 12 cm (5 in). A brilliant little rufous-and-lilac forest kingfisher with red bill and legs, white throat, blue-black wings, a white-and-blue blaze at the side of the neck, and a black V-mark on the back. ***Confusion species:*** Philippine Dwarf Kingfishers are similar to the rufous-backed form of the Oriental Dwarf Kingfisher (59), but nowhere do the two species occur on the same island; the Oriental Dwarf differs mainly in having bright orange-yellow underparts. In the southern Philippine islands the Philippine Dwarf overlaps broadly with the Silvery Kingfisher (67: a blue-black and white bird) and the Variable Dwarf Kingfisher (63: blue upperparts), and in the northern islands with the Philippine Pectoral Kingfisher (68: blue upperparts).

Voice A high-pitched squeak.

Geographical variation Three subspecies.
   C. m. melanurus Luzon and Polillo Islands.
   C. m. samarensis Samar and Leyte Islands. Back darker than in *melanurus* and head more intensely lilac-washed; larger, darker blue spots in the wing-coverts; wing and bill about 10% longer.
   C. m. platenae Basilan and Mindanao Islands. Like *melanurus*, but it lacks a blue spot above the white neck blaze, the wing-covert speckles are lilac, and the wings are fringed with chestnut. The same size as *samarensis*.

Habitat and range A scarce bird of dense primary lowland forest, up to 600 m in altitude, known only from Luzon, Mindanao, Samar and Leyte, and Polillo (east of Luzon) and Basilan (west of Mindanao).

Food Insects.

Habits It is a poorly known, solitary, shy bird that keeps well down in the forest substage. Nest and breeding habits have not been described.

Description *C. m. melanurus* Sexes alike. ***Adult:*** head rufous, strongly suffused with lilac at the sides and on the hindneck; lores buffy; sometimes a few blackish feathers at the front of the forehead; and a white blaze at the side of the neck with a dark blue patch above it. Mantle violet-rufous, with a black line between it and the rufous scapulars; back, rump and uppertail-coverts rufous; short tail rufous with concealed blackish sides. Wings black, the coverts minutely spotted with bright blue. Chin and throat white; breast and flanks bright lilac-rufous; belly whitish; undertail-coverts and underwing-coverts rufous. Bill scarlet; eye dark brown, orbital skin black; legs and feet red, only three toes. ***Juvenile:*** duller than the adult, with much less lilac; bill orange with a pale tip. ***Measurements:*** wing of male 54-58, of female 54-58; tail of male 19-20, of female 17-20; bill of male 33-35, of female 32-35; tarsus of male 9-10, of female 9-10.

References Forshaw (1983), Fry (1980a,b).

61 CELEBES DWARF KINGFISHER

Ceyx fallax

Plate 20

Dacelo fallax Schlegel, 1866, Ned. Tijdschr. Dierk., 3, p. 187, Celebes.

Field identification Length 12 cm (5 in). The only *Ceyx* kingfisher in Sulawesi, where its red bill, rufous-brown back and lilac cheeks distinguish it from the two other small kingfishers, the Blue-eared (75) and the River (76). *At rest:* red bill, blue-speckled blackish head top, rufous-lilac cheeks and ear-coverts, dark rufous back, bright blue rump, and yellow-rufous underparts are distinctive. *Confusion species:* in flight the blue rump makes it look like Blue-eared and River Kingfishers, which are, however, riverside birds (not forest-dwellers) and are larger.

Voice Not described.

Geographical variation Two subspecies.
   C. f. fallax Sulawesi, Indonesia.
   C. f. sangirensis Sangihe Island, between Sulawesi and Philippines. Blue bars on the crown are larger and more lustrous than in *fallax*; superciliary area black, not violet; wings and rump more violaceous. About 10% larger.

Habitat and range Lowland forest from sea level up to 1000 m, in Sulawesi and Sangihe Islands. The bird does not seek the proximity of water. It is doubtless resident.

Food A grasshopper and an 11-cm lizard have been recorded.

Habits Solitary or in pairs, keeping low down in the forest, and evidently behaving in much the same way as better-known *Ceyx* species. *Nesting:* only one nest has been found: a tunnel in an earthen bank set back from a river, in October (Watling 1983).

Description *C. f. fallax* Sexes alike. *Adult:* forehead and crown black, each feather with a glossy blue tip. Lore buff; superciliary area, cheeks, moustachial area and sides of neck lilac; ear-coverts rufous. A buffy-white blaze on the side of the neck; hindneck, mantle and scapulars dark rufous-brown; back, rump and uppertail-coverts brilliant cobalt-blue; tail black. Wings brown-black, the lesser and median coverts tipped with glossy lilac; greater coverts, tertials and secondaries broadly edged with dark rufous. Chin and throat cream, breast dark orange, flanks, belly, undertail-coverts and underwing-coverts paler orange. The breast and uppertail-coverts generally have a strong violaceous wash. Bill red; eye dark brown; legs and feet orange-red; fourth toe vestigial, not nailed, with a single bone <2 mm long. *Juvenile:* upperparts darker and duller than on the adults; the plumage lacks the violaceous wash; bill blackish with a pale tip. *Measurements:* wing of male 56-59, of female 57-61; tail of male 19-22, of female 21-22; bill of male 28-38, of female 34-37; tarsus of male 8-10, of female 9-10.

References Forshaw (1983), Fry (1980b).

62 MADAGASCAR PYGMY KINGFISHER

Ceyx madagascariensis

Plate 20

Alcedo madagascariensis Linnaeus, 1766, Syst. Nat., ed. 12, I, p. 179, Madagascar.

Field identification Length 12 cm (5 in). One of only two kingfishers in Madagascar, both small. It is a rufous bird with red bill, white neck blaze and mainly white underparts, and can never be mistaken for the Madagascar Malachite (66), a purple, azure and orange kingfisher.

Voice A high-pitched squeak.

Geographical variation Two subspecies.

C. m. madagascariensis Madagascar up to about 1800 m, except for the arid southwest.

C. m. dilutus Known from a single specimen taken in the early 1970s at Sakaraha in arid southwest Madagascar; a pale bird with hardly any lilac wash.

Habitat and range Preferred habitats are much like those of African Pygmy Kingfishers (58) in Africa: dry grassy woodland, scrub, and the edges and interior of wet evergreen forest. This species is scarce in the west of Madagascar, but common in the east and also in Ambre Mountain and Sambirano River regions. It appears to be sedentary.

Food Largely frogs; also a variety of insects, larvae, spiders, shrimps, and small lizards.

Habits From what little is on record, the habits of this bird seem to be typically those of its genus. **Nesting:** burrows are excavated in earth banks. Two tunnels were 5 cm in diameter and 30-35 cm long. The clutch is of four eggs. **Laying month:** November.

Description *C. m. madagascariensis* Sexes alike. **Adult:** bright foxy-rufous, except for blackish primaries, white chin and throat, centre of breast, belly and undertail-coverts, and a white oblong on the side of the neck. There is a strong violet or lilac wash on the lower back, rump, hindcheeks, sides of the neck and hindneck. Bill red; eye dark brown; legs and feet red. **Juvenile:** like the adult but duller, with less violet wash; bill blackish with a pale tip. **Measurements:** wing of male 54-60, of female 55-61; tail of male 24-29, of female 24-29; bill of male 29-34, of female 28-32; tarsus of male 9-11, of female 9-11. Weight: male 17-21, female 17-22.

References Benson *et al.* (1976), Forshaw (1983), Fry (1980a,b), Milon *et al.* (1973), Rand (1936).

63 VARIABLE DWARF KINGFISHER   Plate 21
Alcedo lepida

Ceyx lepidus Temminck, 1836, Planch. Col., 100, pl. 595, Amboina.

Geographical variation From the Philippines to the Solomons, the range of this little kingfisher embraces hundreds of islands, and its 14 subspecies vary greatly. The bill is black, red, black-and-red or black-and-yellow, somewhat flattened either laterally or dorsoventrally. There are various combinations of blue or black upperparts with blue or silvery rump and rufous, yellow or white underparts. In one subspecies (*dispar*) male and female are quite different in head markings; in all the others the sexes are alike.

Field identification Length 14 cm (5½ in). With such variety, common characters are not easy to pinpoint, but all subspecies whistle sibilantly, perch low down in the shaded interior of forest, and characteristically fly slowly but with rapid wingbeats. No single plumage feature is diagnostic. In the Philippines, Variable Dwarf Kingfishers have pale blue and dark blue phases and are red-billed; the only other red-billed small kingfishers there, Oriental Dwarf and Philippine Dwarf (59, 60), have violet-rufous (not blue) crowns. Variable is the only red-billed small kingfisher in the Moluccas. The mainland New Guinea form is black-billed and differs from the only other small kingfisher there, the Little (74), in having orange (not white) underparts. Another New Guinea species with black bill and rufous underparts is the Azure Kingfisher (72), which is much larger and has uniformly dark blue upperparts, whereas Variable has a brilliant blue rump contrasting with blackish head and wings. East of mainland New Guinea, from New Britain and New Hanover to the easternmost Solomon Islands, the seven subspecies of Variable

Dwarf Kingfishers are sympatric with the Bismarck Kingfisher (73: three times as heavy; rump dark blue, not silvery), the River Kingfisher (76: barred crown, rufous ear-coverts), and the Little Kingfisher (underparts white, not yellow). On San Cristóbal Island, southeast Solomons, the Variable Dwarf Kingfisher has white underparts and thereby resembles the Little Kingfisher, which, however, occurs no closer than Guadalcanal Island.

Voice A shrill, wheezy 'tzeeip', sometimes uttered almost continuously in flight.

Subspecies Some of the 14 races, particularly in the Philippines and Moluccas, recall typical *Ceyx* kingfishers (59, 60, 61) in their dorsoventrally flattened bill and in plumage. Others, with laterally flattened black bills, are like *Alcedo* kingfishers. Authorities have been divided about the generic allocation of this and the Silvery Kingfisher (67), which are three-toed like *Ceyx* but have *Alcedo* bill shape and colour (Schodde 1977; Forshaw 1983). Contrary to our former treatment (Fry 1980a), we now place them in *Alcedo*, partly out of convenience.

A. l. lepida Southern Moluccas: Ceram and adjacent islands except Buru. Bill red; head and wings black, washed and spotted with dark blue; frontal spot orange; malar stripe blue-black; back to uppertail-coverts brilliant ultramarine-blue, rump silvery-blue; chin and throat yellowish-white, remaining underparts rich orange.

A. l. cajeli Buru Island, west of Ceram. Like *lepida*, but bill stout, throat white, blackish head and wings almost without dark blue; back to uppertail-coverts brilliant silvery-blue; frontal spot and underparts yellow-orange.

A. l. uropygialis Northern Moluccas. Darker, less blue above than *lepida*; underparts darker; bill more slender.

A. l. wallacii Sula Islands, northwest of Buru. Like *lepida*, but blue spots on head and wings paler; back to rump brilliant pale cobalt-blue, uppertail-coverts ultramarine-blue.

A. l. margarethae Southern Philippines: Negros, Cebu, Tablas, Banton, Romblon, Sibuyan, Siquijor, Mindanao, Basilan, Jolo and Balimbing. *Pale phase:* like *lepida*, but upperparts pale cobalt-blue, brightest and silvery on rump; supraloral area darker chestnut; malar stripe orange; belly paler yellow. *Dark phase:* the same, but blues are ultramarine.

A. l. solitaria Mainland New Guinea, Aru Islands, Western Papuan Islands, islands in Geelvink Bay, Karkar Island and D'Entrecasteaux Archipelago. Differs from *lepida* in having the bill black, frontal spot yellowish-white, and rump brilliant ultramarine-blue (not silvery).

A. l. sacerdotis New Britain and Rooke Island. Like *lepida*, but upper mandible dusky red (lower mandible red); rump as in *solitaria*; belly and undertail-coverts very pale orange-yellow.

A. l. dispar Admiralty Islands. **Male:** like *lepida*, but mantle to rump brilliant pale silvery-blue, uppertail-coverts darker, wings more ultramarine; breast dark rufous; legs and feet red. **Female:** head orange, with blue-black restricted to a stripe on the hindcrown and an area in front of the white neck blaze; lore and small area around front of eye black; chin and throat white.

A. l. mulcata New Hanover, New Ireland and Lihir Islands. Like *lepida*, but bill black.

A. l. meeki Bougainville, Buka, and from Choiseul to Santa Ysabel Islands (Papua New Guinea and Solomons). Bill black; frontal spot, neck blaze and underparts pale yellowish-buff on male, more orange-yellow on female. Head and wings blue-black, spangled with pale blue; lower mantle to uppertail-coverts pale blue, silvery on rump; legs and feet flesh-pink.

A. l. collectoris Vella Lavella to Gatukai Islands, Solomons. Bill red, stouter than in *lepida*; upperparts darker blue than *lepida*, and back and rump brilliant purple-blue.

A. l. nigromaxilla Guadalcanal, Solomons. Like *collectoris*, except that upper mandible is mainly black and lower mandible mainly orange-red.

A. l. malaitae Malaita, Solomons. Known only from one specimen described in 1935: a bird like *nigromaxilla*, but much paler above and below, and with the lower mandible yellow (Forshaw 1983).

A. l. gentiana San Cristóbal, Solomons. Bill black; frontal spot and entire underparts white.

Habitat and range Variable Dwarf Kingfishers frequent primary and secondary rainforest, monsoon forest, overgrown plantations, and thick growth fringing streams. They feed away from water, but often visit forest streams to bathe. In forests throughout their vast range from the central Philippines and Sula Islands to the eastern Solomon Islands they are common birds, keeping to the substage and mid-stage, and ranging from sea level up to 1000 m on Karkar and Bougainville, 1200 m on Guadalcanal and 1300 m in mainland New Guinea. A ringing study showed that they are sedentary; some were retrapped at the ringing site up to 6½ years later (Bell 1981).

Food Dragonflies, grasshoppers, locusts, spiders and small frogs.

Habits Dwarf kingfishers are solitary and shy. A bird forages by sitting on a low perch, searching below, around and even above it, bobbing the head and occasionally briefly cocking the tail – movements that can be surprisingly vigorous. Dragonflies and similar insects are taken on the wing in swift, direct, darting flight low over forest pools (Coates 1985). The birds bathe several times a day, dive-bombing into water and rebounding to the perch several times until well soaked, and then preening (Coates 1985). **Nesting:** the clutch of two eggs is laid at the end of a short burrow dug by both parents in some perpendicular earthen face: a stream-bank, the side of a pit, earth in the roots of

a fallen tree, and on Bougainville Island sometimes in termitaria. *Laying months:* New Guinea (Brown River), November; New Britain, about September; Bougainville, September.

Description *A. l. lepida* Sexes alike. *Adult:* frontal spot orange, surrounded by black; forehead, crown, malar area, cheeks, ear-coverts and hindneck glossy blue-black, each feather shaft-streaked with pale blue and tipped with bright blue. A long wedge of white on the side of the neck. Mantle, scapulars and wings glossy deep blue, the wing-coverts spangled with bright blue spots like the crown. Upper back to uppertail-coverts brilliant ultramarine-blue, brightest on the rump. Chin and throat white or yellowish-white; remaining underparts and underwing-coverts rich orange, with a small dark blue patch at the side of the breast, confluent with the closed wing. Bill red; eye dark brown; legs and feet orange-yellow, only three toes. *Juvenile:* upperparts slightly less blue, more blackish than on adults; bill orange, with dusky base and pale tip. *Measurements:* wing of male 59-65, of female 59-67; tail of male 21-25, of female 22-25; bill of male 33-40, of female 33-40; tarsus of male 9-11, of female 9-11. Weight (*A. l. uropygialis* and *solitaria*): male 11-21, female 13-24.

References Coates (1985), Forshaw (1983).

64 WHITE-BELLIED KINGFISHER   Plate 22
Alcedo leucogaster

Halcyon leucogaster Fraser, 1843, Proc. Zool. Soc. London, pt II, p. 4, Clarence, Fernando Póo.

Field identification Length 13 cm (5 in). A small, ultramarine-blue, chestnut and white forest kingfisher, distinguished by its red bill and mainly white underparts. The upperparts are deep glossy ultramarine, the crown not crested nor strongly banded; sides of head and body are rich rufous-chestnut, contrasting sharply with white in the midline from chin to belly. *Confusion species:* the African Dwarf Kingfisher (57), a tiny bird, is immediately

told by its rufous head. The Malachite Kingfisher (65) can occur in the same habitats as White-bellied, although it is generally by water; it has noticeably long crown feathers banded black and pale blue, and its underparts are more uniform rufous with pale throat and belly.

Voice Not known.

Geographical variation We recognise four

subspecies, although more have been described.

A. l. leucogaster From southwest Nigeria to south Cameroon, Bioko Island, Gabon and northwest Angola.

A. l. bowdleri South Mauritania (Guidimaka), southwest Mali (Mandingo Mountains), and Guinea to south Ghana. Rufous area from nostril to above the eye and ear is broader than in *leucogaster*; malar feathers lack dusky tips. A storm-blown bird caught in north Nigeria was intermediate in character, nearer to *bowdleri* than to *leucogaster*.

A. l. nais Principe Island. Superciliary area blue, not rufous; crown paler and bluer than in *leucogaster*, the feathers longer and distinctly banded with black and glossy blue; scapulars with more conspicuous ultramarine edges; breast pale rufous; belly white only in the middle. Juveniles have the crown and malar area strongly black-barred, and the breast dusky.

A. l. leopoldi Congo Basin, from east Congo across Zaïre to southwest Uganda (Sango Bay, Mabira Forest) and northwest Zambia (Salujinga, Isombu). Paler than *leucogaster*; crown barred black and greenish-blue; superciliary area blue, not rufous.

Habitat and range White-bellied Kingfishers are birds of dense primary and secondary forest, keeping mainly within 2 m of ground level, in shade. They occur in tangled vegetation along streams, in wooded swampy glades, along rushing bouldery streams, in mangrove swamps and tidal estuaries, open undergrowth in dry forest, *Marquesia* thickets, and gallery forests. On Principe Island they keep to quite open, dry vegetation and occur in secondary forest, gardens and cocoa plantations and occasionally at ponds. Ranging from Mauritania to Lake Victoria and from Bioko and Principe to Canzele, Quiculango and Cuanza Norte in Angola, from sea level up to 1200 m, they seem to be generally rather uncommon, but are numerous in Gabon, Principe Island and southwest Mali. They are not migratory.

Food Fish and insects about equally: dragonflies, damselflies, aquatic insect larvae, roaches, beetles, termites, ants, wasps, crabs, spiders, earthworms, frogs, tadpoles, lizards and fish.

Habits An unobtrusive, solitary bird which perches low down, intently watching the ground or a stream, from time to time bobbing the head and quickly cocking the tail. Its flight is fast, direct and low. **Nesting:** burrows are dug into streambanks and sloping ground. The clutch is of two eggs. **Laying months:** Cameroon, July, October; Principe Island, December-January; Gabon, December or earlier.

Description *A. l. leucogaster* Sexes alike. **Adult:** frontal spot rufous; narrow superciliary band rufous with lilac tinge; forehead and crown blue-black, the feathers subtly barred with glossy ultramarine-blue. Lore dusky; malar area, cheeks and ear-coverts wine-chestnut; a white blaze on the side of the neck; hindneck to tail ultramarine, the rump more brilliant. Wings blackish, the coverts tipped with glossy ultramarine. Sides of the breast and flanks rufous-chestnut; remaining underparts snowy-white. Bill orange-red, browner on the culmen; eye dark brown; legs and feet red. **Juvenile:** like the adult, but mantle spangled with blue; crown more strongly barred; bill black. **Measurements:** wing of male 54-65, of female 55-63; tail of male 21-26, of female 21-26; bill of male 31-37, of female 31-35; tarsus of male 8-10, of female 8-10. Weight (*C. l. bowdleri*): males average 14.5, females 14.7.

References Forshaw (1983), Fry *et al.* (1988a,b), Fry and de Naurois (1984).

Alcedo cristata Pallas, 1764, in Vroeg's Cat., Adumbr., p. I, Cape of Good Hope.

Field identification Length 13 cm (5 in). This is much the commonest small water-side kingfisher of Africa. It is distinguished by its red bill (black on juveniles), black-and-pale-blue striped forehead and crown with long feathers which usually lie flat but sometimes fan out from the sides of the crown, deep blue upperparts and rufous cheeks and underparts. **Confusion species:** from the African Pygmy Kingfisher (58) it can be told by its blue (not rufous) eyebrow and rufous (not violet) cheeks and ear-coverts: both have red bill and legs and a white neck blaze; the African Pygmy has a more uniform crown and underparts, and its crown feathers are not long. Juvenile Malachite Kingfishers are dusky brown where adults are rufous; they are distinguished from juvenile African Pygmy Kingfishers by the lack of violet on the cheeks and neck and by the dusky (not orange) breast. Adult Malachites differ from White-bellied Kingfishers (64) in having a more variegated crown and in lacking a clear-cut white midline from breast to belly.

Voice A short, shrill 'seek' or 'kweek', often repeated. The song, uttered in duet, is 'ii-tiii-cha-cha, chui chui tuiichui chui', ending with a chuckle.

Geographical variation Four or five subspecies have been recognised in mainland Africa (Clancey 1990); we recognise three, and also a distinctive one on São Tomé Island (Fry and de Naurois 1984), formerly made a race of White-bellied Kingfisher or treated as a full species (Forshaw 1983).

A. c. galerita Senegal to about Ghana.

A. c. thomensis São Tomé Island. Crown feathers shorter, dark blue, not so conspicuously banded; malar area with dusky bars; rufous frontal spot small; rump purple-blue; cheeks and underparts darker rufous than in *galerita*; underparts uniform. Juveniles have black ear-coverts, cheeks, malar area and neck (with a white blaze) and brown-black breast and mantle. Large: wing 57-64 mm, tail 26-30 mm, bill 34-38 mm.

A. c. cristata From about Nigeria east to Sudan, Uganda and Kenya, and south to south Angola, southwest Zambia, Mozambique and South Africa. Underparts much paler rufous than in *galerita*, and belly pale buff or whitish.

A. c. stuartkeithi Ethiopia and adjacently in Sudan (Blue Nile) and Somalia. Like *galerita*, but rump and vent slightly paler (Dickerman 1989).

Habitat and range This kingfisher inhabits reeds and rank vegetation fringing ponds and slow-flowing rivers throughout all sub-Saharan Africa except for arid parts of Somalia, Kenya, Namibia and Botswana. It frequents marshes, dams, sheltered shores, tidal estuaries, papyrus-beds, mangrove, gravel-pits, sewage ponds and forested waterways. It is common, even abundant, in low-lying equatorial savanna country, reaching a density of four pairs per kilometre of Lake Naivasha's shoreline. At higher latitude and altitude it becomes less abundant, although often common and widespread. Above 2000 m it is uncommon, but it occurs as high as 3000 m in East Africa. Malachite Kingfishers are sparse in the tropical rainforest belt, common on São Tomé, Pemba, Zanzibar and Mafia Islands, frequent north to about 15°N, from Senegal River valley to Khartoum and Kassala, but they do not reach the Red Sea nor Somalia east of 46°E (Webbi Shebelle valley), nor northeast Kenya (where they are, however, common on Lake Turkana).

Migration Strictly sedentary on Lake Naivasha, this kingfisher seems to be partially migratory at high latitudes and even on the Equator in Gabon, where, at M'Passa, it is present only from December to March. In north Nigeria it is commoner in June-November than at other seasons. In south Malaŵi adults are sedentary but young birds disperse widely; they are often killed at night by flying into windows, in South Africa mainly in May-August. At Barbersban, Transvaal,

Malachite Kingfishers are uncommon visitors from about March to September.

Food Water-beetles, water boatmen, aquatic insect larvae, small prawns and crabs, tadpoles, small frogs and fish. Some prey are taken on land – mantises, beetles, grasshoppers and lizards. Birds studied on Lake Naivasha each ate 15-20 fish (*Tilapia grahami*) daily, and when breeding twice that number, with a further 60-70 fed daily to five nestlings.

Habits Malachite Kingfishers live solitarily or in pairs; they are territorial birds and not particularly shy. Perching low over water on a reed, twig, stump or rock, an individual searches intently for prey, and suddenly raises and lowers its crest, the long feathers disarrayed and often blown forwards; diving steeply into the surface with a small splash, the hunter bobs up immediately and carries its prey crosswise or head-first in its bill back to the perch, where it is immobilised by beating and swallowed whole. Sometimes these birds hunt along seashores, perching on rocks. Malachite Kingfishers mist-netted and handled almost always perform a curious display: with the bill slightly open and the long, banded forehead feathers sticking straight up or falling sideways, the head is turned stiffly from side to side in a series of tremulous jerks; no noise is uttered. *Nesting:* both sexes dig the burrow, choosing a stream-bank, pit, road cutting, earth mound or, less commonly, soil compacted in the roots of a fallen tree, or the side of an Aardvark lair. Burrows are 25-120 cm long, straight or curving a little to one side, and slightly inclining; often the pair starts to dig two or three adjacent burrows at once, but only one is finished for use. Three or four clutches of 3-6 eggs are laid in quick succession, in a season lasting 4-6 months. In Kenya a pair reared nine young from three broods in four months, and a captive pair in Malaŵi, which first nested when only six months old, raised 14 young from four broods in 4½ months. **Laying months:** West Africa, April-December, in general later in the north than in the south; Uganda, March, May, July, October-November; south Kenya and east Tanzania, April-May, July, October, December; Zambia, all months except July, but mainly February-March and June-September; Malaŵi and south Mozambique, September-June; Zimbabwe and South Africa, August-February, mainly September-October.

Description *A. c. galerita* Sexes alike. *Adult:* forehead black in midline with large rufous frontal spot. Forehead and crown feathers long, particularly at the sides, and strikingly banded with black and pale blue or greenish-blue. Ear-coverts, cheeks and malar area rufous, sharply demarcated from the white chin and throat and from the white blaze at the side of the neck. Hindneck and remaining upperparts glossy ultramarine-blue. The white throat merges into deep orange-rufous on the breast, flanks, belly and undertail-coverts. Bill red; eye dark brown; legs and feet orange-red. *Juvenile:* like the adult, but duller, duskier, and black-billed. Feathers of forehead and crown are broader, shorter, the blues greenish, with wider black banding; mantle and wing-coverts sooty-black, spangled with bright blue. All rufous parts are suffused with brown – the frontal spot buffy, and cheeks, malar area and breast speckled with black. Some birds (e.g. in Landana, Angola) have the cheeks and malar area heavily black-speckled and the neck and breast brownish-black. The black bill starts to turn red at about three months. **Measurements:** wing of male 53-60, of female 55-59; tail of male 23-27, of female 23-27; bill of male 30-36, of female 31-37; tarsus of male 8-10, of female 8-10. Weight: 12-18.

References Forshaw (1983), Fry *et al.* (1988), Fry and de Naurois (1984), Meadows (1977).

Alcedo vintsioides

Alcedo Vintsioides Eydoux and Gervais, 1836, Voyage de la 'Favorite', in Mag. Zool. Bot., p. 30, pl. 74, Madagascar.

Field identification Length 13 cm (5 in). *At rest:* the strikingly crested black-and-green-barred crown, dark blue upperparts, rufous underparts and blackish bill, and in flight the brilliant azure lower back and rump, are all diagnostic. **Confusion species:** Madagascar Pygmy Kingfishers (62), the only other kingfisher in the Malagasy Region, differ in all of the above respects. The two share only white neck blaze, white chin and red legs.

Voice A shrill, high-pitched monosyllable.

Geographical variation *Alcedo vintsioides* ('Vintsy' is the old Malgache name for kingfisher) is a close relative of *A. cristata* (65) in Africa. It has two subspecies.
   A. v. vintsioides Madagascar. Blues purplish.
   A. v. johannae Comoro Islands. Blues paler and greener than in *vintsioides*.

Habitat and range Somewhat less reliant upon water than is its African counterpart, the Madagascar Malachite Kingfisher is nonetheless a far more aquatic bird than the Madagascar Pygmy Kingfisher. It ranges from sea level up to 1800 m, living in tree- and reed-fringed waterways in open country, swamps, paddyfields, coconut plantations, mangrove, sea coasts, estuaries, tide-pools, and streams and clearings in forest. Sometimes it occurs far from water, and in arid southwest Madagascar it has been seen in coastal scrub. Elsewhere in Madagascar, and in the Comoros (where it is the only kingfisher), it is a common bird. On Grand Comoro, a volcanic island without permanent streams, it keeps mainly to the coast and a crater lake. So far as is known it is sedentary.

Food Small fishes, frogs and marine and freshwater crustaceans; aquatic insects, also grasshoppers, bugs, flies and beetles.

Habits A solitary bird with foraging behaviour much like that of the African Malachite (Benson 1960; Benson *et al.* 1976). An individual watched on the Grand Comoro coast sat on rocks exposed at low tide 10 m away from a low rocky cliff, and repeatedly flew to seize small crabs hiding in crevices in the cliff, carrying them back to the rocks to eat (Louette 1983). **Nesting:** nest burrows about 5 cm wide and 40 cm long are excavated by both sexes in an earth bank by a stream or path. Male and female incubate the 3-6 eggs and care for the young. **Laying months:** Comoros, October; Madagascar, November. The breeding season evidently extends to April (Rand 1936).

Description *A. v. vintsioides* Sexes alike. **Adult:** forehead, eyebrow and hindneck evenly banded black and pale green-blue; feathers of the forecrown and particularly the hindcrown are long, broad, floppy and round-ended, striped black and blue, with a pale green border and large subterminal black patch. A small rufous frontal line or spot; malar area deep rufous with a few dusky feather tips, sharply demarcated from the white chin and throat; ear-coverts rich rufous with a purple-blue area behind, and cheeks rich rufous with a white neck blaze behind. Mantle, wings and tail deep ultramarine, back and rump paler, bright azure-blue; underparts below throat rich rufous, paler on belly. Bill black with brown-red base; eye dark brown; legs and feet orange-red. **Juvenile:** like the adult but duller; mantle, scapulars and wing-coverts blacker, spangled with bright blue; rufous parts browner, and in particular breast and belly are buff rather than rufous. Bill blackish. **Measurements:** wing of male 57-61, of female 56-64; tail of male 25-29, of female 24-29; bill of male 31-37, of female 31-37; tarsus of male 9-10, of female 9-10. Weight: male 16.5-21, female 18-22.

References Benson (1960), Benson *et al.* (1976), Forbes-Watson (1969), Forshaw (1983), Fry (1980b), Rand (1936).

Alcedo argentata

Ceyx argentata Tweeddale, 1877, Ann. Mag. Nat. Hist., (4) 20, p. 533, Dinagat, Philippine Islands.

Field identification Length 14 cm (5½ in). A very small, black-and-white kingfisher confined to forest streams in the southern Philippines. Unmistakable: blackish, with black bill, white spots around the crown, white neck blaze, white back and rump, large white throat-patch, and white mark on the blackish belly. Legs red. Frontal spot, neck blaze and throat are pale rufous on young birds. **Confusion species:** the Variable Dwarf Kingfisher (63) has a red bill and orange underparts; the Philippine Pectoral Kingfisher (68) has black-and-red bill and orange underparts with blue breast-bands.

Voice A high-pitched 'cheet', in flight.

Geographical variation Birds from Bohol, Leyte and Samar Islands, *A. a. flumenicola*, differ from the nominate subspecies in having the flanks and breast purplish-blue, and the loral spot, neck blaze and throat pale yellow-cream. They are about 10% smaller than *A. a. argentata*.

Habitat and range A strictly aquatic kingfisher, inhabiting streams and small rivers in primary rainforest or, in cleared countryside, rivers with well-timbered banks and dense overhanging growth. It is fairly common along streams in remnant dipterocarp and secondary forests in Mindanao, and is known to occur on Negros, Panay, Basilan, Cebu, Dinagat, Siargao, Bohol, Leyte and Samar Islands.

Food The diet is known to include small fishes and crabs.

Habits From what little has been recorded, its feeding habits seem to be like those of the River Kingfisher (76). No nests have been found, nor breeding behaviour described.

Description *A. a. argentata* Sexes alike. **Adult:** head black, with a small white frontal spot, and scattered crescentic white or very pale blue feather tips mainly at the sides of the crown and hindneck; white blaze on the side of the neck. Scapulars and wings black, the median coverts with large, crescentic white or bluish-white tips. Upper back to uppertail-coverts white, most feathers narrowly tipped with pale azure-blue. Tail black. Chin, throat and upper breast white, sharply demarcated from the surrounding black. Lower breast, flanks and undertail-coverts black, washed with dull blue; belly the same, with a small white patch in the centre. Bill black; eye dark brown; legs and feet orange-red, only three toes. **Juvenile:** like the adult, but frontal spot and neck blaze warm buff or pale rufous, and chin to upper breast creamy-buff. **Measurements:** wing of male 60-66, of female 61-68; tail of male 21-26, of female 23-25; bill of male 37-42, of female 36-41; tarsus of male 9-11, of female 9-11.

Reference Forshaw (1983).

68 PHILIPPINE PECTORAL KINGFISHER   Plate 23
Alcedo cyanopecta

Ceyx cyanopectus Lafresnaye, 1840, Revue Zool., p. 33, type locality unknown (= Luzon, Philippines).

Field identification Length 13 cm (5 in). A handsome small Philippines kingfisher, with pale-spangled dark blue upperparts, brilliant azure back and rump, and rufous underparts with one (female) or 1-2 (male) distinct ultramarine breast-bands. The bill is black, in northern islands with the lower mandible red. ***Confusion species:*** Variable Dwarf Kingfishers (63), which overlap with Philippine Pectorals only on Sibuyan, Negros and Cebu Islands, are rather similar but have all-red bill and all-rufous underparts. Silvery Kingfishers (67) overlap with Philippine Pectoral Kingfishers on Panay, Negros and Cebu Islands, and are readily distinguished by their all-black bill, large white throat-patch and blackish underparts. Philippine Dwarf Kingfishers (60), which occur together with Philippine Pectorals only on Luzon and Polillo, are quite different, being mainly rufous. Another red-billed kingfisher, the Oriental Dwarf (59), found with the present species on Mindoro and Panay, differs even more on account of its rufous head and yellow underparts.

Voice A thin, high-pitched monosyllable.

Geographical variation There are two subspecies.
   A. c. cyanopecta Northern Philippines: Luzon, Polillo, Mindoro, Marinduque, Masbate, Sibuyan and Ticao Islands.
   A. c. nigrirostris Central Philippines: Panay, Negros and Cebu Islands. Upperparts paler and more spangled, and underparts darker rufous than in *cyanopecta*. Entire bill black. Males and females have a single breast-band, incomplete on females.

Habitat and range This kingfisher lives on rivers and streams with thickly forested banks, but near the coast it also inhabits *Nipa* palm swamps and mangrove. Northern and central Philippines only.

Food Aquatic insects and small fishes.

Habits A solitary bird which perches on rocks and low overhanging riverside branches, to feed by diving headlong into water. ***Nesting:*** the only nest described in the literature was a burrow in a riverbank, with newly hatched chicks in May, in Luzon (Whitehead 1899).

Description *A. c. cyanopecta* **Adult male:** forehead and ear-coverts blackish; lores and frontal spot orange-rufous; forehead, crown, hindneck, cheeks and malar region black, the feathers with bright ultramarine tips, making crescentic spots on the hindcrown. A white blaze on the neck, orange-washed behind. Scapulars, wings and tail blue-washed black, the wing-coverts tipped with bright blue. Mantle to uppertail-coverts brilliant blue. Chin creamy-white, throat pale rufous; breast orange-rufous, crossed above and below by rich cobalt bands, narrow in the midline and broad and confluent at the sides. Flanks cobalt, belly and undertail-coverts orange-rufous, underwing-coverts orange-rufous mixed with blue. Upper mandible greyish-black, lower mandible red; eye dark brown; legs and feet red, only three toes. **Adult female:** like the male, but only one ultramarine pectoral band, often broken in the midline. **Juvenile:** like the adults, except that the underparts are orange-rufous, with a patch of purple-blue at the side of the breast. **Measurements:** wing of male 58-61, of female 59-62; tail of male 20-24, of female 22-26; bill of male 35-43, of female 34-40; tarsus of male 10-11, of female 10-11.

Reference Forshaw (1983).

69 CAERULEAN KINGFISHER   Plate 23
Alcedo coerulescens

Alcedo coerulescens Vieillot, 1818, Nouv. Dict. Hist. Nat., 19, p. 401, Timor (error for Java).

Field identification Length 13 cm (5 in). A small, grey-blue and white kingfisher found from west Java east to Sumbawa Island, Indonesia. ***At rest:*** upperparts blue, with white frontal spot and neck blaze; underparts pure white, with a broad caerulean-blue breast-band. Bill black, with some brown-red at the base of the lower mandible. *In flight:* a typical riverine kingfisher, with a brilliant silvery- or azure-blue line from back to rump and white underwings. *Confusion species:* the three other small kingfishers in its range (59, 75, 76) are all readily distinguished by having rufous in their plumage. Blue-banded Kingfishers (70), overlapping on Java, are much larger and darker.

Voice A high-pitched, penetrating 'tieh', often repeated.

Geographical variation None.

Habitat and range Caerulean Kingfishers inhabit waters in low-lying open country-side: streams, canals, fishponds, flooded paddyfields, swamps, tidal estuaries, and mangrove. They are quite common, and ascend up to about 800 m. The range is Sumatra, Java, the Kangean Islands, Bali, Lombok and Sumbawa Islands, Indonesia; there is an old record from Krakatau, between Java and Sumatra. In Sumatra they are rare visitors but may breed, and are said to be common at one locality (van Marle and Voous 1988).

Food Aquatic insects and crustaceans, and small fishes.

Habits These kingfishers occur singly, in pairs, and as families, fishing from some low perch at the edge of open waters. *Nesting:* the only nest described in the literature was an inclining burrow exca-vated by both birds of a pair into a steep bank by a paddyfield (Hoogerwerf and Siccama 1938). Several clutches have been found, however, of 3-6 eggs. *Laying months:* Java, April-June, August, October.

Description *Adult male:* upperparts grey-ish azure-blue, variegated, most feathers with dark blue-grey bases and bright blue tips; blues darkest on the ear-coverts and hindneck, brightest on the back, and bril-liant silvery-azure on the rump. Loral patch white; a conspicuous white blaze at the side of the neck. Chin, throat, belly, underwing-coverts and undertail-coverts white; breast azure-blue, well demar-cated; flanks blue where concealed by the folded wings, otherwise white. Bill black-ish, with some brown-red at the base of the lower mandible; eye dark brown; legs and feet dark red-brown. *Adult female:* blues duller and slightly greener than on the male; breast-band narrower and less distinctly demarcated. *Juvenile:* blues duller and greyer than on the adults; breast-band indistinct, more grey than blue. *Measurements:* wing of male 60-63, of female 60-64; tail of male 24-27, of female 24-28; bill of male 35-40, of fe-male 31-38; tarsus of male 8-10, of female 9-10.

Reference Forshaw (1983).

70 BLUE-BANDED KINGFISHER   Plate 23
Alcedo euryzona

Alcedo cryzona (sic) Temminck, 1830, Planch. Col., 86; *Alcedo euryzona*, ibid., index, 1838-1839, Java.

Field identification Length 17 cm (6½ in). A shy, robust bird of forested waterways, common only in parts of Borneo; larger than the River Kingfisher (76), and sex-ually dimorphic. Males are blackish, with a brilliant silvery-azure band from mantle to rump, white neck blaze, blue breast, sharply demarcated white throat, and white belly. Females are rather duller, less boldly pied, and with the throat yellowish-washed but other 'white' parts orange-rufous. The strong bill is black, with red in the lower mandible of the female. *In flight:* it looks like a large, very dark River Kingfisher with the silver-blue back-band in striking contrast. *Confusion species:* the River Kingfisher, a winter visitor to most of the Blue-banded's range, is smaller, paler, greener above, with a more slender bill, rufous (not black) ear-coverts and rufous (not blue) breast.

Voice A monosyllable often given in flight, louder but less shrill than River Kingfisher's calls.

Geographical variation Two subspecies, females varying more than males.

A. e. euryzona Java. Male with sides of the throat, underwing-coverts and undertail-coverts variably tinged with buff or yellow; female with well-demarcated blue breast.

A. e. peninsulae Sumatra, Borneo, peninsular Malaysia and Thailand, and Burma. Male with pectoral band mottled, and white parts not so yellowish-tinged; female with dark orange breast, contrasting strongly with whitish throat and weakly with rufous belly.

Habitat and range In Borneo, Blue-banded Kingfishers are fairly common on streams and small rivers in primary rainforest, as in the headwaters and tributaries of Temburong and Sangatta Rivers; they have also been found 100 m away from riversides, in forest. From sea level they ascend to 1250 m in Borneo and 1500 m in Java, where they are, however, scarce. Resident but uncommon in Sumatra (van Marle and Voous 1988); in peninsular Malaysia it is an uncommon bird of mangrove and forested streams up to 850 m; and in Thailand and Burma it is rare, encountered only a few times, as far north as the southern Shan states.

Food Fishes, crustaceans, insects and lizards (Forshaw 1983).

Habits Because they are shy – 'a wild, restless bird, always on the move' (Forshaw 1983) – and in most of their range decidedly scarce, Blue-banded Kingfishers are poorly known. From all accounts habits are much like those of River Kingfishers. *Nesting:* birds dig their nest burrows into the banks of small streams in dense forest, in Malaysia mainly at altitudes of 300-600 m (Forshaw 1983). Three eggs comprise the set. *Laying months:* Malaysia (Perak), February, June; Java, March-April.

Description *A. e. euryzona* **Adult male:** feathers of forehead, crown and hindneck black, with narrow blue tips; ear-coverts uniform blue-washed black; feathers of cheeks and malar area blackish with broad blue tips. A small white or buffy loral spot, and a long white or creamy neck blaze. Mantle to uppertail-coverts brilliant blue, silvery-azure on the rump. Scapulars, wings and tail blue-washed black, the wing-coverts spangled with small blue spots. Chin and throat white, creamy at the sides; breast blue, tinged greenish below, with blackish feather bases showing through; remaining underparts white, the undertail-coverts usually tinged with yellowish-buff and tipped with dusky grey. Underwing-coverts yellowish or buffy-white. Bill grey-black; eye dark brown; legs and feet orange-brown. **Adult female:** upperparts like the male's but dark brown rather than blue-black, except for the azure band from mantle to rump, which is just as vivid. Loral spot rufous; neck blaze orange-rufous; throat pale orange at the sides; underparts below the breast, including the underwing-coverts, orange-rufous. Upper mandible grey-black, lower mandible orange-red. *Juvenile:* like the adults, but duller; males with the lower underparts pale rufous. Bill blackish. **Measurements:** wing of male 87-92, of female 86-90; tail of male 35-41, of female 35-38; bill of male 47-56, of female 48-54; tarsus of male 12-13, of female 11-13. Weight (*A. e. peninsulae*): 34-38.

Reference Forshaw (1983).

Alcedo quadribrachys

Alcedo quadribrachys 'Temm.', Bonaparte, 1850, Consp. Genera Avium, 1, p. 158, Guinea.

Field identification Length 16 cm (6-6½ in). A dark blue-and-chestnut river kingfisher of the rainforest zone of west and equatorial Africa. *At rest:* upperparts dark ultramarine-blue with a lighter blue or brilliant cobalt band from mantle to rump; a small buffy-white loral spot and large neck blaze; white throat, and dark chestnut underparts. The bill is black. *In flight:* dark blue with paler back and rump; underwing-coverts rufous. *Confusion species:* the White-breasted and Malachite Kingfishers (64, 65) have the same combination of ultramarine-blue and rufous, but they are smaller, red-billed, with white breast (64) or banded crown (65). Half-collared Kingfisher (77), which overlaps with Shining-blue only in easternmost Angola and on Mwombezhi River in Solwezi, Zambia, is distinguished by being paler, with a white (not rufous) loral spot and a larger blue mark at the side of the breast.

Voice In flight a high-pitched 'cheep' or 'tschut', repeated rapidly up to six times. Frightened nestlings make a fizzling noise.

Geographical variation Two subspecies, differing in hue.
   A. q. quadribrachys Senegambia to about west-central Nigeria. Mantle to uppertail-coverts bright purple-blue.
   A. q. guentheri Southwest Nigeria to Lake Victoria, south to Angola and northwest Zambia. Mantle and back brilliant cobalt-blue, rump pale azure-blue.

Habitat and range Living on open waters in the forest zone, this kingfisher keeps mainly in the shade of the vegetation fringing rivers, lakes and ponds. It occurs at the coast, in lagoons, estuaries and mangrove, and inland it inhabits reedbeds and emergent woody growth, papyrus swamps, reservoirs, and slow-running streams and rivers in primary forest and in open savanna country and farmland. Shining-blue Kingfishers occur in Gambia,

Guinea-Bissau, Sierra Leone, and Mali (Niger, Bafing, Sankarani and Baoulé Rivers); they range from Ivory Coast through south Nigeria and Cameroon just to Sudan (Aloma Plateau, Yambio), Kenya (once, Kakamega Forest), Rwanda (Akagera River near Kagitumba, Rubyiro River), Burundi (once, upper Kayangozi River), northwest Zambia, and Angola (Cabinda, Cuango River, Foz de Chiluango, Luando, Carmona). They are found at up to 850 m in altitude in Cameroon and 1800 m in Zaïre, and are uncommon in savanna but common in forested country. Some 50 pairs were counted on 48 km of Nsukawkaw River in Ghana (Grimes 1987); they are numerous on forested streams in Gabon and at 700 m in Bwamba, Uganda.

Migration Seasonal occurrences at some places in Nigeria suggest migration, but could also be explained by the dispersal of young birds. Everywhere else the species is sedentary.

Food Mainly fishes, up to 6 cm long; also small crabs and aquatic insect larvae.

Habits Shining-blue Kingfishers are shy birds that live solitarily or in pairs, fishing from a perch 1-2 m high in reeds or waterside trees. Like River Kingfishers (76), they plunge steeply into water, and at night roost in tangled vegetation low over a stream. *Nesting:* breeding habits are not well known. This kingfisher is evidently a monogamous, territorial, solitary nester. Both birds of the pair dig the 40-cm burrow in a perpendicular stream-bank or the side of a gravel-pit or forest saw-pit up to 1 km from water. The clutch is of 5-6 eggs. *Laying months:* Nigeria, about September; Cameroon, about November; Gabon, probably December-March; Congo, March; Uganda, December, February, April-July (mainly May).

Description *A. q. quadribrachys* **Adult male:** a small buffy loral spot, large creamy neck blaze orange-tinged behind, and creamy chin and throat; otherwise all head feathers are black with glossy ultramarine tips, making the crown look faintly banded. Scapulars dark ultramarine-blue; wings like the crown; tail blue-black; mantle to uppertail-coverts brilliant purplish-blue. Breast, underwing-coverts and lower underparts chestnut; a small purple-blue quarter-collar at the side of the breast. Bill black; eye dark brown; legs and feet waxy orange-red. **Adult female:** like the male, but some dark red at the base of the lower mandible. **Juvenile:** like

the adult, but breast paler orange, with the feathers tipped dark blue, and dusky mottling forming a breast-band; crown paler blue than on adult; bill with whitish tip; legs and feet pale pink. **Measurements:** wing of male 75-85, of female 73-83; tail of male 33-38, of female 35-38; bill of male 47-53, of female 44-51; tarsus of male 10-11, of female 10-11. Weight: male 33-36, female 32-40.

References Forshaw (1983), Fry et al. (1988).

72 AZURE KINGFISHER   Plate 24
Alcedo azurea

Alcedo azurea Latham, 1801, Index Orn., Suppl., p. 32, Norfolk Island (error for New South Wales).

Field identification Length 18 cm (7 in). A black-billed, riverside kingfisher, deep ultramarine above and rufous below, with a small white or buffy loral spot, large white neck blaze and white throat. **Confusion species:** Little Kingfishers (74) are much smaller and lack any rufous in the underparts. River Kingfishers (76), which overlap with Azure in Halmahera and New Guinea, are paler, with rufous ear-coverts and brilliant azure-blue back and rump.

Voice A shrill, high-pitched piping 'pseet', repeated several times in flight.

Geographical variation We recognise six subspecies, with trifling differences in hue and size.
 A. a. azurea East Australia from about Cooktown to Tasmania. Chin and throat buffy-white, rest of underparts rufous, flanks tinged with violet.
 A. a. ruficollaris North Australia from about Cooktown to Kimberley Division. Like *azurea*, but colours richer. Wing and tail 10% shorter but bill longer than in *azurea*.
 A. a. lessonii Aru Islands, most of lowland New Guinea, and Fergusson Island (D'Entrecasteaux Archipelago). Underparts paler than in *azurea*, upperparts slightly darker, flanks less violaceous.

 A. a. ochrogaster Islands in Geelvink Bay, and north New Guinea east to Karkar Island; also Admiralty Islands. Underparts paler than in *lessonii*; bill deeper, and pale-tipped.
 A. a. affinis Northern Moluccas: Halmahera and Batjan Islands. Blue paler and brighter than in *lessonii*, tip of bill reddish, and wing 5 mm longer.
 A. a. yamdenae Tanimbar Islands, Indonesia. Like *affinis* but slightly smaller than *lessonii*.

Habitat and range It is a widespread resident in lowland New Guinea and on islands and archipelagos from Halmahera and Tanimbar Islands to Admiralty and Fergusson Islands. It is quite widespread in tropical Australia, but further south it becomes more coastal until, in Tasmania, it is virtually confined to the (west) coast. Its habitat in New Guinea is the wooded margins of creeks, rivers and lakes, estuaries, mangrove, sago swamps, forest pools and secondary growth at up to 1520 m of altitude (Coates 1985). In Australia it occurs in densely vegetated coastal watercourses, mangrove, *Melaleuca* swamps, tidal creeks and lagoons, and wooded rivers in the lowlands and foothills. A pair's territory varies from 200 to 1600 m of suitable river or shoreline.

Migration For the most part Azure

Kingfishers are sedentary, but juveniles disperse widely and non-breeding adults wander locally. They are summer migrants to the Rutherglen district, Victoria (Blakers et al. 1984).

Food Fishes, frogs, tadpoles, crustaceans, water-beetles; also occasional locusts and spiders.

Habits A true fisher, this species takes nearly all of its food by plunging into water from a low overhanging perch. Conspicuous yet rather shy, it is an essentially solitary bird, although sometimes seen in pairs and family parties. From time to time, when searching for prey, it bobs the head and body and momentarily cocks the tail. **Nesting:** both birds of a pair dig the tunnel, 40-60 cm long, in a stream-bank or sometimes the soil in an uprooted tree. The burrow inclines slightly and ends in an unlined cavity where the clutch of up to seven eggs, usually 4-5, is laid. Both parents incubate the eggs and feed the chicks, respectively for 20-22 and 21-28 days. In Victoria the species is double-brooded. **Laying months:** in north Australia the breeding season is December-April and in the south August-January (Forshaw 1983).

Description A. a. azurea **Adult male:** upperparts uniform deep ultramarine-blue, except for a narrow rufous loral line and a large white neck blaze. Chin and throat white, often tinged with buff; remaining underparts including underwing-coverts orange-rufous, except for a large ultramarine patch at the side of the breast and a strong violet wash on the flanks. Bill black, with the very tip white; eye dark brown; legs and feet orange-red, only three toes. **Adult female:** a trifle duller than the male, with less violet on the flanks. **Juvenile:** duller and rather paler than the adult; back and rump paler blue than wings and tail; crown, sides of the breast and scapulars blackish; large whitish tip to the bill. **Measurements:** wing of male 74-80, of female 73-79; tail of male 30-35, of female 30-35; bill of male 44-55, of female 44-54; tarsus of male 10-13, of female 10-12. Weight: male 29-32, female 31-35.

Reference Forshaw (1983).

73 BISMARCK KINGFISHER
Alcedo websteri

Plate 24

Alcyone websteri Hartert, 1898, in C. Cayley Webster, Through New Guinea, p. 371, New Hanover.

Field identification Length 22 cm (8½ in). This is a medium-sized, short-tailed fishing kingfisher, confined to lowland forest waterways in the Bismarck Archipelago, Papua New Guinea. **At rest:** it is uniformly dark greenish-blue above, with a creamy neck blaze, and creamy-white below with a large blue patch and blue crescents at the side of the breast. **Confusion species:** two other *Alcedo* species occur in the Bismarcks, the Little and River Kingfishers (74, 76). The former resembles the Bismarck Kingfisher in plumage, but its blues are much richer and it is only a quarter the weight of the Bismarck. The latter is distinguished by its rufous underparts and brilliant azure rump.

Voice Not known.

Geographical variation None.

Habitat and range It occurs on lowland forest streams and rivers in Rooke, Umboi, New Britain, New Ireland, New Hanover and Lihir Islands, and is locally not uncommon.

Food Fishes, crayfish, shrimps, and 'large green insects'.

Habits From what little is on record, it seems to have the same habits as its close relative the Azure Kingfisher (72). No nests have been found.

Description Sexes alike. **Adult:** a few tiny whitish speckles in the lore, and a large creamy white neck blaze; otherwise the entire upperparts, a large patch at the side of the breast, and the flanks where concealed by the folded wing, are uniform dark grey-greenish blue, brightest on the crown and rump, and with black feather bases showing through in the forehead and breast-patch. The underparts and underwing-coverts are creamy-white to very pale orange, paler on throat and belly than on breast and flanks; where the blue patch borders the breast, creamy feathers have wide dusky blue outer margins, mak-

ing conspicuous half-crescents. Bill waxy black with a whitish tip; eye and orbital skin black; legs and feet grey-brown, only three toes. **Juvenile:** not described. **Measurements:** wing of male 90-95, of female 89-94; tail of male 34-40, of female 37-43; bill of male 50-58, of female 49-55; tarsus of male 13-15, of female 13-15. Weight: male 54-57, one female 67.

References Coates (1985), Forshaw (1983).

74 LITTLE KINGFISHER
Alcedo pusilla

Plate 24

Ceyx pusilla Temminck, 1836, Planch. Col., 100, pl. 595, f. 3, Lobo Bay, New Guinea.

Field identification Length 11 cm (4½ in). The smallest *Alcedo* and one of the three tiniest kingfishers in the world, this dark blue and white gem cannot really be mistaken for any other bird in its range. Variable Dwarf Kingfishers (63, subspecies *gentianus*) and Caerulean Kingfishers (69) are very similar, but do not overlap with it; Bismarck Kingfishers (73) share its range and have similar plumage, but are much bigger – four times the Little's weight.

Voice A high-pitched, repeated 'tsee' or 'tzweeip' in flight. Near the nest more varied calls are uttered, and 'tsee' calls are interspersed with ticking notes (Coates 1985). Hungry nestlings have churring or buzzing calls.

Geographical variation About ten subspecies have been recognised; we admit seven. They vary in hue, size and pectoral-band characters, and in colour of undertail-coverts.
A. p. pusilla New Guinea, Australia except for the range of *ramsayi*, Torres Strait, Kai, Aru, Western Papuan, Fergusson and Goodenough Islands.
A. p. ramsayi Northern Territory, Australia, from Groote Eylandt and Melville Island west to Anson Bay. Blues lighter and brighter than in *pusilla*, and on juveniles washed with grey-green. Blue breast-patches form a broken pectoral band.

A. p. halmaherae Northern Moluccas: Batjan and Halmahera Islands. Like *pusilla*, but paler.
A. p. masauji Bismarck Archipelago: New Britain, New Ireland, New Hanover. Like *pusilla*, but darker, with a complete pectoral band.
A. p. bougainvillei Western Solomons: Bougainville, Santa Ysabel, Choiseul, and Florida Islands. Slightly paler than *pusilla*, wing-coverts green-washed, breast feathers fringed with blue and sometimes forming a scaly pectoral band. Larger, particularly the bill (wing 52-59 mm, tail 19-24 mm, bill 33-37 mm).
A. p. richardsi Central Solomons: from Vella Lavella to Vangunu Islands. Like *bougainvillei*, but with a constant, stronger pectoral band, and blue undertail-coverts.
A. p. aolae Known only from a single bird described from Guadalcanal, Solomon Islands, in 1915. Like *richardsi* but pectoral band incomplete; undertail-coverts white with blue tips.

Habitat and range A bird of coasts and coastal lowlands, occurring at up to 540 m in New Guinea and 750 m in Atherton highlands, Queensland. It inhabits wooded pools, forest streams, mangrove, *Melaleuca* and *Nipa* swamps, forested tidal creeks, and the substage of alluvial forest. In Halmahera it is practically confined to mangrove, and in some small islands is strictly coastal also. Little

Kingfishers range from Halmahera to the eastern Solomon Islands, around Australia's Top End and around Cape York Peninsula south to Archer River in the west and Chester River in the east. It is sedentary, and locally common.

Food Fishes, shrimps and aquatic beetles.

Habits A true fisher, this species feeds by diving into water from some low perch, returning with prey to the same perch. Its flight is swift, low down and direct. *Nesting:* nest burrows are made in river-banks, soil in the roots of a fallen tree, rotting mangrove stumps, terrestrial termitaria, and on Goodenough Island possibly in arboreal termitaria (Bell 1970b). One tunnel in a decaying mangrove trunk was 3 cm wide and 15 cm long, and ended in an egg chamber 10 cm high and 13 cm wide. Both parents feed the brood – once with two 5-cm fish per young per hour – and young birds dive clumsily for fish nine days after leaving the nest (Miller 1932). At another nest the young were fed every five minutes, by each parent alternately, fishing in a swamp 300 m from the tree-stump nest (Coates 1985). *Laying months:* Queensland, November, February; Papua New Guinea, February.

Description *A. p. pusilla* Sexes alike. *Adult:* upperparts deep ultramarine-blue, but for a large white frontal patch and neck blaze. Underparts pure white, except for a wide area of ultramarine at the sides of the breast and flanks (the latter normally concealed under the folded wings). Underwing-coverts mainly white, but small anterior ones dusky. Bill black; eye brown-black, orbital skin black; legs and feet dark pinkish grey-brown, only three toes. *Juvenile:* like the adult, but blue parts have a greenish wash; forecrown, cheeks, malar region and ear-coverts black; crown with indistinct bars; sides of breast blackish, breast feathers (except in midline) with dusky fringes; loral spot buffy and neck blaze pale rufous. *Measurements:* wing of male 49-53, of female 49-54; tail of male 18-23, of female 18-22; bill of male 28-33, of female 29-32; tarsus of male 7-9, of female 7-9. Weight: male 10-14, female 10-12.

References Coates (1985), Forshaw (1983).

75 BLUE-EARED KINGFISHER
Alcedo meninting

Plate 25

Alcedo Meninting Horsfield, 1821, Trans. Linn. Soc. London, 13, pt 1, p. 172, Java.

Field identification Length 17 cm (6½ in). This is a small, short-tailed fishing kingfisher with brilliant blue back and rump, contrasting ultramarine upperparts, orange-rufous underparts, rufous or buffy loral spot, white neck blaze and creamy-white throat. The head top is quite strongly banded with dark blue, the ear-coverts are blue, and the wing-coverts are spangled with paler blue. **Confusion species:** its range overlaps with those of four other *Alcedo* species (and approaches close to those of two more: 72, 74). Distinctions are as follows. Caerulean Kingfisher (69) is small and lacks rufous. Blue-banded (70) is large and has a wide blue breast-band or (females, Burma to Sumatra and Borneo) dark brown upperparts. Great Blue Kingfisher (78) is much larger – 1½ times as long – with olive upperparts and pale-spotted wings. River Kingfisher (76) is very like the Blue-eared, but slightly larger, with rufous ear-coverts, aquamarine rather than ultramarine crown and wings, paler rufous underparts, and a paler line from back to rump. Young Blue-eared Kingfishers have rufous ear-coverts and can be very difficult to distinguish from young Rivers. In the Andaman Islands, Blue-eared Kingfishers have the upperparts the same shade of green-blue as the River. Some extralimital races of River Kingfisher have ultramarine upperparts and blue ear-coverts.

Voice Like that of the River Kingfisher.

Geographical variation There is slight

variation in hue and size. Ten subspecies were recognised by Forshaw (1983), but differences are trivial and we have reduced them to six.

A. m. meninting Sumatra, Java, Bali, Lombok; Banggai and Sula Islands (east of Sulawesi), and possibly Sulawesi; Nias and Batu Islands (west of Sumatra).

A. m. verreauxii Malay Peninsula north to about 10°N, Borneo, Palawan and Sulu Islands (west Philippines), Bangka and Belitung Islands (between Sumatra and Borneo), Riau Archipelago (off Singapore), and Pagi Islands (west of Sumatra). Upperparts slightly darker.

A. m. scintillans Peninsular Burma and Thailand, from about 16°N to 10°N, where it intergrades with *verreauxii*. Paler than *meninting*.

A. m. coltarti From Indochina and about 16°N in Burma and Thailand, to Nepal and eastern India. Blues greener than in *scintillans*, and wing-coverts more spangled.

A. m. philipsi Sri Lanka and adjacent parts of Kerala. Like *coltarti*, but upperparts deep royal-blue, underparts darker, and wing-coverts with larger spots. 5% larger than other races.

A. m. rufigaster Andaman Islands. Like *scintillans*, but upperparts paler, more aquamarine than ultramarine, and underparts paler rufous.

Habitat and range Blue-eared Kingfishers inhabit forest streams, channels in dense mangrove growth, bamboo forest, evergreen and wet deciduous forests, creeks and estuaries. In such habitats they are widespread, although unevenly distributed and seldom at all common, from Sri Lanka and Kerala through Orissa to Nepal, Bengal, Bangladesh, Burma and Thailand to Vietnam, Malaysia and Indonesia east to Palawan, Kalimantan and Lombok. They occupy numerous islands, including the Andamans, and are present in Banggai and Sula Islands and possibly Sulawesi. Everywhere they are sedentary.

Food They eat fish and crustaceans, and significantly more insects than do River Kingfishers (Forshaw 1983).

Habits Solitary and shy, Blue-eared Kingfishers sit patiently at a streamside perch, scanning around, from time to time bobbing the head, flicking the tail up, and plunging into water. Sometimes a bird is more active, flying from perch to perch, seemingly to catch flying insects (Forshaw 1983). **Nesting:** burrows are dug in sloping or perpendicular earth banks, always in forest, generally by streams. Two tunnels, 5 cm wide and 55-60 cm long, ended in chambers 10-12 cm high and 12-14 cm wide; some burrows are 1 m long. Both sexes rear the young. In India some pairs are double-brooded (Baker 1934). **Laying months:** Sumatra, April; Andaman Islands, July. In northern India the breeding season is about April-August, mainly May-June, in Kerala about January, in Burma about April-July, in west Malaysia about February-May, and in Borneo about December-August.

Description *A. m. meninting* **Adult male:** frontal spot rufous; a large white blaze at the side of the neck, washed yellow posteriorly; chin and throat cream-white. Head and neck ultramarine-blue, closely banded with darker blue. The rest of the upperparts including wings and tail are glossy dark blue, with a brilliant pale blue band down the centre of the back and rump. Upperwing-coverts have mid-blue tips and sometimes the black feather bases show through. Breast to undertail-coverts, and underwing, dark rufous. Bill black with reddish-brown base; eye dark brown; legs and feet orange-red. **Adult female:** like the male, but with a greater area of reddish-brown in the bill. **Juvenile:** like the adults, but duller, with rufous ear-coverts and cheeks, and dusky tips to the breast feathers. Bill brown-black, with the tip white. **Measurements:** wing of male 61-71, of female 62-71; tail of male 23-30, of female 25-29; bill of male 39-47, of female 39-43; tarsus of male 9-11, of female 9-10. Weight: 16-18.5.

Reference Forshaw (1983).

76 RIVER KINGFISHER (Eurasian Kingfisher) Plate 25
Alcedo atthis

Gracula atthis Linnaeus, 1758, Syst. Nat., ed. 10, I, p. 109, Egypt.

Field identification Length 16 cm (6-6½ in). In Europe, North Africa, the Middle East, and Asia north of Nepal and Hainan, this is the only small blue kingfisher and as such it is quite unmistakable. *At rest:* northern races (Britain to Japan, south to Sri Lanka, Sumatra, Northern Moluccas and Philippines) have green-blue upperparts with pale azure-blue back and rump, rufous loral spot and ear-coverts, green-blue malar stripe, white neck blaze and throat, rufous underparts, and black bill with some red at the base. Races resident east and west of New Guinea are bluer above, with partly blue ear-coverts. *In flight:* when a River Kingfisher darts past low over the water its greenish and rufous plumage can always be discerned, but the most striking feature is the brilliant 'kingfisher-blue' band from mantle to tail. *Confusion species:* from the Himalayas to the Solomons, River Kingfishers can be mistaken for six other blue-and-rufous kingfishers (63, 68, 70, 72, 75, 78). However, any bird with rufous ear-coverts is either a River or a juvenile Blue-eared (75). River Kingfishers resident in Lesser Sunda Islands have blue-and-rufous ear-coverts. Those resident from Sulawesi to eastern Solomons have blue ear-coverts and blue (not green-blue) upperparts: they can be distinguished from the Blue-eared Kingfisher (which occurs in that region only on Banggai and Sula Islands) only by their smaller loral spot and slightly paler underparts; juveniles have the breast scalloped, forming a vague pectoral band. Some rufous-eared River Kingfishers winter in northern Sulawesi and Halmahera, where they occur alongside the local blue-eared subspecies. In Halmahera and New Guinea the resident River Kingfisher can be told from Variable Dwarf Kingfisher (63) by its greenish-blue (not ultramarine) upperparts and less conspicuous loral spot, and from Azure and Bismarck Kingfishers (72, 73) by its brilliant azure line on back and rump. In Ethiopia migrant River Kingfishers may occasionally penetrate the range of the Half-collared Kingfisher (77); they can be distinguished from it by their rufous (not blue) ear-coverts.

Voice There is no song. The flight call is a short shrill whistle, 'chee', repeated two or three times. Agitated birds emit a harsh, chipped 'shrit-it-it'. Begging nestlings make a churring noise.

Geographical variation Upperparts vary from green-blue to bright blue and purple-blue; ear-coverts are rufous or blue; underparts pale or dark rufous; and there is a 10% size variation. There are seven subspecies.

A. a. ispida Breeds from south Norway, Ireland and Spain to west USSR (about Leningrad) and Romania; it winters south to south Portugal and Iraq.

A. a. atthis Breeds from northwest Africa and south Italy to Bulgaria, occasionally in Turkey, Iraq and Iran, and commonly in Afghanistan, northwest India, north Sinkiang, and Siberia from Omsk to Krasnoyarsk; it is a winter visitor south to Egypt, northeast Sudan, Yemen, Oman and Pakistan. Crown greener, chin and throat white, underparts paler rufous than in *ispida*; slightly larger, particularly the bill.

A. a. bengalensis South and east Asia: India (except the northwest and south) to Malay Peninsula, Indochina, Hainan, China, Korea, Japan, from Sakhalin to Lake Baikal, and east Mongolia; winters south to Sumatra, Java, Borneo, north Sulawesi, Sula Islands, Halmahera and the Philippines. Brighter than the above races, and smaller (wing 68-76 mm, tail 26-37 mm, bill 37-46 mm).

A. a. taprobana Sri Lanka and India south of Cauvery River. Upperparts bright blue, not green-blue; the same size as *bengalensis*.

A. a. floresiana Lesser Sunda Islands: Bali to Timor and Wetar. Like *taprobana*, but blues darker; ear-coverts rufous with some blue feathers.

A. a. hispidoides Sulawesi, Moluccan and Western Papuan Islands; coastal eastern New Guinea from Sepik and Aroa

Rivers to D'Entrecasteaux and Louisiade Archipelagos (east to Woodlark and Misima Islands), and coastal Bismarck Archipelago (Long, Tolokiwa, Umboi, Sakar, New Britain, Watom, Duke of York, New Ireland, New Hanover, Tabar, Lihir, Tanga, Feni, Mussau, Emira, Manus in Admiralty Islands, also Nissan, Buka and north Bougainville – Coates 1985). Colours deeper than in *floresiana*, blues purple-tinged on hindneck and rump; earcoverts blue.

A. a. solomonensis Solomon Islands, east to San Cristóbal. Intergrades with *hispidoides*, but even more purple-tinged; ear-coverts blue; larger than the above three subspecies (wing 72-80 mm, tail 29-34 mm, bill 39-47 mm).

Habitat and range In Europe and Asia this kingfisher inhabits clear, slow-flowing streams and rivers and lakes with reedy and shrubby banks. It keeps to bulrushes, papyrus, reeds and bushes with overhanging branches, by open water, channels and marshes, and it feeds in the shallows. In winter it is more coastal, feeding in estuaries, harbours, ponds and along rocky seashores. Tropical populations frequent the sluggish lower reaches of rivers, often thickly wooded, and mangrove creeks, coastlines, swamps, wet grassland and ornamental gardens. The vast breeding range encompasses Europe and Asia north to 60°N, south to Morocco, north Iran, Sri Lanka and Java, and Indonesia and Melanesia east to Solomon Islands. In northwest Africa, River Kingfishers are common winter visitors, and also scarce breeding residents, on the Moroccan coastal plains south to River Sous and in Tunisia south to Gafsa. They have nested at Biskra, Tamanart and Reghaia in north Algeria, and have also bred rarely in Libya, Lebanon, Sinai and Iraq.

Population Subject to decimation in hard winters, and to persecution, and very sensitive to river pollution, kingfishers fortunately remain common in many regions. Some estimates of breeding pairs, mainly in the 1970s, are: Britain 5,000-9,000, France 1,000-10,000, Belgium 450, Netherlands 90-325, West Germany 1,000-1,200, Denmark 100-200, Sweden 200 and Switzerland 200 (Cramp 1985). That totals about 10,000-15,000 pairs; less heavily industrialised countries prob-

ably have greater densities, so in the whole of Europe east to the Urals there might be as many as 100,000 pairs, with perhaps twice that figure in Asia with Melanesia. Some 16 pairs on 32 km of River Thames, England, were reduced by the severe winter of 1962/63 to a single pair in the following summer.

Migration All birds emigrate after breeding in those regions where freezing conditions in winter are the rule, but the majority of migrants keep within the breeding range of the species. British birds move no more than 250 km (Morgan and Glue 1977), and Spanish ones are mainly sedentary (Martin and Pérez 1991). Some Belgian and French breeders migrate at least 500 km and Czechoslovakian ones 1500 km; but in USSR summer visitors to Perm', say, or the Ob, Yenisei and Lena headwaters, must have travelled at least 3000 km. Autumn movements are pronounced on many Mediterranean shores, as well as over Malaysian mountains, birds moving mainly at night. Kingfishers visit North Africa from September to April, and Sudan from October to March.

Food Minnows, sticklebacks, bullhead, roach, trout, dace, chub, perch, pike and stoneloach, up to 125 mm long (average 23 mm), are the main prey in Europe. This species also catches aquatic insects – dragonfly nymphs (and, rarely, adult dragonflies), water-bugs and water-beetles – and takes a few small molluscs and amphibians and, in winter, crustaceans. On seasonal average, about 60% of food items are fishes. In mid-winter one bird ate 13-21 minnows daily, averaging 46 g in total (Boag 1982).

Habits Like other kingfishers, this one perches 1-2 m above the water, on sedges, posts, twigs or riverbanks, looking stumpy, large-headed, short-tailed and short-legged, bill and tail pointing down as the bird sits intently for long periods. Now and then it turns around, briefly cocks the tail and, the better to gauge distance, bobs its head and body when food is detected. It plunges steeply down, and seizes its prey usually no deeper than 25 cm under the surface. Under water the wings open, and the eyes are open with the protective third eyelid drawn over them from the front corner. The bird rises beak-first from the surface and flies back to its perch (one bird took only 1.16 seconds to dive from a 1-m-high perch, catch a fish 12 cm below the surface, and return to the perch). At the perch the fish is juggled until held near its tail, beaten against the perch several times to left and right, manoeuvred (not tossed) until it is held lengthways, then quickly swallowed head-first. A few times each day, a small greyish pellet of fish bones and insect sclerites is regurgitated. River Kingfishers bathe a lot, especially when nesting, by plunging repeatedly onto water, then preening vigorously in bouts that can total two hours daily; after preening they stretch both wings, 'wrists' upward, and yawn. The flight is swift and direct, 40-45 km/h, low over water or trees, with rapid, even beats. They roost solitarily in rank waterside vegetation, reeds, hollows in trees, or in their nest. **Nesting:** resident birds pair in the autumn but retain separate territories, generally of at least 1 km of stream; territories gradually merge in the spring. Kingfishers are aggressively territorial, advertising by calling in flight and displaying at a perch in the middle of the territory. In display a bird sits silently, very upright, with wings drooping, neck outstretched and bill agape, before chasing an interloper away; or the territory-holder crouches, stretches forward, and sways the body from side to side. Having attracted a mate the male courtship-feeds her, copulation usually following. Two or three broods are reared in quick succession, and the female sometimes lays in an adjacent nest hole before her first brood has flown (Svensson 1978). Burrows are excavated by both birds of the pair, in stone-free sandy soil in a low stream-bank, or sometimes a sand-pit, quarry or earth cutting 500 m from water. Holes are 6-7 cm wide, usually 60-90 cm long (range 15-137 cm), straight, gently inclining, and end in a chamber 9-10 cm wide. Up to ten eggs compose the clutch, usually 6-7; in most clutches one or two

eggs fail to hatch because the parent cannot cover them. Both sexes incubate by day, but only the female at night. An incubating bird sits trance-like, facing the tunnel; it invariably casts a pellet, breaking it up with the bill (Boag 1982). The period is 19-20 days, and young are in the nest for a further 24-25 days, often more. Their first dives into water, about four days after leaving the nest, are all too often disastrous, the fledgling becoming waterlogged and drowning. **Laying months:** Britain, March-July, mainly April; Sweden, mainly May; northwest Africa, March-April; Kashmir, April-July; Malaysia, January-June; Papua New Guinea, June.

Description *A. a. ispida* **Adult male:** forehead, crown, hindneck and malar area banded with blue-green and bright, shining blue. Lores dusky, with a narrow rufous frontal line above; cheeks and ear-coverts pale rufous. Chin, throat and neck blaze white tinged with yellowish-buff. Wings greenish; scapulars and upperwing-coverts green with bright blue tips. Mantle and rump and a narrow connecting line are brilliant cobalt-blue, with uppertail-coverts a deeper bright blue and tail dark blue. Breast orange-rufous, the colour paling towards the underwing- and undertail-coverts. Bill black, gape red; eye dark brown; legs and feet red. **Adult female:** like the male, but lower mandible orange-red with a black tip. **Juvenile:** like the adult, but duller and greener above, paler below, with narrow dusky margins to the breast feathers. The bill has a whitish tip; legs and feet are at first blackish. **Measurements:** wing of male 76-81, of female 76-81; tail of male 35-43, of female 32-40; bill of male 40-48, of female 40-48; tarsus of male 10-11, of female 10-11. Weight: male 37-42, female 34-44.

References Boag (1982), Cramp (1985), Forshaw (1983), Fry *et al.* (1988).

Alcedo semitorquata

Alcedo semitorquata Swainson, 1823, Zool. Illustr., 3, text to pl. 151, Great Fish River.

Field identification Length 18 cm (7 in). A medium-sized kingfisher of African waters with banded dark blue crown, dark greenish-blue back, white throat and neck blaze, yellowish-buff or pale orange underparts, and dark blue half-collar at the side of the breast. ***Confusion species:*** it differs from the Shining-blue Kingfisher (71), which overlaps it in northwest Zambia, in having a white (not rufous) frontal line between bill and eye, white (not pale orange) throat, green-blue (not ultramarine) scapulars and wings, and much paler, more yellowish, underparts. Malachite Kingfishers (65) are smaller, crested, and red-billed. A few River Kingfishers (76) could winter in its Ethiopian range; they have a greener crown, smaller patch at the side of the breast, and rufous (not blue) ear-coverts.

Voice 'Tseep', and a 'sip-ip-ip-ip-prep' of alarm, indistinguishable from the voice of the River Kingfisher.

Geographical variation There are slight regional variations in body size and bill size (Clancey 1951, 1978a), but we do not recognise any subspecies.

Habitat and range Half-collared Kingfishers frequent a variety of waterways, from slow-flowing secluded channels through reedbeds to woodland streams and fast-flowing perennial rivers with emergent vegetation and well-timbered banks; they also inhabit reedy lakeshores, coastal lagoons, and densely bushed estuaries. In East Cape they sometimes fish along the seashore. North of Rift Valley in Ethiopia they are quite common, but in Sudan have been found only in Boma. In Kenya they breed in Kitovu Forest and occur regularly in the Taveta area. They are widespread in northwest Tanzania, and range from northeast Tanzania through southeast Africa to Natal and Cape Province west to Cape Town. In Cape Province they are uncommon, confined to coastal lowlands. From Zambia and Zimbabwe they range westward,

through north Botswana and Caprivi Strip to south Angola, reaching the Atlantic coast at Capangombe.

Migration Mainly resident, the species is a regular visitor to Begemdir and Simien Provinces, Ethiopia, in February-August. In some parts of South Africa it is commoner in summer than in winter, for instance at Rondevlei, and it occurs in Kruger Park only in wet summers.

Food Fishes 3-7 cm long (*Alestes*, *Tilapia*, *Barbus*), and crabs; also frogs, aquatic insects, and occasionally a butterfly caught in flight.

Habits A timid bird, it is often not seen until it retreats in fast direct flight low over the water. Like the River Kingfisher, it often calls in flight, and it forages from low waterside perches in just the same manner. Rarely, it hovers momentarily to scan for prey. ***Nesting:*** it nests in riverbanks, burrow dimensions and parental behaviour being like those of River Kingfishers. On average, a nestling eats 50 g of food a day; parents later withhold food to induce them to quit the nest. In Tanzania first departures are after sunrise, the youngster leaving the nest in the immediate wake of a parent (Moreau 1944). Although the first flight is strong, some young soon fall into the water and perish. ***Laying months:*** Tanzania, January-May and (mainly) October; Zambia, February-March, June, August-October; Zimbabwe, July-March, mainly September and October; South Africa, September-March.

Description ***Adult male:*** lores blackish, narrow frontal line white or buffy, and a large creamy-white blaze on the side of the neck; otherwise the head is banded with bright cobalt-blue and black, with a greenish wash on the forehead and particularly rich blue on ear-coverts and hindneck. Mantle to rump brilliant cobalt-blue, mauve-washed on the uppertail-coverts. Tail dark blue. Scapulars and wings bright blue, green-tinged. Chin yellowish, throat white; remaining under-parts including underwing-coverts rich ochre-buff, with a large half-crescentic deep blue patch at the side of the breast. Bill black; eye dark brown; legs and feet vermilion-red. **Adult female:** like the male, but with some red at the base of the lower mandible. **Juvenile:** duller and paler than the adult; breast feathers tipped dark grey, giving a scaly appearance. Legs and

feet blackish, turning red on subadults. **Measurements:** wing of male 78-86, of female 80-85; tail of male 36-43, of female 37-43; bill of male 45-52, of female 44-51; tarsus of male 10-12, of female 10-12. Weight: 35-40.

References Forshaw (1983), Fry *et al.* (1988), Moreau (1944).

78 GREAT BLUE KINGFISHER
Alcedo hercules

Plate 25

Alcedo hercules Laubmann, 1917, Verh. Orn. Ges. Bayern, 13, p. 105, *nom. nov.* for *Alcedo grandis* Blyth, pre-occupied.

Field identification Length 22 cm (8½ in). The largest *Alcedo* kingfisher; its very size prevents confusion with the two other species in its range. **At rest:** upperparts appear blackish-brown, tinged with green-blue, the crown noticeably banded and the wings speckled; mantle to uppertail-coverts brilliant azure-blue; throat and neck blaze creamy; underparts and underwing-coverts rich dark rufous. **Confusion species:** one-third larger than River Kingfisher (76), the Great Blue is a darker bird distinguished by its blackish-blue (not rufous) ear-coverts. It differs from Blue-eared Kingfisher (75) in its greater size, greenish-blue (not ultramarine) upperparts, and in lacking a large pale frontal spot. It is very like female Blue-banded Kingfisher (70), but that southerly species does not overlap in range.

Voice The flight call, seldom used, is like that of River Kingfisher, but louder and less shrill (Baker 1927).

Geographical variation None.

Habitat and range Great Blue Kingfishers inhabit forested streams in deep ravines and hilly country, rivulets in dense ever-green jungle, and streams running be-tween forest and well-treed farmland. They live at altitudes of up to 1200 m, but occur mainly between 625 and 1000 m. From Sikkim and Bhutan, the species ranges through northern Bangladesh, Assam, Burma and northwest Thailand, to

Yunnan and Hainan. It is a scarce bird, not well known, yet evidently not migratory. Mountfort (1988) regards it as a candidate for the Red Data Book.

Food Fish and insects.

Habits A shy, solitary bird, which dives for fish like River Kingfishers but differs from them in hunting from a perch low down in bushes overhanging the water, rather than from exposed vantage points such as a post or leafless branch (Forshaw 1983). **Nesting:** several nests found by Baker (1934) were burrows in perpendicular faces of forest ravines, or in banks by trickles of water in deep forest. Tunnels in hard earth were 8 cm wide and 45-60 cm long, and ended in chambers 15-20 cm across and 10-13 cm high; one tunnel in a sandy stream-bank was 2 m long. Burrows are straight, inclining a little, then declin-ing slightly into the egg chamber. Clutches are of 4-6 eggs. **Laying months:** northeast India, March-June.

Description Adult male: lore black with narrow, buffy frontal line above; chin and throat yellowish-white, boldly demar-cated from the dark head; large neck blaze yellowish-white. Feathers of the rest of the head are dull black, with crescentic glossy bright blue tips. Scapulars and wings greenish- or bluish-black, the upperwing-coverts shaft-streaked with azure-blue and tipped with cobalt. Mantle to uppertail-coverts brilliant cobalt-blue, tinged with purple at the sides of the rump and uppertail-coverts. Tail dark ultramarine-blue. Breast rich dark rufous, with a large patch of blackish-blue at the side; the rest of the underparts and underwing-coverts are rufous. Bill black; eye reddish-brown; legs and feet red. **Adult female:** like the male, but with red

at the base of the lower mandible. **Juvenile:** not known. **Measurements:** wing of male 96-102, of female 95-103; tail of male 41-48, of female 45-49; bill of male 54-59, of female 48-59; tarsus of male 12-13, of female 13-14.

References Baker (1934), Forshaw (1983).

79 AMERICAN PYGMY KINGFISHER
Chloroceryle aenea

Plate 26

Alcedo aenea Pallas, 1764, in Vroeg's Cat., Adumbr., p. I, no. 54, Surinam.

Field identification Length 13 cm (5 in). A tiny forest kingfisher, dark glossy green above, rich rufous below, with white belly and undertail-coverts, the female with a broad green breast-band. **Confusion species:** the Green-and-rufous Kingfisher (80) has very similar plumages, in both sexes, but is four times the weight. The Green Kingfisher (81) is also much bigger than the American Pygmy, 2-4 times its weight, and is white-collared.

Voice A weak 'tik' or 'dzit', often repeated a few times; a scratchy 'tsweek'; a dry 'cht, cht' like two pebbles struck together; and a weak, descending chatter.

Geographical variation Two subspecies are recognised.
  C. a. aenea The northern half of South America, intergrading with *stictoptera* in central Costa Rica. Two lines of small white spots in the secondary coverts.
  C. a. stictoptera From central Costa Rica to south Mexico (Yucatán, Veracruz, Puebla). 3-4 lines of small white spots in the secondary coverts; a large patch of white feathers hidden below the uppertail-coverts.

Habitat and range American Pygmy Kingfishers inhabit dense forests with small streams and pools, rivers where the edges are thickly overhung with woody vegetation, mangrove thickets and gallery forests. This is a widespread bird, entirely sedentary, and ascends from sea level to 2600 m. From Puebla and Sierra Madre del Sur in Mexico, this kingfisher ranges through Yucatán Peninsula, Guatemala,

Honduras, Nicaragua, Costa Rica and Panama to Colombia and about Guayaquil in Ecuador; and east of the Andes throughout northern South America, including Trinidad, south to Acre, Bolivia, and Minas Gerais to about Rio de Janeiro. In many regions American Pygmy Kingfishers are given as 'common', but in many others as 'uncommon' and 'scarce'. Like many forest birds, particularly small ones that are not very vocal, they are in fact more abundant than appears, as a regular netting programme may show: at one locality in central Brazil we netted all four green kingfishers during a ten-week study, in the proportion of 1 Amazon to 4 Green-and-rufous to 4 Green to 9 American Pygmy Kingfishers (Fry 1970). Interestingly, those densities are inverse to the species' weights, which we found to be exactly in the ratio 8 : 4 : 2 : 1 (respectively Amazon, Green-and-rufous, Green, and American Pygmy). This suggests that undisturbed Amazon rainforest supports nearly the same biomass of each kingfisher, and that the four species may minimise mutual competition by feeding on different prey size-ranges.

Food Small fishes, tadpoles, and insects.

Habits This kingfisher perches patiently low over water, searching for food, which it obtains by splashing into the shallows or plunging steeply into deeper water. In addition, it feeds by hawking – flying out in pursuit of a passing insect, which is caught on the wing. A solitary bird, it is not particularly shy; it is quiet and unobtrusive, although it can be quite active, frequently changing foraging stations. **Nesting:** both birds of a pair excavate the nest burrow, a tunnel 30-40 cm long in a riverbank, earth heap, gravel-pit or cutting; sometimes they use arboreal termitaria. **Laying months:** El Salvador and Surinam, May; Trinidad, May to August or September.

Description *C. a. aenea* **Adult male:** upperparts dark glossy green with gold reflections, the tail a bluer green. Lore black; neat, narrow rufous frontal line above it; a thin line of white below the eye. A very narrow rufous hindneck-collar, connecting with rufous throat and chin. Upperwing-coverts and tertials tipped with gold (which soon wears off); secondary coverts and inner secondaries each with three small gold spots. Breast and flanks rich rufous; centre of belly and undertail-coverts white; wing-lining buffy-orange. Bill black, with pale yellowish base to the lower mandible; eye dark brown; legs and feet dark grey. **Adult female:** like the male but for a dark green breast-band, its feathers with white tips. **Juvenile:** like the adults, but underparts paler and duller; spots in wing buffy and more profuse; males with soft green-black streaks on breast and flanks; females with the breast-band narrow, often broken. **Measurements:** wing of male 53-60, of female 53-60; tail of male 30-38, of female 33-39; bill of male 29-33, of female 29-33; tarsus of male 7-9, of female 7-9. Weight: male 10-16, female 12-16.

References Forshaw (1983), Fry (1970, 1980a).

80 GREEN-AND-RUFOUS KINGFISHER

Chloroceryle inda

Plate 26

Alcedo inda Linnaeus, 1766, Syst. Nat., ed. 12, I, p. 179, India occidentali (error for Guiana).

Field identification Length 24 cm (9½ in). A large kingfisher of clearwater rivers in forested areas, dark glossy green above, rich rufous below, the wings finely speckled with white, particularly on females; females also have a broad green-and-white breast-band. **Confusion species:** the American Pygmy Kingfisher (79) has very similar plumages but is only half the size and a quarter of the weight. Its rufous belly distinguishes the Green-and-rufous from the smaller Green (81) and much larger Amazon Kingfishers (82).

Voice A songbird-like 'chip-chip-chip' and twittering notes.

Geographical variation In the Guianas and east Brazil from Pará and Amapá to Santa Catarina, males have the wing- and tail-coverts more obviously tipped with minute buffy spots than is the case elsewhere in the range. They are sometimes treated as a separate subspecies, but the character is variable and we do not recognise any subspecies.

Habitat and range Green-and-rufous Kingfishers inhabit densely vegetated edges of forest rivers, streams and streamlets inside the forest, swamp forest, creeks and mangrove. The species ranges from southeast Nicaragua, Costa Rica and Panama to the Gulf of Guayaquil and, east of the Andes, the northern half of South America with Trinidad and Tobago, south on the Atlantic coast to Santa Catarina, Brazil. It is a lowland bird, occurring from the coast up to about 400 m in altitude. In some regions it is rather local and uncommon, in others it is plentiful. It seems to be entirely sedentary.

Food Fishes including several characid species, and crabs.

Habits Working for some weeks on the forested banks of Suiá Missu River in central Brazil, we were lucky enough to encounter – and handle – all four species of green kingfishers several times, the Green and Amazon mainly on the riverside, and the American Pygmy Kingfisher and the present one mainly a few hundred metres into the forest. Despite that, we learned little of consequence about their habits, except to confirm that, when fishing from overhanging branches, they all behave much like typical Old World fishers: waiting patiently, from time to time bobbing the head and flicking the tail up, diving steeply for prey, and when alarmed flying away quickly low over the water. Little more than that appears to be on record for Green-and-rufous Kingfishers (Forshaw 1983). *Nesting:* few nest burrows have been found, all in stream-banks, and none adequately described. There are 3-5 eggs in the clutch.

Description *Adult male:* forehead and lores blackish-green with a few tiny rufous spots, and a narrow rufous line above the lore. Crown, ear-coverts and hindneck dark glossy green; a thin line of white below the eye. Chin, throat and malar area pale yellow-buff, changing to bright foxy-rufous on the side of the neck; a narrow hindneck-collar is pale yellow-buff. The remaining upperparts are dark glossy green, the mantle almost black next to the collar, the upperwing-coverts neatly tipped with white, and the tertials and secondaries with evenly spaced small white spots which make four rows in the closed wing. Uppertail-coverts with some small buff-white spots. Below the throat the underparts are rich dark rufous, the underwing- and undertail-coverts rather paler. White spots on the inner webs of the tail feathers are conspicuous on the dark grey underside of the tail. Bill black, with pale yellowish under the lower mandible; eye dark brown; legs and feet dark grey. *Adult female:* like the male, but a broad breast-band of green-tipped white feathers; forehead, upperwing-coverts and rump are more conspicuously spotted, and crown and back are lightly pale-spotted also. *Juvenile:* like the adult female, but wing-coverts and back to uppertail-coverts are more copiously spotted; males have a narrow buff-and-green breast-band. *Measurements:* wing of male 91-99, of female 94-101; tail of male 58-66, of female 53-62; bill of male 48-55, of female 50-58; tarsus of male 10-13, of female 10-12. Weight: male 46-60, female 53-62.

References Forshaw (1983), Fry (1980a).

81 GREEN KINGFISHER   Plate 26
Chloroceryle americana

Alcedo americana Gmelin, 1788, Syst. Nat., I, pt I, p. 451, Cayenne.

Field identification Length 20 cm (8 in). One of four tropical American green kingfishers, the male with bright rufous breast, and the female without any rufous but with green upper breast and cream lower breast. *At rest:* dark green upperparts; two rows of white spots in the wing are usually visible; large white or cream throat patch crossed by a narrow stripe; flanks strongly barred with dark green. *In flight:* wings and tail are heavily spotted with white, as in the other three *Chloroceryle* species. *Confusion species:* American Pygmy Kingfishers (79) are much smaller, both sexes with rufous flanks. Green-and-rufous Kingfishers (80) are larger than the Green, and both sexes have rufous bellies. Amazon Kingfishers (82) are similar to the Green, but 1½ times its size and 2-3 times its weight; they have streaked flanks (barred on the Green), and their folded wings do not show any white spots.

Voice The commonest calls are a clicking like two pebbles being struck together, and a long series of rapid, subdued ticking notes that sound songbird-like. Creaking, scratchy notes have been described.

Geographical variation There is clinal variation in green hue, the prominence of white spots in wing and tail, in flank and undertail-covert characters, and in size. We admit five subspecies.
   C. a. americana Northern South America east of the Andes, from Venezuela to north Bolivia and in Brazil,

Rondônia, Amazonás, Pará and Bahía. Birds on Trinidad and Tobago have the bill slightly stouter.

C. a. mathewsii Intergrading with *americana*, it ranges further south, east of the Andes, to north Argentina, south to Mendoza and La Plata. Upperparts lighter green than in *americana*, female's breastband less pronounced; bill more slender. Slightly larger, and tail 10% longer.

C. a. hachisukai Southernmost Arizona, southwest New Mexico and southwest Texas, to Nayarit, Chihuahua and Coahuila Provinces of Mexico. Greens with yellowish-bronze cast; wing-coverts, secondaries and tail more heavily spotted than in *americana*, and bill 10% longer.

C. a. septentrionalis Ranges between *hachisukai* and *americana*, intergrading with both, and meeting the latter in west Venezuela. Larger white spots in wing and tail than *americana*; less green on flanks and undertail-coverts. Wing 8% longer; bill 10% longer.

C. a. cabanisii North Chile and Peru west of the Andes, merging broadly through west Ecuador and Colombia with *americana*. Large white spots in secondaries; undertail-coverts white in Peru, greenspotted in Ecuador. Wing 5%, bill 10%, and tail up to 15% longer than in *americana*.

Habitat and range This is the commonest and most widespread of the four *Chloroceryle* kingfishers, found in almost all open freshwater and brackish habitats, from southwest USA, through Central America, Trinidad and Tobago, and the northern half of South America, south to north Chile (to near Arica) and the Mendoza and Buenos Aires regions of Argentina. It frequents shaded rivulets, muddy puddles in dried-out arroyos, deep turbid rivers, flooded scrub forest, still dark pools in evergreen forest, coastal lagoons, mangroves, marshes, small rocky watercourses and choked drainage channels, from coastal lowlands up to 1500 m in Colombia, 2500 m in Costa Rica and 2800 m in Mexico. Everywhere the species is sedentary.

Food Small fishes, crustaceans including prawns *Penaeus aztecus* and palaemonids, and insects including dragonfly nymphs, bugs, ants and other Hymenoptera.

Habits Usually seen solitarily or in pairs, Green Kingfishers are strongly territorial, and as the breeding season approaches territorial bickering is commonplace. Sometimes fighting birds fall into the water and float downstream before parting their interlocked bills (Forshaw 1983). They feed by searching from some waterside perch, occasionally bobbing the head and at the same moment flirting the tail up, and plunging steeply into the water. Occasionally a bird hovers briefly 4-6 m over the surface, scanning for prey (Betts and Betts 1977). **Nesting:** nest burrows are dug by both birds of a pair. As with many other kingfishers, the burrow is in a perpendicular riverbank, often half hidden behind vegetation; it is 5-6 cm wide and 1 m long, straight, and inclining to an unlined chamber where the 3-6 eggs are laid. The female incubates at night, and the pair takes turns during the day, with change-overs accompanied by calling. Chicks leave the nest about 27 days after hatching. **Laying months:** Texas, April; Mexico, March, and probably from January to May; Costa Rica, April; Panama, about November to February; Argentina, November.

Description *C. a. americana* **Adult male:** lore and forehead blackish, a minute white crescent under the eye, and a narrow white hindneck-collar; otherwise the upperparts are burnished dark green, with bronze reflections on the crown. Quite large white spots in the primaries, secondaries and secondary coverts form one minor and two major lines in the folded wing (less apparent in worn plumage). Chin and throat, backwards to the hindneck-collar, white, crossed by a narrow green line. Breast bright rufous; belly white in the middle but with wide black-green bars at the sides and on the flanks. Underwing-coverts dull green and white; undertail-coverts barred dark green and white; underside of tail dark grey, with conspicuous white spots on inner webs of the feathers. Bill black, horn-coloured at the base of the lower mandible; eye dark brown; legs and feet dark grey. **Adult female:** upperparts as on the male; throat creamy or pale buff; upper breast glossy gold-green with some white feather tips; lower breast creamy-buff; remaining underparts as on the male. **Juvenile:** like the adult female but duller, less bronzy, with fine buff spots on crown and wing-coverts. *Measurements:* wing of male 76-84, of female 78-83; tail of male 50-60, of female 51-59; bill of male 35-48, of female 36-45; tarsus of male 9-11, of female 9-11. Weight: male 29-40, female 33-55.

References Forshaw (1983), Fry (1980a).

82 AMAZON KINGFISHER   Plate 26
Chloroceryle amazona

Alcedo amazona Latham, 1790, Index Orn., I, p. 257, Cayenne.

Field identification Length 30 cm (12 in). A large tropical American fisher, resplendent in glossy dark green and white, the male with a wide rufous breast-band. *At rest:* the upperparts are green and the head shaggily crested, with a narrow white hindneck-collar. Wings not spotted; a long, white malar stripe, divided from the white throat by a narrow green line from mandible to the side of the breast; belly and undertail-coverts white; from in front, the tail looks blackish with small white ladder-steps. Breast rufous on males, green and white on females. *In flight:* this large kingfisher looks glossy green in the sun but blackish in the shade, with only indistinct white spots in the wings. *Confusion species:* both sexes of the Green Kingfisher (81) have similar plumages, but they are much smaller and told by the conspicuous rows of white spots in the closed wings, and barred (not striped) flanks.

Voice The main call is a loud, harsh 'tek', often repeated to sound like a football-rattle; also frog-like notes. The song, or a song-like call, uttered as a greeting and in similar contexts, is a series of clear notes, first accelerating and rising in pitch, then decelerating and falling away.

Geographical variation Central American birds are a little larger than South American ones and usually lack the minute white frontal spot. The variation is clinal, and too trivial for subspecies to be assigned.

Habitat and range Much more of a lowland species than the Green Kingfisher, it keeps mainly below 1200 m, frequenting broad, placid rivers, winding channels, and wooded lagoons. A scarce bird in many regions of Central America, it is common in the eastern lowlands of Guatemala, the Belize River where there are rapids and large deep pools (Russell 1964), and in Panama. In South America, Amazon Kingfishers are widespread and quite common throughout their range, which is south just to Ecuador and to central Argentina (Buenos Aires, La Rioja). In Cordobá, Argentina, it is the only kingfisher which follows streams up into the highlands (Forshaw 1983); elsewhere, it has been found as high as 1780 m in Guatemala and 2500 m in Venezuela. Despite some early records of vagrants in Trinidad, the species is sedentary.

Food Fishes up to 12 cm long, and some prawns *Penaeus aztecus.*

Habits Fishing behaviour is like that of *Alcedo* kingfishers; besides hunting from a perch, Amazon Kingfishers occasionally hover momentarily over open water to search for fish. The rarely heard song is given by a bird perching upright on top of a tree, with the wings open and the bill pointing skyward (Skutch 1957). *Nesting:* burrows are dug by both sexes in riverbanks, erosion gullies, road cuttings and other vertical faces, generally near water. Befitting such a large kingfisher, nest burrows are long, up to 1.6 m, and inclining a little, straight or gradually bending to left or right, 8-10 cm in diameter, and ending in a chamber about 25 cm wide, 45 cm long and 16 cm high. The 3-4 eggs are incubated for 22 days, by the female at night and the male for much of the day. Both sexes feed the nestlings, which leave the nest at 29-30 days of age. After feeding the brood, the parent emerges backwards and often tumbles into the water to wash itself. **Laying months:** Honduras and Panama, February; Costa Rica, February, May; Trinidad, once, about May.

Description *Adult male:* upperparts glossy, uniformly dark bronzy green; a minute white fleck in front of the eye and thin white crescent below the eye, and a narrow white hindneck-collar. Inner webs of the primaries, secondaries and tail feathers have regular white marks; there are also some small white marks on the outer webs of the outermost tail feathers. A long malar band connecting the lower mandible and the hindneck-collar is white; chin and throat are white, separated from the malar area by a broken narrow dark green line. Breast rich rufous, with dark green sides; belly, underwing-and undertail-coverts white; flanks white, heavily streaked with dark green. Bill black, with horn-coloured area on underside of the lower mandible; eye dark brown; legs and feet dark grey. *Adult female:* like the male, but breast white with bottle-green sides nearly meeting in the midline above the belly. *Juvenile:* like the adult female, but with buff spots in the upperwing-coverts and a large yellowish area in the bill; males have the breast washed with rufous-buff. *Measurements:* wing of male 128-138, of female 127-140; tail of male 70-84, of female 73-88; bill of male 66-72, of female 67-74; tarsus of male 13-15, of female 13-15. Weight: male 98-120, female 125-140.

References Forshaw (1983), Fry (1980a), Skutch (1957).

83 CRESTED KINGFISHER (Greater Pied Kingfisher) Plate 27
Megaceryle lugubris

Alcedo lugubris Temminck, 1834, Planch. Col., 92, pl. 548, Japan.

Field identification Length 41-43 cm (16-17 in). Unmistakable except in the Himalayas and mountains and forested foothills between Tenasserim and Yunnan, where Pied Kingfishers (87) also occur. *At rest:* a very large, shaggily-crested kingfisher with snowy-flecked dark grey head, back, wings and tail, a broad white collar, and white underparts with black-speckled moustachial streak and breast (the breast often with rufous wash or patches on males) and grey-barred flanks. When the crest is fully erect the forehead feathers are vertical; in side view the crest then looks blackish with two large white patches in it. *In flight:* heavy-looking, with copious white spots in wings and tail; males have white and females pale cinnamon underwing-coverts. *Confusion species:* Crested Kingfishers are much larger than Pieds and differ from them mainly in lacking any large, solid-black areas: Pied Kingfishers have black ear-coverts, narrow black breast-bands, black 'wrists', black wingtips and half of the tail black.

Voice Rather silent, but when disturbed they fly off with loud, indignant 'kek' notes. Also a loud 'ping', deep croaks, and rapidly repeated raucous grating notes.

Geographical variation There are three subspecies, varying a little in hue and size.
M. l. lugubris Japan: Honshū, Shikoku and Kyūshū; vagrant to Korea.
M. l. guttulata From near Peking to central Vietnam, westward to northeast Afghanistan. Upperparts and breast darker, white spots in the crest and back and wings larger but less copious than in *lugubris*. Smaller (except for the bill), but west Himalayan birds are the same size as the nominate race.
M. l. pallida Hokkaidō (Japan) and adjacent south Kuril Islands (USSR). Upperparts paler grey than in *lugubris*.

Habitat and range Crested Kingfishers move down into the mouths of rivers in winter (at least on the south coast of Honshū), but they are principally birds of turbulent rivers and wild streams in forested mountains. From extreme northeast Afghanistan, on Kamdesh River, they range through the Himalayas in Kashmir,

Nepal, Bhutan and Assam, where they are locally quite numerous on well-wooded waterways at about 500-1000 m, and much less common up to 2000 m. Shunning rivers with bare, open banks, they prefer swift, rocky or gravelly streams running through forest, particularly near the confluence with a larger river. Frequent in north Burma, these kingfishers are widespread along forest streams up to 2800 m; to the south and east they are much less common, in south Burma, north Thailand, Laos, and Vietnam south to about 14°N. In China they occur up to 2000 m, keeping mainly to torrential streams in forested uplands, north to southern Hopeh Province and west to Shensi, Szechwan and possibly to Lanchow. Crested Kingfishers are better known in Japan; they are locally common on wide, fast mountain streams at up to 1400 m in Shikoku and Honshū, but are scarce in Hokkaidō, where they have reportedly declined sharply during this century. They occur in Kyūshū, but are not known to breed there.

Migration There is some altitudinal migration in Japan and the Himalayas, a few birds appearing in low-lying plains in winter. However, the paucity of reports of winter movements in general suggests that the Crested is the cold-hardiest of all kingfishers and tolerates wintry conditions at high elevations, so long as streams remain unfrozen. In Hokkaidō, some winter around hot springs in the Kitami Hills. Vagrants in Korea, 80 years ago, were all between November and February, suggesting winter wandering from Honshū. A few pairs may have bred in Lam Tsun valley, Hong Kong, 40 years ago, but the species is presently regarded as an irregular passage migrant there, reported in all months but mainly in April-May.

Food Fish up to 15 or 18 cm long, and crayfish.

Habits Shy birds, Crested Kingfishers are markedly territorial, hunting solitarily in a territory of about 4 km². They spend much time perching on a rock or overhanging branch, occasionally bobbing the head, raising the crest, cocking the tail, and diving obliquely for a fish. Unlike Pied Kingfishers, they do not dive from hovering flight. In retreat, the flight is swift,

heavy-looking, with fast even wingbeats and slight irregular undulation. **Nesting:** burrows are dug by both birds of the pair in a sandy bank at least 2 m high, by a stream, or in a ravine or other vertical bank in forest up to 1.5 km away from water. Burrows are 10-15 cm wide and 2-3 m long. The 4-7 eggs are incubated only by the female. Both parents feed the young, which take 40 days before they are ready to leave the nest (Forshaw 1983). **Laying months:** Japan, about April-July; Nepal, mainly March-April.

Description *M. l. lugubris* **Adult male:** a small white spot in front of the eye and narrow crescentic white mark under the eye. Forehead and crown feathers long and erectile. When the crest is flat, the head top appears blackish-grey with copious white spots; but when it is erected the crest has three blackish parts with two almost pure white patches of shorter feathers between them – blackish feathers sticking up vertically in front, then a white patch, blackish feathers at an angle on the hindcrown, a white nape-patch, and blackish hindneck (Forshaw 1989). Mantle, back and scapulars barred black and white in equal widths. Greater coverts barred or spotted with white, other wing-coverts spotted, secondaries and primaries barred. Tail black with 6-8 white bars. Chin and throat white, separated by a white-speckled blackish moustachial line from a broad white collar encircling the neck; the moustachial line joins a black-speckled breast-band, often with pale rufous-orange feathers mixed through it. Belly, undertail- and underwing-coverts white; flanks boldly barred with grey. Bill black with yellowish tip and pale bluish basal half; eye dark brown; legs and feet dark olive-grey. **Adult female:** like the male, but without any rufous in the breast, and with bright pinkish-cinnamon underwing-coverts. **Juvenile:** like the adult female, but sides of neck, breast, flanks and undertail-coverts washed with pale rufous. **Measurements:** wing of male 186-194, of female 185-194; tail of male 108-111, of female 107-117; bill of male 67-80, of female 65-75; tarsus of male 15-17, of female 15-17. Weight (*M. l. guttulata*): 230-280.

References Forshaw (1983, 1989).

Megaceryle maxima

Alcedo maxima Pallas, 1769, Spic. Zool., 6, p. 14, Cape of Good Hope.

Field identification Length 42-46 cm (16½-18 in). Quite the largest kingfisher in Africa, where it cannot be confused with anything else. It is a heavy-set bird, with big, shaggily-crested blackish head and very large shiny black bill. Commonly it gives only a fleeting view: when unexpectedly flushed from woody riverside growth, it gives a raucous call and, flying low over water, disappears around a bend of the river. Upperparts are slaty-black, finely speckled with white; throat and sides of the neck are white. The male has a chestnut breast, dusky-barred whitish belly, and barred white undertail-coverts; the female has a blackish breast and chestnut belly, undertail- and underwing-coverts.

Voice When disturbed from its perch it usually gives a harsh, loud 'kek' or 'chik', sometimes repeated as 'kek, kek-kek-kek'. The greeting call is 'kek', repeated quickly to become a loud rattle, falling slightly in pitch, then becoming regular and monotonous with 3-4 'kek's per second. Both sexes call 'kek'; or one rattles and the other gives single 'kek's.

Geographical variation Two races occupy practically the whole of sub-Saharan Africa between them, one in wooded savannas and one in the rainforest zone. The latter is darker, and intergrades with the former along thousands of kilometres of savanna/forest interface. Southern African birds are slightly larger than equatorial ones.

M. m. maxima Open country from Senegambia to west Ethiopia and from south Angola to Mozambique, eastern South Africa and the coastal strip west to Cape Town.

M. m. gigantea Forest from Liberia to north Angola and west Tanzania. It is darker than the nominate race, its upperparts not so heavily spotted, and its underparts with heavier bars.

Habitat and range It inhabits perennial rivers with wooded banks in forest and savanna regions, dams and lakes with plenty of overhanging woody growth along the edges, coastal lagoons, and mangroves. Sometimes it occurs along thickly wooded, dried-up streambeds with a few stagnant pools; on rapids; in flooded woodland; and at ornamental garden ponds. It is often found on rocky and sandy seashores and in estuaries, fishing up to 100 m from the shore. It occurs throughout all West African coastal countries from Senegambia to Angola, including Bioko Island; and Central African Republic, Zaïre, Rwanda, Burundi, Tanzania, Zambia, Malaŵi, Zimbabwe and Mozambique. It resides also in south Mali, Burkina Faso, southwest Niger, south Chad, south Sudan (records north to Khartoum), west Ethiopia, Uganda except the northeast, southwest Kenya, northernmost Namibia and Caprivi Strip, north Botswana, and locally throughout South Africa excepting northern Cape Province. In East Africa it lives at up to 2700 m altitude.

Population Frequent to common in the South African coastal zone from Cape Town to Mozambique, and common throughout southern Africa north of Okavango and Vaal and Cunene Rivers (but uncommon higher than 1500 ·m). Widespread and common in Tanzania; once recorded in Somalia, in extreme south; in Sudan common on upper Dinder River and Setit River, and south of Bahr el Arab; frequent or common in the Congo Basin and west Ethiopia; frequent and locally common in Nigeria; frequent in Senegal; uncommon in Gambia. One pair in South Africa required 4.3 km of river for its home range. There is evidence that this kingfisher is adversely affected by pesticides draining into its rivers from adjacent farmland.

Migration Little evidence of seasonal movement, except that it emigrates from northwest Ethiopia in October-December. Perhaps a dry-season visitor at Serti, Nigeria.

Food In Liberia and South Africa mainly river crabs, and in Zaïre mainly fish. In South Africa, small crabs *Potamon perlatus* are eaten whole, but ones with a carapace width of 35-45 mm are dismembered first. It eats mosquito fish *Gambusia affinis*, also frogs, clawed toads and occasional centipedes and small reptiles. Nearly fledged young are fed fish up to 18 cm long.

Habits Solitary or in pairs. Shy; often it shuns open perches and uses shady foliage. When flushed, it usually calls and flies away low over water or treetops. A pair keeps to one stretch of a river, perching in trees, on rocks, the ground, telegraph wires, and bridge parapets. Hovering is not common, although it does sometimes hover over tidal pools and other wide expanses of water without ready perches. Fishing is mainly from a branch overhanging a secluded stretch of water; it perches 2-4 m high, scans the water intently, then dives in at a steep or shallow angle, generally immersing completely. Crabs are carried to a stout branch or boulder, juggled until held in the tip of the beak, and vigorously whacked with a swinging movement to right and left, until the pincers are knocked off. Fish are swallowed head-first, occasionally tail-first. Some minutes after a successful dive, the bird often flies to a new feeding station; it changes station 2-5 times an hour, flying 7-8 km each day in the process. After fishing in the sea it dives into fresh water to cleanse itself. *Nesting:* monogamous, solitary-breeding. The nest is an unlined cavity at the end of a hole excavated up to 5 m above water level in a riverbank. The entrance is about 11 cm high and 15 wide, and the tunnel 2 m long, straight and horizontal or sometimes declining or inclining. An 8.5-m-long tunnel is on record, as well as nests up to 1.6 km from flowing water. The hole is dug by both sexes, in seven days, using bills and feet to scrape loosened soil backwards. In time the chamber becomes foul with dropped food, decomposed pellets, and liquid excrement. In a clutch of three eggs, two probably hatch at the same time and the third 1-2 days later. The parents remove eggshells, dropping them on to water and diving on to them to sink them. At one nest with two young a fish was brought every 150 minutes; the male stopped bringing food on the 30th day and the female on the 35th. Both young flew on the 37th day; they started diving into water within a few hours, but were still being fed by the female three weeks later. *Laying months:* South Africa, September-January; Zimbabwe, August-March, mainly September and October; Zambia, March-April, June-August (mainly August); East Africa, June-July, May, July-October; Ethiopia, August; northeast Zaïre, January-March; Cameroon, December; Liberia, December-January; Mali, March; Senegambia, November-February.

Description *M. m. maxima* **Adult male:** forehead, crown, nape and hindneck blackish, with small white spots and streaks on crown. Lores and cheeks black; often a small white spot in front of the eye. Back blackish, each feather with pairs of white spots on the edges, giving a regular white-spotted or white-barred effect. Tail blackish, rather short and square-tipped, and with 6-8 regularly spaced narrow white bars. Chin and throat white; moustachial stripe blackish with a white area behind it under the cheeks and on the sides of the neck. Breast rich coppery-brown; belly and undertail-coverts white with bold, irregular dusky bars. Underside of tail silvery-grey with white bars; underwing-coverts white. Bill black; eye dark brown; legs and feet dark grey or blackish. **Adult female:** like male, but breast black, or densely spotted with black on a white background, and belly, flanks, undertail-coverts, axillaries and underwing-coverts rich copper-brown. **Juvenile:** male like adult male, but with black speckles on the sides of the breast and some rufous feathers on the flanks. Female like adult female, but with the breast less densely spotted and with some rufous fringing, the marks mainly crescentic and at the sides, leaving a whitish band between breast and belly. **Measurements:** wing of male 190-208, of female 194-206; tail of male 105-124, of female 105-124; bill, from tip to front of nostril, 65-86.5, and to feathers, on male 81-94, on female 80-94; tarsus of male 15-18, of female 15-19. Weight: male 275-426, female 255-398.

References Forshaw (1983), Fry (1980a,b), Fry *et al.*(1988).

85 RINGED KINGFISHER

Megaceryle torquata

Plate 28

Alcedo torquata Linnaeus, 1766, Syst. Nat., ed. 12, I, p. 180, Martinique and Mexico.

Field identification Length 40 cm (16 in). Unmistakable in South America, where the only other kingfishers are all green-backed. It is a huge, shaggily-crested, slate-grey kingfisher with a broad white collar and deep rufous underparts. Males have the breast rufous and undertail- and underwing-coverts white; females have a grey band across the upper breast, and rufous undertail- and underwing-coverts. ***Confusion species:*** only the Belted Kingfisher (86). The breeding ranges of the two species do not overlap, except possibly in the lower Rio Grande valley, Texas/Mexico (Mcgrew 1971). In winter, migratory Belted Kingfishers penetrate the range of the sedentary Ringed Kingfisher, south to Panama, north Colombia and Venezuela, Lesser Antilles Islands, Tobago and Trinidad. Belted Kingfishers are much smaller; males lack rufous, and females have rufous restricted to the flanks, sides of the breast and in a narrow band across the lower breast.

Voice A loud monosyllabic 'kek' or 'klek', sometimes doubled as 'klek-klek', which may be repeated. The alarm is a rattling 'klek-klek-klek-klek-klek...'.

Geographical variation Three subspecies, only weakly differentiated.

M. t. torquata The mainland tropical population from south Sinaloa Province (Mexico) and lower Rio Grande (Texas/Mexico), throughout Central and South America to south Peru, Uruguay and about Tandil and Mar del Plata, Argentina; also Margarita Island (Venezuela) and Trinidad.

M. t. stictipennis Caribbean, Guadeloupe, Dominica, Martinique, and possibly St Kitts and Grenada. White spots in the secondaries extend from the inner to the outer webs.

M. t. stellata Breeds from about Concepción (Chile) and Río Negro and Neuquén (Argentina) to Tierra del Fuego. Partially migratory (see below). Like *stictipennis*, but undertail-coverts more strongly spotted and barred with grey.

Habitat and range From the lower Rio Grande, south Sinaloa and Guadeloupe, Ringed Kingfishers range to Tierra del Fuego, except for north Chile and west-central Argentina (between about Tucumán, Mendoza and Río Cuarto). They frequent wide, slow-flowing rivers, lowland lakes, marshes, estuaries, brackish coastal lagoons, mangrove and sometimes open beaches. Other habitats include ricefields, reservoirs, canals, water-gardens in cities such as Rio de Janeiro, and Chilean fiords (Johnson 1967). Individuals have been seen fishing on reefs 1 km offshore, but Ringed Kingfishers usually fish in heavily wooded places. Although found as high as 1100 m in Honduras, 1300 m in Panama and 1500 m in Guatemala (Lake Atitlán), they are uncommon much above 500 m. They are widespread and generally plentiful throughout lowlands, but rare in Guadeloupe and Trinidad.

Migration A summer visitor from November to March to Isla Grande (Tierra del Fuego); winters north to Valparaíso and Buenos Aires. Otherwise it is sedentary.

Food Mainly fish, up to about 20 cm long; also a few frogs, salamanders, reptiles and insects.

Habits Usually encountered solitarily, they are rather shy birds which, when disturbed, seldom fly more than 200 m and then perch out of sight. Sometimes they take short-cuts overland between waterways, flying low over the trees. When fishing, a bird uses one perch, often a stout overhanging branch, for up to two hours, raising the crest and now and then cocking the tail, diving steeply, carrying the fish back to the perch to stun it by beating, swallowing it whole, then either staying or flying to another favourite perch some way off. ***Nesting:*** solitary, although on Orinoco River, Venezuela, several colonies of 4-5 pairs have been reported, and once a colony of 150 pairs (Cherrie 1916).

Burrows, 15 cm wide, 10 cm high, and 2.3-2.7 m long, are excavated by both birds of the pair, generally in riverbanks but occasionally in erosion gulleys and road cuttings well away from water. The 3-6 eggs are brooded by male and female in turn, each sitting for nearly 24 hours and changing over in the early morning. The incubating bird takes an unrelieved half-hour break in the afternoon (Skutch 1972). The incubation period is 22 days or more, and the chicks, which are fed by both parents, are fully feathered at 24 days and quit the nest when 35 days old, flying strongly up to 70 m on the very first attempt. *Laying months:* Texas, about March; Tamaulipas, Mexico, about January; Belize, April-May; Panama, about March-May; Surinam, February, June; Trinidad, April; Guyana, August; southern Chile, about November.

Description *M. t. torquata* **Adult male:** the entire head is bluish slate-grey, but for a small white frontal spot, a narrow semicircle of white just below the eye, and a broad white collar around the neck. Side of upper breast, mantle to uppertail-coverts, scapulars and wings blue-grey; uppertail- and wing-coverts, also secon-

daries and tertials, have minute white tips. Primaries blackish; primaries and secondaries with large white marks on their inner webs. Tail blackish, the feathers with blue-green edges, white tips, and about five evenly spaced white spots on each web; below, the tail is blackish with five white ladder-rungs. Centre of breast to belly deep rufous; undertail-coverts white with some grey bars; underwing-coverts white. Bill grey-black, paler towards the base, and pale horn-coloured at the base of the lower mandible; eye dark brown; legs and feet dark grey. **Adult female:** like the male, but underwing- and undertail-coverts deep rufous, and a blue-grey band across the upper breast with a narrow white line below it. **Juvenile:** like the female, but upperparts streaky and underparts paler, the grey upper breast washed with rufous, and the underwing-coverts partly white. **Measurements:** wing of male 187-201, of female 188-199; tail of male 105-120, of female 115-125; bill of male 77-88, of female 68-78; tarsus of male 15-17, of female 15-17. Weight: male 254-330, female 274-325.

Reference Forshaw (1983).

86 BELTED KINGFISHER   Plate 28
Megaceryle alcyon

Alcedo Alcyon Linnaeus, 1758, Syst. Nat., ed. 10, I, p. 115, South Carolina.

Field identification Length 28-33 cm (11-13 in). Unmistakable in North America (except in lower Rio Grande Valley, Texas). A winter visitor to Central America, the Caribbean and northwest South America, where it can be mistaken for the Ringed Kingfisher (85). It is a very large, shaggily-crested, grey and white kingfisher with a broad white collar and grey breast-band; additionally, females have rufous sides (usually concealed under the folded wing) and a narrow rufous band across the lower breast. **Confusion species:** Ringed Kingfishers are much larger, 2-3 times as heavy, and are readily distinguished by their deep rufous bellies.

Voice The call is a loud, far-carrying, harsh rattle, 'kekity-kek-kek-kek-tk-ticky-kek'; also harsh 'caar' notes and, in courtship flight, high-pitched squeaks.

Geographical variation None (Forshaw 1983).

Habitat and range Belted Kingfishers live on lakes, swift mountain streams, coasts, mangrove, tidal creeks and swamps, rivers and garden ponds, at all elevations from sea level up to 2500 m in the Rockies. They need clear, still waters for fishing, and elevated perches such as trees, telegraph wires and posts; but they have been recorded fishing 1 km offshore. In countryside providing these requirements, they are common and widespread birds, ranging north to Aleutian Islands, Seward Peninsula and Fairbanks in Alaska, north-central Saskatchewan, central Manitoba, central Ontario, east Ungava Bay in Quebec, Labrador and Newfoundland. They breed south throughout USA to south California, south Texas, and the northern coast of the Gulf of Mexico, and in winter range to Panama, north Colombia (very rare) and the coastal lowlands of Venezuela and Guyana (scarce), and they occur commonly throughout the Caribbean to Trinidad. Vagrants have been found in the Azores, Netherlands (Gelderland, December 1899), Iceland (Vestmannaeyjar, September 1901), Ireland (Co. Mayo, December 1978 to February 1979; Mullarney 1981; Co. Down, October 1980; Co. Clare and Co. Tipperary, October 1984 to March 1985), and England (Cornwall, November 1908, and October or November 1979 to December 1981).

Population In New Brunswick densities reach ten birds on every 1600 m of farmland streams (White 1953), and on Lake Hasca, Minnesota, 14 nesting pairs occupied an area of 65 km^2 (Cornwell 1963).

Migration A partial migrant to Central America and the West Indies, with sporadic records of birds wintering almost throughout the breeding range. A summer visitor to Alaska, but a few regularly winter along the coasts of Unalanaska and Shumagin Islands (Aleutians and Alaska Peninsula); some winter also on the coasts and in the interior of British Columbia, South Newfoundland, Nova Scotia, and Washington State. The main wintering grounds are the southern half of USA, Central America south to Panama, and the West Indies south to Trinidad. Although there are no breeding records in the Bahamas, a few birds regularly oversummer on New Providence and other islands there. Non-breeding migrants visit the West Indies, Guatemala and Panama from September to early April, and Trinidad from mid October to late April. In autumn migrants coast south along the shores of Lake Michigan at a peak rate of 12 per hour, and conversely in spring they move north on the west shore of Lake Huron at a rate of up to 15 birds per hour (Salyer and Lagler 1946). Migrants are common along the Atlantic seaboard.

Food Mainly fish, particularly brook trout, freshwater sculpin, three-spined and nine-spined sticklebacks and Atlantic salmon; also lake chub, white sucker, common shiner, black-nosed dace, minnow, banded killfish, mummichogs, yellow perch, horny-headed chub and mud minnow. Food fishes are up to 14 cm long, averaging 9 cm. Crayfish and other crustaceans are sometimes taken, as are frogs, salamanders, lizards, water-shrews, young sparrows, quail chicks, dragonfly nymphs, grasshoppers, moths and butterflies (some caught on the wing), and, in winter, berries.

Habits Most fishes are caught less than 60 cm below the surface, seized about one-third of their length back, with the kingfisher's wings spread under water to brake the dive and the third eyelid covering the eye. Dives are oblique or almost vertical, usually from a stout perch but sometimes from hovering flight up to 15 m above the water surface. Birds regularly forage up to 8 km from their nest. Fish are beaten against the perch to stun them, and swallowed whole; by contrast, invertebrates are sometimes dismembered while being beaten, and crayfish claws which fall off are not retrieved. Belted Kingfishers live singly or in pairs; unlike their congeners they are not shy. At night they roost high up in a leafy tree near water, using small, supple twigs. As with all other coraciiform birds, pellets cast up during the night litter the ground below a regular roosting spot. **Nesting:** territorial when breeding, this kingfisher marks its spring arrival with conspicuous, noisy chasing flights around its territory. Pairs nest solitarily, and the male courtship-feeds its mate. Where well-drained vertical banks by water are plentiful that site is almost always used for the nest burrow. Otherwise, earth cuttings, embankments, mounds, gravel-pits, mud-slides made by Beavers, impacted soil in the roots of a fallen tree, and even sawdust heaps and tree holes are used (Forshaw 1983), sometimes far from water. Tunnels are 1-2 (once 5) m long, inclining a little, with a hump or lip before the egg chamber. Completed clutches are usually of 6-7 eggs, and the average brood is of four young. There is a single brood, although replacement clutches may be laid. The incubation period is 23-24 days and the nestling period 30-35 days. **Laying months:** Ontario, April-July; New York State, May-June; Louisiana, April-June.

Description Adult male: the entire head is bluish slate-grey, but for a small white frontal spot, a narrow semicircle of white just below the eye, and a broad white collar around the neck. Upper breast, mantle to uppertail-coverts, scapulars and wings are blue-grey; the uppertail- and wing-coverts, also secondaries and tertials, have minute white tips. Primaries blackish with white spots above, slaty below, the feathers with white tips and about seven evenly spaced white spots on each

web. Belly, flanks, underwing- and undertail-coverts are white. Bill greyish-black; eye dark brown; legs and feet dark grey. **Adult female:** differs from the male in having a rufous band across the lower breast, rufous sides to the upper breast, and rufous flanks. **Juvenile:** like the adult female, but the grey breast-band is washed with rufous, strongly so on females. **Measurements:** wing of male 151-168, of female 154-168; tail of male 79-91, of female 83-96; bill of male 50-60, of female 54-60; tarsus of male 12-15, of female 12-14. Weight: male 113-173, female 142-178.

References Cornwell (1963), Forshaw (1983), Salyer and Lagler (1946), White (1953).

87 PIED KINGFISHER (Lesser Pied Kingfisher)   Plate 28
Ceryle rudis

Alcedo rudis Linnaeus, 1758, Syst. Nat., ed. 10, I, p. 116, Egypt.

Field identification Length 25 cm (10 in). Practically unmistakable anywhere in its great range: the Pied Kingfisher is even more readily identified because it is common, noisy, conspicuous and quite gregarious and tame. Rarely for a kingfisher, the plumage is black and white only — there is no colour. **At rest:** a thrush-sized bird with the usual upright or slanting kingfisher posture, large head, long dagger-like black bill, untidily crested hindcrown, rather short tail, black-and-white-speckled upperparts, and mainly white underparts. An irregular black patch, from just in front of the eye through the ear-coverts, meets the black hindneck; above it there is an irregular white eyebrow. Crown blackish; the crest is often sleeked flat, the long feathers forming a point over the hindneck. Although the feathers can be — and commonly are — raised on the hindcrown, the forecrown is uncrested. From behind, the tail looks black with white sides and narrow white tip; from below or in front it looks white with the distal half mainly black. Feet black. Females have a conspicuous black patch at each side of the white breast, not quite meeting in the middle; males have

more extensive patches, sometimes meeting, and also a narrow dusky line across the breast, below the patches. **In flight:** head and back appear heavily speckled but mainly blackish, and the wing mainly white, with a large black patch at the bend and black ends to primaries and outer secondaries. The bird commonly hovers, keeping station with flaying wings and looking intently down; the tail looks black-ended. Hovering individuals can usually be sexed easily by the breast marks. Flanks streaked with black. Underside of wing mainly white. **Confusion species:** the Crested Kingfisher (83) is much larger (nearly four times the weight of the Pied), more shaggily crested, without a white eyebrow, and with a broad band of blackish spots across the breast; wing-lining pink-brown (not white). It is a bird more of mountain rivers than of lowland lakes.

Voice A vocal kingfisher, often heard before it is seen. The commonest call is a high-pitched, chattering, rather squeaky 'kwik', repeated at irregular intervals, and given in flight and at perch. A threat call — uttered frequently, since territorial interactions are commonplace – is a high-pitched, staccato 'chicker-kerker', given irregularly. Something like it is used also during communal courtship displays. There is no song. A 'kittle-te-ker' is uttered when a bird flies from its perch, and is repeated every 1-2 seconds during flight. Several other special-function calls have been described (Douthwaite 1978).

Geographical variation Four races are recognised, differing slightly in size and in the amount of black, particularly on the flanks.

C. r. rudis Distributed throughout sub-Saharan Africa, and occurs commonly north in the Nile valley to its delta; central and southern Turkey, and Israel through Mesopotamia to the northern half of the Persian Gulf. In the 19th century a few vagrants occurred in the west Mediterranean, and today it is an uncommon winter visitor to Cyprus. Vagrants have been reported in Greece (five records), USSR and Poland.

C. r. travancoreensis Southwest India. Upperparts blacker than in *rudis*, with smaller white markings; black spots (rather than streaks) on flanks, at sides of throat and sometimes in middle of throat. The bill is up to 10 mm longer than in *rudis*.

C. r. leucomelanura Inhabits the rest of India, Sri Lanka, northeast Afghanistan, Kashmir and Himalayan foothills to Thailand and Indochina. It is like *travancoreensis*, but not quite so dark nor heavily black-spotted, and the bill is smaller (the same length as in *rudis*).

C. r. insignis Hong Kong, Hainan and southeast China. Like *leucomelanura*, but the bill averages 5 mm longer.

Habitat and range Pied Kingfishers are particularly at home at the margins of large expanses of fresh and brackish water: they like small and large lakes, broad placid rivers, sheltered estuaries, dams and reservoirs. But they tend to be much less abundant on fast-flowing rivers, narrow streams, and East African soda lakes. Despite being such successful hunters by the use of hovering – occasionally as far as 3 km out on Lake Kariba – they rely heavily on the availability of perches such as waterside trees, low banks, stakes, dead branches, reeds, papyrus, fences, huts along the shoreline,

dugout canoes, motorboats and fishing tackle. They are especially fond of single posts a few metres offshore; sometimes a line of four or five posts marking a channel will serve as vantage points for the same number of Pied Kingfishers. They range up to 1800 m in Kashmir and 2500 m in Rwanda, but in the eastern Himalayas they ascend only to 900 m. In general the species is commoner in low-lying country, where birds fish in marshes and paddy-fields and can be very numerous in estuaries, coastal lagoons, mangrove, and along both sandy and rocky coasts. In such habitats this fine kingfisher ranges throughout sub-Saharan Africa, including Bioko, Zanzibar, Pemba and Mafia Islands, but it is absent from arid parts of east Ethiopia, Somalia, Namibia, west Botswana and Cape Province. It occurs commonly along the South African coast west to Cape Town. If it occurs at all in arid regions it is restricted to large permanent rivers, such as Webbi Shebelle, Juba, Cunene and Orange Rivers. It lives along the Nile north to Sohag (north Egypt). It is absent from Sinai, but is found from the Gaza Strip to Turkey, and east through Syria and Iraq to southwest Iran. Then from northeast Afghanistan and Kashmir it is distributed without significant break throughout the Indian subcontinent to Sri Lanka, Burma, Thailand, the whole of Indochina, Hainan, Hong Kong, and south China north to about the Yangtze River system.

Population We would guess this to be among the three most numerous species of kingfishers in the world, the other two being River Kingfisher (76) and Mangrove Kingfisher (47). Pied Kingfishers are abundant in the brackish Sundarbans swamps of West Bengal, and in the Kazinga Channel connecting Lake George and Lake Edward in Uganda the density varies between nine and 16 individuals per km; 70 birds were found along 17 km of lake shorelines in Uganda's Kigezi District, and 100 on 32 km of Lake Victoria's shores. On waters in Rwanda, Zambia and Malaŵi an average of two birds per km is perhaps more typical for the species. After stocking of Kigezi District with commercial fish in the 1930s Pied Kingfishers became more abundant, and their density also increased when fish-farming started in Burundi in the 1950s. They are reported to survive endosulfan spraying in the short term (spraying to control tsetse-flies, which also kills fish), but locally they have been badly affected by the application of poisons used to kill fish and Red-billed Queleas *Quelea quelea* in Africa.

Migration Resident, probably mainly sedentary; but there are many reports of seasonal changes in abundance at given localities, and a few, mainly in Africa, of large-scale movements actually observed (although some may have been merely localised roosting movements). A bird ringed at Gambela, Ethiopia, was recovered 760 km away at Lake Kyogo, Uganda.

Food In Africa the Pied Kingfisher is almost exclusively a fish-eater; in India, at least according to a major study in the Bengal coastal Sundarbans, it feeds on fish, crustaceans and aquatic insects. Around Lake Victoria the prey is almost solely fish of three kinds, *Engraulicypris argenteus*, *Haplochromis* spp. and *Barbus* spp., of average length 6 cm and weight 4 g, although the kingfisher can take a fish of 26 g. Each bird consumes some 44 g of fish daily. Much the same fishes are eaten in Botswana: *Haplochromis* spp. and other cichlids, and *Barbus paludinosus*. Many fish species are taken in the Kosi Estuary in Zululand, *Gilchristella aestuarius* the most abundantly, but *Ambassis natalensis* providing the bird with more energy; from Kosi comes this fisher's biggest-fish record, a *Hyporhamphus knysnaensis* 133 mm long. In a study in Zambia numerous fish species were found to be taken, the principal ones being cichlids, *Barbus* and *Alestes*; and at Lake St Lucia in Natal Pied Kingfishers catch mainly the 1-2-g *Sarotherodon mossambicus* and a dozen other fish species, both surface-shoalers and deep-water-shoalers. In some places the fish diet is supplemented throughout the year with aquatic insects and crustaceans. Kingfishers living in swampy shallows at Namwala on the Kafue Flats in Zambia take a great many dragonfly larvae (24% of all prey items) and a few water-bugs and water-beetles. In tropical Africa the birds also catch in flight a good many winged insects: dragonflies, termites *Macrotermes* and grasshoppers *Ruspolia flavovirens*. Similarly, in Kashmir, termites and grasshoppers caught on the wing feature regularly in the diet of Pied Kingfishers, and in the Sundarbans aquatic insects compose 26% of prey and crabs and crayfish 17%. Fishes taken in the Sundarbans are mainly *Mugil parsa* and species of *Ambassis*, *Puntius* and *Mystus*. Pied Kingfishers (and some other kingfishers) can partly digest fish bone, although not insect and crustacean chitin. Diet studies that rely on analysis of stomach contents or of regurgitated pellets may therefore exaggerate somewhat the proportions of insect and crustacean prey.

Habits In several respects the Pied Kingfisher has scored firsts in the evolution of fishing within the Alcedinidae/Cerylidae. Like other kingfishers, it fishes by diving from a perch; but it also regularly hunts by hovering, plunging down to catch its prey like a miniature gannet. It hovers far more than does any other kind of kingfisher: in calm weather 20% of dives are from hovering flight, but when it is windy or choppy hovering accounts for 80% of the feeding.

Hover-hunting releases it from the reliance of all other kingfishers on shorelines with their perching-places; Pied Kingfishers can and do hunt out to sea and far offshore in Africa's great lakes. Another first is its ability to handle prey away from a perch: this kingfisher has been known to catch two fish in one dive, to eat a crab at sea, and often to swallow fish less than 2 cm long on the wing, without first having to return to a firm perching-place to beat them. Pied Kingfishers shun shade (except that of open foliage when they are resting in the heat of midday) and perch in the open. At a foraging post, the bird intently scans the water and suddenly dives fast at a steep or shallow angle, hitting the water surface with quite a loud splash and rising a split-second later with its prey. The fish is carried straight back to the bird's post, gripped crosswise behind the operculum.

Its head and tail are whacked hard against the substrate, and then it is swallowed head-first; according to size, *Tilapia* fish up to 9 cm long are whacked up to 113 times before they are eaten.

After post-fishing, the bird flies low over the surface to a desired hunting station, where it rises 2-10 m high and hovers for up to 10 seconds, with the trunk held nearly vertically, the bill pointing down and the wings beating fast and vigorously. The kingfisher may drop a little, hover again and then plunge down, or fly to another station. It hawks actively on the wing for termites, and occasionally hunts on dry land, dropping into grass like a woodland kingfisher to catch an insect. The species is adaptable, soon learning to raid a new fish farm. When the sardine *Limnothrissa miodon*, a pelagic fish which rises to the surface at dawn and dusk, was introduced to Lake Kariba, Pied Kingfishers started to exploit it by hunting far offshore at those times. They also take crusts of bread thrown out for them. These kingfishers fly with rapid, uneven beats, interspersed with occasional short glides; the flight is direct, without undulation, at a measured speed of 50 km/h. When alarmed or excited, a perched individual flicks its tail up and down. The crest is often flirted, lying flat or sticking up untidily on the hindcrown at an angle of 45°. Bathing is quite frequent: the bird makes several rapid, shallow dives onto the water surface, then preens itself thoroughly at perch.

At night Pied Kingfishers roost usually gregariously, with up to 220 individuals gathering in a few square metres of papyrus interspersed with some woody vegetation, or in a clump of low trees on an islet on a large fallen tree in the water; roosting also takes place in holes in a large sandstone cliff, in ambatch clumps, date palms, or even on the ground. Pellets of indigestible matter are cast up during the night, and by day. Indeed it seems probable that the bird has to empty its stomach before it resumes hunting, since in Zambia day-long foraging was found to be broken by three one-hour resting periods, in the early morning, the forenoon and the early afternoon. Pellets are silvery-grey when composed mainly of fish bones or blackish if full of insect sclerites, and crumbly. They average 13 × 25 mm (maximum 16 × 50 mm).

Pied Kingfishers live in pairs or loosely knit family parties. There are nearly twice as many males as females and they are essentially monogamous. But, at least in Uganda and Kenya, where their curious society has been studied in depth by H.U. Reyer (see Bibliography), one pair in three has a helper or helpers – occasionally as many as four. A helper is always male; he is either the one-year-old son of one or both of the nesting pair (primary helper), or he is unrelated, himself a non-nester or a failed nester (secondary helper). A breeding pair rarely has more than a single primary helper, but can have several secondary helpers. Pairs with poor feeding prospects – poor, because they have had to settle in an area with second-rate food resources – tend to have more helpers than do pairs with plentiful food. A primary helper accompanies the nesting pair from the start and participates in all breeding duties. During the courtship and incubation periods the breeding male feeds its mate, and the primary helper feeds them both, bringing a fish and relinquishing it to either parent after a brief tussle at a perch, on the ground or (rarely) to a recipient in flight. Usually it is the breeding male who receives the fish, and as often as not he gives it in turn to his mate incubating inside the nest. Primary helpers join in mobbing any large mammal or reptile which comes near the nest, diving towards it, calling, and circling slowly with flapping flight alternating with gliding; intruders are often successfully driven away. Primaries join their parents and one or two other nesting groups in communal displays, in which up to 12 birds noisily chase through the air, land on bare ground, face each other with the body upright and wings half spread, and turn around; this sometimes leads to fighting, with bill-grappling and wing-grabbing. Primaries help to feed the nestlings.

Secondary helpers appear any time after the eggs have hatched, usually within a few days. At first the breeding birds drive a secondary away, but they soon accept him; he helps only by bringing food, given more often to the breeding female than to her nestlings. R. Victor tells us that in eastern Nigeria Pied Kingfishers are commonly kept as pets. Fishermen's children take two or three older nestlings from their nest, keep them in fish basket-traps and feed them with scraps of raw fish. They become very tame after only a week and are released to ride around on the children's wrists or to roam freely in the fishing camp. Many go back to the wild; some less fortunate ones end up as an optional extra in fish pepper soup.

Nesting: nesting is solitary or colonial, and breeding is without helpers or (generally) with them. Nesting holes are excavated by both parents and any primary helper in an earthen bank. A colony has rather scattered nests, on average 5 m apart; there are usually fewer than 20 nests, but once 30 in a sea-cliff in Sierra Leone and 100 nests at a Zambian site. The pair defends the burrow and its immediate vicinity, calling vigorously, fanning their tails and half-raising their wings. Copulation is preceded by displaying and courtship-feeding, usually near the nest. The male feeds his mate for about three weeks, starting in the nest-digging period. They both dig the nest, by jabbing with opened beak and kicking out loosened soil backwards with the legs. Excavation takes from 11 days to 11 months (on average, 26 days). The sandy or clayey cliff or bank becomes riddled with holes, mostly 'false starts' or 'cock nests' without a completed egg chamber. Definitive nest burrows are generally straight, horizontal or inclining, 1-2.5 m long, including the unlined egg chamber measuring about 45 cm long, 24 cm wide and 15 cm high, but becoming wider and lower as the nestlings dig earth from the walls with their beaks for sanitation. The clutch size is 1-7 eggs, most often five; eggs average 29.2 × 23.5 mm. **Laying months:** in the more northerly parts of its range the species nests in spring or summer. In the northern tropics it breeds in winter (September-March), as it does in the southern tropics (April-August); at equatorial latitudes it nests in any month. Egypt, March-May; Senegambia, September-April; Ghana and Nigeria, November-March; Ethiopia, December-May; Uganda, Kenya and Tanzania, all months but mainly March-July; Zambia, February-December (mainly June); Malaŵi, June-September; Zimbabwe, July-November (mainly September-October); South Africa, August-November; Kashmir, March-June; India, all months but mainly February-April, southeast India mainly November-April; Sri Lanka, March-May; Burma, October-December;

Thailand, December-March; southeast China and Hong Kong, February-May.

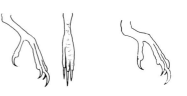

Left feet of Carmine Bee-eater (left) and Pied Kingfisher

Description *C. r. rudis* **Adult male:** forehead, crown and hindneck black, streaked with white, crest streaky, black and white; eyebrow white, narrow immediately above the eye, but broadly and patchily white at the sides of the crown, and making a conspicuous white patch near the nostril. Hindneck black; sides of neck striped black and white. Lores and ear-coverts black, joining hindneck; mantle to uppertail-coverts black, the feathers broadly fringed with white; rump feathers white with wide subterminal black bands; tail distally black, tipped with white, proximally white barred with black. Chin, throat and sides of neck white; a broad black band across the breast, often almost broken in the middle; below it a white band 5 mm wide and underneath that a 2-mm black band; belly, undertail-coverts and underwing-coverts all white. Bill black with blue-grey gape; eye dark brown; legs and feet dark grey or blackish. **Adult female:** differs from the male in lacking the narrow black band across the lower breast; her breast-band is narrower, and generally broken in the midline. **Juvenile:** like the adult female, but feathers of the lores, chin, throat and breast are fringed with brown, and the breast-band is greyish-black. The bill is shorter. **Measurements:** wing of male 133-147, of female 135-149; tail of male 66-74, of female 68-80; bill of male 48-67, of female 48-65; tarsus of male 11-14, of female 11-13. Weight: male 68-100, female 71-110.

References Douthwaite (1973, 1976, 1978, 1982), Fry (1980a,b), Fry *et al.* (1988), Jackson (1984), Junor (1972), Mukherjee (1973), Pring-Mill (1974), Reyer (1980a,b, 1984, 1986a,b), Reyer and Westerturp (1985), Tjømlid (1973), Whitfield and Blaber (1978).

Nyctyornis amicta

Merops amicta Temminck, 1824, Planch. Col., 52, pl. 310, Bencoolen, Sumatra.

Field identification Length 27-31 cm (11-12 in). Adults are unmistakable, bright green birds with pink-lilac forehead and a scarlet beard of long, lax feathers from lores to upper belly. *At rest:* seen from in front, a further character is the long, square-ended tail, yellow with a solid black tip. Resting birds sit very still, often in a rather stooped posture, tail straight down, shoulders hunched, head a little forwards and down, red beard feathers hanging slightly; despite the brilliant colours they can be difficult to spot. When a bird calls it puffs the beard out. *In flight:* the pink and red can generally be seen, but otherwise it is a rather undistinguished green forest bird with rounded wings, a quite long and full tail, and flapping flight with swoops, glides and chases which lack the grace and lightness of *Merops* bee-eaters. *Confusion species:* juveniles are plain green with the tail dusky yellowish below; their stout decurved black bill, with a horn-coloured patch at the base of the lower mandible, serves to distinguish them from barbets, parrots, broadbills or leafbirds.

Voice The commonest call is a loud, gruff, hoarse 'chachachacha', 'quo-qua-qua-qua' or 'kak, kak-ka-ka-ka-ka' on a descending scale, tailing off. Usually quiet, birds at other times call incessantly, answering each other. Another call is a very deep guttural 'kwow' or 'kwok', which can be answered with a rattling 'kwakwakoogoogoo'.

Geographical variation None.

Habitat and range This splendid bee-eater inhabits lowland evergreen dipterocarp forest, primary or logged, from sea level up to 1350 or 1500 m in altitude. The birds keep mainly to the middle storey and lower part of the canopy, where there are gaps allowing sunlight to penetrate, but come to the ground to nest. They favour flooded woods, and forest near streams, swamps and lagoons, and sometimes occur in large well-treed gardens. Red-bearded Bee-eaters are fairly plentiful in primary and dense secondary forests throughout their range, which is from the Dawna Hills and Salween River in Burma to about Bangkok in Thailand, south through the Malayan Peninsula to Johore Bahru, Malaysia; Penang Island; Sumatra, Bangka, and Borneo. In peninsular Malaysia and Thailand they are much less widespread than formerly, because so much dipterocarp forest has been lost to agriculture. The species is sedentary.

Population A density of about two individuals per 20 ha has been found in peninsular Malaysia and about four per 20 ha of primary lowland forest in Borneo.

Food Insects hawked in flight: cicadas, crickets, large beetles, termites, ants, wasps, hornets, carpenter bees and other bees.

Habits While its diet is much the same as among *Merops* bee-eaters, the foraging behaviour of Red-bearded Bee-eaters is different. They hunt solitarily or in pairs, sitting quietly partly hidden from view in foliage in the forest canopy, from time to time giving chase to a passing insect, and returning with it to a different concealed perch. In pursuit of prey they use a fast flapping flight, twisting and turning nimbly between the treetops, and return to the perch with undulating glides alternating with brief flapping. Often they hunt next to a clearing, giving room for manoeuvre during the chase. Like kingfishers but unlike most bee-eaters, they perch almost motionless for long periods, occasionally calling. As it calls, a bird stretches forward, puffs the long throat feathers out, and bobs the head up and down with each note, with the crown feathers raised; it may also jump a few steps sideways along the perch, then turn around to face the other way. When giving the rattling call, it wags the tail backwards and forwards through a small arc. On clear nights these birds sometimes call within two hours of dusk. Two males, once seen courting a female, held their tails down then fanned them and wagged them forwards under the perch, making them conspicuous with the black-and-yellow pattern; one male repeatedly took flight and dived low over the other two birds. **Nesting:** nest burrows are excavated in perpendicular earth banks: road cuttings, sawyers' pits, low cliffs by a stream, once in an archaeological dig. Multiple holes are dug next to each other, but only one is completed and used. They average about 1.2 m long; the clutch comprises 3-5 eggs, evidently incubated by both parents. **Laying months:** Borneo, January-February; Pahang, Malaysia, August and about January; Perak, Malaysia, February; Burma, about March.

Description Adult male: a narrow line of pale blue feathers behind the nostrils and around the base of the lower mandible; forehead and forecrown intense lilac-pink with a pearly sheen; lores, malar area and throat bright red, the lower throat feathers long and lax, with their dark green bases showing through here and there. A narrow line of feathers around the eye is bright blue. Hindcrown, hindneck, ear-coverts,

cheeks, sides of the neck and all remaining upperparts are bright green. Breast bright green, hidden in the middle by the long throat feathers; belly and undertail-coverts pale green, obscurely streaked with white; underside of wings uniformly warm buff. Tail green above, but below brownish-yellow with a broad black tip. Bill black, with the base of the lower mandible grey, inside of mouth yellowish; iris yellow, orange or red-orange; legs and feet olive-brown. **Adult female:** like the male, but with a narrow band of red across the forehead, and behind it the area of pink-lilac is smaller than on the male, stopping short at a line between the eyes. **Juvenile:** a few pale blue feathers at the base of the beak; otherwise green, with yellowish on the belly and dusky yellowish on the underside of the tail; underwing-coverts buff. Eye grey-brown or dull yellow. **Measurements:** wing of male 122-134, of female 116-129; tail of male 103-122, of female 101-116; bill of male 49-59, of female 42-51; tarsus of male 15-17, of female 15-17. Weight: male 68-92, female 61-70.

References Forshaw (1987), Fry (1984).

89 BLUE-BEARDED BEE-EATER   Plate 29
Nyctyornis athertoni

Merops athertoni Jardine and Selby, 1830, Illustr. Orn., 2, pl. 58 and text, India.

Field identification Length 31-34 cm (12½-13½ in). The largest bee-eater; an unobtrusive bird of lowland forest clearings and open hill forests in south and southeast Asia, unmistakable when a good view is obtained owing to its pale blue forehead and beard. Head and upperparts are green, the belly buff with soft green streaks, and the tail rather long, square-ended and dusky yellow below. The beard is a line of large, lax feathers from chin to lower breast; the bird looks full-throated even when the beard lies flat, but when it calls, hunch-shouldered and head lowered, the beard feathers droop down or are puffed out. A rather quiet and inactive bird, usually in pairs, hard to spot perching among greenery 5-15 m above the ground. It is slender, large-headed

with decurved slender black bill, and short-winged. **In flight:** it looks long-tailed, somewhat heavy and barbet- or trogon-like, with several fast beats and then a short glide on rounded wings. It can sail quite slowly, and swoops up to perch from a deep gliding undulation. **Confusion species:** Red-bearded Bee-eaters (88) and Blue-beards overlap only by about 60 km between Moulmein and Kyaikkaimi on the Tenasserim coast of Burma. An unaccompanied juvenile Red-bearded (which lacks any red) could be mistaken for a juvenile Blue-bearded, but the latter is told by its blue throat.

Voice A gruff 'gga gga ggr gr' or 'kor-r-r, kor-r-r', not loud, but audible for 100-200 m in forest; rather like a roller.

Geographical variation Peninsular Indian birds have clearer, lighter greens than Himalayan and southeast Asian ones. From west to east there is a cline of increasingly rich coloration, particularly on Hainan Island, whose population is usually treated as distinct.

N. a. athertoni India to Indochina.

N. a. brevicaudata Hainan. Greens yellowish, throat a richer blue, belly deeper buff and heavily striped with green. Slightly smaller and shorter-tailed than *athertoni*: wing 131-141 mm, tail 120-130 mm, bill 46-50 mm.

Habitat and range Blue-bearded Bee-eaters inhabit thick forest but keep to clearings, by a stream, road, treefall, rock outcrop, or open growth on a ridge. They occur at all elevations from sea level to 1600 m and rarely to 2200 m, where they can be found in moss forest as well as in thin deciduous woods; but they are commonest in thickly forested foothills with steep slopes, ravines and streams. They are quite common in the Himalayan foothills from Kandaghat in Himachal Pradesh and Dehra Dun, through Nepal, Sikkim and Bhutan to Assam, and sparingly distributed in Burma (Kachin, Chin Range, Shan States, Kawthoolei). Absent from Yunnan, they are uncommon in north Thailand except in the National Parks, absent from Thailand's central and peninsular regions, and only locally at all common in Laos, Cambodia, Cochinchina, Hainan, and around the Gulf of Tongking. South of the Himalayas they range throughout Bangladesh, and occur locally in West Bengal, Bihar, Orissa, Madhya Pradesh and Andra Pradesh, and very locally in the Western Ghats from Tapti River and the Satpura hills to western Maharashtra, Mysore, Kerala, and Patni hills in Tamil Nadu.

Migration Reported seasonal fluctuations in abundance in Nepal, Burma, India's Eastern Ghats (Price 1979), and in southwest Thailand (Forshaw 1987) may be more apparent than real, or could indicate some local vertical migrations. In general the species seems to be sedentary.

Food Insects, mainly honeybees of two or three species, carpenter bees, several families of wasps including some huge ones 4 cm long, weevils, scarab, passalid and other beetles up to 4 cm long, dragonflies, and possibly fly pupae (Fry in prep.). Woodlice and wood-boring beetles were found in the gizzard of a bird collected as it flew from a hollow in a dead tree (Baker 1927).

Habits How this bee-eater forages is a bit of a mystery. We watched pairs for several hours in Khao Yei National Park, Thailand, in 1990, expressly to observe foraging behaviour, but they sat stolidly and refused to feed. According to one careful naturalist this species feeds little on the wing, but clambers about in trees with slow, awkward movements to search leaves and flowers for insects; an individual perched on a house roof caught bees as they flew right up to it, which 'confirms the belief that bees mistake the bird's blue "beard" for a flower' (Smythies 1953). A large insect caught in flight is carried back and beaten against the perch, the parts knocked off not being retrieved; only the abdomens of some large beetles seem to be eaten (Fry 1984). Baker's observation, above, suggests that the birds enter hollows to search for invertebrates; yet our analysis of pellets from nests shows a diet of bees, wasps and beetles which we think must all have been caught on the wing. Blue-bearded Bee-eaters occur in pairs, which spend much time perching inactively 10 m up in a leafy tree, half shaded and not easily seen among the foliage, or in full sun at the top of a flowering tree such as *Erythrina*, *Salmalia*, *Macaranga* or *Bombax*. Sometimes they sit close to large nectar-bearing blossoms and (as we observed in Khao Yei) seem to prod them, perhaps looking for insects. Every few seconds a resting bird lifts the tail-tip about 2 cm then depresses it, more in the manner of a kingfisher than like the smooth forwards-and-backwards wagging of the vertically-downward tail typical of *Merops* bee-eaters. Perching in the sun, they do not lift the mantle feathers or use any of the other sunbathing postures of *Merops*. No courtship behaviour has been observed in the wild, but a captive bird, when given a cricket, flew with it to perch next to its mate, when both called, fanned their tails and bowed repeatedly for about a minute (Todd 1977). Similar behaviour has been observed once from a wild pair and is probably food-showing, perhaps culminating in courtship-feeding. Males frequently feed incubating females (Baker 1934). **Nesting:** nest excavation, by both sexes, begins a month or more before egg-laying. Nests are always solitary, although the chosen site – banks by jungle paths, road cuttings, cliff faces in ravines and landslips – is peppered with 4-12 tunnels which are either previous years' nest holes or incomplete 'false starts'. Burrows are round in section, 7.5-9.5 cm in diameter, 1.3-3.0 m long, straight, level or slightly inclining; they end in an egg chamber 20 cm wide and 13 cm high. Although unlined, the chamber soon acquires a deep litter of insect remains from crumbled pellets regurgitated by roosting birds long before egg-laying starts. The six eggs are laid on the litter, which soon collects in the tunnel, too, up to the entrance, and serves to distinguish the true nest from unused, uncompleted ones. **Laying months:** Assam, February-May and August; in Nepal nesting is in April-May but mainly October; Burma, April, with breeding from March to October; Thailand, about April-May.

Description *N. a. athertoni* Sexes alike. **Adult:** forehead pale blue, merging above the eyes into bright green. Lores, head and entire upperparts bright yellowish-green, fading or bleaching to bluish-green on the crown, mantle and tertials before they are moulted. Beard feathers on chin and throat are long and broad, with radiating barbs, dark blue in the feather centre and bright pale blue at the sides and tip. Malar area and sides of throat and breast are yellowish-green; belly and flanks yellowish-buff, softly striped with olive-green; underwing- and undertail-coverts yellowish-buff. Underside of tail dusky mustard-yellow, the feather shafts pale yellow. Bill blackish-brown, with a lead-grey area at the base of the lower mandible; eye bright yellow-orange; legs and feet greenish-grey. **Juvenile:** like the adult. **Measurements:** wing of male 133-143, of female 131-140; tail of male 130-137, of female 126-137; bill of male 45-52, of female 46-53; tarsus of male 18-19, of female 18-19. Weight: male 85-93, female 70-91.

References Forshaw (1987), Fry (1984).

90 CELEBES BEE-EATER (Purple-bearded Bee-eater)   Plate 29
Meropogon forsteni

Meropogon forsteni 'Temm'., Bonaparte, 1850, Consp. Genera Avium, 1, p. 164, Celebes.

Field identification Length 25-26 cm (10 in), excluding tail-streamers of up to 6 cm (2½ in). Restricted to Sulawesi Island (formerly spelt Celebes), Indonesia, where only one other bee-eater occurs, this species is readily distinguished by its purple-blue head and breast (mainly green on juveniles), dark green back, wings and tail-streamers, and brown hindneck and belly. **At rest:** the long purple throat feathers hang over the breast, and with neck and nape feathers form a ruff or cape which can be sleeked down or fluffed out, making the bird look either slender or thick-necked and full-throated. The ruff is often raised high at the back of the neck, and the throat feathers can point almost forwards below the bill. The tail is held straight down, and can be swung forwards under the perch; from in front it is chest-

nut. In poor light the bird appears blackish. **In flight:** it looks mainly green, with broad rounded wings (green above, pale buff below) and a longish green tail with short to medium-long streamers. When the bird banks in flight, its spread tail is mainly chestnut. **Confusion species:** Blue-tailed Bee-eaters (105), the other species in Sulawesi, differ in being gregarious, long-winged, aerial birds with bright green head, yellow chin, rufous throat, and pale blue rump and tail.

Voice A quiet, shrill, high-pitched 'szit', 'peet' or 'sip-sip'.

Geographical variation None.

Habitat and range Celebes Bee-eaters are distributed locally but not uncommonly in north, central and southeast Sulawesi, inhabiting clearings in undisturbed and mature secondary forest, from sea level up to 2000 m. They occur on the edges of montane and elfin moss forests, and in the lowlands where forest abuts upon well-timbered farmland. There are early records from Tondano Mahawu Massif, Masarang Crater, Mongondo, the Mengkoka and Takala ranges, Rurukan, Masembo, Tanke Salokko and Wawo. Recently the species has been found to be fairly plentiful in Tangkoko and Ambang Mountain Reserves, with further records in Dumoga-Bone, Lore Lindu and Morowali Reserves and in several forests in central Sulawesi.

Migration There is apparently some movement towards the coast for the rainy season, and back to the interior to nest in the dry season.

Food Airborne insects: bees and wasps (including little honeybees *Apis indica*, and *Dielis javanica*), beetles (*Euchlora*, *Macronota*, *Glycyphana*) and dragonflies.

Habits Found solitarily, in pairs or family parties, this fine bee-eater forages in the open at mid- and upper-canopy levels, perching on treetops and exposed outer branches, from where it makes short sallies after passing insects. Using a few favoured perches, a bird searches in all directions for prey, twisting and turning its slender-billed head, the neck and throat ruff sleeked or plumped and often looking almost Elizabethan; the tail is wagged backwards and forwards about the downward-pointing position, constantly and emphatically, like an inverted metronome. Sighting a passing insect, the bird makes a short pursuit with an audible flutter of wings, flapping and gliding in deep undulations as it returns to the perch, where the prey is swiped a few times before being swallowed. *Nesting:* nest burrows are dug in the steep banks of forest streams, in cliffs, landslips and road cuttings. One tunnel was 9 cm wide, 3.5 cm high, 90 cm long, and straight and horizontal. *Laying months:* occupied nests have been found in April, July, September and December, recently fledged youngsters in September and October, and a juvenile in January.

Description *Adult male:* lores and upper ear-coverts dull black; forehead, crown and cheeks dark purple-blue; hindneck and narrow line down the side of the breast chocolate or dark vinous-brown. Remaining upperparts dark green, including the streamered central pair of tail feathers, but the rest of the tail is russet or chestnut, with green outer webs to the outer two feathers. Chin, throat, breast and forebelly dark purple-blue; hindbelly dark grey with a greenish wash; flanks green; undertail-coverts cinnamon, broadly edged with green. Underwing-coverts silvery-grey and axillaries white. Underside of tail russet. Bill black; eye dark brown; legs and feet dark grey. *Adult female:* like the male, except that the purple-blue of the breast does not extend to the forebelly (Forshaw 1987). *Juvenile:* forehead and chin feathers black with green tips; lores and ear-coverts dark brown; rest of head and neck dull green; breast feathers purple-blue with broad green edges and tips. In other respects the plumage is like that of the adult female, but the central tail feathers are not streamered and the bill is short. *Measurements:* wing of male 111-120, of female 110-116; tail of male 140-164 and of female 127-161 (including streamers of up to 61 mm, probably longer on males than females); bill of male 44-48, of female 43-48; tarsus of male 12-14, of female 12-14.

References Forshaw (1987), Fry (1984).

Merops breweri

Meropogon Breweri Cassin, 1859, Proc. Acad. Nat. Sci. Philadelphia, p. 34, Ogobai River, Gabon.

Field identification Length 25-28 cm (10-11 in), excluding tail-streamers of 8 cm (3 in). Unmistakable: the only bee-eater with black head, green upperparts and buff underparts. It is much larger than the two other forest-dwelling bee-eaters in its range, the Blue-headed and the Black (92, 93). Young birds have chin and throat black but crown and ear-coverts greenish. *At rest:* rather tame and approachable; at close range the bright crimson eye and rich chestnut band across the lower breast are easy to see, but chestnut does not usually show in the tail. The throat is full-looking. *In flight:* wings rounded; slow sailing flight. Overhead, the black throat and rich buff underwing-coverts and belly are good features. When seen low down in pursuit of flying insects the chestnut sides and green centre of the tail are obvious.

Voice Rather a silent bird. The call usually heard is the alarm, 'wic', repeated every few seconds. A bird bringing food to the nest gives a quiet 'pfuruk-p'r'k'. A greeting or recognition call which is occasionally given when an individual lands beside its mate is 'churruk-churruk' and a soft musical trilling.

Geographical variation None.

Habitat and range A forest-edge bird. Black-headed Bee-eaters are not found deep in rainforest nor generally in open lightly wooded savannas, but they live in between: in open secondary growth and plantations, along sunny paths and around clearings and dwellings in forest, particularly near rivers and streams. They occur on wooded islands in the Congo River and its tributaries, along wooded riverbanks, and in and near gallery forest (narrow strips of forest along streams in grassy valleys). In Nigeria they inhabit moist thickets and disturbed woods with spindly trees and lianes, also open woody growth around cultivated plots, particularly where dug-over fields or roadside drain-

age cuts provide suitable nest sites; they have been found only in farmland/oil-palm-plantation/forest mosaic on Igalaland Plateau, at an altitude of 300-350 m. In 1952 three were found at two localities in Ghana which were later inundated by the rising Lake Volta, and that remains the only record west of southeast Nigeria. Another outlying population is near Bamingui and on Haute Pata near Ndélé in northern Central African Republic. The main range is further south in the forested Congo Basin: Cabinda, Gabon, Congo, and Zaïre from Kinshasa to Bandundu on Kasai River, to about 23°E on Congo River, north to Bangui on Oubangi River, and east to Bambili on Uele River and Banalia on Aruwimi River. There are records in northeast Zaïre on Bomokandi River near Etiga, and just across the border, in Sudan, in Bangangai Forest (50 km west-northwest of Yambio).

Population This bee-eater is scarce over much of its range but is locally common, around Bwamanda in northwest Zaïre for instance, and near Ndélé in Central African Republic. It is resident.

Food Honeybees, carpenter bees and many other sorts of bees, ants and wasps form about half of the diet, and the other half consists of chafers, dung-beetles, numerous other beetles, dragonflies, cicadas, butterflies and hawkmoths (Fry and Gilbert 1983). Some of the hymenopteran prey are very large insects. Possibly small grubs are taken also.

Habits The Black-headed Bee-eater is solitary or occurs in pairs or trios or, soon after breeding, in family parties of up to six birds. Once a flock of 40 was seen, in Cabinda. It is a rather silent and sluggish bird, easily overlooked as it perches in open leafy places against a backdrop of shaded greenery. But when an insect passes, the bird gives fast pursuit, snaps it up in flight and returns to its perch — mainly at mid and low levels at the edge of woods – to batter it vigorously. Apart from dashes after insects, the flight is slow, with alternate gliding and brief flapping on quite rounded wings. Sometimes vegetation is so tangled that the bird has little clear airspace for pursuit of prey. Insects are occasionally snatched from the herb layer, the bird checking in flight but not landing. **Nesting:** this bee-eater is not conspicuously territorial. Two or sometimes three adults attend the nest, which they excavate in sloping heaps of soft earth by roadsides or in bare or grassy flat sandy ground in fields; one nest was in the base of a termite-mound. Two or three pairs and trios of birds can nest a few metres apart, but nests are in general solitary. The burrow is 1-2 m long, straight, declining a little, with a large oval egg chamber angled to one side at the end; the clutch is of 2-3 white eggs. **Laying months:** in Nigeria and Zaïre nest-digging is usually in January, egg-laying in February, hatching in March, and fledging in April; a nest near Bwamanda, Zaïre, had eggs in March.

Description Sexes alike. **Adult:** head, neck and throat black, not glossy. Mantle,

back, scapulars, wings, rump and streamered central tail feathers bright grass-green, with ends of the tertials bluish in worn plumage. The outer vane of the outermost tail feather is green, and the rest of the tail dark cinnamon with a green tip. Breast, underwing-coverts, flanks, belly and undertail-coverts are rich burnished ochreous-buff with a lime-green wash, merging with the black throat via a narrow cinnamon breast-band. Bill black, inside of mouth pink; iris brilliant crimson; legs and feet dark grey, soles pale yellow, nails black. **Juvenile:** like the adult, but the black feathers are broadly fringed with bright green on forehead, crown, hindneck, side of the neck and side of the breast; some young birds have a distinct green moustachial streak. The central tail feathers are not elongated. **Measurements:** wing of male 113-124, of female 115-123; tail of male 146-181, of female·145-174; bill of male 44-55, of female 43-50; tarsus of male 14-16, of female 14-16. Weight: one individual weighed 54 g.

References Forshaw (1987), Fry (1984), Fry and Gilbert (1983), Fry *et al*. (1988).

92 BLUE-HEADED BEE-EATER   Plate 30
Merops muelleri

Meropiscus Mülleri Cassin, 1857, Proc. Acad. Nat. Sci. Philadelphia, p. 37, Muni River, Gaboon.

Field identification Length 19 cm (7½ in), excluding streamers, which in one subspecies are up to 12 mm long on females and 15 mm on males (the other subspecies has a square-ended tail, without streamers). A small, silent, confiding bee-eater of primary and old secondary forest growth, readily distinguished by the combination of dark rufous back and wings, small scarlet patch on the chin, and dark purplish-blue head, breast and tail. **At rest:** from below, the scarlet chin-patch is obvious, surrounded and accentuated by black; sometimes the stiff red barbs separate and stand out. Neck and breast are deep blue, the colour paling towards the vent and undertail-coverts; underside of tail black. West of Cameroon, the top of

the head – hard to see from below – is deep purple-blue. Further east the forehead is white, forecrown pale blue and hindcrown dark blue. The tail, pointing straight down, is constantly wagged back and forth through a small arc. Very young birds have the chin and throat olive-blue, with only a few reddish-brown feathers under the beak. **In flight:** the entire wing appears rufous, especially in direct or transmitted sunlight. **Confusion species:** the Black Bee-eater (93), with much the same range, can be confused in poor light. Its red throat-patch is larger, its belly has pale blue streaks, and the rump and undertail-coverts are conspicuously pale azure-blue; in flight, seen from below, its primaries also appear rufous. The only other scarlet-throated bee-eaters in Africa are the Red-throated (98) and the White-fronted (99), gregarious birds, green above with dark buff breast, and inhabiting dry savanna country.

Voice Silent. Infrequently a weak, high-pitched, squeaky or tinkling 'tsee-sup' or 'ptii-ouit' repeated 3-5 times. Birds perching shoulder to shoulder give a quiet 'sip' or 's'lip'. An annoyance call, given by a bird disturbed by a squirrel, is 'slip' notes running into a short trill. Also a woodpecker-like 'triiii triiii'.

Geographical variation There are two subspecies, meeting near Douala in Cameroon with little or no intergradation. They differ in forehead colour, tail shape, and significantly in weight.

M. m. mentalis West Africa, from Mali to west Cameroon. Forehead and crown dark purple-blue, cheeks dark purple-blue surrounded by black, belly and undertail-coverts pale blue, and central tail feathers in the form of short, slightly club-ended streamers.

M. m. muelleri Central Africa, from Cameroon to west Kenya. Has a capped appearance, with the forehead white, merging into pale blue on the crown. Cheeks, and whole side of the head, solid black; rufous on the wings, back and rump is less intense than in *mentalis*; belly and undertail-coverts dark blue; tail square-cut, without streamers. Measurements not significantly different from *mentalis*, but a lighter bird, weighing 17.5-25 g (females near to laying, up to 30 g).

Habitat and range Keeps to forest areas with dappled sunlight and not too impenetrable shade: glades and small clearings within forest and at its edges, and open spaces where a large tree has fallen or a broad track passes through. At Kakamega, Kenya, it keeps mainly to semi-deciduous, secondary forest, sometimes coming out into sunny adjacent farmland with plenty of scattered trees. The main range is the rainforest zone of Zaïre, from Uele River south along Congo River to Kwamouth and to 6°S in Kasai, about Kananga, and east to the Western Rift. Barely known from Uganda, Rwanda or Burundi, but there is an outlying population on Mt Elgon and in what remains of Kakamega Forest, Kenya. It inhabits high primary for-

ests in Gabon and Cameroon (but whether in Congo Republic is uncertain), and ranges through southern Nigerian forests to about Ibadan; it occurs at up to 1200 m on Bioko. It reappears on Mt Nimba in Ivory Coast, Liberia and Guinea, occurring westwards through Liberia and Sierra Leone, and also inhabits dense gallery forests along Bafing River, south of the well-watered Mandingo Mountains, in Mali. Whether it occurs in Guinea, linking the Sierra Leone and Mali populations, is not yet known.

Migration None. The species appears to be entirely sedentary.

Population Quite common on Bioko Island and in Gabon, but almost everywhere else in its range it seems to be scarce. It is decidedly rare in Ivory Coast, and known from only four places in Nigeria. Probably it is only one-third as common as the Black Bee-eater. The population on Mt Elgon and in Kakamega Forest may number no more than a few hundreds.

Food Little known: a regurgitated pellet contained a worker honeybee, a large fly and a small ichneumon-fly.

Habits Blue-headed Bee-eaters hunt from a perch, by sallying low down, seizing the prey in flight, and wheeling back. Like flycatchers, they regularly use the same perches: exposed dead branches high up in primary forest, or sometimes within 4 m of the ground, or in a small sunny clearing in old secondary forest. Venomous insects are held in the tip of the bill and beaten to left and right, then the insect's tail is rubbed against the perch and the insect quickly swallowed. They live in pairs and trios, in the same place year-round, the third bird presumably being a helper-at-the-nest. One trio in Kakamega Forest was a female with two males, both of which courtship-fed her; that was in mid March, and egg-laying was imminent. ***Nesting:*** very few nests have been found; three in Cameroon forests were an oval chamber at the end of a 55-cm tunnel in a sawyer's pit, and holes in wayside banks, with two eggs in January and two nestlings in February. In Gabon, a pair dug a 60-cm burrow by a forest path in October and there were flying young in February.

Description *M. m. mentalis* Sexes alike except for eye colour: wine-red in the male, red-brown in the female. ***Adult:*** mantle, wings and rump vary from russet to rich chestnut, and the blues of head, breast and uppertail-coverts from greenish mid-blue to purplish dark blue. Secondaries rufous, tipped blackish. Closed tail blue above; all concealed parts of the feathers are black. Bill black; legs and feet greyish-black. ***Juvenile:*** chestnut parts less rich, yellower than on the adult, and blue parts are more a dusky turquoise, with an olive wash on the head and mantle. ***Measurements:*** no difference between the sexes. Wing 86-91; tail 75-92; bill to feathers 30-32, to skull 34-37; tarsus 10-12. Weight: 24-30 (females near to laying, up to 33).

References Brosset and Erard (1986), Fry (1984), Fry *et al.* (1988).

93 BLACK BEE-EATER   Plate 30
Merops gularis

Merops gularis Shaw, 1798, Naturalists' Miscell., 9, text to pl. 337, Sierra Leone.

Field identification Length 20 cm (8 in). A bird of rainforest edges and lush secondary growth in West and Central Africa, perching quite high above the ground, hence usually seen from below. *At rest:* black, with scarlet throat and, equally conspicuous, bright cobalt-blue belly and undertail-coverts. The tail is square-cut, without streamers. *In flight:* wings quite pointed but not very long, the primaries and secondaries dark rufous with blackish tips. When seen on the level, the brilliant cobalt- or azure-blue rump is most conspicuous. *Confusion species:* Blue-headed Bee-eaters (92) have much the same habitats and range, but the crown is purple-blue or whitish, the hindneck purple-blue (not black), the mantle and wings chestnut (not black) and the rump not in strong contrast.

Voice A very silent bird. The flight call is 'wic'. We have not been able to verify the old claim that it has a shrill 'tzik-tzik-tzik' and a pleasant quavering song.

Geographical variation There are two subspecies, one with and one without a superciliary stripe.

M. g. gularis From Sierra Leone to southeast Nigeria. With the forehead blue, and a distinct bright cobalt-blue superciliary stripe. Some southeast Nigerian and west Cameroon birds are intermediate between this and *australis*.

M. g. australis From southeast Nigeria to northeast Zaïre, south to north Angola.

No superciliary stripe; forehead black, sometimes with a few blue feathers; the light azure-blue streaks on breast and even the belly are sometimes scarlet-tipped. Wing 5 mm longer than in the nominate subspecies.

Habitat and range Black Bee-eaters are sometimes found deep in rainforest, but the usual habitat is high forest edge adjacent to natural or cultivated clearings and waterways and roads. They occur in well-timbered farmland, secondary forest, oil-palm-dominated forest, and in humid savanna woodland, also in gallery forest growing in the bottom of grassy valleys in savanna country. They perch sometimes at head height but mainly up to 25 m high, on dead branches, treetops and telegraph wires. The species is widespread, quite common here and there, but nowhere really abundant unless in Bwamba Forest, Uganda. It is not found on Mt Elgon, nor in Kakamega Forest in Kenya, on Bioko Island or in Mandingo Mountains in Mali; but otherwise its range almost completely embraces that of the Blue-headed Bee-eater. Where the two species occur in the same general area, the Black Bee-eater seems to be at least three times commoner; it is the bird of secondary forest, whereas Blue-headed inhabits primary forest. In Guinea the Black Bee-eater inhabits the area between Guékedou and Macenta. It is scarce west of River Jong in Sierra Leone but commoner east of it and southeast of Tingi Plateau; and it is widespread and quite common in Liberia and Ivory coast. Absent from Benin, it is locally common on either side, in the forest zones of Ghana and Nigeria, north to Lokoja. In the lowlands of Cameroon it is rather common, from coastal forests up to 1500 m, and it ranges throughout the Congo Basin north to Oubangi River and Uele River, east to western Uganda, south to Kivu, Lulua River and Kasai River at about 7°S, and to Angola where it ranges along Cuango River to Cabinda, Cuanza Norte and northern Luanda Provinces.

Migration Mainly resident and sedentary, but in Sierra Leone and Liberia, also perhaps in Ivory Coast, Black Bee-eaters seem to move between coastal districts and the interior, withdrawing from the coast at the height of the rains in May-August and appearing on Mt Nimba (Liberia) only at that season to breed. Near Bo, Sierra Leone, they are present only in February-May. On Mt Nimba they occur all year but are scarce in November and December and common in February, when numerous flocks of up to 30 birds cross mountain ridges, flying westward.

Food Airborne insects, mainly honeybees, ants and other venomous Hymenoptera, also dragonflies, butterflies, bugs, beetles, crickets, grasshoppers, tabanids and other large flies.

Habits Black Bee-eaters forage by keeping watch from an elevated perch in unobstructed airspace, intently turning and cocking the head, then giving fast flight after an insect. Whether or not the pursuit is successful, the bird returns to the same perch, or a new one, with a more sailing, less dashing flight; in longer flight there is marked undulation. The birds feed solitarily, in pairs, or in small flocks, often high up at the side of the forest canopy. They are very quiet, and not particularly approachable. A resting bird perches with the tail straight down, constantly moving it back and forth through a small arc. **Nesting:** over most of its range it is a solitary nester, a pair digging the burrow into a low bank, shallow ditch or tree-planting hole. In Sierra Leone and Liberia, however, it is gregarious all year and breeds in small colonies, using sandy riverbanks and roadside embankments; some 12 birds had two nests between

them at a locality in Liberia in March 1979, and eight nest holes two years later (Colston and Curry-Lindahl 1986). Burrows are 40-50 cm long. The clutch is of two eggs (in Gabon). **Laying months:** Liberia, March; Gabon, November-January; in Ghana and Nigeria nest-digging commences in January and eggs are laid from March to May; records from Zaïre are from January to April in Ituri, about June at Basongo on Kasai River, and possibly in September at Lukolela on Congo River.

Description *M. g. gularis* Sexes alike. *Adult:* a narrow line of feathers across the forehead is azure-blue, joining a short, narrow but distinct superciliary stripe of the same colour; the rest of the head is jet-black. Hindneck, mantle, back and scapulars black. Rump and uppertail-coverts, which are long and reach within 25 mm of the tip of the tail, are brilliant azure-blue, the same vivid colour so common in kingfishers. Tail black, the central two feathers broadly edged greenish. Outer two primaries black, other primaries dark rufous with blackish outer webs and tips, secondaries dark rufous with blackish tips, which form a broad black band along the trailing edge of the wing. Upperwing-coverts and inner secondaries narrowly edged with greenish, and tertials broadly tipped with greenish-blue. Underside of wings and tail are black. Chin and throat scarlet, the feathers with radiating non-interlocking barbs. Breast black, with small bright azure-blue streaks that become larger towards the belly; belly and undertail-coverts, which are as long as the uppertail-coverts, are bright azure-blue. In worn, sun-bleached plumage, the exposed black parts have a greenish tinge and the tertials and central tail feathers are grey-blue. Bill black; eye dark red or crimson; legs and feet purplish-black. *Juvenile:* like the adult but duller, with black parts tinged with dull green; chin and sides of the throat greenish-black, centre of throat the same or pale orange; breast black, without any blue streaks; belly and undertail-coverts dull blue. *Measurements:* wing of male 87-94, of female 87-92; tail of male 68-74, of female 69-72; bill of male 34-39, of female 34-39; tarsus of male 10-12, of female 10-12. Weight: male 23-33, female 22-32.

References Brosset and Erard (1986), Colston and Curry-Lindahl (1986), Forshaw (1987), Fry (1984), Fry et al. (1988).

94 SWALLOW-TAILED BEE-EATER
Merops hirundineus

Plate 30

Merops hirundineus Lichtenstein, 1793, Cat. Rer. Nat. Rar., Hamburg, p. 21, no. 213, no locality, = Oranje River, South Africa, ex Levaillant.

Field identification Length 20-22 cm (8-8½ in). The deeply forked tail, blue, quite long, narrow-based and straight-edged, is an excellent field character, easily seen even at a distance on perched and flying birds, and serving to distinguish this species from all other bee-eaters and indeed from all other birds. *At rest:* mainly a green bird, rather long-billed, with yellow throat and narrow purple gorget. Tail white-tipped when seen from behind, rather uniformly grey from in front. *In flight:* wings rufous, with green upperwing-coverts and conspicuous black trailing edge.

Voice Quite a vocal bird, particularly in flocks, but the voice is subdued. Calls are like those of Little Bee-eater (95) and Blue-breasted Bee-eater (96), but less sibilant, drier, and with a rolling quality: 'tip, tip', 'dip-dip-dip', 'diddle-iddle-ip' and 'dreee-dreee'.

Geographical variation Four subspecies are recognised, differing trivially in hue, and more obviously in forehead, eyebrow and tail colour (blue or green).

M. h. hirundineus From the Benguela coast and Malanje highlands of north Angola, through Namibia east of Namib Desert to Orange River in South Africa, east through the highveld to the western slopes of the Drakensberg Mountains, and throughout Botswana and highveld Zimbabwe. Forehead and eyebrow green.

M. h. furcatus East of the above subspecies, in lowveld: southeast Zaïre, Zambia, Malaŵi, lowveld Zimbabwe, Mozambique, and Tanzania north to the southwest corner of Lake Victoria; a single old record from Vanga in Kenya. Like the nominate form, but greens are darker and bronzier, the throat deeper yellow, and the gorget broader and deeper blue.

M. h. chrysolaimus West Africa, from Senegambia to about 21°E in southern Chad; a single record from Gouraye in Mauritania. Forehead and eyebrow bright blue, and tail green (middle feathers green-blue).

M. h. heuglini South Sudan from Boro River in west Bahr el Ghazal, through upper Nile and Equatoria Provinces to Gila River and Omo Valley in southwest Ethiopia, the upper Uele drainage in Zaïre, and in north Uganda the Kidepo Valley National Park, Moroto, Kabalega Falls and the northern shores of Lake Albert; a single old record from north Ethiopia, between Taccazze River and Gash River. Its range may meet that of *chrysolaimus*; it differs only in having darker blue gorget and uppertail-coverts.

Habitat and range Swallow-tailed Bee-eaters are birds of natural, relatively undisturbed woodlands. In West Africa they inhabit mature *Isoberlinia* woodland where there are plenty of open grassy clearings; in southern Africa they occur chiefly in the equivalent *Baikiaea*, *Colophospermum* ('mopane') and *Brachystegia* savanna woodlands, and also in *Combretum* thickets ('jesse'), river floodplains with plenty of bushes and timber, pasture and cultivated land with scattered trees, and arid plains dotted with acacias. They like burnt-over ground, in Zimbabwe perching on telegraph wires or eucalyptus trees to forage for insects attracted to the new young growth that burning promotes. The species ranges above 1000 m in southern Africa and is quite common above 1500 m in Namibia, but elsewhere it is a bird of hot lowlands.

In West Africa the range is much as that of Blue-bellied Rollers (119), both being birds wedded essentially to *Isoberlinia* woodland: the bee-eater ranges from southern Senegal, Gambia and northern Guinea through Mali (north to 15°N), Ivory Coast (south to about Tomodi), southwest Burkina Faso, Ghana (scarce in the north, where it doubtless breeds; migrants recorded in small numbers south to the coastal plains), Togo, Benin, the central belt of Nigeria, probably north Cameroon (no records yet), south Chad and northwest Central African Republic. The Sudan and southern tropical ranges have been given above. South of the Limpopo the species just enters northwest Transvaal, and vagrants have been reported from a dozen localities, south to Oudtshoorn and Uitenhage.

Population It is not uncommon in hot, low-lying parts of Malaŵi, but nearly everywhere else is scarce and local. Densities of two individuals per km² have been reported near Lusaka, Zambia, and at Lamto, Ivory Coast.

Migration The species seems to be migratory throughout its range, although its movements are not well understood. In West Africa it is resident in the north, but some move south for the dry season; for instance, in Ghana it occurs on the Accra Plains from September to February. It is present in Katanga, southeast Zaïre, only from May to November. In Zimbabwe it is commoner in April-September than in October-March, when it seems that most birds migrate to nest around the Kalahari sandveld to the west or in lowland Mozambique sandveld to the southeast.

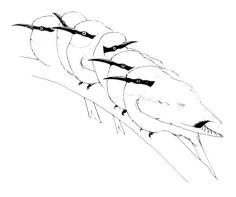

Swallow-tailed Bee-eaters preparing to roost

Food Honeybees, other hymenopterans, cicadas, shieldbugs, grasshoppers, dragonflies, flies, beetles and butterflies, all taken on the wing. Around gardens in Harare, Zimbabwe, these bee-eaters feed almost exclusively on honeybees.

Habits Swallow-tailed Bee-eaters live in pairs or small flocks. When not nesting they roam widely and are flighty, staying in one spot to hunt for food for only a few minutes before moving on. They can be hard to follow. Up to six birds can be seen hawking for insects, spaced out high up in adjacent trees or along telegraph wires, making flycatching sorties at treetop level, then moving away together. In idle moments they sunbathe with mantle feathers lifted and with the head twisted side-up to the sun, looking broken-necked. Two or three individuals greet each other by standing erect on the perch, excitedly calling and quivering the fanned tail, then chasing each other in flight, still calling. Unless nesting, they roost at night shoulder to shoulder in tight-packed ranks of 10-30 birds, in a leafy tree. **Nesting:** they nest singly or with two or three pairs close to each other, digging burrows into level or shelving ground with bare, sandy patches, or into low banks, high sand cliffs, sand mounds, and ditches; one nest was in the side of an Aardvark tunnel. Burrows are 80-100 cm long and the clutch is of 2-4 eggs. A nest helper – a third adult – has been reported only once. **Laying months:** Gambia, May-July; Ghana, July; Tanzania, April; Angola, July-August; southwest Zaïre, August; Namibia, October-January; Zambia, September-December; Zimbabwe, October-December; Malaŵi, October-November; Mozambique, September-November.

Description *M. h. hirundineus* Sexes nearly alike. **Adult male:** forehead and crown bronzy-green, paler at the sides; nape, mantle and closed wings bronzy-green; rump and uppertail-coverts bright caerulean-blue. The tail is blue, greyish-blue on the middle feathers and green-tinged on the outer webs of the others, which become dusky towards the white tip. Primaries and secondaries are mainly rufous, with whitish tips and a broad black subterminal band; outer vanes of the outer primaries are olive-green. Mask black.

Chin and throat bright chrome-yellow; a short white streak below the black ear-coverts; gorget dark purplish-blue; breast green; belly, flanks and undertail-coverts pale blue; underwing-coverts pale rufous. Bill black; eye orange or crimson; legs and feet dull dusky mauve. *Adult female:* slightly paler than the male, with narrower gorget and less deeply forked tail. *Juvenile:* like the adult, but duller; chin and throat are greenish-white, and there is no gorget. The eye is dark brown. *Measurements:* wing of male 92-101, of female 93-98; tail of male 90-104, of female 90-102; bill of male 31-37, of female 31-35; tarsus of male 10-12, of female 10-12. Weight: male 18-23, female 18-27.

References Forshaw (1987), Fry (1984), Fry *et al.* (1988), Harwin and Rockingham-Gill (1981).

95 LITTLE BEE-EATER   Plate 31
Merops pusillus

Merops pusillus P.L.S. Müller 1776, Natursyst., Suppl., p. 95, Senegal.

Field identification Length 15-17 cm (6-6½ in). The smallest bee-eater, and one of the commonest. Tame, vocal and lively; in pairs or family parties, seen mainly hawking low down in shrubby grassland. **At rest:** green, with vivid yellow throat, black mask, red eye, wide black gorget becoming ruddy on the breast and buffy on the belly. Sits upright, with the tail pointing straight down and wagging a little backwards and forwards. From in front the tail is pale rufous, conspicuously black-tipped. **In flight:** wings mainly rufous-buff, with wide black trailing edge; tail green in the middle, rufous at the sides, and black-tipped (except in the middle). **Confusion species:** very similar to the Blue-breasted Bee-eater (96), which is larger and has a white wedge on the side of the neck, at the corner of the yellow throat; the breast is deep blue in some races, but black, like Little Bee-eaters, in others. The Cinnamon-chested Bee-eater (97) is brighter and much larger, with a white mark on the side of the neck, large black gorget, deep orange breast, and greener wings and tail. Other yellow-throated bee-eaters in Africa are the Swallow-tailed (94: deeply forked tail), European (109: chestnut crown and mantle), the yellow-throated Sudanese form of the Little Green (103: tail-streamers, green belly), and a rare variant of the Red-throated (98: no gorget, blue undertail-coverts).

Voice Vocal; the commonest call is a quiet 'sip' or 'slip', repeated when greet-ing an incoming bird: 'sip-sip-sip'. In high-intensity greeting display there is also a song: a high-pitched, sibilant 'siddle-iddle-ip, d'jeee', lasting about 1 second. Sometimes 'd'jeee' is uttered on its own. A pair of birds foraging on its own may call only a few times an hour, but a small flock calls constantly. Alarm: 'ts'p, ts'p, ts'p'.

Geographical variation We recognise five subspecies. Forehead and eyebrow are green or blue, and there are trivial differences in hue, gorget size, and colour of the narrow line between throat and gorget.
   M. p. meridionalis Uganda (except northwest) and west Kenya, south to Angola and Natal. Forehead green; short, narrow, bright blue superciliary stripe; very narrow blue-white line between throat and gorget.
   M. p. argutus The southern border of the range of *meridionalis*, from southwest Angola to southwest Zimbabwe, and Botswana. Paler than *meridionalis*, with a slightly smaller gorget.
   M. p. cyanostictus Intergrades with *meridionalis* in the highlands of Kenya, and ranges from there through arid east and north Kenya to north Somalia and east Ethiopia. Forehead and wide superciliary stripe bright blue; narrow purple-blue line between throat and gorget.
   M. p. ocularis Upper Uele River in Zaïre and northwest Uganda to Equatoria Province of Sudan, northwest Ethiopia and Eritrea. Like *meridionalis*, but paler below, and eyebrow slightly less pronounced.

Intergrades with *cyanostictus* in a corridor 200 km wide.

M. p. pusillus Ranges from Senegambia to 29°E in Sudan, north in Mali to 17°N and south in Zaïre to 4°N. Forehead and eyebrow green; no blue line between throat and gorget, or sometimes a very narrow line of deep blue.

Habitat and range Little Bee-eaters occupy the whole of sub-Saharan Africa, except parts of northeast Ethiopia, Djibouti, Somalia east of about 46°E, some heavily forested coasts in West Africa, the forested northern half of the Congo Basin, and Namibia, western Botswana, Cape Province, Orange Free State and Lesotho. Throughout that vast range they are widespread in grassy savannas and bushy open country of all types, from coasts to up to nearly 3000 m in altitude, not very common far away from water, but plentiful in wet or humid areas. They inhabit drier parts of marshes with waist-high grasses and sedges interspersed with *Mimosa pigra* shrubs; lakeshores, riverbanks, reedbeds, farmland, lightly and sometimes heavily wooded elephant-grass savannas, grassy clearings in forest, bushy sand-dunes, arid pasture-land with *Salvadora persica*, treeless plains and grassy, bouldery hillsides. Like many other birds, this species is attracted to recently burnt country when new grass begins to grow. In Ethiopia it is common in montane grassland up to 2750 m, and frequent in lowland *Acacia/Commiphora/Chrysopogon* semi-desert.

Population Near Lusaka, Zambia, a density of 4.0 birds per km^2 of grazed *Acacia* woodland was recorded (Ulfstrand and Alerstam 1977); near Zaria, Nigeria, we estimated in 1966 that 580 individuals inhabited 100 km^2 of wooded farmland with numerous villages. Extrapolating to the entire range of the species, 14,800,000 km^2, gives a total population of 60-86 million birds (Fry 1984).

Migration From all parts of its range come reports of seasonal changes in abundance, and in places this bee-eater seems to be entirely absent at one time of year but plentiful at another. No overall picture of long-distance migration emerges, however, and most of the reports probably refer to local movements, of up to 100 km

perhaps, as the land dries out and birds concentrate in such areas as stay wet.

Food Hymenoptera and other flying insects, from 4.5 to 30 mm long and mostly less than 2 g in weight. We examined remains of 1,500 insects eaten: there were about 115 species, mainly bees, ants, digger-wasps, spider-hunting wasps, vespid wasps, ichneumon-flies, chalcid and scoliid wasps, dragonflies, tsetse-flies, other flies and beetles; also crickets, pygmy mole-crickets, bugs, butterflies, mayflies, lacewings, termites and cockroaches.

Little Bee-eater foot scratching over wing

Habits Little Bee-eaters hunt low down, keeping watch from a grass stem or shrub 1 m high by a bare patch of ground, or up to 10 m high in a tree in grassy woodland, dashing after a passing insect, snapping it up and gliding back with it to its perch. An individual makes up to some 40 forays an hour, but only one-third are successful. These bee-eaters are monogamous, breeding solitarily, and keeping in pairs year-round. In the evening, however, they go to roost gregariously, up to ten birds jammed together on a leafy twig, shoulder to shoulder, usually all facing the same way. Young may stay with their parents for several months. The species is quite vocal and active; in between bouts of feeding, the birds sunbathe at the perch using a variety of postures, ruffling the mantle feathers or tilting the head sharply to one side. They also dust-bathe, and sometimes splash onto water. **Nesting:** burrows are dug by both birds of the pair in a riverside sand cliff about 1 m high, sometimes in 5-m cliffs, also in the sides of ditches and plough furrows or in flat or sloping ground. Where Aardvarks are common, a favourite site is the ceiling just inside the entrance to their lairs. Burrows are 50-70 cm long and end in an unlined oval egg chamber. There are 4-6 eggs, with one clutch a year. **Laying months:** in the northern tropics egg-laying is from March to June, about the beginning of the wet season, and in general breeding is later at higher latitudes. In Nigeria laying is about March at 9°N, April at 11°N, May at 12°N, and early June at 13-14°N. In East Africa the species breeds year-round, peaking in September. In the southern tropics it lays mainly in September-November, with a few records up to December (Malaŵi) and February (Zimbabwe).

Description *M. p. meridionalis* Sexes alike. **Adult male:** forehead, crown, hindneck, mantle, back, rump, uppertail-coverts, central pair of tail feathers, tertials and upperwing-coverts all grass-green. Lores and ear-coverts black, forming a mask. Above the eye there is a short, bright, light blue stripe. Chin and throat vivid yellow, sharply demarcated from the black gorget, which changes to rich cinnamon on the upper breast, rufous-buff on the lower breast and dark buff on the belly and flanks; undertail-coverts pale buff. Underwing-coverts pale cinnamon. Inner primaries and secondaries rufous, with black tips forming a broad band along the trailing edge of the wing. Tail feathers, except for the middle pair, cinnamon-rufous with black tips. Bill black; eye blood-red or pale orange (perhaps a sexual difference); legs and feet dark grey-brown. **Juvenile:** like the adult, but without the black gorget. Chin and throat are pale yellowish-buff, merging into pale buffy-green on the breast, which is faintly streaked. Eye brown or red-brown. **Measurements:** wing of male 76-84, of female 75-85; tail of male 57-67, of female 57-68; bill of male 26-30, of female 25-30; tarsus of male 9-11, of female 9-11. Weight: male 10-18, female 11-17.

References Douthwaite (1986), Douthwaite and Fry (1982), Forshaw (1987), Fry (1984), Fry *et al.* (1988), Jones (1979).

96 BLUE-BREASTED BEE-EATER
Merops variegatus

Plate 31

Merops variegatus Vieillot 1817, Nouv. Dict. Hist. Nat., 14, p. 25, Malimba.

Field identification Length 19 cm (7½ in) (Ethiopian subspecies), 17 cm (6½ in) (other subspecies). Brighter, larger, and larger-headed than the Little Bee-eater (95) and distinguished by the gorget being purple-blue (not black), except in Zambia and adjacent parts of Angola and Tanzania, where the gorget can be black. The Blue-breasted Bee-eater has a white mark on the side of the neck, visible only at close quarters; but at a distance it makes the yellow throat look larger and brighter. It inhabits wetter and more montane country than the Little Bee-eater. The large Ethiopian highlands subspecies differs from the Cinnamon-chested Bee-eater (97) in having the forehead and gorget blue (not green and black).

Voice Like the voice of Little Bee-eater, but harder, less sibilant, and with slight trilling: 'pip', 'tup-tup', 'trrip'. Courting birds give what is almost a song, 'trrrp p'ti p'ti p'ti'.

Geographical variation Four subspecies. In Ethiopia Blue-breasted Bee-eaters are large, with blue gorget and forehead, strikingly like Cinnamon-chested Bee-eaters. The two forms have often been united under the name *M. oreobates*, but we believe that the Ethiopian population is more akin to the small lowland forms of Blue-breasted.

M. v. variegatus From south Cameroon through Gabon to Kasai (Zaïre) and adjacent north Angola, intergrading with the next subspecies near the Equator. Eyebrow the same green as the crown; gorget blue.

M. v. loringi From southeast Nigeria (Obudu Plateau, Mambilla Plateau), through Cameroon montane districts at altitudes between 1100 and 2100 m, to north Zaïre and Uganda and to Kisumu in Kenya. Eyebrow blue, gorget blue.

M. v. bangweoloensis Central Angola and east Angola above 1000 m (Bié Plateau), Zambia, and west Tanzania. Eyebrow green (or if blue, very small); gorget black, sooty on some birds but usually suffused with blue.

M. v. lafresnayii Highlands of Ethiopia between 1000 and 3200 m, and adjacent southeast Sudan (including Boma hills, above 1800 m). Forehead and broad eyebrow blue, gorget blue, underparts suffused with rufous, wings and tail with less rufous than in the above races. Juveniles have a strong green wash on the breast. Large: wing 93-102 mm, tail 76-86 mm, bill 31-37 mm.

Habitat and range The range is the wet lowlands of the Congo Basin (Gabon, Congo, Zaïre), Uganda, Burundi, Rwanda and northwest Zambia; also upland parts of Cameroon and Ethiopia, with the species just entering Nigeria and Sudan. In addition, it occurs in extreme west Kenya, extreme north and east Angola, and on Bié Plateau in Angola at about 1500 m. It inhabits humid savannas with elephant-grass, near to forest, well-watered bushy plains, grassy hills with scattered trees, forest clearings, swamps, reedy lake-shores, beds of reedmace and papyrus, cattle pasture, coffee farms and gum plantations. In Ethiopia, it occurs at lower altitudes in humid forests and at higher altitudes in more open juniper and *Podocarpus* woods, also in suburban habitats, as around Addis Ababa.

Population It is common in Ethiopia, south and west Uganda, and in parts of Zambia (Balovale District, Lake Bangweulu), but in most other parts of its range it is local or rather uncommon. A density of 30 individuals in an area of 3 ha was once recorded in Cameroon.

Migration Mainly sedentary. An old record of many concentrated near Entebbe, Uganda, in July and August only, suggests some migration; and it visits open country in northeast Gabon in December only.

Food Mainly honeybees and other Hymenoptera; also (in order of decreasing importance) beetles, flies, dragonflies, bugs, and grasshoppers. A pellet from the shores of Lake Victoria, Kenya, contained the digested remains of a small cichlid fish.

Habits This bird is not as well known as the Little Bee-eater, but its everyday behaviour and breeding habits seem to be much the same. The two species commonly occur together. *Nesting:* Blue-breasted Bee-eaters breed in solitary pairs, excavating their burrows in grassy hillsides in Cameroon (once a cold windy summit at 2200 m), where grass-burning seems to stimulate them to start digging, in earth banks in Ethiopia, and in shelving lakeside ground in Zambia. *Laying months:* Ethiopia, January-April; Cameroon, February-March; Gabon, August-September; Zaïre, March; Tanzania, October-December; Zambia, September-October.

Description *M. v. variegatus* Sexes alike. *Adult:* upperparts grass-green; mask black, chin and throat bright yellow becoming white at the side of the neck; large, oblong gorget purple-blue, breast cinnamon, belly greenish-buff or pale green. Secondaries pale rufous with broad black tips, primaries olivaceous and black-tipped. Central tail feathers green, others rufous with narrow green edges and the distal third black. Bill black; eye orange-red; legs and feet blackish. *Juvenile:* like the adult, but without a gorget; chin and throat yellowish-buff, becoming faintly streaky light green on the breast. *Measurements:* wing of male 82-88, of female 80-88; tail of male 60-66, of female 58-64; bill of male 30-33, of female 29-33; tarsus of male 10-11, of female 10-11. Weight: 20-25.

References Forshaw (1987), Fry (1984), Fry *et al.* (1988), Gartshore (1984).

Merops oreobates

Melittophagus oreobates Sharpe, 1892, Ibis, p. 320, Mount Elgon.

Field identification Length 20 cm (8 in). A boldly marked bee-eater of mountain forest edges, and wooded habitats above about 1600 m in East and east-central Africa. In pairs or small parties; quite common in wooded suburbs of highland cities such as Nairobi. Although bright-coloured and boldly marked, it can readily be confused with two other species. *At rest:* entire upperparts from forehead to wings and tail bright green. In worn plumage, tertials are bluish. Chin and throat bright daffodil-yellow, bordered by black above (lores, cheeks, ear-coverts) and below (a broad, black gorget across the upper breast). The yellow throat-patch extends backwards, becoming white, and forming an acute white angle on the sides of the neck. Breast cinnamon-brown, becoming dark buff on belly and undertail-coverts. Eye pale orange or deep red-brown. The bird perches upright with the tail pointing down: seen from in front, the tail is blackish with the basal half orange-brown, and with a 3-mm-deep whitish tip; from behind, it is green when closed, but when fanned (while the bird stretches, or greets another one) the outer feathers show black with warm brown bases. *In flight:* the upperwings are mainly green, but secondaries and inner primaries are rufous with broad black ends and narrow white tips: the impression is of green wings with rufous feather bases, and a broad, black trailing edge. *Confusion species:* the Little Bee-eater (95) is very similar, but much smaller, more solitary, and inhabits hot, low-lying grasslands. It lacks the white flash on the side of the neck, and has narrower black bands in wing and tail; some Little Bee-eater subspecies have pale blue eyebrows. The two species are almost segregated altitudinally. The Blue-breasted Bee-eater (96) poses greater problems. Its lowland populations, which inhabit grassy hillsides and marshes, have purple gorgets in Zambia but black gorgets in East Africa, where they are almost identical to Cinnamon-chested although smaller. Its highland subspecies, common in Ethiopia in the same habitats as Cinnamon-chested Bee-eaters occupy further south, has a purple-blue forehead, superciliary stripe and gorget; it is the same size as Cinnamon-chested, juveniles are very alike, and the two have often been regarded as conspecific. The many sight reports of Cinnamon-chested in south Ethiopia, from lower River Omo to Illubabor salient, around Lake Shala and Lake Shambo and east to Nuara, are probably all referable to Blue-breasted Bee-eaters.

Voice A long 'tzee-ip' or a treble 'tee-si sip' given when a bird alights next to its mate (the homologue of the 's'lip' of the much commoner Little Bee-eater). The song is much like that of the Little Bee-eater, 'siddle-iddle-ip-d'jeee'.

Geographical variation None.

Habitat and range A highland bird, occurring most commonly between 1800 and 2300 m, but down to 730 m (Bangangai Forest, Sudan) and up to 3000 m. It inhabits humid forest, wooded hillsides, forest edges, clearings overgrown with elephant-grass and bracken, cedar forest, eucalyptus plantations, gardens and plantations with shade trees and plenty of weed growth. It occurs in Bangangai Forest (Sudan, 04°51′N, 27°45′E), and highlands of East Africa, from Lolibat and Nangeya Mountains (Sudan/Uganda border), Mt Elgon (Uganda/Kenya border), Nyiru and Kulal, Mathews Range, Cherangani hills, Mt Marsabit, Maralal, Meru, highlands of west and central Kenya, to Crater Highlands of Tanzania, Arusha National Park, Mt Kilimanjaro, Pare Mountains, West Usambaras, and East Ulugurus; in mountains of Zaïre from northwest of Lake Mobutu (Lake Albert), through the Ruwenzoris and south Ugandan highlands, Rwanda and Burundi, to about 5°S on the west side of Lake Tanganyika and on the east side to Kifunzo, Gombi Stream Game Reserve and Mt Mahari.

Population It is common in the highlands of Equatoria, southernmost Sudan, above about 1875 m, also in similar habitat in East Africa between 1600 and 2300 m. In Bwamba Forest, Uganda, it is fairly common between 1560 and 2200 m. In eastern Zaïre it is common between 1875 and 2200 m, especially in the Ruwenzori Range, but it is scarce in northwest Rwanda.

Migration Sedentary, an altitudinal migrant, and a local wanderer. A breeding visitor, from October to April, at Lengibere (2750 m) and Mau Narok (3000 m) in Kenya. Resident all year at some sites, near Nairobi for instance, but at others it disperses away after breeding.

Food As much as 95-99% of the diet is honeybees, at least at two places where studies were made in Kenya. Other insects eaten include wasps, ants, flies, beetles, moths and many butterflies.

Habits It usually occurs in pairs, but ten or more pairs may congregate to breed. Up to 20 birds flock together to feed on swarming bees. It hunts from a low branch, fence, or treetop, perching alertly, upright, with the tail pointing down and wagging irregularly fore and aft through a small arc; then suddenly it darts out in hot pursuit of a flying insect, seizes it with an audible snap of the bill, and gracefully sails back to perch, where the prey is whacked and rubbed against the branch and quickly eaten whole. Up to six birds perch shoulder to shoulder in a row on a twig or wire; in the late afternoon groups come down to sandy soil to dust themselves or sunbathe. Helpers have not been reported, but three individuals sometimes collaborate to dig a nest; pairs visit adjacent nests. Breeding colonies are dense or else loosely associated, once ten nests in a 50-m-long road cutting. *Nesting:* the nest burrow, 60-70 cm long and inclining slightly, is excavated by both sexes in a vertical or sloping cliff face. The egg chamber at the end is offset to one side, and its floor is 4 cm below the tunnel floor. Eggs are white, and slightly glossy; always two in Kenya, often three in

Tanzania. Incubation is mainly by the female, in spells of 15-40 minutes, and sometimes by the male. Fledged young return to their nest burrow to roost for one or two weeks; they remain with their parents for several weeks. This species is often parasitised by Greater Honeyguides *Indicator indicator*. *Laying months:* laying in Uganda and west Kenya is mainly in December-January, and in central Kenya (Nairobi) in August-April (mainly November-December). The species is double-brooded, the only African bee-eater to be so.

Description Sexes alike. *Adult:* scattered frontal feathers and an indistinct superciliary stripe are deep blue; upperparts bright grass-green; tertials darker green, broadly tipped with dull greenish-blue. Outer primaries green, broadly edged with cinnamon-buff basally on the inner webs; undersides of the secondaries cinnamon-buff. Lores, and from base of bill to ear-coverts, black; throat and chin golden-yellow, paling to white towards side of neck; a broad black band across the foreneck, sometimes washed deep blue, is separated from the yellow throat by a very narrow, purple-blue line. Upper breast rich cinnamon, merging into orange-rufous on lower breast and dark buff on belly; lower breast usually tinged with greenish-yellow; undertail-coverts buff washed with pale green. Underwing-coverts deep cinnamon. Central tail feathers green, others subterminally banded with black and tipped with white. Bill black; iris red; legs brownish-grey. *Juvenile:* chin and upper throat paler yellow; lower throat and foreneck dull green, streaky, with a slightly scalloped appearance; breast green, belly feathers cinnamon-buff, broadly shaft-streaked with green, merging into dull bluish-green on the undertail-coverts. Bill black; iris brown; legs pale grey. *Measurements:* male and female the same. Wing 98-106; tail 77-94; bill to feathers 32-39, to skull 42-48; tarsus 11-12. Weight: male 20-38, female 17-28.

References Forshaw (1987), Fry (1984), Fry *et al.* (1988), van Someren (1956).

Merops bullocki

Merops Bulocki Vieillot, 1817, Nouv. Dict. Hist. Nat., 14, p. 13, Sénégal.

Field identification Length 20-22 cm (8-8½ in). A common, gregarious, open-woodland bee-eater found from Senegal to west Ethiopia, where it is the only one with a red throat, making it unmistakable. *At rest:* nearly always two or several together, often perching shoulder to shoulder; they are instantly told by their green upperparts, scarlet chin and throat, warm buff hindneck, breast and belly, and conspicuous ultramarine thighs and undertail-coverts. The tail is moderately long, but without streamers; when fanned, in common greeting display or when clinging to a cliff face, it looks more buff-ochre than green. Up to 1% of individuals have the throat bright yellow, not red; in low evening sunlight normal red-throated birds can also look yellow-throated. *In flight:* they usually call 'wip...wip'. The wings are green above with a broad black trailing-edge band, and pale buff below. *Confusion species:* the closely related White-fronted Bee-eater (99) overlaps only in Virunga National Park, Zaïre, where its white forehead and throat and deep 'gaaa' call immediately distinguish it. Black Bee-eaters (93) have red throats but are black and pale blue birds of high forest. Rosy Bee-eaters (110), overlapping in south Nigeria, with pink-red throats, have grey backs and pink bellies. Red-throated Bee-eaters of the yellow-throated morph can be told from other yellow-throated species (94, 95, 96, 97) by the lack of a dark gorget.

Voice The commonest call of perched and flying birds is 'wip', sharper and louder in anxiety: 'wit' or 'weep'. In greeting, an excited trilling cadence, 'trrrr-trrr-trrr-trr-trr-trr-tr-teu' or 'tee-tee-peu-peu-pirri-pirri-prrrrrp-teu-teu'. Excitement and general alarm, a chattering 'tic-ic-ic-ic-ic-ic'; hawk-alarm, a short fast 'prrrrr'ng'. Eight or nine other calls are known (Fry 1984).

Geographical variation There are two subspecies, with green facial features to the west of Central African Republic and blue to the east; which subspecies occurs in CAR is uncertain.

M. b. bullocki From Senegal to 20°E in the Chari River drainage, Chad.

M. b. frenatus Southwest Sudan from Songo to the western Lolibat foothills, and southward across the Zaïre and Ugandan borders to Virunga National Park and north Lake Albert; also along the Sudan/Ethiopia border from Wad Medani to just west of Lake Tana and south to Sobat, Akoba and Gila River. Like the nominate subspecies, but the forehead, eyebrow and malar streak are pale blue, not green.

Habitat and range Red-throated Bee-eaters inhabit bushy pastures and lightly wooded savannas dissected by small rivers and seasonal streams. In most of their range they are highly sedentary birds, seldom found more than 3 km from the vertical sandy or lateritic riverbanks and erosion gullies where they nest colonially and centre their lives year-round. They like well-timbered farmland, and gardens, the edges of woods around a marsh or field, parkland, and the edges of gallery forest in valleys; sometimes they occur in dry *Combretum* scrub. The range of *frenatus* is given above. Further west, the species ranges from the Senegal and Gambia Rivers to Mopti in Mali, the River Niger headwaters in Guinea, southern Burkina Faso, northern Ivory Coast and Ghana (south to Kete Kratchi), western-most Niger, Benin (reaching the coast near Cotonou), the whole of Nigeria north of Ibadan, Lokoja, Makurdi and Takum, north Cameroon, southern Chad east to Am Timan, and north Central African Republic (Carroll 1988). It occurs above 1000 m in altitude only in central Nigeria and west Ethiopia.

Population Shortly before nesting started, 520 individuals were counted in nine colonies in an area of 25 km² in Nigeria. From that figure we estimate a total African population of 1.75 million before and 3.5 million after breeding.

Migration Long-term ringing studies have shown this bee-eater to be quite sedentary in several regions (and also sometimes to live for at least 12 years). At the periphery of its range, however, there may be some migration, as indicated by a few records at Enugu and Lagos in Nigeria, while birds which nest on the upper Gambia River move downstream about February to spend the wet season, July-October, on the middle reaches.

Red-throated Bee-eater de-stinging bee

Food Red-throated Bee-eaters feed on flying insects by hawking from a cliff perch or the side of a small tree, taking insects one by one and carrying them back to the perch to beat them and, in the case of a stinging bee or wasp, to rub its tail-end against the perch until the venom and sting are discharged. One-quarter of the prey is worker honeybees *Apis mellifera*; small *Trigona* sweat-bees compose 16%, and the remainder includes a great variety of other hymenopterans (ichneumon-flies, chalcidoids, ruby-tailed wasps, velvet-ants, true wasps, spider-hunting wasps, digger wasps, potter wasps, and at least ten other genera of bees) and of beetles, with a few bugs, flies, dragonflies, damsel-flies, moths, butterflies, termites and grasshoppers. Nestlings are given larger items: cicadas, grasshoppers, crickets, hawk-moths and butterflies, as well as some large bees and wasps.

Habits Perching alertly about 3 m above open ground, a bird gives chase to passing insects about 30 times an hour, and successfully makes a capture once in every three sorties. With dashing flight it chases its prey for about 15 m, snaps it up, and glides back to its perch. There the bird holds a bee by its thorax and deals its head

a violent blow against the branch; quickly transferring its grip to the insect's tail, the bird closes its eyes and rubs it rapidly against the perch five or ten times; a couple more sharp raps to the head, and the bee is tossed into the mouth and swallowed. The whole immobilising and devenoming sequence takes 5-10 seconds. Occasionally a bird glides towards the ground to glean an insect from low herbage, momentarily hovering as it does so. Rarely, these bee-eaters forage aloft in continuous flight, not returning to perch, and probably they then feed on tiny soft-bodied insects. Three to eight times a day a Red-throated Bee-eater regurgitates a neat, odourless, oval blackish pellet about 3 cm long; pellets litter the ground under favourite daytime perches and night roosts in a clump of leafy trees. A small proportion of nesting bee-eaters do not catch their own prey; instead they wait at the nesting colony and harry 'honest' birds returning with food for their young, forcing them to drop the insect, which the 'thief' promptly seizes and carries into its own nest. Between bouts of foraging, the birds spend much time sunbathing, generally socially, either facing away from the sun and sharply lifting the mantle feathers in a crescentic ruff, or sitting in a broken-necked posture under the midday sun, the head turned aside, bill agape, neck feathers ruffled, and sunward eye closed. Sometimes an individual suns itself on the ground or clinging to a cliff, spreadeagling itself with the head thrown back so that the crown is pressed against the mantle. Preening, scratching and stretching – the spread tail drawn to one side under one downstretched wing – are interpolated with sunbathing. Often the birds water-bathe, splashing momentarily head-first into the surface (which gives rise to reports of Red-throated Bee-eaters fishing), then vigorously preening. In the late afternoons they commonly come to the ground, a sandy riverbed in front of the nesting cliff, and with much calling they sunbathe or shuffle around picking up and fiddling with small bits of dead leaves and twigs. Grit is eaten (to help the muscular gizzard to break up insects), and shiny fragments of snail shells are carried up to the nest.

Social behaviour: strongly gregarious at all seasons, Red-throated Bee-eaters have complicated, human-village-like societies. They are essentially monogamous and pair for life, but many pairs have one or more adult helpers-at-the-nest. Most colonies contain between five and 50 active nests, but with 'false-start' burrows and previous seasons' nests there may be 100 or more holes in 2 m^2 of riverbank face. Males chase and try to copulate with unguarded females; but conversely they have to spend much time guarding their own mates against other opportunist males. Females for their part lay as many eggs as they can in neighbouring nests, so that others unwittingly have the responsibility of raising foster-nestlings.

Dense colonial living leads to almost constant bickering between nesting neighbours. A perched bird threatens an incomer with head stretched forward, bill wide open, mantle feathers fluffed, and vehement calling. Aerial pursuits are common, and sometimes two individuals fight in the air, grappling with their bills and falling interlocked to the ground, where they may struggle for some minutes. Whenever a bird alights next to a mate or relative there is noisy greeting, both of them stretching the head up, raising the crown feathers, and fanning and vibrating the tail. Several birds may display at once, and then settle, perching shoulder to shoulder. At night a breeding group roosts in the nest in cool weather, or the entire colony sleeps in a leafy tree, a row of six or seven fluffed-up birds jammed tightly together, all facing the same way but looking headless, beaks tucked deep between the shoulders.

Courtship involves an inconspicuous head-bobbing display, and much more conspicuous courtship-feeding of a female by her mate and by any male helpers. Feeding is often followed by copulation (by the mate or even by a helper, who is generally the pair's adult son). Burrow ownership is demonstrated by a brief 'head-dip and flutter' display by a bird clinging to the cliff by its nest entrance. Having a helper at the nest reduces the female's burden and considerably enhances rearing success. After the brood leaves the nest there is a 'weaning' period of about six weeks, during which young birds, closely attended by the adults, perfect the art of catching and de-stinging bees. Instead of dispersing, some youngsters then remain with their parents all year and in the following breeding season help them with all nesting chores – dig-

ging, defence, incubating, and feeding the young. Most nest helpers are thus the elder brothers (sometimes sisters) of the brood they assist to rear. Sometimes a breeding bird whose mate dies, or whose nest fails, abandons breeding and attaches itself to a related pair within the colony as a helper for the rest of the season. A breeding unit – pair plus one or sometimes up to five helpers – forms close ties with two or three other units within the colony. The birds in such a 'friendly' group, called a clan, visit each other's nests, although a pair defends its burrow entrance vigorously from all other comers not in the clan. Clan membership is forged not at the nesting cliff but on the feeding grounds 1-2 km away. There the clan stakes out a corporate territory and defends it from other clans. Within such a territory, clan members space themselves out and hunt essentially solitarily, keeping contact by voice. In the late afternoon clan members return together to the nest cliff. After roosting at night in their nests, the members assemble in the morning and depart for their feeding territory in a flock; other clans daily go their separate ways. Clan membership is stable over long periods, altered by births, deaths, and 'marriage' from outside. Red-throated Bee-eater society, like human society, is based on family and friends, with increasingly distant and tenuous social relationships further afield, complicated at every level by the conflict between selfish and cooperative behaviour.

Nesting: this bee-eater uses perpendicular cliffs, not (or only very rarely) flat or sloping ground. A small part of the cliff face is riddled with a hundred burrows – many of them unused – with entrances about 20 cm apart. Birds dig new nests each year, either among last year's burrows or on the same stretch of cliff within 100 m of them. However high the cliff, nest holes are always excavated near the top. Sometimes a colony of Red-throated Bee-eaters nests at one end of a larger colony of Carmine Bee-eaters (111). With use the tunnel entrance becomes A-shaped, the occupants' feet wearing two channels. Tunnels average 80 cm long, and incline at 20° for two-thirds of their length, then, after a shallow hump, decline into the egg chamber. There is a single clutch, of 3-4 eggs, often parasitised by Greater Honeyguides *Indicator indicator*.

Incubation and nestling periods are 20 and 28 days respectively. Helpers share all nesting duties with both parents. *Laying months:* nests are dug about September when the ground is still moist and soft, and eggs laid in February (occasionally January, March and April).

Description *M. b. bullocki* Sexes alike. *Adult:* forehead and crown green, hindneck warm buff, and remainder of the upperparts green with the secondaries black-tipped, the central tail feathers green and the outer ones bronze-buff with green tips and outer edges. The tertials often bleach to dull blue. Lores, ear-coverts and cheeks black. Chin and throat bright red (rarely, yellow); many individuals have a narrow green line between the black mask and red throat. Breast, flanks and belly are buffy light brown; thighs, vent and undertail-coverts deep ultramarine-blue. Underwing-coverts pale buff, and underside of the tail slaty when closed and cinnamon with slaty feather tips when open. Bill black, inside of mouth pink; eye dark brown; legs and feet dark grey. *Juvenile:* like the adult, but reds and blues are much less intense, and there is always a green stripe under the mask. *Measurements:* wing of male 96-106, of female 98-103; tail of male 84-96, of female 85-92; bill of male 33-39, of female 32-36; tarsus of male 10-12, of female 10-12. Weight: male 21-29, female 20-30.

References Crick (1987), Fry (1984), Fry *et al.* (1988).

99 WHITE-FRONTED BEE-EATER   Plate 32
Merops bullockoides

Merops Bullockoides A. Smith, 1834, S. Afr. Quart. J. 2, (2), p. 320, Marico River.

Field identification Length 22-24 cm (8¹/₂-9¹/₂ in). This is the east and southern African counterpart of the Red-throated Bee-eater (98). Unmistakable throughout its wooded-grassland range, the White-fronted Bee-eater is a strongly gregarious, vocal bird with white forehead, chin and malar stripe, pointed-feathered mealy-buff crown and hindneck, green back, wings and tail, scarlet throat, dark buff breast and belly, and purple-blue upper- and undertail-coverts. *In flight:* a broad black trailing edge to the wing is conspicuous. *Confusion species:* White-fronted Bee-eaters breed in Virunga National Park, Zaïre, where vagrant Red-throated Bee-eaters have occurred; the latter can be told by their smaller size, treble 'wik' flight calls, blue forehead, red chin and green rump. White-fronted Bee-eaters just overlap with another red-throated species, the Black Bee-eater (93), in east Zaïre, south Congo and north Angola; Black Bee-eaters are high-forest birds with mainly black plumage. Note also that two pink-throated bee-eaters overlap (110, 111). In Kenya, a few individual White-fronted Bee-eaters have been found with yellow, not red, throats; they can be told from other yellow-throated bee-eater species by the absence of a black gorget.

Voice The commonest call is a nasal, muffled 'gaaa' or 'gaauu'; sometimes faintly disyllabic, 'waaru', or slightly rolled, 'krrrt' or 'karara'. The alarm is a sharp 'waark'.

Geographical variation Birds from the southern highlands of Tanzania are darker green and red, with hindneck and belly washed with cinnamon; they have been separated subspecifically as *M. b. randorum*.

Habitat and range Habitats are like those of Red-throated Bee-eaters: dry watercourses, eroded gullies, bushy pastures, and perennial rivers and seasonal streams with wooded banks. Somewhat local in Kenya (where restricted to the southwest), this species is in most other parts of its range widespread and common, with a density about the same as that of the Red-throated Bee-eater. In Kenya it is commonest between 1400 and 2000 m, near the Rift Valley; elsewhere it is a bird mainly of hot lowlands. From the southern borders of the forested Congo Basin, it ranges on the Atlantic seaboard from Libreville (Gabon) to about Porto Alexandre (Angola), across to the Indian Ocean seaboard between Tanga (Tanzania) and Durban. Absent from much of west Tanzania, it is common on the west side of Lake Tanganyika and ranges north through Kivu to Semliki and Virunga and through Masai and the Eastern Rift to Kerio and Turkwell Rivers (southwest Lake Turkana). In the south it extends to the Okavango valley and Lake Ngami, Botletle River, Makarikari Pan, Transvaal (rare at 27°S), Orange Free State (Modder, Vet and Vaal Rivers) and to Tugela River in Natal.

Population White-fronted Bee-eaters are particularly common in Zambia and Zimbabwe, along the Luangwa, Zambezi, Kafue, Hunyani and many other rivers. There are thought to be over 1,000 colonies in Zimbabwe.

Migration There is quite distant dispersal, which has led to records at Swakopmund and lower Fish River (Namibia), Durban (Natal) and Malindi (Kenya), but no evidence of true migration (Irwin 1981).

Food Honeybees compose about half of the prey, and a large variety of other bees and wasps much of the other half. Beetles, bugs, flies, dragonflies, damselflies, grasshoppers, termites, moths and butterflies together form 12% of the diet, which is exclusively of flying insects.

Habits From ten years of teamwork in Kenya, even more is known about this than about the previous bee-eater. In habits, behaviour and social organisation the two species are very alike. White-fronted Bee-eaters forage in stable, clan-defended territories, sometimes as far as 7 km from the colony site. A bird makes 300 feeding sorties a day: about 30 of these are slow glides to seize prey from the ground without alighting; of the rest, half are fast pursuits of insects flying past and half are glides with a brief hover to snap up an insect from low herbage. A few insects are taken from the surface of water, and in continuous flight high in the air. **Nesting:** this bee-eater breeds in dense colonies sited in cliffs of riverbanks or erosion gullies. There are generally 10-20 active nests, but sometimes as many as 150 nests with 450 birds. The species is monogamous, with multiple helpers at most nests. A male guards his mate by keeping close to her all the time; all the same, in unguarded moments she will be chased by foreign males on average between three and eight times during the entire breeding season, and some chases end in enforced copulations. Unpaired females are pursued far more, and they (and some paired females) know which nest holes have laying females and opportunistically lay their own egg(s) in them when the owner is absent: to prevent such parasitisation, a rightful female stays in her nest for up to 94% of the time on laying days; nonetheless, about 7% of all eggs in a colony are laid parasitically, and one clutch in six is parasitised by neighbouring bee-eaters (others are parasitised by honeyguides). Breeding success (the production of flying young) is twice as great when parents have helpers as when they have none. **Laying months:** Kenya, all months, with a major peak in October-February and a minor one in April-June; Zambia and Angola, August-September; Zimbabwe, mainly September, also August and (after unseasonal rain) February and April; South Africa, September-October.

Description Sexes alike. **Adult:** forehead white, forecrown buffy-white, hindcrown and hindneck bronzy-buff. Mask black; the chin and a broad stripe below the mask are white. Remaining upperparts are dark bluish-green, but the uppertail-coverts are ultramarine-blue, the secondaries black-tipped and primaries dusky-tipped. Throat scarlet, breast and belly dark buff; thighs, part of the flanks, vent and undertail-coverts ultramarine-blue. Underwing-coverts buff; the underside of the tail is black. Bill black; eye dark brown; legs and feet dark grey. **Juvenile:** like the adult, but red and blue parts are paler. **Measurements:** wing of male 111-120, of female 110-121; tail of male 90-101, of female 90-103; bill of male 34-40, of female 35-40; tarsus of male 11-13, of female 11-13. Weight: male 28-38, female 31-35.

References Emlen (1990), Emlen and Wrege (1986, 1988, 1989, 1991), Fry (1984), Fry *et al.* (1988).

Merops revoilii Oustalet, 1882, in Révoil, Faune et Flore des Pays Çomalis, Oiseaux, p. 5, pl. 1, Somaliland.

Field identification Length 16-18 cm (6½-7 in). A slender, pallid, often leggy and unkempt-looking bee-eater of the Horn of Africa, not gregarious; safely distinguished by its white throat and buff breast. **At rest:** upperparts green; eyebrow and upper- and undertail-coverts pale blue; chin and throat white; breast and belly cinnamon-buff. Forehead and crown feathers are spiky. To shed heat the bird stands with 'wrists' parted from the breast and bare pink thighs exposed. **In flight:** the wings lack the black trailing edge of many other bee-eaters. **Confusion species:** the most lightweight of all bee-eaters, the Somali is about the size of the Little Bee-eater (95), which differs in having a yellow throat and black gorget. White-throated Bee-eaters (101), which overlap near Lake Turkana (north Kenya) and perhaps in northwest Somalia, are larger, gregarious, streamer-tailed, black-crowned and black-gorgeted. (A single specimen is known of a White-fronted Bee-eater (99) with a white, not red, throat; it looks very like a large Somali, but has dark purple-blue, not pale blue, upper- and undertail-coverts.)

Voice The call, seldom used, is said to be a loud, clear descending trill, 'twee-twee-twee-tee'.

Geographical variation None.

Habitat and range Somali Bee-eaters frequent open thorn scrubland, yellowed grassy plains with scattered trees and bushes, waterless steppe but also the environs of desert wells, coastal dunes, irrigated fields, thorn fences around cultivation, palm groves, and sometimes quite dense *Commiphora* bushland. They range from sea level up to about 1000 m in Kenya and 1500 m in Ethiopia. In the more arid parts of its range, this species is commoner than the Little Bee-eater. It is plentiful in northwest Somalia around Hargeisa, in east Ethiopia in the Webbi Shebelle and Ganale Dorya valleys east of 40°E, and on the eastern plateau of Kenya below 1000 m, from the eastern shores of Lake Turkana through Marsabit to Archers Post and down the Tana valley to the coast. It is also common in Mandera, northeast Kenya, and from there through Wajir to north Uaso Nyiro River. It is widespread but not so common in the rest of Somalia, north to Cape Gardafui and south to the lower Juba valley. In the last 25 years Somali Bee-eaters have extended from the Tana to the Galana and upper Voi River valleys and East and West Tsavo National Parks, with records in northeast Tanzania and at Dar es Salaam. There is also a sight record from Namrah, Saudi Arabia, although the species is basically sedentary.

Habits The diet is not known, but the bird makes short forays from a low perch and doubtless catches a range of small flying insects. It feeds throughout the hottest part of the day, perching about 3 m up on an *Acacia* and commonly adopting the leggy heat-shedding posture mentioned above. **Nesting:** very few nest burrows have been reported: two in the side of an earthen well shaft, one a straight declining tunnel 60 cm long in an earth mound around the roots of a fallen date palm, one in a low bank cut by a road-grader, and one with four eggs in April (Clarke 1985). **Laying months:** Somalia, March-April (and fledglings in early October); Kenya, about May-June.

Description Sexes alike. **Adult:** forehead feathers narrow and pointed, grey with green-yellow tips in the centre of the forehead and turquoise tips at the sides; a narrow, pale blue eyebrow. Crown glossy, mealy-green, hindneck buffy-green, mantle bronzy-green, upper back and wings green with most feathers (particularly the tertials) wearing or bleaching bluish; lower back and rump bright cobalt-blue, uppertail-coverts darker blue and tail bluish-green. Mask black. Chin and throat white, the feathers thin and incoherent;

breast, belly and flanks cinnamon-buff, underwing-coverts pale fawn, undertail-coverts pale blue; underside of tail shiny pale grey. Bill black; eye reddish-brown; legs and feet greyish-black. *Juvenile:* like the adult but duller. *Measurements:* wing of male 75-81, of female 73-80; tail of male 62-71, of female 63-70; bill of male 28-36, of female 26-34; tarsus of male 9-11, of female 9-11. Weight: male 12-15, female 11-14.

References Forshaw (1987), Fry (1984), Fry *et al.* (1988).

101 WHITE-THROATED BEE-EATER   Plate 32
Merops albicollis

Merops albicollis Vieillot, 1817, Nouv. Dict. Hist. Nat., 14, p. 15, Sénégal.

Field identification Length 19-21 cm (8 in), excluding tail-streamers which can exceed 12 cm (4¾ in). This is a small, delicately coloured, highly gregarious bee-eater, with a strikingly patterned somewhat shrike-like face and a pleasant trilling voice. It nests in sub-desert steppe, but winters in the rainforest zone. *At rest:* unmistakable: black crown, mask and large oblong gorget, offset by a broad white supercilium, white throat, and red eye; rich ochreous hindneck, green back and wings, blue tertials, rump and tail, pale green breast and white belly. The neat black cap is often emphasised by the bird raising its crown feathers. Tail-streamers are the longest of any of the bee-eaters, adding to the graceful appearance of this slender, beautiful bird. *In flight:* the somewhat round-tipped wings appear more ochreous than green, and have black trailing edges equally conspicuous seen from above or below.

Voice Flight calls, 'prrp' and 'pruik', are like those of European Bee-eaters (109), but more treble and repeated more often. Calling flocks produce a pleasant medley of far-carrying sound, an excited trilling babble which lasts 5-10 seconds and then stops rather abruptly. Variations of the 'pruik' note are commonly given by perched birds, alone or interacting socially.

Geographical variation There is a cline of increasing wing length from West Africa (98 mm) through Sudan (100 mm) to Arabia (103 mm), and eastern birds are also somewhat longer-billed than western ones; however, we do not recognise any subspecies.

Habitat and range Few birds have a greater contrast between breeding and winter habitats. White-throated Bee-eaters nest in sparsely wooded sub-desert steppe, arid thorn scrub, and wide sandy wadis, laghs and dunes practically devoid of vegetation. But they winter in the rainforest region, hawking socially for food from the topmost branches of emergent forest trees or in clearings, well-timbered suburban gardens, plantations, wooded farms, the edges of gallery forest, cut-about secondary growth, and orchard-like moist derived savanna woodlands with open, grassy spaces. On migration they can occur in practically all habitats between the extremes of desert and rainforest, and they range up to 3000 m (in East Africa); however, they keep mainly below 1400 m and pause to feed principally in bushy savannas. An abundant bird in its winter quarters, this species' breeding range is a surprisingly narrow belt across Africa and the Red Sea. It is widespread in the interior of south Mauritania and in north Senegal along the Senegal River from coastal dunes upstream. It nests in southwest and south Mali (Lakamine, Bla, San, Goundam, Ti-n-Ekkart, north to Tabankort), in Niger (Lagane, north of Nguigmi; and probably abundantly throughout the sahel zone), at Malamfatori in northeast Nigeria, between Gardian and Arada in Chad, commonly in north Sudan from Bir Abu Za'ima and El Ga'a to Omdurman, Shendi and Port Sudan, in Ethiopia at Massawa and Awash, near Djibouti, and in Kenya near Ileret and Ferguson's Gulf, in the Olorgesailie area and on Lake Magadi. In Arabia this bee-eater breeds commonly on the Tihama between Al Lith and Lahej.

The wintering range is the rainforest zone from lower Senegambia to Uganda, south to Cabinda and the lower Congo River, the Ituri, Rwanda, Burundi (to 4°S), southwest Kenya and occasionally northwest and east Tanzania (south to Rufiji River). Migrants occur everywhere between the Sahara and the Congo Basin, all over Ethiopia and Kenya, and in south and north (but not central) Somalia east to Cape Gardafui. Vagrants have been found in Zambia (Kafue), South Africa (Kalahari Gemsbok National Park) and United Arab Emirates (Jebel Ali near Dubai).

Migration Being an abundant, vocal and aerial bird, migrations of White-throated Bee-eaters are highly visible. With much regularity migrants visit Lake Turkana (for instance) from late February to early September and northeast Nigeria from late April to late October. At Kaduna, Nigeria, spring passage is in the second and third weeks of May and autumn passage from the second week of October until mid November. Some individuals must move well over 2000 km (those that winter in Cabinda, for example). They fatten for the spring journey, increasing their weight by 15%. They breed at the edge of the Sahara in the season of expected rain, and great numbers die if instead they encounter sand storms and temperatures in excess of 45°C.

Food Mainly airborne insects, especially flying ants. About 30% of the prey are other hymenopterans, beetles, bugs, grasshoppers, flies, dragonflies, butterflies, termites and lacewings. Supplementary food includes sand-living animals such as antlion larvae and 4-cm-long skinks, and in winter some vegetable matter (see below).

Habits Forays, mostly short but sometimes quite lengthy, are made from fences, stakes and thorn trees in the desert, but from perches 10-20 m high in the wintering grounds. A flock often feeds by flying out from the topmost branches of some forest giant 70 m tall. They regularly wait on the lower branches of oil-palms for squirrels to discard skin strips of the oily fruit, which they catch in mid-air (Fry 1964; Pettet 1969), a most unexpected and remarkable thing for a bee-eater to do. Year-round, whenever a bird alights next to others, there is excited trilling with

all the birds sitting upright, the crown feathers raised and the tail fanned and vibrating. In courtship, which begins on the wintering grounds in spring, a vociferously calling individual alternates high-winged gliding with shallow wingbeats, looking deep-chested, then it alights next to its mate and the two salute each other with raised wings; facing each other with wings folded and calling loudly, they stand upright, raise the crests high, and bob up and down by flexing the legs, then make as if to devenom an imaginary bee by rubbing it on the perch at the partner's feet. **Nesting:** White-throated Bee-eaters breed in loose colonies, with up to 250 nest burrows dug into bare sandy ground at a density of up to eight nests per ha. The birds are monogamous and nearly all pairs have up to five helpers-at-the-nest with the average number being much higher than in any other bee-eater. Most burrows are dug in flat or shelving sand in the lee of a small tussock or next to camel-droppings or a stick; they are straight, 1-2 m long, and decline at an angle of 20-24° to the horizontal, so that the floor of the egg chamber is about 40-60 cm below the ground surface. The completed clutch numbers 6-7 eggs; the young are fed principally by their parents but, importantly, also by the helpers. **Laying months:** Senegal and Mauritania, July-August; Mali, July; Niger, about July; Nigeria, May-June; Sudan, July-August; Ethiopia, June; Kenya, Lake Magadi, March, Lake Turkana, April-May. As a rule egg-laying is in June at 15°N and August at 18°N.

Description Sexes alike. **Adult:** forehead and broad superciliary stripe white; crown black; lores and ear-coverts black; hindneck rich ochreous-buff; mantle, back, scapulars and upperwing-coverts gold-green or bluish-green, merging into greyish-blue on the tertials, rump, uppertail-coverts and tail. Primaries and secondaries are rich ochreous-buff, the outer webs washed with green, and all but the outer primaries broadly black-tipped. Chin and throat are white, washed with pale yellow, the deep gorget is black, the breast pale green, flanks (where concealed by folded wings) pale yellowish-green, belly silky-white, undertail-coverts very pale blue, and underwing-coverts warm buff. Bill black; eye crimson; legs and feet light brown. **Juvenile:** like the adult, but the green parts are olivaceous, the hindneck less rufescent, the chin and throat pale yellow, and all black and olive-green head and body feathers are narrowly pale-tipped; the eye is brownish-red. On very young birds the central tail feathers are no longer than the others. *Measurements:* wing of male 95-105, of female 95-104; tail of male 65-82, of fe-male 64-74, with streamers up to 122 mm longer on males and 85 mm on females; bill of male 31-39, of female 31-42; tarsus of male 10-12, of female 10-12. Weight: male 23-25, female 20-28.

References Forshaw (1987), Fry (1984), Fry *et al.* (1988).

102 BOEHM'S BEE-EATER   Plate 33
Merops boehmi

Merops (Melittophagus) boehmi Reichenow, 1882, Orn. Centralsbl., 7-8, p. 62, Bumi, Tanganyika Territory.

Field identification Length 16 cm (6½ in), excluding tail-streamers of up to 7 cm (2¾ in). A small green bee-eater with rufous crown and throat, no black gorget, and long tail-streamers. Juveniles are like the adults, but lack streamers. *At rest:* the narrow blue cheek line is easy to see; from in front the tail is conspicuously black-tipped. *In flight:* looks lightly built, and rather round-winged. *Confusion species:* Swallow-tailed Bee-eaters (94) have green crown, yellow throat, blue gorget, and forked blue tail. Blue-cheeked Bee-eaters (104) are much larger, gregarious, with light blue forehead and yellow chin, and Madagascar Bee-eaters (105) are also large and gregarious, with white forehead, chin and cheeks; both species fly high but Boehm's does not.

Voice A vocal bird but the voice is quiet. Calls are very like those of the Little Bee-eater (95); the contact call is 'sip' or 'slip', and is repeated and elaborated into a short song, 'siddle-iddle-ip, d'jee'. The greeting call, given by a perched bird when its mate arrives, is a dry, rolling 'drreee'.

Geographical variation None.

Habitat and range Boehm's Bee-eater has a somewhat circumscribed and unusual range for an African bird. It is confined to two regions, one between Lake Rukwa in Tanzania and the middle Kafue River in Zambia, and the other running from coast-al Tanzania through Malaŵi to lower Zambezi River. The preferred habitat is park-like: woods and large shade trees separated by cultivation or areas of short-grass sward, with thickets of thornbushes and adjacent riparian evergreen forest. It occurs in shrubland, low woodland, burnt-over ground, large sandy glades in *Brachystegia* forest, wooded farmland, around villages and in roadside vege-tation. The two regions, highland in the west and lowland in the east, lie 400 km apart, with the two populations' nearest approach at Mbesuma in Zambia and Bana near Nkhotakota on Lake Malaŵi. The western population ranges between 900 and 1400 m altitude, from Lake Rukwa and Lake Tanganyika (north to Uvinza in Tanzania and Lake Suse in Zaïre), to Lake Mweru and Lake Retenue in Zaïre, east Lunga River at 13°S and the middle and upper Kafue valley in Zambia; Boehm's Bee-eater has been found near Livingstone but not yet in Zimbabwe. To the east, it occurs from southern Malaŵi, where it ranges up to 900 m, to the lower Zambezi, up to Cabora Dam and down to Manica e Sofala and Revue River in Mozambique, and from northern Malaŵi to Ruvuma River on the Tanzania/Mozambique border, north to Uluguru lowlands, Kilosa, the lowlands between East and West Usambaras, and near the coast between Pugu Hills and Lindi. Why it does not range far more extensively in suitable-looking country to the north, west and south is unknown. Within its range, density varies considerably. In general it is not common; but it is locally plentiful in low-lying land around Lake Malaŵi and in

Lilongwe and Lengwe National Parks, Malawi, and is quite common in southeast Tanzania, at Lake Suse, and in parts of the lower Zambezi valley. The species is resident and mainly sedentary, but there are some local movements and it vacates its breeding grounds near Mopeia in central Mozambique in November-December.

Food Boehm's Bee-eater eats honeybees and other hymenopterans in large part, and flies, beetles, grasshoppers, stick-insects, butterflies, cicadas and other bugs. Flies form a proportion of the diet, 17% numerically, which is high for a bee-eater.

Boehm's Bee-eater sunning

Habits Flightless ants have been found in regurgitated pellets, and they must have been taken from the ground, although we have never seen Boehm's Bee-eater foraging in that manner. It feeds by keeping watch from a long spindly branch 2-3 m high at the edge of a woodland clearing, and making forays after a passing insect, chasing it for up to 12 m through the trees or in a low swoop over the ground. When an insect is snapped up, it is carried back to the perch and beaten to left and right before being tossed into the throat and swallowed; a stinging insect is rubbed against the perch until it discharges its venom. In between bouts of feeding the bird perches inactively in dappled shade for long periods, irregularly wagging its down-pointing tail backward and forward and sunbathing with the mantle feathers lifted. **Nesting:** helpers-at-the-nest have not been noticed in this bee-eater. It nests solitarily and monogamously. Males courtship-feed females. Both sexes dig the nest burrow, in shady, well-drained, flat or gently sloping bare ground; sometimes two or three holes are started, but only one is completed and used. Once there were five burrows along 25 m of a sandy path, probably the work of only a single pair of birds. The nest hole is 75-103 cm long, gently declining and nearly straight. *Laying months:* Zambia, August-September; Malawi, September-October.

Description Sexes alike. *Adult:* forehead, crown and nape chestnut; hindneck, mantle, scapulars, back and rump grass-green; wings and tail grass-green, with blackish tips to the primaries and secondaries and the tail feathers (except the central two, which are attenuated into long, blackish streamers). The mask is black, and a narrow but distinct line under it is pale blue. Chin, throat and upper breast are warm ochre or pale rufous, and lower breast, flanks, belly and undertail-coverts pale green. Wings are warm buff below, and the underside of the tail is grey. Bill black; eye crimson-red; legs and feet light brown. *Juvenile:* like the adult, but paler and duller, the throat yellow-buff tinged with green, the eye red-brown or dark brown, and the tail-streamers short or absent. *Measurements:* wing of male 78-82, of female 77-81; tail of male 63-69, of female 63-69, with streamers up to 70 mm longer; bill of male 28-32, of female 29-31; tarsus of male 10-11, of female 10-11. Weight: 14-20.

References Forshaw (1987), Fry (1984), Fry *et al.* (1988).

Merops orientalis

Merops orientalis Latham, 1801, Index Orn., Suppl., p. 33, India (= Mahratta).

Field identification Length 16-18 cm (6½-7 in). This diminutive bee-eater is the smallest of the streamer-tailed species except perhaps for Boehm's (102). It is a fairly approachable bird that perches low down, makes short forays after passing insects, and is quiet-voiced. Always green-bodied, the throat and crown colours vary throughout the great range from Senegal to Vietnam. **At rest:** a bright golden-green or dark green bird, with a thin black gorget stripe (wide and diffuse in Arabia), black mask, red eye, long narrow tail-streamers (short and pointed in parts of Arabia), and chin and throat that are green across northern Africa but yellow in parts of Sudan, bright blue in Arabia, pale green-blue in India, and green in southeast Asia (where the cap and hindneck are rufous, not bronzy-green). **In flight:** the somewhat rounded wings, green when closed, show rufous above and below, and have a conspicuous black band across the trailing edge. **Confusion species:** in Africa, Swallow-tailed Bee-eaters (94) are similarly green birds with a narrow gorget and the same black-bordered rufous-and-green wings, but they lack streamers and are fish-tailed. In the Orient, the most similar bee-eater is the Blue-throated (107), a larger, long-winged, more aerial and gregarious bird, which can be distinguished by its lack of a transverse gorget-band.

Voice A quiet, pleasing trill with a slightly rolling or buzzing quality, 'trrr trrr trrr trrr'; also a staccato 'ti-ic' or 'ti-ti-ti' of alarm.

Geographical variation The seven subspecies differ in hue (golden-green to bluish-green), cap and hindneck colour (green or rufous), throat colour (green, yellow, or blue), gorget depth, and tail-streamer length.
M. o. viridissimus Senegal to Ethiopia. Yellowish-green; streamers up to 96 mm long. Birds from the Ennedi Massif in Chad to Port Sudan are often yellow-throated; Forshaw (1987) has given new evidence to suggest that they are merely *viridissi-*
mus in worn plumage, and not a separate race as has been claimed.
M. o. cleopatra The Nile valley north of Wadi Halfa and Lake Nasser as far as El Faiyum. Greens not as bronzy as the nominate subspecies; streamers up to 86 mm long.
M. o. cyanophrys Southwest and southeast Arabia: Red Sea coastal plains and hinterland from Medina to Aden, the Hadhramaut, Dhofar (Oman), north Oman and United Arab Emirates; also common further north, in the Dead Sea valley; Jordan. Forehead and eyebrow azure-blue, chin and throat caerulean-blue; gorget-band deep but not very sharply defined; crown olive-green, hindneck rufescent. Other green parts bluer, less bronzy or golden-hued, than in *viridissimus*. Streamers short and pointed, up to 23 mm.
M. o. najdanus Central Saudi Arabia: Riyadh, Wadi Rima, Kharj, Khafs, Rub'ayina. Like *cyanophrys*, but greens paler and yellower, and gorget-band narrower.
M. o. beludschicus From Shatt Al Arab and through the Iranian coastal lowlands and the Makran to lowland Pakistan, west Rajasthan and Punjab. Like *viridissimus*, but cap and hindneck golden-green, chin and throat pale blue becoming pale green next to the gorget, which is a thin streak only 1-2 mm deep; streamers up to 60 mm.
M. o. orientalis From Gujarat and Delhi to Assam, south to Sri Lanka. Greens darker and less yellowish than in *beludschicus*; streamers up to 71 mm.
M. o. ferrugeiceps Intergrades with *orientalis* in Assam and extends from there to Burma and Vietnam. Cap, hindneck and mantle glossy rufous; a narrow stripe over the mask is green and another under it is pale blue. Otherwise like *viridissimus*, but sides of the breast are washed with rufous; streamers up to 63 mm.

Habitat and range In Africa, Arabia, southwest Asia and large parts of India this is an arid-country bird, inhabiting open sandy and gravelly country dotted with thorn trees such as *Acacia* and *Zizyphus*, with or without a ground covering of grasses. It is a bird of desert palm groves, thickets, small cultivated fields and thorn hedges, clumps of *Salvadora* shrubs on sand-dunes, municipal gardens and roadside telephone wires. Elsewhere in India, where they occur up to 2000 m in altitude, Little Green Bee-eaters belong to open country with light forest, shrublands and cultivation, grassy plains and foothills with villages and pasture; in southeast Asia they frequent similar but much wetter open country, up to 1550 m. They are found up to 1250 m in Africa, north to south Mauritania, the Adrar hills on the Mali/Algeria border, Aïr, the Ennedi hills in Chad, Port Sudan, and the whole of the Nile valley and delta, and south to north Nigeria, southwest Chad, south Sudan and (rarely) in northwest Kenya. They occur in Israel and Jordan, central and southern Arabia, and continuously from Iran, through the Indian subcontinent to south China, Thailand south to Bangkok, and the whole of Indochina.

Population Little Green Bee-eaters are common birds throughout much of their range. We regularly count them on a 200-km journey along the north coast of Oman, perched in ones and twos on roadside wires; in summer there are at least 160 pairs.

Migration Little Green Bee-eaters are resident and partially migrant in Africa, occurring at the southernmost fringes of their range only in the dry season (October-April) and being commonest at the northern fringes in the Sahara in the wet season (June-August). They are mainly resident in Jordan and Israel, and occur at Wadi Sawawin in northwest Saudi Arabia only in November-January. Although resident in Oman, they are commoner in winter than in summer, and some probably migrate over the Gulf. In India as in Africa this bee-eater is partially migrant, withdrawing from the north in winter and from areas of heaviest rainfall during the monsoon; it is subject to some altitudinal movement. Seasonal changes in abundance have also been noted in Pakistan, Nepal and Thailand.

Food Flying insects; most prey items are

Hymenoptera, mainly ants, and small halictine bees, ichneumons, honeybees of all four species, and many families of wasps. Numerous beetles are eaten, and dragonflies, termites, Microlepidoptera, butterflies, and many kinds of small bugs and flies.

Habits Little Green Bee-eaters occur generally in pairs, with two pairs sometimes close enough to share the wire between adjacent telegraph poles. Nesting is solitary in Africa but often colonial in Asia; roosting is gregarious everywhere. The birds sit alertly on a wire or small tree, give fast chase to a passing insect, snap it up (often close to the ground), then flap and glide in a more leisurely way back to the perch to eat it. In India they forage from the backs of cattle, and have also been seen taking caterpillars plucked in flight from cotton crops. ***Nesting:*** helpers-at-the-nest have not been reported. Although no systematic studies have been made, this bee-eater seems to be monogamous and weakly territorial. In India it usually breeds solitarily, but colonies of up to 30 pairs have been reported. Nesting is often adjacent to colonies of other bee-eaters. Nest burrows are excavated into firm, bare soil, the surface flat, gently sloping, or forming a cliff about 0.5 m high. Burrows in cliffs are horizontal, but in flat ground they slope down at an angle of 20-30°. They are 0.5-2 m long, and several 'false starts' and previous seasons' nests are often nearby. The clutch is of 4-8 eggs, usually six. ***Laying months:*** throughout the range egg-laying is from March to early June. There is only one clutch.

Description *M. o. viridissimus* **Adult male:** bright glossy green, yellowish-tinged, with black mask and narrow gorget-band, and blackish tips to primaries and particularly secondaries; crown, hindneck and closed wings are a more bronzy-green. There is often a narrow pale blue line immediately below the mask, and the throat is sometimes yellow. Undertail-coverts bluish. In worn plumage the tertials commonly fade to blue. Bill black, mouth pink; eye crimson; legs and feet dark grey. **Adult female:** eye and throat not quite so bright as on the male, gorget-band usually narrower and tail-streamers shorter. **Juvenile:** like the adults, but paler green, with feathers of the upperparts pale-tipped, giving a finely scalloped look; belly very pale, almost white; no black gorget; tail-streamers short. **Measurements:** wing of male 87-96, of female 84-92; tail of male 122-169, of female 118-158; bill of male 27-33, of female 27-33; tarsus of male 9-11, of female 9-11. Weight (*M. o. beludschicus*): male 19-20, female 17-27.

References Forshaw (1987), Fry (1984), Fry *et al.* (1988).

104 BLUE-CHEEKED BEE-EATER   Plate 33
Merops persicus

Merops persicus Pallas, 1773, Reise Versch. Prov. Russ. Reichs, 2, p. 708, Caspian Sea.

Field identification Length 24-26 cm (9¹/₂-10 in), excluding tail-streamers of up to 11 cm (4¹/₂ in). *At rest:* a large bee-eater, very slender and long-winged, gregarious, entirely bright burnished green except for black mask, pale blue or whitish forehead, eyebrow and cheek stripe, yellow chin and rufous throat. Eye bright red. Very vocal, and usually quite approachable. *In flight:* a particularly graceful bee-eater, because of its long wings and tail and its effortless gliding and long swoops. The wings have only a vestigial, narrow, dusky trailing-edge band, and the underwing is conspicuously coppery-rufous. **Confusion species:** high-flying migrants can be hard to distinguish from European Bee-eaters (109) and almost impossible to tell from Madagascar Bee-eaters (105) in Africa and from Blue-tailed (105) in northwest India. At perch the combination of blue-white forehead, yellow chin, rufous throat and green rump and tail renders Blue-cheeked Bee-eaters unmistakable. Madagascar Bee-eaters, overlapping from Ethiopia to Angola and Mozambique, have the chin and cheeks white and the crown dark olive-brown. Blue-tailed Bee-eaters, overlapping between Rawalpindi and Delhi, and Delhi and Gujarat, have the forehead and eyebrow green and rump and tail blue.

Voice A pleasant rolling 'diririp', like the European Bee-eater's 'pruik' but harder, shorter and more definitely polysyllabic; also a mellow interrogative 'tetew ' and, in alarm, a sharp 'dik-dik-dik'. A greeting call, given at perch with the wings briefly raised, the head held high and the tail fanned and vibrated, is 'diripp-dirippdiripp'.

Geographical variation One subspecies in Asia, another in Africa. Madagascar and Blue-tailed Bee-eaters are often treated as belonging to *Merops persicus*. Blue-cheeked and Blue-tailed Bee-eaters do not, however, hybridise where they meet on breeding grounds in northwest India, and so they are separate species. Madagascar Bee-eaters could be regarded as a third full species, or united with Blue-cheeked or with Blue-tailed; we prefer the third course (Fry 1984). This complex of bee-eaters (104, 105) varies mainly in respect of facial colours and rump colour.

M. p. persicus Breeds from the Nile delta to Rajasthan and north to Lake Balkhash, and winters in eastern and southern Africa. Upperparts grass-green; male streamers 45-67 mm longer than the tail.

M. p. chrysocercus Breeds on the fringes of the western Sahara and winters in West Africa, south of 15°N. Upperparts golden-green; male streamers 70-104 mm longer than the tail. Overall, it is slightly smaller than *persicus*.

Habitat and range A desert-edge bird, this bee-eater breeds in sandy or gravelly wastes with clumps of saltbush *Salvadora persica* and scattered *Acacia*, *Zizyphus* and other thorn trees. It likes to forage from telephone wires, but in their absence makes use of low bushes, fences and walls, and spends much time resting on flat ground near its nests. It winters in bushy grassland and cultivated open woodlands, seldom far from water and generally below 1500 m in altitude; also on open lakeshores with reeds and papyrus, in wooded swamps and over coastal plains with mangrove. Blue-cheeked Bee-eaters breed behind the Mauritanian coast at 17-18°N and discontinuously from Dakar (Senegal), and probably Gambia, to the west and east shores of Lake Chad. They nest in Morocco (Wadi Dra, Tafilalet) and Algeria (Beni Abbès, Figuig, Wadi N'Ça, Biskra), the Nile delta, and probably Djibouti. They breed occasionally in Israel, and widely in south Turkey east of the Taurus Mountains, in Mesopotamia (Syria, Iraq), lowland Iran, the Batinah coast of Oman, all of Pakistan except Peshawar, Rawalpindi and Lahore Provinces, in India east to about Delhi, in Armenia, north to Baku in Azerbaijan, on the lower Volga at Ganyushkino and adjacently in Kazakhstan, in the lower Ural and Embe valleys, on the eastern shores of the Caspian, around Aral Sea, all along Syr Darya River, near Tashkent, and east to the Ili delta on Lake Balkhash. The species winters in West African savannas from the coasts of Gambia and Sierra Leone to Nigeria, and from north Sudan, Eritrea (Ethiopia) and Somalia, through East Africa to Mozambique, Angola, Congo, and south and east Zaïre; it is rare in Natal, Transvaal, north Botswana and north Namibia, and vagrant to Cape Town.

Population In its arid breeding grounds in Asia this is one of the commonest birds, with colonies of hundreds in Syria and thousands in Iraq. In Oman it is abundant in summer north of Khaburah, breeding in fields and wadis within 5 km of the sea, in isolated pairs and colonies of tens and hundreds; it promptly occupies sites being excavated for a new building, and sometimes nests alongside European Bee-eaters in old field wells.

Migration Blue-cheeked Bee-eaters migrate mainly by day, in flocks sometimes with European Bee-eaters, passing over at great height. They follow geographical leading lines (coasts, major rivers, mountain ranges). Although they concentrate at capes such as Gardafui in Somalia, sea-crossings and desert-crossings seem to be on a broad front. The birds arrive on their breeding grounds in late March and April and depart mainly in August; migrants visit East Africa from October to April and southern Africa from November to April. Emigration is mainly by way of the Ethiopian Rift Valley and northwest

Somalia, and from January to May great numbers fly down the Nile and cross the north Somali coast.

Food Bees and wasps feature importantly, but this bird is more a dragonfly-eater than a bee-eater. Even on their desert nesting grounds they eat numerous dragonflies and damselflies; also many kinds of small and large bees and wasps, ants, cicadas, water-scorpions and other bugs, grasshoppers, locusts, mantises, beetles, moths and butterflies.

Blue-cheeked Bee-eater sunning

Habits A highly gregarious bird at all times, this bee-eater forages by making fast flights from a treetop or telegraph wire. It swoops towards the ground, or gains height rapidly with even wingbeats, glides towards its prey on outstretched wings and then abruptly twists to take a larger item from below, seizing it in the tips of the mandibles and returning in long swoops to the perch; there the insect is beaten, and a stinging one is rubbed against the perch until it discharges its venom. Sometimes birds forage high in the air, in continuous flight. The species roosts communally in tamarisks, date palms, *Casuarina* groves, reedbeds and tall leafy trees, individuals sleeping shoulder to shoulder. In Mauritania a roost in a large *Prosopis* tree can number 1,500 birds (Lamarche 1988). They sunbathe using the 'mantle-ruffle', 'broken-necked' and 'spreadeagle' postures, and occasionally water-bathe. **Nesting:** nest burrows, dug by both birds of the pair, are often solitary but usually in colonies, either in flat sandy ground almost bare of cover, or in low banks, commonly shared by

European Bee-eaters. A common greeting ceremony (see Voice, probably also a part of courtship), with both wings briefly raised high, makes the coppery underwings very conspicuous. Whether any pairs have helpers-at-the-nest is not known. In a large colony disputes are common, two birds lunging towards each other, calling, giving chase, and sometimes struggling with interlocked bills. Nests are commonly less than 1 m apart. In banks, burrows are straight and horizontal; in flat ground they decline shallowly, at about 20°. They are generally 1-1.5 m long, but in yielding soil sometimes up to 3 m long. The clutch is of 4-8 eggs, usually six. **Laying months:** northwest Africa, Niger and Mali, May-June; Egypt, May; Senegal and Mauritania, May-October; Turkmenia, Pakistan and India, May-July; Oman, April-May.

Description *M. p. persicus* **Adult male:** forehead white, forecrown and superciliary area pale blue; mask black, with a pale blue line below it. Chin yellow, throat russet. The rest of the head, upper-parts and underparts are bright green, but tips of primaries and secondaries are dusky, and the entire underwing is russet. Underside of the tail silvery-grey. By late summer the tertials and edges of the flight feathers have bleached, and with wear the whole plumage becomes more olivaceous. Bill black; eye claret-red; legs and feet dark grey. **Adult female:** like the male, but tail-streamers shorter, and the eye is often orange-red. **Juvenile:** much duller than the adult, greens bluer, chin yellowish-buff, throat rusty-buff, forehead and eyebrow greenish, and all feathers with pale bluish tips giving an overall scaly appearance. Eye dark brown; tail-streamers short. **Measurements:** wing of male 146-163, of female 134-156; tail of male 83-91, of female 82-90, excluding streamers; bill of male 43-51, of female 42-49; tarsus of male 12-14, of female 12-14. Weight: male 45-56, female 45-51, average 49.

References Forshaw (1987), Fry (1984), Fry *et al.* (1988).

105 MADAGASCAR BEE-EATER and BLUE-TAILED BEE-EATER
Merops superciliosus

Plate 34

Merops superciliosus Linnaeus, 1766, Syst. Nat., ed. 12, I, p. 183, Madagascar.

Field identification Length 23-26 cm (9-10 in), excluding tail-streamers of up to 7 cm (2¾ in). We treat these two forms as a single species, which is very closely related with the Blue-cheeked Bee-eater (104) but slightly smaller; voices and behaviour of all three are the same. Madagascar Bee-eaters (which broadly overlap with Blue-cheeked Bee-eaters wintering in East and southern Africa) are distinguished by the white forehead, eyebrow, chin and cheeks, olive-brown or olive-green cap, and otherwise bronzy-green plumage; underwing-coverts are a paler rufous than on Blue-cheeked, and facial features are a little like those of the White-fronted Bee-eater (99), which can readily be told by its ultramarine 'pants' and by voice. Madagascar is the sole bee-eater in the Malagasy region. Blue-tailed Bee-eaters overlap with the Blue-cheeked in northwest India, and can be distinguished by their green (not blue-white) forehead and eyebrow and their blue (not green) rump and tail. Further east, the only other green-crowned *Merops* bee-eaters are juvenile Blue-throated (107) and Bay-headed (108) and adult Rainbow Bee-eater (106). A solitary young Blue-throated Bee-eater would be difficult to separate from a young Blue-tailed, but the latter looks scaly and is buff-throated. Bay-headed Bee-eater has an all-yellow throat and is much smaller. Rainbow Bee-eater, which overlaps with the Blue-tailed in eastern New Guinea, has a black tail and gorget-bar on the adult; juveniles of the two are alike, but Rainbow is smaller and less scaly.

Voice Not known to differ from that of Blue-cheeked Bee-eaters.

Geographical variation See under Blue-cheeked Bee-eater.

M. s. philippinus North Pakistan and India to Indochina, the Philippines, Sulawesi and Papua New Guinea. Pale blue streak below mask; chin yellow; rump and tail blue.

M. s. superciliosus Madagascar, Comoro Islands, Somalia and East African seaboard, occasionally breeding in west Kenya and Zimbabwe. Forehead and eyebrow white or bluish, crown dark olive-brown, chin yellowish-white, and broad area below mask white; rump and tail green.

M. s. alternans Breeds on lower Cunene River (Namibia/Angola border) and on the desert littoral north to near Lucira. Like the nominate subspecies, but the crown is greener (and entirely green on 30% of birds), chin and cheeks whiter, and the body greens brighter and less bronzy.

Habitat and range In Madagascar and the Comoro Islands this species frequents open, dissected country, farmland, rice-fields and plantations. In Africa it occurs in coastal plains, rivers, swamps, lake-shores, open woods, bushy savannas, desertic coastal lowlands, and mangrove. Asiatic habitats are wetter, and Blue-tailed Bee-eaters are often in rain-soaked areas and near standing water: wooded lake-shores, river valleys, flooded ricefields, oil-palm plantations, coconut groves, large gardens, parks, gamesfields, and forest edges by open ground. Madagascar Bee-eaters breed on Mayotte and probably other Comoro Islands and are widespread in Madagascar from Sambavu to Tuléar, and from the lowlands up to 1500 m. They breed on Pemba Island north of Zanzibar, and probably on Lamu and the adjacent Kenya coast, and around Mogadishu, Somalia. They are common and widespread in the Guban area of north Somalia. In Tanzania and Kenya they breed or have bred at Malindi, on the Galana River, near Dar es Salaam, on Mafia Island, near Kisumu on the upper Tana and probably the Athi River, also on the Omo in south Ethiopia and in the Awash valley. In Mozambique they nest numerously from Masambeti (Beira) to Bazaruto and Santa Carolina Islands; they have nested on the Zambezi at Mana Pools and near Victoria Falls. The Angolan coastal population ranges south to Ondagua and east to the Okavango valley. Blue-tailed Bee-eaters breed throughout the hot lowlands of the Indian subcontinent, northwest to Delhi and Bannu (near the Afghanistan border), Peshawar, Lahore, Ferozepore and Gujarat. (Blue-cheeked Bee-eaters also nest at Delhi and Bannu, and both species may breed throughout the Punjab.) They breed in eastern Sri Lanka, in Bengal, Bangladesh, Nepal and Assam, east to Yunnan, Kwangsi-Chuang and west Kwangtung Provinces of China (but not Hong Kong nor Hainan), and south through Burma, Thailand and Indochina to north Malaysia (at Padang Kemunting, Penang Island). The species is common throughout lowland Sulawesi, where a few nesting colonies are known, and is widespread in the Philippines although nests have not been found. It breeds in eastern New Guinea and in New Britain, in natural and man-formed grasslands.

Migration Madagascar Bee-eaters have long been held to migrate between Madagascar and Africa, but on present evidence that may not be so. They occur year-round in Madagascar and in Somalia, and are found erratically all year on the Kenya coast, mainly in August and September. On Zanzibar they occur principally in May-November, on Pemba in June-March, at Dar es Salaam in March-August, at Mikindani in July-August, in Tsavo in February-March, inland in Kenya and Tanzania in May-September, and in east Zaïre in April-August. Passage migrants pass through Malaŵi and Zambia for six weeks in August-October. Most records in Transvaal are in October-April. In autumn Blue-tailed Bee-eaters move from north into south India and Sri Lanka. Similarly, southeast Asian birds withdraw wholly from the northern regions. They winter from the central Burmese plains, lower Irrawaddy, north Tenasserim and Andaman Islands south to Nicobar Islands, peninsular Malaysia, Borneo, Sumatra, Java and the Lesser Sundas east to Timor; probably some winter also in Sulawesi and the Philippines.

Food In the Malagasy region these bee-eaters are known to take grasshoppers, cicadas, bugs, wasps, beetles, flies and butterflies. In India they prey mainly on dragonflies, bees and wasps; one study found that 55% of items were the honey-bees *Apis florea* and *A. cerana*, and 45% were the large dragonfly *Crocothemis servillea*, hornets *Vespa orientalis*, carpenter bees *Xylocopa dissimilis*, and several other wasps, beetles and flies. Dragonflies are the prey most commonly fed to nestlings. At Kuala Lumpur, Malaysia, 96% of prey items are Hymenoptera (two species of honeybees, hornets, ants and ichneumons) and, curiously enough, 3-cm fishes *Gambusia affinis* are known to be eaten on occasion. Near Penang, Malaysia, 68% of the diet by weight were dragonflies, and the rest hymenopterans and beetles.

Habits Like those of Blue-cheeked Bee-eaters. *Nesting:* burrows are excavated solitarily or colonially in dry loamy or sandy soils. Sites chosen are open flat areas such as coastal dunes, clay-pans, abandoned village football-fields and air-strips. Vertical surfaces are often used also: riverbanks, road cuttings, sea-cliffs of volcanic tuff, and crumbling mud walls. Most colonies contain about 10-30 active nests; sometimes there are hundreds. Burrows are 8 cm wide and 1-2 m long, with an egg chamber 20 cm wide and 13 cm high. The clutch is of 5-7 eggs, but only 2-3 in Madagascar. *Laying months:* Angola, October-December; Somalia, Ethiopia and northwest Kenya, April-May; Tana River, August; Kenya coast, November-December; Tanzania, March, June-September; Zimbabwe, September-December; Mozambique, October; Madagascar, September-October; Asia north of the Equator, February-May; Indonesia, February-May and September-November.

Description *M. s. philippinus* Sexes alike. *Adult:* forehead to mantle bronzy-green, washed with brown; scapulars, back and wing-coverts a clearer green; tertials bluish, rump and tail blue; central tail feathers blue, but streamers blackish; primaries dark olive and tips of secondaries blackish. Mask black, usually with a narrow line of pale blue bordering it above and below. Chin pale yellow, throat rufous, breast and sides of neck olive-green, belly and flanks pale olive-green sometimes washed with blue, undertail-coverts very pale blue. Underwing-coverts cinnamon-buff; underside of tail grey. Bill black, mouth pink; eye claret; legs and feet pinkish-brown, nails black. *Juvenile:* like the juvenile Blue-cheeked Bee-eater. *Measurements:* wing of male 127-140, of female 124-138; tail of male 80-89, of female 82-89, excluding streamers of up to 71 mm on males and 50 mm on females; bill of male 40-47, of female 39-46; tarsus of male 12-14, of female 12-13. Weight: (*M. s. philippinus*) male 29-42, female 31-45, average 37; (*M. s. superciliosus*) male 42-48, female 38-43, average 43.

References Forshaw (1987), Fry (1984), Fry *et al.* (1988).

106 RAINBOW BEE-EATER   Plate 34
Merops ornatus

Merops ornatus Latham, 1801, Index Orn., Suppl., p. 35, New South Wales.

Field identification Length 19-21 cm (7½-8 in). Unmistakable in Australia, where it is the only bee-eater: a colourful green, blue, rufous and yellow bird with black frontal marks and a streamered black tail, gregarious and vocal. *Confusion species:* on its wintering grounds it may overlap with Bay-headed Bee-eater (108) on Java and Bali, and it meets Blue-tailed Bee-eaters (105) in the region from Lombok and Sulawesi to New Guinea and New Britain. The former has rufous head top, mask and mantle and greenish tail without streamers; the latter is larger, with far more rufous in the throat, no black gorget-band, and a bluish (not black) tail. Juvenile Rainbow and Blue-tailed Bee-eaters are very alike, and best told by size and by any accompanying adults.

Voice A pleasant rolling 'prrrp, prrrp', 'preee' or 'drrrt', like the calls of Blue-tailed and European Bee-eaters (109) but a little harder and less melodious. Alarm a 'dip-dip'; predator-alarm a rapid, loud 'clip-lip-lip-lip'. Other calls are an agitated 'peer...peer' (territorial defence), 'cleep, cleep' (calling young), and 'tookie tookie' (before entering the nest).

Geographical variation None.

Habitat and range Breeding Rainbow Bee-eaters inhabit all manner of open countryside, and their local distribution seems to be determined primarily by the need for suitable nest sites and only secondarily by water and vegetation that provide insect food. They range throughout the greater part of Australia (not Tasmania) but are absent from *Spinifex*, mallee and saltbush associations except south of Kanowna and southeast of Everard Range. They like flat or undulating sandy pasture, arable land and lightly wooded savannas, and commonly occur around towns and homesteads, nesting in busy city parks and gardens, and everywhere readily using telephone wires. They nest on a number of inshore islands, including Rottnest, the Southwestern Isles in Torres Strait and probably the Pellew group, and they breed abundantly also around Port Moresby and in Ramu valley, Papua New Guinea. Principal wintering grounds are in New Guinea, in lowlands and forest clearings up to 2000 m. Migrants reach all islands west to Lombok (perhaps also Bali and Java), north to Sulawesi, the north Moluccan and Talaud Islands, islands in Geelvink Bay, Wuvulu, Ninigo, Hermit, Manus, Mussau, Bismarck Archipelago, Lihir Island and occasionally Nissan and the northern Solomons. Vagrants have occurred in Caroline and Marianas Islands and in the Ryukyus (Japan). A few birds oversummer in the eastern Lesser Sundas (Moa, Leti, Wetar Islands), where juveniles also occur, but whether they nest there, or in New Britain, awaits discovery.

Population Over most of the breeding range this bee-eater is frequent to abundant. In 1982, 2.5 km^2 of King's Park, Perth, supported 76 nesting birds. Near Port Moresby, also in 1982, there were up to 33 individuals per km^2 at the start of the breeding season.

Migration Rainbow Bee-eaters are found commonly year-round in northern Australia, south to about 26°S on the coast and to about 18°S in the interior. Further south they are summer visitors, with first arrivals in late September, main immigration in October, and departure during March. Great numbers cross Torres Strait to winter in New Guinea. Around Darwin, Northern Territory, there is a striking increase in March-May (Thompson 1984) and in March and April flocks of thousands pass over Innisfail, Queensland, often at night (Gill 1970). Migrants arrive in Port Moresby in mid March, and northbound passage over New Guinea remains strong until late April, some birds crossing the central mountains by way of passes up to 4000 m in altitude, travelling by day and on moonlit nights. Earliest and latest dates in Indonesia are 28 March and 21 September. In September over 850 birds per hour cross Thursday Island in Torres Strait. On several waterless islands in Torres Strait much mortality of spring migrants has been found in September (Garnett 1985), with dehydrated corpses still perched in macabre rows in the roosting bushes: 'dozens huddled side by side, and when the branch was moved the corpses fell off or simply spun to hang upside down by their clinging toes' (in Fry 1984).

Food Airborne insects, up to 95% Hymenoptera: honeybees *Apis mellifera*, wasps *Ropalidia romandi*, sweat-bees *Trigona*, carpenter bees *Xylocopa*, colletid bees *Palaeorhiza*, ants, ichneumons, six other families of wasps, and a few beetles, bugs, flies, grasshoppers, butterflies, dragonflies and spiders.

Habits Pairs and small flocks hunt by spacing themselves out around a stand of trees or along a wire and scanning alertly for passing insects. The bird launches itself from a distance of 5-50 m, flying swiftly towards its prey, follows it with fast twists and turns, snaps it up, and sails back to the perch with undulating flaps and effortless glides. A flock sometimes forages on high, wheeling and swooping. Resting birds sunbathe with the mantle feathers raised fan-wise. They sometimes water-bathe by splashing onto an unruffled surface, and afterwards preen vigorously. In the late afternoon small flocks come to the ground, eat bits of grit and play with an insect shard or bit of dry leaf, tossing it up a few centimetres, catching it, later dropping it. In the evening large numbers gather excitedly at a roost, in a eucalypt, *Casuarina* or mangrove; a roost of migrants can number 500 or more birds. **Nesting:** Rainbow Bee-eaters are monogamous and evidently pair for life. They nest in solitary pairs in loose or dense colonies; about one pair in seven has a nest helper or helpers (at one nest, 4-6 helpers were noted). Solitarily breeding pairs are territorial, defending a territory defined by trees at the corners and with the nest and favourite perches near the centre. Birds forage well away from their territory. Nests are generally in flat or sloping ground, and high perpendicular sand cliffs are not so often used (but one colony nested in 2-m-tall sand cliffs facing an exposed beach with heavy surf). Tunnels are 0.5-2 m long. A typical clutch of five eggs takes six days to lay. Incubation starts with the second or third egg, and lasts for 24 days; females incubate for twice as long as males, unless there is a helper. All eggs hatch within 36 or even 24 hours, and the young grow quickly until they exceed the parental weight at 26 days, then they lose weight until they leave the nest four days later. Nestlings about to fly evoke much interest among adults, several of which encourage them to leave by giving a special call. **Laying months:** Papua New Guinea, September; Australia, Mount Isa district, Queensland, August to about November and again in January-March (Carruthers 1975); southern Australia, mid November to mid December.

Description *Adult male:* forehead and forecrown green, hindcrown and hindneck burnished rufous; a narrow bright green superciliary stripe; mask black, bordered below by a wide, pale blue stripe; chin pale yellow, and gorget black, triangular, 20 mm wide and 10-12 mm deep in the midline; behind the chin a bright rufous area connects the blue cheek stripe and the gorget. Mantle and breast bronzy-green, folded wing a slightly bluer green; back, rump, upper- and undertail-coverts bright pale blue. Tail black, feather edges bluish; streamers are less than 1 mm wide but have spatulate tips 1.5 mm wide. Tertials bluish; primaries and secondaries rufous, with green-edged outer webs and broad black tips; underwing-coverts rufous. Bill black; eye red-brown; legs and feet frosted black. *Adult female:* like the male, but with less russet in the hindneck, usually a narrow blue line under the gorget, and shorter, thicker streamers (2 mm wide) which are not spatulate. *Juvenile:* much duller than the adults, rather uniformly olive-green above and pale green below, with a black mask but without a black gorget or the russet and pale blue marks of the adult; tail blackish-green; eye brown. *Measurements:* wing of male 104-120, of female 108-150; tail of male 73-80, of female 73-79, excluding streamers of up to 71 mm on males and 24 mm on females; bill of male 33-41, of female 33-40; tarsus of male 11-13, of female 11-13. Weight: male 21-33, female 20-31.

References Calver, Saunders and Porter (1987), Forshaw (1987), Fry (1984).

107 BLUE-THROATED BEE-EATER   Plate 34
Merops viridis

Merops viridis Linnaeus, 1758, Syst. Nat., ed. 10, I, p. 117, Java.

Field identification Length 20-23 cm (8-9 in), excluding tail-streamers of up to 9 cm (3½ in). Quite a large bee-eater of east and southeast Asia, lacking a black gorget, and with black mask, red eye, dark chestnut cap and mantle, dark green wings, brilliant pale blue rump, blue tail with long streamers, green breast paling to light blue undertail-coverts, and pale blue or pale green throat; gregarious and vocal. *In*

flight: the underside of the wings is pale rufous with a dusky trailing edge. *Confusion species:* adults are readily distinguished from the Blue-tailed Bee-eater (105) by their chestnut crown and mantle, and from the smaller Bay-headed Bee-eater (108) by their blue-green throat without a gorget-bar. Juveniles of all three species are green-crowned and any unaccompanied by adults could present problems: juvenile Blue-throated Bee-eaters have dark green upperparts, black mask, brilliant blue rump, blue tail and pastel-blue underparts.

Voice A fast, short trill, repeated quietly once or twice, 'brk, brk', and in flight a loud 'prrrp' six times in 2 seconds. Alarm a sharp 'chip'.

Geographical variation There are two subspecies.

M. v. viridis Range of the species except for the Philippines. Cap and mantle dark chestnut, chin and throat blue.

M. v. americanus Philippines. Cap and mantle rufous, chin and throat pale green, with a pale blue line below the mask. About 7% larger.

Habitat and range They feed largely over the canopy of lowland forest, but also frequent beach scrub, dunes, pasture, sandy clearings, marshes, grassland, mangrove, parks, suburban gardens, agricultural and even industrial areas. Very much a lowland species, this common bee-eater is restricted to altitudes below 800 m, except on migration when it occurs as high as 1560 m (in Malaysia). Blue-throated Bee-eaters breed in China in Kwangsi-Chuang, Kwangtung and Fukien Provinces, and in Yunnan north to about 25°N, in Kiangsi to 27°N and in Chekiang to 29°N. They breed in Hainan, but are absent from Taiwan and Hong Kong. They occur throughout Vietnam and Cambodia, and in Thailand east of 101°E and in the Peninsula. In Malaysia breeding colonies are known in nearly all provinces. The species ranges through Singapore, Sumatra, Java, Borneo and the Philippines.

Migration The Philippines population, being racially distinct, is probably sedentary there. Sumatran and Javan birds are probably sedentary, too, but mainland populations are migratory. North of about 15°N Blue-throated Bee-eaters are summer visitors; south of that latitude, in peninsular Malaysia, coastal plains colonies are vacated in September and flocks migrate across the open lowlands of Selangor from late July until October. Heading for Sumatra, they cross the Malacca Straits at Cape Rachado in mid August, and return in February-April.

Inland in the Peninsula there is a considerable influx into hill-forest areas, where birds remain until April, and northbound migrants cross Fraser's Hill and Cameron Highlands during three weeks in April-May.

Food The diet is very like that of other bee-eaters: mainly hymenopterans, with some dragonflies, bugs, flies and beetles, all taken in flight. Occasionally these birds catch small lizards and fish (Fry 1984). When there are young in the nest, adults bring them mainly large dragonflies and themselves eat the majority of bees, wasps and other insects that they catch.

Habits With dashing pursuit flights, this bee-eater forages from tall trees, power cables and telephone lines, returning with each insect to the perch to beat and desting it. Hunting stances are usually high up, 7 m or higher in trees. Flocks often also hunt aloft, hawking for small, soft insects, which seem to be swallowed at once. The birds congregate at hatches of flying termites and ants, and also at fires, where they prey on fleeing insects. Nesting individuals forage up to 24 km from the colony. Body care, roosting and breeding behaviours are the same as in Blue-tailed Bee-eaters. On hot, still days flying birds sometimes hang their legs down, exposing the thinly feathered thighs, as a means of shedding heat. That there are helpers-at-the-nest has not been conclusively established. *Nesting:* some pairs nest solitarily, but generally they congregate into huge colonies sprawling over a hectare or more of beach dunes or open sandy ground inland. There are 900 nests at Padang Kemunting, Penang, and colonies of several thousand birds elsewhere in Malaysia. Flat-ground burrows are 1 m apart, 1-1.5 m long, and decline shallowly. Burrows in perpendicular banks are closer together, and horizontal; some in Borneo were 3-4.5 m long. *Laying months:* Borneo, February-April; peninsular Malaysia, May-June; Java, January, May and September-October; Philippines, June; Hainan, June.

Description *M. v. viridis* Sexes alike. *Adult:* forehead to mantle rich dark rufous-chestnut; back, scapulars and wings grass-green, the tertials becoming blue with age, and primaries and secondaries dusky-tipped; rump and uppertail-coverts pale azure-blue. Tail greyish-blue, the tips of the streamers blackish. Mask black; chin and throat bright blue, paler towards the mask, and abruptly demarcated from the rich green breast. Belly green, paling towards flanks and vent; undertail-coverts very pale blue. Underside of the wing pale rufous and of the tail steel-grey. Bill black; eye red; legs and feet frosted dark grey. *Juvenile:* upperparts dark green, with upperwing-coverts and tertials bluish-edged; mask black, eye dark brown; chin pale buff, throat pale blue, merging into pale green

on the breast and pale bluish-buff on the undertail-coverts. Tail-streamers do not protrude until the young bird is about three months old. *Measurements:* wing of male 108-119, of female 108-117; tail of male 67-78, of female 73-79, excluding streamers of up to 90 mm on males and 50 mm on females; bill of male 36-43, of female 35-41; tarsus of male 12-14, of female 12-14. Weight: male 36-41, female 34-36.

References Bryant and Hails (1983), Forshaw (1987), Fry (1984).

108 BAY-HEADED BEE-EATER   Plate 35
Merops leschenaulti

Merops Leschenaulti Vieillot, 1817, Nouv. Dict. Hist. Nat., 14, p. 17, Java (error for Sri Lanka).

Field identification Length 18-20 cm (7-8 in). A gregarious bee-eater of Asian grasslands, and the only species of *Merops* outside Africa without tail-streamers. **At rest:** rather like a diminutive European Bee-eater (109). Slender, long-winged, square- or slightly fish-tailed, with rufous cap and mantle, green wings and tail, pale yellow throat, narrow black-and-rufous gorget (only black in Java), and pale green breast and belly. The mask is black (or rufous in Java and Andaman Islands) and the eye red. **In flight:** when the bird is directly overhead, its underparts look pale yellowish, the wing-lining rufous, the tail grey, and primaries and secondaries grey with broad black tips. **Confusion species:** European Bee-eaters are larger, with golden rump and scapulars, and most of the inner part of the wing rufous; the two species may overlap in India between Dehra Dun and Nepal.

Voice Very vocal: 'pruik' or 'churit' or 'djewy' and slight variations, much like the calls of European Bee-eaters but briefer and not quite so melodious.

Geographical variation The three subspecies vary in the extent of rufous in the ear-coverts and throat.
    M. l. leschenaulti Range of the species except Andaman Islands, Java and Bali.

Mask black, lower throat rufous.
    M. l. andamanensis Andaman Islands. Like the nominate subspecies, but mask rufous (blackish where it borders the cheek) and side of the breast rufous; larger, and long-tailed (on average the wing is 3 mm, tail 12 mm, and bill 2.4 mm longer).
    M. l. quinticolor Java and Bali; also in Sumatra, where it may be a migrant from Java or Malaysia (with most records in August-March) and where it has occasionally nested (van Marle and Voous 1988). Like *leschenaulti*, but mask rufous, lower throat yellow, tail blue, and the wing 7% shorter.

Habitat and range The habitat is forested hills with large grassy clearings maintained by annual burning, well-wooded open countryside, grassy orchards and parks, pasture, cultivated land near remnant forest, plantations, beach scrub, and (favourite nesting areas) the wooded banks of rivers and hill streams, and hill roads, railways and mule paths with earth cuttings. The combination of patchy forest and grassland seems ideal for this bee-eater, which forages over forest canopy as well as around isolated trees in savanna. It ranges from sea level commonly up to 800 m and locally up to 1500 m (Sri Lanka, India's Western Ghats, Java) and 1600 m

(Nepal). It is widespread in Sri Lanka, plentiful in drier areas, and numerous in Travancore and parts of the Western Ghats, north to Goa and Belgaum and again near Jagalbed (Bombay). In the east it ranges locally south to about Jagdalpur and Godavari River, and further to the north it is very common in the Himalayan foothills, from 78°E in Uttar Pradesh, east through Nepal, Sikkim, Bhutan, Bengal, Bangladesh and Assam to north Burma (Nmai valley), then south through Burma, Thailand and Indochina to Malaysia. These bee-eaters are absent from lowlands around Gulf of Tongking, and occur only in the west of North Vietnam. In Malaysia they breed south to Besut in Trengganu and Chemor in Perak. They occur in the Andamans, Great and Little Cocos and Strait Islands. On Java and Bali they are fairly common. They appear to be colonising Sumatra in the wake of deforestation, and a few are now breeding in the east.

Migration Bay-headed Bee-eaters are mainly summer visitors in north Burma, north India and Nepal, although a few reside there year-round. In the south of their range they are found all year, but numbers are augmented in winter. At middle latitudes the species is resident in general, but vacates some areas at the wettest time of year: for instance, it is common in Khao Yei National Park (Thailand) in winter, some breeding there in spring, but it is absent in June-August.

Food The diet is known to include social wasps and two species of honeybees, dragonflies, grasshoppers, butterflies and termites, all caught on the wing.

Habits This bee-eater makes forays from telegraph wires and small trees, but on the whole feeds high up, often from the tops of emergent forest trees. It bathes by gliding low and splashing down onto still water, returning to a perch to preen. It has several sunbathing postures, and a small flock comes to the ground in the evening to pick up grit. Flocks sometimes appear to feed high in the air, wheeling around with graceful, quite slow gliding and flapping flight. In winter, small flocks that have foraged separately over the forest assemble at a favourite forest-edge area about an hour before nightfall and are particularly vocal, gliding slowly around, greeting each other vociferously, and sitting shoulder to shoulder; at last the whole company, typically of 200 birds, departs unhurriedly in failing light for a traditional roosting tree a few kilometres away, sometimes close to human habitation.

Nesting: this bee-eater nests solitarily or in groups of six or eight pairs; occasionally colonies of hundreds of nests have been found. Nest helpers have not yet been detected. Burrows are from 45 cm long in hard ground to 3 m long in sand. Flat-ground nests decline quite steeply and then level off, and burrows in cliffs slope gently upward for 50 cm before becoming horizontal. Both birds of the pair excavate, incubate, and provide for the young. In Sri Lanka the clutch is of 4-5 eggs, in north India usually six. **Laying months:** Burma, April; Sri Lanka, March-May; Malaysia, about January-April; Sumatra, February; Java, May and July-October.

Description *M. l. leschenaulti* Sexes alike. **Adult:** forehead to mantle rufous; scapulars, tertials and wings green, the coverts with paler edges and tips; primaries greenish-black; secondaries rufous, with black tips and outer webs broadly margined with green. Back, rump and uppertail-coverts bright pale blue; tail green. Ear-coverts black, or black below and rufous above; lore and connecting line below eye black. Chin and throat pale yellow, turning sharply to rufous on the lower throat. A very narrow black gorget borders the rufous; below it, the upper breast is bright yellow, the lower breast bright green, the belly pale blue-green, and the undertail-coverts pale greenish-blue. Underwing-coverts rufous; undersides of tail, primaries and secondaries grey. Bill black; eye red; legs and feet brownish-grey. **Juvenile:** like the adult, but forehead, forecrown and mantle green, hindcrown mottled green and rufous, and hindneck rufous; the lower throat is pale yellow (not rufous), and the gorget-bar is dusky and indistinct. Breast and belly paler and more olivaceous than on the adult. **Measurements:** wing of male 103-111, of female 104-112; tail of male 73-82, of female 74-81; bill of male 34-41, of female 35-40; tarsus of male 10-12, of female 11-12. Weight: 26-33.

References Forshaw (1987), Fry (1984).

Merops apiaster

Merops Apiaster Linnaeus, 1758, Syst. Nat., ed. 10, I, p. 117, Southern Europe.

Field identification Length 23-25 cm (9-10 in). Unmistakable in its northern breeding range, and in Africa immediately told by its combination of chestnut cap and yellow throat. This is one of the loveliest bee-eaters, strongly gregarious, with vivid but harmonious colours, an attractive voice and graceful flight. It is quite large and robust, sleek, long-winged and pointed-tailed. No other bee-eater has golden-yellow scapulars and rump, nor the inner half of the wing bright rufous. Females are slightly paler than males and can often be told in the field by their paler scapulars and less rufous wings. Juveniles are mainly green and lack any chestnut or gold in the plumage, but their pale yellow throats and silvery-green scapulars make them as distinctive as the adults.

Voice Used at all times and seasons, the call is a liquid, throaty, melodious 'prruip', 'pruik' or 'kruup'; 14 other calls are known (Fry 1984). At a distance and *en masse* the 'pruik' call has a distinctive purring, rolling quality, like the voices of White-throated, Blue-cheeked, Madagascar and Rosy Bee-eaters (101, 104, 105, 110).

Geographical variation None.

Habitat and range European Bee-eaters like warm bushy country with rivers, pastureland, sandy soils and scattered trees. Northern breeding limits in Europe coincide with the 21°C July isotherm, but the bird is at its most abundant in even hotter areas, where it inhabits sunny plains and hillsides, dissected steppes, wooded riverbanks in semi-desert, open cork-oak woods, olive groves, cereal fields, grassland and Mediterranean shrublands. It needs riverbanks, sandpits and gullies for nesting, and freely uses telephone wires for perching. Migrants occur in practically all open habitats up to 3000 m. Wintering birds in Africa avoid rainforest and inhabit wooded savannas, lakeshores, rivers and farmland. The species breeds uncommonly in South Africa and Namibia, and commonly in northwest Africa from west Morocco to Libya. It nests on all larger Mediterranean islands, throughout Spain and Portugal, in southwest France, Italy, southeast and east Europe, Turkey, Lebanon, Palestine, Iraq, Iran, north Oman, Afghanistan, at high altitudes (900-2100 m) in Pakistan and Kashmir, and northwards in USSR to Ryazan, the Pry, Moksha and Tsna Rivers, Shilovo, Gorodishche, Syzran, Laishevo, Spassk, Dzhambeity Province, Aral Sea, Il'ich, and the south shores of Lake Balkhash. It is absent from much of Turkmenistan and Uzbekistan, and probably breeds in Dzungaria (China: Sinkiang). In northwest Europe it nests sporadically north to Scotland, Sweden and Finland.

Population A widespread and common bird, its world population is about 4 million pre-breeding and 13 million post-breeding (Fry 1984).

Migration It winters exclusively in Africa, mainly between Lake Victoria and Transvaal and west to Angola, and less commonly in West Africa from Sierra Leone to Ivory Coast. Ringing recoveries suggest that in autumn west European birds move southwestwards (probably to West Africa) and that east European ones move southeastwards and cross or skirt around the east end of the Mediterranean (probably heading down the Nile to southern Africa). One individual ringed in Ryazan, southeast of Moscow, was recovered 20 months later in Zimbabwe, nearly 8000 km away. Bee-eaters migrate by day, and sometimes at night, in high-flying vocal flocks. They follow leading topographical lines, and autumn migration is spectacular in Gibraltar, in the Tisza valley near Szeged in Hungary and at Chokpak Pass in Kazakhstan. In the 1920s millions were thought to cross Uganda and Kenya in spring, but nowadays they seem to be much less abundant there. They are also now much less common than formerly in Malta, on both passages, perhaps because of continued persecution there. Arrival in Camargue, France, is in April and in Burgenland, Austria, in May. Autumn passage at Gibraltar is from mid August to late September but peaks in the second week of September, when tens of thousands cross the Strait. European Bee-eaters that breed in southern Africa, in the austral summer, migrate north and south more or less in time with the wintering immigrants from Eurasia. They winter in central Africa, from 15°S north to the Equator (Brooke and Herroelen 1988). Southwest Cape birds arrive in September and lay in October; as soon as the young fledge they all migrate 150 km inland into the mountains, in December, then move into central Africa in March-April (Underhill 1990). In Ryazan (USSR), France and the Cape, migrant European Bee-eaters return to exactly the same site year after year; there is an 80% return in Ryazan.

Food Airborne insects, mainly Hymenoptera. Bee-eaters living near flowering grassland and cloverfields take mainly bumble-bees; elsewhere honeybees predominate, drones being favoured over workers. Over 300 species of insect prey have been identified, including mayflies, dragonflies, grasshoppers, mantises, termites, bugs, stoneflies, lacewings, scorpionflies, moths, butterflies, caddisflies and numerous kinds of beetles (Fry 1984). Caterpillars and spiders suspended on silk are occasionally taken, and so are a few non-flying arthropods on the ground or herbage, and once even earthworms (Earlé 1991). Most insects eaten are 10-15 mm long.

Habits This bee-eater forages mainly by hawking from a telegraph wire or tree, in pursuits over a few metres (sometimes 100 m): two-thirds of sallies are successful. It also freely hunts aloft, gracefully sailing around at some height, making sudden twists and dashes to catch small insects such as ants and termites, which are evidently swallowed on the spot. Hunting is mostly within 1 km of the nest, but can be up to 12 km away. Pairs roost in the nest until the eggs hatch, when the female alone broods them at night. At other times the birds sleep gregariously on the leeward sides of tall trees, six or seven packed together facing the same way. During the day they often sunbathe with

European Bee-eater wing-stretching

the mantle feathers raised acutely in a ruff or looking broken-necked, the head to one side, bill ajar, skyward eye closed. When hot, they fly with legs dangling and bare thighs exposed. They water-bathe by splashing onto a still surface two or three times, then they perch and preen. During bouts of preening the bird scratches its head with a fast scrabbling action of its foot, reaching over the wing; then it may yawn, or stretch both forewings above the back, 'wrists' nearly touching, or else stretch one wing at a time, downward and backward, spreading the tail wide under the wing to the same side. When a bird alights next to its mate, they both perch upright, call excitedly, and fan and vibrate the tail: a commonplace greeting ceremony. *Nesting:* European Bee-eaters nest in small colonies of up to eight pairs; occasional colonies in Hungary and Yugoslavia hold hundreds of nests. The birds pair for life (but the species is much shorter-lived than tropical bee-eaters). 20% of pairs have a helper, nearly always male. Males courtship-feed females, displaying at the perch with one or both wings briefly raised up. Favourite nest sites are cliffs and steep banks of dry loamy clay, firm sand or soft sandstone; often burrows are dug into level ground. There is a single clutch, of 4-10 eggs, usually 5-6, laid at intervals of about 24 hours. The incubation period is 20 days and the nestling period 30-31 days. **Laying months:** northwest Africa, April-May; Europe and the Middle East, May-June; Uzbekistan, June-July; South Africa, October-November.

Description *Adult male* (summer): forehead white at the bill, merging into chestnut on the forecrown by way of pale yellow then pale green; a short yellowish or bluish eyebrow. Crown, hindneck and mantle chestnut; scapulars, lower back and rump tawny golden-yellow. Uppertail-coverts mainly green; tail green, with short, broad, blackish streamers. In the wing tertials are green, secondaries, greater, median and inner lesser coverts rufous, and primaries, primary coverts, alula and outer lesser coverts are green or green-blue; primaries and particularly secondaries have black tips 15 mm deep, forming a conspicuous trailing-edge band. Mask black; chin and throat bright yellow; a narrow black gorget; breast turquoise-blue, paling towards the undertail-coverts. Wing-lining pale rufous; undersides of primaries, secondaries and tail feathers grey. Autumn and winter plumages each differ slightly (Fry 1984). Bill black, mouth pink; eye crimson; legs and feet frosted purplish-brown. **Adult female:** like the male, but yellow scapulars and lower back are tinged greenish, the inner lesser wing-coverts not so bright green, the rufous median and greater coverts edged with green, and the whole underparts paler than on the male. **Juvenile:** dull olive-green where adults are chestnut or rufous; forehead dull pale green, scapulars pale silvery-green, rump green; chin and throat pale yellow; no black gorget; breast and belly duller than on the adult; no tail-streamers. **Measurements:** wing of male 144-160, of female 141-152; tail of male 85-95, of female 81-88, excluding streamers of up to 24 mm on males and 18 mm on females; bill of male 37-45, of female 36-44; tarsus of male 13-15, of female 13-15. Weight: male 48-78, female 44-72; seasonal averages of males vary from 54 to 61, with females 4 g lighter.

References Brooke and Herroelen (1988), Cramp (1985), Fry (1984), Fry *et al.* (1988), Lessels (1990), Lessells and Krebs (1989), Underhill (1990).

110 ROSY BEE-EATER
Merops malimbicus

Plate 36

Merops malimbicus Shaw, 1806, Naturalists' Miscell., 17, text to pl. 701, Malimba, Portuguese Congo.

Field identification Length 22-25 cm (9-10 in), excluding streamers of 4 cm (1½ in). A tropical west African bee-eater which forages mainly above the forest canopy and nests in vast colonies in shelving sandbanks in the great rivers. **At rest:** upperparts slate-grey, underparts vivid pink with a conspicuous white line below the black mask, eye red, tail dusky carmine with short streamers. **In flight:** wings are plain dark grey above and below, and rump a paler grey; the pink underparts and in particular the white cheek stripe are readily visible at a distance. **Confusion species:** sometimes mistaken for Carmine Bee-eater (111), which is, however, radically different with its crimson back and wings, blue-green cap, pale blue rump and undertail-coverts, lack of white cheek stripe, and 'klunk-klunk' calls. Two other white-cheeked bee-eaters which could be seen within the range of the Rosy near the Gabon/Congo/north Angola coast are the White-fronted (99) and Madagascar (105).

Voice A rather hoarse 'crrrp' or 'chick-k', not unlike the 'pruik' of the European Bee-eater (109), especially when emanating from a large flock. Alarm 'wic'.

Geographical variation None.

Habitat and range Like the other larger *Merops* bee-eaters, this one is an aerial species which makes dashing sorties after an insect from a riverside perch or treetop but also spends much time hawking in continuous flight, often high in the air. It feeds around and above the forest canopy and the tops of trees in moist derived savanna, riverine forest and woodland and gallery forest. Nests, on low-water sandbars in rivers a kilometre or so wide, can be quite far from trees; like some desert bee-eaters, the Rosy tends to rest on sand by its burrow entrance. It hawks low and high over large expanses of water: rivers, lakes, reservoirs and brackish lagoons, and along sea-coasts, where it sometimes nests. It ranges from Ivory Coast (where rare, west to 5°W) through southern Ghana, Togo, Benin and Nigeria (where common), but has not yet been found in Cameroon. It is common in Gabon, Congo, Cabinda, and forested lowlands along Congo River upstream to about 24°E, Sanga and Oubangi Rivers north to 2½°N, and Kasai River and its tributaries in south-central Zaïre, east to 23°E and south nearly to the Angolan border. Nesting colonies are known in Nigeria on the Niger River at 5°48'E (Pategi), 5°55'E, 6°00'E, on Simanka River near Ibi at 9°45'E, at Nzam near Onitsha about 6°30'N, and probably Loko at 7°50'E on Benue River; much smaller breeding colonies have been found at Malimba, on the coast 80 km north of Congo River mouth, and recently near the coast at Gamba, 2°45'S in Gabon.

Population Most of the few colonies which have been found are spectacularly large, with an estimated 8,000, 8,000, 18,500 and 23,700 nest holes, while one colony in 1933 may have been even larger. Allowing for 'false-start' nests and for the likelihood of nest helpers, 23,700 nest holes represent between 25,000 and 50,000 adult birds.

Migration After nesting on large Nigerian rivers in April-June, the birds disperse rapidly, a few travelling upstream on River Niger to 10°N (where there are records in August-September) but most moving south into the rainforest zone, coastal mangrove and (in Ghana) coastal savannas, where they arrive in late June and remain until early April. They are particularly common in the forest zone from September to March. Rosy Bee-eaters are found all year on upper Congo River (although they are not known to breed there) and are partially migratory on the lower Congo, moving to the coast where they breed at Malimba in May-August and Gamba up to October.

Food Mainly flying ants (70% of the insects caught, but perhaps only 10% of the diet by weight), and honeybees and other Hymenoptera (28%). The remaining 2% are dragonflies, damselflies, termites, grasshoppers, crickets, flies, butterflies, beetles and squash-bugs, all taken on the wing.

Habits Ants are caught mainly in continuous wheeling flight and swallowed immediately. Larger prey (fast-flying *Charaxes* butterflies, water-beetles up to 16 mm long, wasps up to 20 mm long) are captured in a rapid sortie from an elevated perch, and brought back to the perch to be de-stung and immobilised. Foraging flocks above the forest in winter number tens or hundreds of birds. Water-bathing is frequent in the evening, a bird gliding across a still surface, splashing down and immediately rising clear; sunbathing has not been recorded. Males courtship-feed females, ceremonially proffering a very small insect: sitting on sand near their nest, male and female face each other and jerk the bill upward through a small arc, to right and left alternately, the female accepting the insect after a few seconds. Whether there are helpers-at-the-nest awaits discovery. Digging birds take their weight on bill and 'wrists', releasing both feet to scrabble sand backwards with a bicycling action. ***Nesting:*** colonies are sited in large shelving sandbars exposed by falling waters of great rivers, in coastal bluffs, and in inland raised beaches backed by forest. Burrows are evenly distributed, with two per m² of bare or grassy sand; one colony was 33 m wide and 330 m long. Burrows average 1.9 m long and decline at about 16° to the horizontal; the egg-chamber floor is 50-55 cm below a level sand surface. Sandbars are submerged by rising waters each year after nesting finishes, so nests cannot be reused; one sandbar was used in four years running. ***Laying months:*** Nigeria, mid May; Angola (Malimba), May; Gabon, about August.

Description Sexes alike. ***Adult:*** forehead and crown dark dove-grey; mantle, back and wings slate-grey; rump slightly paler grey, with a purple tinge; tail dull carmine, but as it grows the exposed parts of the folded tail rapidly bleach to dark grey. Mask black; chin and a broad line through the cheek white; throat, breast and belly bright pink-red; undertail-coverts grey. Underwing-coverts sooty-grey with a mauve wash; undersides of primaries, secondaries and tail feathers shiny black. Bill black; eye red or red-brown; legs and feet yellowish-brown. ***Juvenile:*** like the adult, but upperparts paler, the smaller feathers narrowly pale-fringed, and tail dark grey-brown with a dull carmine wash; mask dark grey, cheeks buffy-white, chin pale grey, throat and breast dusky pink, belly dusky pink-buff; eye dark brown; no tail-streamers. *Measurements:* wing of male 128-145, of female 123-141; tail of male 74-83, of female 76-81, excluding streamers of up to 47 mm on males and 35 mm on females; bill of male 39-47, of female 38-44; tarsus of male 11-14, of female 11-14.

References Fry (1984), Fry *et al.* (1988).

111 CARMINE BEE-EATER
Merops nubicus

Plate 36

Merops nubicus Gmelin, 1788, Syst. Nat., I, pt I, p. 464, Nubia.

Field identification Length 24-27 cm (9½-10½ in), discounting streamers of up to 12 cm (4¾ in). A large, long-tailed bee-eater in bright crimsons and carmines, strongly gregarious and aerial, with a characteristic but un-bee-eater-like voice. *At rest:* crown greenish-blue; chin and throat greenish-blue or vivid pink, mask and large bill black, trunk, wings and tail crimson, rump and undertail-coverts pale blue. *In flight:* from above, the pale blue rump is in strong contrast to the red wings and tail; from below, wings are buffy and the tail grey, and the powder-blue undertail-coverts are almost as good a feature as the vivid pink breast. *Confusion species:* unmistakable in good view and when the voice has been learned, but Carmines have been mistaken for Rosy Bee-eaters (110), which are grey-backed birds with white cheeks.

Voice Flight call a short, bass, throaty 'klunk', 'chung', 'tunk' or 'terk', sometimes slightly rolled: 'krrunk'. It is usually given twice, and less often repeated up to six times. Also a loud, clipped 'rik-rik-rik-rak, rak-rik-rak-rik' and a harsh 'tirriktirrik-tirrik' of alarm.

Geographical variation Two subspecies, differing in throat colour and slightly in size. They are sometimes treated as separate species (Forshaw 1987), although morphological differences are trivial and biological differences non-existent.

M. n. nubicus Northern tropics of Africa, north and east Kenya, northeast Tanzania. Chin and throat greenish-blue. Average weights increase from 43 g in Ethiopia to 51 g in Chad and 55 g in Nigeria.

M. n. nubicoides Southern tropics of Africa, northeast to west Tanzania and Burundi; vagrant to southwest Kenya (three records). Chin and throat carmine-pink (on juveniles pale pink, or rarely pale blue). Wing and bill 2-5% longer and tail-streamers about 25 mm longer than in *nubicus*. Average weights vary from 54 g in Zambia to 57 g and 64 g in Zimbabwe.

Habitat and range Carmine Bee-eaters frequent open wooded and bushy savannas, floodplains with oxbows, woods and cultivation, dry grassy plains, arid *Acacia* steppe, swamps with scattered dead trees, lakeshores and coastal mangrove. They forage widely in the airspace above these habitats and are attracted from considerable distances to bush fires and to herds of ungulates. For nesting they need high, fresh-cut sand cliffs, preferably almost free of vegetation on the cliff face; such sites are typical of large, meandering rivers. In the northern tropics the breeding range is north to a line between Senegal River, Khartoum and Eritrea and south to Gambia, north Ghana, Lokoja in central Nigeria, Uele River in north Zaïre, Ileret, Audache and Lokichokio in north Kenya, and Juba and Shebelle Rivers in Somalia; they breed at altitudes of up to 1000 m. Carmine Bee-eaters are absent from the Horn of Africa, east of 46°E. In winter northern birds extend south to north Sierra Leone, the northern half of Ivory Coast, Enugu in Nigeria, central Cameroon, north Uganda, Kenya and northeast Tanzania (south to Rufiji River). In the southern tropics these bee-eaters breed north to the Cunene and Okavango headwaters in Angola, the Lungwebungu in west Zambia and Luangwa valley and perhaps Lake Bangweulu in north Zambia, Chikwawa in Malawi and Ruenya River in Mozambique; and south to Chobe River, Kasane and Lianshulu in north Botswana, near Bulawayo and Nuanetsi and Lundi Rivers in south Zimbabwe, and Pungwe River in Mozambique. Nesting is up to 1500 m in altitude. In the austral winter they spread into northeast Namibia, Transvaal, Swaziland and northeast Natal and into north Angola, south Zaïre, Burundi, the Lake Kivu area and west Tanzania.

Population The exact location of breeding colonies changes from year to year, as old cliffs crumble away and new ones are cut. Over 130 sites are known, perhaps 10% of all African colonies (Fry 1984). Colonies generally hold between 100 and 1,000 nests, occasionally up to 10,000. From these figures, we think that a total population of 5 million Carmine Bee-eaters is a possibility.

Migration After breeding in the southern tropics in September-November, this bee-eater disperses widely, at first mainly southward for up to 650 km. A few non-breeding visitors are in Transvaal in August-September and many in December-March. In March they return northward through Zimbabwe, mainly in the eastern lowveld, and the species 'winters' in March-August throughout the savannas of Angola, Zambia, Malawi, south Zaïre and west Tanzania. Similar movements are mirrored in the northern tropics, where the birds breed in February-April at lower latitudes (where they are resident) and April-June in higher latitudes (where they are summer visitors); migrants or nomads appear just to the south of the breeding range, south to Sierra Leone and northeast Tanzania, in winter (August-February).

Food Three major studies gave different results, showing that Carmine Bee-eaters in Mali ate mainly locusts and grasshoppers, in Nigeria flying ants and in Zimbabwe honeybees. All three are 'correct', for this bird travels far to exploit any flying insect wherever it is locally plentiful: a hatch of ants or termites, an emergence of cicadas or shieldbugs, a migration of dragonflies or butterflies, and a disturbance of insects in grass by fire or by a herd of antelopes. In the Niger River Inundation

zone in Mali, locusts are the staple food of Carmine Bee-eaters, which migrate and breed in time with the movements of desert locusts *Schistocerca gregaria*, migratory locusts *Locusta migratoria* and at least ten other kinds.

Habits Doubtless because of their predilection for grasshoppers and locusts, Carmine Bee-eaters commonly use wild and domestic mammals, large ground-birds, people and vehicles as beaters to flush insects from grass. Bee-eaters sit on the backs of walking Ostriches, bustards, storks, herons, cranes, ibises, Secretarybirds, cattle, sheep, goats, camels, antelopes, donkeys, zebras, Elephants and Warthogs, and dash out to snap up any insect put to flight. They fly alongside or behind a galloping oryx, keep station with travelling cars, trucks and tractors, and fly slowly behind a person walking through grass, from time to time swooping down for a grasshopper. A column of smoke from a bush fire attracts flocks of Carmine Bee-eaters from afar; they hawk in and out of the smoke and near to the flames, in pursuit of insects (in Gambia their Mandinka name means 'cousin to the fire'). Ever an opportunist, this bee-eater sometimes even catches fish; but much more often the birds glide low over water and suddenly dive onto the surface, even submerging, in order to bathe. *Nesting:* Carmines breed in large, dense colonies; sometimes they dig their nest burrows in level ground, but as a rule perpendicular sandy cliffs are used. Some colonies are of only a few nests, but generally there are over a hundred, and sometimes thousands, at a density of about 60 holes per m² of cliff face. The same site can be used for many years; or a colony shifts 1 km or more along its river each year. In some areas holes are excavated four or five months before laying starts. Tunnels are more or less straight and horizontal, 1-2 m long (once 3.7 m) and 6 cm across. The clutch is of 2-3 eggs at low and 3-5 eggs at higher latitudes. Occupied holes quickly accumulate a noisome carpet of blackish insect sclerites from trodden-in pellets, and they smell strongly of ammonia. *Laying months:* February-June throughout the northern tropics, in general later at high than at low latitudes; September-October, sometimes November, in the southern tropics.

Description *M. n. nubicus* Sexes alike. **Adult:** mask black; forehead, forecrown, chin and upper throat beryl-green (viewed down-light) or blue (against the light), becoming increasingly washed with dark olive-turquoise towards the hindcrown and lower throat (against the light the throat can look mainly blackish). Behind those parts there is an abrupt transition to vivid carmine-pink on hindneck, mantle and breast; scapulars and wings are crimson-red, with tertials broadly edged with greenish-blue, and primaries and secondaries tipped black. Back, rump and uppertail-coverts pale azure-blue; tail crimson, with the streamers mainly blackish. Forebelly carmine, paler than the breast and sometimes slightly buffy; lower belly and undertail-coverts pale azure-blue; underwing-coverts cinnamon-buff. Underside of tail and of primaries and secondaries silvery-grey. Bill black; eye blood-red or red-brown; legs and feet frosted grey. **Juvenile:** forehead and crown blue with dusky mottling, changing to earth-brown on hindneck and upper mantle; lower mantle rufous; scapulars and tertials light olive-brown with blue feather edges; rump greyish-blue; wings and tail dull crimson washed with brown, the wing-coverts with pink fringes and tail feathers with greenish edges. Chin and throat feathers dark grey with blue fringes, breast pale pink mottled with buff, belly very pale pink, vent and undertail-coverts pale greyish-blue. **Measurements:** wing of male 145-157, of female 142-158; tail of male 92-107, of female 92-101, excluding streamers of up to 95 mm on males and 80 mm on females; bill of male 38-46, of female 38-46; tarsus of male 13-15, of female 13-15. Weight: 34-59.

References Forshaw (1987), Fry (1984), Fry *et al.* (1988).

112 RUFOUS-CROWNED ROLLER (Purple Roller)   Plate 37
Coracias naevia

Coracias naevia Daudin, 1800, Traité d'Ornithol., 2, p. 258, Sénégal.

Field identification Length 35-40 cm (14-15½ in). The largest roller; a stocky bird usually seen on a large solitary tree. **At rest:** at a distance it looks rather plain, brownish with a large white superciliary stripe and a small white patch on the nape. Crown rufous (northern tropics) or olive-green (southern tropics), back dull olive-green, closed wings mainly rufous. Underparts pale purple-pink, covered with fine white streaks. Tail dark, quite long and full, square-ended. **In flight:** looks dark, with pinkish throat and breast. Primaries and secondaries blue-black; wing-coverts blue and purple above, whole wing conspicuously silvery-pink below. Wings quite long but round-ended; flies with regular, rapid, shallow wingbeats. Like all rollers, it is easily provoked into 'rolling': a fast, noisy descent, veering away from the target at the last instant. **Confusion species:** this is the only roller without large areas of pale blue in the plumage. At a distance it can look rufous-purple, like broad-billed rollers (120, 121), which differ in having short yellow bills and no white eyebrow.

Voice Less strident than other rollers. Main call is a muffled 'ga', 'kaa' or 'grair', singly, or repeated at an even rate varying from 28 calls in 5 seconds to 20 in 8 seconds. The song has short 'i' or 'chik' syllables mixed with the call notes, a clucking 'g, g, igigidigou' or 'i-ka-i-ka-i-kaa-i-i-i-*kair-kair-kair*'. In rolling display, 'gaa-aaa-aaaah'. Voices have been likened to those of White-bellied Bustards *Eupodotis senegalensis*, plantain-eaters *Crinifer* spp. and Green Wood-Hoopoes *Phoeniculus purpureus*.

Geographical variation Two subspecies.
    C. n. naevia ('Rufous-crowned Roller'). Northern tropics of Africa, south to Tanzania; vagrant to South Yemen. Crown rufous; underparts pink-brown.
    C. n. mosambica ('Purple Roller'). Southern tropics, north to Zaïre and Zambia. Crown olive-green; underparts

purple-brown; no white on the inner webs of the primaries. Larger: wing 175-198 mm, tail 135-152 mm; 15% heavier.

Habitat and range This fine large roller is a bird of open savanna woodlands, where it keeps to the larger trees. It favours hot lowlands below 1300 m, but also occurs up to 3000 m in altitude. Generally rather uncommon, it is commonest (or most readily encountered) in tilled farmland where large shade trees have been left standing; it also inhabits broken country with rocky and shrubby hillsides, and arid, thorny acacia savannas. It often perches on telephone wires. Somewhat nomadic, it occurs in south Mauritania and Mali; north Guinea, Ivory Coast and Ghana; Burkina Faso, Togo and Benin; south Niger; Nigeria north of the rainforest zone; south Chad; north Central African Republic; west and south Sudan (Darfur hills, Kordofan, Bahr el Ghazal, Equatoria, also in south Blue Nile Province); Ethiopia except the west and northeast; parts of north Somalia; Kenya except for the most arid areas; northeast Zaïre; Uganda; north Tanzania. A separate population inhabits southern Africa: Angola, north Namibia, Botswana, Transvaal, Zimbabwe, south Zaïre, Zambia south of 10°S, south Malaŵi and southwest Mozambique.

Migration In the northern tropics it is mainly sedentary in the southern soudanian and northern guinean woodland zones, mainly a wet-season visitor (May-September) to the sahelian zone, and mainly a dry-season visitor (November-March) to southern guinean woodlands. In Gambia it is resident, but also a visitor in September-June, with conspicuous passage in May and June. In Ivory Coast it is fairly common in the dry season, October-May, south to the forest border, but in the rains (June-September) much scarcer, and absent south of 9°N. In East Africa it is nomadic but tends to move south in winter; it was abundant in southeast Kenya in March-July 1984, when there was severe drought in the northeast. In Namibia and Botswana it is commoner in November-April, the wet season, than in May-October, the dry season; in Zimbabwe it is commonest in May-December; and in Zambia it is mainly a non-breeding visitor from May (sometimes March) to October.

Food Mainly locusts, grasshoppers and mantises; also ants, beetles, scorpions, and small lizards, snakes, rodents and young birds.

Habits Food is taken on the ground, the bird keeping watch from a tree or wire and flying down fast to alight and grab the prey in the bill. Rufous-crowned Rollers occur in pairs, but male and female forage well apart – sometimes independently. Rather sluggish and stolid birds, they are less vocal than other rollers and the flight is less buoyant. They are territorial and aggressively drive away other rollers, crows and small hawks. In territorial advertisement, at any time of year but mainly in the breeding season, a roller flies up well above the treetops, repeating the 'gaa' call every second or so, then it dashes down at speed in rolling flight, rocking to left and right about the body axis. **Nesting:** eggs are laid in a cavity such as a woodpecker hole, natural tree hole, cavity in a tall sand or chalk streambank or inaccessible rock cliff, a pipe, or a hole in masonry or a ground termitarium. The clutch, of 2-4 eggs (usually 3-4), is laid 15-60 cm from the nest entrance, on bare earth, stone or wood, or on any chips and fragments that may already have accumulated. **Laying months:** Mauritania, August-October; Senegal and Gambia, August-September; Nigeria, June; Ethiopia, April-August; Uganda, May; Kenya, February, March, May and November; Zimbabwe, September-December (mainly October); Namibia, May-June.

Description *C. n. naevia* Sexes alike. **Adult:** forehead and eyebrow white; crown rufous, tinged with olive-green; ear-coverts and sides of neck dark pinkish-brown; a half-concealed tuft of hindcrown feathers is white. Mantle, scapulars and tertials olive-green; inner median and lesser upperwing-coverts bright lilac, outer ones purple; alula and primary coverts purple; greater coverts wine-brown. Primaries and secondaries blackish, dark blue on the outer webs and paling to white at the base of the inner webs. Back lilac, rump pale purple, uppertail-coverts dark purple. Tail ultramarine, except the central two feathers which are bluish olive-green. Lore black, chin white; throat and breast pink, heavily streaked with white; belly mauve-pink, streaked with white; flanks pale lilac; undertail-coverts blue-lilac. Undersides of flight feathers silvery-grey; underwing-coverts pale pink. Bill black; eye dark brown; legs and feet olive-brown. *Juvenile:* like the adult, but duller, and olive-green where adults are pink, pink-brown or lilac; upperwing-coverts mainly

olive; tail feathers with olive-green tips and edges. *Measurements:* wing of male 178-188, of female 165-189; tail of male 126-138, of female 123-137; bill (to skull) of male 40-49, of female 37-46; tarsus of male 20-25, of female 22-25. Weight: 125-163.

Reference Fry *et al.* (1988).

113 INDIAN ROLLER
Coracias benghalensis

Plate 37

Corvus benghalensis Linnaeus, 1758. Syst. Nat., ed. 10, 1, p. 106, Benghala (= Madras).

Field identification Length 30-34 cm (12-13½ in). A south Asiatic roller, quite large, chunky and broad-winged, which is unlikely ever to be confused with either of the other two rollers in its range. Somewhat muddy-looking (for a roller) when perched, it is gorgeous when it spreads its wings. *At rest:* a large-headed, short-necked and short-legged bird with bluish crown, brown back, azure and purple wings and tail, pinkish throat and breast with profuse white streaks, and pale blue belly. The tail is not streamered, and its azure sides can be hard to see. *In flight:* it is instantly recognisable from above and below by the purple wings with a broad brilliant azure band crossing the wingtip: a highly visible feature shared by no other roller. *Confusion species:* the European Roller (118), which migrates through the range of Indian Rollers, has solid black primaries, an entirely blue head, and in flight silhouette is longer-necked and longer-tailed. Dollarbirds (122) are black-ish, with a round pale window in the primaries, rather than the Indian Roller's bright blue wingtip-band.

Voice The contact call is a harsh mono-syllable, varying from a short 'chack' to a longer, harsh 'tschow'. In territorial rolling display, given at all seasons but particularly when breeding, strident 'kaarsch' calls are repeated at ever greater frequency and volume as a bird rockets down upon an intruder. 'Kaarsch' notes are uttered with the bill slightly agape; other notes uttered with the bill closed lack the 'sch' and sound muffled. Two birds perched side by side sometimes give a staccato chattering.

Geographical variation Three subspecies, intergrading in India; the southeast Asian one is so distinct that it has sometimes been treated as a different species.

C. b. benghalensis From east Iraq to Bangladesh (where it intergrades with *affinis*), and from north Pakistan to north Maharashtra (where it intergrades with *indica*).

C. b. indica Andhra Pradesh and south Maharashtra to Sri Lanka. Hindneck brighter rufous, crown and upperwing-coverts darker blue, and mantle, scapulars and tertials browner and less olive-tinged. Smaller: male wing 175-188 mm and tail 118-125 mm.

C. b. affinis Intergrades with the nominate subspecies between 87° and 92°E (Bihar/Assam), ranging to Hainan, Indochina and peninsular Thailand. Forehead blue-green (not pink-buff); hind-neck brown; chin and throat dark violet with inconspicuous blue streaks; breast purple-brown; forebelly purple-brown

(not pale blue); uppertail-coverts azure; tail (except central pair of feathers) pale blue with a violet basal half. Longer-bodied than *benghalensis*.

Habitat and range This is a common and conspicuous bird of open cultivated areas, plantations, coconut and date palm groves, light deciduous forest, dry *Prosopis* and *Acacia* woodlands, pasture, stubblefields, parks, and buildings standing in extensive grounds with lawns and trees. Indian Rollers make free use of roofs, parapets and telephone wires; in north Oman they are 'roundabout birds' – every verdant roundabout has its pair. They range from near Baghdad through north Oman, United Arab Emirates and south Iran to the entire Indian subcontinent, Maldive and Laccadive Islands and Sri Lanka north to Lahore, Punjab, Nepal, Sikkim, Bangladesh and Assam, through Burma and Thailand to Laos, Cambodia, Vietnam and also Hainan Island, south to the Malaysian border near Kota Bharu. They are vagrant to Kuwait, Syria, eastern Saudi Arabia and Masirah Island (Oman).

Migration Throughout its range it is subject to ill-understood local movements, mainly juvenile dispersal, but amounting to regular migration at least in Oman. There, although present year-round, it is much commoner in winter than in summer: 370 were counted on 250 km of roadside wires in November, and in November-January 200 can congregate on a new-cut 50-ha fodder field.

Food Large arthropods and small vertebrates: grasshoppers, crickets, earwigs, mantises, termites, bugs, moths, caterpillars, wasps, ants, beetles, and occasionally scorpions, spiders, toads, lizards, snakes, mice, shrews, fish and young birds.

Habits Indian Rollers keep watch from a lone tree, telegraph wire, street lamp, haystack or piece of farm equipment, and descend in quite a leisurely way to alight on the ground and snatch the prey, which is generally beaten and killed on the spot. They attend haymaking tractors so closely, flying to the ground for insects or catching them on the wing, that they are occasionally caught up in the machinery and killed. They often hover momentarily a

Sunbathing with mantle feathers raised

metre above intended prey, and they have been known to dive and submerge in water for fish and frogs, like a kingfisher. 'Lazy' and 'lethargic' are among the terms that have been applied to this and other *Coracias* rollers. But this species really comes to life at a bush fire, where in pursuit of insects it darts recklessly into hot smoke; recalling the Carmine Bee-eater's (111) local name 'cousin to the fire', the Indian Roller in Sri Lanka is called 'the one who inhales smoke'. The species hunts solitarily or in pairs and is aggressively territorial for much of the year, although a large flock of migrants can forage without hostility. Birds feed from some exposed perch all day, even in temperatures above 40°C; they generally continue to forage almost to nightfall, and sometimes feed at night on insects attracted to street lights. Despite their aggressiveness and rolling display flights often directed alarmingly at a human being, Indian Rollers seem to be widely tolerated and even welcomed as garden birds. In Kerala they are killed for their supposed medicinal value: roller broth is given as a cure for whooping cough. Territorial displays are like those of other rollers, a half-minute patrolling flight at treetop or third-floor height often ending in a fast rolling flight directed at an intruder. One circuitous, undulating, semi-rolling flight lasted 48 seconds, and 120 'kaarsch' notes were uttered. Frequently a bird launches itself abruptly from some elevated perch at a person, fox or slow-moving vehicle; it accelerates in a shallow dive, calling more and more vehemently, and rolling the body steeply from side to side about its long axis. However, we cannot corroborate the 'fantastic evolutions – tumbling, somersaulting [and] looping the loop' of Ali and Ripley (1970) or the 'twisting and turning . . . somersaulting and tumbling' of de Zylva (1984). **Nesting:** the clutch of 3-5 round white eggs is laid on a simple foundation of feathers, grass bents, rags and bits of wood, in a cavity in masonry, a roof overflow pipe, under eaves or in a tree or palm. In Sri Lanka a favoured place is the hollow opening at the top of a dead coconut palm that has lost its fronds. Incubation, mainly by the female, lasts for 17-19 days. **Laying months:** Oman, April-May; Sri Lanka, March-May; Kerala, January-March; northern India, mainly March-April; Burma, mainly April-May.

Description *C. b. benghalensis* Sexes alike. **Adult:** forehead pink-buff, tinged with lilac; lores darker; bare skin before and behind eye yellow; crown dark dull blue-green in centre and bright blue at sides. Hindneck, mantle, scapulars and tertials dull dark olive-brown, with a strong vinous wash on the hindneck; back and rump bright turquoise; uppertail-coverts ultramarine with greenish tips. The central two tail feathers are dull dark grey-olive, and the rest of the tail is brilliant azure-blue with an ultramarine base and 18-mm-broad ultramarine tip. Ear-coverts are dark rufous-brown with pale shaft-streaks; chin pink-buff; throat lilac and breast vinous-brown, both with creamy shaft-streaks; belly, flanks and undertail-coverts bright pale turquoise. In the wing, marginal coverts are purple, lesser and greater coverts and alula grey-blue, primary coverts brilliant azure; primaries and secondaries ultramarine with brilliant azure bases, the outer six primaries with blackish-blue tips and a 3-cm-deep brilliant azure-blue penultimate band. Wing feathers are glossy, the blue colours structural and varying in hue and intensity with the angle of incidence of light. Underwing ultramarine, with azure coverts and wingtip. Bill black, tinged with brown, the base of lower mandible dull orange; eye grey-brown, orbital skin yellow; legs and feet yellow-brown. **Juvenile:** like the adult, but crown greener, hindneck browner, back more drab, throat vinous-buff, belly greenish-blue, and lesser upperwing-coverts bluish-brown. **Measurements:** wing of male 184-200, of female 175-190; tail of male 129-145, of female 118-132; bill of male 44-47, of female 39-45; tarsus of male 26-27, of female 24-27. Weight: 166-176.

Reference Cramp (1985).

114 CELEBES ROLLER (Purple-winged Roller)   Plate 40
Coracias temminckii

Garrulus Temminckii Vieillot, 1819, Nouv. Dict. Hist. Nat., 29, p. 435, India (= Sulawesi).

Field identification Length 30-34 cm (12-13$\frac{1}{2}$ in). The only roller in Sulawesi other than the Dollarbird (122), which occasionally winters there. **At rest:** large, long-tailed, black-billed; cap and uppertail-coverts brilliant pale blue, back dark olive, rump, tail and wings dull purple, neck and underparts purplish-grey. **In flight:** forewing brilliant purple; wings otherwise dull purple without a 'dollar' in the primaries; the rest of the bird looks blackish with contrasting blue cap and uppertail-coverts. **Confusion species:** Dollarbirds are immediately told by their red bill, black forehead, undistinguished uppertail-coverts and, in flight, large pale blue 'dollars' in the wing.

Voice A variety of harsh 'krark' notes alternating with or followed by an upslurred grating 'tjorraa' (Watling 1983).

Geographical variation None.

Habitat and range Lightly wooded, cultivated lowlands from the coast up to 1000 m in Sulawesi and its offshore islands of Manterawu, Bangka, Lembeh, Muna and Butung. Sedentary, so far as is known.

Food Unknown. Probably like the food of the Indian Roller (113), but the very deep, powerful hooked bill suggests that it eats larger prey than does that species.

Habits Although this is a plentiful bird, little has been noted about its habits except that in general they appear not to differ from those of the Indian Roller. *Laying months:* nestlings found in September and eggs in November.

Description Sexes alike. *Adult:* forehead and crown bright pale blue, slightly olive-washed in the centre of the crown; hindneck dull purplish-black; mantle, back, scapulars and tertials dark olive-brown; rump purple; uppertail-coverts brilliant azure-blue; tail purplish-black. Lesser wing-coverts bright purple; rest of upperwing dull purple. Throat to undertail-coverts dark purple-grey; underwing-coverts bright purple; underside of primaries, secondaries and tail glossy purplish-black. Bill black; eye dark brown; legs and feet yellowish-brown. *Juvenile:* like the adult, but duller. *Measurements:* wing of male 181-191, of female 178-190; tail 123-137; bill (to skull) 42-49, depth 18-19.5; tarsus 25-26.

References Stresemann (1940), White and Bruce (1980).

115 RACKET-TAILED ROLLER
Coracias spatulata

Plate 37

Coracias spatulata Trimen, 1880, Proc. Zool. Soc. London, p. 31, near Victoria Falls.

Field identification Length 28-30 cm (11-12 in), with streamers adding up to 8 cm (3 in). This is a slender blue-and-brown roller peculiar to mature 'miombo' and 'mopane' woodlands in southern Africa. *At rest:* the white forehead and eyebrow, drab greenish crown, rufous-brown back, dark blue 'wrists', blue tail and pale-streaked light blue underparts are like those of Lilac-breasted (116) and European Rollers (118), but the distinctive feature of this species is its blob-tipped tail-streamers. A variable-sized patch at the side of the breast is pink-brown streaked with blue-white; juveniles have the whole breast and throat pink, streaked with white, and, east and occasionally west of Malaŵi, so have the adults. *In flight:* the upperwing is mainly purple, with a brilliant pale azure-blue stripe across the base of the primaries and secondaries, and rufous median coverts (blue on all confusion species); the underwing is pale blue, sharply demarcated from the purple-black tip and trailing-edge border. The flight is light and purposeful, slightly undulating, with regular shallow beats. *Confusion species:* the spatulate tail-streamers are diagnostic.

Otherwise this bird is like three other rollers. Lilac-breasted Rollers, with their pink throat and breast and blue belly, are very like the Racket-tail east of Malaŵi, but the latter can be told by its underparts being white-streaked and by its spatulate tail; elsewhere the two species differ additionally in that the Racket-tailed is blue-breasted. Juveniles of both species have white-streaked throat and breast, and until their streamers have grown they can be distinguished only by Racket-tails having dark rufous-brown (not pale grey-blue) greater wing-coverts and purple (not pale blue) primary coverts. European Rollers lack tail-streamers, have black blobs at the tail-corners, clear pale blue head and neck, and black primaries and secondaries without a visible azure stripe across their bases. Purple Rollers (112: so called in the range of Racket-tails) are large, with olive-green backs and unstreamered dark tails; a perched bird in front view can resemble a Racket-tail of the pink-breasted race, but the latter has a pale blue belly.

Voice A loud, harsh 'cha' or tchek' given by male and female together and repeated

2-4 times a second for several seconds, running into a screeching, explosive 'kaairssh, kaairssh, kaairssh . . .' as the bird rockets earthwards. The 'cha' note, given on the wing and at perch, has also been described as a puppy-like yelp, 'yeeow, yeeow'.

Geographical variation There are two distinct subspecies, with a broad zone of hybridisation between them (Clancey 1969).
C. s. spatulata Angola to Zambia, Zimbabwe and south Mozambique. Ear-coverts, throat and breast pale blue.
C. s. weigalli Extreme south Tanzania, and Mozambique south to the Zambezi. Ear-coverts, throat and breast pink. A 200-km-wide zone of hybridisation runs from Dar es Salaam through Malaŵi to Mozambique south of the Zambezi; occasional pink-breasted hybrids occur in Zambia and Zimbabwe, west to Victoria Falls.

Habitat and range Racket-tailed Rollers inhabit mature, undisturbed, dry dense woodlands with little or no understorey, dominated by *Brachystegia* trees ('miombo'), *Colophospermum* ('mopane'), and *Baikiaea*; they also frequent dry *Acacia* savannas. They range from Bié Plateau in southwest Angola, through Malanje and Lunda Provinces to Zambia, Malaŵi, Zimbabwe, Mozambique (except the very south), southeast Zaïre, and south Tanzania. They are widespread and fairly common in Zambia and Zimbabwe, widespread but uncommon in Tanzania (found north to Busondo and Kikore), and uncommon to frequent but local in Malaŵi (up to 1300 m). They are found in northeast Namibia (the Caprivi Strip) and occur rarely in northeast Botswana, Swaziland and adjacent South Africa (Ndumu).

Migration None; this roller is essentially sedentary, if locally nomadic.

Food Locusts, grasshoppers, beetles, maggots, scorpions and lizards (Ginn *et al.* 1989).

Habits Racket-tailed Rollers perch rather lower down than other rollers, in the mid-storey, scan the ground, and swoop down to seize prey there. They hunt solitarily or in pairs, but sometimes flocks of six or seven birds occur. Like other rollers they are strongly territorial, advertising their territory by flying up above the treetops and then plunging down, gathering speed, screeching raucously, and as they level out rolling or rocking rapidly left and right about the long axis. They sweep back to perch, or rise on closed wings until momentum is lost, tilt forwards, fall head-first with the wings still closed, and repeat the display. **Nesting:** the nest is an unlined cavity, often an old barbet or woodpecker hole, about 6 or 7 m up a tree trunk or limb; 2-4 eggs are laid, usually 3-4. Little more is known. **Laying months:** Zimbabwe, September-December, mainly October; Zambia, the same but not December; Malaŵi, October-November.

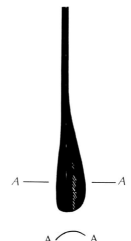

Section at A – A showing shape of outermost rectrix

Description *C. s. spatulata* Sexes alike. **Adult:** forehead and broad superciliary line white, the feathers long, thin and whiskery; crown and nape drab olive, mantle rufescent-olive; back, scapulars, tertials and greater wing-coverts rufous-brown; rump and uppertail-coverts dark ultramarine-blue. Tail forked (central feathers up to 26 mm shorter than the fifth one), purplish-black, the outer three feathers mainly azure-blue, the outermost attenuated into a blackish streamer 2-3 mm wide, with a spatulate tip which is strongly concave below and 10-11 mm wide when flattened. Lore and small patch behind eye are black. Chin bluish-white; ear-coverts, foreneck and underparts brilliant azure-blue, the throat and breast with white shaft-streaks; side of breast pale puce, softly streaked with bluish-white. Lesser wing-coverts, alula and primary coverts purple-blue; inner median coverts rufous-brown, outer ones blue; inner greater coverts mauve, outer ones blue; primaries and secondaries purple-black with basal halves azure. Underside of wing pale azure-blue, sharply demarcated from a broad glossy purple band around the tip and hind edge. Underside of tail pale blue. Bill black; eye dark brown or yellowish-brown; legs and feet dull yellowish. *Juvenile:* like the adult, but duller;

outer tail feather not attenuated nor lengthened; ear-coverts tinged with lilac; throat and breast pinkish; throat, breast and belly with broad white streaks. *Measurements:* wing of male 157-179, of female 155-168; tail of male 120-147, of female 136-144, excluding streamers of up to 78 mm on both sexes; bill (to skull) of male 33-39, of female 31-36; tarsus of male 20-24, of female 21-23. Weight: 88-111.

Reference Fry *et al.* (1988).

116 LILAC-BREASTED ROLLER (Lilac-throated Roller)   Plate 38
Coracias caudata

Coracias caudata Linnaeus, 1766, Syst. Nat., ed. 12, I, p. 160, Angola.

Field identification Length 28-30 cm (11-12 in), with streamers adding up to 8 cm (3 in). An eastern and southern African roller of dry thornbush country, with lilac throat and pale azure belly, and the breast either lilac or azure. **Confusion species:** Abyssinian Rollers (117) are similar, including the streamers, but the throat is pale blue, not pink. The two species overlap in a corridor running from north Ethiopia to east-central then southwest Ethiopia and the Lake Turkana basin. Most Racket-tailed Rollers (115) are readily distinguished by their spatulate streamers and their blue throat and breast; but east (and sometimes west) of Malaŵi they have the throat and breast pink with fine white streaks, and can then be told only by their racket tail, darker greater-coverts area and dark blue primary coverts. For differences between juveniles, see Racket-tailed Roller.

Voice Call, in flight and at perch, is a loud, guttural 'rak, rak'. In the rolling display flight, 'rak' is repeated rapidly and leads up to a raucous, harsh 'kaaa, kaarsh, kaaaarrsh'.

Geographical variation Two subspecies, meeting in Kenya without intergradation, differing mainly in the extent of lilac.
C. c. caudata ('Lilac-breasted Roller') Central Kenya to the Atlantic coast and

northern South Africa. Crown to mantle olive-green; throat and breast lilac, the throat heavily and the breast lightly streaked with white.
C. c. lorti ('Lilac-throated Roller') East and north Kenya to Red Sea coasts of Ethiopia and Somalia. Crown to mantle green-blue; throat lilac, heavily streaked with white, but breast azure-blue. Some individuals have a small lilac patch between the breast and belly.

Habitat and range This species inhabits *Acacia* country with well-spaced trees, rolling bushy gamelands, riverside woods and light forest, cultivated land and sometimes large gardens (but it does not associate at all closely with human habitation). It also occurs in pure grassland, where, in the absence of trees, it uses any elevated perches it can find, such as fences and telegraph wires. In such habitats the species ranges more or less continuously throughout eastern and southern Africa, from the Red Sea coasts of Ethiopia and northwest Somalia to the Angola coast and northern South Africa. It is found throughout Ethiopia except in the northwest, in the hot, low Rift Valley and up to 3000 m in the highlands, but has not yet been reported in Sudan. It occurs in northwest and south Somalia, southeast Uganda, Katanga and adjacent parts of Kasai in Zaïre, throughout Rwanda,

Burundi, Tanzania, Angola, Zambia, Malaŵi, Mozambique, Zimbabwe and Botswana, in the northeast half of Namibia, in Swaziland, and in South Africa south to north Cape, the whole of Transvaal (but scarce south of 26°S), and Natal in thornveld exceptionally as far south as Ladysmith. In Kenya, *caudata* occurs north to Tana River, Chanler's Falls, Ngao and Marsabit, and *lorti* is found around Lake Turkana, in the northeast, and breeds south to Garsen on the lower Tana.

Population It is at its greatest density in east Kenya: 16 were once counted along a 250-km stretch of road, which is a density equivalent to four per km². It is abundant in Somalia, frequent to common in Ethiopia, common in Uganda, Kenya and Tanzania, locally common in Zambia, common in Malaŵi, frequent in Zimbabwe (but sparse in the eastern highlands above 1600 m), and common north of 26°S in Transvaal. It is a common breeding resident on Zanzibar Island, and has been seen on Pemba.

Migration The nominate race is resident, although in Zimbabwe, Zambia and on Zanzibar some disperse for quite some distance after breeding. *C. c. lorti* is a breeding visitor to northwest Somalia from late April to mid September, after which there is a mass migration to wintering grounds in south Somalia; a few winter in northwest Somalia. Those breeding in south Somalia and northeast Kenya are partial migrants for a few hundred kilometres southward within Kenya; they then occur with nominate *caudata* along Tana River and in Tsavo East National Park, from December to March.

Food Arthropods and small vertebrates: locusts, grasshoppers, crickets, beetles, moths, butterflies, ants, spiders, scorpions, centipedes, snails, frogs, small reptiles and birds. Insects include noxious forms such as the grasshopper *Phymateus viridipes* and hairy caterpillars.

Habits Not very well known, but Lilac-breasted Rollers appear to be much like European Rollers (118) in their general behaviour. They occur singly or in pairs, and are vocal, pugnacious and strongly territorial. They feed by searching from an elevated perch for prey on the ground, then swooping down in a fast glide, landing abruptly next to the prey and seizing it with the bill, sometimes with a fluttering pounce; either the prey is eaten on the ground, or the bird returns to its perch and beats it there before swallowing it whole or partly dismembered. The species is attracted to bush fires, where fleeing insects are easily caught. 'Rolling' is a territorial advertisement. The bird flies strongly upwards to 10 or 12 m, then tips forward and falls with closed wings, quickly gaining speed by flapping. Flying very fast, it levels out and rolls to right and left four or five times in a couple of seconds and sweeps up again with closed wings, losing speed, until it tips forward a second time and repeats the roll. It invariably calls when rolling. **Nesting:** the nest is a flat pad made of a few pieces of grass, in a cavity up to 5 m up in a dead baobab, coconut, casuarina or *Terminalia* tree; nest holes have also been found in the side of termite-mounds, and the species will use nestboxes. The eggs, 2-4 in southern Africa (usually 2-3) and 3-4 in Somalia, are incubated by both sexes for 22-24 days. Nestlings are naked at hatching, and covered in grey down at five days; at 19 days they are fully feathered and greyish-brown (Cockburn 1989). **Laying months:** Somalia, April-June; Ethiopia, March and August-September; north Uganda and west Kenya, March and September; Tanzania (except northeast), September-October; coastal Kenya, July, October-November; Zambia, August-November (mainly October-November); Malaŵi, September-November; Zimbabwe, August-December (mainly October); South Africa, August-December.

Description *C. c. caudata* Sexes alike. **Adult:** forehead and sides of forecrown white. Crown and nape glossy olive-green, merging over the mantle into warm brown on the back, scapulars and tertials; rump dark blue; uppertail-coverts azure-blue. Central tail feathers dusky bluish-olive, the next feather dusky blue, and the outer four feathers brilliant azure-blue with dusky tips and small penultimate dark blue patches; the outermost tail feather is narrowed into a black streamer 90 mm long. Lores and narrow line behind eye black. Chin white; cheeks and ear-coverts lilac-rufous; throat and breast lilac, streaked with white; rest of underparts azure-blue. Upperwing-coverts greyish-blue, but largest alula feather dark purple-blue, primary coverts brilliant azure, and marginal and lesser coverts dark blue. Primaries and secondaries have the proximal half brilliant azure and the distal half dark purple-blue on the outer web and black on the inner. Bill brownish-black; eye sepia; legs and feet yellowish olive-green. *Juvenile:* forehead buffy; no distinct superciliary stripe; crown and nape brown with blue or green wash. Outermost tail feather not elongated into a streamer. Throat and breast buffy-pink, usually with a few lilac feathers mixed in, and with broader and more diffuse white streaks than on the adult. *Measurements:* wing of male 160-177, of female 157-167; tail (to fifth feather) of male 103-122, of female 99-116, streamers up to 82 mm longer on male and 74 mm on female; bill (to skull) of male 32-40, of female 35-39; tarsus of male 22-26, of female 20-23. Weight: male 87-129 (Botswana) and 92-135 (Kenya), female 93-114 (Botswana) and 93-135 (Kenya).

References Fry *et al.* (1988), van Someren (1956).

117 ABYSSINIAN ROLLER
Coracias abyssinica

Plate 38

Coracias abyssinica Hermann, 1783, Tabl. Affin. Anim., p. 197, Abyssinia.

Field identification Length 28-30 cm (11-12 in), with streamers adding up to 12 cm (5 in). Abyssinian Rollers are much the commonest roller of villages, cultivation, gardens and woodland in drier parts of Africa's northern tropical savannas. *At rest:* very like the European Roller (118), but bluer, more lightly built, and with a forked tail with very long streamers. Back rufous-brown, whole head, tail and underparts pale blue. *In flight:* forewing azure-blue with the leading edge purple; hindwing ultramarine and wingtip blackish. *Confusion species:* very like the Lilac-throated Roller (116), which overlaps with Abyssinian in a wide corridor in northeast Ethiopia and along the Rift Valley to Lake Turkana; distinctions to look for are in the throat, ear-covert, crown and hindneck colours. European Rollers are also much like Abyssinian but larger, with blackish (not ultramarine) primaries and secondaries, and without long tail-streamers; Abyssinian Rollers have whiter foreheads and faces. Juvenile Abyssinian do not have streamers and are very like juvenile European, but they are smaller, noisier, shorter-winged, look bluer, and have a more agile flight.

Voice The flight call is an abrupt, loud 'rack' or 'gak', and a perched bird utters an explosive screech 'aaaarh' from time to time. In aerial display the flight call is repeated rapidly to become a strident 'ra-ra-ra-ra-gaa-gaa-gaa-aaaaaar, aaaaar' as the bird barrels down upon an intruder.

Geographical variation None, except for a cline of increasing streamer length from west to east.

Habitat and range This roller lives in dry woodland with well-spaced trees, and readily takes to human habitation. It is particularly common where there are houses with spacious gardens, trees and open ground; it readily nests on buildings, and tolerates people, pets and vehicles. Abyssinian Rollers are also common in farmland, on pasture, tilled ground, cereal crops and cassava fields; and they occur in arid thorn-scrub savannas, around marshes, in clearings in dense woods, and pure grassland with telephone wires or the odd tree to provide a hunting post. They like to hunt along roadsides and on burnt-over ground, and are attracted to bush fires to feed on fleeing insects. Abyssinian Rollers range north to about 15°N, the edge of the Sahara, but in Mauritania they occur to 18°N (Tagant) with a vagrant at Nouadhibou (21°N), in Niger to 18°N (Aïr: Téouar), in Chad to 16°N (Ennedi) and in

Ethiopia to 17°N. In Sudan they range north to Khartoum, with vagrants at Port Sudan and in the northwest near Ain Zuwayyah. They are accidental also in Libya (Kufra Oasis) and south Egypt (Nile). From Senegal and Guinea they range to Ethiopia, and south to the borders of the rainforest zone; they breed in north Uganda and northwest Kenya, and regularly wander south, mainly along the Rift Valley, to about 1½°N, once to 2°S. A few occur in Rhamu-Mandera in northeast Kenya, and there are records of vagrants in Somalia to 47°E. Vagrants have turned up in Angola (Cabinda) and in South Yemen, where, indeed, a few have nested.

Migration Across the northern tropics this roller is resident in soudanian savannas. Further north it is mainly a summer wet-season visitor to the sahelian zone, above about 15°N; and to the guinean savannas in the south mainly a winter dry-season visitor. It visits Gambia in September-July, north Sierra Leone in December-May, north Ivory Coast from late November to early April, and Uganda in October-May. Pronounced passage occurs on the east shore of Lake Albert in October-November and in Gambia in January-March and July-August.

Food Grasshoppers, crickets, beetles and caterpillars.

Habits Abyssinian Rollers live in pairs or in well-spaced family parties, with male and female generally hunting at least 50 m apart. They feed like other rollers, scanning the ground from a tree, rooftop or telephone wire, flying down, gliding the last few metres, alighting and seizing the prey in the bill, or sometimes hopping clumsily after it. Some insects are caught in flight. Up to 20 individuals gather at a bush fire or around a herd of antelopes, and feed on the insects that are put up. A roller will even exploit a wheatear when it accidentally disturbs grasshoppers. These rollers are highly territorial. A perched bird challenges an incomer by calling 'aaaaar-aaaaar', with the body horizontal, head lowered and half-spread tail raised straight up; then it may give chase. In territorial advertisement a bird rises in the air to 10-20 m high, then suddenly stalls, plunges down on closed wings, levels out and flies fast for 50 m, shrieking and rolling rapidly from side to side about the body axis; then it uses its momentum to sweep up again on closed wings and repeats the sequence. Raucous flights, without rolling, are often directed aggressively at a human being's head, the bird veering away at the last moment, missing by 1-2 m. **Nesting:** the 3-6 eggs, usually four, are laid on a few bits of vegetable matter in a small cavity in masonry, under eaves, in a tree, palm trunk, or termite-hill. **Laying months:** Mauritania, Senegal and Gambia, April-July; Mali, February-April; Nigeria, March-June; Ethiopia, May to about October; Kenya, about April-May.

Description Sexes alike. **Adult:** chin, forehead and above eye white; the rest of the head and neck light blue, richer towards the hindneck. Mantle, scapulars and tertials rufous-brown; back, rump and uppertail-coverts ultramarine. Tail long, forked, with the central two feathers dusky bluish-brown, and the outer five with dark blue bases and increasing amounts of brilliant azure-blue; the long thin streamers are black. Throat, breast, belly, flanks and undertail-coverts pale blue, the throat lightly streaked with white. Lesser wing-coverts purple, all other upperwing- and underwing-coverts brilliant azure; primaries and secondaries ultramarine, with azure bases which in the upperwing are mainly concealed under the coverts. Bill brownish-black; eye pale brown; legs and feet yellow-brown or yellowish olive-brown. **Juvenile:** like the adult, but duller, with crown, hindneck, chin and breast washed with olive-brown, back, scapulars and tertials darker, and purple-blues in the wing not so sharply delineated from the pale blues. It lacks tail-streamers. **Measurements:** wing of male 151-171, of female 152-167; tail of male 124-135, of female 152-167, excluding streamers up to 181 mm longer than the central feathers on males and 115 mm on females; bill (to skull) of male 41-45, of female 36-41; tarsus of male 22-24, of female 20-23. Weight: 99-140.

Reference Fry et al. (1988).

Coracias garrulus

Coracias garrulus Linnaeus, 1758, Syst. Nat., ed. 10, I, p. 107, Sweden.

Field identification Length 31-32 cm (12½ in). The only roller in its breeding range, except for marginal overlap with the Indian Roller (113) in Iran, but several similar species inhabit its African wintering grounds. European Rollers are rather crow- or jay-like birds, called 'Blue Crows' in several European languages. *At rest:* there is a short black streak through the eye and white about the base of the bill, but otherwise the whole head, neck and underparts are uniformly bright light blue; mantle, scapulars and tertials rufous-brown; wings purple and light blue; and tail dark with pale blue sides. *In flight:* primaries and secondaries are solid black above, ultramarine below; upperwing-coverts and wing-lining are pale blue. *Confusion species:* in the Middle East this roller is readily distinguished from Indian Rollers by its solid blue head and neck (Indian Rollers have a greenish cap, brown neck and white-striped throat), black (not blue) primaries and secondaries, absence of a brilliant pale blue band near the wingtip, and tail with black blobs at the corners but no terminal blue band. In flight neck and tail look longer than on Indian Rollers. In Africa, adult Racket-tailed (115), Lilac-breasted (116) and Abyssinian Rollers (117) are told by their tail-streamers. Otherwise, Racket-tails are like European, but have a gradual, not abrupt, distinction between hindneck and mantle colours and have dark blue primaries and secondaries with a bright azure-blue wingbar. Young and streamer-moulted adult Abyssinian are very like European Rollers, but they have ultramarine (not black) uppersides to the primaries and secondaries, a brighter rufous back, and a cleaner-looking, solid pale blue forewing (European Rollers have pale blue primary coverts, greenish grey-blue greater and median coverts, and dark blue alula).

Voice A short gruff 'rack', a chattering 'rack rack rackrak ak', a screeching 'aaaarrr' of warning (rhymes with 'air'), and in rolling display flight a loud 'ra-ra-

ra-ra-raa-raa-aaaaaar, aaaaar', crescendo, lasting up to 3 seconds.

Geographical variation There are two subspecies, with only slight colour differences.

C. g. garrulus Northwest Africa, Asia Minor, Europe, and southwest Siberia.

C. g. semenowi Iraq, Iran (except the northwest, where the nominate race breeds), east to Kashmir and north to Turkmeniya, south Kazakhstan and west Sinkiang (China). Like *garrulus*, but head and neck paler blue, back browner, rump paler purple, underparts (particularly the throat) paler and greener blue, and marginal band of purple-blue in the forewing narrower.

Habitat and range In their breeding range European Rollers are birds of warm, sunny lowlands, and they shun the unstable maritime climates of northwest Europe. They do not seek open water and avoid treeless steppe and plains; otherwise they occur in practically all open habitats from sea level up to 600 m (occasionally up to 1000 m in Europe and 2000 m in Morocco). They particularly favour oak forests and old pinewoods with heathery clearings, and are locally common in mixed farmland, orchards, broad river valleys and dry, dissected thorn plains. From north Morocco, Algeria and Tunisia they range through Spain and east Portugal (north to 42½°N) to south France, Sardinia, Sicily and lowland Italy, then rather more commonly from Istria to Estonia and to Gulf of Corinth (Greece), and from there to Siberia, Sinkiang and Kashmir. Rollers formerly inhabited Sweden, Denmark and west Germany; a few still breed in east Germany. They breed south to 31°N in Morocco, to Cyprus, Palestine, the Euphrates, and the central Makran foothills of west Pakistan. In Africa European Rollers winter in arid thornbush country, dry wooded savannas, sisal fields, smallholdings in derived savannas near the rainforest zone, and in montane forest clearings. Scarce in West Africa, they winter from Ethiopia to Angola and South Africa, most abundantly in coastal lowlands from south Somalia to Tanzania, and in a broad belt from coastal Angola through northeast Namibia and Botswana to Zimbabwe, Transvaal and south Mozambique.

Population Despite continuing withdrawal from northern Europe, marked decreases in parts of southern Europe and sustained persecution in Italy, Oman and elsewhere, European Rollers still number millions. From roadside counts it has been estimated that 500,000-700,000 winter in Tsavo National Park and 2-3 million throughout east Kenya, where they outnumber all other *Coracias* rollers five to seven times (Brown and Brown 1973); they are just as abundant in parts of Tanzania, Namibia and Botswana. On passage, 500 birds were once seen along 50 km of roadside wires in Atbara (Sudan) in October, hundreds at Zeila (Somalia) in October, 5,000 at Dodoma (Tanzania) in December, and 40,000-50,000 at Balad (Somalia) on one day in April. They nest at a density of about 15 pairs per 100 km^2, but in prime oak or pinewood habitats concentrations of four, six and nine breeding pairs in 1 km^2 have been found (Cramp 1985).

Migration European Rollers winter exclusively in Africa, mainly in the east and south. Ringing recoveries suggest that they travel the 10,000 km from east Europe to central Africa at an average speed of 67 km per day, and return in spring at 110 km per day (Glutz and Bauer 1980). In the first half of April there is a spectacular mass movement northward along the coasts of Tanzania, Kenya and Somalia, with tens or hundreds of thousands passing a given locality in a matter of hours (Ash and Miskell 1980; Feare 1983). They fly high, at 300-500 m, widely and evenly spaced in a column several kilometres wide, travelling at about 48 km/h. From Cape Gardafui (Somalia) they cross 600 km of sea to make a landfall in Dhofar (Oman); large numbers are known then to cross a further 600 km of unremitting desert in the interior of Oman. In Oman resting and feeding migrants are gregarious, forming loose flocks of 10-30 individuals seen commonly from mid April to mid May, occasionally in thousands; there is a more protracted and less numerous passage in autumn. European Rollers stay in southern Africa from October to April or May, and visit southwest Cape Province from December to February. Vagrants have been found north to the Faeroes, and in the Azores, Madeira, Canaries, Aldabra, Seychelles and Novaya Zemlya.

Food Hard insects, mainly beetles; also grasshoppers, locusts, crickets, cicadas, mantises, wasps, bees, ants, termites, flies, butterflies and caterpillars. Animals other than insects comprise about 3% of prey: scorpions, millipedes, centipedes, spiders, worms, molluscs, frogs, lizards, snakes, small mammals and birds.

Habits European Rollers occur mainly in ones and twos; on their breeding grounds they are aggressively territorial and drive other birds away, but migrants flock together densely. They spend much time perching on a telegraph wire or treetop, scanning the ground. Seeing an insect, a bird drops straight down or more often flies down at a shallow angle ending in a glide, alights and grabs it in the bill. Small items are eaten on the spot, and large ones taken back to the perch to be beaten until immobilised. Several neat, brownish pellets are regurgitated daily. In Africa the birds are attracted from afar to bush fires and to swarms of locusts or termites. European Rollers do not hop along a perch but always fly to change station, however short the distance. Flight is easy and buoyant, with regular, rather rapid and shallow beats. They sometimes hop clumsily on the ground after an insect. In 'rolling' territorial displays on their breeding grounds, males fly with deep wingbeats high above the trees, giving a slow series of 'rak' calls. Ascending almost vertically, they suddenly tip forward and dive down steeply, flapping strongly, gathering speed, levelling out and as they do so rolling the body to left and right about its long axis. 'Rolling' is accompanied by a raucous 'rairrairrairrairr . . .', accelerando and crescendo, like a football rattle (Cramp 1985). Rising high in the air again, a bird may repeat the display a few times without pause. **_Nesting:_** nests are in natural or woodpecker holes in trees, usually an old pine or oak, mainly 5-10 m up; they are unlined. Occasional pairs use cavities in masonry, or dig tunnels 60 cm long in a sandy bank. The 2-6 (usually four) eggs are incubated mainly by the female, who starts before the clutch has been completed. Incubation lasts about 18 days, and the fledging period is 26-27 days. *Laying months:* May-July, mainly mid June to mid July.

Description *C. g. garrulus* Sexes alike. *Adult:* forehead and chin and sometimes the sides of the forecrown are white; lores and a small triangle of bare skin behind the eye are black. The rest of the head, neck and underparts are bright pale blue, the throat and breast shaft-streaked with white. Mantle rufous-brown, sharply demarcated from the blue hindneck; scapulars, tertials and inner greater wing-coverts also rufous-brown; back, rump and uppertail-coverts ultramarine. Central two tail feathers dark olive-grey, remaining tail feathers greenish azure-blue with darker bases; the outermost tail feather projects a few millimetres and is black-ended (ultramarine below). Marginal wing-coverts purple; lesser, median and greater coverts blue-grey; primary coverts and base of primaries brilliant azure-blue; rest of primaries and secondaries black above, purple-blue below. Wing-lining pale blue; tail below mainly pale blue. Bill brownish-black; eye light brown; legs and feet yellow-brown. *Juvenile:* like the adult, but duller: head and tail olivaceous-green, breast and lesser wing-coverts strongly washed with rufous; tail lacks black corners; cheeks, chin, throat and breast narrowly streaked with white. *Measurements:* wing of male 194-210, of female 189-201; tail of male 116-123, of female 112-124; bill of male 28-33, of female 26-34; tarsus of male 23-26, of female 23-25. Weight: (Europe) male 127-160, female 130-154; (Africa) 103-140.

References Cramp (1985), Fry *et al.* (1988).

119 BLUE-BELLIED ROLLER — Plate 39
Coracias cyanogaster

Coracias cyanogaster Cuvier, 1817, Règne Anim., I, p. 401, Sénégal.

Field identification Length 28-30 cm (11-12 in), excluding streamers of 6 cm (2¼ in). An unmistakable roller restricted to mature savanna woodland, from Gambia to northeast Zaïre. *At rest:* the whole head, neck, breast and upper mantle are buffy- or chalky-white, and the belly and undertail-coverts are dark ultramarine-blue: both features unique among rollers. The back is brown and wings and tail blue. There are short streamers. *In flight:* the white head and dark blue belly are easily seen. Wings are dark blue with a distinctive, broad pale azure stripe at the base of the flight feathers.

Voice A dry, clicking 'ga-ga-gaa-ga . . . ', uttered at a rate of 3-5 notes per second, for up to 5 seconds; rather like the call of the Broad-billed Roller (121).

Geographical variation None.

Habitat and range Blue-bellied Rollers are practically confined to undisturbed West African savanna woodlands dominated by *Isoberlinia* trees (which are related to the widespread *Brachystegia* of the southern tropics). This tree is typical of the moist guinean zone. They also inhabit derived savanna woods close to the borders of the rainforest zone, plantations, burnt-over clearings in rainforest near its northern edges, the borders of gallery forests and dense woodland abutting onto wet grassland, and *Borassus* palm groves near marshes and streams. From Senegal, Gambia, Guinea and north Sierra Leone, they range through south Mali and Burkina Faso, Ivory Coast and Ghana (except for the rainforest zone), Togo, Benin, Nigeria, north Cameroon, south Chad, Central African Republic and northeast Zaïre, to south Sudan from Kajo Kaji to Maridi. In Mauritania they are found only in the Guidimaka area, and in Niger have been seen in 'W' National Park, Gaya and Bengou.

Population Blue-bellied Rollers are frequent to abundant in the west of their range, but become increasingly scarce in the east. In the *Isoberlinia* woods of south Ivory Coast they reach a density of ten birds per 15 ha near Lamto; but they are scarce in the north guinean woodlands, occurring north only to Fergessedougou and Odienne. They are uncommon in Ghana and Nigeria.

Migration This fine roller is resident in the south of its range, where numbers are supplemented by visitors in the dry season, from October to February and particularly in December-January. Conversely, at that season some birds withdraw from northern parts of the range; in north Ghana all do, and the species is absent from September to January.

Food In Ivory Coast they eat mainly grasshoppers (30% of prey), beetles (chafers, scarabs, weevils, longhorns: 28%), winged termites and ants (16%) and bugs (10%). They also take wasps, mantises, ant-lion larvae, millipedes, earthworms, small skinks and snakes, and occasionally oil-palm nuts.

Habits Blue-bellied Rollers occur in pairs or small groups. In southern Ivory Coast they live all year in groups of 3-6 birds, and exceptionally up to 20, which interact socially with each other all day, calling, chasing, flying and roosting together. The flight is direct, not undulating, with rapid, even, shallow beats, looking quite leisurely. A bird perches in the open, high up the side of a tall tree, and when it spots prey on the ground it flies down, ending in a fast glide. Most food is caught on the ground, but about 20% of items are taken on the wing. This species is monogamous or polygamous, and territorial. Males appear greatly to outnumber females.

Courtship involves fast chases on the wing, with the following bird breaking away and rocketing earthwards, rolling from side to side about its body axis, calling raucously all the while. Not all pairs or groups attempt to nest in any one year. **Nesting:** nests and eggs have not been described. They are in a cavity about 10 m up in a tree or palm, often too fragile for a person to climb. **Laying months:** Senegal and Gambia, April-July; south Ivory Coast, February-September.

Description Sexes alike. **Adult:** lores and a small mark behind the eye are black; otherwise the entire head and neck, upper mantle, chin, throat and breast are pale pinkish-fawn, almost white about the face. Lower mantle, scapulars and tertials are dark brown; back, rump and uppertail-coverts glossy ultramarine; tail azure, with the tip darker blue. Belly, flanks and undertail-coverts glossy dark ultramarine. Wings glossy dark blue, with an azure stripe 2-3 cm wide across the base of the primaries and secondaries. Underwing azure, with the distal halves of all flight feathers blue-black; underside of the tail azure-blue. Bill black; eye light brown; legs and feet dark olive-green. **Juvenile:** like the adult, but duller; no streamers. **Measurements:** wing of male 173-191, of female 169-187; tail of male 104-125, of female 91-112, excluding streamers of up to 6 cm on both sexes; bill (to skull) of male 42-46, of female 36-40; tarsus of male 24-28, of female 24-27. Weight: male 112-178, female 110-150.

References Fry *et al.* (1988), Thiollay (1971, 1978, 1985). We have not yet been able to consult the recent paper on this roller's social and sexual behaviour by Moynihan (1990) (but see review by J. Dumbacher in *Auk* 108, 1991: 457-458).

120 BLUE-THROATED ROLLER
Eurystomus gularis

Plate 39

Eurystomus gularis Vieillot, 1819, Nouv. Dict. Hist. Nat., 29, p. 426, Sierra Leone.

Field identification Length 25 cm (10 in). Broad-billed rollers – two rufous species in Africa and Madagascar and two blue ones in Asia and Australia – are smaller than *Coracias* rollers, with short, very broad, bright yellow or red bills. They are long-winged, buoyant, aerobatic fliers which feed exclusively on the wing and often look falcon-like. *At rest:* Blue-throated Rollers are treetop birds restricted to the equatorial and West African rainforest zone: dumpy, large-headed and thick-necked, dark chestnut with bright yellow bill, blue throat and tail and purple-blue wings (often hardly any purple can be seen in the closed wing). Juveniles have largely bluish underparts. *In flight:* looks thickset, quite long-winged, with falcon-like silhouette and flight action. The wings above are dark purple with chestnut-rufous coverts; below they are dark blue and lilac-rufous, lacking the strong contrast of *Coracias* rollers. The tail is pale blue with a dark blue tip, and is shallowly forked. *Confusion species:* the Broad-billed Roller (121) is very similar, but is larger, with paler underparts which are lilac (not chestnut). Main differences are that the Broad-bill has the throat lilac (not blue), vent and undertail-coverts pale blue (not dark brown), uppertail-coverts grey-blue (not blue-black), and greater coverts ultramarine-blue (not chestnut).

Voice A shrill chatter of squawks repeated about 17 times in 5 seconds.

Geographical variation Two subspecies.
E. g. gularis Guinea to south Nigeria.
E. g. neglectus South Cameroon to Lake Victoria and northwest Angola, intergrading with *gularis* between Cross River (Nigeria) and Mt Cameroon. Upperparts a richer chestnut; uppertail-coverts washed with purple-blue and underparts washed with lilac. Larger: wing up to 170 mm.

Habitat and range Blue-throated Rollers keep to high treetops and hunt above the canopy of primary and secondary forest, oil-palm plantations, cocoa farms, gallery-forest strips and remnant patches of forest in derived savannas. They like forest clearings, riversides, and giant emergent trees. Common throughout, they range from Sierra Leone and adjacent parts of Guinea, through Liberia and southern parts of Ivory Coast, Ghana, Nigeria and Cameroon, to Gabon, Congo, Cabinda, Angola (Cuanza Norte and north Lunda), Zaïre except Katanga, Rwanda, and south Uganda east to Kampala. The species is not migratory.

Food Flying ants (*Crematogaster,*

Oecophylla) form 90% of the diet, and the rest is termites, beetles, bugs, bees, crickets, cockroaches and flies. A very few moths, centipedes, frogs and small fruits are eaten also.

Habits Blue-throated Rollers perch solitarily or in pairs, 10-40 m up in the forest, sitting on a bare branch often at the very top of the canopy. Sometimes they sit for long periods, calling from time to time; at other times they are active, hawking for insects and chasing away a variety of other bird species that have entered their territory. Foraging starts in earnest in the late afternoon, when rollers quit their territories and gather in flocks of 10-20 birds, both Blue-throated and Broad-billed Rollers, to feed on ants and termites as they fly in millions after rain. With powerful but graceful flight, wheeling, stooping and chasing acrobatically around the treetops, the birds catch large numbers of insects, eating them on the wing, and feed actively almost until nightfall. At dusk two birds were found to have eaten 714 and 748 insects, which weighed nearly 40 g (Thiollay 1970). Pairs nest solitarily; territorial defence and courtship involve a great deal of noisy aerial chasing. *Nesting:* The 2-3 eggs are laid in an unlined cavity, usually at least 10 m up in a dead tree at the edge of a forest clearing. *Laying months:* Ivory Coast, February-March; Ghana, February-April; Nigeria, April and evidently September; Gabon, about January; Zaïre, about April (Medje) and October (Lukolela).

Description *E. g. gularis* Sexes alike. *Adult:* upperparts from forehead to rump, scapulars, tertials, and lesser, median and greater wing-coverts all cinnamon-chestnut. Uppertail-coverts, central pair of tail feathers and tail-tip blue-black; sides of the tail bright pale blue. Lores and chin dusky; throat pale blue in the centre, grading through lilac to cinnamon on the breast, sides of the neck and ear-coverts. Belly, flanks and undertail-coverts dark cinnamon, the last with dark blue tips. Primaries and secondaries dark blue with blackish tips and black inner webs; primary coverts dark blue. Underwing-coverts cinnamon, washed with lilac and tipped with purple; underside of primaries and secondaries dark azure-blue, and underside of tail pale blue with a dusky tip. Bill bright yellow; eye hazel-brown; legs and feet olive-green. *Juvenile:* like the adult, but duller, above somewhat scaly, the feathers dark grey with brown-rufous edges; chin, throat and upper breast rufous-brown, lower breast dull blue-grey, flanks pale grey, belly bluish, undertail-coverts pale blue. Bill yellowish with the culmen dark brown; legs and feet grey-brown. *Measurements:* wing of male 154-163, of female 148-158; tail of male 92-97, of female 89-98, depth of fork 13-19; bill (to skull) of male 26-28, of female 23-29, width 23-25; tarsus of male 13-16, of female 13-16. Weight: male 82-110, female 88-108.

References Fry *et al.* (1988), Thiollay (1970, 1971, 1978).

121 BROAD-BILLED ROLLER   Plate 39
Eurystomus glaucurus

Coracias·glaucurus P.L.S. Müller, 1776, Natursyst., Suppl., p. 86, Madagascar.

Field identification Length 29-30 cm (11½ in). A rather small and compact roller found throughout all but the driest parts of Madagascar and tropical Africa, and readily told from other African rollers (except the Blue-throated, 120) by its predominantly dark rufous plumage and stubby bright yellow bill. *At rest:* rufous-chestnut above, deep lilac below, with a short, stout, very wide yellow bill, and mainly blue tail. It tends to perch solitarily near the top of an isolated tall tree. Adults have pale blue undertail-coverts, and juveniles have the underparts below the breast entirely dull blue. *In flight:* a chunky, falcon-like rufous bird with rather short, shallowly-forked tail and quite long blue-black and rufous wings lacking the strikingly contrasted azure and purple patterns of *Coracias* rollers. The yellow bill is readily apparent from afar. It feeds on the wing; flight easy, powerful and dashing. *Confusion species:* Blue-throated Rollers overlap with the Broad-bill in the equatorial and West African rainforest zone; they are smaller, with a small blue patch in the throat, rufous (not lilac) breast and belly, rufous (not pale blue) undertail-coverts, and blackish (not pale blue) uppertail-coverts. The Broad-billed is the only roller in the Malagasy region.

Voice At rest, typically 4-6 guttural, nasal, snarling or growling notes uttered in 3-4 seconds: '(g)iaow, grrrd, grrrd-grrrd, g-r-g'; a long rattling 'g-r-r-r-r-r-r-r-r-d' or 'kik-k-k-k-k-k-k-k-r-r-r-r-r'. The sequence is repeated a few times, with pauses of 2-3 seconds. In flight an excited screaming chatter, somewhat falcon-like: 'crik-crik-crik-crik', increasing in volume.

Geographical variation There are three subspecies in Africa (other authors recognise more), varying mainly in hue and size, and another one in Madagascar with the same plumage but much larger.

E. g. afer From Senegal through Nigeria to Sudan. Central uppertail-coverts brown and lateral ones pale greenish-blue.

E. g. aethiopicus Ethiopia, intergrading with *afer* in Sudan and with *suahelicus* in Uganda and Kenya. Like *afer*, but rufous and lilac parts brighter, and larger, with the wing averaging 7% longer.

E. g. suahelicus Intergrades with *afer* and *aethiopicus* between latitude 5°N and the Equator, ranging southward to Angola, Transvaal and Zululand. Rufous and lilac parts brighter than in *aethiopicus*; sides of head strongly washed with lilac; uppertail-coverts all blue. Slightly larger than *afer*.

E. g. glaucurus Madagascar, wintering in eastern Africa. Like *suahelicus*, but vent and undertail-coverts dark grey-blue (not pale blue), and about 16% larger: wing 190-220 mm, tail 101-126 mm.

Habitat and range Broad-billed Rollers inhabit large clearings and the borders of rivers in the rainforest zone, thick savanna woodland, farmland with scattered trees, wooded hillsides, grassy plains with a few clumps of trees, and palm groves and *Acacia* woods along watercourses in dry country; in short, all types of country with tall trees, particularly near water. They range throughout the tropics, north generally to about 13°N, or 14°N in Senegal and Kordofan and 16°N in Ethiopia, and south to Botswana (Okavango), Namibia (Caprivi Strip), Zimbabwe, the Transvaal lowveld, Mozambique and Swaziland. However, the species is absent from most of Eritrea, southeast Ethiopia, Somalia (except the lower Juba and Shebelle valleys), and north and much of east Kenya.

Population Frequent to common throughout their range, they are sometimes abundant: in savanna-forest mosaic countryside near Lamto, Ivory Coast, the mean density is 570 adults in 25 km^2, or about one per 4 ha.

Migration Madagascan birds are non-breeding visitors to the savannas of east Zaïre and perhaps Tanzania from February to November. They occur on passage in Tanzania, Malawi, east Zambia, northeast Zimbabwe and Mozambique, mainly in April and October. African populations are wet-season breeding visitors in the north and south of their range. For instance, in the sahelian zone in Mali, south Niger and northeast Nigeria they occur from April-May to October-November, and south of it, in the soudanian zone, from May-June to September-October. In southern Africa, south of 10°S, they visit Zambia from September to April and Zimbabwe and South Africa from September to March or early April. Within some 10° of the Equator some individuals are present in all months, but they move so as to vacate regions when the rainfall is greatest, about May-September north of the Equator and November-March south of it. In East Africa movements are complex; for example, rollers visit Tsavo East National Park mainly in November-May, most of Tanzania in October-April, but Arusha National Park mainly in August-January. Daytime migration is not often very evident, but flocks migrate through Gambia in November and December, and up to 500 birds have been seen moving south in Sudan in August.

Food Largely swarming ants (*Crematogaster, Oecophylla*) and termites (*Macrotermes, Pseudacanthotermes*), which form 80% of the insects taken. The rest is beetles and bugs of 14 families including cicadas, also grasshoppers, crickets, mantises, cockroaches, bees, wasps, flies and spiders.

Habits Broad-billed Rollers spend most of the day sitting solitarily or in pairs on some tall treetop, hardly feeding at all, but calling often and aggressively chasing away hornbills, crows, hawks, parrots, and other rollers. In the late afternoon they vacate their territory and join others of their species in hunting for hatches of winged ants and termites. Locating a swarm, a flock of up to 280 rollers feeds silently but excitedly, dashing around in buoyant, wheeling flight with fast, straight or curving glides and erratic twists and turns. Six to ten insects are caught in the bill per minute; feeding until nightfall, each roller takes 200-800 insects. These rollers drink like a swallow, by flying in a straight line for several hundred metres over unruffled water, dipping the bill in a few times; they also dive into water, presumably to bathe. They are monogamous and highly territorial. Territories are well demarcated, and contain several regularly used perches which are defended to a distance of 300 m. **Nesting:** the nest is an unlined cavity high up in the trunk or a major limb of a baobab, locust-bean, mahogany or other tall tree; 2-3 eggs are laid. One year, 147 pairs of these rollers near Lamto in Ivory Coast produced 206 fledglings; about 200 other adults failed to nest (Thiollay 1971, 1978). **Laying months:** in south Ivory Coast, March-May, but in the north and in Senegal, Burkina Faso, Ghana and Nigeria, May-July; Ethiopia, March, October-November; Uganda, January-April (mainly March-April); Kenya and Zambia, September-November; Malawi, September, December; Zimbabwe, September-December (mainly October-November); South Africa, October-December.

Description *E. g. afer* Sexes alike. **Adult:** forehead to rump, scapulars, lesser and median upperwing-coverts, and central uppertail-coverts all rich cinnamon-rufous. Lateral uppertail-coverts and central two tail feathers dull blue; other tail feathers are azure-blue with black tips and a dark blue penultimate band. Eyebrow, ear-coverts and throat pale lilac; narrow orbital ring of feathers, lores and chin lilac-rufous; breast and belly lilac; flanks, vent and undertail-coverts pale blue. Primaries, secondaries, primary and greater coverts dark blue. Underwing-coverts lilac and pale grey-blue; under-sides of primaries and secondaries pale blue and silver-grey. Underside of tail glossy pale blue with a dusky tip. Bill bright yellow; eye hazel or dark brown; legs and feet olive, soles dull yellow. *Juvenile:* like the adult, but cinnamon parts are tinged with brown and dark blue feathers are edged with blue-green; the lores are blackish, ear-coverts, chin and throat brown, and breast and belly dull

blue. The bill is yellow, with the culmen brown. *Measurements:* wing of male 166-180, of female 165-175; tail (central feathers) of male 85-89, of female 84-93, the outer feathers about 13 mm longer on males and 7 mm on females; bill (to skull) of male 27-32, of female 27-32, width 20-23; tarsus of male 17-18, of female 17-18. Weight: male 94-114, female 84-130; West African birds average 104 and East African ones 116.

References Fry *et al.* (1988), Thiollay (1970, 1971, 1978, 1985).

122 DOLLARBIRD

Plate 40

Eurystomus orientalis

Coracias orientalis Linnaeus, 1766, Syst. Nat., ed. 12, I, p. 159, 'India orientali', = Java.

Field identification Length 25-28 cm (10-11 in), but up to 34 cm (13½ in) in the Solomons. The only roller in Australia, New Guinea, the Sundas, Philippines, China, Korea, Manchuria and Japan. *At rest:* a stocky, dark greenish-blue or pur-plish bird with a large head, short thick neck, short legs, short-looking tail, and short but very broad, stout red bill. Juveniles are dusky blue with dark bills. It is active at dusk, when it looks blackish and in profile can be taken for a falcon, nightjar or owl. *In flight:* an oval pale blue or silvery window half way along the outer six primaries, the 'dollar', makes it unmistakable in good light. The wings are broad but long, and can look either pointed or round-tipped, and the tail is square-ended. *Confusion species:* in twi-light the 'dollars' are nightjar-like, but nightjars are narrower-winged, longer-tailed, and much less dashing in flight. The Dollarbird overlaps with Indian Roller (113) in India, Sri Lanka, Thailand and Indochina and with Celebes Roller (114) in Sulawesi, but is readily told by its 'dol-lars', stubby red bill and red legs.

Voice Rather silent, but occasionally it utters a raucous, hoarse, rasping 'chak', repeated after a few seconds; also a fast, accelerating series, 'krak-kak-kak' or 'kek-ek-ek-ek-ek-ek-k-k-k'. Two birds sitting

side by side sometimes give a clattering 'keta-keta-keta-keta . . .', sounding like castanets.

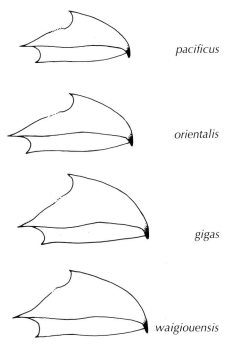

pacificus

orientalis

gigas

waigiouensis

Geographical variation Twelve subspe-cies have been recognised; we admit nine. The three Asiatic mainland ones are alike in plumage, but vary in wing, tail and bill sizes; *E. o. irisi* of Sri Lanka is similar, and *E. o. gigas* of the Andamans is alike in plumage but larger-billed. The Australian bird is paler. The three races of New Guinea, the Bismarck Archipelago and the Solomons are more purplish than the Asiatic forms, with larger bills and (in two forms) much longer tails.

E. o. abundus India (north Cachar), Nepal, north Assam, and from north China to the lower Amur and east to Manchuria; winters in India, peninsular Malaysia, Indochina, Sumatra, southern China and Japan. Wing average 193 mm, tail average 94 mm; bill depth 12-15 mm (average 13.4). Birds from north Thailand ('*deignani*') are intermediate in all characters between *abundus* and the nominate subspecies.

E. o. orientalis Southern Himalayas south to Madras, south Assam, Burma, Thailand, Indochina, Ryukyu Islands, peninsular Malaysia, Sumatra, Java, Borneo and the Philippines; winters in southeast India, the Philippines, north Sulawesi, and Halmahera. Primaries and secondaries with less purple wash than in *abundus*. Wing shorter but tail longer than in *abundus*: wing 172-200 mm (average 187); tail 92-111 mm (average 100). Bill depth 13.5-17.5 mm (average 15.8).

E. o. gigas Rutland and South Andaman Islands. Like *orientalis*, but tail longer (101-111 mm, average 107) and bill much larger (width 27-30 mm, average 28; depth 16-18 mm, average 17).

E. o. laetior Kerala north to Wynaad, west Mysore (Coorg) and west Tamil Nadu (Nilgiri). Face and crown slightly blacker than in *orientalis* and blues brighter and more purplish. Wing the same size as in *orientalis*; tail longer (97-118 mm, average 104).

E. o. irisi South-central Sri Lanka. Always rare, none was seen between 1890 and 1950, when a pair was found breeding and was shot. Rollers were rediscovered in Sinharaja Forest in 1979 and photographed at the nest in 1980, since when there have been many sight records. Like *laetior*, but smaller: wing 180-182 mm, tail 97-98 mm.

E. o. pacificus Australia: near Pilbara, from Broom to Melville and Wessel Islands, Melville Bay and Groote Eylandt, in the Leichhardt valley and on Mt Isa, on lower Flinders and Norman Rivers, and from Banks and Prince of Wales Islands through Cape York Peninsula to Melbourne; vagrant to eastern South Australia, west Tasmania, the west coast of New Zealand, and Micronesia (Palau, Yap, Pohnpei). Lores black; forehead, crown and ear-coverts olive-brown (these parts are blackish in the preceding races); hindneck, mantle and back paler and greyer than in *orientalis*; chin pale brown (not blackish); breast, belly and undertail-coverts greyish blue-green, much paler than in *orientalis*. Wing 190-200 mm (average 196), tail 89-101 mm (average 95). Birds from Sulawesi and Lombok to the Tanimbar group ('*connectens*') are intermediate between *orientalis* and *pacificus*.

E. o. waigiouensis New Guinea, Karkar, Bagabag, Western Papuan Islands, Jobi, Rook and Trobriand Islands, D'Entrecasteaux and Louisiade Archipelagos. Like *orientalis*, but blues purplish rather than greenish; purple in the wings is brighter and more extensive and the 'dollar' is better demarcated. Wing 190-200 mm (average 196), tail 89-101 mm (average 94.5); bill depth 16-19 mm (average 17.0).

E. o. crassirostris Bismarck Archipelago. Like *waigiouensis*, but bill orange-red, usually (but not always) tipped with black, and tail long. Wing 198-208 mm (average 202), tail 111-121 mm (average 116); bill depth 17-19 mm (average 17.7), bill width 26-31 mm (average 29).

E. o. solomonensis Bougainville, Buka and Feni (Anir) Islands, and probably Nissan Island. Like *waigiouensis*, but bill orange-red, and tail much longer. Wing 183-204 mm (average 196), tail 124-138 mm (average 129); bill measurements the same as in *crassirostris*.

Habitat and range Dollarbirds inhabit secondary evergreen forest, cultivated forest clearings, rubber and coffee plantations, and at high latitudes deciduous woodland, wooded riverbanks, and cleared areas with remnant scattered old trees. The range, detailed above, is from northwest India to Manchuria, Japan, Hainan, Taiwan, southeast Asia, the Andamans, Indonesia, Philippines, Sundas, Solomons and Australia; there are distinct populations in southwest India and Sri Lanka. They keep mainly to hot lowlands and foothills, breeding to altitudes of 500 m in

Kerala, 1000 m in the Himalayas and about 1400 m in southeast Asia and New Guinea. Migrants ascend to 2500 m in Queensland and have been found dead on ice at 4500 m in Irian Jaya.

Population In Australian eucalypt woodland densities vary from five to 14 individuals per km^2, and along creeks and streams territories are about 750 m apart.

Migration Most tropical populations are resident. Chinese and Japanese birds are summer visitors in April-September, wintering south to Malaysia; some winter in Japan and south China. Australian ones are summer visitors in September-March, and winter north to New Guinea, New Britain, Witu Islands, Kai Islands, Moluccas and Sulawesi; a few winter in northern Australia. Adults migrate soon after the young leave the nest, and the young depart later. Passage across Torres Strait is in March-May and October-November, and Australian breeders occupy New Guinea, where they are commoner in the north than in the south, in March-November. Migrants travel mainly by day, ones and twos passing high in the air every few seconds, but several have also been netted at night crossing Fraser's Hill, Malaysia, in October and November.

Food Mainly hard insects taken on the wing, particularly beetles; also crickets, mantises, grasshoppers, cicadas, shieldbugs, moths and termites. A few insects and occasional lizards are taken on the ground.

Habits Dollarbirds live solitarily or in pairs. For much of the day they sit inactively on a dead branch emerging from the forest canopy or an equally exposed site in a large tree in cleared land. They also use telephone wires, perching upright, wagging the tail up and down after alighting or when about to fly, but otherwise sitting stolidly, moving only the head. From time to time they fly out after a passing insect, but they feed mainly in the late afternoon and evening. Non-breeding birds often congregate at that hour and hawk actively at dusk, also before, during and after rain and in disturbed weather at any time of day. They fly swiftly, repeatedly quartering a piece of ground where insects are swarming, with strong falcon-like flapping and long fast glides. At other times flight is slower and leisurely. A bird pursuing an insect manoeuvres with speed and dexterity, like some giant swallow. Larger insects are brought back to a perch to be beaten; beetles' wing-cases are commonly broken off and dropped, and the ground below a favourite perch becomes strewn with them. In hot weather the birds sometimes come to the ground, spread the wings, raise the head and tail, and pant with the bill open. The territorial and courtship display flight can last for several minutes, with almost constant calling: a bird rises high above its territory, nose-dives at speed, rolls rapidly from side to side as it levels out, flies powerfully up again, and repeats the sequence many times in a series of steep wave-crests and rolling dives. **Nesting:** the 3-4 eggs are laid in an unlined woodpecker or barbet hole or natural hollow, 8-20 m up in the trunk or a stub of a living or dead tree. A nest is often occupied in several successive years. **Laying months:** north India, March-May; Kerala, September-May (mainly March-April); Japan, April-May; Sumatra, March; Papua New Guinea, about October-February; Bougainville, about July-September; Australia, October-January.

Description *E. o. abundus* Sexes alike. *Adult:* forehead, lores, crown, moustachial region and chin blackish-brown; ear-coverts and nape very dark olive-brown; hindneck dark olive-brown; mantle, scapulars, back and rump bluish-olive. Central tail feathers blackish with dark blue bases; outer ones blackish with purple-blue edges and greenish-blue bases. Upperwing-coverts and tertials olivaceous green-blue, secondaries black with purple-blue edges. Primary coverts purple; primaries blackish with purple edges and brilliant pale blue bases to all except the innermost three, forming a pale round patch in the spread wing 35 mm in diameter. Throat purple with narrow blue streaks; breast, flanks, belly, undertail-coverts and underwing-coverts green-blue, the breast with a greyish wash. Underside of tail, primaries and secondaries glossy purple and black, the primaries with brilliant pale blue bases. Bill vermilion, tipped with black; eye dark brown; legs and feet vermilion. *Juvenile:* like the adult, but upperparts duller and darker, particularly the mantle, scapulars and upperwing-coverts; bases of primaries much less brilliant blue, in the spread wing forming a 'dollar' which is not nearly so well defined as on the adult; throat-patch ill-defined, greenish with a few light blue streaks. Upper mandible blackish, lower mandible with some orange-red; legs and feet dull dark red.

Measurements: wing of male 186-198, of female 193-196; tail of male 91-98, of female 89-99; bill (to skull) of male 27-33, of female 30-35, width at gape 23.5; tarsus of male 19-21, of female 19-21. Weight: 120-178.

References Ali and Ripley (1970), Coates (1985), Ripley (1942), Scholtes (1980), White and Bruce (1986).

123 AZURE ROLLER   Plate 40
Eurystomus azureus

Eurystomus azureus G. R. Gray, 1860, Proc. Zool. Soc. London, 1860, p. 346, Batjan.

Field identification Length 27–30 cm (10½–12 in). The Azure is the resident roller of the Northern Moluccan Islands, where the only other rollers are occasional Dollarbirds (122) of both the southeast Asian subspecies *orientalis* and the Australian subspecies *pacificus* which reach Halmahera in 'winter'. Azure Rollers can be distinguished from the Dollarbird by their blackish forehead and crown and otherwise uniformly bright purple-blue plumage; they are larger, and longer-tailed.

Voice Not described.

Geographical variation None. This bird was formerly treated as a subspecies of the Dollarbird; we agree with Mees (1965), Scholtes (1980) and White and Bruce (1986) that its differences are so distinctive that it should be kept as a separate species.

Habitat and range It inhabits plantations, woodland and the edges of forest in the Northern Moluccan islands of Halmahera, Ternate, Tidore and Batjan. An uncommon bird, there is no evidence that it is migratory.

Habits Barely reported, presumably very like those of the Dollarbird. Azure Rollers, being larger and bigger-billed than Dollarbirds, probably take larger prey, although their food is not certainly known.

Neither is anything known of their breeding habits.

Description Sexes alike. *Adult*: except for the large, well-defined pale blue 'dollar' in the primaries, the plumage is dark purple-blue throughout, rather uniform, but tending to purple-washed black on the forehead, lores and forecrown and to black on the distal half of the tail, the undertail-coverts and the tips of the upperwing-coverts. The purple is richest on rump, tail, breast, belly, primary coverts, secondary coverts, and the edges of the primaries; the blackish-purple throat has a few glossy bright blue streaks. Pale blue-and-white patches on the inner webs of the outermost two primaries and both webs of the next five primaries form a 'dollar' 45 mm across. Bill vermilion; eye dark brown; legs and feet red. *Juvenile:* like the adult, but head, throat, mantle and breast are less glossy and not so intense a shade of purple; the throat lacks any pale streaks, and the 'dollar' is all pale blue, without the adult's white parts. Bill dusky brown, with some red on the lower mandible and at the gape; legs and feet dark red-brown. *Measurements:* wing 204-212, average 209; tail 111-117, average 114; bill (to feathers) 24-28, (to skull) 35-38, width at gape 27-29.5, depth 17-20 (average 18); tarsus 20.

References Mees (1965), Scholtes (1980), White and Bruce (1986).

BIBLIOGRAPHY

Adamson, A M (1939) Review of the fauna of the Marquesas Islands and discussion of its origin. *Bull. Bernice P. Bishop Mus.*, 159: 1-93.

Ali, S, and Ripley, S D (1970) *Handbook of the Birds of India and Pakistan*, Vol. 4. Oxford University Press, Bombay.

Andrew, D G (1990) Shearwaters, sirens and halcyons. *Brit. Birds*, 83: 334-335.

Ash, J S, and Miskell, J E (1980) A mass-migration of Rollers *Coracias garrulus* in Somalia. *Bull. Br. Orn. Club*, 100: 216-218.

Baker, E C S (1927) *The Fauna of British India: Birds*. Vol. 4, 2nd edn. Taylor & Francis, London.

Baker, E C S (1934) *The Nidification of Birds of the Indian Empire*. Vol. 3. Taylor & Francis, London.

Baker, R H (1951) The avifauna of Micronesia: its origin, evolution and distribution. *Univ. Kansas Publs Mus. Nat. Hist*, 3: 1-359.

Beehler, B M (1978) Upland birds of northeastern New Guinea. *Wau Ecol.Inst., Hbk.* 4.

Bell, H L (1970a) Field notes on birds of the Nomad River Sub-district, Papua. *Emu*, 70: 97-104.

Bell, H L (1970b) Additions to the avifauna of Goodenough Island, Papua. *Emu*, 70: 179-182.

Bell, H L (1980) Foraging ecology, territoriality and seasonality of the Common Paradise Kingfisher at Brown River, Papua New Guinea. *Corella*, 4: 113-126.

Bell, H L (1981) Information on New Guinea kingfishers, Alcedinidae *Ibis*, 123: 51-61.

Bell, H L (1982) A bird community of lowland rain forest in New Guinea. 1. Composition and density of avifauna. *Emu*, 82: 24-41.

Benson, C W (1960) The birds of the Comoro Islands: results of the British Ornithologists' Union Centenary Expedition 1958. *Ibis*, 103B: 5-106.

Benson, C W, Colebrook-Robjent, J F R, and Williams, A (1976) Contribution à l'ornithologie de Madagascar. *Oiseau et Rev. fr. Orn.*, 46: 209-242.

Betts, B J, and Betts, D L (1977) The relation of hunting site changes to hunting success in Green Herons and Green Kingfishers. *Condor*, 79: 269-271.

Blakers, M, Davies, S J J F, and Reilly, P N (1984) *The Atlas of Australian Birds*. RAOU/ University of Melbourne Press, Melbourne.

Boag, D (1982) *The Kingfisher*. Blandford Press, Poole.

Bourne, W R P, Mackrill, E J, and Yésou, P (1988) The Yelkouan Shearwater *Puffinus (puffinus?) yelkouan*. *Brit. Birds*, 81: 306-319.

Brooke, R K, and Herroelen, P (1988) The nonbreeding range of southern African bred European Bee-eaters *Merops apiaster*. *Ostrich*, 59: 63-66.

Brosset, A, and Darchen, R (1967) Une curieuse succession d'hôtes parasites des nids de *Nasutitermes*. *Biol. Gabonica*, 3: 153-168.

Brosset, A, and Erard, C (1986) *Les Oiseaux des Régions Forestières du Nord-Est du Gabon*. Société National de Protection de la Nature, Paris.

Brown, L H, and Brown, B E (1973) The relative numbers of migrant and resident rollers in eastern Kenya. *Bull. Br. Orn. Club*, 93: 126-130.

Bryant, D M, and Hails, C J (1983) Energetics and growth patterns of three tropical bird species. *Auk*, 100: 425-439.

Bryant, D M, and Bryant, V M T (1988) Assimilation efficiency and growth of nestling insectivores. *Ibis*, 130: 268-274.

Burton, P J (1978) Notes on some waders and kingfishers in Sarawak. *Sarawak Mus. J.*, 26: 195-204.

Calver, M C, Saunders, D A, and Porter, B D (1987) The diet of nestling Rainbow Bee-eaters, *Merops ornatus*, on Rottnest Island, Western Australia, and observations on a non-destructive method of diet analysis. *Aust. Wildl. Res.*, 14: 541-550.

Carroll, R W (1988) Birds of the Central African Republic. *Malimbus*, 10: 177-200.

Carruthers, R K (1975) Banding and observations of Rainbow Bee-eaters. *Aust. Bird Bander.*, 13: 71-74.

de Castro, J J, and de Castro, M (1990) The Blue-breasted Kingfisher *Halcyon malimbica* in south-west Ethiopia. *Scopus*, 14: 22.

Cherrie, G K (1916) A contribution to the ornithology of the Orinoco region. *Mus. Brooklyn Inst. Arts Sci. Bull.*, 2: 133a-374.

Chinner, D W (1977) Observations on the effect of increased rainfall on birdlife in central Australia. *S. Aust. Orn.*, 27: 188-192.

Clancey, P A (1951) The characters of a new race of *Alcedo semitorquata* Swainson from the low country of Portuguese East Africa. *Ostrich*, 22: 176-178.

Clancey, P A (1965) Comments on the status of the Mangrove Kingfisher *Halcyon senegaloides* Smith in South Africa. *Ostrich*, 36: 93-94.

Clancey, P A (1969) On the status of *Coracias weigalli* Dresser, 1890. *Ostrich*, 40: 156-162.

Clancey, P A (1978) Miscellaneous taxonomic notes on African birds. Further comments on variation in *Alcedo semitorquata* Swainson, 1823; On *Alcedo leucogaster leopoldi* (Dubois), 1905. *Durban Mus. Novit.*, 11 (16): 272-281.

Clancey, P A (1984) Miscellaneous taxonomic notes on African birds, 64: An undescribed equatorial rainforest race of the Pygmy Kingfisher; On the validity of *Halcyon senegaloides ranivorus* Meinertzhagen, 1924. *Durban Mus. Novit*, 13 (14): 169-187.

Clancey, P A (1990) Comment on the geographical variation of the Malachite Kingfisher *Corythornis cristatus* of the Afrotropics. *Bull. Br. Orn. Club*, 110: 137-138.

Clarke, G (1985) Bird observations from northwest Somalia. *Scopus*, 9: 24-42.

Coates, B J (1985) *The Birds of Papua New Guinea*. Vol. I. Dove Publs, Alderley.

Cockburn, J (1989) Breeding biology of Lilac-breasted Roller. *Honeyguide*, 35: 118.

Colston, P R, and Curry-Lindahl, K (1986) *The Birds of Mount Nimba, Liberia*. British Museum (Natural History), London.

Cornwell, G W (1963) Observations on the breeding biology and behaviour of a nesting population of Belted Kingfishers. *Condor*, 65: 426-431.

Cramp, S (ed.) (1985) *The Birds of the Western Palearctic*. Vol. 4. Oxford University Press, Oxford.

Crawford, D N (1979) Effects of grass and fires on birds in the Darwin area, Northern Territory. *Emu*, 79: 150-152.

Crick, H Q P (1987) Intra-specific robbery by Red-throated Bee-eaters. *Ostrich*, 58: 140-141.

Diamond, J M (1972) Avifauna of the Eastern Highlands of New Guinea. *Publ. Nuttall Orn. Club*, 12: 1-438.

Diamond, J M, and Marshall, A G *(1977)* Niche shifts in New Hebridean birds. *Emu*, 77: 61-72.

Dickerman, R W (1989) Notes on the Malachite Kingfisher *Corythornis (Alcedo) cristata. Bull. Br. Orn. Club*, 109: 158-159.

Douthwaite, R J (1973) Pied Kingfisher *Ceryle rudis* populations. *Ostrich*, 44: 89-94.

Douthwaite, R J (1976) Fishing techniques and foods of the Pied Kingfisher on Lake Victoria in Uganda. *Ostrich*, 47: 153-160.

Douthwaite, R J (1978) Breeding biology of the Pied Kingfisher *Ceryle rudis* on Lake Victoria. *J. East Africa Nat. Hist. Soc.*, 31 (166): 1-12.

Douthwaite, R J (1982) Changes in Pied Kingfisher (*Ceryle rudis*) feeding related to endosulfan pollution from tsetse fly control operations in the Okavango delta, Botswana. *J. Appl. Ecol.*, 19: 133-141.

Douthwaite, R J (1986) Effects of drift sprays of endosulfan, applied for tsetse-fly control, on breeding Little Bee-eaters in Somalia. *Environm. Pollut.* (ser. A), 41: 11-22.

Douthwaite, R J, and Fry, C H (1982) Food and feeding behaviour of the little bee-eater *Merops pusillus* in relation to tsetse fly control by insecticides. *Biol. Conserv.*, 23: 71-78.

Earlé, R A (1991). Bee-eaters taking earthworms on the ground. *Brit. Birds*, 84: 61-62.

Elgood, J H, Fry, C H, and Dowsett, R J (1973) African migrants in Nigeria. *Ibis*, 115: 1-45 and 375-411.

Emlen, S T (1990) White-fronted Bee-eaters: helping in a colonially nesting species. Pp 489-526 in P B Stacey and W D Koenig (eds.), *Cooperative Breeding in Birds*, Cambridge University Press, Cambridge.

Emlen, S T, and Wrege, P H (1986) Forced copulations and intra-specific parasitism: two costs of social living in the white-fronted bee-eater. *Ethology*, 71: 2-29.

Emlen, S T, and Wrege, P H (1988) The role of kinship in helping decisions among white-fronted bee-eaters. *Behav. Ecol. Sociobiol.*, 23: 305-315.

Emlen, S T, and Wrege, P H (1989) A test of alternate hypotheses for helping behavior in white-fronted bee-eaters of Kenya. *Behav. Ecol. Sociobiol.*, 25: 303-319.

Emlen, S T, and Wrege, P H (1991) Breeding biology of White-fronted Bee-eaters at Nakuru: the influence of helpers on breeder fitness. *J. Anim. Ecol.*, 60: 309-326.

Emlen, S T, Wrege, P H, Demong, N J, and Hegner, R E (1991) Flexible growth rates in nestling White-fronted Bee-eaters: a possible adaptation to short-term food shortage. *Condor*, 93: 591-597.

Feare, C J (1983) Mass spring migration of European Rollers *Coracias garrulus* in eastern Tanzania. *Bull. Br. Orn. Club*, 103: 39-40.

Forbes-Watson, A D (1969) Notes on birds observed in the Comoros on behalf of the Smithsonian Institution. *Atoll Res. Bull.*, 128: 1-23.

Forshaw, J M (1983-) *Kingfishers and Related Birds* Vol. 1 (1983): *Alcedinidae Ceryle* to *Cittura*. Vol. 2 (1985): *Alcedinidae Halcyon* to *Tanysiptera*. Vol. 3 (1987): *Todidae, Momotidae, Meropidae*. Vol. 4 (1991): [*Coraciidae**]. Lansdowne Editions, Sydney.

* We were not able to consult this volume before the present work went to press in October 1991.

Forshaw, J M (1989) Focus: 'Greater' shots all timed to perfection. *Birds Internat.*, 1 (3): 47-51.

Frith, H J (1976) *Reader's Digest Complete Book of Australian Birds*. Reader's Digest Services, Sydney.

Fry, C H (1964) White-throated Bee-eater eating oil-palm nut fibres. *Bull. Niger. Orn. Soc.*, 1(3): 16.

Fry, C H (1970) Ecological distribution of birds in north-eastern Mato Grosso State, Brazil. *An. Acad. brasil. Ciênc.*, 42: 275-318.

Fry, C H (1978) Alcedinidae to Upupidae. In D W Snow (ed.), *An Atlas of Speciation in African Non-passerine Birds*. British Museum (Natural History), London.

Fry, C H (1980a) The evolutionary biology of kingfishers (Alcedinidae). *The Living Bird*, 18: 113-160.

Fry, C H (1980b) The origin of Afrotropical kingfishers. *Ibis*, 122: 57-74.

Fry, C H (1983) Red mandibles in the Woodland Kingfisher superspecies. *Malimbus*, 5: 91-93.

Fry, C H (1984) *The Bee-eaters*. T and A D Poyser, Calton.

Fry, C H, and Gilbert, D J (1983) Food of the Black-headed Bee-eater. *Bull. Br. Orn. Club,* 103: 119-123.

Fry, C H, Keith, S, and Urban, E K (1988) *The Birds of Africa*. Vol. 3. Academic Press, London.

Fry, C H, and de Naurois, R (1984) *Corythornis* systematics and character release in the Gulf of Guinea islands. *Proc. V Pan-Afr. Orn. Congr.*, 47-61.

Garnett, S (1984) Mortality and group cohesion in migrating Rainbow Bee-eaters. *Emu*, 85: 267-268.

Gartshore, M E (1984) Notes on the nesting of two little-known species of bee-eaters in Cameroon. *Malimbus*, 6: 95-96.

Gill, H B (1964) The White-tailed Kingfisher *Tanysiptera sylvia. Emu*, 63: 273-276.

Gill, H B (1970) Birds of Innisfail and hinterland. *Emu*, 70: 105-116.

Gilliard, E T, and LeCroy, M (1967) Results of the 1958-1959 Gilliard New Britain Expedition. 4. Annotated list of birds of the Whiteman Mountains, New Britain. *Bull. Amer. Mus. Nat. Hist.*, 135: 173-216.

Ginn, P J, McIlleron, W G, and Milstein, P le S (1989) *The Complete Book of Southern African Birds*. Struik Winchester, Cape Town.

Giraudoux, P, Degauquier, R, Jones, P J, Weigel, J, and Isenmann, P (1988) Avifaune du Niger: état des connaissances en 1986. *Malimbus*, 10: 1-140.

Glutz von Blotzheim, U N, and Bauer, K M (1980) *Handbuch der Vögel Mitteleuropas.*, Vol 9. Akademische Verlagsgesellschaft, Wiesbaden.

Greig-Smith, P W (1978a) Behaviour of Woodland Kingfishers in Ghana. *Ostrich*, 49: 67-75.

Greig-Smith, P W (1978b) Observations on the Striped Kingfisher *Halcyon chelicuti. Bull. Niger. Orn. Soc.*, 14: 14-23.

Greig-Smith, P W (1979) Selection of feeding areas by Senegal Kingfishers *Halcyon senegalensis. Z. Tierpsychol.*, 49: 197-209.

Grimes, L G (1987) *The Birds of Ghana*. Br. Orn. Union, London.

Hanmer, D B (1979) The Pigmy Kingfisher *Ispidina picta* in Malaŵi. *Honeyguide*, 98: 17-19.

Hanmer, D B (1980) Mensural and moult data of eight species of kingfisher from Moçambique and Malaŵi. *Ostrich*, 51: 129-150.

Hanmer, D B (1984) Aberrant Woodland Kingfishers—a follow-up. *Safring News*, 13: 58-70.

Hanmer, D B (1989) Even more aberrant Woodland Kingfishers. *Safring News*, 18: 43-46.

Harrison, C J O (1961) Notes on some eggs and nests attributed to the Stork-billed Kingfisher *Pelargopsis capensis* (Linn). *Bull. Br. Orn. Club*, 81: 141-143.

Harrison, C J O, and Frith, C B (1970) Nests and eggs of some New Guinea birds. *Emu*, 70: 173-178.

Harwin, R M, and Rockingham-Gill, D V (1981) Aspects of the biology of the southern races of the Swallow-tailed Bee-eater. *Honeyguide*, 106: 4-10.

Holyoak, D T (1974a) Les oiseaux des Iles de Société. *Oiseau et Rev. fr. Orn.*, 44: 153-184.

Holyoak, D T (1974b) Undescribed land birds from the Cook Islands, Pacific Ocean. *Bull. Br. Orn. Club*, 94: 145-150.

Holyoak, D T (1975) Les oiseaux des Iles Marquises. *Oiseau et Rev. fr. Orn.*, 45: 341-366.

Holyoak, D T, and Thibault, J C (1977) *Halcyon gambieri gambieri* Oustalet, an extinct kingfisher from Mangareva, South Pacific Ocean. *Bull. Br. Orn. Club*, 97: 21-23.

Hoogerwerf, A (1970) On the ornithology of Udjung Kulon. *Nat. Hist. Bull. Siam Soc.*, 23: 447-500.

Hoogerwerf, A, and Siccama, R H (1938) De avifauna van Batavia en omstreken (cont.) *Ardea*, 27: 41-92.

Inglisa, M, and Taglianti, A V (1987) Rinvenimento di tre nidi intercomunicanti di Gruccione *Merops apiaster*. *Avocetta*, 11: 167-168.

Jackson, S (1984) Predation by Pied Kingfishers and Whitebreasted Cormorants on fish in the Kosi Estuary system. *Ostrich*, 55: 113-132.

Jenkins, J M (1983) The native forest birds of Guam. *Orn. Monogr.*, 31: 1-61.

Johnson, T H, and Stattersfield, A J (1990) A global review of island endemic birds. *Ibis*, 132: 167-180.

Jones, P J (1979) The moult of the Little Bee-eater in northwestern Botswana. *Ostrich*, 50: 183-185.

Jones, P J (1980) The timing of wing moult in the Grey- hooded Kingfisher in Nigeria. *Ostrich*, 51: 99-106.

Jones, P J (1984) The status of the Pygmy Kingfisher *Ceyx picta* in north-eastern Nigeria. *Malimbus*, 6: 11-14.

Junor, F J R (1972) Offshore fishing by the Pied Kingfisher *Ceryle rudis* at Lake Kariba. *Ostrich*, 43: 185.

King, W B (1981) *Endangered Birds of the World: The ICBP Red Data Book*. Smithsonian Institution, Washington.

Lamarche, B (1988) *Liste commentée des oiseaux de Mauritanie*. Etudes Sahariennes et Ouest-Africaines I, 4 et spécial: 1-162.

Lessells, C M (1990) Helping at the nest in European Bee-eaters: who helps and why? Pp 357-368 in J Blondel, A Gosler, J D Lebreton and R McCleery (eds), *Population Biology of Passerine Birds*, Springer-Verlag, Berlin.

Lessels, C M, and Avery, M I (1989) Hatching asynchrony in European Bee-eaters *Merops apiaster. J. Anim. Ecol.*, 58: 815-835.

Lessells, C M, and Krebs, J R (1989) Age and breeding performance of European Bee-eaters. *Auk*, 106: 375-382.

Lessells, C M, and Ovenden, G N (1989) Heritability of wing length and weight in European Bee-eaters (*Merops apiaster*). *Condor*, 91: 210-214

Louette, M (1983) Unreported hunting behaviour of the Madagascar Malachite Kingfisher *Corythornis vintsioides* on Grand Comoro. *Scopus*, 7: 21-22.

Mackay, R D (1980) A list of the birds of the Baiyer River Sanctuary and adjacent areas. *New Guinea Bird Soc. Newsletter*, 167-168: 24-38.

Majnep, I S, and Bulmer, R (1977) *Birds of my Kalam Country.* Auckland/Oxford University Press, Auckland.

van Marle, J G, and Voous, K H (1988) *The Birds of Sumatra.* Br. Orn. Union, London.

Marshall, S D (1989) Nest sites of the Micronesian Kingfisher on Guam. *Wilson Bull.*, 101: 472-477.

Martin, J A, and Pérez, A (1990) Movimientos del Martín Pescador (*Alcedo atthis*, L.) en España. *Ardeola*, 37: 13-18.

Mayr, E, and Rand, A L (1937) Results of the Archbold Expeditions. 14, Birds of the 1933-1934 Papuan Expedition. *Bull. Amer. Mus. Nat. Hist.*, 73: 1-248.

McClure, H E (1974) *Migration and Survival of the Birds of Asia.* U.S. Army Medical Component, SEATO, Bangkok.

McGrew, A D (1971) Nesting of the Ringed Kingfisher in the United States. *Auk*, 88: 665-666.

Meadows, B S (1977) The food of a Malachite Kingfisher *Alcedo cristata* holding a territory on a fishless river. *Scopus*, 1: 24-25.

Medway, Lord, and Wells, D R (1976) *The Birds of the Malay Peninsula*, vol. 5. Witherby, London.

Mees, G F (1965) The avifauna of Misool. *Nova Guinea, Zool.*, 31: 139-203.

Mees, G F (1977) Additional records of birds from Formosa (Taiwan). *Zool. Meded. Leiden*, 51: 243-264.

Mees, G F (1982) Birds from the lowlands of southern New Guinea (Merauke and Koembe). *Zool. Verh. Leiden*, 191: 1-188.

Mees, G F (1991) The type locality of *Halcyon coromanda rufa* Wallace. *Bull. Br. Orn. Club*, 111: 49-51.

Miller, R S (1932) Some notes on the Little Kingfisher. *Emu*, 31: 257-259.

Milon, P, Petter, J J, and Randrianasolo, G (1973) Oiseaux. Faune de Madagascar, 35: 1-263.

Milstein, P le S (1962) The Angola Kingfisher *Halcyon senegalensis. Ostrich*, 33: 2-12.

Moon, G (1989) Kingfishers in the spotlight. *Birds Internat.*, 1 (4): 63-71.

Moreau, R E (1944) The Half-collared Kingfisher (*Alcedo semitorquata*) at the nest. *Ostrich*, 15: 161-177.

Mountfort, G (1988) *Rare Birds of the World.* Collins/ICBP, London and Cambridge.

Moynihan, M (1990) Social, sexual and pseudosexual behavior of the Blue-bellied Roller, *Coracias cyanogaster*: the consequences of crowding or concentration. *Smithson. Contrib. Zool.*, 491: 1-23.

Mukherjee, A K (1973) Food-habits of water-birds of the Sundarban, 24 Parganas district, West Bengal, India. *J. Bombay Nat. Hist. Soc.*, 72: 422-447.

de Naurois, R (1980) Le statut de *Halcyon malimbica dryas* Hartlaub (Ile du Prince, Golfe de Guinée). *Bull. I.F.A.N.* 42 (A,3), 608-618.

Parry, V A (1970) *Kookaburras.* Lansdowne Press, Melbourne.

Parry, V A (1973) The auxiliary social system and its effect on territory and breeding in kookaburras. *Emu*, 73: 81-100.

Pratt, H D, Engbring, J, Bruner, P L, and Berrett, D G (1980) Notes on the taxonomy, natural history and status of the resident birds of Palau. *Condor*, 82: 117-131.

Pratt, H D, Engbring, J, Bruner, P L, and Berrett, D G (1987) *A Field Guide to The Birds of Hawaii and the Tropical Pacific.* Princeton University Press, Princeton.

Price, T (1979) The seasonality and occurrence of birds in the Eastern Ghats of Andhra Pradesh. *J. Bombay Nat. Hist. Soc.*, 76: 380-422.

Prigogine, A (1973) The migratory movements of the Pigmy Kingfisher *Ceyx picta natalensis* in the Republic of Zaïre. *Bull. Br. Orn. Club*, 93: 82-89.

Pring-Mill, F (1974) Report of Oxford University expedition to Kashmir 1974. (The feeding behaviour of kingfishers on the Dal Lakes at Srinagar, Kashmir). *Bull. Oxford Univ. Explor. Club*, 23: 1-49.

Ralph, C J, and Ralph, C P (1973) A note on *Dacelo gigas*. *Victorian Nat.*, 90: 132.

Ralph, C J, and Ralph, C P (1977) Some observations on the winter distribution of the New Zealand Kingfisher. *Notornis*, 24: 82-93.

Rand, A L (1936) The distribution and habits of Madagascar birds. *Bull. Amer. Mus. Nat. Hist.*, 72: 143-499.

Rand, A L (1954) A Philippine kingfisher uses a tool. *Silliman J.*, 1: 83-85.

*****Remsen, J V** (1991) Community ecology of Neotropical kingfishers. *Univ. Calif. Publ. Zool.*, 124: 1-128.

Reyer, H U (1980a) Flexible helper structure as an ecological adaptation in the Pied Kingfisher (*Ceryle rudis rudis* L.). *Behav. Ecol. Sociobiol.*, 6:219- 227.

Reyer, H U (1980b) Sexual dimorphism and co-operative breeding in the Striped Kingfisher. *Ostrich*, 51: 117-118.

Reyer, H U (1984) Investment and relatedness: a cost/benefit analysis of breeding and helping in the Pied Kingfisher (*Ceryle rudis*). *Anim. Behav.*, 32: 1163-1178.

Reyer, H U (1986a) Breeder-helper interactions in the Pied Kingfisher reflect the costs and benefits of co-operative breeding. *Behaviour*, 82: 277-303.

Reyer, H U (1986b) The adaptive significance of cooperative breeding in the Pied Kingfisher (*Ceryle rudis*). *Proc. XVIII Int. Orn. Congr.*, 1037.

---

* We were not able to consult this volume before the present work went to press in October 1991.

Reyer, H U, and Westerterp, K (1985) Parental energy expenditure: a proximate cause of helper recruitment in the Pied Kingfisher (*Ceryle rudis*). *Behav. Ecol. Sociobiol.*, 17: 363-369.

Reyer, H U, Migongo-Bake, W, and Schmidt, L (1988) Field studies and experiments on distribution and foraging of Pied Kingfishers at Lake Nakuru (Kenya). *J. Anim. Ecol.*, 57: 595-610.

Ripley, S D (1942) The species *Eurystomus orientalis. Proc. Biol. Soc. Wash.*, 55: 169-176.

Russell, S M (1964) A distributional study of the birds of British Honduras. *Orn. Monogr.*, 1: 1-95.

Salyer, J C, and Lagler, K F (1946) The Eastern Belted Kingfisher *Megaceryle alcyon alcyon* (Linnaeus) in relation to fish management. *Trans. Amer. Fish. Soc.*, 76: 97-117.

Schodde, R (1977) Contributions to Papuasian ornithology. 6. Survey of the birds of southern Bougainville Island, Papua New Guinea. *C.S.I.R.O., Div. Wildl. Res. Tech. Pap.*, 34: 1-103.

Scholtes, C J L (1980) Revisie van *Eurystomus orientalis* (L.). Leiden: RMNH., mss 20 pp.

Sibley, C G, Ahlquist, J E, and Monroe, B L (1988) A classification of the living birds of the world based on DNA-DNA hybridization studies. *Auk*, 105: 409-423.

Skinner, N J (1968) Two-stage northerly local migration of the Grey-headed Kingfisher *Halcyon leucocephala. Bull. Niger. Orn. Soc.*, 5: 88-91.

Skutch, A F (1957) Life history of the Amazon Kingfisher. *Condor*, 59: 217-219.

Skutch, A F (1972) Studies of tropical American birds. *Publs Nuttall Orn. Club*, 10: 1-228.

Smythies, B E (1953) *The Birds of Burma*, 2nd edn. Oliver & Boyd, Edinburgh.

Smythies, B E (1981) *The Birds of Borneo*. Sabah Society and Malayan Nature Society, Kuala Lumpur.

Snow, D W (1978) *An Atlas of Speciation in African Non-Passerine Birds*. Brit. Mus. (Nat. Hist.), London.

van Someren, V G L (1956) Days with birds. *Fieldiana, Zool.*, 38: 1-520.

Storr, G M (1973) List of Queensland birds. *Spec. Publs W. Aust. Mus.*, 5: 1-117.

Stresemann, E (1914) Die Vögel von Seran (Ceram). *Novit. Zool.*, 21: 25-153.

Stresemann, E (1940) Die Vögel von Celebes. *J. Orn.* 88: 389-487.

Stronach, N (1989) Notes on the ecology and nesting of the Spangled Kookaburra *Dacelo tyro* in southern New Guinea. *Bull. Br. Orn. Club,* 6: 115-117.

Svensson, S (1978) Kungsfiskaren *Alcedo atthis* i Klippantrakten, Skåne —förekomst och biologi. *Vår Fågelvärld*, 37: 97-112.

Taylor, R H (1966) Seasonal and altitudinal distribution of kingfishers in the Nelson district. *Notornis*, 13: 200-203.

Thibault, J C (1973) Notes ornithologiques polynesiennes. *Alauda*, 41: 111-119.

Thiollay, J M (1970) L'exploitation par les oiseaux des essaimages de fourmis et termites dans une zone de contact savanne-forêt en Côte d'Ivoire. *Alauda*, 38: 255-273.

Thiollay, J M (1971) Les guêpiers et rolliers d'une zone de contact savane-forêt en Côte d'Ivoire. *Oiseaux et R.F.O.*, 41: 148-162.

Thiollay, J M (1978) Ecologie de migrateurs tropicaux dans une zone préforestière de Côte d'Ivoire. *Terre et Vie*, 27: 268-296.

Thiollay, J M (1985) Stratégies adaptives comparées des rolliers sédentaires et migrateurs dans une savane guinéene. *Rev. Ecol. (Terre et Vie)*, 40: 355-378.

Thompson, H A F (1984) The status of kingfishers and their allies (Coraciiformes) in the Darwin Area, N.T., 1974-1982. *Nth. Terr. Nat.*, 7: 18-29.

Tjømlid, S A (1973) Food preferences and feeding habits of the Pied Kingfisher *Ceryle rudis. Orn. Scand.*, 4: 145-151.

Todd, W (1977) Sexing bee-eaters. *Avicult. Mag.*, 83: 177.

Tubb, J A (1945) Field notes on some New Guinea birds. *Emu*, 44: 249-273.

Ulfstrand, S, and Alerstam, T (1977) Bird communities of *Brachystegia* and *Acacia* woodlands in Zambia. *J. Orn.*, 118: 156-174.

Underhill, L G (1990) Movements, site-faithfulness and biometrics of European Bee-eaters *Merops apiaster* in the southwestern Cape. *Ostrich*, 61: 80-84.

Watling, R (1983) Ornithological notes from Sulawesi. *Emu*, 83: 247-261.

White, H C (1953) The Eastern Belted Kingfisher in the Maritime Provinces. *Fish. Res. Board Canada Bull.*, 97: 1-44.

White, C M N, and Bruce, M D (1986) *The Birds of Wallacea*. Br. Orn. Union, London.

Whitehead, J (1899) Field notes on birds collected in the Philippine Islands in 1893-1896, Part III. *Ibis*, 7,5: 381-399.

Whitfield, A K, and Blaber, S J M (1978) Feeding ecology of piscivorous birds at Lake St Lucia. *Ostrich*, 49: 185-198.

Woodall, P F (1991) Morphometry, diet and habitat in the kingfishers (Aves: Alcedinidae). *J. Zool., Lond.*, 223: 79-90

Wrege, P H, and Emlen, S T (1991) Breeding seasonality and reproductive success of White-fronted Bee-eaters in Kenya. *Auk*, 108: 673-687.

de Zylva, T S U (1984) *Birds of Sri Lanka*. Trumpet Publs, Sri Lanka.

INDEX

abundus, Eurystomus orientalis 306
Abyssinian Roller **38**, 100, 296
abyssinica, Coracias **38**, 100, 296
abyssinica, Halcyon chloris 56, 177
acis, Tanysiptera galatea 114
Actenoides 8
Actenoides bougainvillei **8**, 24, 40, 109
Actenoides concretus **2**, 28, 112
Actenoides hombroni **2**, 28, 110
Actenoides lindsayi **2**, 28, 111
Actenoides monachus **1**, 26, 107
Actenoides princeps **1**, 26, 107
acteon, Halcyon leucocephala 46, 150
admiralitatis, Halcyon saurophaga 60, 184
aenea, Chloroceryle **26**, 11, 76, 224
aenea, Chloroceryle aenea 76, 224
aethiopicus, Eurystomus glaucurus 303
afer, Eurystomus glaucurus 303
affinis, Alcedo azurea 214
affinis, Coracias benghalensis 98, 289
African Dwarf Kingfisher **20**, 8, 13, 64, 195
African Mangrove Kingfisher **12**, 48, 159
African Pygmy Kingfisher **20**, 8, 13, 64, 196
Alaudo 154
alberti, Halcyon chloris 58, 178
albicilla, Halcyon chloris 56, 177
albicollis, Merops **32**, 88, 265
albiventris, Halcyon **11**, 46, 152
albiventris, Halcyon albiventris 46, 152
albonotata, Halcyon **14**, 52, 168
Alcedinidae 6, 8, 21, 22
Alcedininae 6
Alcedo 8
Alcedo argentata **23**, 8, 70, 209
Alcedo atthis **25**, 3, 4, 11, 74, 219
Alcedo azurea **24**, 11, 72, 214
Alcedo coerulescens **23**, 8, 70, 210
Alcedo cristata **22**, 8, 68, 206
Alcedo cyanopecta **23**, 8, 70, 209
Alcedo euryzona **23**, 8, 70, 211
Alcedo hercules **25**, 11, 74, 223
Alcedo lepida **21**, 8, 66, 202
Alcedo leucogaster **22**, 8, 68, 204
Alcedo meninting **25**, 11, 74, 217
Alcedo pusilla **24**, 11, 72, 216
Alcedo quadribrachys **24**, 11, 72, 213
Alcedo semitorquata **25**, 11, 74, 222
Alcedo vintsioides **22**, 8, 68, 208
Alcedo websteri **24**, 11, 72, 215
alcyon, Megaceryle **28**, 11, 80, 234
Alcyone 3, 215
alfredi, Halcyon winchelli 162
alternans, Merops superciliosus 274
amabilis, Lacedo pulchella 127
amauroptera, Halcyon **9**, 42, 140
Amazon Kingfisher **26**, 11, 76, 228
amazona, Chloroceryle **26**, 11, 76, 228
American Pygmy Kingfisher **26**, 11, 76, 224
americana, Chloroceryle **26**, 11, 76, 226
americana, Chloroceryle americana 76, 226
americanus, Merops viridis 92, 278

amicta, Nyctyornis **29**, 82, 241
amoena, Halcyon chloris 58, 178
anachoreta, Halcyon saurophaga 184
andamanensis, Merops leschenaulti 94, 279
aolae, Alcedo pusilla 216
apiaster, Merops **35**, 94, 281
archboldi, Dacelo tyro 36, 130
argentata, Alcedo **23**, 8, 70, 209
argentata, Alcedo argentata 70, 209
argutus, Merops pusillus 253
armstrongi, Halcyon chloris 176
Aru Paradise Kingfisher **4**, 32, 117
Atelornis crossleyi 8
Atelornis pittoides 7, 8
athertoni, Nyctyornis **29**, 82, 242
athertoni, Nyctyornis athertoni 82, 243
atiu, Halcyon tuta 62, 191
atthis, Alcedo **25**, 3, 11, 74, 219
atthis, Alcedo atthis 74, 219
australasia, Halcyon **18**, 60, 188
australasia, Halcyon australasia 60, 188
australis, Merops gularis 84, 249
azela, Halcyon chloris 176
Azure Kingfisher **24**, 11, 72, 214
Azure Roller **40**, 16, 24, 104, 308
azurea, Alcedo **24**, 11, 72, 214
azurea, Alcedo azurea 72, 214
azureus, Eurystomus **40**, 3, 104, 308
azureus, Eurystomus orientalis 3

badia, Halcyon **10**, 44, 146
Banded Kingfisher **6**, 36, 127
bangsi, Halcyon coromanda 142
bangweoloensis, Merops variegatus 86, 256
Bar-headed Wood Kingfisher 107
Barbets 6
Bay-headed Bee-eater **35**, 22, 24, 94, 279
Beach Kingfisher **18**, 13, 60, 183
Belted Kingfisher **28**, 5, 11, 13, 80, 234
beludschicus, Merops orientalis 90, 269
bengalensis, Alcedo atthis 219
benghalensis, Coracias **37**, 98, 289
benghalensis, Coracias benghalensis 98, 289
bennetti, Halcyon chloris 178
Biak Paradise Kingfisher 114
Bismarck Kingfisher **24**, 11, 72, 215
Black Bee-eater **30**, 84, 249
Black-capped Kingfisher **10**, 13, 44, 147
Black-headed Bee-eater **30**, 84, 246
Black-sided Kingfisher **13**, 50, 161
Blue-and-white Kingfisher 164
Blue-banded Kingfisher **23**, 8, 70, 211
Blue-bearded Bee-eater **29**, 82, 242
Blue-bellied Kingfisher 145
Blue-bellied Roller **39**, 16, 19, 102, 300
Blue-breasted Bee-eater **31**, 4, 86, 255
Blue-breasted Kingfisher **12**, 48, 155
Blue-cheeked Bee-eater **33**, 15, 22, 90, 271
Blue-crowned Motmot 7
Blue-eared Kingfisher **25**, 11, 74, 217
Blue-headed Bee-eater **30**, 84, 247
Blue-headed Ground-roller 7, 8, 9
Blue-headed Wood Kingfisher 107
Blue-tailed Bee-eater **34**, 14, 22, 92, 273

Blue-throated Bee-eater **34**, 22, 92, 277
Blue-throated Roller **39**, 22, 102, 301
Blue-winged Kookaburra **7**, 38, 131
boanensis, Tanysiptera galatea 114
Boehm's Bee-eater **33**, 15, 90, 267
boehmi, Merops **33**, 90, 267
borneanus, Actenoides concretus 112
bougainvillei, Actenoides **8**, 24, 40, 109
bougainvillei, Actenoides bougainvillei 40, 109
bougainvillei, Alcedo pusilla 72, 216
bowdleri, Alcedo leucogaster 205
Brachypteracias leptosomus 8
Brachypteracias squamigera 8
Brachypteraciidae 6, 7
brachyura, Halcyon chloris 58, 178
brevicaudata, Nyctyornis athertoni 243
breweri, Merops **30**, 84, 246
Broad-billed Roller **39**, 16, 102, 303
Brown-headed Paradise Kingfisher **4**, 32, 121
Brown-hooded Kingfisher **11**, 46, 152
Brown-winged Kingfisher **9**, 42, 140
browningi, Tanysiptera galatea 114
brunhildae, Tanysiptera galatea 114
Bucerotiformes 6
Buff-breasted Paradise Kingfisher **4**, 32, 118
bullocki, Merops **32**, 88, 259
bullocki, Merops bullocki 88, 259
bullockoides, Merops **32**, 88, 262
burmanica, Halcyon capensis 137

cabanisii, Chloroceryle americana 227
Caerulean Kingfisher **23**, 8, 70, 210
cajeli, Alcedo lepida 66, 203
canacorum, Halcyon sancta 185
Cancrophaga 146
capensis, Halcyon **9**, 42, 137
capensis, Halcyon capensis 42, 137
capucinus, Actenoides monachus 26, 107
Carmine Bee-eater **36**, 4, 5, 15, 96, 240, 285
carolinae, Tanysiptera **3**, 30, 116
caudata, Coracias **38**, 100, 294
caudata, Coracias caudata 100, 294
Celebes Bee-eater **29**, 82, 244
Celebes Dwarf Kingfisher **20**, 8, 64, 201
Celebes Flat-billed Kingfisher 122
Celebes Green Kingfisher **1**, 26, 107
Celebes Roller **40**, 24, 104, 291
Celebes Stork-billed Kingfisher **9**, 42, 139
cervina, Dacelo leachii 38, 131
Ceryle 4
Ceryle rudis **28**, 3, 11, 80, 236
Cerylidae 6, 8, 21, 22
Cerylinae 6
Ceyx 3, 8, 13
Ceyx erithacus **20**, 8, 64, 198
Ceyx fallax **20**, 8, 11, 64, 201
Ceyx lecontei **20**, 8, 64, 195
Ceyx madagascariensis **20**, 8, 64, 201
Ceyx melanurus **20**, 8, 64, 200
Ceyx pictus **20**, 8, 64, 196
Chattering Kingfisher 190
chelicuti, Halcyon **12**, 48, 154
chelicuti, Halcyon chelicut 48, 154

Chestnut-bellied Kingfisher **14**, 13, 52, 149, 170
chimaera, Uratelornis 8
chloris, Halcyon **16, 17**, 56, 58, 175
chloris, Halcyon chloris 56, 176
Chloroceryle aenea **26**, 11, 76, 224
Chloroceryle amazona **26**, 11, 76, 228
Chloroceryle americana **26**, 11, 76, 226
Chloroceryle inda **26**, 11, 76, 225
chloroptera, Halcyon chloris 176
Chocolate-backed Kingfisher **10**, 44, 146
chrysocercus, Merops persicus 271
chrysolaimus, Merops hirundineus 84, 251
cinnamomina, Halcyon **17**, 24, 58, 181
cinnamomina, Halcyon cinnamomina 24, 58, 182
Cinnamon-chested Bee-eater **31**, 86, 257
Cittura cyanotis **5**, 34, 122
cleopatra, Merops orientalis 269
cliftoni, Dacelo leachii 38, 131
Clytoceyx 8
Clytoceyx rex **5**, 8, 34, 125
coerulescens, Alcedo **23**, 8, 70, 210
Collared Kingfisher 175
collaris, Halcyon chloris 177
collectoris, Alcedo lepida 203
colona, Halcyon chloris 177
coltarti, Alcedo meninting 218
Common Paradise Kingfisher **3**, 30, 113
concretus, Actenoides **2**, 28, 112
concretus, Actenoides concretus 28, 112
connectens, Eurystomus orientalis 306
Coracias 23
Coracias abyssinica **38**, 100, 296
Coracias benghalensis **37**, 98, 289
Coracias caudata **38**, 100, 294
Coracias cyanogaster **39**, 102, 300
Coracias garrulus **38**, 100, 298
Coracias naevia **37**, 98, 287
Coracias spatulata **37**, 98, 292
Coracias temminckii **40**, 104, 291
Coraciidae 6, 8, 21
Coraciiformes 6, 22
coromanda, Halcyon **9**, 42, 141
coromanda, Halcyon coromanda 141
Corvus 289
Corythornis 8
crassirostris, Eurystomus orientalis 306
Crested Kingfisher **27**, 22, 78, 229
cristata, Alcedo **22**, 8, 68, 206
cristata, Alcedo cristata 68, 206
Crossley's Ground-roller 9
crossleyi, Atelornis 8
Cuckoo-roller 6, 7, 10
Cyanalcyon 169
cyanogaster, Cracias **39**, 102, 300
cyanoleuca, Halcyon senegalensis 48, 158
cyanopecta, Alcedo **23**, 8, 70, 209
cyanopecta, Alcedo cyanopecta 70, 210
cyanophrys, Merops orientalis 90, 269
cyanopteryx, Halcyon capensis 137
cyanostictus, Merops pusillus 86, 253
cyanotis, Cittura **5**, 34, 122
cyanotis, Cittura cyanotis 34, 122
cyanoventris, Halcyon **10**, 44, 145

Dacelo 4, 8
Dacelo gaudichaud **6**, 36, 128
Dacelo leachii **7**, 38, 131
Dacelo novaeguineae **7**, 38, 133
Dacelo tyro **6**, 36, 130
Dacelonidae 6, 8, 21, 23
Daceloninae 6
dammeriana, Halcyon australasia 188
danae, Tanysiptera **4**, 32, 121
davisoni, Halcyon chloris 176
deignani, Eurystomus orientalis 306
dichrorhyncha, Halcyon melanorhyncha 42, 139
dilutus, Ceyx madagascariensis 202
diops, Halcyon **13**, 50, 164
dispar, Alcedo lepida 66, 203
Dollarbird **40**, 104, 305
doris, Tanysiptera galatea 115
dryas, Halcyon malimbica 156

Earthworm-eating Kingfisher 8
elisabeth, Halcyon macleayii 166
ellioti, Tanysiptera galatea 30, 115
emiliae, Tanysiptera galatea 30, 115
enigma, Halcyon chloris 176
eremogiton, Halcyon chelicuti 154
erithacus, Ceyx **20**, 8, 64, 198
erithacus, Ceyx erithacus 64, 198
erromangae, Halcyon chloris 179
erythrorhamphus, Actenoides princeps 26, 108
Eurasian Kingfisher 219
European Bee-eater **35**, 3, 4, 5, 15, 21, 22, 94, 281
European Kingfisher 3
European Roller **38**, 21, 100, 298
Eurystomus 23
Eurystomus azureus **40**, 3, 104, 308
Eurystomus glaucurus **39**, 102, 303
Eurystomus gularis **39**, 102, 301
Eurystomus orientalis **40**, 3, 104, 305
euryzona, Alcedo **23**, 8, 70, 212
euryzona, Alcedo euryzona 70, 211
eutreptorhyncha, Halcyon melanorhyncha 139
excelsus, Actenoides bougainvillei 40, 109
eximia, Halcyon chloris 179

fallax, Ceyx **20**, 8, 11, 64, 201
fallax, Ceyx fallax 64, 201
farquhari, Halcyon **14**, 52, 170
ferrugeiceps, Merops orientalis 90, 269
ferrugineus, Ceyx pictus 197
flavirostris, Halcyon torotoro 172
floresiana, Alcedo atthis 219
floresiana, Halcyon capensis 138
flumenicola, Alcedo argentata 70, 209
forbesi, Halcyon malimbica 156
Forest Kingfisher **14**, 52, 166
forsteni, Meropogon **29**, 82, 244
frenatus, Merops bullocki 88, 259
fulgida, Halcyon **8**, 40, 136
fulgida, Halcyon fulgida 136
funebris, Halcyon **15**, 54, 174
furcatus, Merops hirundineus 251
fusca, Halcyon smyrnensis 144
fuscopilea, Halcyon senegalensis 158

galatea, Tanysiptera **3**, 30, 113
galatea, Tanysiptera galatea 30, 114
Galbuliformes 6
galerita, Alcedo cristata 206
Gambier Kingfisher 24
gambieri, Halcyon 24, 190, 191, 194
gambieri, Halcyon tuta 24, 62, 191
Garrulus 291
garrulus, Coracias **38**, 100, 298
garrulus, Coracias garrulus 100, 298
gaudichaud, Dacelo **6**, 36, 128
gentiana, Alcedo lepida 66, 203
gertrudae, Halcyon **19**, 24, 62, 193
Giant Kingfisher **27**, 22, 78, 231
gigantea, Halcyon capensis 42, 138
gigantea, Megaceryle maxima 231
gigas, Eurystomus orientalis 306
glaucurus, Eurystomus **39**, 102, 303
glaucurus, Eurystomus glaucurus 102, 303
Glittering Kingfisher 136
godeffroyi, Halcyon **19**, 24, 62, 194
Golden Bee-eater 3
gouldi, Halcyon capensis 138
gracilirostris, Halcyon fulgida 136
Gracula 219
Great Blue Kingfisher **25**, 11, 74, 223
Great-billed Kingfisher 139
Greater Pied Kingfisher 229
Green Kingfisher **26**, 11, 22, 76, 226
Green-and-rufous Kingfisher **26**, 11, 76, 225
Grey-headed Kingfisher **11**, 20, 46, 149
Ground-rollers 6, 7, 8, 9, 24
guentheri, Alcedo quadribrachys 213
gularis, Eurystomus **39**, 102, 301
gularis, Eurystomus gularis 102, 302
gularis, Halcyon smyrnensis 44, 144
gularis, Merops **30**, 84, 249
gularis, Merops gularis 84, 249
guttulata, Megaceryle lugubris 229

hachisukai, Chloroceryle americana 227
Halcyon 3, 4, 8
Halcyon albiventris **11**, 46, 152
Halcyon albonotata **14**, 52, 168
Halcyon amauroptera **9**, 42, 140
Halcyon australasia **18**, 60, 188
Halcyon badia **10**, 44, 146
Halcyon capensis **9**, 42, 137
Halcyon chelicuti **12**, 48, 154
Halcyon chloris **16**, **17**, 56, 58, 175
Halcyon cinnamomina **17**, 24, 58, 181
Halcyon coromanda **9**, 42, 141
Halcyon cyanoventris **10**, 44, 145
Halcyon diops **13**, 50, 164
Halcyon farquhari **14**, 52, 170
Halcyon fulgida **8**, 40, 136
Halcyon funebris **15**, 54, 174
Halcyon gambieri 190, 191, 194
Halcyon gertrudae **19**, 24, 62, 193
Halcyon godeffroyi **19**, 24, 62, 194
Halcyon lazuli **14**, 52, 165
Halcyon leucocephala **11**, 46, 149
Halcyon leucopygia **14**, 52, 169
Halcyon macleayii **14**, 52, 166

Halcyon malimbica **12**, 48, 155
Halcyon megarhyncha **15**, 54, 173
Halcyon melanorhyncha **9**, 42, 139
Halcyon miyakoensis 24
Halcyon nigrocyanea **13**, 50, 161
Halcyon pileata **10**, 44, 147
Halcyon pyrrhopygia **18**, 60, 189
Halcyon recurvirostris 185
Halcyon ruficollaris 191
Halcyon sancta **18**, 60, 185
Halcyon saurophaga **18**, 60, 183
Halcyon senegalensis **12**, 48, 157
Halcyon senegaloides **12**, 48, 159
Halcyon smyrnensis **10**, 3, 44, 143
Halcyon torotoro **15**, 54, 171
Halcyon tuta **19**, 24, 62, 190
Halcyon venerata **19**, 62, 192
Halcyon winchelli **13**, 50, 162
Half-collared Kingfisher **25**, 11, 74, 222
halmaherae, Alcedo pusilla 216
hercules, Alcedo **25**, 11, 74, 223
heuglini, Merops hirundineus 251
hirundineus, Merops **30**, 84, 251
hirundineus, Merops hirundineus 84, 251
hispidoides, Alcedo atthis 74, 219
Hombron's Wood Kingfisher **2**, 28, 110
hombroni, Actenoides **2**, 28, 110
Honeyguides 6
Hook-billed Kingfisher **5**, 8, 12, 34, 123
Hoopoes 6
Hornbills 6
humii, Halcyon chloris 56, 176
hyacinthina, Halcyon leucocephala 150
hydrocharis, Tanysiptera **4**, 32, 117

imperator, Clytoceyx rex 125
incincta, Halcyon macleayii 52, 166
inda, Chloroceryle **26**, 11, 76, 225
Indian Roller **37**, 98, 289
indica, Coracias benghalensis 289
insignis, Ceryle rudis 237
intermedia, Dacelo leachii 38, 132
intermedia, Halcyon capensis 42, 137
interposita, Halcyon australasia 60, 188
irisi, Eurystomus orientalis 306
isoptera, Halcyon capensis 138
ispida, Alcedo atthis 219
Ispidina 195

Jacamars 6
Java Kingfisher **10**, 44, 145
javana, Halcyon capensis 138
jobiensis, Melidora macrorrhina 124
johannae, Alcedo vintsioides 208
juliae, Halcyon chloris 58, 179

kalbaensis, Halcyon chloris 177
kempi, Dacelo leachii 131
Kookaburra 8, 12

Lacedo 4, 8
Lacedo pulchella **6**, 36, 127
laetior, Eurystomus orientalis 306
lafresnayii, Merops variegatus 86, 256

laubmanniana, Halcyon chloris 176
Laughing Kookaburra **7**, 5, 8, 20, 38, 133
Lazuli Kingfisher **14**, 52, 165
lazuli, Halcyon **14**, 52, 165
Lazuline Kingfisher 165
leachii, Dacelo **7**, 38, 131
leachii, Dacelo leachii 38, 131
lecontei, Ceyx **20**, 8, 64, 195
leopoldi, Alcedo leucogaster 205
lepida, Alcedo **21**, 8, 66, 202
lepida, Alcedo lepida 66, 203
Leptosomidae 6
leptosomus, Brachypteracias 8
Leptosomus discolor 7
leschenaulti, Merops **35**, 94, 279
leschenaulti, Merops leschenaulti 94, 279
Lesser Paradise Kingfisher 117
Lesser Pied Kingfisher 236
Lesser Sundas Kingfisher 188
Lesser Yellow-billed Kingfisher **15**, 54, 171
lessonii, Alcedo azurea 72, 214
leucocephala, Halcyon **11**, 46, 149
leucocephala, Halcyon leucocephala 46, 150
leucogaster, Alcedo **22**, 8, 68, 204
leucogaster, Alcedo leucogaster 68, 205
leucomelanura, Ceryle rudis 237
leucopygia, Halcyon **14**, 52, 169
leucura, Tanysiptera sylvia 32, 118
Lilac Kingfisher **5**, 34, 122
Lilac-breasted Roller **38**, 100, 116, 294
Lilac-throated Roller 116, 294
linae, Halcyon coromanda 142
lindsayi, Actenoides **2**, 28, 111
lindsayi, Actenoides lindsayi 28, 111
Little Bee-eater **31**, 86, 253
Little Green Bee-eater **33**, 90, 269
Little Kingfisher **24**, 11, 72, 216
Long-tailed Ground-roller 7, 8, 9
loringi, Merops variegatus 255
lorti, Coracias caudata 100, 294
lugubris, Megaceryle **27**, 78, 229
lugubris, Megaceryle lugubris 78, 229

macleayii, Halcyon **14**, 52, 166
macleayii, Halcyon macleayii 52, 166
macmillani, Halcyon sancta 185
macrocarus, Ceyx erithacus 198
macrorrhina, Melidora **5**, 34, 123
macrorrhina, Melidora macrorrhina 34, 124
Madagascar Bee-eater **34**, 22, 92, 273
Madagascar Malachite Kingfisher **22**, 8, 68, 208
Madagascar Pygmy Kingfisher **20**, 8, 22, 64, 201
madagascariensis, Ceyx **20**, 8, 64, 201
madagascariensis, Ceyx madagascariensis 202
major, Halcyon coromanda 142
mala, Halcyon chloris 178
malaccensis, Halcyon capensis 42, 137
Malachite Kingfisher **22**, 8, 68, 206
malaitae, Alcedo lepida 203
malimbica, Halcyon **12**, 48, 155
malimbica, Halcyon malimbica 156
malimbicus, Merops **36**, 96, 283
Mangrove Kingfisher **16**, **17**, 21, 56, 58, 175, 191
manuae, Halcyon chloris 179

margarethae, *Alcedo lepida* 66, 203
margarethae, *Tanysiptera galatea* 114
marina, *Halcyon chloris* 179
Marquesas Kingfisher **19**, 24, 62, 194
masauji, *Alced pusilla* 216
mathewsii, *Chloroceryle americana* 227
matthiae, *Halcyon chloris* 56, 178
mauke, *Halcyon tuta* 191
maxima, *Megaceryle* **27**, 78, 231
maxima, *Megaceryle maxima* 78, 231
meeki, *Alcedo lepida* 66, 203
Megaceryle alcyon **28**, 11, 80, 234
Megaceryle lugubris **27**, 78, 229
Megaceryle maxima **27**, 78, 231
Megaceryle torquata **28**, 80, 233
megarhyncha, *Halcyon* **15**, 54, 173
megarhyncha, *Halcyon megarhyncha* 54, 173
melanodera, *Halcyon chloris* 58, 178
melanops, *Lacedo pulchella* 36, 127
melanorhyncha, *Halcyon* **9**, 42, 139
melanorhyncha, *Halcyon melanorhyncha* 42, 139
melanurus, *Ceyx* **20**, 8, 64, 200
melanurus, *Ceyx melanurus* 64, 200
Melidora 8
Melidora macrorrhina **5**, 34, 123
Melittophagus 257, 267
meninting, *Alcedo* **25**, 11, 74, 217
meninting, *Alcedo meninting* 74, 218
mentalis, *Merops muelleri* 84, 248
meridionalis, *Merops pusillus* 86, 253
Meropidae 6, 8, 21
Meropiscus 247
Meropogon 8, 246
Meropogon forsteni **29**, 82, 244
Merops albicollis **32**, 88, 265
Merops apiaster **35**, 94, 281
Merops boehmi **33**, 90, 267
Merops breweri **30**, 84, 246
Merops bullocki **32**, 88, 259
Merops bullockoides **32**, 88, 262
Merops gularis **30**, 84, 249
Merops hirundineus **30**, 84, 251
Merops leschenaulti **35**, 94, 279
Merops malimbicus **36**, 96, 283
Merops muelleri **30**, 84, 247
Merops nubicus **36**, 96, 285
Merops oreobates **31**, 86, 257
Merops orientalis **32**, 90, 269
Merops ornatus **34**, 92, 275
Merops persicus **33**, 90, 271
Merops pusillus **31**, 86, 253
Merops revoilii **32**, 88, 264
Merops superciliosus **34**, 92, 273
Merops variegatus **31**, 86, 255
Merops viridis **34**, 92, 277
mexicanus, *Todus* 7
meyeri, *Tanysipter galatea* 114
Micronesian Kingfisher **17**, 181
mindanensis, *Halcyon winchelli* 162
minor, *Dacelo novaeguineae* 133
minor, *Halcyon coromanda* 142
minor, *Tanysiptera galatea* 114
Miyako Kingfisher 24

miyakoensis, *Halcyon* 24, 182
miyakoensis, *Halcyon cinnamomina* 24, 182
mizorhina, *Halcyon coromanda* 141
modesta, *Cittura cyanotis* 122
Moluccan Kingfisher **13**, 50, 164
momota, *Momotus* 7
Momotidae 6
Momotus momota 7
Monachalcyon 107
monachus, *Actenoides* **1**, 26, 107
monachus, *Actenoides monachus* 26, 107
mosambica, *Coracias naevia* 98, 287
moseleyi, *Actenoides lindsayi* 28, 111
motleyi, *Ceyx erithacus* 198
Motmots 6, 7
Mountain Yellow-billed Kingfisher **15**, 54, 173
Moustached Kingfisher **8**, 24, 40, 109
muelleri, *Merops* **30**, 84, 247
muelleri, *Merops muelleri* 84, 248
mulcata, *Alcedo lepida* 66, 203

naevia, *Coracias* **37**, 98, 287
naevia, *Coracias naevia* 98, 287
nais, *Alcedo leucogaster* 68, 205
naïs, *Tanysipter galatea* 30, 114
najdanus, *Merops orientalis* 269
natalensis, *Ceyx pictus* 64, 197
neglectus, *Eurystomus gularis* 102, 302
nesoeca, *Halcyon capensis* 138
nesydrionetes, *Halcyon winchelli* 50, 163
New Britain Kingfisher **14**, 52, 168
Niau Kingfisher **19**, 24, 62, 193
nigriceps, *Tanysiptera* 118
nigriceps, *Tanysiptera sylvia* 32, 118
nigrirostris, *Alcedo cyanopecta* 70, 210
nigrocyanea, *Halcyon* **13**, 50, 161
nigrocyanea, *Halcyon nigrocyanea* 50, 161
nigromaxilla, *Alcedo lepida* 203
nigrorum, *Halcyon winchelli* 163
novaeguinae, *Dacelo novaeguineae* 38, 133
novaeguineae, *Dacelo* **7**, 38, 133
novaehiberniae, *Halcyon chloris* 178
nubicoides, *Merops nubicus* 96, 285
nubicus, *Merops* **36**, 96, 285
nubicus, *Merops nubicus* 96, 285
Numfor Paradise Kingfisher **3**, 30, 116
nusae, *Halcyon chloris* 178
Nyctyornis amicta **29**, 82, 241
Nyctyornis athertoni **29**, 82, 242
nympha, *Tanysiptera* **4**, 32, 120

obiensis, *Tanysiptera galatea* 114
occipitalis, *Halcyon chloris* 56, 177
ochracea, *Halcyon torotoro* 54, 172
ochrogaster, *Alcedo azurea* 214
ocularis, *Merops pusillus* 253
odites, *Halcyon australasia* 188
Olive-backed Kingfisher 174
oreobates, *Merops* **31**, 86, 255, 257
Oriental Dwarf Kingfisher **20**, 8, 64, 198
orientalis, *Eurystomus* **40**, 104, 305
orientalis, *Eurystomus orientalis* 104, 306
orientalis, *Halcyon albiventris* 152
orientalis, *Merops* **33**, 90, 269

orientalis, Merops orientalis 90, 269
orii, Halcyon chloris 58, 177
ornata, Halcyon chloris 58
ornatus, Merops **34**, 92, 275
osmastoni, Halcyon capensis 137
owstoni, Halcyon chloris 177

Pacific Kingfisher **19**, 24, 62, 190
pacificus, Eurystomus orientalis 104, 306
pallida, Megaceryle lugubris 229
pallidiventris, Halcyon leucocephala 46, 150
palmeri, Halcyon chloris 176
pavuvu, Halcyon chloris 178
pealei, Halcyon chloris 58, 179
Pelargopsis 8
pelewensis, Halcyon cinnamomina 58, 182
pelingensis, Halcyon coromanda 142
peninsulae, Alcedo euryzona 70, 212
peristephes, Actenoides concretus 112
persicus, Merops **33**, 90, 271
persicus, Merops persicus 90, 271
Philippine Dwarf Kingfisher **20**, 8, 64, 200
Philippine Pectoral Kingfisher **23**, 8, 70, 209
philippinus, Merops superciliosus 92, 274
philipsi, Alcedo meninting 218
Piciformes 6
pictus, Ceyx **20**, 64, 196
pictus, Ceyx pictus 8, 64, 197
Pied Kingfisher **28**, 5, 11, 13, 19, 20, 22, 80, 236
pilbara, Halcyon chloris 177
pileata, Halcyon **10**, 44, 147
pittoides, Atelornis 8
platenae, Ceyx melanurs 64, 200
Polynesian Kingfisher 190
prentissgrayi, Halcyon albiventris 153
princeps, Actenoides **1**, 26, 107
princeps, Actenoides princeps 26, 107
Puerto Rican Tody 7
Puffbirds 6
pulchella, Lacedo **6**, 36, 127
pulchella, Lacedo pulchella 36, 127
Purple Roller 287
Purple-bearded Bee-eater 244
Purple-winged Roller 291
pusilla, Alcedo **24**, 11, 72, 216
pusilla, Alcedo pusilla 72, 216
pusillus, Merops **31**, 86, 253
pusillus, Merops pusillus 86, 254
pyrrhopygia, Halcyon **18**, 60, 189

quadribrachys, Alcedo **24**, 11, 72, 213
quadribrachys, Alcedo quadribrachys 72, 213
quadricolor, Halcyon nigrocyanea 50, 161
quinticolor, Merops leschenaulti 94, 279

Racket-tailed Roller 98, 292
Rainbow Bee-eater **34**, 4, 22, 92, 275
ramsayi, Alcedo pusilla 72, 216
randorum, Merops bullockoides 262
recurvirostris, Halcyon sancta 185
recurvirostris, Halcyon sancta 60, 185, 186
Red-backed Kingfisher **18**, 12, 60, 189
Red-bearded Bee-eater **29**, 82, 241
Red-breasted Paradise Kingfisher **4**, 32, 120

Red-throated Bee-eater **32**, 5, 19, 88, 259
regalis, Actenoides princeps 26, 108
Regent Kingfisher **1**, 26, 107
regina, Halcyon chloris 179
reichenbachii, Halcyon cinnamomina 24, 182
revoilii, Merops **32**, 88, 264
rex, Clytoceyx **5**, 34, 125
rex, Clytoceyx rex 34, 125
richardsi, Alcedo pusilla 72, 216
riedelii, Tanysiptera galatea 30, 114
Ringed Kingfisher **28**, 233
River Kingfisher **25**, 3, 5, 11, 13, 21, 74, 80, 219
rosseliana, Tanysiptera galatea 30, 114
Rosy Bee-eater **36**, 19, 96, 283
Ruddy Kingfisher **9**, 12, 42, 141
rudis, Ceryle **28**, 3, 11, 80, 236
rudis, Ceryle rudis 80, 237
rufa, Halcyon coromanda 142
ruficollaris, Alcedo azurea 72, 214
ruficollaris, Halcyon 191
ruficollaris, Halcyon tuta 24, 62, 191
rufigaster, Alcedo meninting 74, 218
Rufous-bellied Kookaburra **6**, 128, 36
Rufous-collared Kingfisher **2**, 8, 28, 112
Rufous-crowned Roller **37**, 98, 287

sabrina, Tanysiptera galatea 30, 114
sacerdotis, Alcedo lepida 66, 203
sacra, Halcyon chloris 179
Sacred Kingfisher **18**, 8, 17, 60, 185
salvadorina, Tanysiptera sylvia 118
samarensis, Ceyx melanurs 200
sancta, Halcyon **18**, 60, 185
sancta, Halcyon sancta 60, 185
sanghirensis, Cittura cyanotis 34, 122
sangirensis, Ceyx fallax 64, 201
santoensis, Halcyon chloris 58, 179
saturatior, Halcyon smyrnensis 144
saurophaga, Halcyon **18**, 60, 183
saurophaga, Halcyon saurophaga 60, 184
Scaly Ground-roller 9
scintillans, Alcedo menting 218
sellamontis, Halcyon megarhyncha 54, 173
semenowi, Coracias garrulus 298
semicaerulea, Halcyon leucocephala 150
semitorquata, Alcedo **25**, 11, 74, 222
senegalensis, Halcyon **12**, 48, 157
senegalensis, Halcyon senegalensis 48, 158
senegaloides, Halcyon **12**, 48, 159
septentrionalis, Chloroceryle americana 227
Shining-blue Kingfisher **24**, 11, 72, 213
Short-legged Ground-roller 9
Shovel-billed Kingfisher **5**, 8, 12, 34, 125
Silvery Kingfisher **23**, 8, 70, 209
simalurensis, Halcyon capensis 138
smithi, Halcyon capensis 138
Silvery Kingfisher **23**, 8, 70, 209
smyrnensis, Halcyon **10**, 3, 44, 143
smyrnensis, Halcyon smyrnensis 44, 144
sodalis, Halcyon capensis 138
solitaria, Alcedo lepida 203
solomonensis, Alcedo atthis 220
solomonensis, Eurystomus orientalis 306
solomonis, Halcyon chloris 178
Somali Bee-eater **32**, 88, 264

Sombre Kingfisher **15**, 54, 174
sordida, Halcyon chloris 56, 177
sororum, Halcyon chloris 178
Spangled Kookaburra **6**, 36, 130
spatulata, Coracias **37**, 98, 292
spatulata, Coracias spatulata 98, 293
Spotted Wood Kingfisher **2**, 28, 111
squamigera, Brachypteracias 8
stellata, Megaceryle torquata 233
stictipennis, Megaceryle torquata 233
stictolaema, Halcyon nigrocyanea 50, 161
stictoptera, Chloroceryle aenea 224
Stork-billed Kingfisher **9**, 8, 42, 137
stresemanni, Halcyon chloris 177
Striped Kingfisher **12**, 12, 19, 48, 154
stuartkeithi, Alcedo cristata 206
suahelicus, Eurystomus glaucurus 102, 303
sulana, Halcyon coromanda 142
superciliosus, Merops **34**, 92, 273
superciliosus, Merops superciliosus 92, 274
Swallow-tailed Bee-eater **30**, 84, 251
sylvia, Tanysiptera **4**, 32, 118
sylvia, Tanysiptera sylvia 32, 118
Syma 8, 171, 173

Tahiti Kingfisher **19**, 62, 192
tannensis, Halcyon chloris 179
Tanysiptera 8
Tanysiptera carolinae **3**, 30, 116
Tanysiptera danae **4**, 32, 121
Tanysiptera galatea **3**, 30, 113
Tanysiptera hydrocharis **4**, 32, 117
Tanysiptera nigriceps 118
Tanysiptera nympha **4**, 32, 120
Tanysiptera riedelii 114
Tanysiptera sylvia **4**, 32, 118
taprobana, Alcedo atthis 219
temminckii, Coracias **40**, 104, 291
teraokai, Halcyon chloris 177
thomensis, Alcedo cristata 68, 206
Timor Kingfisher **18**, 60, 188
Todidae 6
Todies 6, 7
Todiramphus 8, 174, 193
Todus 7, 196
Todus mexicanus 7
torotoro, Halcyon **15**, 54, 171
torotoro, Halcyon torotoro 54, 172
torquata, Halcyon malimbica 156
torquata, Megaceryle **28**, 80, 233
torquata, Megaceryle torquata 80, 233
torresiana, Halcyon chloris 179
Toucans 6
travancoreensis, Ceryle rudis 237
tringorum, Halcyon australasia 188

tristami, Halcyon chloris 56, 177
Trogoniformes 6
Trogons 6
Tuamotu Kingfisher 193
tuta, Halcyon **19**, 24, 62, 190
tuta, Halcyon tuta 24, 62, 191
tyro, Dacelo **6**, 36, 130
tyro, Dacelo tyro 36, 130

Ultramarine Kingfisher **14**, 52, 169
Uratelornis chimaera 7, 8
uropygialis, Alcedo lepid 203
utupuae, Halcyon chloris 58, 178

vagans, Halcyon sancta 185
Variable Dwarf Kingfisher **21**, 8, 21, 66, 202
variegatus, Merops **31**, 86, 255
variegatus, Merops variegatus 86, 255
venerata, Halcyon **19**, 62, 192
venerata, Halcyon venerata 62, 192
verreauxii, Alcedo meninting 218
vicina, Halcyon chloris 58, 178
vidali, Halcyon chloris 176
vintsioides, Alcedo **22**, 8, 68, 208
vintsioides, Alcedo vintsioides 68, 208
viridis, Merops **34**, 92, 277
viridis, Merops viridis 92, 278
viridissimus, Merops orientalis 90, 269
vitiensis, Halcyon chloris 58, 179
vociferans, Halcyon albiventris 46, 152
vulcani, Tanysiptera galatea 114

waigiouensis, Eurystomus orientalis 306
waigiuensis, Melidora macrorrhina 124
wallacii, Alcedo lepida 203
websteri, Alcedo **24**, 11, 72, 215
weigalli, Coracias spatulata 98, 293
wellsi, Halcyon megarhyncha 173
White-bellied Kingfisher **22**, 8, 68, 204
White-breasted Kingfisher **10**, 20, 44, 143
White-collared Kingfisher 175
White-fronted Bee-eater **32**, 5, 20, 88, 262
White-mantled Kingfisher 168
White-rumped Kingfisher **8**, 40, 136
White-tailed Paradise Kingfisher 118
White-throated Bee-eater **32**, 15, 88, 265
White-throated Kingfisher 143
Winchell's Kingfisher **13**, 50, 162
winchelli, Halcyon **13**, 50, 162
winchelli, Halcyon winchelli 50, 162
Woodland Kingfisher **12**, 4, 20, 48, 157
Woodpeckers 6

yamdenae, Alcedo azurea 214
youngi, Halcyon venerata 62, 192